D1430025

How to Use This Book

Teach Yourself Visual C++ in 21 Days has two major goals: teaching you to program in C++ and teaching you to create Windows applications using Visual C++. No prior programming experience is required. However, knowing how to program in other languages, such as Basic or Pascal, certainly helps. This book is not for the faint-hearted, because learning to program in C++ and to write Windows applications in C++ are two nontrivial tasks!

The book contains 21 chapters—one for each study day. The material is somewhat fast-paced because of the goals of the book. Each chapter contains a Q&A section, a quiz section, and an exercise section. A review session is presented at the end of each week. In the back of the book there is an offer for the companion disk, which includes the source code and the project files.

Special Features of This Book

Teach Yourself Visual C++ in 21 Days contains some special features to guide you on your journey. Syntax sections help you master a specific Visual C++ topic. Each section provides concrete examples and a full explanation of the Visual C++ concept. To get a feel for the style of the syntax sections, look at the following example. (Don't try to understand the material; you haven't even reached Day 1!)

The Single-Alternative *if* Statement

The general syntax for the single-alternative if statement is

```
if (condition)
    statement;
```

for a single executable statement, and

```
if (tested_condition) {
    <sequence of statements>
}
```

for a sequence of executable statements.

Examples:

```
if (numberOfLines < 0)
    numberOfLines = 0;
if ((height - 54) < 3) {
    area = length * width;
    volume = area * height;
}
```

Other features of this book include Notes, Warnings, and DO/DON'T boxes.

Note: A note provides extra information about the topic currently being discussed.

Warning: A warning alerts you to a hazard regarding the topic currently being discussed.

A DO/DON'T box gives you tips on what to do and what not to do.

DO	DON'T

DO read the rest of this section. It provides an explanation of the workshop section at the end of the day.

DON'T skip any of the quiz questions or exercises. If you can finish the day's workshop, you are ready to move on to new material.

Numerous examples are provided with explanations to help you learn how to program. Each day ends with a Q&A section containing answers to common questions related to the day's material. There is also a workshop at the end of each day which contains a quiz and exercises. The quiz tests your knowledge of the concepts presented that day. If you want to check your responses, or in case you're stumped, the answers are in Appendix B, "Answers."

You won't learn Visual C++ by just reading this book, however. If you want to be a programmer, you've got to write programs. Following each set of quiz questions is a set of exercises. It is recommended that you attempt each exercise. Writing Visual C++ code is the best way to learn the Visual C++ programming language.

Conventions Used in This Book

This book uses various typefaces to help you differentiate between Visual C++ code and regular English, and also to help you identify important concepts. Actual Visual C++ code is typeset in a special monospace font. Placeholders—terms used to represent what you actually type within the code—are typeset in an *italic monospace* font. New or important terms are typeset in *italic*.

Sometimes, the listings have a line that is too long to print in the book. When a line needs to be split, the second line is prefaced with the ➡ character. When you see two lines like this, type them in as one line.

NEW ➡ TERM Some key new terms are highlighted with the New Term icon. A glossary is also included at the end of the book if you need to look up any confusing computer terms.

One last note: the listings in this book are available from the author for those readers who want to save the time of typing them. Please use the form in the back of the book to order your disk copy.

Hopefully, this book will enable you to take the bold step into the world of programming. It is an exciting world that gives you more control over what your machine does. Happy programming!

Teach Yourself Visual C++™
in 21 Days

Teach Yourself
Visual C++™
in 21 Days

Namir Clement Shammas

SAMS
PUBLISHING

A Division of Prentice Hall Computer Publishing
11711 North College, Carmel, Indiana 46032 USA

To my dear new friends, David and Janice Benson

Trademarks

Publisher
Richard K. Swadley

Associate Publisher
Jordan Gold

Acquisitions Manager
Stacy Hiquet

Development Editor
Dean Miller

Senior Editor
Tad Ringo

Production Editor
Nancy Albright

Editorial Coordinators
Bill Whitmer
James R. Welter II

Editorial Assistants
Sharon Cox
Molly Carmody

Technical Reviewer
Greg Guntle

Marketing Manager
Greg Wiegand

Cover Designer
Dan Armstrong

**Director of Production
and Manufacturing**
Jeff Valler

Production Manager
Corinne Walls

Imprint Manager
Kelli Widdifield

Book Designer
Michele Laseau

Production Analyst
Mary Beth Wakefield

**Proofreading/Indexing
Coordinator**
Joelynn Gifford

Graphics Image Specialists
Dennis Sheehan
Tim Montgomery
Sue VandeWalle

Production
Lisa Daugherty
Mitzi Gianakos
Dennis Clay Hager
Carla Hall-Batton
Howard Jones
Sean Medlock
Mike Mucha
Wendy Ott
Linda Quiqley
Michelle Self
Tonya Simpson
Barbara Webster
Dennis Wesner
Donna Winter

Indexers
Michael Hughes
Suzanne Snyder

Overview

How to Use This Book i

Week 1 at a Glance

1   Getting Started 3
2   C++ Program Components 29
3   Operators and Expressions 59
4   Managing I/O 91
5   The Decision-Making Constructs 105
6   Loops 127
7   Arrays 149

Week 1 in Review   **187**

Week 2 at a Glance

8   User-Defined Types and Pointers 193
9   Strings 227
10 Advanced Functions Parameters 259
11 Object-Oriented Programming and C++ Classes 293
12 Basic Stream File I/O 331
13 Programming Windows Using the MFC Library 355
14 Creating Basic MFC Applications 381

Week 2 in Review   **413**

Week 3 at a Glance

15 Basic Windows 419
16 MFC Controls 449
17 Grouped Controls 487
18 List Boxes 519
19 Scroll Bars and Combo Boxes 561
20 Dialog Boxes 601
21 MDI Windows 635

Week 3 in Review   **653**

Appendixes
   A   Controls Resource Script 661
   B   Answers 679

Glossary   **713**

Index   **723**

Contents

How to Use This Book i

Week 1 at a Glance

1   Getting Started 3

    The Basics of C++ Programs 4

    Loading the Visual C++ Workbench 5

    An Overview of the Visual C++ Workbench 5

    The File Option 5

        The New Selection 6

        The Open Selection 6

        The Close Selection 7

        The Save Selection 7

        The Save As Selection 7

        The Save All Selection 8

        The Print Selection 8

        The Page Setup Selection 8

        The Exit Selection 8

        The Most Recent Files Selections 8

    The Edit Option 8

        The Undo Selection 8

        The Redo Selection 9

        The Cut Selection 9

        The Copy Selection 9

        The Paste Selection 9

        The Delete Selection 9

        The Find Selection 9

        The Replace Selection 11

        The Find Matching Brace Selection 12

        The Read Only Selection 12

    The View Option 12

        The Line Selection 12

        The Mixed Source/Asm Selection 12

        The Next Error Selection 12

        The Previous Error Selection 12

The Toggle Bookmark Selection 13
The Next Bookmark Selection 13
The Previous Bookmark Selection 13
The Clear All Bookmarks Selection 13
The Toolbar Selection 13
The Status Bar Selection 13
The Syntax Coloring Selection 13
The Project Option 14
The AppWizard Selection 14
The New Selection 14
The Open Selection 14
The Edit Selection 14
The Close Selection 14
The Compile File Selection 15
The Build Selection 15
The Rebuild All Selection 15
The Stop Build Selection 15
The Execute Selection 15
The Scan Dependencies Selection 16
The Scan All Dependencies Selection 16
The Load Workspace Selection 16
The Save Workspace Selection 16
The Most Recent Projects Selections 16
The Browse Option 16
The Go to Definition Selection 16
The Go to Reference Selection 17
The Next Selection 17
The Previous Selection 17
The Pop Context Selection 17
The Open Selection 17
The ClassWizard Selection 17
The Debug Option 17
The Tools Option 18
The Options Option 18
The Project Selection 18
The Debug Selection 18
The Directories Selection 18
The Editor Selection 18
The Workspace Selection 19

The Tools Selection 19

The Color Selection 19

The Fonts Selection 19

The Window Option 19

The Help Option 19

The QuickWin Applications 19

Your First C++ Program 21

Exiting the Workbench 25

Summary 25

Q&A 26

Workshop 27

Quiz 27

Exercise 28

2   C+ + Program Components 29

Predefined Data Types in Visual C++ 30

Naming Items in Visual C++ 32

The *#include* Directive 32

Declaring Variables 33

Declaring Constants 35

Using Macro-Based Constants 36

Using Formal Constants 38

Declaring and Prototyping Functions 39

Local Variables in Functions 42

Static Variables in Functions 44

Inline Functions 45

Exiting Functions 47

Default Arguments 47

Function Overloading 50

Summary 53

Q&A 54

Workshop 55

Quiz 55

Exercise 57

3   Operators and Expressions 59

Arithmetic Operators 60

Arithmetic Expressions 63

Increment Operators 64

Assignment Operators 66

The *sizeof* Operator 69

Typecasting 72
Relational and Logical Operators 75
Boolean Expressions 77
Bit-Manipulation Operators..81
The Comma Operator 83
    Operator Precedence and Evaluation Direction 84
Summary 86
Q&A 87
Workshop 88
    Quiz 88
    Exercises 90

4   **Managing I/O** **91**
Formatted Stream Output...92
Stream Input 94
The *printf* Function 96
Summary 102
Q&A 103
Workshop 103
    Quiz 103
    Exercises 104

5   **The Decision-Making Constructs** **105**
The Single-Alternative *if* Statement...........................106
The Dual-Alternative *if-else* Statement 108
    Potential Problems with the *if* Statement 110
The Multiple-Alternative *if-else* Statement 111
The *switch* Statement 114
Nested Decision-Making Constructs...........................119
Summary 120
Q&A 122
Workshop 123
    Quiz 123
    Exercises 125

6   **Loops** **127**
The *for* Loop 128
Open Loops Using the *for* Loops 132
The *do-while* Loop 134
The *while* Loop 137
Skipping Loop Iterations 138

Exiting Loops 141

Nested Loops 142

Summary 143

Q&A 144

Workshop 146

    Quiz 146

    Exercises 147

7   Arrays 149

Declaring Single-Dimensional Arrays 150

Using Single-Dimensional Arrays 151

Initializing Single-Dimensional Arrays 154

Array Parameters in Functions 157

Sorting Arrays 161

Searching Arrays 165

Multidimensional Arrays 172

Initializing Multidimensional Arrays 176

Multidimensional Array Parameters 178

Summary 182

Q&A 183

Workshop 184

    Quiz 184

    Exercise 186

Week 1 in Review   187

Week 2 at a Glance

8   User-Defined Types and Pointers 193

Type Definition in C++ 194

Enumerated Data Types.. 195

Structures 199

Unions 203

Reference Variables 204

Overview of Pointers 206

Pointers to Existing Variables 206

Pointers to Arrays 209

    The Pointer Increment/Decrement Method 212

Pointers to Structures 214

Pointers and Dynamic Memory 217

Far Pointers... 221

Summary 221

Q&A 223

Workshop 224

  Quiz 224

  Exercises 225

9   Strings 227

C++ Strings 228

String Input 229

Using the STRING.H Library 230

Assigning Strings 230

The Length of a String 232

Concatenating Strings 233

String Comparison 237

Converting Strings 242

Reversing Strings 243

Locating Characters 246

Locating Strings 248

Summary 253

Q&A 255

Workshop 256

  Quiz 256

  Exercises 257

10   Advanced Functions Parameters 259

Passing Arrays as Arguments 260

Using Strings as Arguments 263

Using Structures as Arguments 265

Passing Arguments by Reference 267

Passing Structures by Reference 268

Passing Structures by Pointers 270

Recursive Functions 271

Passing Pointers to Dynamic Structures 274

Pointers to Functions 278

Summary 288

Q&A 289

Workshop 289

  Quiz 290

  Exercise 291

11 Object-Oriented Programming and C++ Classes 293

Basics of Object-Oriented Programming 294

Classes and Objects 294

Messages and Methods 295

Inheritance 295

Polymorphism 296

Declaring Base Classes 296

The Sections of a Class 297

Constructors 301

Destructors 303

Examples of Constructors and Destructors 304

Declaring a Class Hierarchy 307

Virtual Functions 312

Rules for Virtual Functions 316

Friend Functions 318

Operators and Friend Operators 321

Summary 326

Q&A 327

Workshop 328

    Quiz 328

    Exercise 329

12 Basic Stream File I/O 331

The C++ Stream Library 332

Common Stream I/O Functions 332

Sequential Text Stream I/O 334

Sequential Binary File Stream I/O 339

Random Access File Stream I/O 347

Summary 352

Q&A 353

Workshop 353

    Quiz 353

    Exercise 354

13 Programming Windows Using the MFC Library 355

Popular Windows Data Types 356

The MFC Hierarchy 359

    The *CObject* Class 359

    The *CMenu* Class 359

    The Document Architecture Subhierarchy..............359

The Frames Windows Subhierarchy 359
The Control Bars Subhierarchy 360
The Views Subhierarchy 360
The Dialog Boxes Subhierarchy 360
The Control Subhierarchy 360
The Graphical Drawing Subhierarchy 360
The Graphical Drawing Objects Subhierarchy 361
Other MFC Subhierarchies 361
MFC Macros 361
The Windows API Functions 362
Invoking Windows API Functions 367
The Windows Messages 370
Responding to Messages 373
Sending Messages 375
User-Defined Messages 376
Summary 378
Q&A 378
Workshop 379
     Quiz 379
     Exercise 379

14   Creating Basic MFC Applications 381
Creating a Minimal MFC Application 382
Extending the Window Operations 387
Responding to Menu Selections 393
Creating Multiple Instances 400
Closing a Window 406
Summary 409
Q&A 410
Workshop 410
     Quiz 411
     Exercise 411

Week 2 in Review   413

Week 3 at a Glance

15   Basic Windows 419
Creating a Read-Only Text Window 420
Scrolling Through Text 426
A Scrolling Window 431

Summary 447

Q&A 447

Workshop 448

    Quiz 448

    Exercise 448

16   MFC Controls 449

The Static Text Control 450

The Edit Control 454

    The *CEdit* Class 454

    Clipboard-Related Editing Functions 456

    Query of Edit Controls 456

    Altering the Edit Controls 460

The Push Button Control 462

    The *CButton* Class 463

    Handling Button Messages 464

    Manipulating Buttons 465

    The Command-Line Calculator 465

Summary 485

Q&A 485

Workshop 486

    Quiz 486

    Exercises 486

17   Grouped Controls 487

The Check Box Control 488

    The *CButton* Class and Check Boxes 489

    Responding to Check Box Messages 490

The Radio Button Control 490

    The *CButton* Class and Radio Buttons 490

The Group Control 491

    The *CButton* Class and Group Boxes 491

The Updated Calculator Application 492

    The Illustrated Aspects 492

    Experimenting with the Application 493

Summary 516

Q&A 516

Workshop 517

    Quiz 517

    Exercise 517

18 List Boxes **519**

The List Box Control 520

The *CListBox* Class 520

Responding to List Box Notification Messages 530

The List Manipulation Tester 531

Handling Multiple-Selection Lists 543

The Multiple-Selection List Tester 544

Summary 558

Q&A 558

Workshop 559

Quiz 559

Exercise 559

19 Scroll Bars and Combo Boxes **561**

The Scroll Bar Control 562

The *CScrollBar* Class 562

Responding to Scroll Bar Notification Messages 566

The Count-Down Timer 566

The Combo Box Control 576

The *CComboBox* Class 577

Responding to Combo Box
Notification Messages 584

Combo Boxes as History List Boxes 584

The COCA Version 4 Application 585

Summary 598

Q&A 598

Workshop 598

Quiz 598

Exercises 599

20 Dialog Boxes **601**

Constructing Dialog Boxes 602

Executing Modal Dialog Boxes 603

Transferring Control Data 610

Data Transfer for Modal Dialog Boxes 613

Transferring Data for Modeless Dialog Boxes 621

Summary 632

Q&A 633

Workshop 634

Quiz 634

Exercises 634

21 MDI Windows **635**

MDI Application Features and Components 636

Building an MDI Application 637

The *CMDIFrameWnd* Class 637

Building MDI Frame Windows 638

The *CMDIChildWnd* Class 638

Building MDI Child Windows 639

Managing MDI Messages 639

A Simple Text Viewer 639

Summary 651

Q&A 651

Workshop 652

Quiz 652

Exercise 652

Week 3 in Review   **653**

Appendixes

A Controls Resource Script **661**

Building Menu Resources 662

Dialog Box Resource 665

DIALOG Option Statements 666

The *STYLE* Statement 666

The *CAPTION* Statement 667

The *MENU* Statement 667

The *CLASS* Statement 668

The *FONT* Statement 668

Dialog Box Control Resources 668

The General Control Resource 668

The *LTEXT* Statement 671

The *RTEXT* Statement 671

The *CTEXT* Statement 672

The *CHECKBOX* Statement 672

The *PUSHBUTTON* Statement 673

The *DEFPUSHBUTTON* Statement 673

The *LISTBOX* Statement 674

The *GROUPBOX* Statement 674

The *RADIOBUTTON* Statement 674

The *EDITTEXT* Statement 675

The *COMBOBOX* Statement 675
The *SCROLLBAR* Statement 676
Summary 676
B   **Answers** **679**
Answers to Day 1, "Getting Started" 680
Answers to Day 2, "C++ Program Components" 680
Answers to Day 3, "Operators and Expressions" 683
Answers to Day 4, "Managing I/O" 685
Answers to Day 5, "The Decision-Making
  Constructs" 686
Answers to Day 6, "Loops" 689
Answers to Day 7, "Arrays" 692
Answers to Day 8, "User-Defined Types
  and Pointers" 694
Answers to Day 9, "Strings" 696
Answers to Day 10, "Advanced Functions
  Parameters" 699
Answers to Day 11, "Object-Oriented Programming
  and C++ Classes" 704
Answers to Day 12, "Basic Stream File I/O" 705
Answers to Day 13, "Programming Windows
  Using the MFC Library" 707
Answers to Day 14, "Creating Basic MFC
  Applications" 708
Answers to Day 15, "Basic Windows" 708
Answers to Day 16, "MFC Controls" 709
Answers to Day 17, "Grouped Controls" 709
Answers to Day 18, "List Boxes" 710
Answers to Day 19, "Scroll Bars and Combo
  Boxes" 710
Answers to Day 20, "Dialog Boxes" 711
Answers to Day 21, "MDI Windows" 711

Glossary **713**

Index **723**

Acknowledgments

I would like to thank the many people at Sams Publishing for encouraging me and working with me on this project. I would like to thank publisher Richard Swadley and associate publisher Jordan Gold for their vital support. Many thanks to acquisitions manager Stacy Hiquet for sharing the vision for this book project. My special thanks to development editor Dean Miller, who gave 100 percent and bent over backward to accommodate the tight schedule and to manage the book size. My appreciation to technical reviewer Greg Guntle for his valuable comments. Finally, I want to thank all those at Sams Publishing who participated in producing this book.

About the Author

Namir Clement Shammas is a software engineer and an expert in object-oriented programming. He has written many articles for leading computer magazines and is responsible for many books on computer programming, including *Turbo Pascal 6 Object-Oriented Programming*, *Windows Programmer's Guide to ObjectWindows Library*, and *Teach Yourself QBasic in 21 Days*.

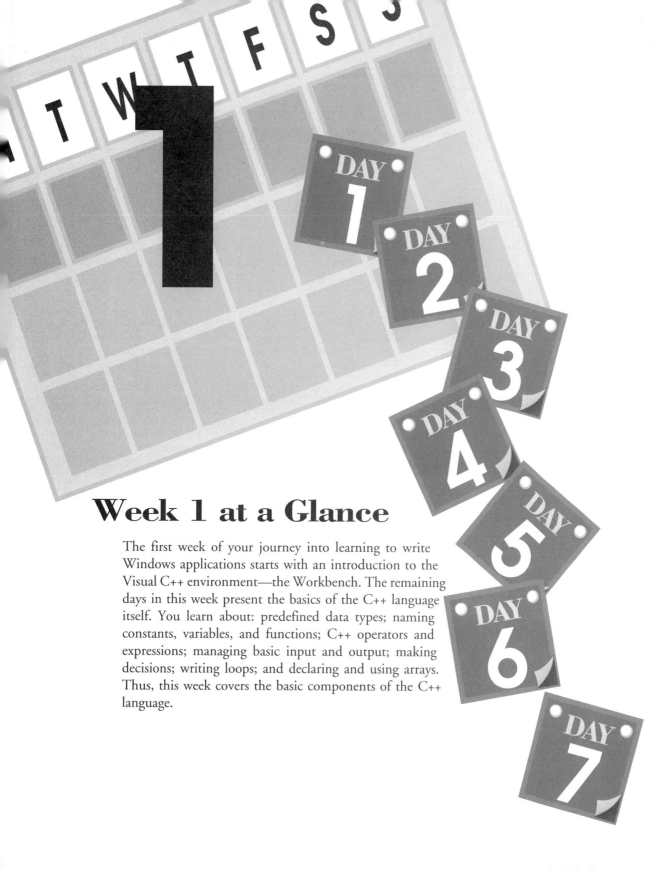

Week 1 at a Glance

The first week of your journey into learning to write Windows applications starts with an introduction to the Visual C++ environment—the Workbench. The remaining days in this week present the basics of the C++ language itself. You learn about: predefined data types; naming constants, variables, and functions; C++ operators and expressions; managing basic input and output; making decisions; writing loops; and declaring and using arrays. Thus, this week covers the basic components of the C++ language.

DAY 1

Getting Started

Welcome to the world of C++ and Windows programming! Your journey into this exciting venture begins today. Most of the information in today's lesson familiarizes you with the Visual C++ Workbench. You learn about the following topics:

- [ ] The basics and history of C++ programs
- [ ] Loading and using the Visual C++ Workbench
- [ ] The QuickWin applications
- [ ] Typing and running your first C++ program

The Basics of C++ Programs

You don't need any previous experience in programming to learn Visual C++ with this book, but if you've programmed before, things will be easier. As with other languages, C++ is made up of declarations and statements that specify exact instructions to be executed when the program runs.

C++ was developed by Bjarn Stroustrup at Bell Labs. The language is meant to succeed and build on the popular C language, mainly by adding object-oriented language extensions.

NEW☞ TERM An *object-oriented language* represents the attributes and operations of objects.

In addition, C++ offers a number of enhancements to C that are not object-oriented. Thus, learning C++ gives you the bonus of becoming very familiar with C. Unlike C, which has been standardized, C++ is still undergoing the standardization process.

Programming in C++ requires that you become aware of the supporting libraries which perform various tasks such as input, output, text manipulation, math operations, file I/O (input/output), and so on. In languages such as BASIC, support for such operations is transparent to programs, because it is automatically available to these programs. As a result, many programs come across as single components that are independent of any other programming components. By contrast, programming in C++ makes you more aware of the dependency on various libraries. The advantage of this language feature is that you are able to select between similar libraries, including ones that you develop. Thus C++ programs are modular. C++ compilers, including Visual C++, use project files and program files. The Visual C++ Workbench uses project files to manage the creation and update of a program.

NEW☞ TERM *Project files* specify the library. *Program files* create an application.

Loading the Visual C++ Workbench

The Visual C++ Workbench is the visual interface for the C++ compiler, linker, debugger, and other tools used to create, manage, and maintain C++ programs. You can load the Workbench by simply clicking on the Visual C++ icon or by double-clicking the MSVC.EXE program from the File Manager. (The file MSVC.EXE is located in the directory \MSVC\BIN.)

The Visual C++ Workbench does not use command-line switches to fine-tune how it loads and operates. Instead, it uses one of its menu options (more about this later in today's lesson).

An Overview of the Visual C++ Workbench

The Visual C++ Workbench is the environment used to develop C and C++ applications. The Workbench is a versatile tool which facilitates developing both MS-DOS and Windows applications as well as libraries. Throughout this book you use the Workbench to learn about programming in C++ and writing Windows applications.

The Visual C++ Workbench has menu options, a tool bar, a status bar, and display area. The built-in editor uses this area to display and edit files in MDI (Multi-Document Interface) windows.

One of the valuable features of the Workbench is the extensive online help. Using the Help option, you can inquire about every aspect of the Workbench, the C++ language, and other aspects of developing programs.

The Visual C++ Workbench contains a menu with ten main options. You don't need to understand what all these options mean exactly. This is just an overview. Each option contains a family of selections which performs a task or sets an option. The next sections introduce you to the menu options of the Visual C++ Workbench.

The File Option

The File option essentially manages loading and saving files, printing, and exiting the Workbench. This option includes the selections in the next subsections.

The New Selection

The **N**ew selection creates a new blank MDI editing window. Each MDI window has a window number, enclosed in angled brackets, and a title (which is the filename). The title of the first new MDI window is UNTITLED.1, the title for the second new MDI window is UNTITLED.2, and so on.

The Open Selection

The **O**pen selection opens an existing file. The selection pops up an Open File dialog box, shown in Figure 1.1, which permits you to select a file. The dialog box allows you to select a file from any existing directory and drive. In addition, the dialog box has a wildcard filenames text box which permits you to choose the set of files to view before selecting an individual file to open. The dialog box also includes a Read Only check box. This control allows you to read a file and protect it from accidentally being altered.

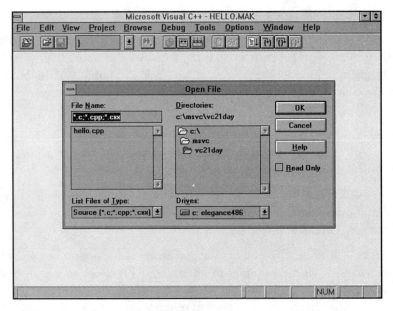

Figure 1.1. The Open File dialog box.

The Close Selection

The Close selection closes the currently edited MDI window. If the contents of that window have not been saved or updated, the Close selection displays a message dialog box. This dialog box asks you if you want to save the contents of the window before closing.

The Save Selection

The Save selection updates the file which is associated with the currently edited window. If you invoke this selection with a new window, the Workbench invokes the Save As dialog box.

The Save As Selection

The Save As selection allows you to save a new window or write the contents of the currently edited window to a different file. The selection invokes the Save As dialog box to allow you to specify the filename as well as the target directory and drive (see Figure 1.2).

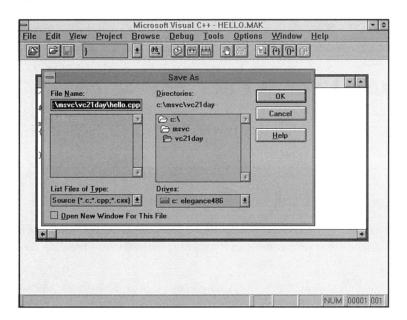

Figure 1.2. The Save As dialog box.

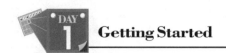

The Save All Selection

The Save All selection quickly saves all the windows in the Workbench. The selection invokes the Save As dialog box to save new windows.

The Print Selection

The Print selection allows you to print part or all of the currently edited window. The selection invokes the Print dialog box which allows you to select the printer, to select printing all or part of the edited text, and to invoke the printer setup. The Print dialog box invokes other dialog boxes for the printer setup.

The Page Setup Selection

The Page Setup selection invokes a dialog box which permits you to specify the header, footer, and the four document margins.

The Exit Selection

The Exit selection allows you to exit the Visual C++ Workbench. If there are edited windows that are not saved, the Workbench gives you the opportunity to save these windows before exiting.

The Most Recent Files Selections

The Visual C++ Workbench remembers the most recent files that you have worked with. The Workbench displays the names of these files in the File option below the Exit selection.

The Edit Option

The Edit option has selections that perform four kinds of operations: undoing changes, cut-and-paste operations, find/replace operations, and toggling read only mode.

The Undo Selection

The Undo selection allows you to undo previous editing tasks. The number of editing tasks which you can undo depends on the size of the Undo buffer (a memory location used to track and store changes in the text). The default size of the buffer is 4K and can be set anywhere from 0 to 64K. The Editor selection in the Options option allows you to alter the size of the Undo buffer.

The Redo Selection

The Redo selection undoes the action carried out by the Undo selection. The Redo selection assists you in restoring part of the edited text if you used the Undo selection too many times.

The Cut Selection

The Cut selection deletes selected text and copies that text to the clipboard (overwriting the previous contents of the clipboard). Consequently, the deleted text can be reinserted using the Paste selection.

The Copy Selection

The Copy selection copies the selected text to the clipboard, overwriting the previous contents of the clipboard. The subsequent invocation of the Paste selection inserts the copied text.

The Paste Selection

The Paste selection inserts the text in the clipboard at the current cursor location. You can move text from one location to another with the Cut and Paste selections. You can duplicate text in one or more windows with the Copy and Paste selections.

The Delete Selection

The Delete selection deletes the selected text or the character at the cursor (if there is no selected text). The deleted text or character is not copied into the clipboard.

The Find Selection

The Find selection allows you to search for text in the currently edited window. The selection invokes the Find dialog box, shown in Figure 1.3. This dialog box allows you to specify the following search options:

☐ The search text (the dialog box uses a combo box control which allows you to specify previous search text)

☐ The search for a whole word (the dialog box offers a check box to toggle the search for a whole word)

☐ The case-sensitive search (the dialog box offers a check box to toggle the case-sensitive search)

☐ The use of regular expressions to search for text using more advanced text patterns

☐ The search direction (the dialog box offers radio buttons to specify the search direction)

The Find dialog box allows you to search for a match one instance at a time, or to set bookmarks on all lines that contain the matching text.

Figure 1.3. The Find dialog box.

The Replace Selection

The Replace selection replaces text in the currently edited window. The selection invokes the Replace dialog box, shown in Figure 1.4. This dialog box allows you to specify the following search options:

☐ The search text (the dialog box uses a combo box control which allows you to specify previous search text)

☐ The replacement text (the dialog box uses a combo box control which allows you to specify previous replacement text)

☐ The search for a whole word (the dialog box offers a check box to toggle the search for a whole word)

☐ The case-sensitive search (the dialog box offers a check box to toggle the case-sensitive search)

☐ The use of regular expressions to search for text using more advanced text patterns

Figure 1.4. The Replace dialog box.

The Replace dialog box replaces all the occurrences of the search text with the replacement text. The dialog box also contains a Find Next command button which allows you to search for text.

The Find Matching Brace Selection

The Find Matching Brace selection empowers you to find matching curly braces—{ and }. C++ uses the braces to define a block of statements.

The Read Only Selection

The Read Only selection toggles the read only mode of text in a window. The Workbench places a check mark to the left of this selection when the read only mode is active.

The View Option

The View option allows you to view quickly various kinds of information. The option contains selections to view a specific line, errors, bookmarks, the toolbar, and the status bar.

The Line Selection

The Line selection invokes a dialog box which prompts you for the line number to view. This selection allows you to make accurate jumps to specific lines. The benefit of this selection is even greater when you are jumping to a distant line in a very large file.

The Mixed Source/Asm Selection

The Mixed Source/Asm selection shows assembly code mixed with C++ statements. This selection is for advanced-level programmers.

The Next Error Selection

The Next Error selection allows you to view the next line which contains an error. If the offending line is located in a file that is not currently in an MDI window, the selection loads that file.

The Previous Error Selection

The Previous Error selection enables you to view the previous line that contains an error. If the offending line is located in a file that is not currently in an MDI window, the selection loads that file.

The Toggle Bookmark Selection

The **T**oggle Bookmark selection toggles the highlight of the line that contains the cursor. When this selection highlights a line, it sets a bookmark at that line. When the selection clears the highlight of a line, that line is no longer marked.

The Next Bookmark Selection

The **N**ext Bookmark selection visits the next line with a bookmark. You can create such lines by either using the Toggle Bookmark selection or by using the Find selection in the Edit option.

The Previous Bookmark Selection

The **P**revious Bookmark selection visits the previous line with a bookmark.

The Clear All Bookmarks Selection

The **C**lear All Bookmarks selection removes all the bookmarks. Use this selection before you employ the **F**ind selection in the **E**dit option to mark lines that match a specific text.

The Toolbar Selection

The **T**oolbar selection toggles the toolbar of the Workbench. When this selection is checked, the toolbar is visible.

The Status Bar Selection

The **S**tatus Bar selection toggles the Status Bar of the Workbench. When this selection is checked, the Status Bar is visible.

The Syntax Coloring Selection

The **S**yntax Coloring selection enables you to select colored syntax for C or C++ programs. The selection displays a cascading menu to select C, C++, or None. The latter choice turns off colored syntax.

The Project Option

The **P**roject option allows you to manage the creation and update of an application. You use various selections in the **P**roject option to compile and run C++ programs.

The AppWizard Selection

The App**W**izard selection assists in creating Windows applications that use the Microsoft Foundation Classes (MFC) library. This selection opens the AppWizard dialog box which allows you to generate a family of MFC project files used with ClassWizard (another powerful tool for creating classes).

The New Selection

The **N**ew selection assists in creating new project files. This selection pops up the New Project dialog box which allows you to specify the name of the project and the type of program (MS-DOS or Windows), and add the files involved in creating the program.

The Open Selection

The **O**pen selection opens an existing project and loads any needed files. Use this selection to complete, update, and run programs in existing projects. This selection automatically closes the currently opened project. The Workbench handles only one project at a time.

The Edit Selection

The **E**dit selection opens an existing project file and enables you to add or remove files from the list of required files. You cannot use this selection to alter the type of file generated by the project file. To do that, use the **P**roject selection in the **O**ptions option.

The Close Selection

The **C**lose selection explicitly closes a project. If you exit the Workbench without closing the current project, that project is automatically reloaded the next time you load the Workbench.

The Compile File Selection

The Compile File selection compiles the statements in the active window. The option saves the contents of that window if need be. The Workbench displays an output window which displays the status of the compilation and any errors generated by the compiler.

NEW☞ TERM C++ allows you to create a program using several components. Each component is stored in a *source file*. The compiler generates .OBJ object files from each source file. The linker creates the .EXE program file by combining the various .OBJ files with run-time library files.

The Build Selection

The **B**uild selection creates the .EXE program file by compiling (or recompiling) the source files. The selection works on only those files that either

☐ Have not yet been compiled

☐ Have been compiled earlier, but their corresponding source codes were changed

The project file stores information which specifies the dependencies of files on other files. This information allows the Build selection to determine the hierarchical level of dependencies between files.

The Rebuild All Selection

The **R**ebuild All selection creates the .EXE program file by systematically recompiling all its components.

The Stop Build Selection

The **S**top Build selection halts the creation of the application as soon as possible.

The Execute Selection

The **E**xecute selection runs the program in the project. This selection recompiles and links the components source file if needed. You use this option to run the programs in this book.

The Scan Dependencies Selection

The Scan **D**ependencies selection updates the list of dependent files for the currently edited file.

The Scan All Dependencies Selection

The Scan **A**ll Dependencies selection updates the list of dependent files for the entire project.

The Load Workspace Selection

The **L**oad Workspace selection enables you to load any one of three workspaces (Edit, Debug, and Custom). A workspace includes the arrangement of windows.

The Save Workspace Selection

The **S**ave Workspace selection enables you to save the current workspace to any one of three workspaces (Edit, Debug, and Custom).

The Most Recent Projects Selections

The Project option includes a list of up to four of the most recent .MAK project files that you worked with. Use these selections to retrieve a project quickly.

The Browse Option

The **B**rowse option contains selections that vary in complexity. Some selections allow you to perform simple tasks, others best serve you later on.

The Go to Definition Selection

The Go to **D**efinition selection jumps to the first location where a name is defined. The selection loads the file which contains the definition, if the definition is not located in any window in the workspace.

The Go to Reference Selection

The Go to **R**eference selection jumps to the first location where a name is referenced. The selection loads the file which contains the reference, if the reference is not located in any window in the workspace.

The Next Selection

The **N**ext selection jumps to the next definition or reference of a name. The action of this selection depends on which of the last two selections was most recently invoked.

The Previous Selection

The **P**revious selection jumps to the previous definition or reference of a name. The action of this selection depends on which selection was most recently invoked—Go to Definition or Go to Reference.

The Pop Context Selection

The Pop **C**ontext selection jumps to the name that you used before the last invocation of the Go to Definition selection or the Go to Reference selection.

The Open Selection

The **O**pen selection opens the Browse window which allows you to browse through the various components of a program. This advanced-level selection serves you later, when you create modular programs.

The ClassWizard Selection

The Class**W**izard selection opens the ClassWizard dialog box. This box assists you in writing Windows programs which use the MFC library.

The Debug Option

The **D**ebug option contains selections that permit you to monitor program execution in order to catch run-time errors. Debugging techniques assign breakpoints to specific statements. The Debug option has selections that enable you to single-step through a program and watch the values of variables.

NEW☞ TERM *Breakpoints* cause the program to temporarily stop, allowing you to inspect various components.

The Tools Option

The Tools option is a flexible menu which you can customize. Its selections are utilities that are invoked from within the Workbench. The default selections are the App Studio, the CodeView for Windows, and the CodeView for MS-DOS. The Workbench Tools selection in the Options option allows you to modify the selections in the Tools option.

The Options Option

The Options option enables you to fine-tune the operations of the compiler, linker, and other aspects of the Visual C++ Workbench.

The Project Selection

The Project selection customizes the compiler, linker, resources, build mode, and project type. This selection invokes the Project Options dialog box which invokes other dialog boxes to customize the action of the compiler, linker, and resources.

The Debug Selection

The Debug selection enables you to customize the debugging of a program.

The Directories Selection

The Directories selection invokes the Directories dialog box which sets the directories for the include files, libraries, executable files, help files, and MFC library source files.

The Editor Selection

The Editor selection pops up the Editor dialog box which sets the options for tab setting, use of scroll bars, saving a file before building it, prompting you before saving a file, and the size of the Undo buffer.

The Workspace Selection

The **W**orkspace selection opens the Workspace dialog box and allows you to set the options for the three workspaces.

The Tools Selection

The **T**ools selection opens the Tools dialog box which permits you to add and remove tools from the Tools option.

The Color Selection

The **C**olor selection pops up the Colors dialog box which permits you to alter the colors used for syntax coloring.

The Fonts Selection

The **F**onts selection brings up the Fonts dialog box which enables you to select the fonts for the edited windows.

The Window Option

The **W**indow option has a group of selections which allow you to tile, cascade, close, and duplicate windows in the workspace. In addition, the Window option allows you to display special windows that view program variables and the CPU registers.

The Help Option

The **H**elp option provides versatile and time-saving online help. The selections of the **H**elp option offer information on the Workbench itself, the build tools, the C/C++ languages, the MFC library, the Windows 3.1 SDK (Software Development Kit), and where to obtain technical information.

The QuickWin Applications

The Visual C++ Workbench allows you to build a special kind of program called a QuickWin application. This application is a cross between an MS-DOS program and a Windows program. The programs in Days 1 through 12 are QuickWin applications which allow you to focus on learning C++ using DOS-like interface and input/output. The QuickWin window is the standard input and output for C++ programs (compiled as QuickWin applications). The QuickWin window has a simple menu with few options and a few selections.

To create a QuickWin application, perform the following steps:

1. Load the Visual C++ Workbench.

2. Choose the **N**ew selection in the **F**ile option.

3. Type in the C++ program in the new window.

4. Choose the Sa**v**e As selection in the **F**ile option. Save the C++ programs with a .CPP extension. The Save As dialog box allows you to select the drive and/ or directory to store the new program.

5. Close the currently edited window using the **C**lose selection in the **F**ile option.

6. Choose the **N**ew selection in the **P**roject option to pop up the project dialog box.

7. Enter the name of the project (use the same name as the .CPP file) and select the QuickWin application (.EXE) item from the Project Type list box. Click on the OK button when you are finished.

8. The Workbench displays the Edit dialog box which allows you to select the file or files that make up a project. The dialog box includes controls for selecting another drive and/or another directory. Use these controls to locate the program you just entered. To add a file to the list of project files, either double-click on that file or select it and then click on the Add button. To remove a file from the list of project files, select that file and click on the Delete button. When you have finished selecting files, click on the Close button.

9. Invoke the **B**uild selection in the **P**roject option. This step compiles and links your program.

10. Choose the E**x**ecute selection in the **P**roject option to run the program. The output appears in a QuickWin window which has the title of the project name.

To view the project files, click on the left icon in the toolbar. This action causes the Workbench to display all your files that make up the project. Double-click on the file you want to view and/or edit.

Note: The programs in this book are located in the directory \MSVC\VC21DAY. Please create the subdirectory VC21DAY and attach it to directory \MSVC.

Your First C++ Program

The first C++ program that I present displays a one-line greeting message. This simple program enables you to see the very basic components of a C++ program.

Listing 1.1 contains the source code for program HELLO.CPP with numbered lines. Do *not* enter the line numbers when you type in the program. These line numbers serve as reference only. The trivial program displays the string `"Hello Programmer!"`. Carry out the following steps to create and run the first C++ program:

1. Load the Visual C++ Workbench, if not already loaded.

2. Pick the **N**ew selection in the **F**ile option.

3. Enter in the new window the program found in Listing 1.1.

4. Choose the Sa**v**e As selection in the **F**ile option. Save the C++ programs as HELLO.CPP in directory \MSVC\VC21DAY.

5. Close the currently edited window, using the **C**lose selection in the **F**ile option.

6. Invoke the **N**ew selection in the **P**roject option. This step pops up the dialog box shown in Figure 1.5.

7. Enter `hello` as the name of the project and select the QuickWin application (.EXE) item from the Project Type list box. Click on the OK button.

8. The Workbench displays the Edit dialog box, shown in Figure 1.6. Select the HELLO.CPP file in directory \MSVC\VC21DAY and double-click on that file.

9. Invoke the **B**uild selection in the **P**roject option to compile and link the HELLO.CPP program.

10. Choose the E**x**ecute selection in the Project option to run the HELLO.EXE program.

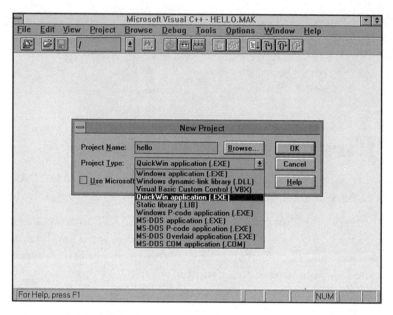

Figure 1.5. The New Project dialog box.

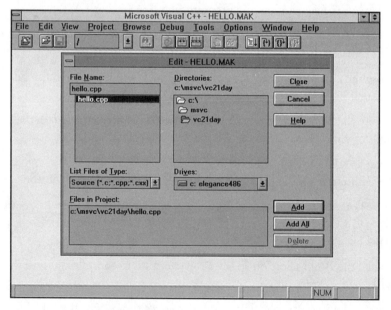

Figure 1.6. The Edit dialog box.

Listing 1.1. Source code for the program HELLO.CPP.

```
1: // a trivial C++ program that says hello
2:
3: #include <iostream.h>
4:
5: main()
6: {
7:    cout << "Hello Programmer!";
8:    return 0;
9: }
```

The output of the program appears in Figure 1.7. Notice that the status bar of the output window has the word Finished to indicate that the program has terminated.

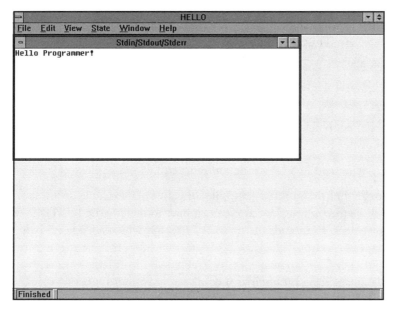

Figure 1.7. The output of the HELLO.EXE program.

 Examine the short code of the C++ program and notice the following characteristics:

☐ C++ uses the `//` characters for comments that run to the end of the line. C++ also supports the C-style comments that begin with the `/*` characters and end with the `*/` characters. Line number 1 contains a comment that briefly describes the program.

NEW☛ TERM *Comments* are remarks that you put in the program to explain or clarify certain parts of the program. The compiler ignores comments.

☐ The C++ program has no reserved keywords which declare the end of a program. In fact, C++ uses a rather simple scheme for organizing a program. This scheme supports two levels of code: global and single-level functions. In addition, the function `main`, which starts in line 5, plays a very special role because run-time execution begins with this function. Therefore, there can be only a single function `main` in a C++ program. You can place the function `main` anywhere in the code.

☐ The C++ strings and characters are enclosed in double and single quotes, respectively. Thus, `'A'` is a single character whereas `"A"` is a single-character string. Mixing C++ single-character strings and characters is not allowed.

NEW☛ TERM Strings can have any number of characters, including no characters—the *empty string*.

☐ C++ defines blocks using the `{` and `}` characters (see examples in lines 6 and 9, respectively).

☐ Every statement in a C++ program must end with a semicolon (`;`).

☐ C++ contains the `#include` compiler directive. An example of this is in line 3, instructing the Visual C++ compiler to include the IOSTREAM.H header file. C++ extends the notion of streams, which already exists in C. IOSTREAM.H provides the operations that support basic stream input and output. The C++ language does not include built-in I/O routines. Instead, the language relies on libraries specializing in various types of I/O.

NEW☛ TERM A *compiler directive* is a special instruction for the compiler. A *header file* contains the declarations of constants, data types, variables, and forward (early) declarations of functions. A *stream* is a sequence of data flowing from part of a computer to another.

☐ The C++ program outputs the string `"Hello Programmer!"` to the standard output stream `cout`, which is the QuickWin window. In addition, the program uses the extractor operator, `<<`, to send the emitted string to the output stream.

☐ The function main must return a value that reflects the error status of the C++ program. Returning the value 0 signals to the operating system that the program terminated normally.

Exiting the Workbench

To exit the workbench, close the current project (using the Close selections in the Project option) and choose the Exit selection in the File option.

Summary

Today's lesson introduces you to the Visual C++ Workbench and presents you with the first C++ program. You learn these basics:

☐ C++ programs are modular and rely on standard and/or custom libraries.

☐ The two ways to load the Visual C++ Workbench are clicking on the Visual C++ icon or double-clicking on the MSVC.EXE file when using the File Manager (or any similar utility).

☐ The Visual C++ Workbench is a versatile environment for developing, maintaining, and debugging C and C++ programs and libraries for MS-DOS and Windows applications.

☐ The File option allows you to manage files, print text, and exit the Workbench.

☐ The Edit option permits you to undo text changes, manage text (cut, paste, copy, and delete), search for text, and replace text.

☐ The View option allows you to view compiler errors, manage bookmarks, toggle the status bar, and toggle the toolbar.

☐ The Project option enables you to manage programs by compiling source files, building projects, running programs, managing workspaces, and managing the dependencies of files.

☐ The Browse option permits you to locate the definition and references of a name.

☐ The Debug option offers choices that allow you to manage breakpoints in source files, single-step program execution, and watch variables.

☐ The Tools option invokes utilities that assist in developing, managing, and maintaining programs.

☐ The Options option fine-tunes projects, directories, the editor, syntax color, fonts, tools, the workspaces, and the debugger.

☐ The Window option allows you to manage windows and open special windows.

☐ The Help option provides versatile online help on a variety of topics, such as the Workbench, the C/C++ language, and the MFC library.

☐ The QuickWin applications are Windows applications providing special windows that act as standard input and output devices. QuickWin applications allow you to write DOS-like programs.

☐ The first C++ program is a simple greeting program that illustrates the basic components of a C++ program. These components include comments, the `#include` directive, and the `main` function.

☐ You exit the Workbench through the Exit selection in the File option.

Q&A

Q. Does C++ use line numbers?

A. No. I am using line numbers in the listings only for the sake of reference.

Q. Does the Workshop's editor monitor what I type?

A. Yes it does. In fact, when you type in a C++ keyword, the Workbench quickly colors that keyword.

Q. What happens if I forget to type the second double quote in the first program?

A. The compiler tells you that there is an error in the program. You need to add the second double quote and build the project.

Q. How do I delete text in the currently edited window?

A. Use the Replace selection in the Edit option and specify nothing for the replacement string.

Workshop

The Workshop provides quiz questions to help you solidify your understanding of the material covered and exercises to provide you with experience in using what you've learned. Try to understand the quiz and exercise answers before continuing on to the next day's lesson. Answers are provided in Appendix B, "Answers."

Quiz

1. What is the output of the following program?

```
1: // quiz program #1
2:
3: #include <iostream.h>
4:
5: main()
6: {
7:   cout << "C++ in 21 Days?";
8:   return 0;
9: }
```

2. What is the output of the following program?

```
1: // quiz program #2
2:
3: #include <iostream.h>
4:
5: main()
6: {
7:   // cout << "C++ in 21 Days?";
8:   return 0;
9: }
```

3. What is wrong with the following program?

```
1: // quiz program #3
2:
3: #include <iostream.h>
4:
5: main()
```

```
6: {
7:    cout << "C++ in 21 Days?"
8:    return 0;
9: }
```

Exercise

Write a program that displays the message I am a C++ Programmer.

DAY
2

C++ Program Components

Day 1 presents the Visual C++ Workbench and a simple C++ program. Today we focus on the basic components of C++ programs, including data types, variables, constants, and functions. You learn about the following topics:

☐ The predefined data types in Visual C++

☐ Naming items in Visual C++

☐ The #include directive

☐ Declaring variables

☐ Declaring constants

☐ Declaring and prototyping functions

☐ Local variables in functions

☐ Static variables in functions

☐ Inline functions

☐ Exiting functions

☐ Default arguments

☐ Function overloading

Predefined Data Types in Visual C++

Visual C++ offers the int, char, float, double, and void data types to represent integers, characters, single-precision floating-point numbers, double-precision floating point numbers, and valueless data, respectively. C++ uses the void type with a function's returned values to indicate that the function acts as a procedure.

C++ adds more flexibility to data types by supporting data type modifiers. The type modifiers are: signed, unsigned, short, and long. Table 2.1 shows the predefined data types in C++ (and includes the type modifiers) along with their sizes and ranges. Notice that the int and unsigned int are system-dependent. The table shows the 16-bit values for these data types.

NEW☞ TERM *Data type modifiers* alter the precision and the range of values.

Table 2.1. Predefined data types in C++.

Data Type	Byte Size	Range	Examples
char	1	–128 to 127	'A','!'
signed char	1	–128 to 127	23
unsigned char	1	0 to 255	200,0x1a
int	2	Depends on system –32768 to 32767 for 16-bit	3000
unsigned int	2	Depends on system 0 to 65535 for 16-bit	0xffff, 65535
short int	2	–32768 to 32767	100
unsigned short int	2	0 to 65535	0xff, 40000
long int	4	–2147483648 to 2147483647	0xfffff -123456,
unsigned long int	4	0 to 4294967295	123456
float	4	3.4E–38 to 3.4E+38 and –3.4E–38 to –3.4E+38	2.35, -52.354, 1.3e+10
double	8	1.7E–308 to 1.7E+308 and –1.7E–308 to –1.7E+308	12.354 -2.5e+100 -78.32544
long double	10	1.2E-4932 to 1.2E+4932 and –1.2E–4932 to –1.2E+4932	8.5e-3000

NEW☞ TERM   C++ supports *hexadecimal numbers.* Such numbers begin with the characters 0x followed by the hexadecimal value. For example, the number 0xff is the hexadecimal equivalent of the decimal number 255.

Naming Items in Visual C++

Visual C++ requires you to observe the following rules with identifiers:

1. The first character must be a letter or an underscore (_).

2. Subsequent characters can be letters, digits, or underscores.

3. The maximum length of an identifier is 247 characters.

4. Identifiers are case-sensitive in C++. Thus, the names `rate`, `RATE`, and `Rate` refer to three different identifiers.

5. Identifiers cannot be reserved words such as `int`, `double`, or `static` (to name just a few).

Here are examples of valid identifiers:

```
X
x
aString
DAYS_IN_WEEK
BinNumber0
bin_number_0
bin0Number2
_length
```

DO	DON'T
DO use descriptive names that have a reasonable length.	
DON'T use identifier names that are too short or too long. Short names yield poor readability and long names are prone to typos.	

The *#include* Directive

Recall that a directive is a special instruction for C and C++ compilers. A directive begins with the # character and is followed by the directive name. Directives are usually placed in the first column of a line. They can be preceded only by spaces or tab characters. The C++ program in Day 1 contains the #include directive. This directive tells the compiler to include the text of a file as if you have typed that text yourself. Thus, the #include directive is a better alternative than cutting text from one file and pasting in another file. Recall from Day 1 that programs use the #include directive to include header files.

The *#include* Directive

The general syntax for the #include directive is

```
#include <filename>
#include "filename"
```

Example:

```
#include <iostream.h>
#include "string.h"
```

The filename represents the name of the included file. The two forms differ in how the #include directive searches for the included file. The first form searches for the file in the special directory for included files. The second form extends the search to involve the current directory.

Declaring Variables

Declaring variables requires you to state the data type of the variable and the name of the variable. The word variable indicates that you can alter the data of these data containers.

NEW☞ TERM *Variables* are identifiers used to store and recall information. You can regard a variable as a labeled data container.

Declaring Variables

The general syntax for declaring variables is

```
type variableName;
type variableName = initialValue;
type var1 [= initVal1], var2 [= initVal2], ...;
```

Example:

```
int j;
double z = 32.314;
long fileSize, diskSize, totalFileSize = 0;
```

C++ allows you to declare a list of variables (that have the same types) in a declarative statement. For example:

```
int j, i = 2, k = 3;
double x = 3.12;
double y = 2 * x, z = 4.5, a = 45.7;
```

The initializing values may contain other variables defined earlier.

DO	DON'T
DO resist using global variables. **DON'T** declare variables, within the same program unit, with names that are different in character case (such as `rate` and `Rate`).	

Let's look at a simple example which uses variables. Listing 2.1 shows the source code for the program VAR1.CPP. The program declares four variables, two of which are initialized during their declarations. The program then assigns values to the uninitialized variables and displays the contents of all four variables. Create the project VAR1 and include the VAR1.CPP file. Build and run the VAR1.MAK project.

Type   Listing 2.1. Source code for the program VAR1.CPP.

```
 1: // C++ program that illustrates simple variables
 2:
 3: #include <iostream.h>
 4:
 5: main()
 6: {
 7:   int i, j = 2;
 8:   double x, y = 355.0 / 113;
 9:
10:   i = 3 * j;
11:   cout << "i = " << i << "\n"
12:        << "j = " << j << "\n";
13:
14:   x = 2 * y;
15:   x = x * x;
16:   cout << "y = " << y << "\n"
17:        << "x = " << x << "\n";
18:   return 0;
19:
20: }
```

Here is a sample session with the program in Listing 2.1:

```
i = 6
j = 2
y = 3.14159
x = 39.4784
```

The program uses the #include directive in line 3 to include the stream I/O header file IOSTREAM.H. The function main appears in line 5. The function contains the declarations of the int-typed variables i, j in line 7, and the double-typed variables x and y in line 8. The declarations initialize the variable j and y. The statement in line 10 multiplies the value in variable j (which is 2) by 3 and stores the result in variable x. The stream output statement in lines 11 and 12 displays the values of variables i and j. The statement includes strings that label the output.

The statement in line 14 doubles the value in variable y and stores it in variable x. The statement in line 15 squares the value in variable x and assigns the result back to variable x. This statement uses the variable x on both sides of the equal sign. The stream output statement in lines 16 and 17 displays the values in variable x and y. The statement in line 18 returns 0 as the result of function main.

Declaring Constants

Many languages such as BASIC (the more recent implementations), Modula-2, Ada, C, Pascal, and C++ support constants. No one can deny that constants enhance the readability of a program by replacing numeric constants with identifiers that are more descriptive. Moreover, using constants enables you to change the value of a program parameter by merely changing the value of that parameter in one location. This capability is certainly easier and less prone to generate errors that may occur when you employ your text editor to replace certain numbers with other numbers.

NEW☞ *Constants* are identifiers that are associated with fixed values. C++ offers
TERM constants in two flavors: *macro-based* and *formal*. The macro-based constants are inherited from C and use the #define compiler directive.

The #*define* Directive

The general syntax for the #define directive is

```
#define constantName constantValue
```

The #define directive causes the compiler to invoke the preprocessor and perform text substitution to replace the macro-based constants with their values. This text replacement step occurs before the compiler processes the statements in the source file.

Consequently, the compiler never sees the macro-based constants themselves—only what they expand to.

Examples:

```
#define ASCII_A 65
#define DAYS_IN_WEEK 7
```

The second type of constant in C++ is the formal constant.

The Formal Constant

The general syntax for the formal constant is

```
const dataType constantName = constantValue;
```

The *dataType* item is an optional item that specifies the data type of the constant values. If you omit the data type, the C++ compiler assumes the int type.

Examples:

```
const unsigned char ASCII_A = 65;
const DAYS_IN_WEEK = 7;
const char FIRST_DISK_DRIVE = 'A';
```

DO	DON'T

DO use uppercase names for constants. This naming style enables you to quickly determine if an identifier is a constant.

DON'T assume that other people who read your code will know what embedded numbers mean. Use declared constants to enhance the readability of your programs.

Using Macro-Based Constants

Let's look at an example that uses macro-based constants. Listing 2.2 shows the source code for program CONST1.CPP. The program prompts you to enter the number of hours, minutes, and seconds since midnight. The program then calculates and displays the total number of seconds since midnight. Create the project CONST1 and include the CONST1.CPP file. Build and run the CONST1.MAK project.

Listing 2.2. Source code for the program CONST1.CPP.

```
1:  // C++ program that illustrates constants
2:
3:  #include <iostream.h>
4:
5:  #define SEC_IN_MIN 60
6:  #define MIN_IN_HOUR 60
7:
8:  main()
9:  {
10:    long hours, minutes, seconds;
11:    long totalSec;
12:
13:    cout << "Enter hours: ";
14:    cin >> hours;
15:    cout << "Enter minutes: ";
16:    cin >> minutes;
17:    cout << "Enter seconds: ";
18:    cin >> seconds;
19:
20:    totalSec = ((hours * MIN_IN_HOUR + minutes) *
21:                SEC_IN_MIN) + seconds;
22:
23:    cout <<"\n\n" << totalSec << " seconds since midnight";
24:    return 0;
25: }
```

Here is a sample session with the program in Listing 2.2:

```
Enter hours: 10
Enter minutes: 0
Enter seconds: 0


36000 seconds since midnight
```

The program uses the `#include` directive in line 3 to include the header file IOSTREAM.H. Lines 5 and 6 contain the `#define` directive that declares the macro-based constants `SEC_IN_MIN` and `MIN_IN_HOUR`. Both constants have the value 60, but each value has a different meaning. The function `main` which starts at line 8 declares four `long`-typed variables: `hours`, `minutes`, `seconds`, and `totalSec`.

The function uses pairs of statements to output the prompting messages and receive input. Line 13 contains the stream output statement which prompts you for the number of hours. Line 14 contains the stream input statement. The identifier `cin` is the name of the standard input stream and uses the *insertion operator* `>>` to read data

37

from the keyboard and to store it in the variable hours. The input and output statements in lines 15 through 18 perform a similar task of prompting for input and obtaining keyboard input.

Line 20 contains a statement which calculates the total number of seconds since midnight and stores the result in variable totalSec. The statement uses the macro-based constants MIN_IN_HOUR and SEC_IN_MIN. As you can see, using these constants enhances the readability of the statement compared to using the number 60 in place of both constants. Line 23 contains a stream output statement which displays the total number of seconds since midnight (stored in variable totalSec), followed by qualifying text to clarify the output.

Using Formal Constants

Now let's look at a new version of the program, one which uses the formal C++ constants. Listing 2.3 shows the source code for program CONST2.CPP. This program works like the CONST1.CPP program. Create the project CONST2 and include the CONST2.CPP file. Build and run the CONST2.MAK project.

 Note: At this point I assume that you are familiar with the process of creating the .CPP source file and the .MAK project file. From now on I will not mention creating these files, unless there is a special set of source files in a project.

 Listing 2.3. Source code for the program CONST2.CPP.

```
1: // C++ program that illustrates constants
2:
3: #include <iostream.h>
4:
5: const SEC_IN_MIN = 60; // global constant
6:
7: main()
8: {
9:   const MIN_IN_HOUR = 60; // local constant
10:
11:   long hours, minutes, seconds;
12:   long totalSec;
13:
14:   cout << "Enter hours: ";
```

```
15:    cin >> hours;
16:    cout << "Enter minutes: ";
17:    cin >> minutes;
18:    cout << "Enter seconds: ";
19:    cin >> seconds;
20:
21:    totalSec = ((hours * MIN_IN_HOUR + minutes) *
22:                SEC_IN_MIN) + seconds;
23:
24:    cout <<"\n\n" << totalSec << " seconds since midnight";
25:    return 0;
26: }
```

2

Here is a sample session with the program in Listing 2.3:

```
Enter hours: 1
Enter minutes: 10
Enter seconds: 20


4220 seconds since midnight
```

The programs in Listings 2.2 and 2.3 are similar. The difference between them is in how they declare their constants. In Listing 2.3, I use the formal C++ constant syntax to declare the constants. In addition, I declare constant SEC_IN_MIN in line 5, outside the function main. This kind of declaration makes the constant global. That is, if there were another function in the program, it would be able to use the constant SEC_IN_MIN. By contrast, I declare the constant MIN_IN_SEC inside the function main. Thus, the constant MIN_IN_SEC is local to the function main.

Declaring and Prototyping Functions

Most programming languages use functions and procedures. C++ does not support formal procedures. Instead, all C++ routines are functions!

NEW☞
TERM
Functions are the primary building blocks that conceptually extend the C++ language to fit your custom programs.

Syntax

Declaring Functions

The general form for the ANSI C style of declaring functions (which is maintained by C++) is

```
returnType functionName(typedParameterList)
```

Examples:

```
double sqr(double y)
{ return y * y; }

char prevChar(char c)
{ return c - 1; }
```

Remember the following rules when declaring C++ functions:

1. The return type of the C++ function appears before the function's name.

2. If the parameter list is empty, you still use empty parentheses. C++ also allows you the option of using the void keyword to explicitly state that the parameter list is void.

3. The typed parameter list consists of a list of typed parameters that use the following general format:

   ```
   [const] type1 parameter1, [const] type2 parameter2, ...
   ```

   This format shows that the individual parameter is declared like a variable—you state the type first and then the parameter's identifier. The list of parameters in C++ is comma-delimited. In addition, you cannot group a sequence of parameters that have the exact same data type. You must declare each parameter explicitly. If a parameter has the const clause, the compiler makes sure that the function does *not* alter the arguments of that parameter.

4. The body of a C++ function is enclosed in braces ({}). There is no semicolon after the closing brace.

5. C++ supports passing arguments either by value or by reference. By default, parameters pass their arguments by value. Consequently, the functions work with a copy of the data, preserving the original data. To declare a reference parameter, insert the & character after the data type of the parameter. A reference parameter becomes an alias to its arguments. Any changes made to the reference parameter also affect the argument. The general form for reference parameters is

   ```
   [const] type1& parameter1, [const] type2& parameter2, ...
   ```

If a parameter has the const clause, the compiler makes sure that the function does not alter the arguments of that parameter.

6. C++ supports local constants, data types, and variables. Although these data items can appear in nested block statements, C++ does not support nested functions.

7. The return keyword returns the function's value.

8. If the function's return type is void, you do not have to use the return keyword, unless you need to provide an exit route in the middle of the function.

NEW☛
TERM C++ dictates that you either declare or define a function before you use it. Declaring a function, which is commonly called *prototyping*, lists the function name, return type, and the number and type of its parameters. Including the name of the parameter is optional. You also need to place a semicolon after the close parenthesis. C++ requires that you declare a function if you call it before you define it.

The following is a simple example of prototyping:

```
// prototype the function square
double sqr(double);

main()
{
  cout << "5^2 = " << sqr(5) << "\n";
  return 0;
}

double sqr(double z)
{ return z * z; }
```

Notice that the declaration of function sqr only contains the type of its single parameter.

Typically, the declaration of a function is global. You may still prototype a function within its client function. This technique conceals the prototype from other functions.

Calling a function requires that you supply its parameter with arguments. The arguments are mapped onto the parameter by the sequence in which the parameters are declared. The arguments must be data types that match or are compatible with those of the parameters. For example, you may have a function volume which is defined as follows:

```
double volume(double length, double width, double height)
{
  return length * width * height;
}
```

To call the function `volume` you need to supply `double`-typed arguments or arguments with compatible types (which in this case are all of numeric data types). Here are a number of sample calls to function `volume`:

```
double len = 34, width = 55, ht = 100;
int i = 3;
long j = 44;
unsigned k = 33;

cout << volume(len, width, ht) << "\n";
cout << volume(1, 2, 3) << "\n";
cout << volume(i, j, k) << "\n";
cout << volume(len, j, 22.3) << "\n";
```

> **Note:** C++ allows you to discard the result of a function. This kind of function call is used when the focus is on what the function does rather than its return value.

Local Variables in Functions

Sound structured programming techniques foster the notion that functions should be as independent and as reusable as possible. Consequently, functions can have their own data types, constants, and variables to give them this independence.

NEW TERM The *local variable* in a function exists only when the host function is called. Once the function terminates, the run-time system removes the local variables. Consequently, local variables lose their data between function calls. In addition, the run-time system applies any initialization to local variables every time the host function is called.

DO	DON'T

DO use local variables to store and alter the values of parameters that are declared with the `const` clause.

DON'T declare a local variable to have the same name of a global variable which you need to access in the function.

Let's look at an example. Listing 2.4 displays the value of the following mathematical function:

$$f(X) = X^2 - 5 X + 10$$

and its slope at the argument 3.5. The program calculates the slope using the following approximation:

$$f'(X) = (f(X + h) - f(X - h)) / 2h$$

where h is a small increment.

Type **Listing 2.4. Source code for the program VAR2.CPP.**

```
 1: // C++ program that illustrates local variables in a function
 2:
 3: #include <iostream.h>
 4:
 5: double f(double x)
 6: {
 7:   return x * x - 5 * x + 10;
 8: }
 9:
10: double slope(double x)
11: {
12:   double f1, f2, incrim = 0.01 * x;
13:   f1 = f(x + incrim);
14:   f2 = f(x - incrim);
15:   return (f1 - f2) / 2 / incrim;
16: }
17:
18: main()
19: {
20:   double x = 3.5;
21:
22:   cout << "f(" << x << ") = " << f(x) << "\n"
23:        << "f'(" << x << ") = " << slope(x) << "\n";
24:
25:   return 0;
26: }
```

Here is a sample session with the program in Listing 2.4:

```
f(3.5) = 4.75
f'(3.5) = 2
```

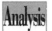 The program in Listing 2.4 declares three functions, namely f (in line 5), slope (in line 10), and main (in line 18). The function f is simple and returns the value of the mathematical function. The function f is void of local variables. By contrast, the function slope declares the local variables f1, f2, and incrim. This function also initializes the latter variable. Line 13 assigns the value of f(x + incrim) to the local variable f1. Line 14 assigns the value of f(x - incrim) to the local variable f2. Line 15 returns the value for function slope using the local variables f1, f2, and incrim. The function main simply displays the values of the mathematical function and its slope when x = 3.5.

Static Variables in Functions

In Listing 2.4, the local variables in function slope lose their values once the function terminates. C++ allows you to declare a local variable as static by simply placing the static keyword to the left of its data type. Static variables are usually initialized. This initialization is performed once, when the host function is called the first time.

NEW☞ TERM There are a number of programming techniques that require maintaining the values of local variables between function calls. These special local variables are called *static variables*.

When the host function terminates, the static variables maintain their values. The compiler supports this language feature by storing static variables in a separate memory location that is maintained while the program is running. You can use the same names for static variables in different functions. This duplication does not confuse the compiler because it keeps track of which function owns which static variables.

Let's look at a simple program. Listing 2.5 uses a function with static variables to maintain a moving average. The program supplies its own data and calls that function several times to obtain and display the current value of the moving average.

 Listing 2.5. Source code for the program STATIC1.CPP.

```
1: // C++ program that illustrates static local variables
2:
3: #include <iostream.h>
4:
5: double mean(double x)
6: {
7:   static double sum = 0;
8:   static double sumx = 0;
```

```
 9:
10:    sum = sum + 1;
11:    sumx = sumx + x;
12:    return sumx / sum;
13: }
14:
15: main()
16: {
17:    cout << "mean = " << mean(1) << "\n";
18:    cout << "mean = " << mean(2) << "\n";
19:    cout << "mean = " << mean(4) << "\n";
20:    cout << "mean = " << mean(10) << "\n";
21:    cout << "mean = " << mean(11) << "\n";
22:    return 0;
23: }
```

Here is a sample session with the program in Listing 2.5:

```
mean = 1
mean = 1.5
mean = 2.33333
mean = 4.25
mean = 5.6
```

 The program in Listing 2.5 declares the function mean which contains static local variables. Lines 7 and 8 declare the static variables sum and sumx, respectively. The function initializes both static variables with 0. The statement in line 10 increments the variable sum by 1. The statement in line 11 increments the variable sumx by the value of parameter x. Line 12 returns the updated moving average, obtained by dividing sumx by sum.

The function main issues a series of calls to function mean. The stream output statements in lines 17 through 21 display the updated moving average. These results are possible thanks to the static local variables sum and sumx in function mean. If static variables are not supported by C++, you must resort to using global variables—a highly questioned programming choice!

Inline Functions

Using functions requires the overhead of calling them, passing their arguments, and returning their results. C++ allows you to use inline functions that expand into their statements. Thus, inline functions offer faster execution speed—especially where speed is critical—at the cost of expanding the code.

The *inline* Function

The general syntax for the `inline` function is

```
inline returnType functionName(typedParameterList)
```

Examples:

```
inline double cube(double x)
{ return x * x * x; }

inline char nextChar(char c)
{ return c + 1; }
```

The alternative to using inline functions is the use of the `#define` directive to create macro-based pseudofunctions. Many C++ programmers (including me) strongly recommend abandoning this method in favor of inline functions. The justification for this inclination is that inline functions provide type checking. Macros created with the `#define` directive do not.

DO	DON'T

DO start by declaring inline functions as ordinary functions when you develop your programs. Non-inline functions are easier to debug. Once your program is working, insert the inline keyword where needed.

DON'T declare inline functions with too many statements. The increase in .EXE program size may not be acceptable.

Here is a simple example of a program that uses inline functions. Listing 2.6 contains the source code for program INLINE1.CPP. The program prompts you for a number. Then the program calculates and displays the square and cube values for your input.

Type

Listing 2.6. Source code for the program INLINE1.CPP.

```
 1: // C++ program that illustrates inline functions
 2:
 3: #include <iostream.h>
 4:
 5: inline double sqr(double x)
 6: {
 7:    return x * x;
 8: }
 9:
10: inline double cube(double x)
```

```
11: {
12:    return x * x * x;
13: }
14:
15: main()
16: {
17:    double x;
18:
19:    cout << "Enter a number: ";
20:    cin >> x;
21:
22:    cout << "square of "  << x << " = " << sqr(x) << "\n"
23:         << "cube of " << x << " = " << cube(x) << "\n";
24:
25:    return 0;
26: }
```

2

Here is a sample session with the program in Listing 2.6:

```
Enter a number: 2.5
square of 2.5 = 6.25
cube of 2.5 = 15.625
```

The program in Listing 2.6 declares the inline functions sqr and cube. Each function heading starts with the keyword inline. The other aspects of the inline functions resemble short normal functions. The function main calls the function sqr and cube to display the square and cube values, respectively.

Exiting Functions

Usually you make an early exit from a function because particular conditions do not allow you to proceed with executing the statements in that function. C++ provides the return statement to exit from a function. If the function has the void type then you employ the statement return and include no expression after the return. By contrast, if you exit a non-void function, the return statement should produce a value that indicates the purpose for exiting the function.

Default Arguments

Default arguments are a language feature that is quite simple and yet very powerful. When you omit the argument of a parameter that has a default argument, that argument is automatically used.

**NEW☞
TERM** C++ permits you to assign *default arguments* to the parameters of a function.

Using default arguments requires that you follow these rules:

1. Once you assign a default argument to a parameter, you must do so for all subsequent parameters in the same parameter list. You cannot randomly assign default arguments to parameters. This rule means that the parameter list can be divided into two sublists: the leading parameters which do not have default arguments, and the trailing parameters which do.

2. You must provide an argument for every parameter that has no default argument.

3. You may omit the argument for a parameter that has a default argument.

4. Once you omit the argument for a parameter with a default argument, the arguments for all subsequent parameters must also be omitted.

> **Note:** The best way to list the parameters with default arguments is to locate them according to the likelihood of using their default arguments. Place the least likely used arguments first and the most likely used arguments last.

Let's look at a simple example which uses a function with default arguments. Listing 2.7 shows the source code for program DEFARGS1.CPP. The program prompts you to enter the X and Y coordinates of two points. Then the program calculates and displays the distance between the two points and between each point and the origin (0, 0).

Type **Listing 2.7. Source code for the program DEFARGS1.CPP.**

```
1: // C++ program that illustrates default arguments
2:
3: #include <iostream.h>
4: #include <math.h>
5:
6: inline double sqr(double x)
7: { return x * x; }
8:
9: double distance(double x2, double y2,
10:                 double x1 = 0, double y1 = 0)
```

```
11: {
12:    return sqrt(sqr(x2 - x1) + sqr(y2 - y1));
13: }
14:
15: main()
16: {
17:    double x1, y1, x2, y2;
18:
19:    cout << "Enter x coordinate for point 1: ";
20:    cin >> x1;
21:    cout << "Enter y coordinate for point 1: ";
22:    cin >> y1;
23:    cout << "Enter x coordinate for point 2: ";
24:    cin >> x2;
25:    cout << "Enter y coordinate for point 2: ";
26:    cin >> y2;
27:
28:    cout << "distance between points = "
29:         << distance(x1, y1, x2, y2) << "\n";
30:    cout << "distance between point 1 and (0,0) = "
31:         << distance(x1, y1, 0) << "\n";
32:    cout << "distance between point 2 and (0,0) = "
33:         << distance(x2, y2) << "\n";
34:
35:    return 0;
36: }
```

Here is a sample session with the program in Listing 2.7:

```
Enter x coordinate for point 1: 1
Enter y coordinate for point 1: 1
Enter x coordinate for point 2: -1
Enter y coordinate for point 2: 1
distance between points = 2
distance between point 1 and (0,0) = 1.41421
distance between point 2 and (0,0) = 1.41421
```

The program in Listing 2.7 includes not one but two header files. Line 4 uses the #include directive to include the MATH.H header file which declares the square root math function, sqrt. The program declares the inline sqr function in line 6. This function returns the square value of the arguments for parameter x. The program also declares the function distance with four double-typed parameters. The parameters x2 and y2 represent the X and Y coordinates, respectively, for the second point, whereas the parameters x1 and y1 represent the X and Y coordinates, respectively, for the first point. Both parameters x1 and y1 have the default argument of 0. The function returns the distance between the two points. If you omit the arguments for x1 and y1, the function returns the distance between the point (x2, y2) and the origin (0, 0). If you omit only the argument for the last parameter, the function yields the distance between the points (x2, y2) and (x1, 0).

The function main prompts you to enter the X and Y coordinates for two points, using the statements in lines 19 through 26. The output statement in lines 28 and 29 calls the function distance, providing it with four arguments, namely, x1, y1, x2, and y2. Therefore, this call to function distance uses no default arguments. By contrast, the statement in lines 30 and 31 calls function distance, supplying it with only three arguments. This call to function distance uses the default argument for the last parameter. The statement in lines 32 and 33 calls function distance, providing it with only two arguments. This call to function distance uses the two default arguments for the third and fourth parameters. I can omit the third argument in the second call to function distance and still compile and run the program.

Function Overloading

Function overloading is a language feature in C++ that has no parallel in either C, Pascal, or BASIC. This new feature enables you to declare multiple functions that have the same name but different parameter lists. The function's return type is not part of the function signature, because C++ allows you to discard the result type. Consequently, the compiler is not able to distinguish between two functions with the same parameters and different return type, when these return types are omitted.

 NEW TERM　A parameter list is also called the *function signature*.

 Warning: Using default arguments with overloaded functions may duplicate the signature for some of the functions (when the default arguments are used). The C++ compiler is able to detect this ambiguity and generate a compile-time error.

DO	DON'T

DO use default arguments to reduce the number of overloaded functions.

DON'T use overloaded functions to implement different operations.

Let's look at a simple program that uses overloaded functions. Listing 2.8 contains the source code for program OVERLOAD.CPP. The program performs the following tasks:

☐ Declares variables that have the char, int, and double types, and initializes them with values

☐ Displays the initial values

☐ Invokes overloaded functions that increment the variables

☐ Displays the updated values stored in the variables

2

Type **Listing 2.8. Source code for the program OVERLOAD.CPP.**

```
1:  // C++ program that illustrates function overloading
2:
3:  #include <iostream.h>
4:
5:  // inc version for int types
6:  void inc(int& i)
7:  {
8:    i = i + 1;
9:  }
10:
11: // inc version for double types
12: void inc(double& x)
13: {
14:   x = x + 1;
15: }
16:
17: // inc version for char types
18: void inc(char& c)
19: {
20:   c = c + 1;
21: }
22:
23: main()
24: {
25:   char c = 'A';
26:   int i = 10;
27:   double x = 10.2;
28:
29:   // display initial values
30:   cout << "c = " << c << "\n"
31:        << "i = " << i << "\n"
32:        << "x = " << x << "\n";
33:   // invoke the inc functions
```

continues

51

Listing 2.8. continued

```
34:     inc(c);
35:     inc(i);
36:     inc(x);
37:     // display updated values
38:     cout << "After using the overloaded inc function\n";
39:     cout << "c = " << c << "\n"
40:          << "i = " << i << "\n"
41:          << "x = " << x << "\n";
42:
43:     return 0;
44: }
```

Here is a sample session with the program in Listing 2.8:

```
c = A
i = 10
x = 10.2
After using the overloaded inc function
c = B
i = 11
x = 11.2
```

The program in Listing 2.8 declares three versions of the overloaded void function inc. The first version of function inc has an int-typed reference parameter, i. The function increments the parameter i by 1. Because the parameter i is a reference to its arguments, the action of function inc(int&) affects the argument outside the scope of the function. The second version of function inc has a double-typed reference parameter, x. The function increments the parameter x by 1. Because the parameter x is a reference to its arguments, the action of function inc(double&) affects the argument beyond the scope of the function. The second version of function inc has a char-typed reference parameter, c. The function increments the parameter c by 1. The reference parameter affects its arguments outside the scope of the function.

The function main declares the variables c, i, and x to have the char, int, and double types, respectively. The function also initializes the variables c, i, and x using the values 'A', 10, and 10.2, respectively. The statement in lines 30 through 32 displays the initial values in variables c, i, and x. The function main invokes the overloaded function inc in lines 34 through 36. The call to function inc in line 34 ends up calling the function inc(char&) because the argument used is a char-typed variable. The call to function inc in line 35 results in calling the function inc(int&) because the argument used is an int-typed variable. The call to function inc in line 36 invokes the function inc(double&) because the argument used is a double-typed variable. The output statement in lines 39 through 41 displays the updated values in variable c, i, and x.

Summary

Today's lesson presents the basic components of C++ programs. These components include data types, variables, constants, and functions. You learn these basics:

☐ The predefined data types in Visual C++ include the int, char, float, double, and void data types. C++ adds more flexibility to data types by supporting data type modifiers. These modifiers alter the precision and the range of values. The type modifiers are: signed, unsigned, short, and long.

☐ Visual C++ identifiers can be up to 247 characters long and must begin with a letter or an underscore. The subsequent characters of an identifier may be a letter, digit, or underscore. C++ identifiers are case-sensitive.

☐ The #include directive is a special instruction to the compiler. The directive tells the compiler to include the contents of the specified file as though you typed it in the currently scanned source file.

☐ Declaring variables requires you to state the data type of the variable and the name of the variable. C++ allows you to initialize a variable when you declare it. You can declare multiple variables in a single declarative statement.

☐ Declaring constants involves using the #define directive to declare macro-based constants, or using the const keyword to declare formal constants. The formal constants require that you specify the constant's type (the default is int, when omitted), the name of the constants, and the associated value.

☐ The general form for defining functions is

```
returnType functionName(parameterList)
{
    <declarations of data items>

    <function body>
    return returnValue;
```

You need to prototype a function if it is used by a client function before the prototyped function is defined. The general form for prototyping functions is

```
returnType functionName(parameterList);
```

You can omit the name of the parameters from the parameter list.

☐ Local variables in a function support the implementation of highly independent functions. Declaring local variables is similar to declaring global variables.

☐ Static variables in functions are declared by placing the keyword `static` before the data type of the variables. Static variables retain their values between function calls. In most cases, you need to initialize static variables. These initial values are assigned to the static variables the first time the program calls the host function.

☐ Inline functions allow you to expand their statements in place, like macro-based pseudofunctions. However, unlike these pseudofunctions, inline functions perform type checking.

☐ You exit functions with the `return` statement. Void functions do not need to include an expression after the `return` keyword.

☐ Default arguments allow you to assign default values to the parameters of a function. When you omit the argument of a parameter that has a default argument, that argument is automatically used.

☐ Function overloading enables you to declare multiple functions that have the same name but different parameter lists (also called the function signature). The function's return type is not part of the function signature, because C++ allows you to discard the result type.

Q&A

Q. Is there a specific style for naming identifiers?

A. There are a few styles that have become popular in recent years. The one I use has the identifier begin with a lowercase character. If the identifier contains multiple words, such as `numberOfElements`, make the first character of each subsequent word an uppercase letter.

Q. Can C++ functions declare nested functions?

A. No. Nested functions actually add a lot of overhead at run-time.

Q. When can I use static global variables?

A. Never! Global variables need not be declared static, because they exist for the entire program's lifetime.

Workshop

The Workshop provides quiz questions to help you solidify your understanding of the material covered and exercises to provide you with experience in using what you've learned. Try to understand the quiz and exercise answers before continuing on to the next day's lesson. Answers are provided in Appendix B, "Answers."

Quiz

1. Which of the following variables is valid and which is not (and why)?

   ```
   numFiles
   n0Distance_02_Line
   0Weight
   Bin Number
   static
   Static
   ```

2. What is the output of the following program? What can you say about the function swap?

   ```
   #include <iostream.h>

   void swap(int i, int j)
   {
     int temp = i;
     i = j;
     j = temp;
   }
   ```

```
main()
{
  int a = 10, b = 3;
  swap(a, b);
  cout << "a = " << a << " and b = " << b;
  return 0;
}
```

3. What is the output of the following program? What can you say about the function swap?

```
#include <iostream.h>

void swap(int& i, int& j)
{
  int temp = i;
  i = j;
  j = temp;
}

main()
{
  int a = 10, b = 3;
  swap(a, b);
  cout << "a = " << a << " and b = " << b;
  return 0;
}
```

4. What is the problem with the following overloaded functions?

```
void inc(int& i)
{
  i = i + 1;
}

void inc(int& i, int diff = 1)
{
  i = i + diff;
}
```

5. Where is the error in the following function?

```
double volume(double length, double width = 1, double
height)
{
  return length * width * height
}
```

6. Where is the error in the following function?

```
void inc(int& i, int diff = 1)
{
  i = I + diff;
}
```

7. What is the error in the following program, and how can you correct it?

```
#include <iostream.h>

main()
{
  double x = 5.2;

  cout << x << "^2 = " << sqr(x);
  return 0;
}

double sqr(double x)
{ return x * x ; }
```

Exercise

Create the program OVERLOD2.CPP by adding a second parameter with default arguments to the overloaded inc functions in program OVERLOAD.CPP. The new parameter should represent the increment value, with a default argument of 1.

DAY
3

Operators and
Expressions

The manipulation of data involves expressions that are made up of operands and operators. C++ supports several kinds of operators and expressions.

NEW☞
TERM   *Operators* are special symbols that take the values of *operands* and produce a new value.

Each category of operators manipulates data in a specific way. Today you learn about the following topics:

- ☐ Arithmetic operators and expressions

- ☐ Increment operators

- ☐ Arithmetic assignment operators

- ☐ Typecasting and data conversion

- ☐ Relational operators and conditional expressions

- ☐ Bit-manipulating operators

- ☐ The comma operator

Arithmetic Operators

Table 3.1 shows the C++ arithmetic operators. The compiler carries out floating-point or integer division depending on the operands. If both operands are integer expressions, the compiler yields the code for an integer division. If either or both operands are floating-point expressions, the compiler generates code for floating-point division.

Table 3.1. C++ arithmetic operators.

C++ Operator	Purpose	Data Type	Example
+	Unary plus	Numeric	x = +y + 3;
-	Unary minus	Numeric	x = -y;
+	Add	Numeric	z = y + x;
-	Subtract	Numeric	z = y - x;
*	Multiply	Numeric	z = y * x;
/	Divide	Numeric	z = y / x;
%	Modulus	Integers	z = y % x;

Let's look at an example that uses the mathematical operators with integers and floating-point numbers. Listing 3.1 shows the source code for program OPER1.CPP. The program performs the following tasks:

☐ Prompts you to enter two integers (one integer per prompt)

☐ Applies the +, -, *, /, and % operators to the two integers, storing the results in separate variables

☐ Displays the result of the integer operations

☐ Prompts you to enter two floating-point numbers (one number per prompt)

☐ Applies the +, -, *, and / operators to the two numbers, storing the results in separate variables

☐ Displays the result of the floating-point operations

3

Type **Listing 3.1. Source code for the program OPER1.CPP.**

```
1:  // simple C++ program to illustrate simple math operations
2:
3:  #include <iostream.h>
4:
5:  main()
6:  {
7:
8:      int int1, int2;
9:      long long1, long2, long3, long4, long5;
10:     float x, y, real1, real2, real3, real4;
11:
12:     cout << "\nType first  integer : ";
13:     cin >> int1;
14:     cout << "Type second integer : ";
15:     cin >> int2;
16:     cout << "\n";
17:     long1 = int1 + int2;
18:     long2 = int1 - int2;
19:     long3 = int1 * int2;
20:     long4 = int1 / int2;
21:     long5 = int1 % int2;
22:     cout << int1 << " + " << int2 << " = " << long1 << '\n';
23:     cout << int1 << " - " << int2 << " = " << long2 << '\n';
24:     cout << int1 << " * " << int2 << " = " << long3 << '\n';
25:     cout << int1 << " / " << int2 << " = " << long4 << '\n';
26:     cout << int1 << " mod " << int2 << " = " << long5 << '\n';
27:     cout << "\n\n";
28:     cout << "Type first  real number : ";
```

continues

Listing 3.1. continued

```
29:     cin >> x;
30:     cout << "Type second real number : ";
31:     cin >> y;
32:     cout << "\n";
33:     real1 = x + y;
34:     real2 = x - y;
35:     real3 = x * y;
36:     real4 = x / y;
37:     cout << x << " + " << y << " = " << real1 << '\n';
38:     cout << x << " - " << y << " = " << real2 << '\n';
39:     cout << x << " * " << y << " = " << real3 << '\n';
40:     cout << x << " / " << y << " = " << real4 << '\n';
41:     cout << "\n\n";
42:     return 0;
43: }
```

Here is a sample session with the program in Listing 3.1:

```
Type first  integer : 10
Type second integer : 5

10 + 5 = 15
10 - 5 = 5
10 * 5 = 50
10 / 5 = 2
10 mod 5 = 0


Type first  real number : 1.25
Type second real number : 2.58

1.25 + 2.58 = 3.83
1.25 - 2.58 = -1.33
1.25 * 2.58 = 3.225
1.25 / 2.58 = 0.484496
```

The program in Listing 3.1 declares a set of int-typed, long-typed, and float-typed variables in the function main. Some of these variables store your input and others store the results of the mathematical operations. The output statement in line 12 prompts you to enter the first integer. The input statement in line 13 obtains your input and stores it in the variable int1. Lines 14 and 15 perform a similar operation to prompt you for the second integer and store it in variable int2.

The program performs the integer math operation in lines 17 through 21 and stores the results of these operations in variables long1 though long5. I declared these variables as long-typed to guard against possible numeric overflow. The output statements in lines 22 through 26 display the integer operands, the operators used, and the results.

The output statement in line 28 prompts you to enter the first floating-point number. The input statement in line 29 obtains your input and stores it in the variable x. Lines 30 and 31 perform a similar operation to prompt you for the second floating-point number and to store it in variable y.

NEW☞ TERM   A floating-point number is also known as a *real number*.

The program performs the floating-point math operation in lines 33 through 36 and stores the results of these operations in variables real1 though real4. The output statements in lines 37 through 40 display the operands, the operators used, and the results.

Arithmetic Expressions

The simplest kinds of expressions are the ones that contain literals, such as

```
-12
34.45
'A'
"Hello"
```

NEW☞ TERM   In general terms, an *arithmetic expression* is part of a program statement which contains a value.

The literal constants -12 and 35.45 are the simplest arithmetic expressions. The next level of arithmetic expressions includes single variables or constants, such as

```
DAYS_IN_WEEK // a constant
i
x
```

The next level of arithmetic expressions contains a single operator with numbers, constants, and variables as operands. Here are a few examples:

```
355 / 113
4 * i
45.67 + x
```

More advanced arithmetic expressions contain multiple operators, parentheses, and even functions, such as

```
(355 / 113) * square(radius)
PIE * square(radius)
(((2 * x - 3) * x + 2) * x - 5
(1 + x) / (3 - x)
```

I discuss the order of executing the operators at the end of today's lesson, after introducing the other types of operators.

Increment Operators

C++ supports the special increment and decrement operators.

Increment (++) and *decrement* (- -) *operators* allow you to increment and decrement, respectively, by one the value stored in a variable.

Increment Operators

The general syntax for the increment operators is

```
variable++  // post-increment
++variable  // pre-increment
```

Example:

```
lineNumber++;
++index;
```

Decrement Operators

The general syntax for the decrement operators is

```
variable--  // post-decrement
--variable  // pre-decrement
```

Example:

```
lineNumber--;
--index
```

This general syntax demonstrates that there are two ways to apply the ++ and - - operators. Placing these operators to the left of their operand changes the value of the operand *before* the operand contributes its value in an expression. Likewise, placing these operators to the right of their operands alters the value of the operand *after* the operand contributes its value in an expression. If the ++ or - - operators are the only operators in a statement, there is no practical distinction between using the pre- or post- forms.

Here are a few simple examples:

```
int n, m, t = 5;

t++; // t is now 6, same effect as ++t
--t; // t is now 5, same effect as t--
t = 5;
n = 4 * t++; // t is now 6 and m is 20
t = 5;
m = 4 * ++m; // t is now 6 and m is 24
```

The first statement uses the post-increment ++ operator to increment the value of variable t. If you write ++t instead, you get the same result once the statement finishes executing. The second statement uses the pre-decrement - - operator. Again, if I write t - - instead, I get the same result. The next two statements assign 5 to variable t and then use the post-increment ++ operator in a simple math expression. This statement multiplies 4 by the current value of t (that is, 5), assigns the result of 20 to the variable n, and then increments the values in variable t to 6. The last two statements show a different outcome. The statement first increments the value in variable t (the value in variable t becomes 6), then performs the multiplication, and finally assigns the result of 24 to the variable m.

Let's look at a simple program that illustrates the feature of the increment operator. Listing 3.2 shows the source code for program OPER2.CPP. The program requires no input from you. It simply displays two integers whose values were obtained using the increment operator.

3

Listing 3.2. Source code for the program OPER2.CPP.

```
 1: /*
 2:    C++ program to illustrate the feature of the increment operator.
 3:    The ++ or -- may be included in an expression.  The value
 4:    of the associated variable is altered after the expression
 5:    is evaluated if the var++ (or var--) is used, or before
 6:    when ++var (or --var) is used.
 7: */
 8:
 9: #include <iostream.h>
10:
11: main()
12: {
13:    int i, k = 5;
14:
15:    // use post-incrementing
16:    i = 10 * (k++); // k contributes 5 to the expression
17:    cout << "i = " << i << "\n\n"; // displays 50 (= 10 * 5)
18:
19:    k--; // restores the value of k to 5
20:
21:    // use pre-incrementing
22:    i = 10 * (++k); // k contributes 6 to the expression
23:    cout << "i = " << i << "\n\n"; // displays 60 (= 10 * 6)
24:    return 0;
25: }
```

Here is a sample session with the program in Listing 3.2:

```
i = 50

i = 60
```

The program in Listing 3.2 has the function `main` which declares two `int`-typed variables, `i` and `k`. The function initializes the variable `k` by assigning it the value 5. Line 16 contains a statement which applies the post-increment operator to the variable `k`. Consequently, the statement multiplies 10 by the initial value in `k`, 5, and assigns the product, 50, to variable `i`. After assigning the result to variable `i`, the program increments the value in variable `k`. The output statement in line 17 displays the value in variable `i`. The statement in line 19 decrements the value in variable `k` back to 5. The statement in line 22 applies the pre-increment operator to the variable `k`. Therefore, the program first increments the value in variable `k` (from 5 to 6) and then multiples 10 by the updated value in `k`. The program assigns the result of the multiplication, 60, to the variable `i`. The output statement in line 23 displays the current value of variable `i`.

Assignment Operators

As a programmer you often come across statements that look like this:

```
IndexOfFirstElement = IndexOfFirstElement + 4;
GraphicsScaleRatio = GraphicsScaleRatio * 3;
CurrentRateOfReturn = CurrentRateOfReturn / 4;
DOSfileListSize = DOSfileListSize - 10;
```

The variable that receives the result of an expression is also the first operand. (Of course, the addition and multiplication are communicative operations. Therefore the assigned variable can be either operand with these operations.) Notice that I chose relatively long names to remind you of your need to shorten the expression without making the names of the variables shorter.

NEW☞ TERM C++ offers *assignment operators* that merge with simple math operators.

You can write the following statements:

```
IndexOfFirstElement += 4;
GraphicsScaleRatio *= 3;
CurrentRateOfReturn /= 4;
DOSfileListSize -= 10;
```

Notice that the name of the variable appears only once. In addition, notice that the statements use the operators +=, *=, /=, and -=. Table 3.2 shows the arithmetic assignment operators. C++ supports other types of assignment operators.

Table 3.2. Arithmetic assignment operators.

Assignment Operator	Long Form	Example
x += y	x = x + y	x += 12;
x -= y	x = x - y	x -= 34 + y;
x *= y	x = x * y	scale *= 10;
x /= y	x = x / y	z /= 34 * y;
x %= y	x = x % y	z %= 2;

Let's look at a program which applies the assignment operators to integers and floating-point numbers. Listing 3.3 shows the source code for program OPER3.CPP. The program performs the following tasks:

☐ Prompts you to enter two integers (one integer per prompt)

☐ Applies a set of assignment and increment operators to the two integers

☐ Displays the new values of the integers

☐ Prompts you to enter two floating-point numbers (one number per prompt)

☐ Applies a set of assignment and increment operators to the two numbers

☐ Displays the new values of the floating-point numbers

Type **Listing 3.3. Source code for the program OPER3.CPP.**

```
1:  // C++ program to illustrate math assignment operators
2:
3:  #include <iostream.h>
4:
5:  main()
6:  {
7:      int i, j;
8:      double x, y;
9:
10:     cout << "Type first  integer : ";
```

continues

Listing 3.3. continued

```
11:     cin >> i;
12:     cout << "Type second integer : ";
13:     cin >> j;
14:     i += j;
15:     j -= 6;
16:     i *= 4;
17:     j /= 3;
18:     i++;
19:     j--;
20:     cout << "i = " << i << "\n";
21:     cout << "j = " << j << "\n";
22:
23:     cout << "Type first  real number : ";
24:     cin >> x;
25:     cout << "Type second real number : ";
26:     cin >> y;
27:     // abbreviated assignments also work with doubles in C++
28:     x += y;
29:     y -= 4.0;
30:     x *= 4.0;
31:     y /=  3.0;
32:     x++;
33:     y--;
34:     cout << "x = " << x << "\n";
35:     cout << "y = " << y << "\n";
36:     return 0;
37: }
```

Here is a sample session with the program in Listing 3.3:

```
Type first  integer : 55
Type second integer : 66
i = 485
j = 19
Type first  real number : 2.5
Type second real number : 4.58
x = 29.32
y = -0.806667
```

 The program in Listing 3.3 contains the function main which declares two int-typed variables (i and j) and two double-typed variables (x and y) in lines 7 and 8, respectively. The output statement in line 10 prompts you to enter the first integer. The input statement in line 11 receives your input and stores it in the variable i. Lines 12 and 13 are similar to lines 10 and 11—they prompt you for the second integer and store it in variable j.

The program manipulates the values in variable i and j using the statements in lines 14 through 19. In line 14, the program uses the += operator to increment the value in variable i by the value in variable j. Line 15 uses the -= operator to decrement the value in variable j by 6. Line 16 applies the *= operator to multiply the value in variable i by 4 and to assign the result back to variable i. Line 17 utilizes the /= operator to divide the value in variable j by 3 and to store the result in j. Lines 18 and 19 apply the increment and decrement operators to variables i and j, respectively. The output statements in lines 20 and 21 display the contents of variables i and j, respectively.

The output statement in line 23 prompts you to enter the first floating-point number. The input statement in line 24 receives your input and saves it in the variable x. Lines 25 and 26 are similar to lines 23 and 24—they prompt you for the second floating-point number and store it in variable y.

The program manipulates the values in variable x and y using the statements in lines 28 through 33. In line 28, the program uses the += operator to increment the value in variable x by the value in variable y. Line 29 uses the -= operator to decrement the value in variable y by 4. Line 30 applies the *= operator to multiply the value in variable x by 4 and to save the result back to x. Line 31 utilizes the /= operator to divide the value in variable y by 3 and to store the result in y. Lines 32 and 33 apply the increment and decrement operators to variable x and y, respectively. The output statements in lines 34 and 35 display the contents of variables x and y, respectively.

The *sizeof* Operator

Frequently your programs need to know the byte size of a data type or of a variable. C++ provides the sizeof operator which takes for an argument either a data type or the name of a variable (scalar, array, record, and so on).

The *sizeof* Operator

The general syntax for the sizeof operator is

```
sizeof({variable_name ¦ data_type})
sizeof {variable_name ¦ data_type}
```

Example:

```
int sizeDifference = sizeof(double) - sizeof(float);
int intSize = sizeof int;
```

DO	DON'T

DO use `sizeof` with the name of the variable instead of its data type. This approach is the safest, because if you alter the data type of the variable, the `sizeof` operator still returns the correct answer. By contrast, if you use the `sizeof` operator with the data type of the variable and later alter the variable's type, you create a bug if you do not update the argument of the `sizeof` operator.

DON'T use numbers to represent the size of a variable. This approach often causes errors.

Let's look at an example which uses the `sizeof` operator with variables and data types. Listing 3.4 contains the source code for program SIZEOF1.CPP. The program displays two similar tables that indicate the sizes of the `short int`, `int`, `long int`, `char`, and `float` data types. The program displays the first table by applying the `sizeof` operators to variables of the above types. The program displays the second table by directly applying the `sizeof` operator to the data types.

Type

Listing 3.4. Source code for the program SIZEOF1.CPP.

```
 1: /*
 2:    simple program that returns the data sizes using the sizeof()
 3:    operator with variables and data types.
 4: */
 5:
 6: #include <iostream.h>
 7:
 8: main()
 9:
10: {
11:     short int aShort;
12:     int anInt;
13:     long aLong;
14:     char aChar;
15:     float aReal;
16:
17:     cout << "Table 1. Data sizes using sizeof(variable)\n\n";
18:     cout << "    Data type        Memory used\n";
19:     cout << "                        (bytes)\n";
20:     cout << "----------------    ----------";
21:     cout << "\n    short int          " << sizeof(aShort);
22:     cout << "\n     integer           " << sizeof(anInt);
23:     cout << "\n   long integer        " << sizeof(aLong);
```

```
24:      cout << "\n      character              " << sizeof(aChar);
25:      cout << "\n        float                " << sizeof(aReal);
26:      cout << "\n\n\n\n";
27:
28:      cout << "Table 2. Data sizes using sizeof(dataType)\n\n";
29:      cout << "     Data type          Memory used\n";
30:      cout << "                          (bytes)\n";
31:      cout << "------------------      -----------";
32:      cout << "\n       short int          " << sizeof(short int);
33:      cout << "\n        integer           " << sizeof(int);
34:      cout << "\n      long integer        " << sizeof(long);
35:      cout << "\n       character          " << sizeof(char);
36:      cout << "\n         float            " << sizeof(float);
37:      cout << "\n\n\n\n";
38:
39:      return 0;
40: }
```

Here is a sample session with the program in Listing 3.4:

```
Table 1. Data sizes using sizeof(variable)

     Data type          Memory used
                          (bytes)
------------------      -----------
       short int             2
        integer              2
      long integer           4
       character             1
         float               4




Table 2. Data sizes using sizeof(dataType)

     Data type          Memory used
                          (bytes)
------------------      -----------
       short int             2
        integer              2
      long integer           4
       character             1
         float               4
```

The program in Listing 3.4 declares five variables in function main. Each variable has a different data type and derives its name from its data type. For example, the variable anInt is an int-typed variable, the variable aLong is a long-typed variable, and so on.

The statements in lines 17 through 25 display the table of data sizes. The output statements in lines 21 through 25 use the `sizeof` operator with the variables.

The statements in lines 28 through 36 also display the table of data sizes. The output statements in lines 32 through 36 use the `sizeof` operator with the data type identifiers.

Typecasting

Automatic data conversion of a value from one data type to another compatible data type is one of the duties of a compiler. This data conversion simplifies expressions and eases the frustration of both novice and veteran programmers. With behind-the-scene data conversion you do not need to examine every expression that mixes compatible data types in your program. For example, the compiler handles most expressions that mix various types of integers or mix integers and floating-point types. You get a compile-time error if you attempt to do something illegal!

NEW☞
TERM   *Typecasting* is a language feature which allows you to specify explicitly how to convert a value from its original data type into a compatible data type. Thus, typecasting instructs the compiler to perform the conversion you want and not the one the compiler thinks is needed!

Typecasting

C++ supports the following forms of typecasting:

`type_cast(expression)`

and

`(type_cast) expression`

Examples:

```
int i = 2;
float a, b;
a = float(i);
b = (float) i;
```

Let's look at an example which illustrates implicit data conversion and typecasting. Listing 3.5 shows the source code for program TYPCAST1.CPP. The program declares variables that have the character, integer, and floating-point data types. Then the program performs two sets of similar mathematical operations. The first set relies on the automatic conversions of data types, performed by the compiler. The second set of operations uses typecasting to explicitly instruct the compiler on how to convert the data types. The program requires no input—it provides its own data—and displays the output values for both sets of operations. The program illustrates that the compiler succeeds in generating the same output for both sets of operations.

Listing 3.5. Source code for the program TYPCAST1.CPP.

```
 1: // simple C++ program that demonstrates typecasting
 2:
 3: #include <iostream.h>
 4:
 5: main()
 6: {
 7:     short shortInt1, shortInt2;
 8:     unsigned short aByte;
 9:     int anInt;
10:     long aLong;
11:     char aChar;
12:     float aReal;
13:
14:     // assign values
15:     shortInt1 = 10;
16:     shortInt2 = 6;
17:     // perform operations without typecasting
18:     aByte = shortInt1 + shortInt2;
19:     anInt = shortInt1 - shortInt2;
20:     aLong = shortInt1 * shortInt2;
21:     aChar = aLong + 5; // conversion is automatic to character
22:     aReal = shortInt1 * shortInt2 + 0.5;
23:
24:     cout << "shortInt1 = " << shortInt1 << '\n'
25:         << "shortInt2 = " << shortInt2 << '\n'
26:         << "aByte = " << aByte << '\n'
27:         << "anInt = " << anInt << '\n'
28:         << "aLong = " << aLong << '\n'
29:         << "aChar is " << aChar << '\n'
30:         << "aReal = " << aReal << "\n\n\n";
31:
32:     // perform operations with typecasting
33:     aByte = (unsigned short) (shortInt1 + shortInt2);
34:     anInt = (int) (shortInt1 - shortInt2);
35:     aLong = (long) (shortInt1 * shortInt2);
36:     aChar = (unsigned char) (aLong + 5);
37:     aReal = (float) (shortInt1 * shortInt2 + 0.5);
38:
39:     cout << "shortInt1 = " << shortInt1 << '\n'
```

continues

Listing 3.5. continued

```
40:          << "shortInt2 = " << shortInt2 << '\n'
41:          << "aByte = " << aByte << '\n'
42:          << "anInt = " << anInt << '\n'
43:          << "aLong = " << aLong << '\n'
44:          << "aChar is " << aChar << '\n'
45:          << "aReal = " << aReal << "\n\n\n";
46:    return 0;
47: }
```

Here is a sample session with the program in Listing 3.5:

```
shortInt1 = 10
shortInt2 = 6
aByte = 16
anInt = 4
aLong = 60
aChar is A
aReal = 60.5


shortInt1 = 10
shortInt2 = 6
aByte = 16
anInt = 4
aLong = 60
aChar is A
aReal = 60.5
```

The program in Listing 3.5 declares the following variables in the function `main`:

☐ The `short`-typed variables `shortInt1` and `shortInt2`

☐ The `unsigned short`-typed variable `aByte`

☐ The `int`-typed variable `anInt`

☐ The `long`-typed variable `aLong`

☐ The `char`-typed variable `aChar`

☐ The `float`-typed variable `aReal`

Lines 15 and 16 assign the integers 10 and 6 to variable `shortInt1` and `shortIn2`, respectively. Lines 18 through 22 perform various mathematical operations and assign the results to variables `aByte`, `anInt`, `aLong`, `aChar`, and `aReal`.

Note: C and C++ treat the char type as a special integer. Each char-typed literal (such as `'A'`), constant, or variable has an integer value that is equal to its ASCII representation. This language feature enables you to store an integer in a char-typed variable and treat a char-type data item as an integer. The statement in line 21 adds the integer 5 to the value of the variable aLong and assigns the result, an integer, to variable aChar. The value of the assigned integer, 65, represents the ASCII code for the letter A.

The output statement in lines 24 through 30 displays the values stored in the variables. Notice that the output for variable aChar is the letter A. If I write the output term for variable aChar as << (int) aChar, I get 65, the ASCII code of the character stored in aChar.

The statements in lines 32 through 37 perform similar operations to the statements in lines 18 through 22. The main difference is that the statements in lines 32 through 37 use typecasting to explicitly instruct the compiler on how to convert the result. The output statement in lines 39 through 45 displays the contents of the variables.

Relational and Logical Operators

Table 3.3 shows the C++ relational and logical operators. Notice that C++ does not spell out the operators AND, OR, and NOT. Rather, it utilizes single and dual character symbols. Also notice that C++ does not support the relational XOR operator. You can use the following #define macro directives to define the AND, OR, and NOT identifiers as macros:

NEW☞
TERM The *relational operators* (less than, greater than, and equal to) and *logical operators* (AND, OR, and NOT) are the basic building blocks of decision-making constructs in any programming language.

```
#define AND &&
#define OR ||
#define NOT !
```

Table 3.3. C++ relational and logical operators.

C++ Operator	Meaning	Example
&&	Logical AND	if (i > 1 && i < 10)
||	Logical OR	if (c==0 || c==9)
!	Logical NOT	if (!(c>1 && c<9))
<	Less than	if (i < 0)
<=	Less than or equal to	if (i <= 0)
>	Greater than	if (j > 10)
>=	Greater than or equal to	if (x >= 8.2)
==	Equal to	if (c == '\0')
!=	Not equal to	if (c != '\n')
? :	Conditional assignment	k = (i<1) ? 1 : i;

Although these macros are permissible in C++, you might get a negative reaction from veteran C++ programmers who read your code. Who said that programming is always objective?

Warning: Do *not* use the = operator as the equality relational operator. This common error is a source of logical bugs in a C++ program. You may be accustomed to using the = operator in other languages to test the equality of two data items. *In C++, you must use the == operator.* What happens if you employ the = operator in C++? Do you get a compiler error? The answer is that you may get a compiler warning. Other than that, your C++ program should run. When the program reaches the expression that is supposed to test for equality, it actually attempts to assign the operand on the right of the = sign to the operand on the left of the = sign. Of course, a session with such a program most likely leads to weird program behavior, or even a system hang!

> **Note:** C++ does not support predefined Boolean identifiers. Instead, the language regards 0 as false and a nonzero value as true. To add clarity to your programs I suggest that you declare global constants TRUE and FALSE and assign them 1 and 0, respectively.

Notice that the last operator in Table 3.3 is the ?:. This special operator supports what is known as the conditional expression.

NEW☞ TERM The *conditional expression* is a shorthand for a dual-alternative simple if-else statement (see Day 5 for more information about the if statement).

For example, the following is an if-else statement:

```
if (condition)
     variable = expression1;
else
     variable = expression2;
```

The equivalent conditional expression is

```
variable = (condition) ? expression1 : expression2;
```

The conditional expression tests the condition. If that condition is true, it assigns *expression1* to the target variable. Otherwise, it assigns *expression2* to the target variable.

Boolean Expressions

Often, you need to use a collection of relational and logical operators to formulate a nontrivial condition. Here are examples of such conditions:

```
x < 0 || x > 11
(i != 0 || i > 100) && (j != i || j > 0)
x != 0 && x != 10 && x != 100
```

NEW☞ TERM *Boolean* (also called *logical*) *expressions* are expressions that involve logical operators and/or relational operators.

DO   **DON'T**

DO double-check to avoid Boolean expressions that are either always true or always false. For example, the expression (x < 0 && x > 10) is always false, because no value of x can be negative and greater than 10 at the same time.

DON'T use the = operator to test for equality.

Let's look at an example that uses relational and logical operators and expressions. Listing 3.6 shows the source code for program RELOP1.CPP. The program prompts you to enter three integers, and then proceeds to perform a battery of tests. The program displays the relational and logical operations, their operands, and their results.

Type   **Listing 3.6. Source code for the program RELOP1.CPP.**

```
 1: /*
 2:     simple C++ program that uses logical expressions
 3:     this program uses the conditional expression to display
 4:     TRUE or FALSE messages, since C++ does not support the
 5:     BOOLEAN data type.
 6: */
 7:
 8: #include <iostream.h>
 9:
10: const MIN_NUM = 30;
11: const MAX_NUM = 199;
12: const int TRUE = 1;
13: const int FALSE = 0;
14:
15: main()
16: {
17:     int i, j, k;
18:     int flag1, flag2, in_range,
19:         same_int, xor_flag;
20:
21:     cout << "Type first  integer : "; cin >> i;
22:     cout << "Type second integer : "; cin >> j;
23:     cout << "Type third  integer : "; cin >> k;
24:
25:     // test for range [MIN_NUM..MAX_NUM]
26:     flag1 = i >= MIN_NUM;
27:     flag2 = i <= MAX_NUM;
28:     in_range = flag1 && flag2;
29:     cout << "\n" << i << " is in the range "
30:         << MIN_NUM << " to " << MAX_NUM << " : "
31:         << ((in_range) ? "TRUE" : "FALSE");
```

```
32:
33:     // test if two or more entered numbers are equal
34:     same_int = i == j ¦¦ i == k ¦¦ j == k;
35:     cout << "\nat least two integers you typed are equal : "
36:          << ((same_int) ? "TRUE" : "FALSE");
37:
38:     // miscellaneous tests
39:     cout << "\n" << i << " != " << j << " : "
40:          << ((i != j) ? "TRUE" : "FALSE");
41:     cout << "\nNOT (" << i << " < " << j << ") : "
42:          << ((!(i < j)) ? "TRUE" : "FALSE");
43:     cout << "\n" << i << " <= " << j << " : "
44:          << ((i <= j) ? "TRUE" : "FALSE");
45:     cout << "\n" << k << " > " << j << " : "
46:          << ((k > j) ? "TRUE" : "FALSE");
47:     cout << "\n(" << k << " = " << i << ") AND ("
48:          << j << " != " << k << ") : "
49:          << ((k == i && j != k) ? "TRUE" : "FALSE");
50:
51:     // NOTE: C++ does NOT support the logical XOR operator for
52:     // boolean expressions.
53:     // add numeric results of logical tests.  Value is in 0..2
54:     xor_flag = (k <= i) + (j >= k);
55:     // if xor_flag is either 0 or 2 (i.e. not = 1), it is
56:     // FALSE therefore interpret 0 or 2 as false.
57:     xor_flag = (xor_flag == 1) ? TRUE : FALSE;
58:     cout << "\n(" << k << " <= " << i << ") XOR ("
59:          << j << " >= " << k << ") : "
60:          << ((xor_flag) ? "TRUE" : "FALSE");
61:     cout << "\n(" << k << " > " << i << ") AND("
62:          << j << " <= " << k << ") : "
63:          << ((k > i && j <= k) ? "TRUE" : "FALSE");
64:     cout << "\n\n";
65:     return 0;
66: }
```

Here is a sample session with the program in Listing 3.6:

```
Type first  integer : 55
Type second integer : 64
Type third  integer : 87

55 is in the range 30 to 199 : TRUE
at least two integers you typed are equal : FALSE
55 != 64 : TRUE
NOT (55 < 64) : FALSE
55 <= 64 : TRUE
87 > 64 : TRUE
(87 = 55) AND (64 != 87) : FALSE
(87 <= 55) XOR (64 >= 87) : FALSE
(87 > 55) AND(64 <= 87) : TRUE
```

Analysis The program in Listing 3.6 declares four global constants. The constants MIN_NUM and MAX_NUM define a range of numbers used in the logical tests. The constants TRUE and FALSE represent the Boolean values. The function main declares a number of int variables which are used for input and various testing. The statements in lines 21 through 23 prompt you for three integers and store them in the variables i, j, and k, respectively.

The statements in lines 26 through 31 deal with testing whether the value in variable i lies in the range of MIN_NUM and MAX_NUM. The statement in line 26 tests if the value in i is greater than or equal to the constant MIN_NUM. The program assigns the Boolean result to the variable flag1. The statement in line 27 tests whether the value in i is less than or equal to the constant MAX_NUM. The program assigns the Boolean result to the variable flag2. The statement in line 28 applies the && operator to the variable flag1 and flag2, and assigns the Boolean result to the variable in_range. The output statement in lines 29 through 31 states what the test is and displays TRUE or FALSE depending on the value in variable in_range. The statement uses the conditional operator ?: to display the string TRUE if in_range has a nonzero value, and to display the string FALSE if otherwise.

The statements in lines 34 through 36 determine whether at least two of the three integers you entered are equal. The statement in line 34 uses a Boolean expression which applies the == relational operators and the ¦¦ logical operators. The statement assigns the Boolean result to the variable same_int. The output statement in lines 35 and 36 states the test and displays the TRUE/FALSE outcome. The output statement uses the conditional operator to display the strings TRUE or FALSE depending on the value in variable same_int.

The statements in lines 39 through 49 perform miscellaneous tests which involve the input values, and display both the test and the results. Please feel free to alter these statements to conduct different tests.

Note: The statements in lines 54 through 60 perform an XOR test and display the outcome. The program uses a simple programming trick to implement the XOR operator. The statement in line 54 adds the Boolean value of the subexpressions (k <= i) and (j >= k). The result is 0 if both subexpressions are false, 1 if only one of the subexpressions is true, and 2 if both subexpressions are true. Since the XOR operator is true only if either subexpression is true, the statement in line 57 assigns TRUE to the variable

xor_flag if the previous value is 1. Otherwise, the statement assigns FALSE
to xor_flag. The statements in lines 61 through 63 perform another
miscellaneous test.

Bit-Manipulation Operators

C++ is a programming language that is suitable for system development. System
development requires bit-manipulating operators.

NEW☛ TERM *Bit-manipulating operators* toggle, set, query, and shift the bits of a byte or a
word.

Table 3.4 shows the bit-manipulating operators. Notice that C++ uses the symbols &
and ¦ to represent the bitwise AND and OR, respectively. Recall that the && and ¦¦
characters represent the logical AND and OR operators, respectively. In addition to the
bit-manipulating operators, C++ supports the bit-manipulating assignment operators, shown in Table 3.5. (Using bit-manipulating operators is part of advanced
programming which involves fiddling with single bits. As a novice C++ programmer
you will most likely not use these operators in the near future.)

Table 3.4. C++ bit-manipulating operators.

C++ Operator	Meaning	Example
&	Bitwise AND	i & 128
¦	Bitwise OR	j ¦ 64
^	Bitwise XOR	j ^ 12
~	Bitwise NOT	~j
<<	Bitwise shift left	i << 2
>>	Bitwise shift right	j >> 3

Table 3.5. C++ bit-manipulating assignment operators.

C++ Operator	Long Form	Example
x &= y	x = x & y	i &= 128
x ¦= y	x = x ¦ y	j ¦= 64
x ^= y	x = x ^ y	k ^= 15
x <<= y	x = x << y	j <<= 2
x >>= y	x = x >> y	k >>= 3

Let me present a C++ program that performs simple bit manipulation. Listing 3.7 contains the source code for program BITS1.CPP. The program requires no input, because it uses internal data. The program applies the ¦, &, ^, >>, and << bitwise operators and displays the results of the bitwise manipulation.

Type **Listing 3.7. Source code for the program BITS1.CPP.**

```
1: // C++ program to perform bit manipulations
2:
3: #include <iostream.h>
4:
5: main()
6: {
7:
8:     int i, j, k;
9:
10:     // assign values to i and j
11:     i = 0xF0;
12:     j = 0x1A;
13:
14:     k = j & i;
15:     cout << j << " AND " << i << " = " << k << "\n";
16:
17:     k = j ¦ i;
18:     cout << j << " OR " << i << " = " << k << "\n";
19:
20:     k = j ^ 0x1C;
21:     cout << j << " XOR " << 0x1C << " = " << k << "\n";
22:
23:     k = i << 2;
24:     cout << i << " shifted left by 2 bits = " << k << "\n";
25:
```

```
26:        k = i >> 2;
27:        cout << i << " shifted right by 2 bits = " << k << "\n";
28:        return 0;
29: }
```

Here is a sample session with the program in Listing 3.7:

```
26 AND 240 = 16
26 OR 240 = 250
26 XOR 28 = 6
240 shifted left by 2 bits = 960
240 shifted right by 2 bits = 60
```

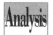

The program in Listing 3.7 declares three int-typed variables, i, j, and k. The statements in lines 11 and 12 assign hexadecimal numbers to the variables i and j, respectively. The statement in line 14 applies the bitwise AND operator to the variables i and j, and stores the result in variable k. The output statement in line 15 displays the operands, the bitwise operator, and the results. The statement in line 17 applies the bitwise OR operator to the variable i and j, and saves the result to variable k. The output statement in line 18 displays the operands, the bitwise operator, and the results. The statement in line 20 applies the bitwise XOR operator using the variable j and the hexadecimal integer 0x1C. The output statement in line 21 displays the operands, the bitwise operator, and the results.

The statements in lines 23 through 27 apply the shift left and shift right operators to variable i. These operators shift the bits of variable i by 2 bits and assign the result to variable k. The effect of the left shift operator is the same as multiplying the value in variable i by 4. Similarly, the effect of the right shift operator is the same as dividing the value in variable i by 4.

The Comma Operator

The comma operator requires that the program completely evaluates the first expression before evaluating the second expression. Both expressions are located in the same C++ statement! What does *located in the same C++ statement* mean exactly? Why utilize this rather unusual operator in the first place? Because the comma operator with its peculiar role does serve a specific and very important purpose in the for loop.

NEW☞
TERM *Loops* are powerful language constructs that enable computers to excel in achieving repetitive tasks. The *comma operator* enables you to create multiple expressions that initialize multiple loop-related variables.

Syntax

The Comma Operator

The general syntax for the comma operator is

```
expression1, expression2
```

Example:

```
for (i = 0, j = 0; i < 10; i++, j++)
```

You learn more about the for loop in Day 6. For now, this example shows you how to apply the comma operator.

Operator Precedence and Evaluation Direction

Now that you are familiar with most of the C++ operators (there are a few more operators that deal with pointers and addresses) there are two related aspects you need to know. First, the precedence of the C++ operators. Second, the direction (or sequence) of evaluation. Table 3.6 shows the C++ precedence of the C++ operators that I have covered so far and also indicates the evaluation direction.

Table 3.6. C++ operators and their precedence.

Category	Name	Symbol	Evaluation Direction	Precedence
Monadic	[ ] ( ) . →		*Left to Right 1*	
	Post-increment	++	Left to right	1
	Post-decrement	--	Left to right	1
	Indirection	*＊*	*Right to Left 2*	
	Address	&	Right to left	2
	Bitwise NOT	~	Right to left	2
	Typecast	(type)	Right to left	2
	Logical NOT	!	Right to left	2
	Negation	-	Right to left	2
	Plus sign	+	Right to left	2
	Pre-increment	++	Right to left	2
	Pre-decrement	--	Right to left	2
	Size of data	sizeof	Right to left	2

Category	Name	Symbol	Evaluation Direction	Precedence
Multiplicative				
	Modulus	%	Left to right	3
	Multiply	*	Left to right	3
	Divide	/	Left to right	3
Additive				
	Add	+	Left to right	4
	Subtract	-	Left to right	4
Bitwise Shift				
	Shift left	<<	Left to right	5
	Shift right	>>	Left to right	5
Relational				
	Less than	<	Left to right	6
	Less or equal	<=	Left to right	6
	Greater than	>	Left to right	6
	Greater or equal	>=	Left to right	6
	Equal	==	Left to right	7
	Not equal	!=	Left to right	7
Bitwise				
	AND	&	Left to right	8
	XOR	^	Left to right	9
	OR	¦	Left to right	10
Logical				
	AND	&&	Left to right	11
	OR	¦¦	Left to right	12

continues

Table 3.6. continued

Category	Name	Symbol	Evaluation Direction	Precedence
Ternary				
	Cond. express.	?:	Right to left	13
Assignment				
	Arithmetic	=	Right to left	14
		+=	Right to left	14
		-=	Right to left	14
		*=	Right to left	14
		/=	Right to left	14
		%=	Right to left	14
	Shift	>>=	Right to left	14
		<<=	Right to left	14
	Bitwise	&=	Right to left	14
		¦=	Right to left	14
		^=	Right to left	14
	Comma	,	Left to right	15

Summary

Today's lesson presents the various C++ operators and discusses how to use these operators to manipulate data. You learn the following:

☐ The arithmetic operators include +, -, *, /, and % (modulus).

☐ The arithmetic expressions vary in complexity. The simplest expression contains a single data item (literal, constant, or variable). Complex expressions include multiple operators, functions, literals, constants, and variables.

☐ The increment and decrement operators come in the pre- and post- forms. C++ allows you to apply these operators to variables that store characters, integers, and even floating-point numbers.

☐ The arithmetic assignment operators allow you to write shorter arithmetic expressions in which the primary operand is also the variable receiving the result of the expression.

☐ The `sizeof` operator returns the byte size of either a data type or a variable.

☐ Typecasting allows you to force the type conversion of an expression.

☐ Relational and logical operators permit you to build logical expressions. C++ does not support a predefined Boolean type and instead considers 0 as false and any nonzero value as true.

☐ Boolean expressions combine relational and logical operators to formulate nontrivial conditions. These expressions allow a program to make sophisticated decisions.

☐ The conditional expression offers you a short form for the simple dual-alternative `if-else` statement.

☐ The bit-manipulation operators perform bitwise AND, OR, XOR, and NOT operations. In addition, C++ supports the << and >> bitwise shift operators.

☐ The bit-manipulation assignment operators offer short forms for simple bit-manipulation statements.

Q&A

Q. How does the compiler react when you declare a variable but never assign a value to it?

A. The compiler issues a warning that the variable is unreferenced.

Q. What is the Boolean expression to check that the value of a variable, call it `i`, is in the range of values (for example, defined by variables `loVal` and `hiVal`)?

A. The expression that determines whether the value in variable `i` is located in a range is

```
(i >= lowVal && i <= hiVal)
```

Q. What is the Boolean expression to check that the value of a variable, call it i, is *inside* the range of values (for example, defined by variables loVal and hiVal)?

A. The expression that determines whether the value in variable i is located inside a range is

```
(i > lowVal && i < hiVal)
```

Workshop

The Workshop provides quiz questions to help you solidify your understanding of the material covered and exercises to provide you with experience in using what you've learned. Try to understand the quiz and exercise answers before continuing on to the next day's lesson. Answers are provided in Appendix B, "Answers."

Quiz

1. What is the output of the following program?

```
#include <iostream.h>

main()
{
  int i = 3;
  int j = 5;
  double x = 33.5;
  double y = 10.0;

  cout << 10 + j % i << "\n";
  cout << i * i - 2 * i + 5 << "\n";
  cout << (19 + i + j) / (2 * j + 2) << "\n";
  cout << x / y + y / x << "\n";
  cout << i * x + j * y << "\n";
  return 0;
}
```

2. What is the output of the following program?

```
#include <iostream.h>

main()
{
  int i = 3;
  int j = 5;

  cout << 10 + j % i++ << "\n";
  cout << --i * i - 2 * i + 5 << "\n";
  cout << (19 + ++i + ++j) / (2 * j + 2) << "\n";
  return 0;
}
```

3. What is the output of the following program?

```
#include <iostream.h>

main()
{
  int i = 3;
  int j = 5;

  i += j;
  j *= 2;
  cout << 10 + j % i << "\n";
  i -= 2;
  j /= 3;
  cout << i * i - 2 * i + j << "\n";
  return 0;
}
```

4. What is the output of the following program?

```
include <iostream.h>

main()
{
  int i = 5;
  int j = 10;
```

```
cout << ((i > j) ? "TRUE" : "FALSE") << "\n";
cout << ((i > 0 && j < 100) ?  "TRUE" : "FALSE") << "\n";
cout << ((i > 0 && i < 10) ? "TRUE" : "FALSE") << "\n";
cout << ((i == 5 && i == j) ? "TRUE" : "FALSE") << "\n";
return 0;
}
```

Exercises

1. Use the conditional operator to write the function `max` which returns the greater of two integers.

2. Use the conditional operator to write the function `min` which returns the smaller of two integers.

3. Use the conditional operator to write the function `abs` which returns the absolute value of an integer.

4. Use the conditional operator to write the function `isOdd` which returns 0 if its integer argument is an odd number and yields 1 if otherwise.

DAY
4

Managing I/O

C++, like its parent language C, does not define I/O operations that are part of the core language. Instead, C++ and C rely on I/O libraries to provide the needed I/O support. Such libraries are mainly aimed at non-GUI (Graphics User Interface) environments such as MS-DOS. These libraries usually work with QuickWin applications, which is why they are of interest in this book. However, because my primary goal is to teach you how to write Windows programs, I keep the discussion of these I/O libraries to a minimum. Today's short lesson looks at a small selection of input and output operations and functions that are supported by the STDIO.H and IOSTREAM.H header files. You learn about the following topics:

- [ ] Formatted stream output
- [ ] Stream input
- [ ] The `printf` function

Formatted Stream Output

C++ brought with it a family of extendable I/O libraries. The language designers recognized that the I/O functions in STDIO.H, inherited from C, have their limitations when dealing with classes (more about classes in Day 11). Consequently, C++ extends the notion of streams. Recall that streams, which already exist in C, are a sequence of data flowing from part of a computer to another. In the programs that I have presented so far you have seen the extractor operator << working with the standard output stream, `cout`. You also saw the inserter operator >> and the standard input stream, `cin`. In this section I introduce you to the stream functions `width` and `precision` which help in formatting the output. The C++ stream libraries have many more functions to further fine-tune the output. However, as I stated earlier, because these functions work for non-GUI interfaces, I don't want to overwhelm you with information that is relevant to Windows programming. The `width` function specifies the width of the output. The general form for using this function with the `cout` stream is

```
cout.width(widthOfOutput);
```

The `precision` function specifies the number of digits for floating-point numbers. The general form for using this function with the `cout` stream is

```
cout.precision(numberOfDigits);
```

Let's look at an example. Listing 4.1 contains the source code for program OUT1.CPP. The program, which requires no input, displays formatted integers, floating-point numbers, and characters using the `width` and `precision` stream functions.

Listing 4.1. Source code for the program OUT1.CPP.

```
1: // Program that illustrates C++ formatted stream output
2: // using the width and precision functions
3:
4: #include <iostream.h>
5:
6: main()
7: {
8:    short     aShort    = 4;
9:    int       anInt     = 67;
10:   unsigned char aByte  = 128;
11:   char      aChar     = '@';
12:   float     aSingle   = 355.0;
13:   double    aDouble   = 1.130e+002;
14:   // display sample expressions
15:   cout.width(3); cout << int(aByte) << " + ";
16:   cout.width(2); cout << anInt << " = ";
17:   cout.width(3); cout << (aByte + anInt) << '\n';
18:
19:   cout.precision(4); cout << aSingle << " / ";
20:   cout.precision(4); cout << aDouble << " = ";
21:   cout.precision(5); cout << (aSingle / aDouble) << '\n';
22:
23:   cout << "The character in variable aChar is "
24:        << aChar << '\n';
25:   return 0;
26: }
```

Here is a sample session with the program in Listing 4.1:

```
128 + 67 = 195
355 / 113 = 3.1416
The character in variable aChar is @
```

The program in Listing 4.1 declares a set of variables which have different data types. The statements in lines 15 through 17 use the stream function width to specify the output width for the next item displayed by a cout statement. Notice that it takes six statements to display three integers. In addition, notice that in line 15 the program uses the expression int(aByte) to typecast the unsigned char type into an int. Without this type conversion, the contents of variable aByte appear as a character instead of a number. If I use the stream output to display integers that have default widths, I can indeed replace the six stream output statements with a single one.

Lines 19 through 21 contain the second set of stream output statements for the floating-point numbers. The statements in these lines contain the stream function precision to specify the total number of digits to display. Again, its takes six C++

statements to output three floating-point numbers. Once more, if I use the stream output to display numbers that have default widths, I can replace the six stream output statements with a single one.

Stream Input

Like the standard output stream, C++ offers the standard input stream, cin. This input stream is able to read predefined data types, such as int, unsigned, long, and char. Typically, you use the inserter operator >> to obtain input for the predefined data types. The programs that I presented so far use the >> operator to enter a single item. C++ streams allow you to chain the >> operator to enter multiple items. In the case of multiple items, you need to observe the following rules:

1. Enter a space between two consecutive numbers to separate them.

2. Entering a space between two consecutive chars is optional.

3. Entering a space between a char and a number (and vice versa) is necessary only if the char is a digit.

4. The input stream ignores spaces.

5. You can enter multiple items on different lines. The stream input statements are not fully executed until they obtain all the specified input.

Note: I postpone discussing the input of character strings for now. Day 9 covers strings and includes the input of strings.

Let's look at a program which illustrates both the input of multiple items and different combinations of data types. Listing 4.2 shows the source code for program IN1.CPP. The program performs the following tasks:

☐ Prompts you to enter three numbers

☐ Calculates the sum of the three numbers

☐ Displays the sum and the average of the three numbers you entered

☐ Prompts you to type in three characters

☐ Displays your input

☐ Prompts you to enter a number, a character, and a number

☐ Displays your input

☐ Prompts you to enter a character, a number, and a character

☐ Displays your input

Listing 4.2. Source code for the program IN1.CPP.

```
1: // Program that illustrates standard stream input
2:
3: #include <iostream.h>
4:
5: main()
6: {
7:    double x, y, z, sum;
8:    char c1, c2, c3;
9:
10:   cout << "Enter three numbers separated by a space : ";
11:   cin >> x >> y >> z;
12:   sum = x + y + z;
13:   cout << "Sum of numbers = " << sum
14:        << "\nAverage of numbers = " << sum / 2 << "\n";
15:   cout << "Enter three characters : ";
16:   cin >> c1 >> c2 >> c3;
17:   cout << "You entered characters '" << c1
18:        << "', '" << c2 << "', and '"
19:        << c3 << "'\n";
20:   cout << "Enter a number, a character, and a number : ";
21:   cin >> x >> c1 >> y;
22:   cout << "You entered " << x << " " << c1 << " " << y << "\n";
23:   cout << "Enter a character, a number, and a character : ";
24:   cin >> c1 >> x >> c2;
25:   cout << "You entered " << c1 << " " << x << " " << c2 << "\n";
26:
27:   return 0;
28: }
```

Here is a sample session with the program in Listing 4.2:

```
Enter three numbers separated by a space : 1 2 3
Sum of numbers = 6
Average of numbers = 3
Enter three characters : ABC
You entered characters 'A', 'B', and 'C'
Enter a number, a character, and a number : 12A34.4
You entered 12 A 34.4
Enter a character, a number, and a character : A3.14Z
You entered A 3.14 Z
```

Analysis The program in Listing 4.2 declares four double-typed variables and three char-typed variables. The output statement in line 10 prompts you to enter three numbers. The input statement in line 11 obtains your input and stores the numbers in variables x, y, and z. You need to enter a space character between any two numbers. You can also enter each number on a separate line. The statement stores the first number you enter in variable x, the second number in variable y, and the third one in variable z. This sequence is determined by the sequence in which these variables appear in line 11. The statement in line 12 calculates the sum of the values in variable x, y, and z. The output statement in lines 13 and 14 displays the sum and average of the numbers that you entered.

The output statement in line 15 prompts you to enter three characters. The input statement in line 16 obtains your input and sequentially stores the characters in variables c1, c2, and c3. Your input need not separate the characters with a space. Thus, you can type in characters such as 1A2, Bob, and 1 D d. The output statement in lines 17 through 19 displays the characters you type in, separated by spaces.

The output statement in line 20 prompts you to enter a number, a character, and a number. The input statement in line 21 sequentially stores your input in variables x, c1, and y. You need to type in a space between the character and either number only if the character can be interpreted as part of either number. For example, if you want to enter the number 12, the dot character, and the number 55, type in 12 . 55. The spaces around the dot ensure that the input stream does not consider it as a decimal part of either floating-point number. The output statement in line 22 displays the values you entered, separated by spaces.

The output statement in line 23 prompts you to enter a character, a number, and a character. The input statement in line 24 sequentially stores your input in variables c1, x, and c2. You need to enter a space between the characters and the number only if the characters can be interpreted as part of the number. For example, if you want to enter the character -, the number 12, and the digit 0, type in - 12 0. The output statement in line 25 displays the values you entered, separated by spaces.

The *printf* Function

As a novice C++ programmer you have a wealth of I/O functions to choose from. In this section I discuss the formatting features of function printf which is part of the standard I/O of C. The function is prototyped in the header file STDIO.H.

The printf function offers much power and presents formatted controls. The general syntax for the individual formatting instruction is

```
% [flags] [width] [.precision] [F ¦ N ¦ h ¦ 1] <type character>
```

The *flags* options indicate the output justification, numeric signs, decimal points, and trailing zeros. In addition, these flags also specify the octal and hexadecimal prefixes. Table 4.1 shows the options for the flags in the format string of the `printf` function.

The *width* option indicates the minimum number of displayed characters. The `printf` function uses zeros and blanks to pad the output if needed. When the width number begins with a 0, the `printf` function uses leading zeros, instead of spaces, for padding. When the * character appears instead of a width number, the `printf` function obtains the actual width number from the function's argument list. The argument that specifies the required width must come before the argument actually being formatted. The following is an example which displays the integer 3 using 2 characters, as specified by the third argument of `printf`:

```
printf("%*d", 3, 2);
```

The *precision* option specifies the maximum number of displayed characters. If you include an integer, the precision option defines the minimum number of displayed digits. When the * character is used in place of a precision number, the `printf` function obtains the actual precision from the argument list. The argument that specifies the required precision must come before the argument that is actually being formatted. The following is an example which displays the floating-point number 3.3244 using 10 characters, as specified by the third argument of `printf`:

```
printf("%7.*f", 3.3244, 10);
```

The F, N, h, and 1 options are sized options used to overrule the argument's default size. The F and N options are used in conjunction with far and near pointers, respectively. The h and 1 options are used to indicate `short int` or `long`, respectively.

Table 4.1. The escape sequence.

Sequence	Decimal Value	Hex Value	Task
\a	7	0x07	Bell
\b	8	0x08	Backspace
\f	12	0x0C	Formfeed
\n	10	0x0A	New line
\r	13	0x0D	Carriage return

continues

Table 4.1. continued

Sequence	Decimal Value	Hex Value	Task
\t	9	0x09	Horizontal tab
\v	11	0x0B	Vertical tab
\\	92	0x5C	Backslash
\'	44	0x2C	Single quote
\"	34	0x22	Double quote
\?	63	0x3F	Question mark
\ooo			1 to 3 digits for octal value
\Xhhh and \xhhh		0xhhh	Hexadecimal value

The printf function requires that you specify a data type character with each % format code. Table 4.2 shows the options for the flags in the format string of printf. Table 4.3 shows the data type characters used in the format string of printf.

**Table 4.2. Options for the flags
in the format string of the printf function.**

Format Option	Outcome
-	Justifies to the left within the specified field
+	Displays the plus or minus sign of a value
blank	Displays a leading blank if the value is positive; displays a minus sign if the value is negative
#	No effect on decimal integers; displays a leading 0X or 0x for hexadecimal integers; displays a leading zero for octal integers; displays the decimal point for reals

Table 4.3. Data type characters utilized in the format string of `printf`.

Category	Type Character	Outcome
Character	c	Single character
	d	Signed decimal int
	i	Signed decimal int
	o	Unsigned octal int
	u	Unsigned decimal int
	x	Unsigned hexadecimal int (the set of numeric characters used is 01234567890abcdef)
	X	Unsigned hexadecimal int (the set of numeric characters used is 01234567890ABCdef) *←LETTERS ARE CAPS*
Pointer	p	Displays only the offset for near pointers as OOOO; displays far pointers as SSSS:OOOO
Pointer to int	n	
real	f	Displays signed value in the format [-]dddd.dddd
	e	Displays signed scientific value in the format [-]d.dddde[+l-]ddd
	E	Displays signed scientific value in the format [-]d.ddddE[+l-]ddd
	g	Displays signed value using either the f or e formats, depending on the value and the specified precision

4

continues

Table 4.3. continued

Category	Type Character	Outcome
	G	Displays signed value using either the f or E formats, depending on the value and the specified precision
String pointer	s	Displays characters until the null terminator of the string is reached

Note: Although the function printf plays no role in the output of Windows applications, its sister function, sprintf, does. The latter function creates a string of characters which contains the formatted image of the output. I discuss the sprintf function in Day 9, and use that function in the latter lessons of this book to create a dialog box that contains messages that include numbers.

Let's look at a simple example. Listing 4.3 shows the source code for program OUT2.CPP. I created this program by editing the OUT1.CPP in Listing 4.1. The new version displays formatted output using the printf function. The program displays the same floating-point numbers using three different sets of format code.

Listing 4.3. Source code for the program OUT2.CPP.

```
1: // C++ program that uses the printf function for formatted output
2:
3: #include <stdio.h>
4:
5: main()
6: {
7:    short    aShort    = 4;
8:    int      anInt     = 67;
9:    unsigned char aByte = 128;
10:   char     aChar     = '@';
11:   float    aSingle   = 355.0;
12:   double   aDouble   = 1.130e+002;
13:   // display sample expressions
14:   printf("%3d %c %2d = %3d\n",
```

```
15:              aByte, '+', anInt, aByte + anInt);
16:
17:    printf("Output uses the %%lf format\n");
18:    printf("%6.4f / %6.4lf = %7.5lf\n", aSingle, aDouble,
19:                                aSingle / aDouble);
20:    printf("Output uses the %%le format\n");
21:    printf("%6.4e / %6.4le = %7.5le\n", aSingle, aDouble,
22:                                aSingle / aDouble);
23:    printf("Output uses the %%lg format\n");
24:    printf("%6.4g / %6.4lg = %7.5lg\n", aSingle, aDouble,
25:                                aSingle / aDouble);
26:
27:    printf("The character in variable aChar is %c\n", aChar);
28:    printf("The ASCII code of %c is %d\n", aChar, aChar);
29     return 0;
30: }
```

Here is a sample session with the program in Listing 4.3:

```
128 + 67 = 195
Output uses the %lf format
355.0000 / 113.0000 = 3.14159
Output uses the %le format
3.5500e+002 / 1.1300e+002 = 3.14159e+000
Output uses the %lg format
  355 / 113 = 3.1416
The character in variable aChar is @
The ASCII code of @ is 64
```

The program in Listing 4.3 declares a collection of variables with different data types. The output statement in lines 14 and 15 displays integers and characters using the %d and %c format controls. Table 4.4 shows the effect of the various format controls in the printf statement at line 14. Notice that the printf function converts the first item in output from an unsigned char to an int.

Table 4.4. Effects of the various format controls in the printf statement at line 14.

Format Control	Item	Data Type	Output
%3d	aByte	unsigned char	Integer
%c	'+'	char	Character
%2d	anInt	int	Integer
%3d	aByte + anInt	int	Integer

The output statement in line 18 displays the variable aSingle, the variable aDouble, and the expression aSingle / aDouble using the format controls %6.4f, %6.4lf, and %7.5lf. These controls specify precision values of 4, 4, and 5 digits, respectively, and minimum widths of 6, 6, and 7 characters, respectively. The last two format controls indicate that they display a double-typed value.

The output statement in line 21 is similar to that in line 18. The main difference is that the printf in line 21 uses the e format instead of the f format. Consequently, the three items in the printf statement appear in scientific notations.

The output statement in line 24 is similar to that in line 18. The main difference is that the printf in line 24 uses the g format instead of the f format. Consequently, the first two items in the printf statement appear with no decimal places, because they are whole numbers.

The output statement in line 27 displays the contents in variable aChar using the %c format control. The output statement in line 28 displays the contents of variable aChar twice: once as a character and once as an integer (the ASCII code of a character, to be more exact). The printf function in line 28 performs this task by using the %c and %d format controls, respectively.

Summary

Today's lesson examines the basic input and output operations and functions that are supported by the IOSTREAM.H and STDIO.H header files. You learn the following:

☐ Formatted stream output uses the precision and width functions to provide some basic formatting output.

☐ Standard stream input supports the insert operator >> to obtain input for the predefined data types in C++.

☐ The format codes involved in the format string of the printf function empower the printf function to control the appearance of the output and even perform type conversion.

INT PRINTF (CONST CHAR * FORMAT [ARGUMENT, ...])

Q&A

Q. How can I chain >> or << operators?

A. Each of these operators returns a special stream data type which can be the input for another similar stream operator.

Q. Why can't I use the stream I/O operators in Windows applications?

A. Windows applications have a fundamentally different way of interacting with you. When a QuickWin program (which emulates a non-GUI MS-DOS application) executes an input statement, it goes into a special mode where it monitors the keyboard input. By contrast, Windows programs (which are GUI applications) are always monitoring the mouse (its movements and its button clicks) and the keyboard and reporting the current status to the part of Windows which monitors events. The vast difference between GUI and non-GUI applications render non-GUI input functions useless in GUI applications.

Workshop

The Workshop provides quiz questions to help you solidify your understanding of the material covered and exercises to provide you with experience in using what you've learned. Try to understand the quiz and exercise answers before continuing on to the next day's lesson. Answers are provided in Appendix B, "Answers."

Quiz

1. What is wrong with the following statement?

```
count << "Enter a number " >> x;
```

2. What happens in the following statement?

```
cout << "Enter three numbers : ";
cin >> x >> y >> x;
```

*[handwritten:] INT FPRINTF (FILE *STREAM, CONST CHAR *FORMAT [, ARGUMENT, ...])*

*[handwritten:] INT SPRINTF (CHAR *STRING, CONST, CHAR *FORMAT [, ARGUMENT, ...])*

Exercises

1. Write the program OUT3.CPP which displays a table of square roots for whole numbers in the range of 2 to 10. Use the MATH.H header file to import the sqrt function which calculates the square root of a double-typed argument. Because I have not discussed C++ loops, use repetitive statements to display the various values. Employ the format controls %3.0lf and %3.4lf to display the number and its square root, respectively.

2. Write the program OUT4.CPP which prompts you for an integer and displays the hexadecimal and octal equivalent forms. Use the printf format controls to perform the conversion between decimal, hexadecimal, and octal numbers.

DAY
5

The Decision-
Making Constructs

The support of different programming languages varies depending on their decision-making constructs.

NEW☞
TERM
Decision-making constructs enable your applications to examine conditions and designate courses of action.

Today's lesson looks at the decision-making constructs in C++ and covers the following topics:

☐ The single-alternative `if` statement

☐ The dual-alternative `if-else` statement

☐ The multiple-alternative `if-else` statement

☐ The multiple-alternative `switch` statement

☐ Nested decision-making constructs

The Single-Alternative *if* Statement

Unlike many programming languages, C++ does not have the keyword `then` in any form of the `if` statement. This language feature may lead you to ask how the `if` statement separates the tested condition from the executable statements. The answer is that C++ dictates that you enclose the tested condition in parentheses.

NEW☞
TERM
An `if` statement is a *single-alternative* statement.

The Single-Alternative *if* Statement

The general syntax for the single-alternative `if` statement is

```
if (condition)
    statement;
```

for a single executable statement, and

```
if (tested_condition) {
    <sequence of statements>
}
```

for a sequence of executable statements.

Examples:

```
if (numberOfLines < 0)
    numberOfLines = 0;

if ((height - 54) < 3) {
    area = length * width;
    volume = area * height;
}
```

C++ uses the open and close braces ({})to define a block of statements. Figure 5.1 shows the flow in a single-alternative if statement.

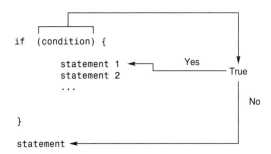

Figure 5.1. The program flow in the single-alternative if statement.

Let's look at an example. Listing 5.1 shows a program with a single-alternative if statement. The program prompts you to enter a nonzero number and stores the input in the variable x. If the value in x is not zero, the program displays the reciprocal of x.

Type **Listing 5.1. Source code for the program IF1.CPP.**

```
1: // Program that demonstrates the single-alternative if statement
2:
3: #include <iostream.h>
4:
5: main()
6: {
7:    double x;
8:    cout << "Enter a non-zero number : ";
9:    cin >> x;
10:   if (x != 0)
11:      cout << "The reciprocal of " << x
12:           << " is " << (1/x) << "\n";
13:   return 0;
14: }
```

Here is a sample session with the program in Listing 5.1:

```
Enter a non-zero number : 25
The reciprocal of 25 is 0.04
```

The program in Listing 5.1 declares the `double`-typed variable `x` in function `main`. The output statement in line 8 prompts you to enter a nonzero number. The input statement in line 9 stores your input in variable `x`. The `if` statement in line 10 determines whether `x` does not equal zero. If this condition is true, the program executes the output statement in lines 11 and 12. This statement displays the value of `x` and its reciprocal, `1/x`. If the tested condition is false, the program skips the statement in lines 11 and 12 and resumes at the statement in line 13.

The Dual-Alternative *if-else* Statement

In the *dual-alternative* form of the `if` statement, the `else` keyword separates the statements used to execute each alternative.

NEW The *dual-alternative* `if-else` statement provides you with two alternate
TERM courses of action based on the Boolean value of the tested condition.

The Dual-Alternative *if-else* Statement

The general syntax for the dual-alternative `if-else` statement is

```
if (condition)
    statement1;
else
    statement2;
```

for a single executable statement in each clause, and

```
if (tested_condition) {
    <sequence #1 of statements>
}
else {
    <sequence #2 of statements>
}
```

for a sequence of executable statements in both clauses.

Example:

```
if (moneyInAccount > withdraw) {
```

```
    moneyInAccount -= withdraw;
    cout << "You withdrew $" << withdraw << "\n";
    cout << "Balance is $" << moneyInAccount << "\n";
}
else {
  cout << "Cannot withdraw $" << withdraw << "\n";
  cout << "Account has $" << moneyInAccount << "\n";
}
```

Figure 5.2. shows the program flow in the dual-alternative if-else statement.

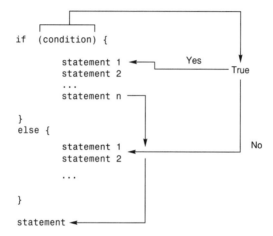

Figure 5.2. The program flow in the dual-alternative if-else statement.

Let's look at an example that uses the dual-alternative if-else statement. Listing 5.2 contains the source code for the program IF2.CPP. The program prompts you to enter a character and then determines whether or not you entered a letter. The program output classifies your input as either a letter or a nonletter character.

Type   **Listing 5.2. Source code for the program IF2.CPP.**

```
1: // Program that demonstrates the dual-alternative if statement
2:
3: #include <iostream.h>
4: #include <ctype.h>
5:
6: main()
7: {
8:   char c;
9:   cout << "Enter a letter : ";
```

continues

Listing 5.2. continued

```
10:    cin >> c;
11:    // convert to uppercase
12:    c = toupper(c);
13:    if (c >= 'A' && c <= 'Z')
14:      cout << "You entered a letter\n";
15:    else
16:      cout << "Your input was not a letter\n";
17:    return 0;
18: }
```

Here is a sample session with the program in Listing 5.2:

```
Enter a character : g
You entered a letter
```

The program in listing 5.2 declares the `char`-typed variable c in line 8. The output statement in line 9 prompts you to enter a letter. The input statement in line 10 obtains your input and stores it in variable c. The statement in line 12 converts the value in the variable to uppercase by calling the function `toupper` (prototyped in the CTYPE.H header file). This character case conversion simplifies the tested condition in the `if-else` statement at line 13. The `if-else` statement determines if the variable c contains a character in the range of A to Z. If this condition is true, the program executes the output statement in line 14. This statement displays a message stating that you have entered a letter. By contrast, if the tested condition is false, the program executes the `else` clause statement in line 16. This statement displays a message stating that your input was not a letter.

Potential Problems with the *if* Statement

There is a potential problem with the dual-alternative `if` statement. This problem occurs when the `if` clause includes another single-alternative `if` statement. In this case, the compiler considers that the `else` clause pertains to the nested `if` statement. (A nested `if` statement is one that contains another `if` statement in the if and/or else clauses—more about nesting in the next section.) Here is an example:

```
if (i > 0)
    if (i = 10)
        cout << "You guessed the magic number";
else
    cout << "Number is out of range";
```

In this code fragment, when variable i is a positive number other than 10, the code displays the message Number is out of range. The compiler treats these statements as though the code fragment meant

```
if (i > 0)
    if (i = 10)
        cout << "You guessed the magic number";
    else
        cout << "Number is out of range";
```

To correct this problem, enclose the nested if statement in a statement block:

```
if (i > 0) {
    if (i = 10)
        cout << "You guessed the magic number";
}
else
    cout << "Number is out of range";
```

The Multiple-Alternative *if-else* Statement

C++ allows you to nest if-else statements to create a multiple-alternative form. This alternative gives a lot of power and flexibility to your applications.

NEW TERM   The *multiple-alternative* if-else statement contains nested if-else statements.

The Multiple-Alternative *if-else* Statement

The general syntax for the multiple-alternative if-else statement is

```
if (tested_condition1)
    statement1; ¦ { <sequence #1 of statement> }
else if (tested_condition2)
    statement2; ¦ { <sequence #2 of statement> }
...
else if (tested_conditionN)
    statementN; ¦ { <sequence #N of statement> }
[else
    statementN+1; ¦ { <sequence #N+1 of statement> }]
```

Example:

```
char op;

int opOk = 1;
double x, y, z;
```

5

```
cout << "Enter operand1 operator operand2: ";
cin >> x >> op >> y;
if (op == '+')
    z = x + y;
else if (op == '-')
    z = x - y;
else if (op == '*')
    z = x * y;
else if (op == '/' && y != 0)
    z = x / y;
else
    opOk = 0;
```

The multiple-alternative if-else statement performs a series of cascaded tests until one of the following occurs:

1. One of the conditions in the if clause or in the else if clauses is true. In this case, the accompanying statements are executed.

2. None of the tested conditions is true. The program executes the statements in the catch-all else clause (if there is an else clause).

Figure 5.3 shows the program flow in the multiple-alternative if-else statement.

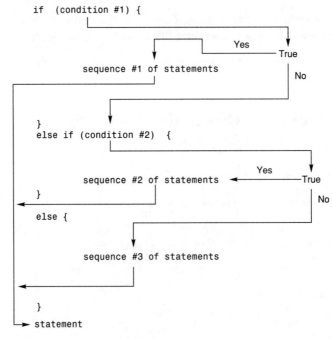

Figure 5.3. The program flow in the multiple-alternative if-else statement.

Let's look at an example. Listing 5.3 shows the source code for program IF3.CPP. The program prompts you to enter a character and uses the multiple-alternative if-else statement to determine whether your input is one of the following:

☐ An uppercase letter

☐ A lowercase letter

☐ A digit

☐ A nonalphanumeric character

 Listing 5.3. Source code for the IF3.CPP program.

```
 1: // Program that demonstrates the multiple-alternative if statement
 2:
 3: #include <iostream.h>
 4:
 5: main()
 6: {
 7:    char c;
 8:    cout << "Enter a character : ";
 9:    cin >> c;
10:    if (c >= 'A' && c <= 'Z')
11:      cout << "You entered an uppercase letter\n";
12:    else if (c >= 'a' && c <= 'z')
13:      cout << "You entered a lowercase letter\n";
14:    else if (c >= '0' && c <= '9')
15:      cout << "You entered a digit\n";
16:    else
17:      cout << "You entered a non-alphanumeric character\n";
18:    return 0;
19: }
```

Here is a sample session with the program in Listing 5.3:

```
Enter a character : !
You entered a non-alphanumeric character
```

The program in Listing 5.3 declares the char-typed variable c in line 7. The output statement in line 8 prompts you to enter a letter. The input statement in line 9 obtains your input and stores it in variable c. The multi-alternative if-else statement tests the following conditions:

1. In line 10, the if statement determines if the variable c contains a letter in the range of A to Z. If this condition is true, the program executes the

output statement in line 11. This statement confirms that you entered an uppercase letter. The program then resumes at line 18.

2. If the condition in line 10 is false, the program jumps to the first `else if` clause in line 12. There the program determines whether the variable c contains a letter in the range of a to z. If this condition is true, the program executes the output statement in line 13. This statement confirms that you entered a lowercase letter. The program then resumes at line 18.

3. If the condition in line 12 is false, the program jumps to the second `else if` clause in line 14. There the program determines whether the variable c contains a digit. If this condition is true, the program executes the output statement in line 15. This statement confirms that you entered a digit. The program then resumes at line 18.

4. If the condition in line 14 is false, the program jumps to the catch-all `else` clause in line 16 and executes the output statement in line 17. This statement displays a message telling you that your input was neither a letter nor a digit.

The *switch* Statement

The `switch` statement offers a special form of multiple-alternative decision-making. It enables you to examine the various values of an integer-compatible expression and choose the appropriate course of action.

The *switch* Statement

The general syntax for the `switch` statement is

```
switch (expression) {
    case constant1_1:
[   case constant1_2: ...]
        <one or more statements>
        break;
    case constant2_1:
[   case constant2_2: ...]
        <one or more statements>
        break;
...
    case constantN_1:
[   case constantN_2: ...]
        <one or more statements>
        break;
```

```
        default:
            <one or more statements>
}
```

Example:

```
OK = 1;
switch (op) {
    case '+':
        z = x + y;
        break;
    case '-':
        z = x - y;
        break;
    case '*':
        z = x * y;
        break;
    case '/':
        if (y != 0)
            z = x / y;
        else
            OK = 0;
        break;
    default:
        Ok = 0;
}
```

The rules for using a switch statement are

1. The switch requires an integer-compatible value. This value may be a constant, variable, function call, or expression. The switch statement does not work with floating-point data types.

2. The value after each case label *must be* a constant.

3. C++ does not support case labels with ranges of values. Instead, *each* value must appear in a separate case label.

4. You need to use a break statement after each set of executable statements. The break statement causes program execution to resume after the end of the current switch statement. If you do not use the break statement, the program execution resumes at the subsequent case labels.

5. The default clause is a catch-all clause.

6. The set of statements in each case label or grouped case labels need not be enclosed in open and close braces.

5

> **Note:** The lack of single `case` labels with ranges of values makes it more appealing to use a multiple-alternative `if-else` statement if you have a large contiguous range of values.

Figure 5.4 shows the program flow in the multiple-alternative `switch` statement.

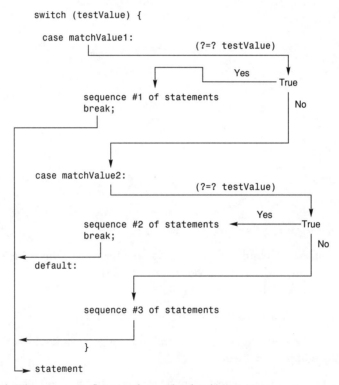

Figure 5.4. The program flow in the multiple-alternative `switch` statement.

Let's look at an example that uses the `switch` statement. Listing 5.4 contains the source code for program SWITCH1.CPP that I obtained by editing Listing 5.3. The new program performs the same task of classifying your character input, this time using a `switch` statement.

**Listing 5.4. Source code
for the SWITCH1.CPP program.**

```
 1: // Program that demonstrates the multiple-alternative switch
    statement
 2:
 3: #include <iostream.h>
 4:
 5: main()
 6: {
 7:   char c;
 8:   cout << "Enter a character : ";
 9:   cin >> c;
10:   switch (c) {
11:     case 'A':
12:     case 'B':
13:     case 'C':
14:     case 'D':
15:     // other case labels
16:       cout << "You entered an uppercase letter\n";
17:       break;
18:     case 'a':
19:     case 'b':
20:     case 'c':
21:     case 'd':
22:     // other case labels
23:       cout << "You entered a lowercase letter\n";
24:       break;
25:     case '0':
26:     case '1':
27:     case '2':
28:     case '3':
29:     // other case labels
30:       cout << "You entered a digit\n";
31:       break;
32:     default:
33:       cout << "You entered a non-alphanumeric character\n";
34:   }
35:   return 0;
36: }
```

Here is a sample session with the program in Listing 5.4:

```
Enter a character : 2
You entered a digit
```

5

117

Analysis   The program in Listing 5.4 declares the char-typed variable c. The output statement in line 8 prompts you to enter a character. The statement in line 9 stores your input in variable c. The switch statement starts at line 10. Lines 11 through 14 contain the case labels for the letter A to D. I omitted the case labels for the rest of the uppercase letters to keep the program short. If the character in variable c matches any value in lines 11 through 14, the program executes the output statement in line 16. This statement confirms that you entered an uppercase letter. (Because I reduced the number of case labels, the program executes the statement in line 16 only if you enter the letters A to D.) The break statement in line 17 causes the program flow to jump to line 35, past the end of the switch statement.

If the character in variable c does not match any of the case labels in lines 11 through 14, the program resumes at line 18 where it encounters another set of case labels. These labels are supposed to represent lowercase characters. As you can see, I reduced the number of labels to shorten the program. If the character in variable c matches any value in lines 18 through 21, the program executes the output statement in line 23. This statement confirms that you entered a lowercase letter. (Because I reduced the number of case labels, the program executes the statement in line 23 only if you enter the letters a to d.) The break statement in line 24 causes the program flow to jump to line 35, past the end of the switch statement.

If the character in variable c does match any of the case labels in lines 18 through 21, the program resumes at line 25 where it encounters another set of case labels. These labels are supposed to represent digits. Again, you can see that I reduced the number of labels to shorten the program. If the character in variable c matches any value in lines 25 through 28, the program executes the output statement in line 30. This statement confirms that you entered a digit. (Because I reduced the number of case labels, the program executes the statement in line 30 only if you enter the digits 0 to 3.) The break statement in line 31 causes the program flow to jump to line 35, past the end of the switch statement.

If the character in variable c does not match any case label in lines 25 through 28, the program jumps to the catch-all clause in line 32. The program executes the output statement in line 33. This statement tells you that you entered a nonalphanumeric character.

Nested Decision-Making Constructs

Often you need to use nested decision-making constructs to manage nontrivial conditions. Nesting decision-making constructs enables you to deal with complicated conditions using a divide-and-conquer approach. The outer-level constructs help you to test preliminary or more general conditions. The inner-level constructs help you deal with more specific conditions.

Let's look at an example. Listing 5.5 shows the source code for program IF4.CPP. The program prompts you to enter a character. Then the program determines if your input is an uppercase letter, a lowercase letter, or a character that is not a letter. The program displays a message which classifies your input.

Listing 5.5. Source code for the program IF4.CPP.

```
 1: // Program that demonstrates the nested if statements
 2:
 3: #include <iostream.h>
 4:
 5: main()
 6: {
 7:   char c;
 8:   cout << "Enter a character : ";
 9:   cin >> c;
10:   if ((c >= 'A' && c <= 'Z') || (c >= 'a' && c <= 'z'))
11:     if (c >= 'A' && c <= 'Z')
12:       cout << "You entered an uppercase letter\n";
13:     else
14:       cout << "You entered a lowercase letter\n";
15:   else
16:     cout << "You entered a non-letter character\n";
17:   return 0;
18: }
```

Here is a sample session with the program in Listing 5.5:

Output

```
Enter a character : a
You entered a lowercase letter
```

5

119

Analysis The program in Listing 5.5 declares the char-typed variable c. The output statement in line 8 prompts you to enter a character. The statement in line 9 stores your input in variable c. The program uses nested if-else statements that begin at lines 10 and 11. The outer if-else statement determines whether or not the variable c contains a letter. If the tested condition is true, the program executes the inner if-else statement in line 11. Otherwise, the program resumes at the else clause of the outer if-else statement and executes the output statement in line 16. This statement tells you that your input was not a letter.

The program uses the inner if-else statement to further examine the condition of the outer if-else statement. The if-else statement in line 11 determines whether or not the variable c contains an uppercase letter. If this condition is true, the program executes the output statement in line 12. Otherwise, the program executes the else clause statement in line 14. These output statements tell you whether you entered an uppercase or a lowercase letter. After executing the inner if-else statement, the program jumps to line 17, past the end of the outer if-else statement.

Summary

Today's lesson presents the various decision-making constructs in C++, including the following:

☐ The single-alternative if statement, such as

```
if (tested_condition)
    statement; ¦ {    <sequence of statements> }
```

☐ The dual-alternative if-else statement, such as

```
if (tested_condition)
    statement1; { <sequence #1 of statements> }
else
    statement1; { <sequence #1 of statements> }
```

☐ The multiple-alternative if-else statement, such as

```
if (tested_condition1)
    statement1; ¦ { <sequence #1 of statement> }
else if (tested_condition2)
    statement2; ¦ { <sequence #2 of statement> }
```

```
    ...
    else if (tested_conditionN)
        statementN; ¦ { <sequence #N of statement> }
    [else
        statementN+1; ¦ { <sequence #N+1 of statement> }]
```

☐ The multiple-alternative switch statement, such as

```
switch (caseVar) {
    case constant1_1:
    case constant1_2:
    <other case labels>
        <one or more statements>
        break;
    case constant2_1:
    case constant2_2:
    <other case labels>
        <one or more statements>
        break;
    ...
    case constantN_1:
    case constantN_2:
    <other case labels>
        <one or more statements>
        break;

    default:
        <one or more statements>
        break;
}
```

You also learn about the following topics:

☐ The if statements require you to observe two rules:

The tested condition must be enclosed in parentheses.

Blocks of statements are enclosed in pairs of open and close braces.

☐ Nested decision-making constructs empower you to deal with complex conditions using a divide-and-conquer approach. The outer-level constructs help you in testing preliminary or more general conditions. The inner-level constructs assist in handling more specific conditions.

Q&A

Q. Does C++ impose any rules for indenting statements in the clauses of an `if` statement?

A. No. The indentation is purely up to you. Typical indentations range from 2 to 4 spaces. Using indentations makes your listings much more readable. Here is the case of an `if` statement with unindented clause statements:

```
if (i > 0)
j = i * i;
else
j = 10 - i;
```

Compare the readability of that listing with this indented version:

```
if (i > 0)
  j = i * i;
else
  j = 10 - i;
```

The indented version is much easier to read.

Q. What are the rules for writing the condition of an `if-else` statement?

A. There are two schools of thought. The first one recommends that you write the condition so that it is more often true than not. The second school recommends avoiding negative expressions (those that use the relational operator `!=` and the Boolean operator `!`). Programmers in this camp translate this `if` statement:

```
if (i != 0)
    j = 100 / i;
else
    j = 1;
```

into the following equivalent form:

```
if (i == 0)
    j = 1;
else
    j = 100 \ i;
```

even though the likelihood of variable `i` storing 0 might be very low.

Q. How do I handle a condition such as the following that divides by a variable that can possibly be zero?

```
if (i != 0 && 1/i > 1)
    j = i * i;
```

A. C++ does not always evaluate the entire tested condition. This partial evaluation occurs when a term in the Boolean expression renders the entire expression false or true, regardless of the values of the other terms. In this case, if variable i is 0, the run-time system does not evaluate the term 1/i > 1. This is because the term i != 0 is false and would render the entire expression false, regardless of what the second term yields.

Q. Is it really necessary to include an else or default clause in multi-alternative if-else and switch statements?

A. Programmers highly recommend the inclusion of these catch-all clauses to ensure that the multiple-alternative statements handle all conditions.

Workshop

The Workshop provides quiz questions to help you solidify your understanding of the material covered and exercises to provide you with experience in using what you've learned. Try to understand the quiz and exercise answers before continuing on to the next day's lesson. Answers are provided in Appendix B, "Answers."

Quiz

1. Simplify the following nested if statements by replacing them with a single if statement:

```
if (i > 0)
  if (i < 10)
     cout << "i = " << i << "\n";
```

2. Simplify the following if statements by replacing them with a single if statement:

```
if (i > 0) {
    j = i * i;
    cout << "j = " << j << "\n";
}
```

```
if (i < 0) {
    j = 4 * i;
    cout << "j = " << j << "\n";
}
if (i == 0) {
    j = 10 + i
    cout << "j = " << j << "\n";
}
```

3. True or false? The following `if` statements perform the same tasks as the `if-else` statement:

```
if (i < 0) {
    i = 10 + i;
    j = i * i;
    cout << "i = " << i << "\n";
    cout << "j = " << j << "\n";
}
if (i >= 0) {
    k = 4 * i + 1;
    cout << "k = " << k << "\n";

}


if (i < 0) {
    i = 10 - i;
    j = i * i;
    cout << "i = " << i << "\n";
    cout << "j = " << j << "\n";
}
else {
    k = 4 * i + 1;
    cout << "k = " << k << "\n";
}
```

4. Simplify the following `if-else` statement:

```
if (i > 0 && i < 100)
    j = i * i;
else if (i > 10 && i < 50)
    j = 10 + i;
```

```
else if (i >= 100)
   j = i;
else
   j = 1;
```

5. What is wrong with the following `if` statement?

```
if (i > (1 + i * i)) {
   j = i * i
   cout << "i = " << i << " and j = " << j << "\n";
}
```

Exercises

1. Write the program IF5.CPP to solve for the roots of a quadratic equation. The quadratic equation is

   $$A\ X^2 + B^X + C = 0$$

   The roots of the quadratic equation are

   ```
   root1 = (-B + √(B² - 4AC)) / (2A)
   root2 = (-B - √(B² - 4AC)) / (2A)
   ```

   If the term in the square root is negative, the roots are complex. If the term in the square root term is zero, the two roots are the same and are equal to `-B/(2A)`.

2. Write the program SWITCH2.CPP, which implements a simple four-function calculator. The program should prompt you for the operand and the operator and display both the input and the result. Include error checking for bad operators and the attempt to divide by zero.

5

DAY
6

Loops

Recall from Day 3 that loops are powerful language constructs that enable computers to excel in achieving repetitive tasks. Computers are able to repeat tasks quickly, accurately, and tirelessly—an area where computers seem to do a better job than humans. Today's lesson presents the following loops in C++:

- ☐ The `for` loop statement
- ☐ The `do-while` loop statement
- ☐ The `while` loop statement
- ☐ Skipping iterations
- ☐ Exiting loops
- ☐ Nested loops

The *for* Loop

The `for` loop in C++ is a versatile loop because it offers both fixed and conditional iterations. The latter feature of the `for` loop deviates from the typical use of the `for` loop in other programming languages, such as Pascal and Basic.

The *for* Loop

The general syntax for the `for` loop statement is

```
for (<initialization of loop control variables>;
     <loop continuation test>;
     <increment/decrement of loop control variables>)
```

Example:

```
for (i = 0; i < 10; i++)
    cout << "The cube of " << i << " = " << i * i * i << "\n";
```

The `for` loop statement has three components, all of which are optional. The first component initializes the loop control variables. (C++ permits you to use more than one loop control variable.) The second part of the loop is the condition which determines whether or not the loop makes another iteration. The last part of the `for` loop is the clause that increments and/or decrements the loop control variables.

Note: The C++ `for` loop allows you to declare the loop control variables. Such variables exist in the scope of the loop.

Let's look at an example. Listing 6.1 contains the source code for program FOR1.CPP. The program prompts you to define a range of integers by specifying its lower and upper bounds. Then the program calculates the sum of integers in the range you specify, as well as the average value.

Listing 6.1. Source code for the program FOR1.CPP.

```
1: // Program that calculates a sum and average of a range of
2: // integers using a for loop
3:
4: #include <iostream.h>
5:
6: main()
7: {
8:     double sum = 0;
9:     double sumx = 0.0;
10:    int first, last, temp;
11:
12:    cout << "Enter the first integer : ";
13:    cin >> first;
14:    cout << "Enter the last integer : ";
15:    cin >> last;
16:    if (first > last) {
17:      temp= first;
18:      first = last;
19:      last = temp;
20:    }
21:    for (int i = first; i <= last; i++) {
22:      sum++;
23:      sumx += (double)i;
24:    }
25:    cout << "Sum of integers from "
26:         << first << " to " << last << " = "
27:         << sumx << "\n";
28:    cout << "Average value = " << sumx / sum;
29:    return 0;
30: }
```

Here is a sample session with the program in Listing 6.1:

```
Enter the first integer : 1
Enter the last integer : 100
Sum of integers from 1 to 100 = 5050
Average value = 50.5
```

6

Analysis   The program in Listing 6.1 declares a collection of int-typed and double-typed variables in function main. The function initializes the summation variables, sum and sumx, to 0. The input and output statements in lines 12 through 15 prompt you to enter the integers that define a range of values. The program stores these integers in the variables first and last. The if statement in line 16 determines whether or not the value in variable first is greater than the value in variable last. If this condition is true, the program executes the block of statements in lines 17 through 19. These statements swap the values in variables first and last, using the variable temp as a swap buffer. Thus, the if statement ensures that the integer in variable first is less than or equal to the integer in variable last.

The program carries out the summation using the for loop in line 21. The loop declares its own control variable, i, and initializes it with the value in variable first. The loop continuation condition is i <= last. This condition indicates that the loop iterates as long as i is less than or equal to the value in variable last. The loop increment component is i++, which increments the loop control variable by 1 for every iteration. The loop contains two statements. The first statement increments the value in variable sum. The second statement adds the value of i (after typecasting it to double) to the variable sumx.

> **Note:** I can rewrite the for loop to move the first loop statement to the loop increment component:
>
> ```
> for (int i = first; i <= last; i++, sum++)
>     sumx += (double)i;
> ```

The output statement in lines 25 through 27 displays the sum and average of integers in the range you specified.

To illustrate the flexibility of the for loop, I created the program FOR2.CPP, shown in Listing 6.2, by editing program FOR1.CPP. The two programs perform the same tasks and interact identically with you. The changes I made are in lines 10 and 21 through 25. Line 10 declares the loop control variable. In line 21 I initialize the variable i using the value in variable first. The for loop is located at line 22. The loop has no initialization part, because I took care of that in line 21. In addition, I removed the loop increment component and compensated for it by applying the post-increment operator to variable i in line 24.

Listing 6.2. Source code for the program FOR2.CPP.

```
1: // Program that calculates a sum and average of a range of
2: // integers using a for loop
3:
4: #include <iostream.h>
5:
6: main()
7: {
8:     double sum = 0;
9:     double sumx = 0.0;
10:    int first, last, temp, i;
11:
12:    cout << "Enter the first integer : ";
13:    cin >> first;
14:    cout << "Enter the last integer : ";
15:    cin >> last;
16:    if (first > last) {
17:      temp= first;
18:      first = last;
19:      last = temp;
20:    }
21:    i = first;
22:    for (; i <= last; ) {
23:      sum++;
24:      sumx += (double)i++;
25:    }
26:    cout << "Sum of integers from "
27:         << first << " to " << last << " = "
28:         << sumx << "\n";
29:    cout << "Average value = " << sumx / sum;
30:    return 0;
31: }
```

Here is a sample session with the program in Listing 6.2:

```
Enter the first integer : 10
Enter the last integer : 100
Sum of integers from 10 to 100 = 5005
Average value = 55
```

Open Loops
Using the *for* Loops

When I introduced you to the C++ `for` loop, I stated that the three components of the `for` loop are optional. In fact, C++ permits you to leave these three components empty!

NEW ☞ When you leave the three components of a loop empty, the result is an *open*
TERM *loop.*

It is worthwhile pointing out that other languages, such as Ada and Modula-2, do support formal open loops and provide mechanisms to exit these loops. C++ permits you to exit from a loop in one of the following two ways:

1. The `break` statement causes the program execution to resume after the end of the current loop. Use the `break` statement when you wish to exit a `for` loop and resume with the remaining parts of the program.

2. The `exit` function (declared in the STDLIB.H header file) allows you to exit the program. Use the `exit` function if you want to stop iterating and also exit the program.

Let's look at an example. Listing 6.3 contains the source code for program FOR3.CPP. The program uses an open loop to repeatedly prompt you for a number. The program takes your input and displays it along with its reciprocal value. Then the program asks you whether or not you wish to calculate the reciprocal of another number. If you type in the letter Y or y, the program performs another iteration. Otherwise, the program ends. If you keep typing Y or y for the latter prompt, the program keeps running— at least until the computer breaks down!

Listing 6.3. Source code for the program FOR3.CPP.

```
1: // Program that demonstrates using the
2: // for loop to emulate an infinite loop.
3:
4: #include <iostream.h>
5: #include <ctype.h>
6:
7: main()
8: {
9:     char ch;
10:     double x, y;
11:
```

```
12:    // for loop with empty parts
13:    for (;;) {
14:      cout << "\nEnter a number : ";
15:      cin >> x;
16:      // process number if non-zero
17:      if (x != 0) {
18:        y = 1/ x;
19:        cout << "1/(" << x << ") = " << y << "\n";
20:        cout << "More calculations? (Y/N) ";
21:        cin >> ch;
22:        ch = toupper(ch);
23:        if (ch != 'Y')
24:          break;
25:      }
26:      else
27:        // display error message
28:        cout << "Error: cannot accept 0\n";
29:    }
30:    return 0;
31: }
```

Here is a sample session with the program in Listing 6.3:

```
Enter a number : 5
1/(5) = 0.2
More calculations? (Y/N) y

Enter a number : 12
1/(12) = 0.0833333
More calculations? (Y/N) y

Enter a number : 16
1/(16) = 0.0625
More calculations? (Y/N) n
```

The program in Listing 6.3 declares the char-typed variable c and two double-typed variables, x and y. The function main uses the for loop, in line 13, as an open loop by eliminating all three loop components. The output statement in line 14 prompts you to enter a number. The input statement in line 15 obtains your input and stores it in variable x. The if-else statement in line 17 determines if the value in variable x is not zero. If this condition is true, the program executes the block of statements in lines 18 through 24. Otherwise, the program executes the else clause statement in line 28. This statement displays an error message.

The statement in line 18 assigns the reciprocal of the value in variable x to variable y. The output statement in line 19 displays the values in variables x and y. The output statement in line 20 prompts you for more calculations, and requires a Y/N (in either

6

uppercase or lowercase) type of answer. The input statement in line 21 stores your single-character input in variable c. The statement in line 22 converts your input into uppercase, using the function toupper (this function is prototyped in the CTYPE.H header file). The if statement in line 23 determines whether or not the character in variable c is not the letter Y. If this condition is true, the program executes the break statement in line 24. This statement causes the program execution to exit the open loop and to resume at line 30.

The *do-while* Loop

The do-while loop in C++ is a conditional loop. Therefore, the do-while loop iterates at least once.

NEW
TERM
A *conditional loop* iterates as long as a condition is true. This condition is tested at the end of the loop.

The *do-while* Loop

The general syntax for the do-while loop is

```
do {
    sequence of statements
} while (condition);
```

Example:

The following loop displays the squares of 2 to 10:

```
int i = 2;
do {
    cout << i << "^2 = " << i * i << "\n";
} while (++i < 11);
```

Let's look at an example. Listing 6.4 shows the source code for program DOWHILE1.CPP which essentially calculates square root values. The program performs the following tasks:

☐ Prompts you to enter a number (if you enter a negative number, the program reprompts you for a number)

☐ Calculates and displays the square root of the number you keyed in

☐ Asks you if you wish to enter another number (if you enter the letter Y or y, the program resumes at step number 1; otherwise, the program ends)

Listing 6.4. Source code for the program DOWHILE1.CPP.

```cpp
 1: // Program that demonstrates the do-while loop
 2:
 3: #include <iostream.h>
 4:
 5: const double TOLERANCE = 1.0e-7;
 6:
 7: double abs(double x)
 8: {
 9:   return (x >= 0) ? x : -x;
10: }
11:
12: double sqroot(double x)
13: {
14:   double guess = x / 2;
15:   do {
16:     guess = (guess + x / guess) / 2;
17:   } while (abs(guess * guess - x) > TOLERANCE);
18:   return guess;
19: }
20:
21: double getNumber()
22: {
23:   double x;
24:   do {
25:     cout << "Enter a number: ";
26:     cin >> x;
27:   } while (x < 0);
28:   return x;
29: }
30:
31: main()
32: {
33:   char c;
34:   double x, y;
35:
36:   do {
37:     x = getNumber();
38:     y = sqroot(x);
39:     cout << "Sqrt(" << x << ") = " << y << "\n"
40:          << "Enter another number? (Y/N) ";
41:     cin >> c;
42:     cout << "\n";
43:   } while (c == 'Y' || c == 'y');
44:   return 0;
45: }
```

Here is a sample session with the program in Listing 6.4:

```
Enter a number: 25
Sqrt(25) = 5
Enter another number? (Y/N) y

Enter a number: 144
Sqrt(144) = 12
Enter another number? (Y/N) n
```

The program in Listing 6.4 declares the global constant TOLERANCE and the functions abs, sqroot, getNumber, and main. The function abs, located in line 7, returns the absolute value of double-typed arguments.

The function sqroot, located in line 12, returns the square root of the parameter x. The function sets the initial guess for the square root to x / 2 in line 14. Then the function uses a do-while loop to refine iteratively the guess for the square root. The condition in the while clause determines if the absolute difference between the square of the current guess and the parameter x is greater than the allowable error (represented by the constant TOLERANCE). The loop iterates as long as this condition is true. The function returns the guess for the square root in line 18. The function sqroot implements Newton's method for iteratively obtaining the square root of a number.

The function getNumber, located in line 21, prompts you for a number and stores your input in the local variable x. The function uses a do-while loop to ensure that you enter a nonnegative number. The while clause in line 27 determines if the value in variable x is negative. As long as this condition is true, the do-while loop iterates. In line 28 the return statement yields the value of x.

The function main, located in line 31, uses a do-while loop to perform the following tasks:

☐ Prompts you for a number by calling function getNumber (the statement in line 37 contains the function call and assigns the result to the local variable x)

☐ Calculates the square root of x by calling function sqroot, and assigns the result to variable y (the statement which contains this function call is in line 38)

☐ Displays the values in variables x and y

☐ Asks you if you want to enter another number (the input statement in line 41 takes your single-character Y/N input and stores it in variable c)

The while clause, located in line 43, determines if the variable c contains either the letter Y or y. The do-while loop iterates as long as this condition is true.

The program in Listing 6.4 illustrates the following uses for the do-while loop:

1. *Iterative calculations.* The loop in function sqroot shows this aspect.

2. *Data validation.* The loop in function getNumber illustrates this aspect.

3. *Program continuation.* The loop in function main shows this aspect.

The *while* Loop

The while loop C++ is another conditional loop that iterates as long as a condition is true. Thus, the while loop may not iterate if the tested condition is initially false.

The *while* Loop

The general syntax of the while loop is

```
while (condition)
    statement; ¦ { sequence of statements }
```

Example:

```
function power(double x, int n)
{
  double pwr = 1;
  while (n-- > 0)
    pwr *= x;
  return pwr;
}
```

Let's look at an example. Listing 6.5 shows the source code for program WHILE1.CPP. This program performs the same operations as program FOR1.CPP, in Listing 6.1. The two programs interact in the same way and yield the same results.

Listing 6.5. Source code for the program WHILE1.CPP.

```
1: // Program that demonstrates the do-while loop
2:
3: #include <iostream.h>
4:
5: main()
6: {
7:     double sum = 0;
8:     double sumx = 0.0;
9:     int first, last, temp, i;
10:
```

continues

6

137

Listing 6.5. continued

```
11:      cout << "Enter the first integer : ";
12:      cin >> first;
13:      cout << "Enter the last integer : ";
14:      cin >> last;
15:      if (first > last) {
16:        temp= first;
17:        first = last;
18:        last = temp;
19:      }
20:      i = first;
21:      while (i <= last) {
22:        sum++;
23:        sumx += (double)i++;
24:      }
25:      cout << "Sum of integers from "
26:           << first << " to " << last << " = "
27:           << sumx << "\n";
28:      cout << "Average value = " << sumx / sum;
29:      return 0;
30: }
```

Here is a sample session with the program in Listing 6.5:

```
Enter the first integer : 1
Enter the last integer : 100
Sum of integers from 1 to 100 = 5050
Average value = 50.5
```

Because the programs in Listing 6.5 and 6.1 are similar, I focus on lines 20 through 24 where the main difference between the two programs lies. The statement in line 20 assigns the value of variable first to variable i. The while loop starts at line 21. The loop iterates as long as the value in variable i is less than or equal to the value in variable last. The variable i plays the role of the loop control variable. The statement in line 22 increments the value in variable sum. The statement in line 23 adds the value in variable i to the variable sumx and also increments the variable i. The statement performs the latter task by applying the post-increment operator to the variable i.

Skipping Loop Iterations

C++ enables you to jump to the end of a loop and resume the next iteration using the continue statement. This programming feature permits your loop to skip iteration for special values, which may cause run-time errors.

Syntax

The *continue* Statement

The general form for using the continue statement is

```
<loop-start clause> {
    // sequence #1 of statements
    if (skipCondition)
        continue;
    // sequence #2 of statements
} <loop-end clause>
```

Example (in a for loop):

```
double x, y;
for (int i = -10; i < 11; i++) {
  x = i;
  if (i == 1)
    continue;
  y = 1/sqrt(x * x - 1);
  cout << "1/sqrt(" << (x*x-1) << ") = " << y << "\n";
}
```

This form shows that the evaluation of the first sequence of statements in the for loop gives rise to a condition tested in the if statement. If that condition is true, the if statement invokes the continue statement to skip the second sequence of statements in the for loop.

Let's look at an example. Listing 6.6 shows the source code for program FOR4.CPP. The program displays the table of values for the function f(X) = $\sqrt{(X^2 - 9)}$ at integer values between -10 and 10. Because the integers between -2 and 2 yield complex results, which the program avoids, the table does not display the complex values for f(X) between -2 and 2.

Listing 6.6. Source code for the program FOR4.CPP.

6

```
 1: // Program that demonstrates using the continue statement
 2: // to skip iterations.
 3:
 4: #include <iostream.h>
 5: #include <math.h>
 6:
 7:
 8: double f(double x)
 9: {
10:   return sqrt(x * x - 9);
11: }
12:
13: main()
14: {
```

Listing 6.6. continued

```
15:    double x, y;
16:
17:    cout << "         X";
18:    cout << "              f(X)\n";
19:    cout << "_____\n\n";
20:    // for loop with empty parts
21:    for (int i = -10; i <= 10; i++) {
22:      if (i > -3 && i < 3)
23:        continue;
24:      x = (double)i;
25:      y = f(x);
26:      cout << "    ";
27:      cout.width(3);
28:      cout << x << "         ";
29:      cout.width(7);
30:      cout << y << "\n";
31:    }
32:    return 0;
33: }
```

Here is a sample session with the program in Listing 6.6:

X	f(X)
-10	9.53939
-9	8.48528
-8	7.4162
-7	6.32456
-6	5.19615
-5	4
-4	2.64575
-3	0
3	0
4	2.64575
5	4
6	5.19615
7	6.32456
8	7.4162
9	8.48528
10	9.53939

Analysis The program in Listing 6.6 declares the function f to represent the mathematical function f(X). The function main declares the double-typed variables x and y in line 15. The output statements in lines 17 through 19 display the table's heading. The for loop in line 21 declares its own control variable and iterates between -10 to 10, in increments of 1. The first statement inside the loop is the if statement located at line 22. This statement determines if the value in variable i is greater than -3 and less than 3. If this condition is true, the program executes the continue statement in line 23. Thus, the if statement enables the for loop to skip error-generating iterations and resume with the next iteration. The statement in line 24 assigns the value in variable i to variable x. The statement in line 25 calls the function f and supplies it with the argument x. The statement then assigns the result to variable y. The output statements in lines 25 through 30 display the values of variable x and y. The statements use the function width for simple formatting.

Exiting Loops

C++ supports the break statement to exit a loop. The break statement makes the program resume after the end of the current loop.

Syntax

The *break* Statement

The general form for using the break statement in a loop is

```
<start-loop clause> {
    // sequence #1 of statements
    if (exitLoopCondition)
        break;
    // sequence #2 of statements
} <end-loop clause>
// sequence #3 of statements
```

Example:

```
// calculate the factorial of n
factorial = 1;
for (int i = 1; ; i++) {
  if (i > n)
     break;
  factorial *= (double)i;
}
```

This form shows that the evaluation of the first sequence of statements in the for loop gives rise to a condition tested in the if statement. If that condition is true, the if statement invokes the break statement to exit the loop altogether. The program execution resumes at the third sequence of statements.

For a good example that uses the break statement, I recommend that you reexamine the FOR3.CPP program in Listing 6.3.

Nested Loops

Nested loops enable you to contain repetitive tasks as part of other repetitive tasks. C++ allows you to nest any kind of loops to just about any level needed. Nested loops are frequently used to process arrays (covered in Day 7).

An example that uses nested loops, Listing 6.7 shows the source code for program NESTFOR1.CPP. The program displays a table for square roots for whole numbers in the range of 1 to 10. The program uses an outer loop to iterate over the above range of numbers, and employs an inner loop to iteratively calculate the square root.

 Listing 6.7. Source code for the program NESTFOR1.CPP.

```
1: // Program that demonstrates nested loops
2:
3: #include <stdio.h>
4:
5: const double TOLERANCE = 1.0e-7;
6: const int MIN_NUM = 1;
7: const int MAX_NUM = 10;
8:
9: double abs(double x)
10: {
11:   return (x >= 0) ? x : -x;
12: }
13:
14: main()
15: {
16:    double x, sqrt;
17:
18:    printf("  X      Sqrt(X)\n");
19:    printf("_____\n\n");
20:    // outer loop
21:    for (int i = MIN_NUM; i <= MAX_NUM; i++) {
22:      x = (double)i;
23:      sqrt = x /2;
24:      // inner loop
25:      do {
26:        sqrt = (sqrt + x / sqrt) / 2;
27:      } while (abs(sqrt * sqrt - x) > TOLERANCE);
28:      printf("%4.1f     %8.6lf\n", x, sqrt);
29:    }
30:    return 0;
31: }
```

Here is a sample session with the program in Listing 6.7:

142

X	Sqrt(X)
1.0	1.000000
2.0	1.414214
3.0	1.732051
4.0	2.000000
5.0	2.236068
6.0	2.449490
7.0	2.645751
8.0	2.828427
9.0	3.000000
10.0	3.162278

The program in Listing 6.7 includes the header file STDIO.H in order to use the `printf` output function with its powerful formatting capabilities. The lines 5 through 7 define the constants `L`, `TOLERANCE`, `MIN_NUM`, and `MAX_NUM`, to represent the tolerance in square root values, the first number in the output table, and the last number in the output table. The program defines the function `abs` to return the absolute number of a `double`-typed number.

The function `main` declares the `double`-typed variables `x` and `sqrt`. The output statements in lines 18 and 19 display the table's heading. Line 21 contains the outer loop, a `for` loop. This loop declares its control variable, `i`, and iterates from `MIN_NUM` to `MAX_NUM`, in increments of 1. Line 22 stores the typecast value of `i` in variable `x`. The statement in line 23 obtains the initial guess for the square root and stores it in variable `sqrt`. Line 25 contains the inner loop, a `do-while` loop which iterates to refine the guess for the square root. The statement in line 26 refines the guess for the square root. The `while` clause in line 27 determines whether or not the refined guess is adequate. The output statement in line 28 displays the formatted values for the variables `x` and `sqrt`.

Summary

6

Today's lesson covers the C++ loops and topics related to loops. You learn about the following:

☐ The `for` loop in C++ has the following general syntax:

```
for (<initialization of loop control variables>;
     <loop continuation test>;
     <increment/decrement of loop control variables>)
```

The `for` loop contains three components: the loop initialization, loop continuation condition, and the increment/decrement of the loop variables.

☐ The conditional loop do-while has the following general syntax:

```
do {
    sequence of statements
} while (condition);
```

The do-while loop iterates at least once.

☐ The conditional while loop has the following general syntax:

```
while (condition)
    statement; ¦ { sequence of statements }
```

The while loop may not iterate if its tested condition is initially false.

☐ The continue statement enables you to jump to the end of the loop and resume with the next iteration. The advantage of the continue statement is that it uses no labels to direct the jump.

☐ Open loops are for loops with empty components. The break statement enables you to exit the current loop and resume program execution at the first statement that comes after the loop. The exit function (declared in STDLIB.H) enables you to make a critical loop exit by halting the C++ program altogether.

☐ Nested loops empower you to contain repetitive tasks as part of other repetitive tasks. C++ allows you to nest any kind of loops to just about any level needed.

Q&A

Q. How can a while loop simulate a for loop?

A. Here is a simple example:

```
                                  int i = 1;
for (int i = 1; i <= 10; i +=2) {  while (i <= 10) {
  cout << i << "\n";                 cout << i << "\n";
                                      i += 2;
                                    }
```

The while loop needs a leading statement that initializes the loop control variable. Also notice that the while loop uses a statement inside it to alter the value of the loop control variable.

Q. How can a `while` loop simulate a `do-while` loop?

A. Here is a simple example:

```
i = 1;                          i = 1;
do {                            while (i <= 10) {
  cout << i << "\n";              cout << i << "\n";
  i += 2;                         i += 2;
} while (i <= 10);              }
```

The two loops have the same condition in their `while` clauses.

Q. How can the open `for` loop emulate the `while` and `do-while` loops?

A. The open `for` loop is able to emulate the other C++ loops by placing the loop-escape `if` statement near the beginning or end of the loop. Here is how the open `for` loop emulates a sample `while` loop:

```
i = 1;                          i = 1;
while (i <= 10) {               for (;;) {
                                  if(i > 10) break;
  cout << i << "\n"               cout << i << "\n"
  i += 2;                         i += 2;
}                               }
```

Notice that the open `for` loop uses a loop-escape `if` statement as the first statement inside the loop. The condition tested by the `if` statement is the logical reverse of the `while` loop condition. Here is a simple example showing the emulation of the `do-while` loop:

```
i = 1;                          i = 1;
do {                            for (;;) {
  cout << i << "\n"               cout << i << "\n"
  i += 2;                         i += 2;
                                  if (i > 10) break;
} while (i <= 10);              }
```

The open `for` loop uses a loop-escape `if` statement right before the end of the loop. The `if` statement tests the reverse condition as the `do-while` loop.

6

Q. In nested for loops, can I use the loop control variable of the outer loops as part of the range of values for the inner loops?

A. Yes. C++ does not object to such use. Here is a simple example:

```
for (int i = 1; i <= 100; i += 5)
    for (int j = i; j <= 100; j++)
        cout << i * j << "\n";
```

Q. Does C++ restrict nesting of the various types of loops?

A. No, you can nest any combination of loops in a C++ program.

Workshop

The Workshop provides quiz questions to help you solidify your understanding of the material covered and exercises to provide you with experience in using what you've learned. Try to understand the quiz and exercise answers before continuing on to the next day's lesson. Answers are provided in Appendix B, "Answers."

Quiz

1. What is wrong with the following loop?

```
i = 1;
while (i < 10) {
  j = i * i - 1;
  k = 2 * j - i;
  cout << "i = " << i << "\n";
  cout << "j = " << << j << "\n";
  cout << "k = " << k << "\n";
}
```

2. What is the output of the following for loop?

```
for (int i = 5; i < 10; i + 2)
    cout << i - 2 << "\n";
```

3. What is the output of the following for loop?

```
for (int i = 5; i < 10; )
    cout << i - 2 << "\n";
```

4. What is wrong with the following code?

```
for (int i = 1; i <= 10; i++)
    for (i = 8; i <= 12; i++)
        cout << i << "\n";
```

5. Where is the error in the following nested loops?

```
for (int i = 1; i <= 10; i++)
  cout << i * i << "\n";
for (int i = 1; i <= 10; i++)
  cout << i * i * i << "\n";
```

6. Where is the error in the following loop?

```
i = 1;
while (1 > 0) {
  cout << i << "\n";
  i++;
}
```

7. The factorial of a number is the product of the sequence of integers from 1 to that number. The following general equation defines the factorial (which uses the symbol !):

```
n! = 1 * 2 * 3 * ... * n
```

Here is a C++ program that calculates the factorial of a number. The problem is that for whatever positive value you enter, the program displays 0 value for the factorial. Where is the error in the program?

```
int n;
double factorial;
cout << "Enter positive integer : ";
cin >> n;
for (int i = 1; i <= n; i++)
  factorial *= i;
cout << n << "!= " << factorial;
```

Exercises

1. Write the program for FOR5.CPP which uses a for loop to obtain and display the sum of odd integers in the range of 11 to 121.

2. Write the program WHILE2.CPP which uses a `while` loop to obtain and display the sum of the squared odd integers in the range of 11 to 121.

3. Write the program DOWHILE2.CPP which uses a `do-while` loop to obtain and display the sum of the squared odd integers in the range of 11 to 121.

DAY 7

7

Arrays

Arrays are among the most popular data structures. They allow programs to store data for processing later on. Most popular programming languages support static arrays. Many languages also support dynamic arrays.

NEW☞
TERM An *array* is a group of variables.

Today, you learn about the following topics related to static arrays:

☐ Declaring single-dimensional arrays

☐ Using single-dimensional arrays

☐ Initializing single-dimensional arrays

☐ Declaring single-dimensional arrays as function parameters

☐ Sorting arrays

☐ Searching arrays

☐ Declaring multidimensional arrays

☐ Using multidimensional arrays

☐ Initializing multidimensional arrays

☐ Declaring multidimensional arrays as function parameters

Declaring Single-Dimensional Arrays

The single-dimensional array is the simplest kind of array. In a single-dimensional array, each variable is individually accessed using a single index.

NEW☞
TERM A *single-dimensional array* is a group of variables that share the same name (which is the name of the array).

A Single-Dimensional Array

The general syntax for declaring a single-dimensional array is

```
type arrayName[numberOfElements];
```

C++ requires you to observe the following rules in declaring single-dimensional arrays:

1. The lower bound of a C++ array is set at 0. C++ does not allow you to override or alter this lower bound.

2. Declaring a C++ array entails specifying the number of members. Keep in mind that the number of members is equal to the upper bound plus one.

The valid range of indices for this general form extends between `0` and `numberOfElements - 1`.

Examples:

```
int intArray[10];
char name[31];
double x[100];
```

Using Single-Dimensional Arrays

Using a single-dimensional array involves stating both its name and the valid index to access one of its members. Depending on where the reference to an array element occurs, it can either store or recall a value. The simple rules to remember are

1. Assign a value to an array element before accessing that element to recall data. Otherwise, you get garbage data.

2. Use a valid index.

DO	DON'T
DO make reasonable checks for the indices which access the arrays.	
DON'T assume that indices are always valid.	

Let's look at an example. Listing 7.1 shows the source code for the program ARRAY1.CPP. The program uses a 30-element numeric array to calculate the average for the data in a numeric array. The program performs the following tasks:

☐ Prompts you to enter the number of actual data points (this value must lie in the range of valid numbers indicated by the prompting message)

☐ Prompts you to enter the data for the array elements

☐ Calculates the average of the data in the array

☐ Displays the average value

7

Listing 7.1. Source code for the program ARRAY1.CPP.

```cpp
1: /*
2:    C++ program that demonstrates the use of one-dimension
3:    arrays.  The average value of the array is calculated.
4: */
5:
6: #include <iostream.h>
7:
8: const int MAX = 30;
9:
10: main()
11: {
12:
13:     double x[MAX];
14:     double sum, sumx = 0.0, mean;
15:     int i, n;
16:
17:     do { // obtain number of data points
18:         cout << "Enter number of data points [2 to "
19:              << MAX << "] : ";
20:         cin >> n;
21:         cout << "\n";
22:     } while (n < 2 ¦¦ n > MAX);
23:
24:     // prompt user for data
25:     for (i = 0; i < n; i++) {
26:         cout << "X[" << i << "] : ";
27:         cin >> x[i];
28:     }
29:
30:     // initialize summations
31:     sum = n;
32:
33:     // calculate sum of observations
34:     for (i = 0; i < n; i++)
35:         sumx += x[i];
36:
37:     mean = sumx / sum; // calculate the mean value
38:     cout << "\nMean = " << mean << "\n\n";
39:     return 0;
40: }
```

Here is a sample session with the program in Listing 7.1:

```
Enter number of data points [2 to 30] : 5

X[0] : 12.5
X[1] : 45.7
```

```
X[2] : 25.6
X[3] : 14.1
X[4] : 68.4

Mean = 33.26
```

 The program in Listing 7.1 declares the global constant MAX as the size of the array used in the program. The function main declares the double-typed array x, in line 13, to have MAX elements. The function also declares other nonarray variables in lines 14 and 15.

The do-while loop, which is located in lines 17 through 22, obtains the number of data points you want to store in the array x. The output statement in lines 18 and 19 prompts you to enter the number of data points. The output indicates the range of valid numbers, which is 2 to MAX. The statement in line 20 obtains your input and stores it in variable n. The while clause validates your input. The clause determines if the value in variable n is less than 2, or is greater than MAX. If this condition is true, the do-while loop iterates again to obtain a correct input value.

The for loop statement, in lines 25 through 28, prompts you to enter the data. The loop uses the control variable i and iterates from 0 to n-1, in increments of 1. The output statement in line 26 prompts you to enter the value for the indicated array element. The input statement in line 27 obtains your input and stores it in the element x[i].

The statement in line 31 assigns the integer in variable n to the double-typed variable sum. The for loop in lines 34 and 35 adds the values in array x to the variable sumx. The loop uses the control variable i and iterates from 0 to n-1, in increments of 1. The statement in line 35 uses the increment assignment operator to add the value in element x[i] to the variable sumx.

The statement in line 37 calculates the mean value and stores it in variable mean. The output statement in line 38 displays the mean value.

 Note: The program in Listing 7.1 shows how to use a for loop to process the elements of an array. The loop continuation test uses the < operator and the value beyond the last valid index. You can use the <= operator followed by the last index. For example, I can write the data input loop as

```
24:      // prompt user for data
25:      for (i = 0; i <= (n - 1); i++) {
26:          cout << "X[" << i << "] : ";
27:          cin >> x[i];
28:      }
```

However, this form is not popular, because it requires an additional operator, whereas the condition i < n does not.

DO	DON'T

DO write the loop continuation expression so that it uses the minimum number of operators. This approach reduces the code size and speeds up loop execution.

DON'T use the <= operator in the loop continuation condition, unless using the operator helps you write an expression that minimizes the number of operations.

Initializing Single-Dimensional Arrays

C++ enables you to initialize arrays and is flexible about the initialization. You need to enclose the list of initializing values in a pair of open and close braces ({}). The list is comma-delimited and may continue on multiple lines. If there are fewer items in the initializing list than there are array elements, the compiler assigns 0 to balance the array elements. By contrast, if the list of initializing values has more items than the number of array elements, the compiler flags a compile-time error.

The next program, Listing 7.2, modifies the last program to supply data internally. Consequently, I eliminate the steps that prompt you for the number of data and the data itself. The program simply displays the array elements (obtained from the initialization list) and the average value for the data. Although this program does not interact with the user, it offers a version that stores data in the source code. You can edit the program periodically to add, edit, and delete data before recalculating a new average value.

Listing 7.2. Source code for the program ARRAY2.CPP.

```
1:  /*
2:     C++ program that demonstrates the use of single-dimensional
3:     arrays.  The average value of the array is calculated.
```

```
 4:    The array has its values preassigned internally.
 5: */
 6:
 7: #include <iostream.h>
 8:
 9: const int MAX = 10;
10:
11: main()
12: {
13:
14:     double x[MAX] = { 12.2, 45.4, 67.2, 12.2, 34.6, 87.4,
15:                         83.6, 12.3, 14.8, 55.5 };
16:     double sum = MAX, sumx = 0.0, mean;
17:     int n = MAX;
18:
19:     // calculate sum of observations
20:     cout << "Array is:\n";
21:     for (int i = 0; i < n; i++) {
22:         sumx += x[i];
23:         cout << "x[" << i << "] = " << x[i] << "\n";
24:     }
25:
26:     mean = sumx / sum; // calculate the mean value
27:     cout << "\nMean = " << mean << "\n\n";
28:     return 0;
29: }
```

Here is a sample session with the program in Listing 7.2:

```
Array is:
x[0] = 12.2
x[1] = 45.4
x[2] = 67.2
x[3] = 12.2
x[4] = 34.6
x[5] = 87.4
x[6] = 83.6
x[7] = 12.3
x[8] = 14.8
x[9] = 55.5

Mean = 42.52
```

Let me focus on the initialization of the array x in Listing 7.2. Line 14 contains the declaration of array x and its initialization. The initializing list, which runs to line 15, is enclosed in a pair of braces and has comma-delimited values. The statement in line 16 declares the variables sum and sumx and initializes these variables to MAX and 0, respectively. The statement in line 17 declares the int-typed variable n and initializes it with the value MAX. The rest of the program resembles parts of the program in Listing 7.1.

7

If you are somewhat dismayed by the fact that you have to count the exact number of initializing values, then I have some good news for you: C++ allows you to size an array automatically using the number of items in the corresponding initializing list. Consequently, you don't need to place a number in the square brackets of the array and can let the compiler do the work for you.

DO	**DON'T**

DO include dummy values in the initializing list, if the initialized array needs to expand later.

DON'T rely on counting the number of items in the initializing list to provide the data for the number of array elements.

Listing 7.3 shows the source code for the program ARRAY3.CPP. This new version uses the feature of automatic array sizing.

Listing 7.3. Source code for the program ARRAY3.CPP.

```
1:  /*
2:    C++ program that demonstrates the use of single-dimensional
3:    arrays.  The average value of the array is calculated.
4:    The array has its values preassigned internally.
5:  */
6:
7:  #include <iostream.h>
8:
9:  main()
10: {
11:
12:     double x[] = { 12.2, 45.4, 67.2, 12.2, 34.6, 87.4,
13:                    83.6, 12.3, 14.8, 55.5 };
14:     double sum,  sumx = 0.0, mean;
15:     int n;
16:
17:     n = sizeof(x) / sizeof(x[0]);
18:     sum = n;
19:
20:     // calculate sum of observations
21:     cout << "Array is:\n";
22:     for (int i = 0; i < n; i++) {
23:         sumx += x[i];
24:         cout << "x[" << i << "] = " << x[i] << "\n";
```

```
25:    }
26:
27:    mean = sumx / sum; // calculate the mean value
28:    cout << "\nNumber of data points = " << n << "\n"
29:         << "Mean = " << mean << "\n";
30:    return 0;
31: }
```

Here is a sample session with the program in Listing 7.3:

```
Array is:
x[0] = 12.2
x[1] = 45.4
x[2] = 67.2
x[3] = 12.2
x[4] = 34.6
x[5] = 87.4
x[6] = 83.6
x[7] = 12.3
x[8] = 14.8
x[9] = 55.5

Number of data points = 10
Mean = 42.52
```

Notice that the program in Listing 7.3 does not declare the constant MAX which appears in the previous version, shown in Listing 7.2. How does the program determine the number of array elements? Line 17 shows that the program calculates the number of elements in array x by dividing the size of the array x (obtained by using `sizeof(x)`) by the size of the first element (obtained by using `sizeof(x[0])`). You can use this method to obtain the size of any array of any data type.

Array Parameters in Functions

C++ allows you to declare function parameters that are arrays. In fact, C++ permits you to either be specific or general about the size of the array parameter. If you want an array parameter to accept arrays of a fixed size, you can specify the size of the array in the parameter declaration. By contrast, if you want the array parameter to accept arrays with the same basic type but have different sizes, use empty brackets with the array parameter.

7

A Fixed-Array Parameter

The general syntax for declaring a fixed-array parameter is

```
type parameterName[arraySize]
```

Examples:

```
int minArray(int arr[100], int n);
void sort(unsigned dayNum[7]);
```

An Open-Array Parameter

The general syntax for declaring an open-array parameter is

```
type parameterName[]
```

Examples:

```
int minArray(int arr[], int n);
void sort(unsigned dayNum[]);
```

DO	DON'T
DO use open-array parameters in functions.	
DON'T forget to check the upper bounds of an open-array parameter in general-purpose functions.	

Let's look at a simple example. Listing 7.4 shows the source code for program ARRAY4.CPP. The program performs the following tasks:

☐ Prompts you to enter the number of data points, which ranges from 2 to 10

☐ Prompts you to enter the integer values for the arrays

☐ Displays the smallest value in the array

☐ Displays the largest value in the array

Listing 7.4. Source code for the program ARRAY4.CPP.

```
1: // C++ program that passes arrays as arguments of functions
2:
3: #include <iostream.h>
4:
5: const int MAX = 10;
6:
```

SAMS
Learning
Center
Sams
SAMS
PUBLISHING

```
 7: main()
 8: {
 9:   int arr[MAX];
10:   int n;
11:
12:   // declare prototypes of functions
13:   int getMin(int a[MAX], int size);
14:   int getMax(int a[], int size);
15:
16:   do { // obtain number of data points
17:     cout << "Enter number of data points [2 to "
18:         << MAX << "] : ";
19:     cin >> n;
20:     cout << "\n";
21:   } while (n < 2 ¦¦ n > MAX);
22:
23:   // prompt user for data
24:   for (int i = 0; i < n; i++) {
25:     cout << "arr[" << i << "] : ";
26:     cin >> arr[i];
27:   }
28:
29:   cout << "Smallest value in array is "
30:         << getMin(arr, n) << "\n"
31:         << "Biggest value in array is "
32:         << getMax(arr, n) << "\n";
33:   return 0;
34: }
35:
36:
37: int getMin(int a[MAX], int size)
38: {
39:   int small = a[0];
40:   // search for the smallest value in the
41:   // remaining array elements
42:   for (int i = 1; i < size; i++)
43:     if (small > a[i])
44:       small = a[i];
45:   return small;
46: }
47:
48: int getMax(int a[], int size)
49: {
50:   int big = a[0];
51:   // search for the biggest value in the
52:   // remaining array elements
53:   for (int i = 1; i < size; i++)
54:     if (big < a[i])
55:       big = a[i];
56:   return big;
57: }
```

7

Here is a sample session with the program in Listing 7.4:

```
Enter number of data points [2 to 10] : 5

arr[0] : 55
arr[1] : 69
arr[2] : 47
arr[3] : 85
arr[4] : 14
Smallest value in array is 14
Biggest value in array is 85
```

The program in Listing 7.4 declares the global constant MAX, in line 5, to size up the array of data. The function main declares the int-typed array arr in line 9.

Line 10 contains the declaration of the int-typed variable n. Lines 13 and 14 declare the prototypes for the functions getMin and getMax which return the smallest and biggest values in an int-typed array, respectively. The prototype of function getMin indicates that it uses a fixed-array parameter. By contrast, the prototype of function getMax indicates that it uses an open-array parameter. I use both kinds of array parameters for the sake of demonstration.

The do-while loop, located in lines 16 through 21, obtains the number of data points you want to store in the array arr. The output statement in lines 17 and 18 prompts you to enter the number of data points. The output indicates the range of valid numbers, which runs between 2 and MAX. The statement in line 19 obtains your input and stores it in variable n. The while clause validates your input. The clause determines if the value in variable n is less than 2, or is greater than MAX. If this condition is true, the do-while loop iterates again to obtain a correct input value.

The for loop statement in lines 24 through 27 prompts you to enter the data. The loop uses the control variable i and iterates from 0 to n-1, in increments of 1. The output statement in line 25 prompts you to enter the value for the indicated array element. The statement in line 26 obtains your input and stores it in the element arr[i].

The output statement in lines 29 through 32 displays the smallest and biggest integers in array arr. The statement invokes the functions getMin and getMax, supplying each one of them with the arguments arr and n.

The program defines function getMin in lines 37 through 46. The function has two parameters: the int-typed, fixed-array parameter a, and the int-typed parameter size. The function declares the local variable small and initializes it with a[0], the first element of parameter a. The function searches for the smallest value in the parameter a using the for loop in line 42. This loop declares the control variable i, and iterates from 1 to size-1, in increments of 1. The loop contains an if statement which assigns the value in element a[i] to variable small, if the latter is greater than element a[i].

The function returns the value in variable small. The function getMin only accepts int-typed arrays that have MAX elements.

The program defines function getMax in lines 48 through 57. This function, which is similar to function getMin, has two parameters: the int-typed, open-array parameter a, and the int-typed parameter size. The function declares the local variable big and initializes it with a[0], the first element of parameter a. The function searches for the smallest value in the parameter a using the for loop in line 53. This loop declares the control variable i, and iterates from 1 to size-1, in increments of 1. The loop contains an if statement which assigns the value in element a[i] to variable big, if the latter is less than element a[i]. The function returns the value in variable big. The function getMax accepts int-typed arrays of any size.

Sorting Arrays

Sorting and searching arrays are the most common nonnumerical operations for arrays. Sorting an array arranges its elements in typically ascending order. The process uses parts or all of the value in each element to determine the precedence of the elements in the array. Searching for data in sorted arrays is much easier than in unordered arrays.

Computer scientists have spent much time and effort studying and creating methods for sorting arrays. Discussing and comparing these methods is beyond the scope of this book. I only mention that my favorite array sorting methods include the QuickSort, Shell-Metzner sort, heap sort, and the new Comb sort. The QuickSort method is the fastest method, in general, but requires some operational overhead. The Shell-Metzner and Comb sort methods do not require similar overhead. The example in this section uses the new Comb sort method which is more efficient than the Shell-Metzner method.

The Comb sort method uses the following steps, given an array A with N elements:

1. Initializes the Offset value, used in comparing elements, to N

2. Sets the Offset value to either 8*Offset/11 or 1, whichever is bigger

3. Sets the InOrder flag to true

4. Loops for values 0 to N-Offset, using the loop control variable i:

   ~~Assigns I + Offset to J.~~ *ASSIGNS OFFSET TO J*

   If A[I] is greater than A[J], swaps A[I] with A[J] and sets the InOrder flag to false

5. Resumes at step 2 if Offset is not 1 and InOrder is false

Let's look at a program that sorts an array of integers. Listing 7.5 shows the source code for program ARRAY5.CPP. The program performs the following tasks:

☐ Prompts you to enter the number of data points

☐ Prompts you to enter the integer values for the array

☐ Displays the elements of the unordered array

☐ Displays the elements of the sorted array

Type

Listing 7.5. Source code for the program ARRAY5.CPP.

```
1: // C++ program that sorts arrays using the Comb sort method
2:
3: #include <iostream.h>
4:
5: const int MAX = 10;
6: const int TRUE = 1;
7: const int FALSE = 0;
8:
9: int obtainNumData()
10: {
11:   int m;
12:   do { // obtain number of data points
13:     cout << "Enter number of data points [2 to "
14:          << MAX << "] : ";
15:     cin >> m;
16:     cout << "\n";
17:   } while (m < 2 || m > MAX);
18:   return m;
19: }
20:
21: void inputArray(int intArr[], int n)
22: {
23:   // prompt user for data
24:   for (int i = 0; i < n; i++) {
25:     cout << "arr[" << i << "] : ";
26:     cin >> intArr[i];
27:   }
28: }
29:
30: void showArray(int intArr[], int n)
31: {
32:   for (int i = 0; i < n; i++) {
33:     cout.width(5);
34:     cout << intArr[i] << " ";
35:   }
36:   cout << "\n";
37: }
```

```
38:
39: void sortArray(int intArr[], int n)
40: {
41:    int offset, temp, inOrder;
42:
43:    offset = n;
44:    do {
45:      offset = (8 * offset) / 11;
46:      offset = (offset == 0) ? 1 : offset;
47:      inOrder = TRUE;
48:      for (int i = 0, j = offset; i < (n - offset); i++, j++) {
49:        if (intArr[i] > intArr[j]) {
50:           inOrder = FALSE;
51:           temp = intArr[i];
52:           intArr[i] = intArr[j];
53:           intArr[j] = temp;
54:        }
55:      }
56:    } while (!(offset = 1 && inOrder == TRUE));
57: }
58:
59: main()
60: {
61:    int arr[MAX];
62:    int n;
63:
64:    n = obtainNumData();
65:    inputArray(arr, n);
66:    cout << "Unordered array is:\n";
67:    showArray(arr, n);
68:    sortArray(arr, n);
69:    cout << "\nSorted array is:\n";
70:    showArray(arr, n);
71:    return 0;
72: }
```

Here is a sample session with the program in Listing 7.5:

```
Enter number of data points [2 to 10] : 10
arr[0] : 55
arr[1] : 68
arr[2] : 74
arr[3] : 15
arr[4] : 28
arr[5] : 23
arr[6] : 69
arr[7] : 95
arr[8] : 22
arr[9] : 33
```

```
Unordered array is:
    55     68     74     15     28     23     69     95     22     33

Sorted array is:
    15     22     23     28     33     55     68     69     74     95
```

The program in Listing 7.5 declares the constants MAX, TRUE, and FALSE in lines 5 through 7. The constant MAX defines the size of the array used in the program. The constants TRUE and FALSE define the Boolean values. The program also defines the functions obtainNumData, inputArray, showArray, sortArray, and main.

The parameterless function obtainNumData, which is defined in lines 9 through 19, prompts you to enter the number of values. The output statement in lines 13 and 14 also specifies the valid range for your input. The statement in line 15 stores your input in the local variable m. The function uses a do-while loop to ensure that it returns a valid number. The loop iterates as long as the value in variable m is less than 2 or greater than MAX. The function returns the value in variable m.

The function inputArray, which is defined in lines 21 through 28, obtains the data for the tested array. The function has two parameters. The open-array parameter intArr passes the input values back to the caller of the function. The parameter n specifies how many values to obtain for parameter intArr. The function uses a for loop, which iterates from 0 to n-1, in increments of 1. Each loop iteration prompts you for a value and stores that value in an element of array intArr.

Note: The function inputArray illustrates that C++ functions treat array parameters as if they are references to their arguments because these parameters affect the values in the arguments beyond the scope of the functions. In reality, the C++ compiler passes a copy of the address of the array argument to the function when dealing with an array parameter. Armed with the address of the array, C++ functions can then alter the values of the array beyond the scope of these functions. This feature is possible, because the function is working with the original array and not a copy.

The function showArray, which is defined in lines 30 through 37, displays the meaningful data in an array. The function has two parameters. The open-array parameter intArr passes the array values to be displayed by the function. The parameter n specifies how many array elements to display intArr (remember that not all of the array elements are used to store your data). The function uses a for loop, which iterates from 0 to n-1, in increments of 1. Each loop iteration displays the value in an array element. The array elements appear on the same line.

The function sortArray, which is defined in lines 39 through 57, sorts the elements of an array using the Comb sort method. The function has two parameters. The open-array parameter intArr passes the array values to be sorted by the function. The parameter n specifies how many array elements to sort. The statements in the function sortArray implement the Comb sort method outlined earlier.

> **Note:** The function sortArray illustrates how array parameters can pass data to and from a function. The function sortArray receives an unordered array, sorts it, and passes the ordered array to the function's caller. The compiler supports this feature by passing a copy of the address of the array to the function. Thus, the function need not explicitly return the array because it is working with the original data and not a copy.

The function main performs the various program tasks by calling the functions mentioned earlier. The function declares the array arr and the simple variable n in lines 61 and 62, respectively. The statement in line 64 calls function obtainNumData to obtain the number of data you want to store in the array. The statement assigns the result of the function obtainNumData to variable n. The statement in line 65 calls the function inputArray to prompt you for the data. The function call passes the arguments arr and n. The output statement in line 66 displays a message which indicates that the program is about to display the elements of the unordered array. The statement in line 67 calls showArray and passes it the arguments arr and n. This function call displays the elements of the array arr on one line. The statement in line 68 calls the function sortArray to sort the first n elements in array arr. The output statement in line 69 displays a message which indicates that the program is about to display the elements of the sorted array. The statement in line 70 calls showArray and passes the arguments arr and n. This function call displays the elements of the ordered array arr on one line.

Searching Arrays

Searching arrays is another important nonnumerical operation. Because arrays can be sorted or unordered, there is a general category of search methods for each. The simplest search method for unordered arrays is the linear search method. The simplest search method for sorted arrays is the versatile binary search method. The search methods for unordered arrays can also be applied to sorted arrays. However, they do not take advantage of the array order.

NEW☞
TERM
The *linear search* method sequentially examines the array elements, looking for an element that matches the search value. If the sought value is not in the array, the linear search method examines the entire array's elements.

NEW☞
TERM
The *binary search* method takes advantage of the order in the array. The method searches for a matching value by using the shrinking intervals approach. The initial search interval includes all the array elements (which contain meaningful data). The method compares the median element of the interval with the search value. If the two match, the search stops. Otherwise, the method determines which subinterval to use as the next search interval. Consequently, each search interval is half the size of the previous one. If the search value has no match in the examined array, the binary method makes far fewer examinations than the linear search method. The binary search method is the most efficient general-purpose search method for sorted arrays.

DO	**DON'T**
DO use the unordered-array search method when you are not sure that the array is sorted.	
DON'T use sorted-array search methods with unordered arrays. The results of such searches are not reliable.	

Let's look at a program that sorts an array of integers. Listing 7.6 shows the source code for program ARRAY6.CPP. I created this program by adding functions and operations to program ARRAY5.CPP. The program performs the following tasks:

☐ Prompts you to enter the number of data points

☐ Prompts you to enter the integer values for the array

☐ Displays the elements of the unordered array

☐ Asks you if you want to search for data in the unordered array (if you type characters other than Y or y, the program resumes at step 8)

☐ Prompts you for a search value

☐ Displays the search outcome (if the program finds a matching element, it displays the index of that element; otherwise, the program tells you that it found no match for the search value)

☐ Resumes at step 4

☐ Displays the elements of the sorted array

☐ Asks you if you want to search for data in the unordered array (if you type characters other than Y or y, the program ends)

☐ Prompts you for a search value

☐ Displays the search outcome (if the program finds a matching element it displays the index of that element; otherwise, the program tells you that it found no match for the search value)

☐ Resumes at step 9

 Listing 7.6. Source code for the program ARRAY6.CPP.

```
1: // C++ program that searches arrays using the linear
2: // and binary searches methods
3:
4: #include <iostream.h>
5:
6: const int MAX = 10;
7: const int TRUE = 1;
8: const int FALSE = 0;
9: const int NOT_FOUND = -1;
10:
11: int obtainNumData()
12: {
13:   int m;
14:   do { // obtain number of data points
15:     cout << "Enter number of data points [2 to "
16:         << MAX << "] : ";
17:     cin >> m;
18:     cout << "\n";
19:   } while (m < 2 || m > MAX);
20:   return m;
21: }
22:
23: void inputArray(int intArr[], int n)
24: {
25:   // prompt user for data
26:   for (int i = 0; i < n; i++) {
27:     cout << "arr[" << i << "] : ";
28:     cin >> intArr[i];
29:   }
30: }
31:
32: void showArray(int intArr[], int n)
33: {
```

continues 167

Listing 7.6. continued

```
34:   for (int i = 0; i < n; i++) {
35:     cout.width(5);
36:     cout << intArr[i] << " ";
37:   }
38:   cout << "\n";
39: }
40:
41: void sortArray(int intArr[], int n)
42: // sort the first n elements of array intArr
43: // using the Comb sort method
44: {
45:   int offset, temp, inOrder;
46:
47:   offset = n;
48:   do {
49:     offset = (8 * offset) / 11;
50:     offset = (offset == 0) ? 1 : offset;
51:     inOrder = TRUE;
52:     for (int i = 0, j = offset; i < (n - offset); i++, j++) {
53:       if (intArr[i] > intArr[j]) {
54:         inOrder = FALSE;
55:         temp = intArr[i];
56:         intArr[i] = intArr[j];
57:         intArr[j] = temp;
58:       }
59:     }
60:   } while (!(offset = 1 && inOrder == TRUE));
61: }
62:
63: int linearSearch(int searchVal, int intArr[], int n)
64: // perform linear search to locate the first
65: // element in array intArr that matches the value
66: // of searchVal
67: {
68:   int notFound = TRUE;
69:   int i = 0;
70:   // search through the array elements
71:   while (i < n && notFound)
72:     // no match?
73:     if (searchVal != intArr[i])
74:       i++; // increment index to compare the next element
75:     else
76:       notFound = FALSE; // found a match
77:   // return search outcome
78:   return (notFound == FALSE) ? i : NOT_FOUND;
79: }
80:
81: int binarySearch(int searchVal, int intArr[], int n)
82: // perform binary search to locate the first
```

```
83:  // element in array intArr that matches the value
84:  // of searchVal
85:  {
86:    int median, low, high;
87:
88:    // initialize the search range
89:    low = 0;
90:    high = n - 1;
91:    // search in array
92:    do {
93:      // obtain the median index of the current search range
94:      median = (low + high) / 2;
95:      // update search range
96:      if (searchVal > intArr[median])
97:        low = median + 1;
98:      else
99:        high = median - 1;
100:   } while (!(searchVal == intArr[median] || low > high));
101:   // return search outcome
102:   return (searchVal == intArr[median]) ? median : NOT_FOUND;
103: }
104:
105: void searchInUnorderedArray(int intArr[], int n)
106: // manage the linear search test
107: {
108:   int x, i;
109:   char c;
110:   // perform linear search
111:   cout << "Search in unordered array? (Y/N) ";
112:   cin >> c;
113:   while (c == 'Y' || c == 'y') {
114:     cout << "Enter search value : ";
115:     cin >> x;
116:     i = linearSearch(x, intArr, n);
117:     if (i != NOT_FOUND)
118:       cout << "Found matching element at index " << i << "\n";
119:     else
120:       cout << "No match found\n";
121:     cout << "Search in unordered array? (Y/N) ";
122:     cin >> c;
123:   }
124: }
125:
126: void searchInSortedArray(int intArr[], int n)
127: // manage the binary search test
128: {
129:   int x, i;
130:   char c;
131:   // perform binary search
132:   cout << "Search in sorted array? (Y/N) ";
133:   cin >> c;
```

continues

Listing 7.6. continued

```
134:    while (c == 'Y' || c == 'y') {
135:      cout << "Enter search value : ";
136:      cin >> x;
137:      i = binarySearch(x, intArr, n);
138:      if (i != NOT_FOUND)
139:        cout << "Found matching element at index " << i << "\n";
140:      else
141:        cout << "No match found\n";
142:      cout << "Search in sorted array? (Y/N) ";
143:      cin >> c;
144:    }
145: }
146:
147: main()
148: {
149:    int arr[MAX];
150:    int n;
151:
152:    n = obtainNumData();
153:    inputArray(arr, n);
154:    cout << "Unordered array is:\n";
155:    showArray(arr, n);
156:    searchInUnorderedArray(arr, n);
157:    sortArray(arr, n);
158:    cout << "\nSorted array is:\n";
159:    showArray(arr, n);
160:    searchInSortedArray(arr, n);
161:    return 0;
162: }
```

Here is a sample session with the program in Listing 7.6:

```
Enter number of data points [2 to 10] : 5

arr[0] : 85
arr[1] : 41
arr[2] : 55
arr[3] : 67
arr[4] : 48
Unordered array is:
    85    41    55    67    48
Search in unordered array? (Y/N) y
Enter search value : 55
Found matching element at index 2
Search in unordered array? (Y/N) y
Enter search value : 41
Found matching element at index 1
Search in unordered array? (Y/N) n
```

```
Sorted array is:
    41    48    55    67    85
Search in sorted array? (Y/N) y
Enter search value : 55
Found matching element at index 2
Search in sorted array? (Y/N) y
Enter search value : 67
Found matching element at index 3
Search in sorted array? (Y/N) n
```

 The program in Listing 7.6 declares the functions obtainNumData, inputArray, sortArray, linearSearch, binarySearch, searchInUnorderedArray, searchInSortedArray, and main. Because the first three functions are identical to those in Listing 7.5, I discuss only the remaining functions.

The linearSearch function performs a linear search to find the first element in array intArr with a value that matches the one in parameter searchVal. The function searches the first n elements in array intArr. The linearSearch function returns the index of the matching element in array intArr, or yields the value of the global constant NOT_FOUND if no match is found. The function uses a while loop to examine the elements in array intArr. The search loop iterates while the value in variable i is less than that in variable n and while the local variable notFound stores TRUE. The statement in line 78 returns the function result using the conditional operator.

The binarySearch function has the same parameters as the linearSearch function and returns the same kind of value. The function uses the local variables low and high to store the current search interval. The function initializes the variables low and high using the values 0 and n-1, respectively. The do-while loop in lines 92 through 100 calculates the index of the median element and compares the median element with the search value. The if statement in line 96 performs this comparison, and its clauses update the value of either variable low or variable high, depending on the outcome of the comparison. The update in either variable shrinks the search interval. The return statement in line 102 yields the function's value based on one last comparison between the search value and the median element of the current search interval.

The function searchInUnorderedArray manages the search in the unordered array. The function accesses the unordered array using the open-array parameter intArr. The function declares local variables which are used to prompt you for and store the search value. The statement in line 116 calls the function linearSearch and passes the argument x (the local variable which stores the search value), intArr, and n. The statement assigns the result of function linearSearch to the local variable i. The if statement in line 117 determines whether or not the value in variable i is not

NOT_FOUND. If this condition is true, the output statement in line 118 shows the index of the matching element. Otherwise, the output statement in line 120 displays a no-match-found message.

The function searchInSortedArray is very similar to the function searchInUnorderedArray. The main difference is that the function searchInSortedArray deals with ordered arrays and therefore calls the binarySearch function to conduct a binary search on the ordered array intArr.

The function main invokes these functions to support the program tasks that I described earlier.

Multidimensional Arrays

In a multidimensional array, each additional dimension provides you with an additional access attribute. Two-dimensional arrays (or matrices, if you prefer) are the most popular kind of multidimensional arrays. Three-dimensional arrays are used less frequently than matrices, and so on.

NEW TERM *Multidimensional arrays* are supersets of the single-dimensional arrays.

Two-Dimensional and Three-Dimensional Arrays

The general syntax for declaring two-dimensional and three-dimensional arrays is

```
type array [size1][size2];
type array [size1][size2][size3];
```

As with simple arrays, each dimension has a lower bound index of 0, and the declaration defines the number of elements in each dimension.

Examples:

```
double matrixA[100][10];
char table[41][22][3];
int index[7][12];
```

It is important to understand how C++ stores the elements of a multidimensional array. Most compilers store the elements of a multidimensional array in a contiguous fashion (that is, as one long array). The run-time code calculates where a sought element is located in that long array. To explain the storage scheme of multidimensional arrays, let me start by employing a convention for referencing the indices of the different dimensions. The following schema specifies the dimension numbering and the concept of high- and low-order dimensions. Here is a six-dimensional array—an extreme case that is a good example:

```
    1    2    3    4    5    6   <-- dimension number
M [20]  [7]  [5]  [3]  [2]  [2]
     higher dimension order -->
```

The first element of the array M is M[0][0][0][0][0][0] and is stored at the first memory location of array M. The array M is stored in a contiguous block of 8400 elements. The location in that contiguous block stores the element at index 1 in the highest dimension number, dimension 6 (that is, M[0][0][0][0][0][1]). The location of the next elements in the contiguous block stores the subsequent elements in dimension 6 until the upper limit of dimension 6 is reached. Reaching this limit bumps the index of dimension 5 by 1 and resets the index of dimension 6 to 0. This process is repeated until every element in a multidimensional array is accessed. You can depict this storage scheme as looking at a gasoline pump meter when refueling your car: the right digits turn the fastest, the left digits turn the slowest.

Here is another example that uses a three-dimensional array, M[3][2][2]:

```
M[0][0][0]        <-- the starting memory address
M[0][0][1]        <-- 3rd dimension is filled
M[0][1][0]
M[0][1][1]        <-- 2nd and 3rd dimensions are filled
M[1][0][0]
M[1][0][1]        <-- 3rd dimension is filled
M[1][1][0]
M[1][1][1]        <-- 2nd and 3rd dimensions are filled
M[2][0][0]
M[2][0][1]        <-- 3rd dimension is filled
M[2][1][0]
M[2][1][1]        <-- all dimensions are filled
```

Let's look at a program example that illustrates basic matrix manipulation. Listing 7.7 shows the source code for the MAT1.CPP program. The program manages a matrix that contains up to 10 columns and 30 rows and performs the following tasks:

☐ Prompts you to enter the number of rows (the program validates your input)

☐ Prompts you to enter the number of columns (the program validates your input)

☐ Prompts you to enter the matrix elements

☐ Calculates and displays the average for each column in the matrix

7

Type Listing 7.7. Source code for the program MAT1.CPP.

```
1: /*
2:   C++ program that demonstrates the use of two-dimension arrays.
3:   The average value of each matrix column is calculated.
4: */
5:
6: #include <iostream.h>
7:
8: const int MAX_COL = 10;
9: const int MAX_ROW = 30;
10:
11: main()
12: {
13:     double x[MAX_ROW][MAX_COL];
14:     double sum, sumx, mean;
15:     int rows, columns;
16:
17:     // get the number of rows
18:     do {
19:       cout << "Enter number of rows [2 to "
20:            << MAX_ROW << "] : ";
21:       cin >> rows;
22:     } while (rows < 2 || rows > MAX_ROW);
23:
24:     // get the number of columns
25:     do {
26:       cout << "Enter number of columns [1 to "
27:            << MAX_COL << "] : ";
28:       cin >> columns;
29:     } while (columns < 1 || columns > MAX_COL);
30:
31:     // get the matrix elements
32:     for (int i = 0; i < rows; i++)  {
33:       for (int j = 0; j < columns; j++)  {
34:           cout << "X[" << i << "][" << j << "] : ";
35:           cin >> x[i][j];
36:       }
37:       cout << "\n";
38:     }
39:
40:     sum = rows;
41:     // obtain the sum of each column
42:     for (int j = 0; j < columns; j++)  {
43:       // initialize summations
44:       sumx = 0.0;
45:       for (i = 0; i < rows; i++)
46:         sumx += x[i][j];
47:       mean = sumx / sum;
48:       cout << "Mean for column " << j
```

```
49:                    << " = " << mean << "\n";
50:       }
51:       return 0;
52: }
```

Here is a sample session with the program in Listing 7.7:

```
Enter number of rows [2 to 30] : 3
Enter number of columns [1 to 10] : 3
X[0][0] : 1
X[0][1] : 2
X[0][2] : 3

X[1][0] : 4
X[1][1] : 5
X[1][2] : 6

X[2][0] : 7
X[2][1] : 8
X[2][2] : 9

Mean for column 0 = 4
Mean for column 1 = 5
Mean for column 2 = 6
```

The program in Listing 7.7 declares the global constants MAX_COL and MAX_ROW in lines 8 and 9, respectively. These constants define the dimensions of the matrix created in the program. The function main declares the matrix x to have MAX_ROW rows and MAX_COL columns. The function also declares other nonarray variables.

The do-while loop, in lines 18 through 22, prompts you to enter the number of rows of matrix x which will contain your data. The output statement in lines 19 and 20 indicates the range of the valid number of rows. The statement in line 21 stores your input in the variable rows.

The second do-while loop, in lines 25 through 29, prompts you to enter the number of columns of matrix x which will contain your data. The output statement in lines 26 and 27 indicates the range of the valid number of columns. The statement in line 28 saves your input in the variable columns.

The nested for loops, in lines 32 through 38, prompt you for the matrix elements. The outer for loop uses the control variable i and iterates from 0 to rows −1, in increments of 1. The inner for loop uses the control variable j and iterates from 0 to columns-1, in increments of 1. The output statement in line 34 displays the index of the matrix element which will receive your input. The statement in line 35 stores your input in the matrix element x[i][j].

The process of obtaining the average of each matrix column starts at line 40. The statement in that line assigns the integer in variable rows to the double-typed variable sum. The program uses another pair of nested for loops in lines 42 through 50. The outer for loop uses the control variable j and iterates from 0 to columns-1, in increments of 1. This loop processes each column. The first statement inside the outer for loop assigns 0 to the variable sumx. The inner for loop is located at line 45. This loop uses the control variable i and iterates from 0 to rows-1, in increments of 1. The inner loop uses the statement in line 46 to add the values of elements x[i][j] to the variable sumx. The statement in line 47 (which is outside the inner for loop) calculates the column average and assigns it to the variable mean. The output statement in lines 48 and 49 displays the column number and its average value.

> **Note:** The for loop in line 42 redeclares its control variable j (not so with the for loop in line 45). Why? The for loop in line 33 also declares the control variable j. However, the scope of that loop is limited to the scope of the outer for loop. Once the first pair of nested loops finishes executing, the loop control variable j is removed by the run-time system.

Initializing Multidimensional Arrays

C++ allows you to initialize a multidimensional array in a manner similar to single-dimensional arrays. You need to use a list of values that appear in the same sequence in which the elements of the initialized multidimensional array are stored. Now you realize the importance of understanding how C++ stores the elements of a multidimensional array. I modified the previous C++ program to use an initializing list that internally supplies the program with data. Consequently, the program does not prompt you for any data. Rather, the program displays the values of the matrix and the average for its columns.

 Listing 7.8. Source code for the program MAT2.CPP.

```
1: /*
2:   C++ program that demonstrates the use of two-dimension arrays.
3:   The average value of each matrix column is calculated.
4: */
```

```
 5:
 6: #include <iostream.h>
 7:
 8: const int MAX_COL = 3;
 9: const int MAX_ROW = 3;
10:
11: main()
12: {
13:     double x[MAX_ROW][MAX_COL] = {
14:                                     1, 2, 3, // row # 1
15:                                     4, 5, 6, // row # 2
16:                                     7, 8, 9  // row # 3
17:                                     };
18:     double sum, sumx, mean;
19:     int rows = MAX_ROW, columns = MAX_COL;
20:
21:     cout << "Matrix is:\n";
22:     // display the matrix elements
23:     for (int i = 0; i < rows; i++)  {
24:       for (int j = 0; j < columns; j++)  {
25:           cout.width(4);
26:           cout.precision(1);
27:           cout << x[i][j] << " ";
28:       }
29:       cout << "\n";
30:     }
31:     cout << "\n";
32:
33:     sum = rows;
34:     // obtain the sum of each column
35:     for (int j = 0; j < columns; j++)  {
36:       // initialize summations
37:       sumx = 0.0;
38:       for (i = 0; i < rows; i++)
39:         sumx += x[i][j];
40:       mean = sumx / sum;
41:       cout << "Mean for column " << j
42:             << " = " << mean << "\n";
43:     }
44:     return 0;
45: }
```

Here is a sample session with the program in Listing 7.8:

```
Matrix is:
   1    2    3
   4    5    6
   7    8    9

Mean for column 0 = 4
Mean for column 1 = 5
Mean for column 2 = 6
```

The program in Listing 7.8 declares the matrix x and initializes it with a list of values. Notice that the program declares the constants MAX_COL and MAX_ROW with values that match the size of the initialized matrix. The declaration statement in lines 13 through 17 shows the elements assigned to each row. The function main also initializes the variable rows and columns with the constants MAX_ROW and MAX_COL, respectively. The function performs this initialization for two reasons: first, the program no longer prompts you to enter values for the variable rows and columns. Second, the program is working with a custom-fit size for matrix x.

The program uses the nested for loops, in lines 21 through 30, to display the elements of the matrix x. The second pair of nested for loops calculates the average for each matrix column. This nested for loop is identical to the one in Listing 7.7.

Multidimensional Array Parameters

C++ allows you to declare function parameters that are multidimensional arrays. As with single-dimensional arrays, C++ allows you to be either specific or general about the size of the array parameter. However, in the latter case, you can only generalize the first dimension of the array. If you wish an array parameter to accept arrays of a fixed dimension, you can specify the size of each dimension of the array in the parameter declaration. By contrast, if you want the array parameter to accept arrays of the same basic type but of different first-dimension sizes, use empty brackets for the first dimension in the array parameter.

A Fixed-Array Parameter

The general syntax for declaring a fixed-array parameter is

```
type parameterName[dim1Size][dim2Size]...
```

Examples:

```
int minMatrix(int intMat[100][20], int rows, int cols);
void sort(unsigned mat[23][55],
          int rows, int cols, int colIndex);
```

An Open-Array Parameter

The general syntax for declaring an open-array parameter is

```
type parameterName[][dim2Size]...
```

Examples:

```
int minMat(int intMat[][100], int rows, int cols);
void sort(unsigned mat[][55],
          int rows, int cols, int colIndex);
```

Let's look at an example. Listing 7.9 shows the source code for program MAT3.CPP. The program performs the same tasks as program MAT1.CPP in Listing 7.7. I created program MAT3.CPP by editing program MAT1.CPP and placing each program task in a separate function. Thus, program MAT3.CPP is a highly structured version of program MAT1.CPP.

Listing 7.9. Source code for the program MAT3.CPP.

```
1: /*
2:   C++ program that demonstrates the use of two-dimension arrays.
3:   The average value of each matrix column is calculated.
4: */
5:
6: #include <iostream.h>
7:
8: const int MAX_COL = 10;
9: const int MAX_ROW = 30;
10:
11: int getRows()
12: {
13:   int n;
14:   // get the number of rows
15:   do {
16:     cout << "Enter number of rows [2 to "
17:          << MAX_ROW << "] : ";
18:     cin >> n;
19:   } while (n < 2 || n > MAX_ROW);
20:   return n;
21: }
22:
23: int getColumns()
24: {
25:   int n;
26:   // get the number of columns
27:   do {
28:     cout << "Enter number of columns [1 to "
29:          << MAX_COL << "] : ";
30:     cin >> n;
31:   } while (n < 1 || n > MAX_COL);
32:   return n;
33: }
34:
```

continues

Listing 7.9. continued

```
35: void inputMatrix(double mat[][MAX_COL],
36:                   int rows, int columns)
37: {
38:   // get the matrix elements
39:   for (int i = 0; i < rows; i++)  {
40:     for (int j = 0; j < columns; j++)  {
41:       cout << "X[" << i << "][" << j << "] : ";
42:       cin >> mat[i][j];
43:     }
44:     cout << "\n";
45:   }
46: }
47:
48: void showColumnAverage(double mat[][MAX_COL],
49:                        int rows, int columns)
50: {
51:   double sum, sumx, mean;
52:   sum = rows;
53:   // obtain the sum of each column
54:   for (int j = 0; j < columns; j++)  {
55:     // initialize summations
56:     sumx = 0.0;
57:     for (int i = 0; i < rows; i++)
58:       sumx += mat[i][j];
59:     mean = sumx / sum;
60:     cout << "Mean for column " << j
61:          << " = " << mean << "\n";
62:   }
63: }
64:
65: main()
66: {
67:     double x[MAX_ROW][MAX_COL];
68:     int rows, columns;
69:     // get matrix dimensions
70:     rows = getRows();
71:     columns = getColumns();
72:     // get matrix data
73:     inputMatrix(x, rows, columns);
74:     // show results
75:     showColumnAverage(x, rows, columns);
76:     return 0;
77: }
```

Here is a sample session with the program in Listing 7.9:

```
Enter number of rows [2 to 30] : 3
Enter number of columns [1 to 10] : 3
```

```
X[0][0] : 10
X[0][1] : 20
X[0][2] : 30

X[1][0] : 40
X[1][1] : 50
X[1][2] : 60

X[2][0] : 70
X[2][1] : 80
X[2][2] : 90

Mean for column 0 = 40
Mean for column 1 = 50
Mean for column 2 = 60
```

The program in Listing 7.9 declares the functions getRows, getColumns, inputMatrix, showColumnAverage, and main. The function getRows prompts you for the number of matrix rows that you will be using. The function returns your validated input. Similarly, the function getColumns returns the validated number of matrix columns.

The function inputMatrix obtains the data for the matrix. The function has three parameters. The parameter mat specifies the matrix parameter (with an open first dimension). The parameters rows and columns specify the number of rows and columns of matrix mat, respectively, that will receive input data.

The function showColumnAverage calculates and displays the column averages for the matrix parameter mat. The parameters rows and columns specify the number of rows and columns of matrix mat, respectively, which contain meaningful data.

This function contains the same statements that appeared in program MAT1.CPP. Program MAT3.CPP uses these functions as shells or wrappers for the statements which perform the various tasks. From a structured programming point of view, program MAT3.CPP is superior to program MAT1.CPP.

The function main declares the matrix x with MAX_ROW rows and MAX_COL columns. The function calls the functions getRows and getColumns to obtain the number of working rows and columns, respectively. The statement in line 73 invokes the function inputMatrix and supplies it with the arguments x, rows, and columns. The statement in line 75 calls function showColumnAverage and passes it the arguments x, rows, and columns.

7

Summary

Today's lesson covers various topics that deal with arrays, including single-dimensional and multidimensional arrays. You learn about the following topics:

☐ Declaring single-dimensional arrays requires you to state the data type of the array elements, the name of the array, and the number of array elements (enclosed in square brackets). All C++ arrays have a 0 lower bound. The upper bound of an array is equal to the number of elements minus 1.

☐ Using single-dimensional arrays requires you to state the array's name and include a valid index, enclosed in square brackets.

☐ Initializing single-dimensional arrays can be carried out while declaring them. The initializing list of data is enclosed in braces and contains comma-delimited data. C++ allows you to include fewer data than the size of the array. In this case, the compiler automatically assigns zeros to the elements which you do not explicitly initialize. In addition, C++ allows you to omit the explicit size of the initialized array and instead use the number of initializing items as the number of array elements.

☐ Declaring single-dimensional arrays as function parameters takes two forms. The first one deals with fixed-array parameters, whereas the second one handles open-array parameters. Fixed-array parameters include the size of the array in the parameter. Arguments for this kind of parameter must match the type and size of the parameter. Open-array parameters use empty brackets to indicate that the arguments for the parameters can be of any size.

☐ Sorting arrays is an important nonnumerical array operation. Sorting arranges the elements of an array in either ascending or descending order. Sorted arrays are much easier to search. For sorting arrays, the new Comb sort method is very efficient.

☐ Searching arrays involves locating an array element which contains the same data as the search value. Searching methods are geared toward unordered or ordered arrays. The linear search method is used for unordered arrays and the binary search method is used for sorted arrays.

☐ Declaring multidimensional arrays requires you to state the data type of the array elements, the name of the array, and the size of each dimension (enclosed in separate brackets). The lower index of each dimension is 0. The upper bound of each dimension in an array is equal to the dimension size minus 1.

- Using multidimensional arrays requires you to state the array's name and include valid indices. Each index must be enclosed in a separate set of brackets.

- Initializing multidimensional arrays can be carried out while declaring them. The initializing list of data is enclosed in braces and contains comma-delimited data. C++ allows you to include fewer data than the total size of the array. In this case, the compiler automatically assigns zeros to the elements which you do not explicitly initialize.

- Declaring multidimensional arrays as function parameters takes two forms. The first one deals with fixed-array parameters, whereas the second one handles parameters with an open first dimension. Fixed-array parameters include the size of each dimension in the array parameter. Arguments for this kind of parameter must match the type and sizes of the parameter. Open-array parameters use empty brackets for only the first dimension to indicate that the arguments for the parameters have varying sizes for the first dimensions. The other dimensions of the arguments must match those of the array parameter.

Q&A

Q. Does C++ permit me to alter the size of an array?

A. No. C++ does not allow you to redimension arrays.

Q. Can I declare arrays with the basic type `void` (for example, `void array[81];`)to create buffers?

A. No. C++ does not allow you to use the `void` type with an array, because the type `void` has no defined size. Use the `char` or `unsigned char` type to create an array that works as a buffer.

Q. Does C++ allow me to redeclare an array?

A. C++ allows you to redeclare an array to change its basic type, number of dimensions, and size if you declare these arrays in nested statement blocks. Here is an example:

```
#include <iostream.h>
const MAX = 100;
const MAX_ROWS = 100;
const MAX_COLS = 20;
```

```
main()
{
  // declare variables here?
  {
    double x[MAX];
    // declare other variables?
    // statements to manipulate the single-dimensional
       array x
  }
  {
    double x[MAX_ROWS][MAX_COLS];
    // declare other variables?
    // statements to manipulate the matrix x
  }
  return 0;
}
```

The function `main` declares the array `x` in the first nested statement block. When program execution reaches the end of that block, the run-time system removes the array `x` and all other variables declared in that block. Then the function redeclares `x` as a matrix in the second block. When program execution reaches the end of the second block, the run-time system removes the matrix `x` and all other variables declared in that block.

Q. Are arrays limited to the predefined types?

A. Not at all. C++ allows you to create arrays using user-defined types (see Day 8).

Workshop

The Workshop provides quiz questions to help you solidify your understanding of the material covered and exercises to provide you with experience in using what you've learned. Try to understand the quiz and exercise answers before continuing on to the next day's lesson. Answers are provided in Appendix B, "Answers."

Quiz

1. What is the output of the following program?

```cpp
#include <iostream.h>
const int MAX = 5;
main()
{
  double x[MAX];
  x[0] = 1;
  for (int i = 1; i < MAX; i++)
    x[i] = i * x[i-1];
  for (i = 0; i < MAX; i++)
    cout << "x[" << i << "] = " << x[i] << "\n";
  return 0;
}
```

2. What is the output of the following program?

```cpp
#include <iostream.h>
#include <math.h>
const int MAX = 5;
main()
{
  double x[MAX];
  for (int i = 0; i < MAX; i++)
    x[i] = sqrt(double(i));
  for (i = 0; i < MAX; i++)
    cout << "x[" << i << "] = " << x[i] << "\n";
  return 0;
}
```

3. Where is the error in the following program?

```cpp
#include <iostream.h>
const int MAX = 5;
main()
{
  double x[MAX];
  x[0] = 1;
  for (int i = 0; i < MAX; i++)
    x[i] = i * x[i-1];
  for (i = 0; i < MAX; i++)
    cout << "x[" << i << "] = " << x[i] << "\n";
  return 0;
}
```

7

Exercise

Write the program ARRAY7.CPP by editing program ARRAY6.CPP and replacing the Comb sort method in function sortArray with an implementation of the Shell-Metzner method.

Week 1 in Review

Before you proceed to the second week of learning about programming with Visual C++, let's look at a special example that evolves at the end of the next two weeks. The example is a simple number-guessing game, shown in Listing R1.1. The program selects a number, at random, between 0 and 1,000 and prompts you to enter a number in that range. If your input is greater than the secret number, the program tells you that your guess was higher. By contrast, if your input is less than the secret number, the program tells you that your guess was lower. If you guess the secret number, the game ends with your victory. The program allows you up to 11 guesses. You can end the game at any prompt by entering a negative integer. In this case, the program stops the game and displays the secret number.

Type Listing R1.1. Source code for program GAME1.CPP.

```
1: #include <stdlib.h>
2: #include <iostream.h>
3: #include <time.h>
4:
5: // declare a global random number generating function
6: int random(int maxVal)
7: { return rand() % maxVal; }
8:
9:
10: main()
11: {
12:     int n, m;
13:     int MaxIter = 11;
14:     int iter = 0;
15:     int ok = 1;
```

continues

Listing R1.1. continued

```
16:
17:
18:    // reseed random-number generator
19:    srand((unsigned)time(NULL));
20:    n = random(1001);
21:    m = -1;
22:
23:    // loop to obtain the other guesses
24:    while (m != n && iter < MaxIter && ok == 1) {
25:      cout << "Enter a number between 0 and 1000 : ";
26:      cin >> m;
27:      ok = (m < 0) ? 0 : 1;
28:      iter++;
29:      // is the user's guess higher?
30:      if (m > n)
31:        cout << "Enter a lower guess\n\n";
32:      else if (m < n)
33:        cout << "Enter a higher guess\n\n";
34:      else
35:        cout << "You guessed it! Congratulations.";
36:    }
37:    // did the user guess the secret number
38:    if (iter >= MaxIter || ok == 0)
39:      cout << "The secret number is " << n << "\n";
40:
41:    return 0;
42: }
```

Here is a sample session with the program in Listing R1.1:

```
Enter a number between 0 and 1000 : 500
Enter a lower guess

Enter a number between 0 and 1000 : 250
Enter a higher guess

Enter a number between 0 and 1000 : -1
Enter a higher guess

The secret number is 399
```

The program in Listing R1.1 declares the function `random` to return a random number in the range of 0 to 1,000. The program also declares the function `main` which conducts the guessing game. The function declares a number of local variables in lines 12 through 15. The statement in line 19 reseeds the random number generator. The statement in line 20 assigns the secret number to the variable n. The statement in line 21 assigns -1 to the variable m which stores your guesses.

The while loop in lines 24 through 36 conducts the game. The while loop determines whether or not the following conditions are all true:

☐ Your guess (stored in variable m) does not match the secret number stored in variable n.

☐ The number of iterations (stored in variable iter) are less than the maximum number of iterations (stored in variable MaxIter).

☐ The variable ok stores 1.

The first statement in the loop prompts you to enter a number between 0 and 1,000. The statement in line 26 obtains your input and stores it in variable m. The statement in line ok assigns 0 to the variable ok if you entered a negative integer. Otherwise, the statement assigns 1 to variable ok. The statement in line 28 increments the variable iter.

The multi-alternative if statement in lines 30 through 35 compares your input with the secret number and displays the appropriate message reflecting your guess.

The if statement in line 38 displays the secret number if you failed to guess it in MaxIter iterations or if you entered a negative integer.

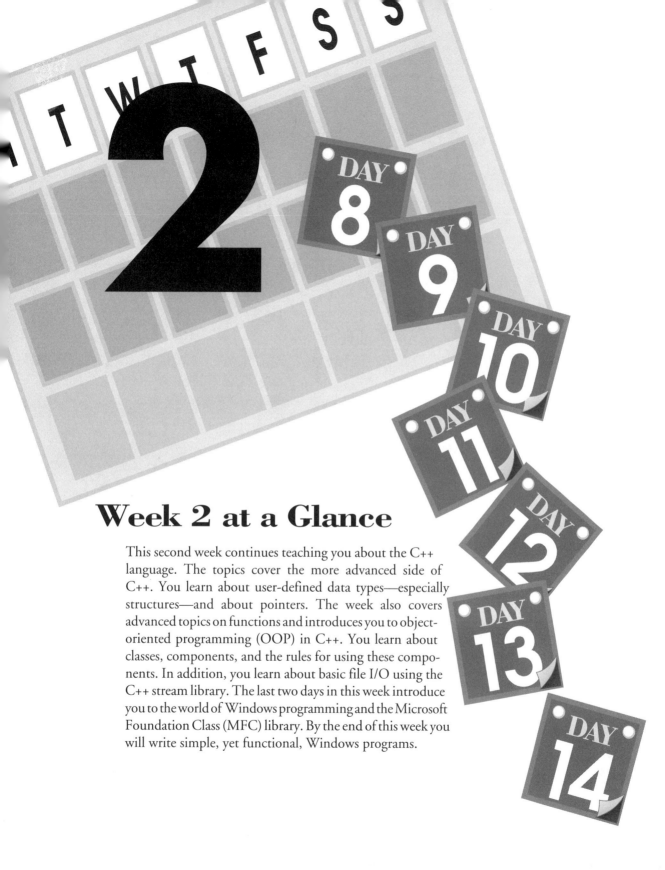

Week 2 at a Glance

This second week continues teaching you about the C++ language. The topics cover the more advanced side of C++. You learn about user-defined data types—especially structures—and about pointers. The week also covers advanced topics on functions and introduces you to object-oriented programming (OOP) in C++. You learn about classes, components, and the rules for using these components. In addition, you learn about basic file I/O using the C++ stream library. The last two days in this week introduce you to the world of Windows programming and the Microsoft Foundation Class (MFC) library. By the end of this week you will write simple, yet functional, Windows programs.

DAY

8

User-Defined
Types and Pointers

Creating user-defined data types is one of the features that are expected of modern programming languages. Today's lesson looks at the enumerated data types and structures that allow you to better organize your data. In addition, this lesson discusses using pointers with simple variables, arrays, structures, and dynamic data. Today, you learn about the following topics:

☐ The type definition using `typedef`

☐ Enumerated data types

☐ Structures

☐ Unions

☐ Reference variables

☐ Pointers to existing variables

☐ Pointers to arrays

☐ Pointers to structures

☐ Using pointers to access and manage dynamic data

☐ Far pointers

Type Definition in C++

C++ offers the `typedef` keyword that enables you to define new data type names as aliases of existing types.

The *typedef* Keyword

The general syntax for using `typedef` is

```
typedef knownType newType;
```

Examples:

```
typedef unsigned word;
typedef unsigned char byte;
type unsigned char boolean;
```

The `typedef` keyword defines a new type from a known one. You can use `typedef` to create aliases that shorten the names of existing data types or define names of data types that are more familiar to you (see the previous second example which `typedef`s a byte type). In addition, the `typedef` statement can define a new type name that better describes how the data type is used. The previous third example illustrates this use of `typedef`. You can also use `typedef` to define the name of an array type.

8

An Array Type Name

The general syntax for defining the name of an array type is

```
typedef baseType arrayTypeName[arraySize];
```

The `typedef` statement defines the *arrayTypeName* whose basic type and size are *baseType* and *arraySize*, respectively.

Examples:

```
typedef double vector[10];
typedef double matrix[10][30];
```

Thus, the identifiers `vector` and `matrix` are names of data types.

Enumerated Data Types

The rule to follow with enumerated data types is that while the enumerated identifiers must be unique, the values assigned to them are not.

NEW☞
TERM   An *enumerated type* defines a list of unique identifiers and associates values with these identifiers.

An Enumerated Type

The general syntax for declaring an enumerated type is

```
enum enumType { <list of enumerated identifiers> };
```

Example:

```
enum Boolean { false, true };
num YesNo { no, yes, dontCare, maybe };
enum weekday { Sunday, Monday, Tuesday,
               Wednesday, Thursday, Friday, Saturday };
```

Here is an example of declaring an enumerated type:

```
enum CPUtype { i8088, i80286, i80386DX, i80386SX,
               i80486DX, i80486SX };
```

C++ associates integer values with the enumerated identifiers. For example, in this type, the compiler assigns 0 to i8088, 1 to i80286, and so on.

C++ is very flexible in declaring an enumerated type. First, the language allows you to explicitly assign a value to an enumerated identifier. Here is an example:

```
enum weekday { Sunday = 1, Monday, Tuesday, Wednesday,
               Thursday, Friday, Saturday };
```

This declaration explicitly assigns 1 to the enumerated identifier Sunday. The compiler then assigns the next integer, 2, to the next identifier Monday, and so on. C++ allows you to explicitly assign a value to each member of the enumerated list. Moreover, these values need not be unique. Here are some examples of the flexibility in declaring enumerated types in C++:

```
// explicit value assignment for every list member
enum colors { black = 1, red = 2, blue = 3, green = 5,
              yellow = 7, white = 11 };

// intermittent value assignment
enum colors { black = 1, red, blue, green = 5,
              yellow = 7, white = 11 };

// duplicate values
enum CPUtype { i8088 = 1, i80286 = 2,
               i80386DX = 3, i80386SX = 3,
               i80486DX = 4, i80486SX = 4 };

enum choiceType { false, true, dontCare = 0 };
```

In the last example, the compiler associates the identifier false with 0 by default. However, the compiler also associates the value 0 with dontCare because of the explicit assignment.

C++ allows you to declare variables that have enumerated types in the following ways:

1. The declaration of the enumerated type may include the declaration of the variables of that type. The general syntax is

   ```
   enum enumType { <list of enumerated identifiers> }
                   <list of variables>;
   ```

   Here is an example:

   ```
   enum weekDay { Sun = 1, Mon, Tue, Wed, Thu, Fri, Sat }
           recycleDay, payDay, movieDay;
   ```

2. The separate declaration of the enumerated type and its variables includes multiple statements to declare the type and the associated variables separately. The general syntax is

   ```
   enum enumType { <list of enumerated identifiers> };
   enumType var1, var2, ..., varN;
   ```

Let's look at an example. Listing 8.1 shows the source code for program ENUM1.CPP. The program implements a simple one-line, four-function calculator that performs the following tasks:

□ Prompts you to enter a number, an operator (+, -, *, or /), and a number

□ Performs the requested operation, if valid

□ Displays the operands, the operator, and the result, if the operation was valid; otherwise displays an error message which indicates the kind of error (either you entered a bad operator, or attempted to divide by 0)

 Listing 8.1. Source code for the program ENUM1.CPP.

```
1: /*
2:   C++ program that demonstrates enumerated types
3: */
4:
5: #include <iostream.h>
6:
7: enum mathError { noError, badOperator, divideByZero };
8:
9: void sayError(mathError err)
10: {
11:   switch (err) {
12:     case noError:
13:       cout << "No error";
14:       break;
15:     case badOperator:
16:       cout << "Error: invalid operator";
17:       break;
18:     case divideByZero:
19:       cout << "Error: attempt to divide by zero";
20:   }
21: }
22:
23: main()
24: {
25:   double x, y, z;
26:   char op;
27:   mathError error = noError;
28:
29:   cout << "Enter a number, an operator, and a number : ";
30:   cin >> x >> op >> y;
31:
32:   switch (op) {
33:     case '+':
34:       z = x + y;
```

continues

197

Listing 8.1. continued

```
35:        break;
36:     case '-':
37:      z = x - y;
38:        break;
39:     case '*':
40:      z = x * y;
41:        break;
42:     case '/':
43:      if (y != 0)
44:         z = x / y;
45:      else
46:         error = divideByZero;
47:      break;
48:     default:
49:         error = badOperator;
50:    }
51:
52:   if (error == noError)
53:     cout << x << " " << op << " " << y << " = " << z;
54:   else
55:     sayError(error);
56:   return 0;
57: }
```

Here is a sample session with the program in Listing 8.1:

```
Enter a number, an operator, and a number : 355 / 113
355 / 113 = 3.14159
```

The program in Listing 8.1 declares the enumerated type `mathError` in line 7. This data type has three enumerated values: `noError`, `badOperator`, and `divideByZero`.

The program also defines the function `sayError` in lines 9 through 21 to display a message based on the value of the enumerated parameter `err`. The function uses the `switch` statement in line 11 to display messages that correspond to the various enumerated values.

The function `main` declares the `double`-typed variables x, y, and z to represent the operands and the result, respectively. In addition, the function declares the `char`-typed variable op to store the requested operation, and the enumerated variable error to store the error status. The function initializes the variable error with the enumerated value `noError`.

The output statement in line 29 prompts you to enter the operands and the operator. The statement in line 30 stores your input in variables x, op, and y, in that order. The function uses the switch statement in line 32 to examine the value in variable op and perform the requested operation. The case labels at lines 33, 36, 39, and 42 provide the values for the four supported math operations. The last case label contains an if statement which detects the attempt to divide by zero. If this is true, the else clause statement assigns the enumerated value divideByZero to the variable error.

The catch-all default clause in line 48 handles invalid operators. The statement in line 49 assigns the enumerated value badOperator to the variable error.

The if statement in line 52 determines whether or not the variable error contains the enumerated value noError. If this condition is true, the program executes the output statement in line 53. This statement displays the operands, the operator, and the result. Otherwise, the program executes the else clause statement which calls the function sayError and passes it the argument error. This function call displays a message which identifies the error.

Structures

C++ supports structures, and these members can be predefined types or other structures.

NEW☛ TERM *Structures* enable you to define a new type that logically groups several fields or members.

A Structure

The general syntax for declaring a structure is

```
struct structTag {
    < list of members >
};
```

Example:

```
struct point {
    double x;
    double y;
};

struct rectangle {
    point upperLeftCorner;
    point lowerRightCorner;
    double area;
};
```

```
struct circle {
    point center;
    double radius;
    double area;
};
```

Once you define a `struct` type, you can use that type to declare variables. Here are examples of declarations that use structures that I declared in the syntax box:

```
point p1, p2, p3;
```

You can also declare structured variables when you define the structure itself:

```
struct point {
    double x;
    double y;
} p1, p2, p3;
```

 NEW **TERM** *Untagged structures* allow you to declare structure variables without defining a name for their structures.

> **Note:** Interestingly, C++ permits you to declare untagged structures. For example, the following structure definition declares the variables p1, p2, and p3 but omits the name of the structure:
>
> ```
> struct {
>     double x;
>     double y;
> } p1, p2, p3;
> ```

C++ allows you to declare and initialize a structured variable. Here is an example:

```
point pt = { 1.0, -8.3 };
```

Accessing the members of a structure uses the dot operator. Here are a few examples:

```
p1.x = 12.45;
p1.y = 34.56;
p2.x = 23.4 / p1.x;
p2.y = 0.98 * p1.y;
```

Let's look at an example. Listing 8.2 shows the source code for program STRUCT1.CPP. The program prompts you for four sets of coordinates that define four rectangles. Each rectangle is defined by the X and Y coordinates of the upper-left and lower-right corners. The program calculates the areas of each rectangle, sorts the rectangles by area, and displays the rectangles in the order of their areas.

Listing 8.2. Source code for the program STRUCT1.CPP.

8

```
1:  /*
2:    C++ program that demonstrates structured types
3:  */
4:
5:  #include <iostream.h>
6:  #include <stdio.h>
7:  #include <math.h>
8:
9:  const MAX_RECT = 4;
10:
11: struct point {
12:   double x;
13:   double y;
14: };
15:
16: struct rect {
17:   point ulc; // upper left corner
18:   point lrc; // lower right corner
19:   double area;
20:   int id;
21: };
22:
23: typedef rect rectArr[MAX_RECT];
24:
25: main()
26: {
27:   rectArr r;
28:   rect temp;
29:   double length, width;
30:
31:   for (int i = 0; i < MAX_RECT; i++) {
32:     cout << "Enter (X,Y) coord. for ULC of rect. # "
33:          << i << " : ";
34:     cin >> r[i].ulc.x >> r[i].ulc.y;
35:     cout << "Enter (X,Y) coord. for LRC of rect. # "
36:          << i << " : ";
37:     cin >> r[i].lrc.x >> r[i].lrc.y;
38:     r[i].id = i;
39:     length = fabs(r[i].ulc.x - r[i].lrc.x);
40:     width = fabs(r[i].ulc.y - r[i].lrc.y);
41:     r[i].area = length * width;
42:   }
43:
44:   // sort the rectangles by areas
45:   for (i = 0; i < (MAX_RECT - 1); i++)
46:     for (int j = i + 1; j < MAX_RECT; j++)
47:       if (r[i].area > r[j].area) {
48:         temp = r[i];
```

continues

Listing 8.2. continued

```
49:        r[i] = r[j];
50:        r[j] = temp;
51:      }
52:
53:   // display rectangles sorted by area
54:   for (i = 0; i < MAX_RECT; i++)
55:     printf("Rect # %d has area %5.4lf\n", r[i].id, r[i].area);
56:   return 0;
57: }
```

Here is a sample session with the program in Listing 8.2:

```
Enter (X,Y) coord. for ULC of rect. # 0 : 1 1
Enter (X,Y) coord. for LRC of rect. # 0 : 2 2
Enter (X,Y) coord. for ULC of rect. # 1 : 1.5 1.5
Enter (X,Y) coord. for LRC of rect. # 1 : 3 4
Enter (X,Y) coord. for ULC of rect. # 2 : 1 2
Enter (X,Y) coord. for LRC of rect. # 2 : 5 8
Enter (X,Y) coord. for ULC of rect. # 3 : 4 6
Enter (X,Y) coord. for LRC of rect. # 3 : 8 4
Rect # 0 has area 1.0000
Rect # 1 has area 3.7500
Rect # 3 has area 8.0000
Rect # 2 has area 24.0000
```

The program in Listing 8.2 includes the header files IOSTREAM. MATH.H, and STDIO.H. The program declares the global constant MAX_RECT to specify the maximum number of rectangles. Line 11 contains the declaration of structure point, which is made up of two double-typed members, x and y. This structure models a two-dimensional point. Line 16 contains the declaration of structure rect which models a rectangle. The structure contains two point-typed members, ulc and lrc, the double-typed member area, and the int-typed member id. The members ulc and lrc represent the coordinates for the upper left and lower right corners which define a rectangle. The member area stores the area of the rectangle. The member id stores a numeric identification number.

The typedef statement in line 23 defines the type recArr as an array of MAX_RECT elements of structure rect.

The function main declares the rectArr-typed array r, the rect-typed structure temp, and the double-typed variables length and width.

The function main uses the for loop in lines 31 through 42 to prompt you for the coordinates of the rectangles, calculate their areas, and assign their id numbers. The output statements in lines 32 and 33, and in lines 35 and 36, prompt you for the X and Y coordinates of the upper left and lower right corners, respectively. The input statements in lines 34 and 37 store the coordinates you enter in members `r[i].ulc.x`, `r[i].ulc.y`, `r[i].lrc.x`, and `r[i].lrc.y`, respectively. The statement in line 38 stores the value of the loop control variable `i` in member `r[i].id`. The statement in line 39 calculates the length of a rectangle using the `x` members of the `ulc` and `lrc` members in the element `r[i]`. The statement in line 40 calculates the width of a rectangle using the `y` members of the `ulc` and `lrc` members in the element `r[i]`. The statement in line 41 calculates the area of the rectangle and stores it in member `r[i].area`.

The nested loops in lines 44 through 51 sort the elements of array `r` using the member `area`. The loops implement the simple bubble sort method (which is useful for very small arrays). The `if` statement in line 47 compares the areas of elements `r[i]` and `r[j]`. If the area of rectangle `r[i]` is larger than that of rectangle `r[j]`, the statements in lines 48 through 50 swap all the members of `r[i]` and `r[j]`. The swap uses the structure `temp`. This task illustrates that you can assign all the members of a structure to another structure in one statement.

The `for` loop in lines 54 and 55 displays the rectangles sorted according to their areas. The output statement in line 55 uses the `printf` function to display the rectangle id numbers and areas.

Unions

The size of a union is equal to the size of its largest member.

NEW☞ TERM   *Unions* are special structures that store members that are mutually exclusive.

Unions

The general syntax for unions is

```
union unionTag {
    type1 member1;
    type2 member2;
    ...
    typeN memberN;
};
```

Example:

```
union Long {
    unsigned mWord[2];
    long mLong;
};
```

Unions offer an easy alternative for quick data conversion. Unions were more significant in the past decades, when the price of memory was much higher and consolidating memory using unions was feasible. Accessing union members involves the dot access operators, just as in structures.

Reference Variables

In Day 2, you learn that you declare reference parameters by placing the & symbol after the parameter's type. Recall that a reference parameter becomes an alias to its arguments. In addition, any changes made to the reference parameter affect its argument. In addition to reference parameters, C++ supports reference variables. You can manipulate the referenced variable by using its alias. As a novice C++ programmer, your initial use of reference variables will most likely be limited. On the other hand, you probably are using reference parameters more frequently. As you advance in using C++, you discover how reference variables can implement programming tricks that deal with advanced class design. This book discusses only the basics of reference variables.

NEW TERM Like reference parameters, *reference variables* become aliases to the variables they access.

A Reference Variable

The general syntax for declaring a reference variable is

```
type& refVar;
type& refVar = aVar;
```

The refVar is the reference variable which can be initialized when declared. You must ensure that a reference variable is initialized or assigned a referenced variable before using the reference variable.

Examples:

```
int x = 10, y = 3;
int& rx = x;
int& ry;
ry = y; // take the reference
```

Here is a simple example that shows a reference variable at work. Listing 8.3 shows the source code for program REFVAR1.CPP. The program displays and alters the values of a variable using either the variable itself or its reference. The program requires no input.

Listing 8.3. Source code for the program REFVAR1.CPP.

8

```
 1: /*
 2:    C++ program that demonstrates reference variables
 3: */
 4:
 5: #include <iostream.h>
 6:
 7: main()
 8: {
 9:    int x = 10;
10:    int& rx = x;
11:    // display x using x and rx
12:    cout << "x contains " << x << "\n";
13:    cout << "x contains (using the reference rx) "
14:         << rx << "\n";
15:    // alter x and display its value using rx
16:    x *= 2;
17:    cout << "x contains (using the reference rx) "
18:         << rx << "\n";
19:    // alter rx and display value using x
20:    rx *= 2;
21:    cout << "x contains " << x << "\n";
22:    return 0;
23: }
```

Here is a sample session with the program in Listing 8.3:

```
x contains 10
x contains (using the reference rx) 10
x contains (using the reference rx) 20
x contains 40
```

 The program in Listing 8.3 declares the int-typed variable x and the int-typed reference variable rx. The program initializes the variable x with 10 and the reference variable rx with the variable x.

The output statement in line 12 displays the value in variable x using the variable x. By contrast, the output statement in line 13 and 14 displays the value in variable x using the reference variable rx.

The statement in line 16 doubles the integer in variable x. The output statement in lines 17 and 18 displays the new value in variable x using the reference variable rx. As the output shows, the reference variable accurately displays the updated value in variable x.

The statement in line 20 doubles the value in variable x by using the reference variable rx. The output statement in line 21 displays the updated value in variable x using variable x. Again, the output shows that the variable x and reference variable rx are synchronized.

Overview of Pointers

Each piece of information, both program and data, in the computer's memory resides at a specific address and occupies a specific number of bytes. When you run a program, your variables reside at specific addresses. With a high-level language such as C++ you are not concerned about the actual address of every variable. That task is handled transparently by the compiler and the run-time system. Conceptually, each variable in your program is a tag for a memory address. Manipulating the data using the tag is much easier than dealing with actual numerical addresses, such as 0F64:01AF4.

NEW
TERM An *address* is a memory location. A *tag* is the variable's name.

C++ and its parent C are programming languages that are also used for low-level systems programming. In fact, many regard C as a high-level assembler. Low-level systems programming requires that you frequently work with the address of data. This is where pointers, in general, come into play. Knowing the address of a piece of data enables you to set and query its value.

NEW
TERM A *pointer* is a special variable which stores the address of another variable or information.

> **Warning:** Pointers are very powerful language components. They can also be dangerous if used carelessly, because they may hang your system! This malfunction occurs when the pointer happens to have a low memory address of some critical data or function.

Pointers to Existing Variables

In this section you learn how to use pointers to access the values in existing variables. C++ requires that you associate a data type (including void) with a declared pointer. The associated data type may be a predefined type or a user-defined structure.

A Pointer

The general syntax for declaring a pointer is

```
type* pointerName;
type* pointerName = &variable;
```

The & operator is the address-of operator and is used to take the address of a variable.

8

Example:

```
int *intPtr; // pointer to an int
double *realPtr; // pointer to a double
char *aString; // pointer to a character
long lv;
long* lp = &lv;
```

You can also declare nonpointers in the same lines that declare pointers:

```
int *intPtr, anInt;
double *realPtr, x;
char *aString, aKey;
```

Note: C++ permits you to place the asterisk character right after the associated data type. You should not interpret this kind of syntax to mean that every other identifier appearing in the same declaration is automatically a pointer:

```
int* intPtr; // pointer to an int
double* realPtr; // pointer to a double
char* aString; // pointer to a character
int *intP, j; // intP is a pointer to int, j is an int
double *realPtr, *doublePtr;  // both identifiers
                              // are pointers to a double
```

DO	DON'T

DO initialize a pointer before you use it, just as you do with ordinary variables. In fact, the need to initialize pointers is more pressing—using uninitialized pointers invites trouble that leads to unpredictable program behavior or even a system hang!

DON'T assume that uninitialized pointers are harmless!

Once a pointer contains the address of a variable, you can access the value in that variable using the * operator followed by the pointer's name. For example, if px is a pointer to the variable x, you can use *px to access the value in variable x.

DO   DON'T

DO include the * operator to the left of a pointer to access the variable whose address is stored in the pointer.

DON'T forget to use the * operator. Without it, a statement ends up manipulating the address in the pointer instead of the data at that address.

Here is a simple example that shows a pointer at work. Listing 8.4 shows the source code for program PTR1.CPP. The program displays and alters the values of a variable using either the variable itself or its pointer. The program requires no input.

Type **Listing 8.4. Source code for the program PTR1.CPP.**

```
1: /*
2:    C++ program that demonstrates pointers to existing variables
3: */
4:
5: #include <iostream.h>
6:
7: main()
8: {
9:    int x = 10;
10:   int* px = &x;
11:   // display x using x and rx
12:   cout << "x contains " << x << "\n";
13:   cout << "x contains (using the pointer px) "
14:        << *px << "\n";
15:   // alter x and display its value using *px
16:   x *= 2;
17:   cout << "x contains (using the pointer px) "
18:        << *px << "\n";
19:   // alter *px and display value using x
20:   *px *= 2;
21:   cout << "x contains " << x << "\n";
22:   return 0;
23: }
```

Here is a sample session with the program in Listing 8.4:

```
x contains 10
x contains (using the pointer px) 10
x contains (using the pointer px) 20
x contains 40
```

The program in Listing 8.4 declares the int-typed variable x and the int-typed pointer px. The program initializes the variable x with 10 and the pointer px with the address of variable x.

The output statement in line 12 displays the value in variable x using the variable x. By contrast, the output statement in lines 13 and 14 displays the value in variable x using the pointer px. Notice that the statement uses *px to access the value in variable x.

The statement in line 16 doubles the integer in variable x. The output statement in lines 17 and 18 displays the new value in variable x using the pointer px. As the output shows, the pointer accurately displays the updated value in variable x.

The statement in line 20 doubles the value in variable x by using the pointer px. Notice that the assignment statement uses *px on the left side of the = operator to access the variable x. The output statement in line 21 displays the updated value in variable x using variable x. Again, the output shows that the variable x and the pointer px are synchronized.

Pointers to Arrays

C++, and its parent language C, support a special use for the names of arrays. The compiler interprets the name of an array as the address of its first element. Thus, if x is an array, the expressions &x[0] and x are equivalent. In the case of a matrix—call it mat—the expressions &mat[0][0] and mat are also equivalent. This aspect of C++ and C make them work as high-level assembly languages. Once you have the address of a data item, you've got its number, so to speak. The knowledge of the memory address of a variable or array enables you to manipulate its contents using pointers.

NEW☞ TERM A *program variable* is a label that tags a memory address. Using a variable in a program means accessing the associated memory location by specifying its name (or tag, if you prefer). In this sense, a variable becomes a name that points to a memory location—a pointer.

C++ allows you to use a pointer to access the various elements of an array. When you access the element x[i] of an array x, the compiled code performs two tasks. First, it obtains the base address of the array x (that is, where the first array element is located). Second, it uses the index i to calculate the offset from the base address of the array. This offset equals i multiplied by the size of the basic array type:

```
address of element x[i] = address of x + i * sizeof(basicType)
```

Looking at the above equation, assume that I have a pointer ptr that takes the base address of array x:

```
ptr = x; // pointer ptr points to address of x[0]
```

I can now substitute x with ptr in the equation and come up with the following:

```
address of element x[i] = ptr + i * sizeof(basicType)
```

In order for C++ and C to become high-level assemblers, they simplify the use of this equation by absolving it from having to explicitly state the size of the basic array type. Thus, you can write the following:

```
address of element x[i] = p + i
```

This equation states that the address of element x[i] is the expression (p + i).

Let me illustrate the use of pointers to access one-dimensional arrays by presenting the next program, PTR2.CPP (Listing 8.5). This program is a modified version of the program ARRAY1.CPP that calculates the average value for data in an array. The program begins by prompting you to enter the number of data and the data itself. Then the program calculates the average of the data in the array. Next, the program displays the average value.

Type **Listing 8.5. Source code for the program PTR2.CPP.**

```
 1: /*
 2:     C++ program that demonstrates the use of pointer with
 3:     one-dimension arrays.  Program calculates the average
 4:     value of the data found in the array.
 5: */
 6:
 7: #include <iostream.h>
 8:
 9: const int MAX = 30;
10:
11: main()
12: {
13:
14:     double x[MAX];
15:     // declare pointer and initialize with base
16:     // address of array x
```

```
17:        double *realPtr = x; // same as = &x[0]
18:        double sum, sumx = 0.0, mean;
19:        int n;
20:        // obtain the number of data points
21:        do {
22:            cout << "Enter number of data points [2 to "
23:                 << MAX << "] : ";
24:            cin >> n;
25:            cout << "\n";
26:        } while (n < 2 || n > MAX);
27:
28:        // prompt for the data
29:        for (int i = 0; i < n; i++) {
30:            cout << "X[" << i << "] : ";
31:            // use the form *(x+i) to store data in x[i]
32:            cin >> *(x + i);
33:        }
34:
35:        sum = n;
36:        for (i = 0; i < n; i++)
37:        // use the form *(realPtr + i) to access x[i]
38:            sumx += *(realPtr + i);
39:        mean = sumx / sum;
40:        cout << "\nMean = " << mean << "\n\n";
41:        return 0;
42: }
```

Here is a sample session with the program in Listing 8.5:

```
Enter number of data points [2 to 30] : 5

X[0] : 1
X[1] : 2
X[2] : 3
X[3] : 4
X[4] : 5

Mean = 3
```

The program in Listing 8.5 declares the double-typed array x to have MAX elements. In addition, the program declares the pointer realPtr and initializes it using the array x. Thus, the pointer realPtr stores the address of x[0], the first element in array x.

The program uses the pointer for *(x + i) in the input statement at line 32. Thus, the identifier x works as a pointer to the array x. Using the expression *(x + i) accesses the element number i of array x, just as using the expression x[i] does.

The program uses the pointer realPtr in the for loop at lines 37 and 38. The expression *(realPtr + i) is the equivalent of *(x + i), which in turn is equivalent to x[i]. Thus, the for loop uses the pointer realPtr with an offset value, i, to access the elements of array x.

The Pointer Increment/Decrement Method

The previous C++ program maintains the same address in the pointer realPtr. Employing pointer arithmetic with the for loop index i, I can write a new program version that increments the offset to access the elements of array x. C++ provides you with another choice that allows you to access sequentially the elements of an array without the help of an explicit offset value. The method merely involves using the increment or decrement operator with a pointer. You still need to initialize the pointer to the base address of an array and then use the ++ operator to access the next array element. Here is a modified version of the last program that uses the pointer increment method. Listing 8.6 shows the source code for the PTR3.CPP program.

Listing 8.6. Source code for the program PTR3.CPP.

```
 1: /*
 2:    C++ program that demonstrates the use of pointers with
 3:    one-dimension arrays.  The average value of the array
 4:    is calculated.  This program modifies the previous version
 5:    in the following way:  the realPtr is used to access the
 6:    array without any help from any loop control variable.
 7:    This is accomplished by 'incrementing' the pointer, and
 8:    consequently incrementing its address.  This program
 9:    illustrates pointer arithmetic that alters the pointer's
10:    address.
11:
12: */
13:
14: #include <iostream.h>
15:
16: const int MAX = 30;
17:
18: main()
19: {
20:
21:      double x[MAX];
22:      double *realPtr = x;
23:      double sum, sumx = 0.0, mean;
24:      int i, n;
```

```
25:
26:    do {
27:        cout << "Enter number of data points [2 to "
28:            << MAX << "] : ";
29:        cin >> n;
30:        cout << "\n";
31:    } while (n < 2 || n > MAX);
32:
33:    // loop variable i is not directly involved in accessing
34:    //    the elements of array x
35:    for (i = 0; i < n; i++) {
36:        cout << "X[" << i << "] : ";
37:        // increment pointer realPtr after taking its reference
38:        cin >> *realPtr++;
39:    }
40:
41:    // restore original address by using pointer arithmetic
42:    realPtr -= n;
43:    sum = n;
44:    // loop variable i serves as a simple counter
45:    for (i = 0; i < n; i++)
46:        // increment pointer realPtr after taking a reference
47:        sumx += *(realPtr++);
48:    mean = sumx / sum;
49:    cout << "\nMean = " << mean << "\n\n";
50:    return 0;
51:
52: }
```

Here is a sample session with the program in Listing 8.6:

```
Enter number of data points [2 to 30] : 5

X[0] : 10
X[1] : 20
X[2] : 30
X[3] : 40
X[4] : 50


Mean = 30
```

The program in Listing 8.6 initializes the realPtr pointer to the base address of array x, in line 22. The program uses the realPtr pointer in the keyboard input statement in line 38. This statement uses *realPtr++ to store your input in the currently accessed element of array x and then to increment the pointer to the next element of array x. When the input loop terminates, the pointer realPtr points past the tail of array x. To reset the pointer to the base address of array x, the program uses the assignment statement in line 42. This statement uses pointer arithmetic to decrease the current address in pointer `realPtr` by n times `sizeof(real)`. The statement resets the address in the pointer `realPtr` to access the array element `x[0]`. The program uses the same incrementing method to calculate the sum of data in the second `for` loop in line 47.

Pointers to Structures

C++ supports declaring and using pointers to structures. Assigning the address of a structured variable to a pointer of the same type uses the same syntax as with simple variables. Once the pointer has the address of the structured variable, it needs to use the `->` operator to access the members of the structure.

Accessing Structure Members

The general syntax for accessing the members of a structure by a pointer is

```
structPtr->aMember
```

Example:

```
struct point {
  double x;
  double y;
};

point p;
point* ptr = &p;

ptr->x = 23.3;
ptr->y = ptr->x + 12.3;
```

Here is a sample program that uses pointers to structures. Listing 8.7 shows the source code for program PTR4.CPP. This program is the version of program STRUCT1.CPP which uses pointers. The program prompts you for four sets of coordinates that define four rectangles. Each rectangle is defined by the X and Y coordinates of the upper-left and lower-right corners. The program calculates the areas of each rectangle, sorts the rectangles by area, and displays the rectangles in the order of their areas.

Type **Listing 8.7. Source code for the program PTR4.CPP.**

```
1: /*
2:   C++ program that demonstrates pointers to structured types
3: */
4:
```

```
5: #include <iostream.h>
6: #include <stdio.h>
7: #include <math.h>
8:
9: const MAX_RECT = 4;
10:
11: struct point {
12:   double x;
13:   double y;
14: };
15:
16: struct rect {
17:   point ulc; // upper left corner
18:   point lrc; // lower right corner
19:   double area;
20:   int id;
21: };
22:
23: typedef rect rectArr[MAX_RECT];
24:
25: main()
26: {
27:   rectArr r;
28:   rect temp;
29:   rect* pr = r;
30:   rect* pr2;
31:   double length, width;
32:
33:   for (int i = 0; i < MAX_RECT; i++, pr++) {
34:     cout << "Enter (X,Y) coord. for ULC of rect. # "
35:          << i << " : ";
36:     cin >> pr->ulc.x >> pr->ulc.y;
37:     cout << "Enter (X,Y) coord. for LRC of rect. # "
38:          << i << " : ";
39:     cin >> pr->lrc.x >> pr->lrc.y;
40:     pr->id = i;
41:     length = fabs(pr->ulc.x - pr->lrc.x);
42:     width = fabs(pr->ulc.y - pr->lrc.y);
43:     pr->area = length * width;
44:   }
45:
46:   pr -= MAX_RECT; // reset pointer
47:   // sort the rectangles by areas
48:   for (i = 0; i < (MAX_RECT - 1); i++, pr++) {
49:     pr2 = pr + 1; // reset pointer pr2
50:     for (int j = i + 1; j < MAX_RECT; j++, pr2++)
51:       if (pr->area > pr2->area) {
52:         temp = *pr;
53:         *pr = *pr2;
54:         *pr2 = temp;
55:       }
```

continues

Listing 8.7. continued

```
56:  }
57:
58:  pr -= MAX_RECT - 1; // reset pointer
59:  // display rectangles sorted by area
60:  for (i = 0; i < MAX_RECT; i++, pr++)
61:    printf("Rect # %d has area %5.4lf\n", pr->id, pr->area);
62:  return 0;
63: }
```

Here is a sample session with the program in Listing 8.7:

```
Enter (X,Y) coord. for ULC of rect. # 0 : 1 1
Enter (X,Y) coord. for LRC of rect. # 0 : 2 2
Enter (X,Y) coord. for ULC of rect. # 1 : 1.5 1.5
Enter (X,Y) coord. for LRC of rect. # 1 : 3 4
Enter (X,Y) coord. for ULC of rect. # 2 : 1 2
Enter (X,Y) coord. for LRC of rect. # 2 : 5 8
Enter (X,Y) coord. for ULC of rect. # 3 : 4 6
Enter (X,Y) coord. for LRC of rect. # 3 : 8 4
Rect # 0 has area 1.0000
Rect # 1 has area 3.7500
Rect # 3 has area 8.0000
Rect # 2 has area 24.0000
```

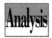

The program in Listing 8.7 declares the pointers pr and pr2 in lines 29 and 30, respectively. These pointers access the structure of type rect. The program initializes the pointer pr with the base address of array r.

The first for loop, which begins at line 33, uses the pointer pr to access the elements of array r. The loop increment part contains the expression pr++, which uses pointer arithmetic to make the pointer pr access the next element in array r. The input statements in lines 36 and 39 use the pointer pr to access the members ulc and lrc. Notice that the statements use the pointer access operator -> to allow pointer pr to access the members ulc and lrc. The statements in lines 40 through 43 also use the pointer pr to access the members id, ulc, lrc, and area, using the -> operator.

The statement in line 46 resets the address stored in pointer pr by MAX_RECT units (that is MAX_RECT * sizeof(double) bytes). The nested loops in lines 48 through 56 use the pointers pr and pr2. The outer for loop increments the address in pointer pr by one before the next iteration. The statement in line 49 assigns pr + 1 to the pointer pr2. This statement gives the pointer pr2 the initial access to the element i + 1 in array r. The inner for loop increments the pointer pr2 by 1 before the next iteration. Thus the nested for loops use the pointers pr and pr2 to access the elements of array r. The if statement in line 51 uses the pointers pr and pr2 to access the area member in comparing the areas of various rectangles. The statements in line 52 through 54 swap the elements of array r, which are accessed by pointers pr and pr2. Notice that the statements use *pr and *pr2 to access an entire element of array r.

The statement in line 58 resets the address in pointer pr by subtracting MAX_RECT -1. The last for loop also uses the pointer pr to access and display the members id and area of the various elements in array r.

This program illustrates that you can completely manipulate an array using pointers only—they are powerful and versatile.

Pointers and Dynamic Memory

The programs presented so far create the space for their variables at compile-time. When the programs start running, the variables have their memory spaces preassigned. There are many applications in which you need to create new variables during the program execution. You need to allocate the memory space dynamically for these new variables at run-time. The designers of C++ have chosen to introduce new operators, that are not found in C, to handle the dynamic allocation and deallocation of memory. These new C++ operators are new and delete. While the C-style dynamic memory functions malloc, calloc, and free are still available, you should use the operators new and delete. These operators are more aware of the type of dynamic data created than functions malloc, calloc, and free.

Syntax

The *new* and *delete* Operators

The general syntax for using the new and delete operators in creating dynamic scalar variables is

```
pointer = new type;
delete pointer;
```

The operator new returns the address of the dynamically allocated variable. The operator delete removes the dynamically allocated memory accessed by a pointer. If the dynamic allocation of operator new fails, it returns a NULL (equivalent to 0) pointer. Therefore, you need to test for a NULL pointer after using the new operator if you suspect trouble.

Example:

```
int *pint;
pint = new int;
*pint = 33;
cout << "Pointer pint stores " << *pint;
delete pint;
```

A Dynamic Array

To allocate and deallocate a dynamic array, use the following general syntax:

```
arrayPointer = new type[arraySize];
delete [] arrayPointer;
```

The operator `new` returns the address of the dynamically allocated array. If the allocation fails, the operator assigns NULL to the pointer. The operator `delete` removes the dynamically allocated array accessed by a pointer.

Example:

```
const int MAX = 10;
int* pint;
pint = new int[MAX];
for (int i = 0; i < MAX; i++)
    *pint[i] = i * i
for (i = 0; i < MAX; i++)
    cout << *(pint + i) << "\n";
delete [] pint;
```

DO	DON'T

DO maintain access to dynamic variables and arrays at all times. Such access does not need the original pointers used to create these dynamic variables and arrays. Here is an example:

```
int* p = new int;
int* q;
*p = 123;
q = p; // q now also points to 123
p = new int; // create another dynamic variable
*p = 345; // p points to 345 whereas q points to 123
cout << *p << " " << *q << " " << (*p + *q) << "\n";
delete p;
delete q;
```

DON'T forget to delete dynamic variables and arrays at the end of their scope.

Using pointers to create and access dynamic data can be illustrated with the next program, PTR5.CPP (Listing 8.8). This program is a modified version of the program ARRAY1.CPP that calculates the average value for data in an array. The program begins by prompting you to enter the actual number of data and validates your input. Then the program prompts you for the data and calculates the average of the data in the array. Next, the program displays the average value.

Listing 8.8. Source code for the program PTR5.CPP.

```
 1: /*
 2:    C++ program that demonstrates the pointers to manage
 3:    dynamic data
 4: */
 5:
 6: #include <iostream.h>
 7:
 8: const int MAX = 30;
 9:
10: main()
11: {
12:
13:     double* x;
14:     double sum, sumx = 0, mean;
15:     int *n;
16:
17:     n = new int;
18:     if (n == NULL)
19:       return 1;
20:
21:     do { // obtain number of data points
22:         cout << "Enter number of data points [2 to "
23:              << MAX << "] : ";
24:         cin >> *n;
25:         cout << "\n";
26:     } while (*n < 2 || *n > MAX);
27:     // create tailor-fit dynamic array
28:     x = new double[*n];
29:     if (!x) {
30:       delete n;
31:       return 1;
32:     }
33:     // prompt user for data
34:     for (int i = 0; i < *n; i++) {
35:         cout << "X[" << i << "] : ";
36:         cin >> x[i];
37:     }
38:
39:     // initialize summations
40:     sum = *n;
41:     // calculate sum of observations
42:     for (i = 0; i < *n; i++)
43:         sumx += *(x + i);
44:
45:     mean = sumx / sum; // calculate the mean value
46:     cout << "\nMean = " << mean << "\n\n";
47:     // deallocate dynamic memory
48:     delete n;
```

continues

Listing 8.8. continued

```
49:       delete [] x;
50:       return 0;
51: }
```

Here is a sample session with the program in Listing 8.8:

```
Enter number of data points [2 to 30] : 5

X[0] : 1
X[1] : 2
X[2] : 3
X[3] : 4
X[4] : 5

Mean = 3
```

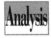

The program in Listing 8.8 uses two pointers for dynamic allocations. Line 13 declares the first pointer, which is used to allocate and access the dynamic array. Line 15 declares the pointer to create a dynamic variable.

The statement in line 17 uses the operator new to allocate the space for a dynamic int variable. The statement returns the address of the dynamic data to the pointer n. The if statement in line 18 determines whether or not the dynamic allocation failed. If so, the function main exits and returns an exit code of 1 (to flag an error).

The do-while loop in lines 21 through 26 prompts you to enter the number of data points. The statement in line 24 stores your input in the dynamic variable accessed by pointer n. The statement uses the pointer reference *n for this access. The while clause also uses *n to access the value in the dynamic variable. In fact, all the statements in the program access the number of data using the pointer reference *n.

The statement in line 28 creates a dynamic array using the operator new. The statement creates a dynamic double-typed array with the number of elements that you specify. This feature shows the advantage of using dynamic allocation to create custom-fit arrays. The if statement in line 29 determines whether or not the allocation of the dynamic array was successful. If not, the statements in line 30 and 31 deallocate the dynamic variable accessed by pointer n and exit the function with a return value of 1.

The for loop in lines 34 through 37 prompts you to enter values for the dynamic array. The statement in line 36 stores your input to the element i of the dynamic array. Notice that the statement uses the expression x[i] to access the targeted element. This form resembles that of static arrays. C++ treats the expression x[i] as equivalent to *(x + i)`. In fact , the program uses the latter form in the second `for` loop in lines 42 and 43. The statement in line 43 accesses the elements in the dynamic array using the form `*(x + i)`.

The last statements in function `main` delete the dynamic variable and array. The statement in line 48 deallocates the space for the dynamic variable accessed by pointer `n`. The statement in line 49 deletes the dynamic array accessed by pointer `x`.

Far Pointers

The architecture of processors such as the family of Intel 80x86 uses segmented memory. Each segment is 64K. Using segments has advantages and disadvantages.

NEW☞
TERM This storage scheme supports two kinds of pointers: near pointers and far pointers. Within a segment you can use *near pointers* to access data in the same segment. The pointers only store the offset address in the segment and thus require fewer bytes to store their address. By contrast, *far pointers* store the segment and offset addresses, and thus require more space. Windows applications use far pointers.

To declare far pointers, insert the keyword `far` (or sometimes `_far`) between the pointer's type and the pointer's name.

Summary

Today's lesson introduces you to user-defined data types and covers the following topics:

☐ You can use the `typedef` statements to create alias types of existing types and define array types. The general syntax for using `typedef` is

```
typedef knownType newType;
```

☐ Enumerated data types enable you to declare unique identifiers that represent a collection of logically related constants. The general syntax for declaring an enumerated type is

```
enum enumType { <list of enumerated identifiers> };
```

☐ Structures enable you to define a new type that logically groups several fields or members. These members can be predefined types or other structures. The general syntax for declaring a structure is

```
struct structTag {
    < list of members >
};
```

☐ Unions are a form of variant structures. The general syntax for unions is

```
union unionTag {
    type1 member1;
    type2 member2;
    ...
    typeN memberN;
};
```

☐ Reference variables are aliases of the variables which they reference. To declare a reference variable, place the & after the data type of the reference variable or to the left of the variable's name.

☐ Pointers are variables which store the addresses of other variables or data. C++ uses pointers to offer flexible and efficient manipulation of data and system resources.

☐ Pointers to existing variables use the & operator to obtain the addresses of these variables. Armed with these addresses, pointers offer access to the data in their associated variables. To access the value using a pointer, use the * operator followed by the name of the pointer.

☐ Pointers access the elements of arrays by being assigned the base address of a class. C++ considers the name of an array as equivalent to the pointer of the base address. For example, the name of the array X is treated as &X[0]. Pointers can be used to sequentially traverse the elements of an array to store and/or recall values from these elements.

☐ Pointers to structures manipulate structures and access their members. C++ provides the -> operator to allow a pointer access to the members of a structure.

☐ Pointers can create and access dynamic data using the operators new and delete. These operators allow you to create dynamic variables and arrays. The new operator assigns the address of the dynamic data to the pointer used in creating and accessing the data. The operator delete assists in recuperating the space of dynamic data when that information is no longer needed.

☐ Far pointers are pointers which store both the segment and offset addresses of an item. Near pointers only store the offset address of an item. Far pointers require more storage than near pointers.

Q&A

Q. Does C++ support pointers to the predefined type void?

A. Yes, void* pointers are considered typeless pointers and can be used to copy data.

Q. Because C++ pointers have types (even void* pointers), can I use typecasting to translate the data accessed by the general-purpose void* pointers to non-void* pointers?

A. Yes, C++ allows you to typecast pointer references. For example:

```
void* p = data;
long *lp = (long*) p;
```

The pointer lp uses the typecast to translate the data it accesses.

Q. What happens if I delete a dynamic array using the delete operator without following it with the empty brackets?

A. The run-time system only deletes the first element of the dynamic array. The other elements remain in memory, as inaccessible data.

Q. Can a structure contain a pointer to itself?

A. Yes. Many structures that model dynamic data structures use this kind of declaration. For example, the following structure models the nodes of a dynamic list with pointer-based links:

```
struct listNode {
  dataType data;
  listNode *next;
};
```

Q. Does C++ allow the declaration of a pointer-to-structure type before declaring the structure?

A. Yes, this feature makes declaring nodes of dynamic data structure possible.

Q. Does C++ allow pointers that access the addresses of other pointers?

A. Yes, C++ supports pointers to pointers (also called *double pointers*). To declare such pointers, use two * characters, as shown in the example below which declares the double pointer p:

```
int x;
int *px = &x;
int **p = &px;
```

Then expression *p accesses the pointer px and the expression **p accesses the variable x.

Workshop

The Workshop provides quiz questions to help you solidify your understanding of the material covered and exercises to provide you with experience in using what you've learned. Try to understand the quiz and exercise answers before continuing on to the next day's lesson. Answers are provided in Appendix B, "Answers."

Quiz

1. What is the error in the following statements?

```
enum Boolean { false, true };
enum State { on, off };
enum YesNo { yes, no };
enum DiskDriveStatus { on , off };
```

2. Is the declaration of the following enumerated type incorrect?

```
enum YesNo ( no = 0, No = 0, yes = 1, Yes = 1 };
```

3. What is the problem with the following program?

```
#include <iostream.h>
main()
{
  int *p = new int;
  cout << "Enter a number : ";
  cin >> *p;
  cout << "The square of " << *p << " = " << (*p * *p);
  return 0;
}
```

Exercises

1. Modify program PTR4.CPP to create program PTR6.CPP, which uses the Comb sort method to sort the array of rectangles.

2. Define a structure which can be used to model a dynamic array of integers. The structure should have a member to access the dynamic data and a member to store the size of the dynamic array. Call the structure intArrStruct.

3. Define a structure which can be used to model a dynamic matrix. The structure should have a member to access the dynamic data, and two members to store the number of rows and columns. Call the structure matStruct.

8

DAY

9

Strings

The examples presented from Day 1 through Day 8 are predominantly numeric, with a few aimed at character manipulation. You may have grown suspicious about the absence of strings in all of these examples. Today's lesson discusses C++ strings. You learn about the following topics:

☐ Strings in C++

☐ String input

☐ Using the standard string library

☐ Assigning strings

☐ Getting the length of strings

☐ Concatenating strings

☐ Comparing strings

☐ Converting strings

☐ Reversing the characters in a string

☐ Locating characters

☐ Locating substrings

C++ Strings

C++ (and its parent language C) have no predefined string type. Instead, C++, like C, regards strings as arrays of characters that end with the ASCII 0 null character ('\0').

NEW☛ TERM   The '\0' character is also called the *null terminator*. Strings that end with the null terminator are sometimes called *ASCIIZ strings*, with the letter Z standing for zero, the ASCII code of the null terminator.

The null terminator *must* be present in all strings and taken into account when dimensioning a string. When you declare a string variable as an array of characters, be sure to reserve an extra space for the null terminator. The advantage of using the null terminator is that you can create strings that are not restricted by any limit imposed by the C++ implementation. In addition, ASCIIZ strings have very simple structures.

 Note: The lesson in Day 8 discusses how pointers can access and manipulate the elements of an array. C and C++ make extensive use of this programming feature in manipulating the characters of a string.

DO	**DON'T**

DO include an extra space for the null terminator when specifying the size of a string.

DON'T declare a string variable as a single-character array. Such a variable is useless!

String Input

The programs that I have presented so far display string literals in output stream statements. Thus, C++ supports stream output for strings as a special case for a non-predefined data type. (You can say the support came by popular demand!) String output using string variables uses the same operator and syntax. With string input, the inserter operator >> does not work well because strings often contain spaces which are ignored by the inserter operator. Instead of the inserter operator you need to use the `getline` function. This function reads up to a specified number of characters.

The *getline* Function

The general syntax for the overloaded `getline` function is

```
istream& getline(signed char* buffer,
                 int size,
                 char delimiter = '\n');

istream& getline(unsigned char* buffer,
                 int size,
                 char delimiter = '\n');
```

The parameter `buffer` is a pointer to the string receiving the characters from the stream. The parameter `size` specifies the maximum number of characters to read. The parameter `delimiter` specifies the delimiting character which causes the string input to stop before reaching the number of characters specified by parameter `size`. The parameter `delimiter` has the default argument of `'\n'`.

Example:

```
#include <iostream.h>
main()
{
```

```
    char name[80];
    cout << "Enter your name: ";
    cin.getline(name, sizeof(name)-1);
    cout << "Hello " << name << ", how are you";
    return 0;
}
```

Using the STRING.H Library

The community of C programmers has developed the standard string library STRING.H that contains the most frequently used string-manipulation functions. The STDIO.H and IOSTREAM.H header file prototype functions also support string I/O. The different C++ compiler vendors have also developed C++-style string libraries. These libraries use classes to model strings (more about classes in Day 11). However, these string libraries *are not standard*, whereas the C-style string routines in STRING.H are part of the ANSI C standard. In the next subsections I present several, but not all, of the functions which are prototyped in the STRING.H header file.

Some of the string functions in STRING.H have more than one version. The extra versions which append the letters _f, f, or _, work with strings that are accessed using far pointers.

Assigning Strings

C++ supports two methods for assigning strings. You can assign a string literal to a string variable when you initialize it. This method is simple and requires using the = operator and the assigning string.

Initializing a String

The general syntax for initializing a string is

```
char stringVar[stringSize] = stringLiteral;
```

Example:

```
char aString[81] = "Visual C++ in 21 days";
char name[] = "Namir Shammas";
```

The second method for assigning one ASCIIZ string to another uses the function strcpy. This function assumes that the copied string ends with the null character.

The *strcpy* Function

The prototype for the function `strcpy` is

```
char* strcpy(char* target, const char* source)
```

The function copies the characters from string source to string target. The function *assumes* that the target string accesses enough space to contain the source string.

Example:

```
char name[41];
strcpy(name,"Visual C++");
```

The variable `name` contains the string `"Visual C++"`.

The function `strdup` allows you to copy the character to another string and allocate required space in the target string.

The *strdup* Function

The prototype for the function `strdup` is

```
char* strdup(const char* source)
```

The function copies the characters in the source string and returns a pointer to the duplicate string.

Example:

```
char* string1 = "The reign in Spain";
char* string2;

string2 = strdup(string1);
```

This example copies the contents of `string1` into `string2` after allocating the memory space for `string2`.

The string library also offers the function `strncpy` to support copying a specified number of characters from one string to another.

The *strncpy* Function

The prototype for the function `strncpy` is

```
char* strncpy(char* target, const char* source, size_t num);
```

The function copies *num* characters from the source string to the target string. The function performs character truncation or padding, if necessary.

Example:

```
char str1[] = "Pascal";
char str2[] = "Hello there";

strncpy(str1, str2, 6);
```

The variable `str1` now contains the string `"Hello "`.

Note: Using pointers to manipulate strings is new to many novice C++ programmers. In fact, you can use pointers to manipulate the trailing parts of a string by assigning the address of the first character to manipulate. For example, if I declare the string `str1` as follows:

```
char str1[41] = "Hello World";
char str2[41];
char* p = str1;

p += 6; // p now points to substring "World" in str
strcpy(str2, p);
cout << str2 << "\n";
```

The output statement displays the string `"World"`. This example shows how using pointers can incorporate an offset number of characters.

The Length of a String

Many string operations require the number of characters in a string. The STRING.H library offers the function `strlen` to return the number of characters, excluding the null terminator, in a string.

Syntax

The *strlen* Function

The prototype for the function `strlen` is

```
size_t strlen(const char* string)
```

The function `strlen` returns the number of characters in parameter `string`. The result type `size_t` represents a general integer type.

Example:

```
char str[] = "1234567890";
unsigned i;
i = strlen(str);
```

These statements assign 10 to the variable i.

Concatenating Strings

Often, you build a string by concatenating two or more strings. The function strcat allows you to concatenate one string to another.

NEW☞
TERM
When you *concatenate* strings you join or link them together.

The *strcat* Function

The prototype for the function strcat is

```
char* strcat(char* target, const char* source)
```

The function appends the contents of the source string to the target string and returns the pointer to the target string. The function *assumes* that the target string can accommodate the characters of the source string.

Example:

```
char string[81];
strcpy(string, "Visual");
strcat(string," C++")
```

The variable string now contains "Visual C++".

The function strncat concatenates a specified number of characters from the source string to the target strings.

The *strncat* Function

The prototype for the function strncat is

```
char* strncat(char* target, const char* source, size_t num)
```

The function appends num characters of the source string to the target string and returns the pointer to the target string.

Example:

```
char str1[81] = "Hello I am ";
char str2[41] = "Thomas Jones";

strncat(str1, str2, 6);
```

The variable `str1` now contains `"Hello I am Thomas"`.

DO	**DON'T**

DO use the function `strncat` to control the number of concatenated characters, when you are unsure of the capacity of the target string.

DON'T assume that the target string is always adequate to store the characters in the source string.

Let's look at a program that uses the `getline`, `strlen`, and `strcat` functions. Listing 9.1 contains the source code for the program STRING1.CPP. The program performs the following tasks:

- [ ] Prompts you to enter a string (your input should not exceed 40 characters)

- [ ] Prompts you to enter a second string (your input should not exceed 40 characters)

- [ ] Displays the number of characters in each of the strings you enter

- [ ] Concatenates the second string to the first one

- [ ] Displays the concatenated strings

- [ ] Displays the number of characters in the concatenated strings

- [ ] Prompts you to enter a search character

- [ ] Prompts you to enter a replacement character

- [ ] Displays the concatenated string after translating all the occurrences of the search character with the replacement character

Type Listing 9.1. Source code for the program STRING1.CPP.

```
1: /*
2:    C++ program that demonstrates C-style strings
3: */
4:
5: #include <iostream.h>
6: #include <string.h>
7:
8: const unsigned MAX1 = 40;
9: const unsigned MAX2 = 80;
10:
11: main()
12: {
13:
14:     char smallStr[MAX1+1];
15:     char bigStr[MAX2+1];
16:     char findChar, replChar;
17:
18:     cout << "Enter first string:\n";
19:     cin.getline(bigStr, MAX2);
20:     cout << "Enter second string:\n";
21:     cin.getline(smallStr, MAX1);
22:     cout << "String 1 has " << strlen(bigStr)
23:         << " characters\n";
24:     cout << "String 2 has " << strlen(smallStr)
25:         << " characters\n";
26:     // concatenate bigStr to smallStr
27:     strcat(bigStr, smallStr);
28:     cout << "Concatenated strings are:\n"
29:         << bigStr << "\n";
30:     cout << "New string has " << strlen(bigStr)
31:         << " characters\n";
32:     // get the search and replacement characters
33:     cout << "Enter search character : ";
34:     cin >> findChar;
35:     cout << "Enter replacement character : ";
36:     cin >> replChar;
37:     // replace characters in string bigStr
38:     for (unsigned i = 0; i < strlen(bigStr); i++)
39:       if (bigStr[i] == findChar)
40:         bigStr[i] = replChar;
41:     // display the updated string bigStr
42:     cout << "New string is:\n"
43:         << bigStr;
44:     return 0;
45: }
```

Here is a sample session with the program in Listing 9.1:

```
Enter first string:
The rain in Spain stays
Enter second string:
 mainly in the plain
String 1 has 23 characters
String 2 has 20 characters
Concatenated strings are:
The rain in Spain stays mainly in the plain
New string has 43 characters
Enter search character : a
Enter replacement character : A
New string is:
The rAin in SpAin stAys mAinly in the plAin
```

The program in Listing 9.1 includes the STRING.H header file for the string manipulation functions. Lines 8 and 9 declare the global constants MAX1 and MAX2 used to size a small string and a big string, respectively. The function main declares two strings, smallStr and bigStr. Line 14 declares the variable smallStr to store MAX1+1 characters (the extra space is for the null character). Line 15 declares the variable bigStr to store MAX2+1 characters. Line 16 declares the char-typed variable findChar and replChar.

The output statement in line 18 prompts you to enter the first string. The statement in line 19 uses the stream input function getline to obtain your input and to store it in variable bigStr. The function call specifies that you can enter up to MAX2 characters. The output statement in line 20 prompts you to enter the second string. The statement in line 21 uses the stream input function getline to obtain your input and to store it in variable smallStr. The function call specifies that you can enter up to MAX1 characters.

The output statements in lines 22 through 25 display the number of characters in variables bigStr and smallStr, respectively. Each output statement calls function strlen and passes it a string variable.

The statement in line 27 concatenates the string in variable smallStr to variable bigStr. The output statement in lines 28 and 29 displays the updated string bigStr. The output statement in lines 30 and 31 displays the number of characters in the updated string variable bigStr. This statement also uses the function strlen to obtain the number of characters.

The statement in line 33 prompts you to enter the search character. The statement in line 34 obtains your input and stores it in variable findChar. The statement in line 35 prompts you to enter the replacement character. The statement in line 36 obtains your input and stores it in variable replChar.

The for loop in lines 38 through 40 translates the characters in string bigStr. The loop uses the control variable i and iterates, in increments of 1, from 0 to strlen(bigstr)-1. The if statement in line 39 determines whether or not character number i in bigStr matches the character in variable findChar. If this condition is true, the program executes the statement in line 40. This statement assigns the character in variable replChar to character number i in variable bigStr. This loop shows how you can manipulate the contents of a string variable by accessing each character in that string.

The output statement in lines 42 and 43 displays the updated string bigStr.

String Comparison

Because strings are arrays of characters, the STRING.H library provides a set of functions to compare strings. These functions compare the characters of two strings using the ASCII value of each character. The functions are strcmp, stricmp, strncmp, and strnicmp.

The function strcmp performs a case-sensitive comparison of two strings, using every character possible.

Syntax

The *strcmp* Function

The prototype for the function strcmp is

```
int strcmp(const char* str1, const char* str2);
```

The function compares strings *str1* and *str2*. The integer result indicates the outcome of the comparison:

```
< 0   when str1 is less than str2
= 0   when str1 is equal to str2
> 0   when str1 is greater than str2
```

Example:

```
char string1[] = "Visual C++";
char string2[] = "Visual Basic";
int i;

i = strcmp(string1, string2);
```

The last statement assigns a *POSITIVE* ~~negative~~ number to the variable i, because the string in variable string1 is ~~less~~ *GREATER* than the string in variable string2.

The function stricmp performs a case-insensitive comparison between two strings, using every character possible.

The *stricmp* Function

The prototype for the function stricmp is

```
int stricmp(const char* str1, const char* str2);
```

The function compares the strings *str1* and *str2* without making a distinction between upper- and lowercase characters. The integer result indicates the outcome of the comparison:

```
< 0   when str1 is less than str2
= 0   when str1 is equal to str2
> 0   when str1 is greater than str2
```

Example:

```
char string1[] = "Visual C++";
char string2[] = "VISUAL C++"
int i;

i = stricmp(string1, string2);
```

The last statement assigns 0 to the variable i, because the strings in variables string1 and string2 differ only in their cases.

The function strncmp performs a case-sensitive comparison on specified leading characters in two strings.

The *strncmp* Function

The prototype for the function strncmp is

```
int strncmp(const char* str1, const char* str2, size_t num);
```

The function compares the *num* leading characters in two strings *str1* and *str2*. The integer result indicates the outcome of the comparison:

```
< 0   when str1 is less than str2
= 0   when str1 is equal to str2
> 0   when str1 is greater than str2
```

Example:

```
char string1[] = "Visual C++";
char string2[] = "Visual Basic"
int i;

i = strncmp(string1, string2, 8);
```

This assigns a ~~negative~~ *POSITIVE* number to the variable i because "Visual C" is ~~less~~ *GREATER* than "Visual B".

The function strnicmp performs a case-insensitive comparison on specified leading characters in two strings.

Syntax

The *strnicmp* Function

The prototype for the function strnicmp is

```
int strnicmp(const char* str1, const char* str2, size_t num);
```

The function compares the *num* leading characters in two strings *str1* and *str2*, regardless of the character case. The integer result indicates the outcome of the comparison:

```
< 0   when str1 is less than str2
= 0   when str1 is equal to str2
> 0   when str1 is greater than str2
```

Example:

```
char string1[] = "Visual C++";
char string2[] = "VISUAL Basic"
int i;

i = strnicmp(string1, string2, 6);
```

This assigns 0 to the variable i because the strings "Visual" and "VISUAL" differ only in the case of their characters.

Let's look at an example that compares strings. Listing 9.2 creates an array of strings and initializes it with data. Then the program displays the unordered array of strings, sorts the array, and displays the sorted array.

Type

Listing 9.2. Source code for the program STRING2.CPP.

```
 1:  /*
 2:  C++ program that demonstrates comparing strings
 3:  */
 4:
 5:  #include <iostream.h>
 6:  #include <string.h>
 7:
 8:  const unsigned STR_SIZE = 40;
 9:  const unsigned ARRAY_SIZE = 11;
10:  const int TRUE = 1;
11:  const int FALSE = 0;
12:
13:  main()
14:  {
```

continues

Listing 9.2. continued

```
15:                          ARRAY_SIZE   STR_SIZE
16:        char strArr[STR_SIZE][ARRAY_SIZE] =
17:            { "California", "Virginia", "Alaska", "New York",
18:                "Michigan", "Nevada", "Ohio", "Florida",
19:                "Washington", "Oregon", "Arizona" };
20:        char temp[STR_SIZE];
21:        unsigned n = ARRAY_SIZE;
22:        unsigned offset;
23:        int inOrder;
24:
25:        cout << "Unordered array of strings is:\n";
26:        for (unsigned i = 0; i < ARRAY_SIZE; i++)
27:          cout << strArr[i] << "\n";
28:
29:        cout << "\nEnter a non-space character and press Enter";
30:        cin >> temp[0];
31:        cout << "\n";
32:
33:        offset = n;
34:        do {
35:          offset = (8 * offset) / 11;
36:          offset = (offset == 0) ? 1 : offset;
37:          inOrder = TRUE;
38:          for (unsigned i = 0, j = offset;
39:                i < n - offset; i++, j++)
40:            if (strcmp(strArr[i], strArr[j]) > 0) {
41:              strcpy(temp, strArr[i]);
42:              strcpy(strArr[i], strArr[j]);
43:              strcpy(strArr[j], temp);
44:              inOrder = FALSE;
45:            }
46:        } while (!(offset == 1 && inOrder));
47:
48:        cout << "Sorted array of strings is:\n";
49:        for (i = 0; i < ARRAY_SIZE; i++)
50:          cout << strArr[i] << "\n";
51:        return 0;
52:    }
```

Here is a sample session with the program in Listing 9.2:

```
Unordered array of strings is:
California
Virginia
Alaska
New York
Michigan
Nevada
```

```
Ohio
Florida
Washington
Oregon
Arizona
Enter a non-space character and press Enter
Sorted array of strings is:
Alaska
Arizona
California
Florida
Michigan
Nevada
New York
Ohio
Oregon
Virginia
Washington
```

9

The program in Listing 9.2 declares the global constants STR_SIZE, ARRAY_SIZE, TRUE, and FALSE in lines 8 through 11. The constant STR_SIZE specifies the size of each string. The constant ARRAY_SIZE indicates the number of strings in the array used by the program. The constants TRUE and FALSE represent the Boolean values employed in sorting the array of strings. The function main declares the array strArr (actually, the variable strArr is a matrix of characters) to have ARRAY_SIZE elements and STR_SIZE characters per elements. Notice that the declaration states the size of each string in the first dimension and the size of the array in the second dimension. The function also initializes the array strArr. The function also declares the variable temp as a swap buffer. Lines 21 through 23 declare miscellaneous variables.

The output statement in line 25 displays the title before showing the elements of the unordered array strArr. The for loop in lines 26 and 27 displays these elements. The loop uses the control variable i and iterates, in increments of 1, from 0 to ARRAY_SIZE-1. The output statement in line 27 displays the string at element i, using the expression strArr[i].

The output and input statements in lines 29 and 30 prompt you to enter a nonspace character. This input allows you to examine the unordered array before the program sorts the array and displays its ordered elements.

The statements in lines 33 through 46 implement the Comb sort method. Notice that the if statement in line 40 uses the function strcmp to compare elements number i and j, accessed using the expressions strArr[i] and strArr[j], respectively. The statements in lines 41 through 43 swap the elements i and j using the function strcpy and the swap buffer temp.

The output statement in line 48 displays the title before showing the elements of the sorted array. The for loop in lines 49 and 50 displays these elements. The loop utilizes the control variable i and iterates, in increments of 1, from 0 to ARRAY_SIZE-1. The output statement in line 50 displays the string at element i, using the expression strArr[i].

Converting Strings

The STRING.H library offers the function _strlwr and _strupr to convert the characters of a string to lowercase and uppercase, respectively. Note that these functions are more commonly called strlwr and strupr (without the leading underscore character) in C text books.

The _strlwr Function

The prototype for the function _strlwr is

```
char* _strlwr(char* source)
```

The function converts the uppercase characters in string *source* to lowercase. Other characters are not affected. The function also returns the pointer to the string *source*.

Example:

```
char str[] = "HELLO THERE";

_strlwr(str);
```

The variable str now contains the string "hello there".

The _strupr Function

The prototype for the function _strupr is

```
char* _strupr(char* source)
```

The function converts the lowercase characters in string *source* to uppercase. Other characters are not affected. The function also returns the pointer to the string *source*.

Example:

```
char str[] = "Visual C++";
_strupr(str);
```

The variable str now contains the string "VISUAL C++".

DO	**DON'T**

DO make copies for the arguments of functions _strlwr and _strupr if you need the original arguments later in a program.

DON'T always assume that applying the function _strlwr and then the function _strupr (or vice versa) to the same variable will succeed in restoring the original characters in that variable.

9

Reversing Strings

The STRING.H library offers the function strrev to reverse the characters in a string.

The *strrev* Function

The prototype for the function strrev is

```
char* strrev(char* str)
```

The function reverses the order of the characters in string str and returns the pointer to the string str.

Example:

```
char string[] = "Hello";

strrev(string);
cout << string;
```

This displays "olleH".

Let's look at a program that manipulates the characters in a string. Listing 9.3 shows the source code for the program STRING3.CPP. The program performs the following tasks:

- ☐ Prompts you to enter a string
- ☐ Displays your input
- ☐ Displays the lowercase version of your input
- ☐ Displays the uppercase version of your input
- ☐ Displays the character you typed in reverse order
- ☐ Displays a message that your input has no uppercase character, if this is true

243

Strings

□ Displays a message that your input has no lowercase character, if this is true

□ Displays a message that your input has symmetrical characters, if this is true

Type **Listing 9.3. Source code for the program STRING3.CPP.**

```
1: /*
2:   C++ program that demonstrates manipulating the
3:   characters in a string
4: */
5:
6: #include <iostream.h>
7: #include <string.h>
8:
9: const unsigned STR_SIZE = 40;
10: const int TRUE = 1;
11: const int FALSE = 0;
12:
13: main()
14: {
15:     char str1[STR_SIZE+1];
16:     char str2[STR_SIZE+1];
17:     int isLowerCase;
18:     int isUpperCase;
19:     int isSymmetrical;
20:
21:
22:     cout << "Enter a string : ";
23:     cin.getline(str1, STR_SIZE);
24:     cout << "Input: " << str1 << "\n";
25:     // copy str1 to str2
26:     strcpy(str2, str1);
27:     // convert to lowercase
28:     strlwr(str2);
29:     isLowerCase = (strcmp(str1, str2) == 0) ? TRUE : FALSE;
30:     cout << "Lowercase: " << str2 << "\n";
31:     // convert to uppercase
32:     strupr(str2);
33:     isUpperCase = (strcmp(str1, str2) == 0) ? TRUE : FALSE;
34:     cout << "Uppercase: " << str2 << "\n";
35:     // copy str1 to str2
36:     strcpy(str2, str1);
37:     // reverse characters
38:     strrev(str2);
39:     isSymmetrical = (strcmp(str1, str2) == 0) ? TRUE : FALSE;
40:     cout << "Reversed: " << str2 << "\n";
41:     if (isLowerCase)
42:       cout << "Your input has no uppercase letters\n";
43:     if (isUpperCase)
```

```
44:        cout << "Your input has no lowercase letters\n";
45:    if (isSymmetrical)
46:        cout << "Your input has symmetrical characters\n";
47:    return 0;
48: }
```

Here is a sample session with the program in Listing 9.3:

```
Enter a string : level
Input: level
Lowercase: level
Uppercase: LEVEL
Reversed: level
Your input has no uppercase letters
Your input has symmetrical characters
```

The program in Listing 9.3 declares the string variables str1 and str2 in function main. Each string stores STR_SIZE + 1 characters (including the null terminator). The function also declares the flags isLowerCase, isUpperCase, and isSymmetrical.

The output statement in line 22 prompts you to enter a string. The statement in line 23 uses the string input function getline to store your input in variable str1. The output statement in line 24 echoes your input.

The statement in line 26 copies the characters in variable str1 to variable str2. The statement in line 26 calls the function strlwr to convert the characters in variable str2. The program manipulates the characters of variable str2, while maintaining the original input in variable str1. The statement in line 29 calls the function strcmp to compare the characters in str1 and str2. The two strings can be equal only if your input has no uppercase characters. The statement uses the conditional operator to assign the constant TRUE to the flag isLowerCase if the above condition is true. Otherwise, the statement assigns FALSE to the flag isLowerCase. The output statement in line 30 displays the characters in variable str2.

The statement in line 32 calls the function strupr and supplies it the argument str2. This function call converts any lowercase character in variable str2 into uppercase. The statement in line 33 calls the function strcmp to compare the characters in str1 and str2. The two strings can be equal only if your input has no lowercase characters. The statement uses the conditional operator to assign the constant TRUE to the flag isUpperCase if that is true. Otherwise, the statement assigns FALSE to the flag isUpperCase. The output statement in line 34 displays the characters in variable str2.

To display the original input in reverse order, the program calls the function strcpy to copy the characters of variable str1 to variable str2 once more. The statement in line 38 calls the function strrev and passes it the argument str2. The statement in line 39 calls the function strcmp to compare the characters in str1 and str2. The two strings can be equal only if your input has symmetrical characters. The statement uses the conditional operator to assign the constant TRUE to the flag isSymmetrical if the above condition is true. Otherwise, the statement assigns FALSE to the flag isSymmetrical. The output statement in line 40 displays the characters in variable str2.

The program uses the if statements in lines 41, 43, and 45 to indicate that your input has special characteristics. The if statement in line 41 comments on the fact that your input has no uppercase letter when the value in variable isLowerCase is TRUE. The if statement in line 43 comments on the fact that your input has no lowercase letter when the value in variable isUpperCase is TRUE. The if statement in line 45 comments on the fact that your input has symmetrical characters when the value in variable isSymmetrical is TRUE.

Locating Characters

The STRING.H library offers a number of functions for locating characters in strings. These functions include strchr, strrchr, strspn, strcspn, and strpbrk. These functions allow you to search for characters and simple character patterns in strings.

The function strchr locates the first occurrence of a character in a string.

Syntax

The *strchr* Function

The prototype for the function strchr is

```
char* strchr(const char* target, int c)
```

The function locates the first occurrence of pattern c in string target. The function returns the pointer to the character in string target which matches the specified pattern c. If the character c does not occur in the string target, the function yields a NULL.

Example:

```
char str[81] = "Visual C++";
char* strPtr;

strPtr = strchr(str, '+');
```

The pointer strPtr points to the substring "++" in string str.

The function strrchr locates the last occurrence of a character in a string.

SAMS
PUBLISHING

The *strrchr* Function

The prototype for the function `strrchr` is

```
char* strrchr(const char* target, int c)
```

The function locates the last occurrence of pattern *c* in string *target*. The function returns the pointer to the character in string *target* which matches the specified pattern *c*. If the character *c* does not occur in the string *target*, the function yields a NULL.

Example:

```
char str[81] = "Visual C++ is here";
char* strPtr;

strPtr = strrchr(str, '+');
```

The pointer `strPtr` points to the substring `"+ is here"` in string `str`.

The function `strspn` yields the number of characters in the leading part of a string that matches any character in a pattern of characters.

The *strspn* Function

The prototype for the function `strspn` is

```
size_t strspn(const char* target, const char* pattern)
```

The function returns the number of characters in the leading part of string *target* that matches any character in the string *pattern*.

Example:

```
char str[] = "Visual C++ 1.0";
char substr[] = "Vailus ";
int index;

index = strspn(str, substr);
```

This statement assigns 7 to variable `index`, because the characters in `substr` found a match in every one of the first seven characters of `str`.

The function `strcspn` scans a string and yields the number of the leading characters in a string that is totally void of the characters in a substring.

9

Syntax

The *strcspn* Function

The prototype for the function strcspn is

```
size_t strcspn(const char* str1, const char* str2)
```

The function scans str1 and returns the length of the leftmost substring that is totally void of the characters of the substring str2.

Example:

```
char strng[] = "The rain in Spain";
int i;

i = strcspn(strng," in");
```

This example assigns 3 (the length of "The" "rain") to the variable i.

The function strpbrk searches a string for the first occurrence of any character in a pattern of characters.

Syntax

The *strpbrk* Function

The prototype for the function strpbrk is

```
char* strpbrk(const char* target, const char* pattern)
```

The function searches the *target* string for the first occurrence of *any character* in the characters of string *pattern*. If the characters in the pattern do not occur in the string *target*, the function yields a NULL.

Example:

```
char* str = "Hello there how are you";
char* substr = "hr";
char* ptr;

ptr = strpbrk(str, substr);
cout << ptr << "\n";
```

This displays "here how are you", because the 'h' is encountered in the string before the 'r'.

Locating Strings

The STRING.H library offers the function strstr to locate a substring in a string.

The *strstr* Function

The prototype for the function strstr is

```
char* strstr(const char* str, const char* substr);
```

The function scans the string *str* for the first occurrence of a string *substr*. The function yields the pointer to the first character in string *str* which matches the parameter *substr*. If the string *substr* does not occur in the string *str*, the function yields a NULL.

Example:

```
char str[] = "Hello there! how are you";
char substr[] = "how";
char* ptr;

ptr = strstr(str, substr);
cout << ptr << "\n";
```

This displays "how are you" because the string search matched "how". The pointer ptr points to the rest of the original string starting with "how".

DO	DON'T

DO use the function strrev before calling function strstr if you want to search for the last occurrence of a string.

DON'T forget to reverse both the main and the search strings when using the strrev function to locate the last occurrence of the search string.

The string library also provides the function strtok which allows you to break down a string into substrings based on a specified set of delimiting characters.

NEW☞
TERM   Substrings are sometimes called *tokens*.

The *strtok* Function

The prototype for the function strtok is

```
char* strtok(char* target, const char* delimiters);
```

The function searches the target string for tokens. A string supplies the set of delimiter characters. The following example shows how this function works in returning the tokens in a string. The function strtok modifies the string target by inserting '\0' characters after each token. Make sure that you store a copy of the original target string in another string variable.

Example:

[handwritten: 1) SKIPS LEADING DELIM 2) TMP STRING UPTO NEXT DELIM 3) SUB-CALLS INC NULL TO CONT WHERE IT LEFT OFF]

```c
#include <stdio.h>
#include <string.h>

main()
{
    char* str = "(Base_Cost+Profit) * Margin";
    char* tkn = "+* ()";
    char* ptr = str;

    printf("%s\n", str);
    // the first call looks normal
    ptr = strtok(str, tkn);
    printf("\n\nis broken into: %s",ptr);
    while (ptr) {
        printf(" %s",ptr);
        // must make first argument a NULL character
        ptr = strtok(NULL, tkn);
    }
    printf("\n\n");
}
```

This example displays the following when the program is run:

(Base_Cost+Profit) * Margin   *[handwritten: BASE_COST PROFIT MARGIN]*

This is broken into `Base_Cost`, `Profit`, `Margin`.

DO	**DON'T**

DO remember to supply `NULL` as the first argument to function `strtok` to locate the next token.

DON'T forget to store a copy of the target string in the function `strtok`.

Let's look at an example that searches for characters and strings. Listing 9.4 shows the source code for the program STRING4.CPP. The program performs the following tasks:

☐ Prompts you to enter the main string

☐ Prompts you to enter the search string

☐ Prompts you to enter the search character

☐ Displays a character ruler and the main string

☐ Displays the indices where the search string occurs in the main string

☐ Displays the indices where the search character occurs in the main string

Listing 9.4. Source code for the program STRING4.CPP.

```
1: /*
2:    C++ program that demonstrates searching for the
3:    characters and strings
4: */
5:
6: #include <iostream.h>
7: #include <string.h>
8:
9: const unsigned STR_SIZE = 40;
10:
11: main()
12: {
13:     char mainStr[STR_SIZE+1];
14:     char subStr[STR_SIZE+1];
15:     char findChar;
16:     char *p;
17:     int index;
18:     int count;
19:
20:     cout << "Enter a string : ";
21:     cin.getline(mainStr, STR_SIZE);
22:     cout << "Enter a search string : ";
23:     cin.getline(subStr, STR_SIZE);
24:     cout << "Enter a search character : ";
25:     cin >> findChar;
26:
27:     cout << "              1         2         3         4\n";
28:     cout << "01234567890123456789012345678901234567890\n";
29:     cout << mainStr << "\n";
30:     cout << "Searching for string " << subStr << "\n";
31:     p = strstr(mainStr, subStr);
32:     count = 0;
33:     while (p) {
34:       count++;
35:       index = p - mainStr;
36:       cout << "Match at index " << index << "\n";
37:       p = strstr(++p, subStr);
38:     }
39:     if (count == 0)
40:       cout << "No match for substring in main string\n";
41:
```

continues

Listing 9.4. continued

```
42:     cout << "Searching for character " << findChar << "\n";
43:     p = strchr(mainStr, findChar);
44:     count = 0;
45:     while (p) {
46:       count++;
47:       index = p - mainStr;
48:       cout << "Match at index " << index << "\n";
49:       p = strchr(++p, findChar);
50:     }
51:     if (count == 0)
52:       cout << "No match for search character in main string\n";
53:     return 0;
54: }
```

Here is a sample session with the program in Listing 9.4:

```
Enter a string : here, there, and everywhere
Enter a search string : here
Enter a search character : e
          1         2         3         4
0123456789012345678901234567890123456789 0
here, there, and everywhere
Searching for string here
Match at index 0
Match at index 7
Match at index 23
Searching for character e
Match at index 1
Match at index 3
Match at index 8
Match at index 10
Match at index 17
Match at index 19
Match at index 24
Match at index 26
```

The program in Listing 9.4 declares the strings `mainStr` and `subStr` to represent the main and search strings, respectively. The program also declares the variable `findChar` to store the search character. In addition, the program declares the character pointer `p` and the `int`-typed variables `index` and `count`.

The output statement in line 20 prompts you to enter a string. The statement in line 21 calls the stream input function `getline` and stores your input in variable `mainStr`. The output statement in line 22 prompts you to enter the search string. The statement in line 23 calls the stream input function `getline` and saves your input in variable subStr. The output statement in line 24 prompts you to enter the search character. The statement in line 25 obtains your input and stores it in variable findChar.

The output statements in lines 27 through 29 display a ruler and your input, aligned under the ruler. The output statement in line 30 informs you that the program is searching for the substring you entered. The search begins at the statement in line 31. This statement calls function strstr to locate the first occurrence of string subStr in the string mainStr. The statement in line 32 assigns 0 to the variable count, which keeps track of the number of times the string mainStr contains the string subStr.

The program uses the while loop in lines 33 through 38 to locate all the occurrences of subStr in mainStr. The condition of the while loop examines the address of pointer p. If that pointer is not NULL, the loop iterates. The first statement inside the loop increments the variable count. The statement in line 35 calculates the index of string mainStr where the last match occurs. The statement obtains the sought index by subtracting the address of pointer p from the address of the first character in variable mainStr (remember that the expression &mainStr[0] is equivalent to the simpler expression mainStr). The statement assigns the result to variable index. The output statement in line 36 displays the value in variable index.

The statement in line 37 searches for the next occurrence of the string subStr in mainStr. Notice that this statement calls strstr and supplies it the pointer p as the first argument. The statement also applies the pre-increment operator to pointer p to store the address of the next character. This action ensures that the call to function strstr finds the next occurrence, if any, and is not stuck at the last occurrence. The if statement outside the while loop examines the value in variable count. If it contains zero, the program executes the output statement in line 40 to inform you that no match was found for the search string.

The output statement in line 42 informs you that the program is now searching for the character you specified in the main string. The process of searching for the character in findChar is very similar to searching for the string subStr. The main difference is that searching for a character involves the function strchr.

Summary

Today's lesson presents C++ strings and discusses string manipulation functions which are exported by the STRING.H header file. You learn about the following topics:

☐ Strings in C++ are arrays of characters that end with the null character (the ASCII 0 character).

☐ String input requires the use of the `getline` stream input function. This function requires that you specify the input variable, the maximum number of input characters, and the optional line delimiter.

☐ The STRING.H header file contains the standard (for the C language) string library. This library contains many versatile functions that support copying, concatenating, converting, reversing, and searching for strings.

☐ C++ supports two methods for assigning strings. The first method assigns a string to another when you declare the latter string. The second method uses the function `strcpy` to assign one string to another at any stage in the program. The string library also offers the function `strdup` to copy a string and allocate the needed space.

☐ The function `strlen` returns the length of a string.

☐ The `strcat` and `strncat` functions permit you to concatenate two strings. The function `strncat` allows you to specify the number of characters to concatenate.

☐ The functions `strcmp`, `stricmp`, `strncmp`, and `strnicmp` allow you to perform various types of string comparisons. The function `strcmp` performs a case-insensitive comparison of two strings, using every character possible. The `stricmp` is a version of function `strcmp` which performs a case-insensitive comparison. The function `strncmp` is a variant of function `strcmp` which uses a specified number of characters in comparing the strings. The function `strnicmp` is a version of function `strncmp` which performs a case-insensitive comparison.

☐ The functions `strlwr` and `strupr` convert the characters of a string into lowercase and uppercase, respectively.

☐ The function `strrev` reverses the order of characters in a string.

☐ The functions `strchr`, `strrchr`, `strspn`, `strcspn`, and `strpbrk` allow you to search for characters and simple character patterns in strings.

☐ The function `strstr` searches for a string in another string. The function `strtok` empowers you to break down a string into small strings which are delimited by a set of characters that you specify.

Q&A

Q. Can a statement initialize a pointer using a string literal?

A. Yes, the compiler stores the characters of the string literal in memory and assigns its address to that pointer. Here is an example:

```
char* p = "I am a small string";
```

In addition, you can overwrite the characters of the string literal using their pointers. However, keep in mind that the pointer p accesses a string with a fixed number of characters.

Q. Can a statement declare a constant pointer to a literal string?

A. Yes, this kind of declaration resembles the one I mentioned previously. However, because the statement declares a constant pointer, you cannot overwrite the characters of the initializing string literal. Here is an example:

```
const char* p = "Version 1.0";
```

Use the constant char pointer to store fixed messages and titles.

Q. Can a statement declare an array of pointers to a set of string literal strings?

A. Yes, this is the easiest method to use an array of pointers to access a collection of messages, titles, or other kinds of fixed strings. Here is an example:

```
char* mainMenu[] = { "File", "Edit", "Search", "View",
                     "Debug", "Options", "Windows", "Help"};
```

Thus the element p[0] accesses the first string, p[1] the second string, and so on.

Q. How can I use strcmp to compare strings, starting at a specific number of characters?

A. Simply add the offset value to the arguments of the function strcmp. Here is an example:

```
char s1[41] = "Visual C++";
char s2[41] = "Visual Basic";
int offset = 7;
int i;
i = strcmp(str1 + offset, str2 + offset);
```

9

Q. How can I use `strncmp` to compare a specific number of characters in two strings, starting at a specific character?

A. Simply add the offset value to the arguments of the function `strcmp`. Here is an example:

```
char s1[41] = "Visual C++";
char s2[41] = "Visual Basic";
int offset = 7;
int num = 3;
int i;
i = strncmp(str1 + offset, str2 + offset, num);
```

Workshop

The Workshop provides quiz questions to help you solidify your understanding of the material covered and exercises to provide you with experience in using what you've learned. Try to understand the quiz and exercise answers before continuing on to the next day's lesson. Answers are provided in Appendix B, "Answers."

Quiz

1. Where is the error in the following program?

```
#include <iostream.h>
#include <string.h>
const in MAX = 10;
main()
{
  char s1[MAX+1];
  char s2[] = "12345678901234567890123456789   0";
  strcpy(s1, s2);
  cout << "String 1 is " << s1
       << "\nString 2 is " << s2;
  return 0;
}
```

2. How can you fix the program in the last question using the function `strncpy` instead of `strcpy`?

3. What is the value assigned to variable `i` in the following statements?

```
char s1[] = "Visual C++";
char s2[] = "Visual Basic";
int i;
i = strcmp(s1, s2);
```

4. What is the value assigned to variable `i` in the following statements?

```
char s1[] = "Visual C++";
char s2[] = "Visual Basic";
int offset = strlen("Visual ");
int i;
i = strcmp(s1 + offset, s2 + offset);
```

5. True or false? The following function correctly returns 1 if a string does not contain lowercase characters, and yields 0 if otherwise:

```
int hasNoLowerCase(const char* s)
{
  char s2[strlen(s)+1];
  strcpy(s2, s);
  strupr(s2);
  return (strcmp(s1, s2) == 0) ? 1 : 0);
}
```

Exercises

1. Write your own version of function `strlen`. Use a `while` loop and a character-counting variable to obtain the function result.

2. Write another version of function `strlen`. This time use a `while` loop and a local pointer to obtain the function result.

3. Write the program STRING5.CPP which uses the function `strtok` to break down the string `"2*(X+Y)/(X+Z) - (X+10)/(Y-5)"` into three sets of tokens, using the token delimiter strings `"+-*/ ()"`, `"( )"`, and `"+-*/ "`.

DAY
10

Advanced
Functions
Parameters

Functions are the basic building blocks that conceptually extend the C++ language to fit your custom applications. C, the parent language of C++, is more function-oriented than C++. This difference is due to the support for classes, inheritance, and other object-oriented programming features (more about the latter in tomorrow's lesson). Nevertheless, functions still play an important role in C++. In today's lesson, you learn about the following advanced aspects of C++ functions:

☐ Passing arrays as function arguments

☐ Passing strings as function arguments

☐ Passing structures by value

☐ Passing structures by reference

☐ Passing structures by pointer

☐ Recursive functions

☐ Passing pointers to dynamic structures

☐ Pointers to functions

Passing Arrays as Arguments

When you write a C++ function that passes an array parameter, you can declare that parameter as a pointer to the basic type of the array.

A Pointer-to-Array Parameter

The general syntax for prototyping a function with a pointer-to-array parameter is

```
returnType function(basicType*, <other parameter types>);
```

The general syntax for defining this function is

```
returnType function(basicType *arrParam, <other parameters>)
```

Example:

```
// prototypes
void ShellSort(unsigned *doubleArray, unsigned arraySize);
void QuickSort(unsigned *intArray, unsigned arraySize);
```

In Day 7 I state that C++ allows you to declare open array parameters using a pair of empty brackets. This kind of declaration is equivalent to using a pointer parameter. C++ programmers use open array form less frequently than the explicit pointer form, even though using the brackets shows the intent of the parameter more clearly.

DO	**DON'T**

DO use const parameters to prevent the host function from altering the arguments.

DON'T forget to include a parameter which specifies the number of array elements to manipulate, when the array-typed arguments are only partially filled with meaningful data.

Let's look at an example. Listing 10.1 shows the source code for the program ADVFUN1.CPP. I created this program by performing minor edits to program ARRAY5.CPP (found in Listing 7.5 of Day 7). The program performs the following tasks:

☐ Prompts you to enter the number of data points

☐ Prompts you to enter the integer values for the array

☐ Displays the elements of the unordered array

☐ Displays the elements of the sorted array

 Listing 10.1. Source code for the program ADVFUN1.CPP.

```
1: // C++ program that sorts arrays using the Comb sort method
2:
3: #include <iostream.h>
4:
5: const int MAX = 10;
6: const int TRUE = 1;
7: const int FALSE = 0;
8:
9: int obtainNumData()
10: {
11:   int m;
12:   do { // obtain number of data points
13:     cout << "Enter number of data points [2 to "
14:         << MAX << "] : ";
15:     cin >> m;
16:     cout << "\n";
17:   } while (m < 2 || m > MAX);
18:   return m;
19: }
20:
21: void inputArray(int *intArr, int n)
22: {
```

```
23:   // prompt user for data
24:   for (int i = 0; i < n; i++) {
25:     cout << "arr[" << i << "] : ";
26:     cin >> *(intArr + i);
27:   }
28: }
29:
30: void showArray(const int *intArr, int n)
31: {
32:   for (int i = 0; i < n; i++) {
33:     cout.width(5);
34:     cout << *(intArr + i) << " ";
35:   }
36:   cout << "\n";
37: }
38:
39: void sortArray(int *intArr, int n)
40: {
41:   int offset, temp, inOrder;
42:
43:   offset = n;
44:   do {
45:     offset = (8 * offset) / 11;
46:     offset = (offset == 0) ? 1 : offset;
47:     inOrder = TRUE;
48:     for (int i = 0, j = offset; i < (n - offset); i++, j++) {
49:       if (intArr[i] > intArr[j]) {
50:         inOrder = FALSE;
51:         temp = intArr[i];
52:         intArr[i] = intArr[j];
53:         intArr[j] = temp;
54:       }
55:     }
56:   } while (!(offset =≠1 && inOrder == TRUE));
57: }
58:
59: main()
60: {
61:   int arr[MAX];
62:   int n;
63:
64:   n = obtainNumData();
65:   inputArray(arr, n);
66:   cout << "Unordered array is:\n";
67:   showArray(arr, n);
68:   sortArray(arr, n);
69:   cout << "\nSorted array is:\n";
70:   showArray(arr, n);
71:   return 0;
72: }
```

Here is a sample session with the program in Listing 10.1:

```
Enter number of data points [2 to 10] : 5

arr[0] : 55
arr[1] : 22
arr[2] : 78
arr[3] : 35
arr[4] : 45
Unordered array is:
    55    22    78    35    45

Sorted array is:
    22    35    45    55    78
```

The program in Listing 10.1 is almost identical to that in Listing 7.5 of Day 7. The new program uses slightly different parameters in functions inputArray, showArray, and sortArray. The first parameter in these functions is a pointer to the int type. The function showArray prefixes the pointer type with const. Such a declaration tells the compiler that the function showArray cannot alter the elements of the arguments for parameter intArray.

Using Strings as Arguments

Because C++ treats strings as arrays of characters, the rules for passing arrays as arguments to functions also apply to strings. The next program contains functions that manipulate strings. Listing 10.2 shows the source code for the program ADVFUN2.CPP. The program prompts you to enter a string. Then the program displays the number of characters you typed (the size of the input string) and the uppercase version of your input.

Listing 10.2. Source code for the program ADVFUN2.CPP.

```
1: /*
2:   C++ program that declares functions with string parameters
3: */
4:
5: #include <iostream.h>
6:
7: const unsigned MAX = 40;
8:
9: char* upperCase(char* str)
10: {
11:    int ascii_shift = 'A' - 'a';
12:    char* p = str;
```

continues

Listing 10.2. continued

```
13:
14:     // loop to convert each character to uppercase
15:     while ( *p != '\0') {
16:         if ((*p  >= 'a' && *p <= 'z'))
17:             *p += ascii_shift;
18:         p++;
19:     }
20:     return str;
21: }
22:
23: int strlen(char* str)
24: {
25:   char *p = str;
26:   while (*p++ != '\0');
27:   return *p - str;
28: }
29:
30: main()
31: {
32:     char aString[MAX+1];
33:
34:     cout << "Enter a string: ";
35:     cin.getline(aString, MAX);
36:     cout << "Your string has " << strlen(aString)
37:         << " characters\n";
38:     // concatenate bigStr to aString
39:     upperCase(aString);
40:     cout << "The uppercase version of your input is: "
41:         << aString;
42:     return 0;
43: }
```

Here is a sample session with the program in Listing 10.2:

```
Enter a string: Visual C++ 1.0
Your string has 14 characters
The uppercase version of your input is: VISUAL C++ 1.0
```

The program in Listing 10.2 declares its own string-manipulating functions: upperCase and strlen. The function upperCase has a single parameter, str, which is a pointer to the char type. This parameter passes the address of an array of characters. The function converts the characters accessed by the pointer string to uppercase, and returns the pointer to the string. The function declares the local variable ascii_shift and the local char-pointer p. The function also initializes the variable ascii_shift with the difference between the ASCII values of the letters A and a. Thus, the ascii-shift variable contains the difference in ASCII codes needed to convert a lowercase character into an uppercase character. The function also initializes the local pointer p with the address in parameter str.

The upperCase function uses the while loop in line 15 to traverse the characters of the string argument. The while clause determines whether the pointer p does not access the null terminator. The if statement in line 16 determines if the character accessed by pointer p is a lowercase letter. If this condition is true, the function executes the statement in line 17. This statement adds the value in variable ascii_shift to the character currently accessed by pointer p. This action converts a lowercase character into uppercase. The statement in line 18 increments the address of pointer p to access the next character. The function returns the address of pointer str.

The function strlen returns the number of characters in the string accessed by the char-pointer parameter str. The function declares the local char-pointer p and initializes it with the address of parameter str. The function uses a while loop with an empty loop statement to locate the null terminator in the string accessed by pointer p. The return statement yields the sought value by taking the difference between the addresses of pointers p and str. The return statement first applies the pre-decrement operator to pointer p to adjust the address of that pointer.

The function main declares the string variable aString. The output statement in line 34 prompts you to enter a string. The statement in line 35 calls the stream input function getline to obtain your input and to store it in variable aString. The output statement in line 36 displays the number of characters you typed. The statement calls the function strlen and passes it the argument aString. The statement in line 39 calls the function upperCase and also passes it the argument aString. The output statement in line 40 displays the uppercase version of your input, which is now stored in variable aString.

Using Structures as Arguments

C++ allows you to pass structures either by value or by reference. In this section I demonstrate passing structures by value. In the next sections I show you how to pass structures by reference. The structure's type appears in the function prototype and heading in a manner similar to that of predefined types.

Listing 10.3 shows the source code for the program ADVFUN3.CPP. The program performs the following tasks:

☐ Prompts you for the X and Y coordinates of a first point

☐ Prompts you for the X and Y coordinates of a second point

☐ Calculates coordinates of the median point between the two points that you entered

☐ Displays the coordinates of the median point

Type **Listing 10.3. Source code for the program ADVFUN3.CPP.**

```
 1: // C++ program which uses a function that passes
 2: // a structure by value
 3:
 4: #include <iostream.h>
 5:
 6: struct point {
 7:   double x;
 8:   double y;
 9: };
10:
11: // declare the prototype of function getMedian
12: point getMedian(point, point);
13:
14: main()
15: {
16:   point pt1;
17:   point pt2;
18:   point median;
19:
20:   cout << "Enter the X and Y coordinates for point # 1 : ";
21:   cin >> pt1.x >> pt1.y;
22:   cout << "Enter the X and Y coordinates for point # 2 : ";
23:   cin >> pt2.x >> pt2.y;
24:   // get the coordinates for the median point
25:   median = getMedian(pt1, pt2);
26:   // get the median point
27:   cout << "Mid point is (" << median.x
28:        << ", " << median.y << ")\n";
29:   return 0;
30: }
31:
32: point getMedian(point p1, point p2)
33: {
34:   point result;
35:   result.x = (p1.x + p2.x) / 2;
36:   result.y = (p1.y + p2.y) / 2;
37:   return result;
38: };
```

Here is a sample session with the program in Listing 10.3:

```
Enter the X and Y coordinates for point # 1 : 1 1
Enter the X and Y coordinates for point # 2 : 5 5
Mid point is (3, 3)
```

Analysis The program in Listing 10.3 declares the structure point which models a two-dimensional point. This structure has two double-typed members, x and y. Line 12 declares the prototype for the function getMedian. The function takes two point-typed parameters which are passed by value.

The function main declares the point-typed variables pt1, pt2, and median in lines 16 through 18, respectively. The output statement in line 20 prompts you to enter the X and Y coordinates for the first point. The statement in line 21 obtains your input and stores the coordinates in the members pt1.x and pt1.y. Lines 22 and 23 repeat the same prompting and input process for the second point. The input statement in line 23 stores the values for the second point in members pt2.x and pt2.y. The statement in line 25 calls function getMedian and passes it the arguments pt1 and pt2. The function receives a copy of the arguments pt1 and pt2. The statement assigns the point-typed function result to the variable median. The output statement in lines 27 and 28 displays the X and Y coordinates of the median point (by displaying the x and y members of the variable median).

The function getMedian declares two point-typed parameters, p1 and p2. In addition, the function declares the local point-typed variable result. The statement in line 35 assigns the average of members p1.x and p2.x to member result.x. The statement in line 36 assigns the average of members p1.y and p2.y to member result.y. Notice that these statements use the dot operator to access the members x and y of the structures p1, p2, and result. This syntax is used when the function passes a copy or a reference of a structure. The return statement yields the value in the local structure result.

Passing Arguments by Reference

C++ enables you to write functions with parameters that pass arguments by reference. This kind of parameter enables you to change the value of the argument beyond the scope of the function. C++ offers two ways to implement such parameters: with pointers and with formal reference parameters. The following sections present functions that pass various kinds of data types by reference.

10

Passing Structures by Reference

You can pass structures to functions either by using pointers or by using formal reference. Many C++ programmers consider either approach as more efficient than passing the structure parameters by copy—you save on the overhead of copying the structure-typed arguments.

Note: Passing a structure by reference allows you to use the dot operator with the reference parameters (as with passing by value). The added advantage is that the reference parameters do not create copies of the original arguments. Thus, they are faster and save memory resources. The downside is that because reference parameters become aliases to their arguments, any changes made to the parameters inside the function affect their arguments. One method to prevent this change is to use const reference parameters. Such parameters tell the compiler that the function cannot assign new values to the reference parameters.

DO	DON'T

DO pass structures either by formal reference or by pointers when both of the following two circumstances apply: the host function does not alter the arguments and the function returns values through these structures.

DON'T pass structures by value unless you need to supply the host function with a copy of the data which will be modified by the function.

Let's look at an example. Listing 10.4 shows the source code for the program ADVFUN4.CPP. The program performs the same tasks as the last program, ADVFUN3.CPP. The new version differs only in its implementation.

Listing 10.4. Source code for the program ADVFUN4.CPP.

```
1: // C++ program which uses a function that passes
2: // a structure by reference
3:
```

```
 4: #include <iostream.h>
 5:
 6: struct point {
 7:   double x;
 8:   double y;
 9: };
10:
11: // declare the prototype of function getMedian
12: point getMedian(const point&, const point&);
13:
14: main()
15: {
16:   point pt1;
17:   point pt2;
18:   point median;
19:
20:   cout << "Enter the X and Y coordinates for point # 1 : ";
21:   cin >> pt1.x >> pt1.y;
22:   cout << "Enter the X and Y coordinates for point # 2 : ";
23:   cin >> pt2.x >> pt2.y;
24:   // get the coordinates for the median point
25:   median = getMedian(pt1, pt2);
26:   // get the median point
27:   cout << "Mid point is (" << median.x
28:        << ", " << median.y << ")\n";
29:   return 0;
30: }
31:
32: point getMedian(const point& p1, const point& p2)
33: {
34:   point result;
35:   result.x = (p1.x + p2.x) / 2;
36:   result.y = (p1.y + p2.y) / 2;
37:   return result;
38: };
```

Here is a sample session with the program in Listing 10.4:

```
Enter the X and Y coordinates for point # 1 : 1 1
Enter the X and Y coordinates for point # 2 : 9 9
Mid point is (5, 5)
```

The program in Listing 10.4 is very similar to that in Listing 10.3. The new program version uses reference parameters in function getMedian. Thus, the prototype and the function's declaration place the & character after the structure type point. Using reference parameters, the call to function getMedian looks very much like the call to the version in Listing 10.3. Likewise, the implementation of function getMedian is similar to the one in Listing 10.3—both versions use the dot operator to access the members x and y in the structure point.

Passing Structures by Pointers

Using pointers is another efficient way to pass structures. As with the reference parameter types, use the const declaration to prevent the implementation from changing the structured variables accessed by the pointer parameters.

The next example is, as you might expect, the version of program ADVFUN3.CPP which uses pointer parameters. Listing 10.5 shows the source code for the new version, program ADVFUN5.CPP.

 Listing 10.5. Source code for the program ADVFUN5.CPP.

```
1: // C++ program which uses a function that passes
2: // a structure by pointer
3:
4: #include <iostream.h>
5:
6: struct point {
7:    double x;
8:    double y;
9: };
10:
11: // declare the prototype of function getMedian
12: point getMedian(const point*, const point*);
13:
14: main()
15: {
16:    point pt1;
17:    point pt2;
18:    point median;
19:
20:    cout << "Enter the X and Y coordinates for point # 1 : ";
21:    cin >> pt1.x >> pt1.y;
22:    cout << "Enter the X and Y coordinates for point # 2 : ";
23:    cin >> pt2.x >> pt2.y;
24:    // get the coordinates for the median point
25:    median = getMedian(&pt1, &pt2);
26:    // get the median point
27:    cout << "Mid point is (" << median.x
28:        << ", " << median.y << ")\n";
29:    return 0;
30: }
31:
32: point getMedian(const point* p1, const point* p2)
33: {
34:    point result;
35:    result.x = (p1->x + p2->x) / 2;
36:    result.y = (p1->y + p2->y) / 2;
```

```
37:    return result;
38: };
```

Here is a sample session with the program in Listing 10.5:

```
Enter the X and Y coordinates for point # 1 : 2 2
Enter the X and Y coordinates for point # 2 : 8 8
Mid point is (5, 5)
```

The program in Listing 10.5 uses pointer parameters in function `getMedian`. The prototype and the implementation of the function uses the `const point*` type for both parameters. The statement in line 25, which calls the function `getMedian`, passes the address of the variable `pt1` and `pt2`, using the `address-of` operator `&`. The implementation of the function `getMedian` uses the `->` operator to access the members `x` and `y` for the pointer parameters `p1` and `p2`.

Recursive Functions

There are many problems that can be solved by breaking them down into simpler and similar problems. Such problems are solved using recursion.

NEW☛
TERM
Recursive functions are functions which obtain a result and/or perform a task by calling themselves. These recursive calls must be limited to avoid exhausting the memory resources of the computer. Consequently, every recursive function must examine a condition which determines the end of the recursion.

NEW☛
TERM
A common example of a recursive function is the *factorial function.* A factorial of a number N is the product of all the integers from 1 to N, with the exclamation point (!) as the mathematical symbol for the factorial function.

The mathematical equation for a factorial is

$$N! = 1 * 2 * 3 * ... * (N-2) * (N-1) * N$$

The recursive version of this equation is

$$N! = N * (N-1)!$$

$$(N-1)! = (N-1) * (N-2)!$$

$$(N-2)! = (N-2) * (N-3)!$$

...

$$2! = 2 * 1!$$

$$1! = 1$$

Recursion entails looping to obtain a result. Most recursive solutions have alternate nonrecursive solutions. In some cases, the recursive solutions are more elegant than the nonrecursive ones. The factorial function is an example of a mathematical function that can be implemented using either recursion or a nonrecursive straight-forward loop.

DO	DON'T
DO include a decision-making statement in a recursive function to end the recursion.	
DON'T use recursion unless its advantages significantly outweigh the alternate nonrecursive solution.	

Let me present an example that implements the recursive factorial function. Listing 10.6 shows the source code for the program ADVFUN6.CPP. The program prompts you to enter two positive integers—the first one must be greater than or equal to the second one. The program displays the number of combinations and permutations obtained from the two integers. The number of combinations is given by the following equation:

$$mCn = m! / ((m - n)! * n!)$$

The number of permutations is given by the following equation:

$$mPn = m! / (m - n)!$$

 Listing 10.6. Source code for the program ADVFUN6.CPP.

```
1: // C++ program which uses a recursive function
2:
3: #include <iostream.h>
4:
5: const int MIN = 4;
6: const int MAX = 30;
7:
8: double factorial(int i)
9: {
10:   if (i > 1)
11:     return double(i) * factorial(i - 1);
12:   else
13:     return 1;
14: }
15:
```

```
16: double permutation(int m, int n)
17: {
18:   return factorial(m) / factorial(m - n);
19: }
20:
21: double combination(int m, int n)
22: {
23:   return permutation(m, n) / factorial(n);
24: }
25:
26: main()
27: {
28:   int m, n;
29:
30:   do {
31:     cout << "Enter an integer between "
32:         << MIN << " and " << MAX << " : ";
33:     cin >> m;
34:   } while (m < MIN ¦¦ m > MAX);
35:
36:   do {
37:     cout << "Enter an integer between "
38:         << MIN << " and " << m << ": ";
39:     cin >> n;
40:   } while (n < MIN ¦¦ n > m);
41:
42:   cout << "Permutations(" << m << ", " << n
43:       << ") = " << permutation(m, n) << "\n";
44:   cout << "Combinations(" << m << ", " << n
45:       << ") = " << combination(m, n) << "\n";
46:
47:   return 0;
48: }
```

Here is a sample session with the program in Listing 10.6:

```
Enter an integer between 4 and 30 : 10
Enter an integer between 4 and 10 : 5
Permutations(10, 5) = 30240
Combinations(10, 5) = 252
```

The program in Listing 10.6 declares the recursive function `factorial`, and the functions `permutation`, `combination`, and `main`. The program also declares the global constants `MIN` and `MAX` which specify the limits of the first integer you enter.

The function `factorial` has a single parameter, the `int`-typed parameter `i`. The function returns a `double`-typed value. The `if` statement in line 10 compares the value of parameter `i` with 1. This comparison determines whether to make a recursive call, in line 11, or return the value 1, in line 13. The recursive call in line 11 invokes the function factorial with the argument i - 1. Thus, the recursive call supplies the function with a smaller (or simpler, if you prefer) argument.

The function permutation takes two int-typed parameters, m and n. The function calls the recursive function factorial twice: once with the argument m and once with the argument m - n. The function permutation returns the ratio of the two calls to function factorial.

The function combination also takes two int-typed parameters, m and n. The function calls the function permutation and passes it the arguments m and n. The function also calls the function factorial and passes it the argument n. The function combination returns the ratio of the values returned by functions permutation and factorial.

The function main declares the int-typed variable m and n. The function uses two do-while loops to prompt you for integer values. The output statement in the first loop prompts you to enter an integer between MIN and MAX. The statement in line 33 stores your input in variable m. The while clause of the do-while loop validates your input. The clause determines if your input is less than MIN or greater than MAX. If this condition is true, the loop iterates again.

The output statement in the second do-while loop prompts you to enter an integer between m and MAX. The statement in line 39 saves your input in variable n. The while clause validates your input. The clause determines if your input is less than MIN or greater than m. If this condition is true, the loop iterates again.

The output statement in lines 42 and 43 displays the permutations of the values in variables m and n. The statement calls function permutation and passes it the argument m and n. The output statement in lines 44 and 45 displays the combinations of the values in variables m and n. The statement calls function combination and passes it the arguments m and n.

Passing Pointers to Dynamic Structures

Implementing a binary tree requires functions that—at least—insert, search, delete, and traverse the tree. All these functions access the binary tree through the pointer of its *root*. Interestingly, operations such as tree insertion and deletion may affect the root itself. In such cases, the address of the root node changes. Consequently, you need to pass a reference to the pointer of the root node. Using a reference to a pointer guarantees that you maintain an updated address of the tree root.

The *binary tree* is among the popular dynamic data structures. Such structures enable you to build ordered collections of data without prior knowledge of the number of data items. The basic building block for a binary tree is a *node*. Every node in a binary tree is the *root* of all subtrees below it. Terminal nodes are the roots of empty subtrees. The binary tree has a special node which is the root of all other nodes. Each node has a *field* (used as a sorting key), optional additional data (called *non-key data*), and two pointers to establish a link with other tree nodes. Dynamic memory allocation enables you to create space for each node and to set up the links between the various nodes dynamically. To learn more about binary tree structure, consult a data structure text book.

NEW TERM

DO   DON'T

DO declare the parameters handling critical pointers to a data structure using the reference to these pointers. This declaration ensures that the addresses of these parameters are updated outside the scope of the function.

DON'T assume that when a function alters the address of a nonreference pointer parameter, the change also affects the address of the argument.

Let's look at an example which inserts and displays dynamic data in a binary tree. Listing 10.7 shows the source code for the program ADVFUN7.CPP. The program supplies its own set of data (a list of names), inserts the data in a binary tree, then displays the data in ascending order.

Type

Listing 10.7. Source code for the program ADVFUN7.CPP.

```
 1: // C++ program which passes parameter to dynamic data
 2:
 3: #include <iostream.h>
 4: #include <string.h>
 5:
 6: const unsigned MAX = 30;
 7:
 8: typedef struct node* nodeptr;
 9:
10: struct node {
11:     char value[MAX+1];
12:     nodeptr left;
13:     nodeptr right;
14: };
15:
```

continues

Listing 10.7. continued

```
16: void insert(nodeptr& root, const char* item)
17: // Recursively insert element in binary tree
18: {
19:    if (!root)  {
20:      root = new node;
21:      strncpy(root->value, item, MAX);
22:      root->left = NULL;
23:      root->right = NULL;
24:    }
25:    else {
26:      if (strcmp(item, root->value) < 0)
27:        insert(root->left, item);
28:      else
29:        insert(root->right, item);
30:    }
31: }
32:
33: void showTree(nodeptr& root)
34: {
35:    if (!root)
36:      return;
37:
38:    showTree(root->left);
39:    cout << root->value << "\n";
40:    showTree(root->right);
41: }
42:
43: main()
44: {
45:    char *names[] = { "Virginia", "California", "Maine", "Michigan",
46:                      "New York", "Florida", "Ohio", "Illinois",
47:                      "Alaska", "Arizona", "Oregon", "Vermont",
48:                      "Maryland", "Delaware", "NULL" };
49:    nodeptr treeRoot = NULL;
50:    int i = 0;
51:
52:    // insert the names in the binary tree
53:    while (strcmp(names[i], "NULL") != 0)
54:      insert(treeRoot, names[i++]);
55:
56:    showTree(treeRoot);
57:    return 0;
58: }
```

Here is a sample session with the program in Listing 10.7:

```
Alaska
Arizona
California
Delaware
Florida
Illinois
Maine
Maryland
Michigan
New York
Ohio
Oregon
Vermont
Virginia
```

The program in Listing 10.7 declares the global constant MAX to specify the maximum number of characters stored by each node in the binary tree. The declaration in line 8 defines the pointer-type nodeptr based on the structure node. The program defines the structure node in lines 10 through 14. The structure contains the member value (which stores a string), the pointer to the left node, left, and the pointer to the right node, right. Both pointers have the nodeptr type.

The program declares the recursive function insert to insert a string in the binary tree. The function has two parameters: root and item. The parameter root is a reference to a nodeptr-typed pointer. This parameter keeps track of the various nodes of the binary tree and updates their addresses as needed. This update occurs when the binary tree inserts a data item.

The if statement in line 19 determines whether or not the parameter root is NULL. If this condition is true, the function executes the statement in lines 20 through 23. The statement in line 20 allocates a new node using the operator new. The statement in line 21 uses the function strncpy to copy up to MAX characters from the parameter item to the member value. The statements in lines 22 and 23 assign NULLs to the left and right node pointers of the newly created node. The statements in line 20 to 24 not only affect the actual root of the tree, but also alter the pointers to the various nodes. The condition in the if statement helps to end the recursive calls.

The else clause in line 25 handles the case when the parameter root is not NULL. The if statement in line 26 determines if the string accessed by pointer item is less than the string in the value member of the currently accessed tree node. If this condition is true, the function makes a recursive call passing the argument root->left and item.

This call inserts the new string in the left subtree, whose root is the current node. Otherwise, the function makes a recursive call passing the argument root->right and item. This call inserts the new string in the right subtree, whose root is the current node.

The recursive function showTree traverses, in order, the nodes of the tree and subtree whose root is the reference parameter root. The function quickly exits if the current value of the parameter root is NULL. This condition indicates that the argument for parameter root is a terminal node. Therefore, this condition ends the recursive call. If the argument for parameter root is not NULL, the function makes a recursive call passing the argument root->left. This call allows the function to visit the left subtree whose root is the current node. Once the left subtree of the current node is visited, the function displays the string stored in the member value of the current node. Then the function makes another recursive call, this time passing the argument root->right. This call allows the function to visit the right subtree whose root is the current node. Once the right subtree of the current node is visited, the function exits.

The function main declares an array of pointers to the internal data, shown in lines 45 through 48. The function also declares the variable treeRoot as the root of the binary tree. The declaration of this variable also initializes the variable to NULL. The function also declares the int-typed variable i and initializes it with 0.

The function main uses the while loop in line 53 to insert the strings in the list of state names. The loop iterates until the current name matches the string "NULL". This string is a special name that I use to track the end of the list. If you modify the program and add more state names, be sure to make the string "NULL" the last item in the list. The statement in line 54 calls the function insert to insert the element names[i] in the binary tree whose root is the pointer treeRoot.

The statement in line 56 calls the function showTree and supplies it the argument treeRoot. The call to this recursive function displays the names of the states in ascending order.

Pointers to Functions

The program compilation process translates the names of variables into memory addresses where data are stored and retrieved. Pointers to addresses can also access these addresses. This translation step holds true for variables and functions alike. The compiler translates the name of a function into the address of executable code. C++ extends the strategy of manipulating variables by using pointers to include functions.

A Pointer to a Function

The general syntax for declaring a pointer to a function is

```
returnType (*functionPointer)(<list of parameters>);
```

This form tells the compiler that the *functionPointer* is a pointer to a function that has the *returnType* return type and a list of parameters.

Examples:

```
double (*fx)(int n);
void (*sort)(int* intArray, unsigned n);
unsigned (*search)(int searchKey, int* intArray, unsigned n);
```

The first identifier, fx, points to a function that returns a double and has a single int-typed parameter. The second identifier, sort, is a pointer to a function that returns a void type and takes two parameters: a pointer to int and an unsigned. The third identifier, search, is a pointer to a function that returns an unsigned and has three parameters: an int, a pointer to an int, and an unsigned.

An Array of Function Pointers

C++ allows you to declare an array of function pointers. The general syntax is

```
returnType (*functionPointer[arraySize])(<list of parameters>);
```

Examples:

```
double (*fx[3])(int n);
void (*sort[MAX_SORT])(int* intArray, unsigned n);
unsigned (*search[MAX_SEARCH])(int searchKey,
                               int* intArray, unsigned n);
```

The first identifier, fx, points to an array of functions. Each member returns a double and has a single int-typed parameter. The second identifier, sort, is a pointer to an array of functions. Each member returns a void type and takes two parameters: a pointer to int and an unsigned. The third identifier, search, is a pointer to an array of functions. Each member returns an unsigned and has three parameters: an int, a pointer to an int, and an unsigned.

As with any pointer, you need to initialize a function pointer before using it. This step is very simple. You merely assign the bare name of a function to the function pointer.

10

Initializing a Function Pointer

The general syntax for initializing a pointer to a function is

```
functionPointer = aFunction;
```

The assigned function must have the same return type and parameter list as the function pointer. Otherwise, the compiler flags an error.

Example:

```
void (*sort)(int* intArray, unsigned n);
sort = qsort;
```

Assigning a Function to an Element

The general syntax for assigning a function to an element in an array of function pointers is

```
functionPointer[index] = aFunction;
```

Once you assign a function name to a function pointer, you can use the pointer to invoke its associated function. Now it should become evident why the function pointer must have the same return type and parameter list as the accessed function.

Example:

```
void (*sort[2])(int* intArray, unsigned n);
sort[0] = shellSort;
sort[1] = CombSort;
```

The Function Pointer Expression

The general syntax for the expression that invokes function pointers is

```
(*functionPointer)(<argument list>);
(*functionPointer[index])(<argument list>);
```

Examples:

```
(*sort)(intArray, n);
(*sort[0])(&intArray, n);
```

Let's look at an example. Listing 10.8 shows the source code for the program ADVFUN8.CPP. The program performs linearized regression on two observed variables: the independent variable X, and the dependent variable Y. The model that relates these two variables is

```
f(Y) = intercept + slope * g(X)
```

The function f(Y) transforms the data for the Y variable. The function g(X)

transforms the data for the X variable. The functions f(Y) and g(X) can be linear, logarithmic, exponential, square root, square, or any other mathematical function. When both f(Y) = Y and g(X) = X, the model becomes this linear regression model:

```
Y = intercept + slope * X
```

The linearized regression (back to the general model) calculates the best values for the slope and intercept for the values of f(Y) and g(X). The regression also provides the correlation coefficient statistic which represents the percent (as a fractional number) of the f(Y) data that is explained by the variation in g(X). A value of 1 represents a perfect fit, and 0 represents a total lack of any correlation between f(Y) and g(X) data.

Listing 10.8 performs linear regression and carries out the following tasks:

☐ Prompts you to enter the number of data (your input must be in the limit indicated by the program)

☐ Prompts you to enter the observed values of X and Y

☐ Prompts you to select the function that transforms the observations for variable X (the program displays a small itemized menu that shows your options, indicating the linear, logarithmic, square, square root, and reciprocal functions)

☐ Prompts you to select the function that transforms the observations for variable Y (the program displays a small itemized menu that shows your options, indicating the linear, logarithmic, square, square root, and reciprocal functions)

☐ Performs the regression calculations

☐ Displays the intercept, slope, and correlation coefficient for the linearized regression

☐ Prompts you to select another set of transformation functions (if you choose to use another set of functions, the program resumes at step 3)

Listing 10.8. Source code for the program ADVFUN8.CPP.

```
1: /*
2:    C++ program that uses pointers to functions to implement
3:    a linear regression program that supports temporary
4:    mathematical transformations.
5: */
6:
7: #include <iostream.h>
```

continues

Listing 10.8. continued

```
 8: #include <math.h>
 9:
10: const unsigned MAX_SIZE = 100;
11:
12: typedef double vector[MAX_SIZE];
13:
14: struct regression {
15:     double Rsqr;
16:     double slope;
17:     double intercept;
18: };
19:
20: // declare function pointer
21: double (*fx)(double);
22: double (*fy)(double);
23:
24: // declare function prototypes
25: void initArray(double*, double*, unsigned);
26: double linear(double);
27: double sqr(double);
28: double reciprocal(double);
29: void calcRegression(double*, double*, unsigned, regression&,
30:                     double (*fx)(double), double (*fy)(double));
31: int select_transf(const char*);
32:
33: main()
34: {
35:     char ans;
36:     unsigned count;
37:     vector x, y;
38:     regression stat;
39:     int trnsfx, trnsfy;
40:
41:     do {
42:         cout << "Enter array size [2.."
43:             << MAX_SIZE << "] : ";
44:         cin >> count;
45:     } while (count <= 1 || count > MAX_SIZE);
46:
47:     // initialize array
48:     initArray(x, y, count);
49:     // transform data
50:     do {
51:         // set the transformation functions
52:         trnsfx = select_transf("X");
53:         trnsfy = select_transf("Y");
54:         // set function pointer fx
55:         switch (trnsfx) {
56:             case 0 :
```

```
57:            fx = linear;
58:            break;
59:          case 1 :
60:            fx = log;
61:            break;
62:          case 2 :
63:            fx = sqrt;
64:            break;
65:          case 3 :
66:            fx = sqr;
67:            break;
68:          case 4 :
69:            fx = reciprocal;
70:            break;
71:          default :
72:            fx = linear;
73:            break;
74:        }
75:        // set function pointer fy
76:        switch (trnsfy) {
77:          case 0 :
78:            fy = linear;
79:            break;
80:          case 1 :
81:            fy = log;
82:            break;
83:          case 2 :
84:            fy = sqrt;
85:            break;
86:          case 3 :
87:            fy = sqr;
88:            break;
89:          case 4 :
90:            fy = reciprocal;
91:            break;
92:          default :
93:            fy = linear;
94:            break;
95:        }
96:
97:        /*  call function with functional arguments
98:                                            ¦      ¦
99:                                            V      V */
100:       calcRegression(x, y, count, stat, fx, fy);
101:
102:       cout << "\n\n"
103:            << "R-square = " << stat.Rsqr << "\n"
104:            << "Slope = " << stat.slope << "\n"
105:            << "Intercept = " << stat.intercept << "\n\n\n";
106:       cout << "Want to use other transformations? (Y/N) ";
107:       cin >> ans;
```

continues

Listing 10.8. continued

```
108:      } while (ans == 'Y' || ans == 'y');
109:    return 0;
110: }
111:
112: void initArray(double* x, double* y, unsigned count)
113: // read data for array from the keyboard
114: {
115:     for (unsigned i = 0; i < count; i++, x++, y++) {
116:         cout << "X[" << i << "] : ";
117:         cin >> *x;
118:         cout << "Y[" << i << "] : ";
119:         cin >> *y;
120:     }
121: }
122:
123: int select_transf(const char* var_name)
124: // select choice of transformation
125: {
126:
127:     int choice = -1;
128:     cout << "\n";
129:     cout << "select transformation for variable " << var_name
130:         << "\n"
131:         << "0) No transformation\n"
132:         << "1) Logarithmic transformation\n"
133:         << "2) Square root transformation\n"
134:         << "3) Square   transformation\n"
135:         << "4) Reciprocal transformation\n";
136:     while (choice < 0 || choice > 4) {
137:         cout << "\nSelect choice by number : ";
138:         cin >> choice;
139:     }
140:     return choice;
141: }
142:
143: double linear(double x)
144: { return x; }
145:
146: double sqr(double x)
147: { return x * x; }
148:
149: double reciprocal(double x)
150: { return 1.0 / x; }
151:
152: void calcRegression(double* x,
153:                     double* y,
154:                     unsigned count,
155:                     regression &stat,
156:                     double (*fx)(double),
157:                     double (*fy)(double))
```

```
158:
159: {
160:     double meanx, meany, sdevx, sdevy;
161:     double sum = (double) count, sumx = 0, sumy = 0;
162:     double sumxx = 0, sumyy = 0, sumxy = 0;
163:     double xdata, ydata;
164:
165:     for (unsigned i = 0; i < count; i++) {
166:         xdata = (*fx)(*(x+i));
167:         ydata = (*fy)(*(y+i));
168:         sumx += xdata;
169:         sumy += ydata;
170:         sumxx += sqr(xdata);
171:         sumyy += sqr(ydata);
172:         sumxy += xdata * ydata;
173:     }
174:
175:     meanx = sumx / sum;
176:     meany = sumy / sum;
177:     sdevx = sqrt((sumxx - sqr(sumx) / sum)/(sum-1.0));
178:     sdevy = sqrt((sumyy - sqr(sumy) / sum)/(sum-1.0));
179:     stat.slope = (sumxy - meanx * meany * sum) /
180:                       sqr(sdevx)/(sum-1);
181:     stat.intercept = meany - stat.slope * meanx;
182:     stat.Rsqr = sqr(sdevx / sdevy * stat.slope);
183:
184: }
```

Here is a sample session with the program in Listing 10.8:

```
Enter array size [2..100] : 5
X[0] : 10
Y[0] : 50
X[1] : 25
Y[1] : 78
X[2] : 30
Y[2] : 85
X[3] : 35
Y[3] : 95
X[4] : 100
Y[4] : 212

select transformation for variable X
0) No transformation
1) Logarithmic transformation
2) Square root transformation
3) Square transformation
4) Reciprocal transformation
```

285

```
Select choice by number : 1

select transformation for variable Y
0) No transformation
1) Logarithmic transformation
2) Square root transformation
3) Square transformation
4) Reciprocal transformation

Select choice by number : 1


R-square = 0.977011
Slope = 0.63039
Intercept = 2.37056


Want to use other transformations? (Y/N) y

select transformation for variable X
0) No transformation
1) Logarithmic transformation
2) Square root transformation
3) Square transformation
4) Reciprocal transformation

Select choice by number : 0

select transformation for variable Y

0) No transformation
1) Logarithmic transformation
2) Square root transformation
3) Square transformation
4) Reciprocal transformation

Select choice by number : 0


R-square = 0.999873
Slope = 1.79897
Intercept = 32.0412


Want to use other transformations? (Y/N) n
```

Analysis   The program in Listing 10.8 declares the global constant MAX_SIZE, which determines the maximum size of the arrays. The program also declares the type vector in line 12. In addition, the program defines the structure regression in lines 14 through 18. This structure stores the statistics of a regression. Lines 21 and

22 define the global function pointers fx and fy. Each pointer deals with a function that takes a double-typed argument and returns a double-typed value. The program uses these global pointers to store the mathematical transformations which you select.

The program also declares the functions initArray, linear, sqr, reciprocal, calcRegression, select_transf, and main. The function initArray prompts you to enter the data for the arrays x and y. The functions linear, sqr, and reciprocal are simple functions that provide the transformations for the data. These functions supplement the mathematical functions, such as sqrt and log, which are prototyped in the MATH.H header file. Each one of these functions has the same parameter and return type as the function pointers fx and fy.

The function calcRegression calculates the regression statistics based on the arrays passed by its array parameters x and y. The function uses the function pointer parameters fx and fy to transform the data in arrays x and y. The statements in lines 166 and 167 use the pointers fx and fy to transform the elements of arrays x and y, respectively.

The function select_transf prompts with a simple itemized menu to select the transformation functions by number. The function returns the value for the transformation code number which you select.

The function main declares the arrays x and y, using the type vector. The function also declares the structure stat which stores the regression statistics. The function main prompts you to enter the number of data points which you want to process. Then, the function calls function initArray to obtain the data for the arrays x and y. Next, the function invokes the function select_trans twice, to select the transformation functions for the data in arrays x and y. The switch statement in line 55 examines the value in variable trnsfx, which contains the index of the transformation value for the array x. The various case labels assign the proper function to the pointer fx. Some of these functions, such as log and sqrt, are prototyped in the MATH.H header file. The switch statement in line 76 performs a similar task to assign the proper function to pointer fy.

The function main then calls the function calcRegression and passes the arguments x, y, count, stat, the function pointer fx, and the function pointer fy. The output statement in lines 102 through 105 displays the regression statistics for the current set of transformation functions. The statement in line 106 asks you if you wish to select another set of transformation functions. The statement in line 107 stores your input in variable ans. The while clause in line 108 determines if the program repeats the process of selecting the transformation functions and calculating the corresponding regression statistics.

Summary

Today's lesson presents simple C++ functions. You learn about the following topics:

☐ You can pass arrays as function arguments using pointers to the basic types. C++ allows you to declare array parameters using explicit pointer types or using the empty brackets. Such parameters enable you to write general-purpose functions that work with arrays of different sizes. In addition, these pointers access the array by using its address, instead of making a copy of the entire array.

☐ Passing strings as function arguments follows the same rules as passing arrays, because C++ strings are arrays of characters.

☐ Passing structures as function arguments enables you to shorten the parameter list by encapsulating various related information in C++ structures. C++ supports passing structures by value. Such parameters pass a copy of their arguments to the host function. Consequently, the changes made to the structure members do not affect the arguments outside the scope of the function.

☐ Passing reference parameters may use pointers or formal references. The formal references become aliases of their arguments. Any changes made to the parameters affect their arguments outside the function. You can declare a constant reference parameter to ensure that the function does not alter the arguments for the reference parameter. Accessing the members of a structured reference parameter uses the dot operator.

☐ Passing structures by pointer gives the host function the address of the structure. The pointer parameter needs to use the -> operator to access the various members of the structure. You can use the const prefix with the pointer parameter to prevent the function from changing the members of the structure, which is accessed by the pointer parameters.

☐ Recursive functions are functions which obtain a result and/or perform a task by calling themselves. These recursive calls must be limited to avoid exhausting the memory resources of the computer. Consequently, every recursive function must examine a condition which determines the end of the recursion.

☐ Passing pointers to dynamic structures often requires passing the reference to the root or head pointers which manage such structures. Today's lesson illustrates how to create functions to insert data in a binary tree and display its data.

☐ Pointers to functions store the address of functions. Such pointers need to have the parameter list and return type defined, in order to access functions with the same prototype. Pointers to functions enable you to select which function you wish to invoke at run-time.

Q&A

Q. How does using a reference parameter impact the design of a function, compared to a value parameter?

A. The reference parameter can also update—unless it is declared as a const parameter—the argument. Thus, the function can use reference parameters as an input/output data conduit and also as an output data conduit.

Q. How can I distinguish between a pointer that passes an array of value and one used to pass back a value through its argument?

A. You need to read the declaration of the function in context. However, you can use a reference parameter to declare a parameter that passes a value back to the caller.

Q. What is the memory resource used in managing calls to recursive functions?

A. The run-time system uses the stack to store intermediate values, including the ones generated by calls to recursive functions. As with other memory resources, stacks have a limited space. Consequently recursive calls with long sequence or memory-consuming arguments drain the stack space and cause a run-time error.

NEW☞ TERM A *stack* is a memory location where information is inserted and removed on a Last-In-First-Out (LIFO) priority.

Workshop

The Workshop provides quiz questions to help you solidify your understanding of the material covered and exercises to provide you with experience in using what you've learned. Try to understand the quiz and exercise answers before continuing on to the next day's lesson. Answers are provided in Appendix B, "Answers."

Quiz

1. Can you use the conditional operator to write the recursive factorial function?

2. What is wrong with the following recursive function?

```
double factorial(int i)
{
  switch (i) {
    case 0:
    case 1:
        return 1;
        break;
    case 2:
        return 2;
        break;
    case 3:
        return 6;
        break;
    case 4:
        return 24;
        break;
    default:
        return double(i) * factorial(i-1);
  }
}
```

3. Convert the following recursive Fibonacci function (this function has the sequence Fib(0) = 0, Fib(1) = 1, Fib(2) = 1, Fib(3) = 2, Fib(4) = 3, and so on) into a nonrecursive version:

```
double Fibonacci(int n)
{
  if (n == 0)
    return 0;
  else if (n == 1 || n == 2)
    return 1;
  else
    return Fibonacci(n - 1) + Fibonacci(n - 2);
}
```

4. True or false? The two versions of the following functions are equivalent:

```
struct stringStruct {
    char source[MAX+1];
    char uprStr[MAX+1];
    char lwrStr[MAX+1];
    char revStr[MAX+1];
```

```
    };

    void convertStr2(const char* str, stringStruct& s)
    {
      strncpy(s.source, str, MAX);
      strncpy(s.uprStr, str, MAX);
      strncpy(s.lwrStr, str, MAX);
      strncpy(s.revStr, str, MAX);
      _strlwr(s.lwrStr);
      _strupr(s.uprStr);
      strrev(s.revStr);
    }

    void convertStr2(const char* str, stringStruct* s)
    {
      strncpy(s->source, str, MAX);
      strncpy(s->uprStr, str, MAX);
      strncpy(s->lwrStr, str, MAX);
      strncpy(s->revStr, str, MAX);
      _strlwr(s->lwrStr);
      _strupr(s->uprStr);
      strrev(s->revStr);
    }
```

Exercise

Create the program ADVFUN9.CPP from ADVFUN8.CPP by replacing the individual function pointers fx and fy with the array of function pointers f. In addition, replace the two function pointer parameters of function calcRegression with a parameter that is an array of function pointers.

Object-Oriented Programming and C++ Classes

Classes provide C++ with object-oriented programming (OOP) constructs. Today's lesson, which marks an important milestone for learning C++, introduces you to building individual classes as well as class hierarchy. You learn about the following topics:

- ☐ The basics of object-oriented programming
- ☐ Declaring base classes
- ☐ Constructors
- ☐ Destructors
- ☐ Declaring a class hierarchy
- ☐ Virtual functions
- ☐ Friend functions
- ☐ Operators and friend operators

Basics of Object-Oriented Programming

We live in a world of objects. Each object has its attributes and operations. Some objects are more animated than others. You can categorize objects into classes. For example, my CASIO Data Bank watch is an object that belongs to the class of the CASIO Data Bank watches.

NEW☞ TERM *Object-oriented programming (OOP)* uses the notions of real-world objects to develop applications.

You can also relate individual classes in a class hierarchy. The class of CASIO Data Bank watches is part of the watch class hierarchy. The basics of OOP include classes, objects, messages, methods, inheritance, and polymorphism.

NEW☞ TERM A `class` defines a category of objects. Each *object* is an instance of a class.

Classes and Objects

An object shares the same attributes and functionality with other objects in the same class. Typically, an object has a unique state, defined by the current values of its attributes. The functionality of a class determines the operations that are possible for the class instances. C++ calls the attributes of class data members and calls the operations of class member functions. Classes encapsulate data members and member functions.

Going back to the CASIO watch example, the buttons in the watch represent the member functions of the class of CASIO watches, and the display represents a data member. I can press certain buttons to edit the date and/or time. In OOP terms, the member functions alter the state of the object by changing its data members.

Messages and Methods

Object-oriented programming models the interaction with objects as events where messages are sent to an object or between objects. The object receiving a message responds by invoking the appropriate method (that's the member function in C++). C++ does not explicitly foster the notion of messages and methods as other OOP languages such as SmallTalk do. However, I find it easier to discuss invoking member functions using the term "message." The terms "methods" and "member functions" are equivalent.

NEW☞
TERM   The *message* is *what* is done to an object. The *method* is *how* the object responds to the incoming message.

Inheritance

In object-oriented languages, you can derive a class from another one.

NEW☞
TERM   With *inheritance*, the derived class (also called the *descendant class*) inherits the data members and member functions of its *parent* and *ancestor classes*.

Deriving a class refines the parent class by appending new attributes and new operations. The derived class typically declares new data members and new member functions. In addition, the derived class also can override inherited member functions when the operations of these functions are not suitable for the derived class.

To apply the concept of inheritance to the CASIO Data Bank watch, consider the following possible scenario. Suppose that the watch manufacturer decides to create a CASIO Data Comm watch that offers the same features of the CASIO Data Bank plus a beeper! Rather than redesigning the new model (that is the new class, in OOP terms) from scratch, the CASIO engineers start with the existing design of the CASIO Data Bank and build on it. This process may well add new attributes and operations to the

11

existing design and alter some existing operations to fit the new design. Thus, the CASIO Data Comm model inherits the attributes and the operations of the CASIO Data Bank model. In OOP terms, the class of CASIO Data Comm watches is a descendant of the class of CASIO Data Bank watches.

Polymorphism

The OOP feature of polymorphism allows the instances of different classes to react in a particular way to a message (or function invocation, in C++ terms). For example, in a hierarchy of graphical shapes (point, line, square, rectangle, circle, ellipse, and so on), each shape has a *Draw* function that is responsible for properly responding to a request to draw that shape.

NEW☞ TERM *Polymorphism* enables the instances of different classes to respond to the same function in ways that are appropriate to each class.

Declaring Base Classes

C++ enables you to declare a class which encapsulates data members and member functions. These functions alter and/or retrieve the values of the data members as well as perform related tasks.

A Base Class

The general syntax for declaring a base class is

```
class className
{
    private:
        <private data members>
        <private constructors>
        <private member functions>
    protected:
        <protected data members>
        <protected constructors>
        <protected member functions>
    public:
        <public data members>
        <public constructors>
        <public destructor>
        <public member functions>
};
```

Example:

```
class point
{
    protected:
        double x;
        double y;
    public:
        point(double xVal, double yVal);
        double getX();
        double getY();
        void assign(double xVal, double yVal);
        point& assign(point& pt);
};
```

The Sections of a Class

The previous syntax shows that the declaration involves the keyword `class`. C++ classes offer three levels of visibility for the various members (that is, both data members and member functions):

☐ The private section

☐ The protected section

☐ The public section

NEW☛ TERM In the *private section*, only the member functions of the class can access the private members. The class instances are denied access to private members. In the *protected section*, only the member functions of the class and its descendant classes can access protected members. The class instances are denied access to protected members. The *public section* specifies members that are visible to the member functions of the class, class instances, member functions of descendant classes, and their instances.

The following rules apply to the various class sections:

1. The class sections can appear in any order.

2. The class sections may appear more than once.

3. If no class section is specified, the C++ compiler treats the members as protected.

4. You should avoid placing data members in the public section, unless such a declaration significantly simplifies your design. Data members are typically

placed in the protected section to allow their access by member functions of descendant classes.

5. Use member functions to set and/or query the values of data members. The members that set the data members assist in performing validation and updating other data members, if need be.

6. The class may have multiple constructors, which are typically located in the public section.

7. The class can have only one destructor, which must be declared in the public section.

8. The member functions (as well as the constructors and destructors) that have multiple statements are defined outside the class declaration. The definition may reside in the same file that declares the class.

NEW⟶ TERM *Constructors* are special members that must have the same name as the host class. *Destructors* automatically remove class instances.

In software libraries, the definition of the member functions referred to in rule 8 typically resides in a separate source file. When you define a member function you must qualify the function name with the class name. The syntax of such a qualification involves using the class name followed by two colons (::) and then the name of a function. For example, consider the following class:

```
class point
{
    protected:
        double x;
        double y;
    public:
        point(double xVal, double yVal);
        double getX();
        // other member functions
};
```

The definitions of the constructor and member functions are

```
point::point(double xVal, double yVal)
{
  // statements
}

double point::getX()
{
  // statements
}
```

Once you declare a class, you can use the class name as a type identifier to declare class instances. The syntax resembles declaring variables.

Let's look at an example. Listing 11.1 shows the source code for the program CLASS1.CPP. The program prompts you to enter the length and width of a rectangle (which is an object). The program then displays the length, width, and area of the rectangle you specified.

Type

Listing 11.1. Source code for the program CLASS1.CPP.

```
1: // C++ program that illustrates a class
2:
3: #include <iostream.h>
4:
5: class rectangle
6: {
7:   protected:
8:     double length;
9:     double width;
10:  public:
11:     rectangle() { assign(0, 0); }
12:     rectangle(double len, double wide) { assign(len, wide); }
13:     double getLength() { return length; }
14:     double getWidth() { return width; }
15:     double getArea() { return length * width; }
16:     void assign(double len, double wide);
17: };
18:
19: void rectangle::assign(double len, double wide)
20: {
21:   length = len;
22:   width = wide;
23: }
24:
25: main()
26: {
27:   rectangle rect;
28:   double len, wide;
29:
30:   cout << "Enter length of rectangle : ";
31:   cin >> len;
32:   cout << "Enter width of rectangle : ";
33:   cin >> wide;
34:   rect.assign(len, wide);
35:   cout << "Rectangle length = " << rect.getLength() << "\n"
36:        << "          width  = " << rect.getWidth() << "\n"
37:        << "          area   = " << rect.getArea() << "\n";
38:   return 0;
39: }
```

11

Here is a sample session with the program in Listing 11.1:

```
Enter length of rectangle : 10
Enter width of rectangle : 12
Rectangle length = 10
         width  = 12
         area   = 120
```

The program in Listing 11.1 declares the class rectangle, which models a rectangle. The class has two double-typed data members, length and width, which store the dimensions of a rectangle. In addition, the class has two constructors: the default constructor and the nondefault constructor. The class also defines the member functions getLength, getWidth, getArea, and assign.

NEW☞
TERM
The *default constructor* creates an instance with 0 dimensions, and the *nondefault constructor* creates an instance with nonzero dimensions.

The function getLength, which is defined in the class declaration, simply returns the value in member length. The function getWidth, which is also defined in the class declaration, merely returns the value in member width. The function getArea which is defined in the class declaration simply returns the value of the result of multiplying the members length and width.

The member function assign, which is defined outside the class declaration, assigns the arguments for its parameters len and wide to the data members length and width, respectively. I simplify the implementation of this function by not checking for negative values.

The function main declares rect as the instance of class rectangle, and the double-typed variables len and wide. The output statement in line 30 prompts you to enter the length of the rectangle. The statement in line 31 obtains your input and stores it in variable len. The output statement in line 32 prompts you to enter the width of the rectangle. The statement in line 33 obtains your input and stores it in variable wide.

The function main assigns the input values to the instance rect using the assign member function. In OOP terms, I can say that the function main sends the assign message to the object rect. The arguments of the message are variables len and wide. The object rect responds by invoking the method (the member function) rectangle::assign(double, double).

The output statement in lines 35 through 37 displays the length, width, and area of the object rect. This statement sends the messages getLength, getWidth, and getArea to the object rect. In turn, the object rect invokes the appropriate methods (or member function, if you prefer) to respond to each one of these messages.

Constructors

C++ constructors and destructors work automatically to guarantee the appropriate creation and removal of class instances.

Constructors

The general syntax for constructors is

```
class className
{
    public:
        className(); // default constructor
        className(className& c); // copy constructor
        className(<parameter list>); // another constructor
};
```

Example:

```
class point
{
    protected:
        double x;
        double y;
    public:
        point();
        point(double xVal, double yVal);
        point(point& pt);
        double getX();
        double getY();
        void assign(double xVal, double yVal);
        point& assign(point& pt);
};
```

NEW☞ TERM A *copy constructor* allows you to create class instances by copying the data from existing instances.

C++ has the following features and rules regarding constructors:

1. The name of the constructor must be identical to the name of its class.

2. You must not include any return type, not even void.

3. A class can have any number of constructors, including none. In the latter case, the compiler automatically creates one for that class.

4. The default constructor is the one that either has no parameters or possesses a parameter list where all the parameters use default arguments. Here are two examples:

```
// class uses parameterless constructor
class point1
{
    protected:
        double x;
        double y;
    public:
        point1();
        // other member functions
};
```

```
// class uses constructor with default arguments
class point2
{
    protected:
        double x;
        double y;
    public:
        point(double xVal = 0, double yVal = 0);
        // other member functions
};
```

5. The *copy constructor* enables you to create a class instance using an existing instance. Here is an example:

```
class point
{
    protected:
        double x;
        double y;
    public:
        point();
        point(double xVal, double yVal);
        point(point& pt);
        // other member functions
};
```

6. The declaration of a class instance (which includes function parameters and local instances) involves a constructor. Which constructor is called? The answer depends on how many constructors you have declared for the class and how you declared the class instance. For example, consider the following instances of the last version of class `point`:

```
point p1; // involves the default constructor
point p2(1.1, 1.3); // uses the second constructor
point p3(p2); // uses the copy constructor
```

Because instance p1 specifies no arguments, the compiler uses the default constructor. The instance p2 specifies two floating-point arguments. Consequently, the compiler uses the second constructor. The instance p3 has the instance p2 as an argument. Therefore, the compiler uses the copy constructor to create instance p3 from instance p2.

DO   DON'T

DO declare copy constructors, especially for classes that model dynamic data structures. These constructors perform what is called a *deep copy* which includes the dynamic data. By default, the compiler creates what is called *shallow copy* constructors, which copy the data members only.

DON'T rely on the shallow copy constructor to copy instances for classes which have members that are pointers.

Destructors

C++ classes may contain destructors that automatically remove class instances.

Destructors

The general syntax for destructors is

```
class className
{
    public:
        className(); // default constructor
        // other constructors
        ~className();
        // other member function
};
```

Example:

```
class String
{
    protected:
        char *str;
        int len;

    public:
        String();
        String(String& s);
        ~String();
        // other member functions
};
```

C++ has the following features and rules regarding destructors:

1. The name of the destructor must begin with a tilde (~). The rest of the destructor name must be identical to the name of its class.

2. You must not include any return type, not even void.

3. A class can have no more than one destructor. In addition, if you omit the destructor, the compiler automatically creates one for you.

4. The destructor cannot have any parameters.

5. The runtime system automatically invokes a class destructor when the instance of that class is out of scope.

Examples of Constructors and Destructors

Let's look at a program that typifies the use of constructors and destructors. Listing 11.2 contains the source code for the CLASS2.CPP program. The program performs the following tasks:

☐ Creates a dynamic array (the object)

☐ Assigns values to the elements of the dynamic array

☐ Displays the values in the dynamic array

☐ Removes the dynamic array

Listing 11.2. Source code for the CLASS2.CPP program.

```cpp
1: // Program demonstrates constructors and destructors
2:
3: #include <iostream.h>
4:
5: const unsigned MIN_SIZE = 4;
6:
7: class Array
8: {
9:   protected:
10:     double *dataPtr;
11:     unsigned size;
12:
13:   public:
14:     Array(unsigned Size = MIN_SIZE);
15:     ~Array()
16:       { delete [] dataPtr; }
17:     unsigned getSize() const
18:       { return size; }
19:     void store(double x, unsigned index)
20:       { dataPtr[index] = x; }
21:     double recall(unsigned index)
22:       { return dataPtr[index]; }
23: };
24:
25: Array::Array(unsigned Size)
26: {
27:   size = (Size < MIN_SIZE) ? MIN_SIZE : Size;
28:   dataPtr = new double[size];
29: }
30:
31: main()
32: {
33:   Array Arr(10);
34:   double x;
35:   // assign data to array elements
36:   for (unsigned i = 0; i < Arr.getSize(); i++) {
37:     x = double(i);
38:     x = x * x - 5 * x + 10;
39:     Arr.store(x, i);
40:   }
41:   // display data in the array element
42:   cout << "Array Arr has the following values:\n\n";
43:   for (i = 0; i < Arr.getSize(); i++)
44:     cout << "Arr[" << i << "] = " << Arr.recall(i) << "\n";
45:   return 0;
46: }
```

11

Here is a sample session with the program in Listing 11.2:

```
Array Ar1 has the following values:

Ar1[0] = 10
Ar1[1] = 6
Ar1[2] = 4
Ar1[3] = 4
Ar1[4] = 6
Ar1[5] = 10
Ar1[6] = 16
Ar1[7] = 24
Ar1[8] = 34
Ar1[9] = 46
```

The program in Listing 11.2 declares the global constant MIN_SIZE, in line 5, which specifies the minimum size of dynamic arrays. The program also declares the class Array in line 7. The class has two data members, dataPtr and size. The member dataPtr is the pointer to the elements' dynamically allocated array. The member size stores the number of elements in an instance of class Array.

The class declares a default constructor. (The constructor actually has a parameter with the default value MIN_SIZE.) The program defines the constructor in lines 25 through 29. The arguments for the parameter Size specify the number of array elements. The statement in line 27 assigns the greater value of parameter Size and the constant MIN_SIZE to the data member size. The statement in line 28 allocates the dynamic space for the array by using the operator new. The statement assigns the base address of the dynamic array to the member dataPtr.

The destructor ~Array removes the dynamic space of the array by applying the operator delete to the member dataPtr.

The member function getSize, which is defined in the class declaration, returns the value in data member size.

The function store, which is defined in the class declaration, stores the value passed by parameter x at the element number specified by the parameter index. I simplify the implementation of this function by eliminating the out-of-range index check.

The function recall, which is defined in the class declaration, returns the value in the element specified by the parameter index. I simplify the implementation of this function by eliminating the out-of-range index check.

The function main declares the object Arr as an instance of class Array. The declaration, located in line 33, specifies that the instance has 10 elements. The function also declares the double-typed variable x. The for loop in lines 36 through 40 stores values in the instance Arr. The loop uses the control variable i and iterates from 0 to `Arr.getSize()-1`, in increments of 1. The loop continuation condition sends the `getSize` message to instance `Arr` to obtain the number of elements in the array. The statements in lines 37 and 38 calculate the value to store in an element of instance `Arr`. The statement in line 39 sends the message `store` to instance `Arr` and passes the arguments x and i. The object `Arr` saves the value in variable x at the element number i.

The output statement in line 42 comments on the output of the `for` loop in lines 43 and 44. The loop uses the control variable i and iterates from 0 to `Arr.getSize()-1`, in increments of 1. The output statement in line 44 displays the element in instance `Arr` by sending the message `recall` to that instance. The message has the argument i.

Declaring a Class Hierarchy

The power of the OOP features of C++ comes from the fact that you can derive classes from existing ones. A descendant class inherits the members of its ancestor classes (that is, parent class, grandparent class, and so on) and also can override some of the inherited functions. Inheritance enables you to reuse code in descendant classes.

A Derived Class

The general syntax for declaring a derived class is

```
class className : [public] parentClass
{
    <friend classes>

    private:
        <private data members>
        <private constructors>
        <private member functions>

    protected:
        <protected data members>
        <protected constructors>
        <protected member functions>

    public:
        <public data members>
        <public constructors>
        <public destructor>
        <public member functions>

        <friend functions and friend operators>
};
```

Example:

The following example shows the class cRectangle and its descendant, class cBox:

```
class cRectangle
{
    protected:
        double length;
        double width;
    public:
        cRectangle(double len, double wide);
        double getLength() const;
        double getWidth(); const;
        double assign(double len, double wide);
        double calcArea();
};

class cBox : public cRectangle
{
    protected:
        double height;

    public:
        cBox(double len, double wide, double height);
        double getHeight() const;
        assign(double len, double wide, double height);
        double calcVolume();
};
```

The class lineage is indicated by a colon followed by the optional keyword public and then the name of the parent class. When you include the keyword public, you allow the instances of the descendant class to access the public members of the parent and other ancestor classes. By contrast, when you omit the keyword public, you deprive the instance of the descendant class from accessing the members of the ancestor classes.

A descendant class inherits the data members of its ancestor classes. C++ has no mechanism for removing unwanted inherited data members—you are basically stuck with them. By contrast, C++ allows you to override inherited member functions. More about this topic later in today's lesson. The descendant class declares new data members, new member functions, and overriding member functions. Again, you can place these members in the private, protected, or public sections as you see fit in your class design.

DO   DON'T

DO reduce the number of constructors by using default argument parameters.

DO use member functions to access the values in the data members. These member functions allow you to control and validate the values in the data members.

DON'T declare all the constructors of a class protected unless you want to force the client programmers (that is, those programs that use the class) to use the class by declaring its descendants with public constructors.

DON'T declare the data members in the public section.

Let's look at an example that declares a small class hierarchy. Listing 11.3 shows the source code for the CLASS3.CPP program. This program declares classes that contain a hierarchy of two simple geometric shapes: a circle and a cylinder. The program requires no input. Instead, it uses internal data to create the geometric shapes and to display their dimensions, areas, and volume.

Listing 11.3. Source code for the CLASS3.CPP program.

```
 1: // Program that demonstrates a small hierarchy of classes
 2:
 3: #include <iostream.h>
 4: #include <math.h>
 5:
 6: const double pi = 4 * atan(1);
 7:
 8: inline double sqr(double x)
 9: { return x * x; }
10:
11: class cCircle
12: {
13:   protected:
14:     double radius;
15:
16:   public:
17:     cCircle(double radiusVal = 0) : radius(radiusVal) {}
18:     void setRadius(double radiusVal)
19:       { radius = radiusVal; }
20:     double getRadius() const
21:       { return radius; }
```

continues

Listing 11.3. continued

```
22:        double area() const
23:           { return pi * sqr(radius); }
24:        void showData();
25: };
26:
27: class cCylinder : public cCircle
28: {
29:    protected:
30:        double height;
31:
32:    public:
33:        cCylinder(double heightVal = 0, double radiusVal = 0)
34:           : height(heightVal), cCircle(radiusVal) {}
35:        void setHeight(double heightVal)
36:           { height = heightVal; }
37:        double getHeight() const
38:           { return height; }
39:        double area() const
40:           { return 2 * cCircle::area() +
41:                      2 * pi * radius * height; }
42:        void showData();
43: };
44:
45: void cCircle::showData()
46: {
47:    cout << "Circle radius       = " << getRadius() << "\n"
48:         << "Circle area         = " << area() << "\n\n";
49: }
50:
51: void cCylinder::showData()
52: {
53:    cout << "Cylinder radius     = " << getRadius() << "\n"
54:         << "Cylinder height     = " << getHeight() << "\n"
55:         << "Cylinder area       = " << area() << "\n\n";
56: }
57:
58: main()
59: {
60:    cCircle Circle(1);
61:    cCylinder Cylinder(10, 1);
62:
63:    Circle.showData();
64:    Cylinder.showData();
65:    return 0;
66: }
```

Here is a sample session with the program in Listing 11.3:

```
Circle radius      = 1
Circle area        = 3.14159

Cylinder radius    = 1
Cylinder height    = 10
Cylinder area      = 69.115
```

The program in Listing 11.3 declares the classes cCircle and cCylinder. The class cCircle models a circle, whereas class cCylinder models a cylinder.

The cCircle class declares a single data member, radius, to store the radius of the circle. The class also declares a constructor and a number of member functions. The constructor assigns a value to the data member radius when you declare a class instance. Notice that the constructor uses a new syntax to initialize the member radius. The functions setRadius and getRadius serve to set and query the value in member radius, respectively. The function area returns the area of the circle. The function showData displays the radius and area of a class instance.

The class cCylinder, a descendant of cCircle, declares a single data member, height, to store the height of the cylinder. The class inherits the member radius needed to store the radius of the cylinder. The cCylinder class declares a constructor and a number of member functions. The constructor assigns values to the radius and height members when creating a class instance. Notice the use of a new syntax to initialize the members—member height is initialized, and member radius is initialized by invoking the constructor of class cCircle with the argument radiusVal. The functions getHeight and setHeight serve to set and query the value in member height, respectively. The class uses the inherited functions setRadius and getRadius to manipulate the inherited member radius. The function area, which overrides the inherited function cCircle::area(), returns the surface area of the cylinder. Notice that this function explicitly invokes the inherited function cCircle::area(). The function showData displays the radius, height, and area of a class instance.

The function main declares the instance Circle, of class cCircle, and assigns 1 to the circle's radius. In addition, the function also declares the instance Cylinder, of class cCylinder, and assigns 10 and 1 to the circle's height and radius, respectively. The function then sends the showData message to the instances Circle and Cylinder. Each object responds to this message by invoking the appropriate member function.

Virtual Functions

As I mentioned previously, polymorphism is an important object-oriented programming feature. Consider the following simple classes and the function `main`:

```
#include <iostream.h>
class cA
{
    public:
        double A(double x) { return x * x; }
        double B(double x) { return A(x) / 2; }
};

class cB : public cA
{
    public:
        double A(double x) { return x * x * x; }
};

main()
{
    cB aB;
    cout << aB.B(3) << "\n";
    return 0;
}
```

Class cA contains functions A and B, where function B calls function A. Class cB, a descendant of class cA, inherits function B, but overrides function A. The intent here is to have the inherited function cA::B call function cB::A, in order to support polymorphic behavior. What is the program output? The answer is 4.5 and not 13.5! Why? The answer lies in the fact that the compiler resolves the expression aB.B(3) by using the inherited function cA::B, which in turn calls function cA::A. Therefore, function cB:A is left out and the program fails to support polymorphic behavior.

C++ supports polymorphic behavior by offering virtual functions.

NEW☛ *Virtual functions*, which are bound at runtime, are declared by placing the
TERM keyword `virtual` before the function's return type.

Once you declare a function `virtual`, you can override it only with virtual functions in descendant classes. These overriding functions must have the same parameter list. Virtual functions can override nonvirtual functions in ancestor classes.

Virtual Functions

The general syntax for declaring virtual functions is

```
class className1
{
     // member functions
     virtual returnType functionName(<parameter list>);
};

class className2 : public className1
{
     // member functions
     virtual returnType functionName(<parameter list>);
};
```

Example:

This example shows how virtual functions can successfully implement polymorphic behavior in classes cA and cB:

```
#include <iostream.h>
class cA
{
     public:
          virtual double A(double x) { return x * x; }
          double B(double x) { return A(x) / 2; }
};

class cB : public cA
{
     public:
          virtual double A(double x) { return x * x * x; }
};

main()
{
     cB aB;
     cout << aB.B(3) << "\n";
     return 0;
}
```

This example displays 13.5, the correct result, because the call to the inherited function cA::B is resolved at runtime by calling cB::A.

<table>
<tr><td>

DO

DO use virtual functions when you have a callable function that implements a class-specific behavior. Declaring such a function as virtual ensures that it provides the correct response that is relevant to the associated class.

DON'T declare a member function as virtual by default. Virtual functions have some additional overhead.

</td><td>

DON'T

</td></tr>
</table>

Let's look at an example. Listing 11.4 shows the source code for the program CLASS4.CPP. The program creates a square and a rectangle, and displays their dimensions and areas. No input is required.

Type

Listing 11.4. Source code for the program CLASS4.CPP.

```
 1: // Program that demonstrates virtual functions
 2:
 3: #include <iostream.h>
 4:
 5: class cSquare
 6: {
 7:   protected:
 8:     double length;
 9:
10:   public:
11:     cSquare(double len) { length = len; }
12:     double getLength() { return length; }
13:     virtual double getWidth() { return length; }
14:     double getArea() { return getLength() * getWidth(); }
15: };
16:
17: class cRectangle : public cSquare
18: {
19:   protected:
20:     double width;
21:
22:   public:
23:     cRectangle(double len, double wide) :
24:         cSquare(len), width(wide) {}
25:     virtual double getWidth() { return width; }
26: };
27:
28: main()
29: {
30:     cSquare square(10);
```

```
31:     cRectangle rectangle(10, 12);
32:
33:     cout << "Square has length = " << square.getLength() << "\n"
34:          << "         and area   = " << square.getArea() << "\n";
35:     cout << "Rectangle has length = "
36:          << rectangle.getLength() << "\n"
37:          << "            and width  = "
38:          << rectangle.getWidth() << "\n"
39:          << "            and area   = "
40:          << rectangle.getArea() << "\n";
41:     return 0;
42: }
```

Here is a sample session with the program in Listing 11.4:

```
Square has length = 10
        and area   = 100
Rectangle has length = 10
           and width  = 12
           and area   = 120
```

 The program in Listing 11.4 declares the classes cSquare and cRectangle to model squares and rectangles, respectively. The class cSquare declares a single data member, length, to store the length (and width) of the square. The class declares a constructor with the parameter len, which passes arguments to the member length. The class also declares the functions getLength, getWidth, and getArea. Both functions getLength and getWidth return the value in member length. Notice that the class declares function getWidth as virtual. The function getArea returns the area of the rectangle, calculated by calling the functions getLength and getWidth. I choose to invoke these functions rather than use the data member length in order to demonstrate how the virtual function getWidth works.

The program declares class cRectangle as a descendant of class cSquare. The class cRectangle declares the data member width and inherits the member length. These members enable the class to store the basic dimensions of a rectangle. The class constructor has the parameters len and wide which pass values to the members len and wide. Notice that the constructor invokes the constructor cSquare and supplies it with the argument len. The constructor initializes the data member width with the value of parameter wide.

The class cRectangle declares the virtual function getWidth. This version returns the value in data member width. The class inherits the member functions getLength and getArea, because their implementation is adequate for the cRectangle.

The function main declares the object square as an instance of class cSquare. The instance square has a length of 10. The function main also declares the object rectangle as an instance of class cRectangle. The instance rectangle has the length of 10 and the width of 12.

The output statement in lines 33 and 34 displays the length and area of the instance square. The statement sends the messages getLength and getArea to the above instance in order to obtain the sought values. The instance square invokes the function getArea which in turn calls the functions cSquare::getLength and cSquare::getWidth.

The output statement in lines 35 through 40 displays the length, width, and area of the instance rectangle. The statement sends the messages getLength, getWidth, and getArea to this instance. The instance responds by calling the inherited function cSquare::getLength, the virtual function cRectangle::getWidth, and the inherited function cSquare::getArea. The latter function calls the inherited function cSquare::getLength and the virtual function cRectange::getWidth to correctly calculate the area of the rectangle.

DO	DON'T

DO declare your destructor as virtual. This ensures polymorphic behavior in destroying class instances. In addition, it is highly recommended that you declare a copy constructor and an assignment operator for each class.

DON'T forget that you can inherit virtual functions and destructors when appropriate for the descendant class. You need not declare shell functions and destructors that simply call the corresponding member of the parent class.

Rules for Virtual Functions

The rule for declaring a virtual function is "once virtual, always virtual." In other words, once you declare a function to be virtual in a class, any subclass that overrides the virtual function must do so using another virtual function (that has the same parameter list). The virtual declaration is mandatory for the descendant classes. At first this rule seems to lock you in. This limitation is certainly true for object-oriented programming languages that support virtual functions but not overloaded functions. In the case of C++, the work-around is interesting. You can declare nonvirtual and overloaded functions that have the same name as the virtual function, but bear a different parameter list. Moreover, you cannot inherit nonvirtual member functions that share the same name with a virtual function. Here is a simple example that illustrates the point:

```cpp
#include <iostream.h>
class cA
{
  public:
    cA() {}
    virtual void foo(char c)
      { cout << "virtual cA::foo() returns " << c << '\n'; }
};

class cB : public cA
{
  public:
    cB() {}
    void foo(const char* s)
      { cout << "cB::foo() returns " << s << '\n'; }
    void foo(int i)
      { cout << "cB::foo() returns " << i << '\n'; }
    virtual void foo(char c)
      { cout << "virtual cB::foo() returns " << c << '\n'; }
};

class cC : public cB
{
  public:
    cC() {}
    void foo(const char* s)
      { cout << "cC::foo() returns " << s << '\n'; }
    void foo(double x)
      { cout << "cC::foo() returns " << x << '\n'; }
    virtual void foo(char c)
      { cout << "virtual cC::foo() returns " << c << '\n'; }
};

main()
{
  int n = 100;
  cA Aobj;
  cB Bobj;
  cC Cobj;

  Aobj.foo('A');
  Bobj.foo('B');
  Bobj.foo(10);
  Bobj.foo("Bobj");
  Cobj.foo('C');
```

11

```
    // if you uncomment the next statement, program does not compile
    // Cobj.foo(n);
    Cobj.foo(144.123);
    Cobj.foo("Cobj");
    return 0;
}
```

This code declares three classes, cA, cB, and cC, to form a linear hierarchy of classes. Class cA declares function foo(char) as virtual. Class cB also declares its own version of the virtual function foo(char). In addition, class cB declares the nonvirtual overloaded functions foo(const char* s) and foo(int). Class cC, the descendant of class B, declares the virtual function foo(char) and the nonvirtual and overloaded functions foo(const char*) and foo(double). Notice that class cC must declare the foo(const char*) function if it needs the function, because it cannot inherit the member function cB::foo(const char*). C++ supports a different function inheritance scheme when there is an overloaded and virtual function involved. The function main creates an instance for each of the three classes and involves the various versions of the member function foo.

Friend Functions

C++ allows member functions to access all the data members of a class. In addition, C++ grants the same privileged access to friend functions. The declaration of friend functions appears in the class and begins with the keyword friend. Other than using the special keyword, friend functions look very much like member functions, except they cannot return a reference to the befriended class because this requires returning the self-reference *this. However, when you define friend functions outside the declaration of their befriended class, you need not qualify the function names with the name of the class.

NEW☞
TERM
Friend functions are ordinary functions that have access to all data members of one or more classes.

Syntax

Friend Functions

The general form of friend functions is

```
class className
{
    public:
        className();
        // other constructors

        friend returnType friendFunction(<parameter list>);
};
```

Example:

```
class String
{
    protected:
        char *str;
        int len;

    public:
        String();
        ~String();
        // other member functions
        friend String& append(String& str1, String& str2);
        friend String& append(const char* str1, String& str2);
        friend String& append(String& str1, const char* str2);
};
```

Friend classes are able to accomplish tasks that are awkward, difficult, and even impossible with member functions.

Let's look at a simple example for using friend functions. Listing 11.5 contains the source code for the CLASS5.CPP program. This program internally creates two complex numbers, adds them, stores the result in another complex number, and then displays the operands and resulting complex numbers.

11

Type Listing 11.5. Source code for the CLASS5.CPP program.

```
 1: // Program that demonstrates friend functions
 2:
 3: #include <iostream.h>
 4:
 5: class Complex
 6: {
 7:     protected:
 8:         double x;
 9:         double y;
10:
11:     public:
12:         Complex(double real = 0, double imag = 0);
13:         Complex(Complex& c) { assign(c); }
14:         void assign(Complex& c);
15:         double getReal() const { return x; }
16:         double getImag() const { return y; }
17:         friend Complex add(Complex& c1, Complex& c2);
18: };
19:
20: Complex::Complex(double real, double imag)
21: {
```

continues

Listing 11.5. continued

```
22:   x = real;
23:   y = imag;
24: }
25:
26: void Complex::assign(Complex& c)
27: {
28:   x = c.x;
29:   y = c.y;
30: }
31:
32: Complex add(Complex& c1, Complex& c2)
33: {
34:   Complex result(c1);
35:
36:   result.x += c2.x;
37:   result.y += c2.y;
38:   return result;
39: }
40:
41: main()
42: {
43:   Complex c1(2, 3);
44:   Complex c2(5, 7);
45:   Complex c3;
46:
47:   c3.assign(add(c1, c2));
48:   cout << "(" << c1.getReal() << " + i" << c1.getImag() << ")"
49:       << " + "
50:       << "(" << c2.getReal() << " + i" << c2.getImag() << ")"
51:       << " = "
52:       << "(" << c3.getReal() << " + i" << c3.getImag() << ")"
53:       << "\n\n";
54:   return 0;
55: }
```

Here is a sample session with the program in Listing 11.5:

```
(2 + i3) + (5 + i7) = (7 + i10)
```

The program in Listing 11.5 declares the class Complex which models complex numbers. This class declares two data members, two constructors, a friend function (the highlight of this example), and a set of member functions. The data members x and y store the real and imaginary components of a complex number, respectively.

The class has two constructors. The first constructor has two parameters (with default arguments) that allow you to build a class instance using the real and imaginary components of a complex. Because the two parameters have default arguments, the constructor doubles up as the default constructor. The second constructor, `complex(complex&)`, is the copy constructor.

The `Complex` class declares three member functions. The function `assign` copies a class instance into another one. The functions `getReal` and `getImag` return the value stored in the members `real` and `imag`, respectively.

The `Complex` class declares the friend function `add` to add two complex numbers. To make the program short, I do not implement complementary friend functions that subtract, multiply, and divide class instances. What is so special about the friend function `add`? Why not use an ordinary member function to add a class instance? The following declaration of the alternate `add` member function answers these questions:

```
complex& add(complex& c)
```

This declaration states that the function treats the parameter `c` as a second operand. Here is how the member function `add` works:

```
complex c1(3, 4), c2(1.2, 4.5);
c1.add(c2); // adds c2 to c1
```

First, the member function `add` works as an increment and not as an addition function. Second, the targeted class instance is always the first operand. This is not a problem for operations like addition and multiplication, but it is a problem for subtraction and division. That is why the friend function `add` works better by giving you the freedom of choosing how to add the class instances.

The friend function `add` returns a class instance. The function creates a local instance of class `Complex` and returns that instance.

The function `main` uses the member function `assign` and the friend function `add` to perform simple complex operations. In addition, the function `main` invokes the functions `getReal` and `getImag` with the various instances of class `Complex` to display the components of each instance.

Operators and Friend Operators

The last program uses a member function and a friend function to implement complex math operations. The approach is typical in C and Pascal, because these languages do not support user-defined operators. By contrast, C++ allows you to declare operators and friend operators. These operators include +, -, *, /, %, ==, !=, <=, <, >=, >, +=, -=, *=, /=, %=, [ ], ( ), <<, and >>. Consult a C++ language reference book for more details on the rules of using these operators. C++ treats operators and friend operators as special member functions and friend functions.

Operators and Friend Operators

The general syntax for declaring operators and friend operators is

```
class className
{
    public:
        // constructors and destructor
        // member functions

        // unary operator
        returnType operator operatorSymbol(operand);
        // binary operator
        returnType operator operatorSymbol(firstOperand,
                                             secondOperand);
        // unary friend operator
        friend returnType operator operatorSymbol(operand);
        // binary operator
        friend returnType operator operatorSymbol(firstOperand,
                                                    secondOperand);
};
```

Example:

```
class String
{
    protected:
        char *str;
        int len;

    public:
        String();
        ~String();
        // other member functions
        // assignment operator
        String& operator =(String& s);
        String& operator +=(String& s);
        // concatenation operators
        friend String& operator +(String& s1, String& s2);
        friend String& operator +(const char* s1, String& s2);
        friend String& operator +(String& s1, const char* s2);
        // relational operators
        friend int operator >(String& s1, String& s2);
        friend int operator =>(String& s1, String& s2);
```

```
         friend int operator <(String& s1, String& s2);
         friend int operator <=(String& s1, String& s2);
         friend int operator ==(String& s1, String& s2);
         friend int operator !=(String& s1, String& s2);
};
```

The functions you write use the operators and friend operators just like predefined operators. Therefore, you can create operators to support the operations of classes that model, for example, complex numbers, strings, arrays, and matrices. These operators enable you to write expressions that are far more readable than expressions that use named functions.

Let's look at an example. Listing 11.6 contains the source code for the CLASS6.CPP program. I created this program by modifying and expanding Listing 11.5. The new program performs more additions and displays two sets of operands and results.

Type   **Listing 11.6. Source code for the CLASS6.CPP program.**

```
 1: // Program that demonstrates operators and friend operators
 2:
 3: #include <iostream.h>
 4:
 5: class Complex
 6: {
 7:    protected:
 8:       double x;
 9:       double y;
10:
11:    public:
12:       Complex(double real = 0, double imag = 0)
13:          { assign(real, imag); }
14:       Complex(Complex& c);
15:       void assign(double real = 0, double imag = 0);
16:       double getReal() const { return x; }
17:       double getImag() const { return y; }
18:       Complex& operator =(Complex& c);
19:       Complex& operator +=(Complex& c);
20:       friend Complex operator +(Complex& c1, Complex& c2);
21:       friend ostream& operator <<(ostream& os, Complex& c);
22: };
23:
24: Complex::Complex(Complex& c)
25: {
26:    x = c.x;
27:    y = c.y;
28: }
29:
```

continues

Listing 11.6. continued

```
30: void Complex::assign(double real, double imag)
31: {
32:   x = real;
33:   y = imag;
34: }
35:
36: Complex& Complex::operator =(Complex& c)
37: {
38:   x = c.x;
39:   y = c.y;
40:   return *this;
41: }
42:
43: Complex& Complex::operator +=(Complex& c)
44: {
45:   x += c.x;
46:   y += c.y;
47:   return *this;
48: }
49:
50: Complex operator +(Complex& c1, Complex& c2)
51: {
52:   Complex result(c1);
53:
54:   result.x += c2.x;
55:   result.y += c2.y;
56:   return result;
57: }
58:
59: ostream& operator <<(ostream& os, Complex& c)
60: {
61:   os << "(" << c.x << " + i" << c.y << ")";
62:   return os;
63: }
64:
65: main()
66: {
67:   Complex c1(3, 5);
68:   Complex c2(7, 5);
69:   Complex c3;
70:   Complex c4(2, 3);
71:
72:   c3 = c1 + c2;
73:   cout << c1 << " + " << c2 << " = " << c3 << "\n";
74:   cout << c3 << " + " << c4 << " = ";
75:   c3 += c4;
76:   cout << c3 << "\n";
77:   return 0;
78: }
```

Here is a sample session with the program in Listing 11.6:

```
(3 + i5) + (7 + i5) = (10 + i10)
(10 + i10) + (2 + i3) = (12 + i13)
```

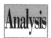

The new class `Complex` replaces the `assign(Complex&)` member function with the operator =. The class also replaces the friend function `add` with the friend operator +:

```
Complex& operator =(Complex& c);
friend Complex operator +(Complex& c1, Complex& c2);
```

The operator = has one parameter, a reference to an instance of class `Complex`, and also returns a reference to the same class. The friend operator + has two parameters (both are references to instances of class `Complex`) and yields a complex class type.

I also took the opportunity to add two new operators:

```
complex& operator +=(complex& c);
friend ostream& operator <<(ostream& os, complex& c);
```

The operator += is a member of class `Complex`. It takes one parameter, a reference to an instance of class `Complex`, and yields a reference to the same class. The other new operator is the friend operator <<, which illustrates how to write a stream extractor operator for a class. The friend operator has two parameters: a reference to class `ostream` (the output stream class) and a reference to class `Complex`. The operator << returns a reference to class `ostream`. This type of value enables you to chain stream output with other predefined types or other classes (assuming that these classes have a friend operator <<). The definition of friend operator << has two statements. The first one outputs strings and the data members of class `Complex` to the output stream parameter os. The friendship status of operator << allows it to access the `real` and `imag` data members of its `Complex`-typed parameter c. The second statement in the operator definition returns the first parameter os.

The function main declares four instances of class `Complex`, c1, c2, c3, and c4. The instances c1, c2, and c4 are created with nondefault values assigned to the data members `real` and `imag`. The function tests using the operators =, +, <<, +=. The program illustrates that you can use operators and friend operators to write code that is more readable and supports a higher level of abstraction.

Summary

Today's lesson introduces you to C++ classes and discusses the following topics:

☐ The basics of object-oriented programming include classes, objects, messages, methods, inheritance, and polymorphism.

☐ You declare base classes to specify the various private, protected, and public members. C++ classes contain data members and member functions. The data members store the state of a class instance, and the member functions query and manipulate that state.

☐ Constructors and destructors support the automatic creation and removal of class instances. Constructors are special members that must have the same name as the host class. You may declare any number of constructors, or none at all. In the latter case, the compiler creates one for you. Each constructor enables you to create a class instance in a different way. There are two special kinds of constructors: the default constructor and the copy constructor. In contrast with constructors, C++ allows you to declare only one parameterless destructor. Destructors automatically remove class instances. The run-time system automatically invokes the constructor and destructor when a class instance comes into and goes out of its scope.

☐ Declaring a class hierarchy enables you to derive classes from existing ones. The descendant classes inherit the members of their ancestor classes. C++ classes are able to override inherited member functions by defining their own versions. If you override a nonvirtual function, you may declare the new version using a different parameter list. By contrast, you cannot alter the parameter list of an inherited virtual function.

☐ Virtual member functions enable your classes to support polymorphic behavior. Such behavior offers a response that is suitable for each class in a hierarchy. Once you declare a function virtual, you can override it only with a virtual function in a descendant class. All versions of a virtual function in a class hierarchy must have the same signature.

☐ Friend functions are special nonmember functions that may access protected and private data members. These functions enable you to implement operations that are more flexible than those offered by member functions.

☐ Operators and friend operators enable you to support various operations, such as addition, assignment, and indexing. These operators enable you to offer a level of abstraction for your classes. In addition, they assist in making the expressions that manipulate class instances more readable and more intuitive.

Q&A

Q. What happens if I declare the default, copy, and other constructors as protected?

A. Client programs are unable to create instances of that class. However, client programs can use that class by declaring descendant classes with public constructors.

Q. Can I use the constructor for typecasting?

A. Yes, you can incorporate this kind of typecasting in the creation of a class instance. For example, if the class `Complex` has the constructor `Complex(double real, double imag)`, you can declare the instance c of class `Complex` as follows:

```
Complex c = Complex(1.7, 2.4);
```

Q. Can I chain messages to an instance?

A. Yes, as long as the chained messages invoke member functions that return a reference to the same class which receives the message. For example, if you have a class `String` with the following member functions:

```
String& upperCase();
string& reverse();
String& mapChars(char find, char replace);
```

you can write the following statement for the instance of class `String` s:

```
s.upperCase().reverse().mapChar(' ', '+');
```

Q. What happens if a class relies on the copy constructor, which is created by the compiler, to copy instances of a class which has pointers?

A. These constructors perform a bit-by-bit copy. Consequently, the corresponding pointer members in both instances end up with the address to the same dynamic data. This kind of duplication is a recipe for trouble!

Q. Can I create an array of instances?

A. Yes, however the accompanying class must have a default constructor. The instantiation of the array uses the constructor mentioned previously.

Q. Can I use a pointer to create an instance of class?

A. Yes, you need to use the operators `new` and `delete` to allocate and deallocate the dynamic space for the instance. Here is an example using the class `Complex`:

```
Complex* pC;
pC = new Complex;
// manipulate the instance accessed by pointer pC
delete pC;

or

Complex* pC = new Complex;
// manipulate the instance accessed by pointer pC
delete pC;
```

Workshop

The Workshop provides quiz questions to help you solidify your understanding of the material covered and exercises to provide you with experience in using what you've learned. Try to understand the quiz and exercise answers before continuing on to the next day's lesson. Answers are provided in Appendix B, "Answers."

Quiz

1. Where is the error in the following class declaration?

```
class String {
      char *str;
      unsigned len;
      String();
      String(String& s);
      String(unsigned size, char = ' ');
      String(unsigned size);
      String& assign(String& s);
      ~String();
      unsigned getLen() const;
      char* getString();
      // other member functions
};
```

2. Where is the error in the following class declaration?

```
class String {
    protected:
      char *str;
      unsigned len;
```

```
    public:
        String();
        String(const char* s);
        String(String& s);
        String(unsigned size, char = ' ');
        String(unsigned size);
        ~String();
        // other member functions
};
```

3. True or false? The following statement which creates the instance s, based on the above declaration of class String, is correct:

```
s = String("Hello Visual C++");
```

4. Looking at program CLASS6.CPP, if you change the declarations of the instances in function main to the following, will the program still compile?

```
Complex c1 = Complex(3, 5);
Complex c2 = Complex(7, 5);
Complex c3 = c1;
Complex c4 = Complex(2, 3);
```

11

Exercise

Create program CLASS7.CPP from CLASS6.CPP by replacing the individual instances c1 to c4 with c, an array of instances.

DAY 12

Basic Stream
File I/O

Today's lesson introduces you to file I/O operations using the C++ stream library. Although the STDIO.H library in C has been standardized by the ANSI C committee, the C++ stream library has not. You have a choice of using file I/O functions in the STDIO.H file and those in the C++ stream library. Each of these two I/O libraries offers a lot of power and flexibility. Today's lesson presents basic and practical operations that enable you to read and write data to files. You learn about the following topics:

☐ Common stream I/O functions

☐ Sequential stream I/O for text

☐ Sequential stream I/O for binary data

☐ Random access stream I/O for binary data

To learn more about the C++ stream library, consult a C++ language reference book, such as Tom Swan's *C++ Primer* (SAMS 1992).

The C++ Stream Library

The C++ stream I/O library is made up of a hierarchy of classes that are declared in several header files. The IOSTREAM.H header file that I have used so far is only one of these. Others include IO.H, ISTREAM.H, OSTREAM.H, IFSTREAM.H, OFSTREAM.H, and FSTREAM.H. The IO.H header file declares low-level classes and identifiers. The ISTREAM.H and OSTREAM.H files support the basic input and output stream classes. The IOSTREAM.H combines the operations of the classes in the previous two header files. Similarly, The IFSTREAM.H and OFSTREAM.H files support the basic file input and output stream classes. The FSTREAM.H file combines the operations of the classes in the previous two header files. There are additional stream library files that offer even more specialized stream I/O. The C++ ANSI committee will define the standard stream I/O library, and this will end any confusion regarding which classes and header files are part of the standard stream library and which ones are not.

Common Stream I/O Functions

In this section I present stream I/O functions that are common to both sequential and random access I/O. These functions include open, close, good, and fail, in addition to the operator !.

The open function enables you to open a file stream for input, output, append, and both input and output. The function also permits you to specify whether the related I/O is binary or text.

The *open* Function

The prototype for the open function is

```
void open(const char* filename,
          int mode,
          int m = filebuf::openprot);
```

The parameter *filename* specifies the name of the file to open. The parameter *mode* indicates the I/O mode. Here is a list of arguments for parameter mode that are exported by the IO.H header file:

in	Open stream for input.
out	Open stream for output.
ate	Set stream pointer to the end of the file.
app	Open stream for append mode.
trunc	Truncate file size to 0 if it already exists.
nocreate	Raise an error if the file does not already exist.
noreplace	Raise an error if the file already exists.
binary	Open in binary mode.

Examples:

```
// open stream for input
fstream f;
f.open("\\AUTOEXEC.BAT", ios::in);

// open stream for output
fstream f;
f.open("\\AUTOEXEC.OLD", ios:out);

// open stream for binary input and output
fstream f;
f.open("INCOME.DAT", ios::in ¦ ios::out ¦ ios::binary);
```

12

Note: The file stream classes offer constructors that include the action (and have the same parameters) of function open.

The close function closes the stream and recuperates the resources involved. These resources include the memory buffer used in the stream I/O operations.

The *close* Function

The prototype for the close function is

```
void close();
```

Example:

```
fstream f;
// open stream
f.open("\\AUTOEXEC.BAT", ios::in);
// process file
// now close stream
f.close();
```

The C++ stream library includes a set of basic functions that check the error status of a stream operation. These functions include the following:

1. The good() function returns a nonzero value if there is no error in a stream operation. The declaration of function good is

   ```
   int good();
   ```

2. The fail() function returns a nonzero value if there is an error in a stream operation. The declaration of function fail is

   ```
   int fail();
   ```

3. The overloaded operator ! is applied to a stream instance to determine the error status.

The C++ stream libraries offer additional functions to set and query other aspects and types of stream errors.

Sequential Text Stream I/O

The functions and operators involved in sequential text I/O are simple—you have already been exposed to most of them in earlier lessons. The functions and operators include the following:

1. The stream extractor operator << writes strings and characters to a stream.

2. The stream inserter operator >> reads characters from a stream.

3. The getline function reads strings from a stream.

The *getline* Function

The prototype for the function getline is

```
istream& getline(signed char* buffer,
                 int size,
                 char delimiter = '\n');

istream& getline(unsigned char* buffer,
                 int size,
                 char delimiter = '\n');
```

The parameter *buffer* is a pointer to the string receiving the characters from the stream. The parameter *size* specifies the maximum number of characters to read. The parameter *delimiter* specifies the delimiting character which causes the string input to stop before reaching the number of characters specified by parameter size. The parameter delimiter has the default argument of '\n'.

Example:

```
fstream f;
char textLine[MAX];
f.open("\\CONFIG.SYS", ios::in);
while (!f.eof()) {
  f.getline(textLine, MAX);
  cout << textLine << "\n";
}
f.close();
```

Let's look at an example. Listing 12.1 shows the source code for the IO1.CPP program. The program performs the following tasks:

☐ Prompts you to enter the name of an input text file

☐ Prompts you to enter the name of an output text file (the program detects if the names of the input and output files are the same, and if so, reprompts you for a different output filename)

☐ Reads the lines from the input files and removes any trailing spaces in these lines

☐ Writes the lines to the output file and also to the standard output window

 Listing 12.1. Source code for the IO1.CPP program.

```
1: // C++ program that demonstrates sequential file I/O
2:
3: #include <iostream.h>
4: #include <fstream.h>
```

12

Listing 12.1. continued

```
 5: #include <string.h>
 6:
 7: enum boolean { false, true };
 8:
 9: const unsigned LINE_SIZE = 128;
10: const unsigned NAME_SIZE = 64;
11:
12: void trimStr(char* s)
13: {
14:   int i = strlen(s) - 1;
15:   // locate the character where the trailing spaces begin
16:   while (i >= 0 && s[i] == ' ')
17:     i--;
18:   // truncate string
19:   s[i+1] = '\0';
20: }
21:
22: void getInputFilename(char* inFile, fstream& f)
23: {
24:   boolean ok;
25:
26:   do {
27:     ok = true;
28:     cout << "Enter input file : ";
29:     cin.getline(inFile, NAME_SIZE);
30:     f.open(inFile, ios::in);
31:     if (!f) {
32:       cout << "Cannot open file " << inFile << "\n\n";
33:       ok = false;
34:     }
35:   } while (!ok);
36:
37: }
38:
39: void getOutputFilename(char* outFile, const char* inFile,
40:                        fstream& f)
41: {
42:   boolean ok;
43:
44:   do {
45:     ok = true;
46:     cout << "Enter output file : ";
47:     cin.getline(outFile, NAME_SIZE);
48:     if (stricmp(inFile, outFile) != 0) {
49:       f.open(outFile, ios::out);
50:       if (!f) {
51:         cout << "File " << outFile << " is invalid\n\n";
52:         ok = false;
53:       }
```

```
54:     }
55:     else {
56:       cout << "Input and output files must be different!\n";
57:       ok = false;
58:     }
59:   } while (!ok);
60: }
61:
62: void processLines(fstream& fin, fstream& fout)
63: {
64:   char line[LINE_SIZE + 1];
65:
66:   // loop to trim trailing spaces
67:   while (fin.getline(line, LINE_SIZE)) {
68:     trimStr(line);
69:     // write line to the output file
70:     fout << line << "\n";
71:     // echo updated line to the output window
72:     cout << line << "\n";
73:   }
74:
75: }
76: main()
77: {
78:
79:   fstream fin, fout;
80:   char inFile[NAME_SIZE + 1], outFile[NAME_SIZE + 1];
81:
82:   getInputFilename(inFile, fin);
83:   getOutputFilename(outFile, inFile, fout);
84:   processLines(fin, fout);
85:   // close streams
86:   fin.close();
87:   fout.close();
88:   return 0;
89: }
```

Here is a sample session with the program in Listing 12.1:

```
Enter input file : sample.txt
Enter output file : sample.out
This is line 1
This is line 2
This is line 3
This is line 4
```

The program in Listing 12.1 declares no classes and instead focuses on using file streams to input and output text. The program declares the functions trimStr, getInputFilename, getOutputFilename, processLines, and main.

The function trimStr shaves the trailing spaces in the strings passed by parameter s. The function declares the local variable i and assigns it the index of the character just before the null terminator. The function uses the while loop in line 13 to perform a backward scan of the characters in string s for the first nonspace character. The statement at line 16 assigns the null terminator character to the character located right after the last nonspace character in the string s.

The function getInputFilename obtains the input filename and opens its corresponding input file stream. The parameter inFile passes the name of the input file to the function caller. The reference parameter f passes the opened input stream to the function caller. The function getInputFilename declares the local flag ok. The function uses the do-while loop in lines 26 through 35 to obtain a valid filename and to open that file for input. Line 27 contains the first statement inside the loop which assigns the enumerated value true to the local variable ok. The output statement in line 28 prompts you for the input filename. The statement in line 29 calls the stream input function getline to obtain your input and to store it in the parameter inFile. The statement in line 30 opens the input file using the stream parameter f. The open statement uses the ios::in value to indicate that the stream is opened for text input. The if statement in line 31 determines whether or not the stream f is successfully opened. If not, the function executes the statements in lines 32 and 33. These statements display an error message and assign the enumerated value false to the local variable ok. The loop's while clause in line 35 examines the condition !ok. The loop iterates until you supply it a valid filename which must successfully be opened for input.

The function getOutputFilename complements the function getInputFilename and has three parameters. The parameter outFile passes the output filename of the function caller. The parameter inFile supplies the function with the input filename. The function uses this parameter to ensure that the input and output filenames are not the same. The parameter f passes the output stream to the function caller. The implementation of function getOutputFilename is very similar to that of function getInputFilename. The main difference is that the function getOutputFilename calls the function stricmp to compare the values in parameter inFile and outFile. The function uses the result of stricmp to determine whether the names of the input and output files are identical. If so, the function executes the statements in the else clause at lines 57 and 58. These statements display an error message and assign false to the local variable ok.

The function processLines reads the lines from the input file stream, trims them, and writes them to the output file stream. The parameters fin and fout pass the input and output file streams, respectively. The function declares the local string variable line and uses the while loop in lines 67 through 73 to process the text lines. The while clause contains the call to function getline which reads the next line in the input stream fin and assigns the input line to variable line. The result of function getline causes the while loop to stop iterating when there are no more input lines. The first statement inside the loop, located at line 68, calls the function trimStr and passes it the argument line. This function call prunes any existing trailing spaces in the local variable line. The statement in line 70 writes the string in variable line to the output file stream. The statement in line 72 echoes the string in line to the standard output window. I place this statement in the program so that you can monitor the progress of the program.

The function main declares the file streams fin and fout, and the string variables inFile and outFile. The statement in line 82 calls function getInputFilename and passes it the arguments inFile and fin. This call obtains the name of the input file and the input stream through the arguments inFile and fin, respectively. The statement in line 83 calls the function getOutputFilename and passes it the arguments outFile, inFile, and fout. This call obtains the name of the output file and the output stream through the arguments outFile and fout, respectively. The statement in line 84 calls function processLines and passes it the arguments fin and fout. This call processes the lines in the input file stream fin and writes the results to the output file stream fout. The statements in lines 86 and 87 close the input and output file streams, respectively.

Sequential Binary File Stream I/O

The C++ stream library offers the overloaded stream functions write and read for sequential binary file stream I/O. The function write sends multiple bytes to an output stream. This function can write any variable or instance to a stream.

The *write* Function

The prototype for the overloaded function write is

```
ostream& write(const signed char* buff, int num);
ostream& write(const unsigned char* buff, int num);
```

The parameter *buff* is the pointer to the buffer that contains the data to be sent to the output stream. The parameter *num* indicates the number of bytes in the buffer that are sent to the stream.

Example:

```
const MAX = 80;
char buff[MAX+1] = "Hello World!";
int len = strlen(buffer) + 1;
fstream f;
f.open("CALC.DAT", ios::out | ios::binary);
f.write((const unsigned char*)*len, sizeof(len));
f.write((const unsigned char*)buff, len);
f.close();
```

The function `read` receives multiple bytes from an input stream. This function can read any variable or from a stream.

The *read* Function

The prototype for the overloaded function `read` is

```
istream& read(signed char* buff, int num);
istream& read(unsigned char* buff, int num);
```

The parameter `buff` is the pointer to the buffer that receives the data from the input stream. The parameter `num` indicates the number of bytes to read from the stream.

Example:

```
const MAX = 80;
char buff[MAX+1];
int len;
fstream f;
f.open("CALC.DAT", ios::in | ios::binary);
f.read((const unsigned char*)*len, sizeof(len));
f.read((const unsigned char*)buff, len);
f.close();
```

Let's look at an example that performs sequential binary stream I/O. Listing 12.2 shows the source code for the IO2.CPP program. The program declares a class that models dynamic numerical arrays. The stream I/O operations enable the program to read and write both the individual array elements and an entire array in binary files. The program creates the arrays `arr1`, `arr2`, and `arr3`, and then performs the following tasks:

☐ Assigns values to the elements of array `arr1` (this array has 10 elements)

☐ Assigns values to the elements of array `arr3` (this array has 20 elements)

☐ Displays the values in array `arr1`

☐ Writes the elements of array `arr1` to the file ARR1.DAT, one element at a time

☐ Reads the elements of arr1 from the file into the array arr2 (the array arr2 has 10 elements—the same size as array arr1)

☐ Displays the values in array arr2

☐ Displays the values in array arr3

☐ Writes, in one swoop, the elements of array arr3 to file ARR3.DAT

☐ Reads, in one swoop, the data in file ARR3.DAT and stores them in array arr1

☐ Displays the values in array arr1 (the output shows that array arr1 has the same size and data as array arr3)

Type **Listing 12.2. Source code for the IO2.CPP program.**

```
1:  /*
2:      C++ program that demonstrates sequential binary file I/O
3:  */
4:
5:  #include <iostream.h>
6:  #include <fstream.h>
7:
8:  const unsigned MIN_SIZE = 10;
9:  const double BAD_VALUE = -1.0e+30;
10: enum boolean { false, true };
11:
12: class Array
13: {
14:    protected:
15:      double *dataPtr;
16:      unsigned size;
17:      double badIndex;
18:
19:    public:
20:      Array(unsigned Size = MIN_SIZE);
21:      ~Array()
22:        { delete [] dataPtr; }
23:      unsigned getSize() const { return size; }
24:      double& operator [](unsigned index)
25:      { return (index < size) ? *(dataPtr + index) : badIndex; }
26:      boolean writeElem(fstream& os, unsigned index);
27:      boolean readElem(fstream& is, unsigned index);
28:      boolean writeArray(const char* filename);
29:      boolean readArray(const char* filename);
30: };
31:
```

continues

341

Listing 12.2. continued

```
32: Array::Array(unsigned Size)
33: {
34:   size = (Size < MIN_SIZE) ? MIN_SIZE : Size;
35:   badIndex = BAD_VALUE;
36:   dataPtr = new double[size];
37: }
38:
39: boolean Array::writeElem(fstream& os, unsigned index)
40: {
41:   if (index < size) {
42:     os.write((unsigned char*)(dataPtr + index), sizeof(double));
43:     return (os.good()) ? true : false;
44:   }
45:   else
46:     return false;
47: }
48:
49: boolean Array::readElem(fstream& is, unsigned index)
50: {
51:   if (index < size) {
52:     is.read((unsigned char*)(dataPtr + index), sizeof(double));
53:     return (is.good()) ? true : false;
54:   }
55:   else
56:     return false;
57: }
58:
59: boolean Array::writeArray(const char* filename)
60: {
61:   fstream f(filename, ios::out | ios::binary);
62:
63:   if (f.fail())
64:     return false;
65:   f.write((unsigned char*) &size, sizeof(size));
66:   f.write((unsigned char*)dataPtr, size * sizeof(double));
67:   f.close();
68:   return (f.good()) ? true : false;
69: }
70:
71: boolean Array::readArray(const char* filename)
72: {
73:   fstream f(filename, ios::in | ios::binary);
74:   unsigned sz;
75:
76:   if (f.fail())
77:     return false;
78:   f.read((unsigned char*) &sz, sizeof(sz));
79:   // need to expand the array
80:   if (sz != size) {
```

```
81:       delete [] dataPtr;
82:       dataPtr = new double[sz];
83:       size = sz;
84:     }
85:     f.read((unsigned char*)dataPtr, size * sizeof(double));
86:     f.close();
87:     return (f.good()) ? true : false;
88: }
89:
90: main()
91: {
92:   const unsigned SIZE1 = 10;
93:   const unsigned SIZE2 = 20;
94:   char* filename1 = "array1.dat";
95:   char* filename2 = "array3.dat";
96:   Array arr1(SIZE1), arr2(SIZE1), arr3(SIZE2);
97:   fstream f(filename1, ios::out ¦ ios::binary);
98:
99:   // assign values to array arr1
100:  for (unsigned i = 0; i < arr1.getSize(); i++)
101:    arr1[i] = 10 * i;
102:
103:  // assign values to array arr3
104:  for (i = 0; i < SIZE2; i++)
105:    arr3[i] = i;
106:
107:  cout << "Array arr1 has the following values:\n";
108:  for (i = 0; i < arr1.getSize(); i++)
109:    cout << arr1[i] << "  ";
110:  cout << "\n\n";
111:
112:  // write elements of array arr1 to the stream
113:  for (i = 0; i < arr1.getSize(); i++)
114:    arr1.writeElem(f, i);
115:  f.close();
116:
117:  // reopen the stream for input
118:  f.open(filename1, ios::in ¦ ios::binary);
119:
120:  for (i = 0; i < arr1.getSize(); i++)
121:    arr2.readElem(f, i);
122:  f.close();
123:
124:  // display the elements of array arr2
125:  cout << "Array arr2 has the following values:\n";
126:  for (i = 0; i < arr2.getSize(); i++)
127:    cout << arr2[i] << "   ";
128:  cout << "\n\n";
129:
130:  // display the elements of array arr3
131:  cout << "Array arr3 has the following values:\n";
```

12

continues

Listing 12.2. continued

```
132:    for (i = 0; i < arr3.getSize(); i++)
133:      cout << arr3[i] << "   ";
134:    cout << "\n\n";
135:
136:    // write the array arr3 to file ARRAY3.DAT
137:    arr3.writeArray(filename2);
138:    // read the array arr1 from file ARRAY3.DAT
139:    arr1.readArray(filename2);
140:
141:      // display the elements of array arr1
142:    cout << "Array arr1 now has the following values:\n";
143:    for (i = 0; i < arr1.getSize(); i++)
144:      cout << arr1[i] << "   ";
145:    cout << "\n\n";
146:    return 0;
147: }
```

Here is a sample session with the program in Listing 12.2:

```
Array arr1 has the following values:
0   10   20   30   40   50   60   70   80   90

Array arr2 has the following values:
0   10   20   30   40   50   60   70   80   90

Array arr3 has the following values:
0   1   2   3   4   5   6   7   8   9   10   11   12   13   14   15   16   17   18   19

Array arr1 now has the following values:
0   1   2   3   4   5   6   7   8   9   10   11   12   13   14   15   16   17   18   19
```

 The program in Listing 12.2 declares a version of class Array that resembles the one in Day 11, Listing 11.2. The main difference is that I use the operator [ ] to replace both the member functions store and recall. This operator checks for valid indices and returns the value in member badIndex if the argument is out of range. In addition to operator [ ], I add the member functions writeElem, readElem, writeArray, and readArray to perform sequential binary file stream I/O.

The function writeElem, defined in lines 39 through 47, writes a single array element to an output stream. The parameter os represents the output stream. The parameter index specifies the array element to write. The function writeElem yields true if the argument for the index is valid and if the stream output proceeds without any error. After writeElem writes an array element, the internal stream pointer advances to the next location.

The function readElem, defined in lines 49 through 57, reads a single array element from an input stream. The parameter is represents the input stream. The parameter index specifies the array element to read. The function readElem returns true if the argument for the index is valid and if the stream input proceeds without any error. After the readElem reads an array element, the internal stream pointer advances to the next location.

The functions writeElem and readElem permit the same class instance to write and read data elements, respectively, from multiple streams.

The function writeArray, defined in lines 59 through 69, writes the entire elements of the array to a binary file. The parameter filename specifies the name of the output file. The function opens an output stream and writes the value of the data member size and then writes the elements of the dynamic array. The writeArray function returns true if it successfully writes the array to the stream. Otherwise, the function yields false. The function opens a local output stream using the stream function open and supplying it with the filename and I/O mode arguments. The I/O mode argument is the expression ios::out ¦ ios::binary which specifies that the stream is opened for binary output only. The function makes two calls to the stream function write: the first to write the data member size, and the second to write the elements of the dynamic array.

The function readArray, defined in lines 71 through 88, reads the entire elements of the array from a binary file. The parameter filename specifies the name of the input file. The function opens an input stream and reads the value of the data member size and then reads the elements of the dynamic array. The readArray function returns true if it successfully reads the array to the stream. Otherwise, the function yields false. The function opens a local input stream using the stream function open and supplying it the filename and I/O mode arguments. The I/O mode argument is the expression ios::in ¦ ios::binary which specifies that the stream is opened for binary input only. The function makes two calls to the stream function read: the first to read the data member size, and the second to read the elements of the dynamic array. Another feature of function readArray is that it resizes the instance of class Array to accommodate the data from the binary file. This means that dynamic array accessed by the class instance may either shrink or expand, depending on the size of the array stored on file.

The member functions in Listing 12.2 indicate that the program performs two types of sequential binary stream I/O. The first type of I/O, implemented in functions readElem and writeElem, involves items that have the same data type. The second type of I/O, implemented in functions readArray and writeArray, involves items that have different data types.

The function main performs the following relevant tasks:

☐ Declares, in line 96, three instances of class Array , namely, arr1, arr2, and arr3 (the first two instances have the same dynamic array size, specified by the constant SIZE1, whereas instance arr3 has a larger size, specified by the constant SIZE2)

☐ Declares, in line 97, the file stream f and opens it (using a stream constructor) to access file ARR1.DAT in binary output mode

☐ Uses the for loops in lines 100 and 104 to assign arbitrary values to the instance arr1 and arr3, respectively

☐ Displays the elements of instance arr1 using the for loop in line 108

☐ Writes the elements of array arr1 to the output file stream f, using the for loop in line 113 to send the writeElem message to instance arr1 and to supply the message with the output file stream f and the loop control variable i

☐ Closes the output file stream by sending the close message to the output file stream f

☐ Opens, in line 118, the file stream f to access the data file ARR1.DAT (this time, the message open specifies a binary input mode)

☐ Reads the elements of instance arr2 (which has not yet been assigned any values) from the input file stream f, using the for loop in line 120 to send the message readElem to instance arr2 and supply the message with the arguments f, the file stream, and i, the loop control variable

☐ Closes the input file stream, in line 122, by sending the close message to the input file stream f

☐ Displays the elements of instance arr2 using the for loop in line 126 (these elements match those of instance arr1)

☐ Displays the elements of instance arr3 by using the for loop in line 132

☐ Writes the entire instance arr3 by sending the message writeArray to instance arr3 (the message writeArray has the filename argument of ARR3.DAT)

☐ Reads the array in file ARR3.DAT into instance arr1, sending the message readArray to instance arr1 and supplying the message with the filename argument of ARR3.DAT

☐ Displays the new elements of instance arr1 using the for loop in line 143

Random Access File Stream I/O

Random access file stream operations also use the stream functions `read` and `write` presented in the last section. The stream library offers a number of stream-seeking functions to enable you to move the stream pointer to any valid location. The function `seekg` is one of such functions.

The *seekg* Function

The prototype for the overloaded function `seekg` is

```
istream& seekg(long pos);
istream& seekg(long pos, seek_dir dir);
```

The parameter *pos* in the first version specifies the absolute byte position in the stream. In the second version, the parameter *pos* specifies a relative offset based on the argument for parameter *dir*. Here are the arguments for the latter parameter:

`ios::beg`	From the beginning of the file
`ios::cur`	From the current position of the file
`ios::end`	From the end of the file

Example:

```
const BLOCK_SIZE = 80;
char buff[BLOCK_SIZE] = "Hello World!";
fstream f("CALC.DAT", ios::in ¦ ios::out ¦ ios::binary);
f.seekg(3 * BLOCK_SIZE); // seek block # 4
f.read((const unsigned char*)buff, BLOCK_SIZE);
cout << buff <<< "\n";
f.close();
```

NEW👉 TERM   A *virtual array* is a disk-based array that stores fixed-size strings on disk.

Let's look at an example that uses random access file stream I/O. Listing 12.3 shows the source code for the IO3.CPP program, and implements a virtual array. The program performs the following tasks:

☐ Uses an internal list of names to create a virtual array object

☐ Displays the elements in the unordered virtual array object

☐ Prompts you to enter a character and press Return

□ Sorts the elements of the virtual array object (this process requires random access I/O)

□ Displays the elements in the sorted virtual array object

 Listing 12.3. Source code for the IO3.CPP program.

```
1: /*
2:    C++ program that demonstrates random-access binary file I/O
3: */
4:
5: #include <iostream.h>
6: #include <fstream.h>
7: #include <stdlib.h>
8: #include <string.h>
9:
10: const unsigned MIN_SIZE = 5;
11: const unsigned STR_SIZE = 31;
12: const double BAD_VALUE = -1.0e+30;
13: enum boolean { false, true };
14:
15: class VmArray
16: {
17:    protected:
18:      fstream f;
19:      unsigned size;
20:      double badIndex;
21:
22:    public:
23:      VmArray(unsigned Size, const char* filename);
24:      ~VmArray()
25:        { f.close(); }
26:      unsigned getSize() const
27:        { return size; }
28:      boolean writeElem(const char* str, unsigned index);
29:      boolean readElem(char* str, unsigned index);
30:      void Combsort();
31: };
32:
33: VmArray::VmArray(unsigned Size, const char* filename)
34: {
35:    char s[STR_SIZE+1];
36:    size = (Size < MIN_SIZE) ? MIN_SIZE : Size;
37:    badIndex = BAD_VALUE;
38:    f.open(filename, ios::in | ios::out | ios::binary);
39:    if (f.good()) {
40:      // fill the file stream with empty strings
41:      strcpy(s, "");;
42:      f.seekg(0);
```

348

```
43:        for (unsigned i = 0; i < size; i++)
44:            f.write((unsigned char*)s, sizeof(s));
45:    }
46: }
47:
48: boolean VmArray::writeElem(const char* str, unsigned index)
49: {
50:    if (index < size) {
51:        f.seekg(index * (STR_SIZE+1));
52:        f.write((unsigned char*)str, (STR_SIZE+1));
53:        return (f.good()) ? true : false;
54:    }
55:    else
56:        return false;
57: }
58:
59: boolean VmArray::readElem(char* str, unsigned index)
60: {
61:    if (index < size) {
62:        f.seekg(index * (STR_SIZE+1));
63:        f.read((unsigned char*)str, (STR_SIZE+1));
64:        return (f.good()) ? true : false;
65:    }
66:    else
67:        return false;
68: }
69:
70: void VmArray::Combsort()
71: {
72:    unsigned i, j, gap = size;
73:    boolean inOrder;
74:    char strI[STR_SIZE+1], strJ[STR_SIZE+1];
75:
76:    do {
77:        gap = (gap * 8) / 11;
78:        if (gap < 1)
79:            gap = 1;
80:        inOrder = true;
81:        for (i = 0, j = gap; i < (size - gap); i++, j++) {
82:            readElem(strI, i);
83:            readElem(strJ, j);
84:            if (strcmp(strI, strJ) > 0) {
85:                inOrder = false;
86:                writeElem(strI, j);
87:                writeElem(strJ, i);
88:            }
89:        }
90:    } while (!(inOrder && gap == 1));
91: }
92:
```

continues

Listing 12.3. continued

```
 93: main()
 94: {
 95:   char* data[] = { "Michigan", "California", "Virginia", "Maine",
 96:                    "New York", "Florida", "Nevada", "Alaska",
 97:                    "Ohio", "Maryland" };
 98:   VmArray arr(10, "arr.dat");
 99:   char str[STR_SIZE+1];
100:   char c;
101:
102:   // assign values to array arr
103:   for (unsigned i = 0; i < arr.getSize(); i++) {
104:     strcpy(str, data[i]);
105:     arr.writeElem(str, i);
106:   }
107:   // display unordered array
108:   cout << "Unsorted arrays is:\n";
109:   for (i = 0; i < arr.getSize(); i++) {
110:     arr.readElem(str, i);
111:     cout << str << "\n";
112:   }
113:   // pause
114:   cout << "\nPress any key and then Return to sort the array...";
115:   cin >> c;
116:   // sort the array
117:   arr.Combsort();
118:   // display sorted array
119:   cout << "Sorted arrays is:\n";
120:   for (i = 0; i < arr.getSize(); i++) {
121:     arr.readElem(str, i);
122:     cout << str << "\n";
123:   }
124:   return 0;
125: }
```

Here is a sample session with the program in Listing 12.3:

```
Unsorted arrays is:
Michigan
California
Virginia
Maine
New York
Florida
Nevada
Alaska
Ohio
Maryland
```

```
Press any key and then Return to sort the array...d
Sorted arrays is:
Alaska
California
Florida
Maine
Maryland
Michigan
Nevada
New York
Ohio
Virginia
```

The program in Listing 12.3 declares the class VmArray. This class models a disk-based dynamic array that stores all its elements in a random access binary file. Notice that the class declares an instance of class fstream, and that there is no pointer to a dynamic array. The class declares a constructor, a destructor, and a number of member functions.

The class constructor has two parameters, namely, Size and filename. The parameter Size specifies the size of the virtual array. The parameter filename names the binary file that stores the elements of a class instance. The constructor opens the stream f using the stream function open and supplies it the argument of parameter filename and the I/O mode expression ios::in ¦ ios::out ¦ ios::binary. This expression specifies that the stream is opened for binary input and output mode (that is, random access mode). If the constructor successfully opens the file stream, it proceeds with filling the file with zeros. The class destructor performs the simple task of closing the file stream f.

The functions writeElem and readElem support the random access of array elements. These functions use the stream function seekg to position the stream pointer at the appropriate array element. The writeElem then calls the stream function write to store an array element (supplied by the parameter str). By contrast, the function readElem calls the stream function read to retrieve an array element (returned by the parameter str). Both functions return Boolean results that indicate the success of the I/O operation.

The VmArray class also declares the Combsort function to sort the elements of the virtual array. This function uses the readElem and writeElem member functions to access and swap the array elements.

The function main performs the following relevant tasks:

☐ Declares the instance arr, of class VmArray (this instance stores 10 strings in the binary file ARR.DAT)

☐ Assigns random values to the elements of instance arr, using the for loop in lines 103 through 106 to assign strings accessed by data[i] to the variable str, then to write the value in str to the instance arr by sending it the message writeElem (the arguments for the message writeElem are the string variable, str, and the loop control variable, i)

☐ Displays the unsorted elements of instance arr using the for loop in line 109 (the statement in line 110 sends the message readElem to the instance arr to obtain an element in the virtual array)

☐ Sorts the array by sending the message Combsort to the instance arr

☐ Displays the sorted elements of instance arr using the for loop in line 120 (the statement in line 121 sends the message readElem to the instance arr to obtain an element in the virtual array)

Summary

Today's lesson gives you a brief introduction to the C++ stream I/O library and discusses the following topics:

☐ Common stream functions include open, close, good, fail, and the operator !. The function open opens a file for stream I/O and supports alternate and multiple I/O modes. The function close shuts down a file stream. The functions good and fail indicate the success or failure, respectively, of a stream I/O operation.

☐ C++ allows you to perform sequential stream I/O for text, using the operators << and >> as well as the stream function getline. The operator << is able to write characters and strings (as well as the other predefined data types). The operator >> is suitable for obtaining characters. The function getline enables your applications to read strings from the keyboard or from a text file.

☐ Sequential stream I/O for binary data uses the stream functions write and read to write and read data from any kind of variables.

☐ Random access stream I/O for binary data uses the seekg function in conjunction with the functions read and write. The seekg function enables you to move the stream pointer to either absolute or relative byte locations in the stream.

Q&A

Q. How can I emulate the random access of lines in a text file?

A. First read the lines in the file as text, obtain the length of the lines (plus the two characters for the end of each line), and store the cumulative length in a special array, call it `lineIndex`. This array stores the byte location where each line starts. The last array element should store the size of the file. To access line number `i`, use the `seek` or `seekg` function to locate the offset value in `lineIndex[i]`. The size of line number `i` is equal to `lineIndex[i+1]` - `lineIndex[i]`.

Q. How do I write a general-purpose routine to copy between an input and an output file stream?

A. You need to use the stream function `gcount()` to obtain the number of bytes actually read in the last unformatted stream input. Here is the function `copyStream`:

```
void copyStream(fstream& fin, fstream& fout,
                unsigned char* buffer, int buffSize)
{
  int n;
  while (fin.read(buffer, buffSize) {
    n = fin.gcount();
    fout.write(buffer, n);
  }
}
```

Workshop

The Workshop provides quiz questions to help you solidify your understanding of the material covered and exercises to provide you with experience in using what you've learned. Try to understand the quiz and exercise answers before continuing on to the next day's lesson. Answers are provided in Appendix B, "Answers."

Quiz

1. True or false? The stream I/O functions `read` and `write` are able to correctly read and write any data type.

2. True or false? The stream I/O functions read and write are able to correctly read and write any data type, as long as the type has no pointer members.

3. True or false? The seek and seekg functions expand the file when you supply them an index that is one byte beyond the current end of file.

4. True or false? The arguments of the functions seek and seekg require no range checking.

Exercise

Create program IO4.CPP by modifying program IO3.CPP. The class VmArray in IO4.CPP should have the function binSearch which conducts a binary search on the members of the sorted array. Add a loop at the end of function main to search in the array arr, using the unordered data of the initializing list. (The members of this list are accessed using the pointer data.)

DAY
13

Programming Windows Using the MFC Library

The Microsoft Foundation Class (MFC) library provides a powerful tool that assists you in developing Windows applications. Without such a library, coding Windows applications becomes a more difficult, frustrating, and increasingly code-intensive process. The MFC library succeeds in combining object-oriented and event-driven programming concepts, and shows how well these two programming disciplines work together. Today's lesson introduces you to the MFC library and some basic information related to Windows, including creating Windows applications using the MFC library. Today you learn about the following:

☐ Popular Windows data types

☐ MFC data-typing conventions

☐ The MFC hierarchy

☐ Windows API functions

☐ Responding to Windows messages

☐ Sending messages

☐ User-defined messages

Although the MFC library provides a good tool for developing Windows applications, you need to know about the underlying Windows API functions.

Popular Windows Data Types

Windows programming comprises a large number of data types. In this section, I focus on the data types that are most relevant for now. Becoming familiar with these data types enables you to better understand the declarations of MFC. The Windows data types include a number of simple ones as well as a group of structures. The simple data types include many that are `typedefs` that declare aliases with more meaningful names. These aliases clarify the declarations of functions and variables. Table 13.1 shows a selection of the most frequently used Windows data types.

Table 13.1. Most frequently used Windows data types.

Data Type	Meaning
char	Signed 8-bit character
int	Signed 16-bit integer
long	Signed 32-bit integer

Data Type	Meaning
short	Signed 16-bit integer
void	Empty value
BOOL	16-bit integer that represents Boolean values
BYTE	Unsigned 8-bit integer
UINT	Unsigned 32-bit integer
DWORD	Unsigned 32-bit integer or segment/offset address
FAR	Data-type attribute used to create
FARPROC	Long pointer to a function
HANDLE	General handle
HDC	Handle to a display context
HWND	Window handler
LONG	Same as the long type
LPSTR	Long pointer to a character string
LPVOID	Long pointer to a void type
PWORD	Pointer to the WORD type
WORD	Unsigned 16-bit integer

In addition to the simple data types shown in Table 13.1, there are many structures that are involved in Windows programming. The POINT and RECT structures are simple yet important. The POINT structure stores the X and Y coordinates of a point and is declared as follows:

```
typedef struct tagPOINT {
    int x;
    int y;
} POINT;
```

The RECT structure defines the coordinates of the upper-left and lower-right corners of a rectangle, and is declared as follows:

```
typedef struct tagRECT {
    int left;
    int top;
```

13

```
        int right;
        int bottom;
} RECT;
```

The left and right members are the X-coordinates for the upper-left and lower-right corners of the rectangle, respectively. The top and bottom fields are the Y-coordinates for the upper-left and lower-right corners of the rectangle, respectively.

The MFC library uses the Hungarian prefix naming convention, shown in Table 13.2. The table also shows examples of variables using this naming convention.

NEW TERM   With the *Hungarian prefix naming convention*, the prefixes hint at the data type associated with a variable, making your code easier to read.

Table 13.2. Hungarian prefix naming convention.

Prefix	Type	Example	Comment
ch	char	chInputChar	8-bit character
b	BOOL	bOk	Boolean value
n	int	nCount	System-dependent integer
w	WORD	wSize	16-bit unsigned integer
l	LONG	lTotalSize	32-bit signed integer
dw	DWORD	dwSumSize	32-bit unsigned integer
p	*	pStr	Pointer
lp	FAR*	lpStr	Far pointer
lpsz	LPSTR	lpszFilename	32-bit pointer to a character string
lpsz	LPCSTR	lpszFilename	32-bit pointer to a constant character string
h	handle	hWnd	Handle to a Windows object
lpfn	callback	lpfnHelp	Far pointer to CALLBACK function

The MFC Hierarchy

The MFC hierarchy includes several subhierarchies that manage different aspects of a Windows application. These subhierarchies include Windows classes, GDI classes, miscellaneous Windows classes, Object Linking and Embedding (OLE) classes, file classes, object I/O classes, exceptions classes, collections classes, and miscellaneous support classes.

The *CObject* Class

The CObject class is the abstract base class for the MFC library, and is the root class for both the MFC library and the descendants that you create. CObject is not a dummy abstract class. Instead, it offers a number of operations that are common to all its descendant classes. These operations include object creation and deletion, support for serialization, diagnostics, and compatibility with collection classes.

The *CMenu* Class

The CMenu class, a descendant of CObject, manages menus. Menu management includes the creation, update, tracking, and removal of a menu resource associated with a window.

The Document Architecture Subhierarchy

The Document Architecture subhierarchy has the class CCmdTarget as its root. This set of classes includes the class CWinApp which is the parent of the custom application classes. Another set of classes in this subhierarchy supports OLE documents.

The Frames Windows Subhierarchy

The Frames Windows subhierarchy has the CFrameWnd class as its root. This group of classes models the basic single-document interface (SDI) window or the more complex multiple-document interface (MDI) windows. The Windows program manager is an example of an MDI-compliant application. The latter windows use the CMDIFrameWnd and CMDIChildWnd to model the frame and child windows in an MDI-compliant application.

13

The Control Bars Subhierarchy

The Control Bars subhierarchy models the tool bar, status bar, dialog bar, and the splitter window. (Windows's File Manager uses the latter control to display the directory tree and the list of files for the currently selected directory.)

The Views Subhierarchy

The Views subhierarchy has the CView class as its root. Views are child windows that can be created inside other windows and provide a special framework for accepting input.

The Dialog Boxes Subhierarchy

The Dialog Boxes subhierarchy includes the general-purpose dialog box class, CDialog, as well as the classes that support the common dialog boxes for selecting files, selecting colors, selecting fonts, printing, and finding and replacing text. The CDialog class models both modal and modeless dialog boxes and is the root of this subhierarchy. Day 20 covers the CDialog class.

The Control Subhierarchy

The Control subhierarchy includes classes which model the static text, command buttons, bitmap buttons, list box, combo boxes, scroll bars, edit controls, and VB (Visual Basic) controls. These visual controls provide an important part of the Windows interface. Days 16 through 19 focus on several of these controls.

The Graphical Drawing Subhierarchy

The CDC class, a descendant of CObject, is the root class for the CDC subhierarchy in the MFC library. The class and its descendants support device-context objects. The CDC class comes with a large number of member functions ready to do business, so to speak. These functions provide tools such as mapping functions, drawing tools functions, and region functions, to name just a few. The CDC class contains member functions that support the functionality offered by the descendants of CDC. Thus, these descendants are basically wrapper classes.

NEW TERM *Regions* are elliptic or polygonal areas within a window that can be supplied with a graphical output.

The Graphical Drawing Objects Subhierarchy

The Graphical Drawing Objects subhierarchy models drawing objects such as pens, brushes, fonts, bitmaps, and palettes. If you plan to write Windows applications that draw graphics objects, you need to work with the classes in this hierarchy.

Other MFC Subhierarchies

The MFC library contains other subhierarchies which I do not cover in this book:

1. The Exceptions subhierarchy offers classes which handle various kinds of run-time errors.

2. The File Services subhierarchy presents classes which deal with files as objects.

3. The Collections subhierarchy contains classes which manage dynamic lists and arrays of objects.

4. The OLE 1.0 Support subhierarchy offers classes to support object linking and embedding.

5. The Run-Time Object Model Support subhierarchy provides information about an object or its base class at run-time.

6. The Simple Value Types subhierarchy models commonly used objects, such as strings, time, rectangles, points, and window sizes.

7. The Structures subhierarchy models information related to the status of a file, printing, memory state, and the creation of a window.

8. The Support Classes subhierarchy provides classes that are involved in transferring data to and from dilaog boxes, and managing the commands generated by the user-interface.

13

MFC Macros

The MFC library also declares a number of macros that support the `CObject` class and all its descendants:

☐ The `RUNTIME_CLASS` macro returns the `CRunTimeClass` structure that matches the named class.

☐ The `DECLARE_DYNAMIC` macro allows access to run-time class data. This macro can be used in each class declaration.

□ The IMPLEMENT_DYNAMIC macro allows access to run-time class data. This macro is used in the class implementation.

□ The DECLARE_SERIAL macro allows serialization and access to run-time class data. This macro can be used in each class declaration.

□ The IMPLEMENT_SERIAL macro allows serialization and access to run-time class data. This macro is used in the class implementation.

The Windows API Functions

If you are familiar with the Windows API functions, you can skip this section. If not, read on. This section is for the reader who is new to programming Windows applications. Windows 3.1 has just over 1,000 API Windows functions, divided into the following three groups:

□ Windows manager interface functions

□ Graphics device interface (GDI) functions

□ System services interface functions

Table 13.3 shows the types of Windows manager interface functions.

NEW☞ TERM *Windows manager interface functions* manage message processing, create a window, move a window, alter a window, and create system output.

Table 13.3. Types of Windows manager interface functions.

API Functions Type	Purpose
Message	Read and process Windows messages in an application's queue.
Window-creation	Create, destroy, alter, and retrieve information about windows.
Display and movement	Show, hide, move, and return information regarding the number and positions of windows on the screen.
Input	Take control of the system devices, disable input from system devices, and specify the special action to be carried out by Windows when an application receives input from the system devices.

API Functions Type	Purpose
Hardware	Alter and query the state of input devices (mouse and keyboard).
Painting	Ready a window for painting and offer practical general graphics functions.
Dialog-box	Create, change, test, and remove dialog boxes and the controls inside the boxes.
Scrolling	Control the scrolling of a window and of the window's scroll bars.
Menu	Create, alter, and remove menus.
Information	Retrieve information about the number and location of windows on a screen.
System	Return information about the system metrics, color, and time.
Clipboard	Perform the exchange of data between Windows applications and the clipboard.
Error	Display system errors and request a response from the user to handle the error.
Caret	Create, remove, display, hide, and change the blink time of the caret.
Cursor	Set, move, show, hide, and restrict the cursor movements.
Hook	Manage system hooks.
Property	Create and retrieve the window's property list.
Rectangle	Set and query the information about rectangles in a window's client area.

NEW☞
TERM *Graphics device interface (GDI) functions* perform device-independent graphics operations for Windows applications.

Graphics device interface (GDI) operations include drawing a wide assortment of lines, text, and bitmapped images on several output devices. Table 13.4 shows the types of GDI functions. The operations of these functions are also implemented in the MFC hierarchy.

13

Table 13.4. Types of graphics device interface (GDI) functions.

API Functions Type	Purpose
Device-context	Create, delete, and restore device contexts that link a Windows application, a device driver, and an output device.
Drawing-tool	Create and remove the drawing tools that GDI utilizes when it generates output on a device.
Color-palette	Provide a device-independent method for accessing colors of a display device.
Drawing-attribute	Influence the output image of a Windows application (which can appear as a brush, line, bitmap, or text).
Mapping	Set and query the GDI mapping mode information.
Coordinate	Convert between custom and screen coordinates, and determine the location of an individual point.
Region	Create, modify, and obtain information about regions.
Clipping	Create, change, and test clipping regions.
Line-output	Create both simple and complex line output using a selected pen drawing tool.
Ellipse and Polygon	Draw ellipses and polygons.
Bitmap	Display bitmaps.
Text	Write text on a device or display surface, obtain text information, change text alignment, and modify text justification.
Fonts	Select, create, delete, and obtain information about fonts.
Metafile	Create, copy, close, remove, retrieve, play, and obtain information about metafiles.

API Functions Type	Purpose
Device-control	Obtain information about a device and alter its initialization.
Printer-control	Obtain the printer's capabilities, and alter its initialization state.
Printer-Escape	Permit an application to access the facilities of a specific device that is not directly available through GDI.
Environment	Set and query the information related to the environment of the output device.

NEW☞
TERM *System services interface functions* access code and data in modules, allocate local and global memory, manage tasks, load program resources, manipulate strings, change the Windows initialization files, offer debugging aid, perform port communication and file I/O, and create sound. Recall that a task is a single Windows application call.

Table 13.5 shows the types of system services interface functions.

Table 13.5. Types of system services interface functions.

API Functions Type	Purpose
Module-management	Set and query information regarding Windows modules.
Memory-management	Manage global and local system memory.
Segment	Allocate, deallocate, lock, and unlock memory segments.
OS interrupt	Permit assembly-language programs to carry out certain DOS and NETBIOS interrupts without directly coding the interrupts.
Task	Change the execution status of a task, retrieve the information related to a task, and obtain the information about the environment within which a task is executing.

continues

13

Table 13.5. continued

API Functions Type	Purpose
Resource-management	Locate and load application resources (limited to cursor, icon, bitmap, string, and font) from a Windows executable file.
String-manipulation	Offer frequently used string manipulation functions, such as string copy, comparison, case conversion, and character test.
Atom-management	Create and manage atoms (unique integer-indices to a string).
Initialization-file	Set and query information from the WIN.INI Windows initialization file or any other private initialization file (usually with an .INI extension).
Communications	Perform serial and parallel communications via the system's ports.
Sound	Create sound and music for the system's sound generator.
Utility macros	Obtain the contents of bytes, words, and long integers. Create unsigned long integers and structures.
File I/O	Create, open, close, read from, and write to files.
Debugging	Assist in catching errors in Windows applications and modules.
Optimization-tool	Manage how the Windows Profiler and Swap software development tools (available in the Microsoft Windows SDK) interact with a Windows application that is being developed.
Application-exec	Allow one Windows application to execute another Windows program.

Invoking Windows API Functions

The value of the MFC hierarchy comes from the fact that it packages most of the Windows API functions using C++ classes. This section presents two Windows API functions as examples of how you can directly call these functions.

The following code fragment includes the Polyline, MessageBeep, and MessageBox API functions. The code's main purpose is to plot a polygon and involves these tasks:

☐ Starts a loop that attempts to draw a polygon

☐ Calls a user-defined routine to obtain a number of points used to create the polygon

☐ Invokes the Boolean function Polyline

☐ If the result of function Polyline is FALSE, calls the API function MessageBeep to sound a beep, then invokes the MessageBox function

The MessageBox function pops up an error message box that asks you whether you want to get a new set of points to plot. The message box shows the Yes and No buttons and the lowercase i icon.

The code for these steps is

```
const MAX_POINTS = 10;
POINT points[MAX_POINTS];
HDC hDC;
int answer = IDNO;
// other declarations
// other statements
do {
    read_points(points); // get the data for the points
    if (!Polyline(hDC, points, MAX_POINTS)) {
        MessageBeep(0); // beep
        // show error message box
        answer = MessageBox(
                    HWindow,                 // window handle
                    "Error! Try again",      // error message
                    "Polygon Plot Error!",   // message box title
                    MB_YESNO |               // message box
                                             // options
                    MB_ICONINFORMATION);

    }
} while (answer == IDYES);
// other statements
```

13

The `Polyline` function is declared as follows:

```
BOOL Polyline(HDC hDC, LPPOINT lpPoints, int nCount)
```

where `hDC` is the handle of the device context. The `lpPoints` is the pointer to a `POINT`-typed array. The `nCount` is the number of points in the array that are used to draw the polygon (there must be at least two).

The `MessageBeep` function is a simple function that is declared as follows:

```
void MessageBeep(WORD wType)
```

The argument value of 0 assigned to the `wType` parameter supplies the only required argument.

The `MessageBox` function is an important API function that enables you to communicate with the end-user of your Windows applications. The declaration of the `MessageBox` function is

```
int FAR PASCAL MessageBox(HWND hWndParent, LPSTR lpText,
                          LPSTR lpCaption, WORD wType)
```

The first parameter is the handle to the parent window. The second and third parameters are the message and caption strings. The last parameter specifies the buttons and the icons that appear in the message box. Table 13.6 shows most of the values for the message box `wType` parameter. In the previous code example, the argument for `wType` is

```
MB_YESNO ¦ MBICONINFORMATION
```

which causes the message box to show the Yes and No buttons and also includes the lowercase i icon.

**Table 13.6. Most of the values
for the message box `wType` parameter.**

Value	Meaning
MB_ABORTRETRYIGNORE	Message box shows three buttons: Abort, Retry, Ignore.
MB_DEFBUTTON1	First button is the default. If no MB_DEFBUTTONx identifier is specified, the message box makes the first button the default.
MB_DEFBUTTON2	Second button is the default.

Value	Meaning
MB_DEFBUTTON3	Third button is the default.
MB_ICONASTERISK	Message box includes an icon with a lower case i in a circle; same as MB_ICONINFORMATION.
MB_ICONEXCLAMATION	Message box includes an exclamation point icon.
MB_ICONHAND	Message box includes a stop sign icon; same as MB_ICONSTOP.
MB_ICONINFORMATION	Message box includes an icon with a lower case i in a circle.
MB_ICONQUESTION	Message box includes a question mark icon.
MB_ICONSTOP	Message box includes a stop sign icon.
MB_OK	Message box contains an OK button.
MB_OKCANCEL	Message box contains the OK and Cancel buttons.
MB_RETRYCANCEL	Message box contains the Retry and Cancel buttons.
MB_YESNO	Message box contains the Yes and No buttons.
MB_YESNOCANCEL	Message box contains the Yes, No, and Cancel buttons.

The MessageBox function returns a value that reflects the user's choice. Table 13.6 shows the identifiers that represent the function's values.

The class CWnd declares the MessageBox member function that is a wrapper for the MessageBox API function. The difference between the two functions is that function CWnd::MessageBox does not have the hWndParent parameter. The wType parameter of function CWnd::MessageBox also uses the values shown in Table 13.6. The result of the function CWnd:MessageBox can also be compared with the values shown in Table 13.7.

13

Table 13.7. Identifiers representing the values returned by the MessageBox function.

Identifier	Meaning
IDABORT	Abort button was pressed.
IDCANCEL	Cancel button was pressed.
IDIGNORE	Ignore button was pressed.
IDNO	No button was pressed.
IDOK	OK button was pressed.
IDRETRY	Retry button was pressed.
IDYES	Yes button was pressed.

The Windows Messages

Windows applications contain various types of objects that interact with each other via messages, in response to events. The Windows metaphor resembles the working office that is made up of employees, managers, departments, and material resources (computers, typewriters, photocopying machines, phones, faxes, and so forth). Each employee (who, for the sake of the discussion, corresponds to a Windows object) has a role to play as defined by his or her job description (which corresponds to a class declaration). The activities of an office are stimulated by events from the outside world, events directed to the outside world, and internal events. To respond to these events, the various employees and departments need to communicate with each other via messages. In a similar manner, the Windows environment and its applications interact with each other and with the outside world (the input and output devices) using messages. These messages can be generated in the following ways:

☐ A user-generated event, such as typing on the keyboard, moving the mouse, and clicking on the mouse button results in user-generated messages.

☐ A Windows application can call Windows functions and result in Windows sending messages back to the application.

☐ A Windows application can send internal messages aimed at specific program components.

☐ The Windows environment can send messages to a Windows application.

☐ Two Windows applications can send dynamic-data exchange (DDE) messages to share data.

Windows 3.1 has these types of message categories:

☐ Windows management messages

☐ Initialization messages

☐ Input messages

☐ System messages

☐ Clipboard messages

☐ System information messages

☐ Control manipulation messages

☐ Control notification messages

☐ Scroll bar notification messages

☐ Nonclient-area messages

☐ MDI messages

Windows management messages are sent by Windows to an application when the state of a window is altered. Table 13.8 shows a selection of Windows management messages.

Table 13.8. A selection of Windows management messages.

Message	Meaning
WM_ACTIVATE	Sent when a window becomes active or inactive
WM_CLOSE	Sent when a window is closed
WM_MOVE	Sent when a window is moved
WM_PAINT	Sent when either Windows or an application requests to repaint part of an application's window
WM_QUIT	Signifies a request to end an application
WM_SIZE	Sent after a window is resized

13

Initialization messages are sent by Windows when an application constructs a menu or a dialog box. Table 13.9 shows the initialization messages.

Table 13.9. Initialization messages.

Message	Meaning
WM_INITDIALOG	Sent right before a dialog box is displayed
WM_INITMENU	Request to initialize a menu
WM_INITMENUPOPUP	Sent right before a pop-up menu is displayed

Input messages are emitted by Windows in response to an input through the mouse, keyboard, scroll bars, or system timer. Table 13.10 shows a selection of input messages.

Table 13.10. A selection of input messages.

Message	Meaning
WM_COMMAND	Sent when you select a menu item
WM_HSCROLL	Sent when you click the horizontal scroll bar with the mouse
WM_KEYDOWN	Sent when a nonsystem key is pressed
WM_KEYUP	Sent when a nonsystem key is released
WM_LBUTTTONDBLCLK	Sent when you double-click on the left mouse button
WM_LBUTTONDOWN	Sent when you press the left mouse button
WM_LBUTTONUP	Sent when you release the left mouse button
WM_MOUSEMOVE	Sent when you move the mouse
WM_RBUTTONDBLCLK	Sent when you double-click the right mouse button
WM_RBUTTONDOWN	Sent when you press the right mouse button
WM_RBUTTONUP	Sent when you release the right mouse button
WM_TIMER	Sent when the timer limit set for a specific timer has elapsed
WM_VSCROLL	Sent when you click the vertical scroll bar with the mouse

System messages are sent by Windows to an application when you access the Windows's Control menu, scroll bars, or size box. Most of the Windows applications do not respond to these messages but rather pass them to the DefWindowProc function for default processing.

Clipboard messages are emitted by Windows to an application when other applications attempt to access a window's clipboard.

System information messages are sent by Windows when a system-level change is made that affects other Windows applications. Among such changes are ones that affect the fonts, color palette, system color, time, and contents of the WIN.INI file.

Control manipulation messages are sent by Windows applications to a control object, such as the push-down button, list box, combo box, and edit control. The control messages result in performing a specific task, and also return a value that indicates the outcome.

Control notification messages notify the parent window of the actions that have occurred within a control attached to that window.

Scroll bar notification messages include the WM_HSCROLL and WM_VSCROLL messages. The scroll bars send these messages to their parent windows when you click the bars.

Nonclient-area messages are sent by Windows to create and update the nonclient area. You are seldom required to override the default responses to these messages in your MFC application.

NEW☞ TERM The *nonclient area* is the area outside the working or client area of a window.

MDI messages are sent by an MDI frame window to a child client window. These messages result in operations such as activating, deactivating, creating, removing, arranging, and restoring client windows.

Responding to Messages

The MFC library uses a special mechanism to determine the response of an application to various messages. This mechanism involves a few macros and a language extension. The extension to C++ allows you to declare (or mark, if you prefer) the message response member functions by placing the keyword afx_msg before the return type of the function. The class that contains at least one message response function must declare the macro DECLARE_MESSAGE_MAP(). This macro initializes the message map that is defined in the implementation part of the program.

13

The following is a typical example of declaring message response functions:

```
class CAppWindow : CFrameWnd {
public:
    CAppWindow();
    // handle painting
    afx_msg void OnPaint();
    // handle resizing a window
    afx_msg void OnSize(UINT nType, int cx, int cy);

protected:
    // handle closing the window
    afx_msg void OnClose();

    DECLARE_MESSAGE_MAP();
};
```

The OnPaint, OnSize, and OnClose member functions respond to the predefined messages WM_PAINT, WM_SIZE, and WM_CLOSE, respectively. The class implementation includes the definitions of these member functions as well as the special message map macros START_MESSAGE_MAP() and END_MESSAGE_MAP(). These special macros contain other macros that map the individual member functions and the messages they respond to. The message map macro for the previous class is

```
BEGIN_MESSAGE_MAP(CAppWindow, CFrameWnd)
    ON_WM_PAINT()
    ON_WM_SIZE()
    ON_WM_CLOSE()
END_MESSAGE_MAP()
```

Notice that the BEGIN_MESSAGE_MAP contains two arguments: the application window class and its parent MFC class. Stating the class involved is required, and becomes more important when you have multiple message response maps for multiple classes. Notice the three ON_WM_xxxx macros. The first macro, ON_WM_PAINT(), specifies that the default member function, OnPaint, responds to the message WM_PAINT. In fact, the MFC library has a large set of predefined message mapping macros that relate various class member functions with WM_xxxx messages. The ON_WM_SIZE() and ON_WM_CLOSE() macros are two additional examples. The ON_WM_SIZE() specifies that the OnSize member function responds to the WM_SIZE message. Likewise, the ON_WM_CLOSE() macro ties the OnClose member function with the WM_CLOSE message.

Note: The previous message map declaration has the message macros listed in the same order of declaring the corresponding member functions. This is required by the Microsoft C++ compiler.

Sending Messages

Windows allows your application to send messages to itself, other applications, or to Windows itself. The Windows API functions SendMessage, PostMessage, and SendDlgItemMessage provide important tools for sending messages. The SendMessage function sends a message to a window and requires that window to handle the emitted message. The SendMessage is declared as follows:

```
DWORD SendMessage(HWND hWnd, WORD wMsg, WORD wParam, LONG lParam)
```

The parameter hWnd is the handle of the window receiving the message. The parameter wMsg specifies the message sent. The parameters wParam and lParam designate additional optional information. You can use the SendMessage function to communicate with other windows and controls.

The PostMessage is similar to SendMessage, except it lacks the sense of urgency—the message is posted in the window's message queue. The message is handled later by the targeted window when it is convenient for that window. The declaration of the Boolean PostMessage function is

```
BOOL PostMessage(HWND hWnd, UINT wMsg,
                 WPARAM wParam, LPARAM lParam)
```

The parameter hWnd is the handle of the window receiving the message. The parameter wMsg specifies the message sent. The parameters wParam and lParam designate additional optional information.

The SendDlgItemMessage function sends a message to a particular item in a dialog box. The declaration of the SendDlgItemMessage function is posted next:

```
LRESULT SendDlgItemMessage(HWND hwndDlg, int idDlgItem,
                           UINT uMsg, WPARAM wParam, LPARAM lParam)
```

The parameter hwndDlg is the handle of the dialog box that contains the targeted control. The parameter idDlgItem indicates the integer identifier of the dialog box item that receives the message. The parameter wMsg specifies the message sent. The parameters wParam and lParam designate additional optional information.

13

The class CWnd declares the SendMessage, PostMessage, and SendDlgItemMessage member functions to send messages to the host window. These member functions are declared as follows:

```
LRESULT SendMessage(UINT message, WPARAM wParam = 0,
                    LPARAM lParam = 0);

BOOL PostMessage(UINT message, WPARAM wParam = 0,
                 LPARAM lParam = 0);
```

```
LRESULT SendDlgItemMessage(int nID, UINT message,
                           WPARAM wParam = 0, LPARAM lParam = 0);
```

User-Defined Messages

MFC allows you to define your own messages. The constant WM_USER is associated with the number of the first message (see Table 13.11). You need to declare constants that represent the offset values for your custom messages. For example, you can use the #define directive to define your own messages:

```
#define WM_USER1 (WM_USER + 0)
#define WM_USER2 (WM_USER + 1)
#define WM_USER3 (WM_USER + 2)
```

Table 13.11 shows the range of Windows messages for Windows 3.1.

Table 13.11. Ranges of Windows messages.

Constant	Value	Message Range	Meaning
		0x0000-0x03FF	Windows messages
WM_USER	0x0400	0x0400-0x7FFF	Programmer-defined window messages
		0x8000-0xBFFF	Reserved for use by Windows
		0xC000-0xFFFF	String messages for use by applications

The user-defined messages specify the commands emitted by menu items or keyboard input. The message mapping macro ON_COMMAND is used to associate the user-defined command with its response member function. The general form for the ON_COMMAND macro is

```
ON_COMMAND(command, command_function)
```

To illustrate how to employ user-defined messages, consider the following messages CM_CALC and CM_STORE declared in the header file USRMSG.H:

```
#define CM_CALC (WM_USER + 0)
#define CM_STORE (WM_USER + 1)
```

The declaration of the window class that responds to these messages is

```
#include <afxwin.h>
#include "usrmsg.h"

class CAppWindow : CFrameWnd
{
public:
    CAppWindow();

    // handle painting
    afx_msg void OnPaint();

    // handle calculation command
    afx_msg void CMCalc();

    // handle store command
    afx_msg void CMStore();

protected:

    // handle closing the window
    afx_msg void OnClose();

    DECLARE_MESSAGE_MAP();
};
```

The corresponding message map is

```
BEGIN_MESSAGE_MAP(CAppWindow, CFrameWnd)
    ON_WM_PAINT()
    ON_COMMAND(CM_CALC, CMCalc)
    ON_COMMAND(CM_STORE, CMStore)
    ON_WM_CLOSE()
END_MESSAGE_MAP()
```

The first ON_COMMAND macro specifies that the CMCalc member function responds to the CM_CALC command message. The second ON_COMMAND macro indicates that the CMStore member function responds to the CM_STORE command message. Again, notice the order of the message macros—they match the order of the declarations of message response member functions.

The MFC library has other message mapping macros that will be presented as the need arises.

13

Summary

Today's lesson presents basic information regarding the Microsoft Foundation Class (MFC) class hierarchy as well as Windows-related information. You learn about the following topics:

☐ Popular Windows data types include simple data types (such as BYTE, WORD, and LONG) and data structures (such as RECT and POINT).

☐ The MFC hierarchy presents the various classes that make up the MFC library.

☐ There are three general categories of Windows API functions: the window manager, GDI, and system services.

☐ Windows API functions that can be invoked include MessageBox, MessageBeep, and Polyline.

☐ There are several categories of Windows messages that you can respond to in your own MFC applications. This is a process that involves declaring descendant MFC classes that contain one or more message response member functions. The latter functions provide the required response.

☐ You can use a few Windows API functions to send messages.

☐ You can define your own messages, send these messages, and then respond to them.

Day 14 presents the basics of building an MFC application and attaching menus to such applications.

Q&A

Q. Does the MFC library consist of simple wrappers for the various Windows API functions?

A. Version 2.0 of the MFC library comes with more sophisticated classes than version 1.0. The new classes have more functionality built into them.

Q. Is the Hungarian notation required by the Visual C++ compiler?

A. No, it is merely a naming convention to make your C++ code clearer. Adapting any naming notation takes time, so try to ease into it.

Q. What is the relationship between Windows messages and C++ messages to an instance?

A. Both use the object metaphor.

Workshop

The Workshop provides quiz questions to help you solidify your understanding of the material covered and exercises to provide you with experience in using what you've learned. Try to understand the quiz and exercise answers before continuing on to the next day's lesson. Answers are provided in Appendix B, "Answers."

Quiz

1. What MB_xxxx constants are needed to create a message box with the Yes, No, and Cancel buttons, and the question mark icon?

2. What MB_xxxx constants are needed to create a message box with the OK button and the exclamation point icon?

3. What value does the MessageBox function return if you click the Yes button in a message dialog box that contains the Yes and No buttons?

4. What value does the MessageBox function return if you click the Cancel button in a message dialog box that contains the Yes, No, and Cancel buttons?

Exercise

Familiarize yourself with the MFC hierarchy using the Quick Reference card included in your Visual C++ package.

13

DAY
14

Creating Basic
MFC Applications

Day 13 provides you with a lot of background information regarding the Microsoft Foundation Class library, Windows API functions, and Windows messages. In today's lesson, you start building simple MFC applications. You learn about the following topics:

☐ Creating a minimal MFC application

☐ Extending the operations of the application's window

☐ Adding a menu to an MFC application

☐ Responding to menu selections

☐ Alternating between different menus

☐ Creating multiple instances of an MFC application

☐ Closing a window

Today's lesson also shows you the power and functionality provided by the MFC library. This functionality includes default characteristics and responses. Building your own MFC application involves extending the basic characteristics and functionality of the MFC.

Creating a Minimal MFC Application

Each MFC application that you create starts with declaring a descendant of class CWinApp. This is a step needed by even the most trivial MFC applications. Extending the other MFC library classes relies on the features of your applications. The entry point for a Windows application is the WinMain function (which is similar to the function main() in a non-Windows C or C++ program). Fortunately, the MFC library supplies a default WinMain function that is suitable for most Windows applications. You can define your own version of WinMain to supply your application a higher level of customization. The applications in this book use the predefined WinMain function. To execute an MFC program, you declare an application instance, as shown in the following general form:

```
_CWindowApp_ _WindowApp_;
```

The _CWindowApp_ class represents the application class that you derive from CWinApp. The _WindowApp_ variable represents the application instance. This instance is created using the class constructor or the inherited class constructor.

When an MFC application starts running, it invokes the member functions in the following order:

1. Invokes the virtual InitApplication member function to initialize the first instances of the MFC application. The code for the member function CWinApp::InitApplication is

```
BOOL CWinApp::InitApplication()
{ return TRUE; }
```

   This member function performs no task—it's simply a dummy function that you override to carry out a special initialization to the application.

2. Calls the virtual InitInstance member function to initialize every other instance of the MFC application. The CWinApp::InitInstance member function is also a dummy function like InitApplication. Every time you create an instance of an MFC application, these two functions are invoked.

3. Invokes the window class constructor to initialize the main window of each instance.

Note: If you plan to carry out additional steps in initializing the instances of an application, you need to declare your own InitInstance in the following general form:

```
BOOL_CWinApp_::InitInstance()
{
    // put statements here
    return boolean_value;
}
```

An Application Class

The general syntax for an application class is

```
class _CWindowApp_ : public CWinApp
{
public:
  // public data members declarations
protected:
// protected data members

// optional constructor
_CWindowApp_(const char* pszAppName,    // application name
             _other_params_)            // additional parameter
```

14

383

```
// other constructors
// class destructors
// other member functions

// overridable data members
virtual BOOL InitInstance();
virtual BOOL InitApplication();  // optional

// other protected member functions

private:
  // private data members
  // other private member functions
};
```

This general template shows that your application classes should declare an InitInstance member function. The declaration of the member function InitApplication is required only to fine-tune the operations of these inherited functions in your MFC application. This fact also applies to declaring other constructor parameters, data members (public, protected, and private), and member functions (public, protected, and private).

Example:

See the program in Listing 14.1.

Let's look at an example. Listing 14.1 shows the source code for the program MINWINAP.CPP. This program is a minimal Windows application. You can move, resize, minimize, and maximize the program's window using either a mouse or the menu selections available in the system menu. To close the window, use the Close selection in the system menu. Other than these operations, the program does nothing! For example, if you click on the mouse, nothing visual happens.

Note: To create any Windows application you need a .DEF file. Listing 14.2 shows the contents of the MINWINAP.DEF file. This file has information that includes the application's name, title, modes of operations, and heap size. All the .DEF files in this book are very similar to MINWINAP.DEF but differ in the application name and title.

To create the MINWINAP.EXE program, create the MINWINAP directory as a child of the \MSVC\VC21DAY directory. Store the files MINWINAP.CPP and MINWINAP.DEF in the \MSVC\VC21DAY\MINWINAP directory. Also use the latter directory to store the MINWINAP.MAK file which is created by the Visual C++ Workbench.

Listing 14.1. Source code in the MINWINAP.CPP file.

```
 1: #include <afxwin.h>
 2:
 3: // Define a window class derived from CFrameWnd
 4: class CAppWindow : public CFrameWnd
 5: {
 6: public:
 7:     CAppWindow()
 8:     { Create(NULL, "Minimal MFC Application",
 9:                   WS_OVERLAPPEDWINDOW, rectDefault); }
10: };
11:
12: // Define an application class derived from CWinApp
13: class CWindowApp : public CWinApp
14: {
15: public:
16:   virtual BOOL InitInstance();
17: };
18:
19: // Construct the CWindowApp's m_pMainWnd data member
20: BOOL CWindowApp::InitInstance()
21: {
22:   m_pMainWnd = new CAppWindow();
23:   m_pMainWnd->ShowWindow(m_nCmdShow);
24:   m_pMainWnd->UpdateWindow();
25:   return TRUE;
26: }
27:
28: // application's constructor initializes and runs the app
29: CWindowApp WindowApp;
```

Listing 14.2. Contents of the MINWINAP.DEF file.

```
1: NAME          MinWinAp
2: DESCRIPTION   'Minimal MFC Windows Application'
3: EXETYPE       WINDOWS
4: CODE          PRELOAD MOVEABLE DISCARDABLE
5: DATA          PRELOAD MOVEABLE MULTIPLE
6: HEAPSIZE      1024
```

Figure 14.1 shows a sample session with program MINWINAP.EXE.

Figure 14.1. A sample session with program MINWINAP.EXE.

Listing 14.1 shows the source code for a minimal MFC application that uses the template that I presented earlier in today's lesson. The program contains the declaration of an application class CWindowApp (a descendant of CWinApp), and a window class CAppWindow (a descendant of CWnd).

Line 1 contains the directive to include the header file AFXWIN.H. This file ensures that all the required Windows and MFC declarations are available to the compiler.

Line 13 contains the declaration of class CWindowApp which contains only the member function InitInstance. This function creates an instance of CAppWindow, which is accessed by the inherited pointer-typed data member m_pMainWnd.

Line 4 contains the declaration of the window class CAppWindow. This class only declares a class constructor to create the class instances using the CFrameWnd::Create member function. The member function CFrameWnd::Create has the following declaration:

```
BOOL Create(
    const char FAR* lpClassName,      // Windows class
                                      // registration name
    const char FAR* lpWindowName,     // title
    DWORD dwStyle = WS_OVERLAPPEDWINDOW, // style attribute
    const RECT& rect = rectDefault,   // location and size
```

```
const CWnd* pParentWnd = NULL,      // parent window
const char FAR* lpMenuName = NULL); // ID of menu
```

The `lpClassName` is the Windows registration class name. This non-OOP name specifies the window category name. The `lpWindowName` parameter specifies the caption or title of the window. The `dwStyle` parameter specifies the style of the created window and has the default value of `WS_OVERLAPPEDWINDOW`. The `rect` parameter defines the location and size of the window and has the default value for `rectDefault`. The `pParentWnd` parameter is the pointer to the parent window and has the default value of `NULL`. The `lpMenuName` parameter defines the name of the menu resource attached to the window. Some menu resources have a numeric ID associated with a constant. To use this kind of menu resource, invoke the macro `MAKEINTRESOURCE` and supply it the numeric ID of the sought menu. This macro translates the numeric ID into a string.

NEW☞
TERM *Resources* are components that are created and compiled outside a Windows application.

The statement in line 29 declares an application instance. This declaration results in executing the MFC program.

Extending the Window Operations

After building a minimal MFC application, let's write a new application that adds a few operations to the application. The next program performs the following main tasks:

☐ Responds to the left button mouse click (when the mouse is inside the application window) by displaying a message box with an OK button

☐ Responds to the right button mouse click by displaying a message box that asks you whether or not you want to close the window

☐ Supports a menu which includes nested menu selections (the menu items, except for Exit, are dummy ones)

Most Windows applications include menus. The MINWINAP.EXE application has only the System menu. This section shows you how to use a resource file to build a menu that can be attached to the application's window. The example loads a menu from a menu resource while creating a window. The next section illustrates more elaborate menu manipulation.

Applications use resources by loading them. Resources only define the appearance of visual objects. They are not responsible for the behavior of these objects. That is the task of the Windows or MFC application. The advantage of using resources is that you can modify them without recompiling the application. For example, you can change the wording of menu items and alter the location of a button. A more dramatic example is the ability to change the language used in the various menus, dialog boxes, and other controls. This enables a software developer to maintain and update a single version of the application easily, while using different versions of the resources for each language. This approach was applied by Apple Computer in making the Apple Macintosh computer work in different languages, including Arabic.

 Note: Appendix A describes the syntax for the menu and dialog box resource scripts. The first section discusses the menu resources.

Listing 14.3 presents the contents of the menu resource file MENU1.RC. The file contains a single menu definition with the OPTIONS name ID. The menu contains three main menu items: File, Edit, and Help. The File and Edit menu items are pop-up menus. The Edit menu options contain the Delete menu item which is also a pop-up menu. The menu items include horizontal separator bars. All the menu names use the ampersand (&) to define the corresponding hot-keys.

The various MENUITEM statements contain CM_*xxxx* constants that define the result of selecting the menu items. The CM_*xxxx* constants are defined in the MENU1.H header file, shown in Listing 14.4. Listing 14.5 shows the source code for the MENU1.CPP program.

Create the directory MENU2 as a subdirectory of \MSVC\VC21DAY and store all the project's files in the new directory. The project's .MAK file should contain the files MENU1.CPP, MENU1.RC, and MENU1.DEF. The latter file resembles file MINWINAP.DEF in Listing 14.2.

 Listing 14.3. Script for the MENU1.RC resource file.

```
1: #include <windows.h>
2: #include <afxres.h>
3: #include "menu1.h"
4:
5: OPTIONS MENU LOADONCALL MOVEABLE PURE DISCARDABLE
```

```
 6: BEGIN
 7:   POPUP "&File"
 8:   BEGIN
 9:     MENUITEM "&New", CM_FILENEW
10:     MENUITEM "&Open", CM_FILEOPEN
11:     MENUITEM "&Save", CM_FILESAVE
12:     MENUITEM "Save&As", CM_FILESAVEAS
13:     MENUITEM SEPARATOR
14:     MENUITEM "E&xit", CM_EXIT
15:   END
16:   POPUP "&Edit"
17:   BEGIN
18:     MENUITEM "&Undo", CM_EDITUNDO
19:     MENUITEM SEPARATOR
20:     MENUITEM "C&ut", CM_EDITCUT
21:     MENUITEM "C&opy", CM_EDITCOPY
22:     MENUITEM "&Paste", CM_EDITPASTE
23:     POPUP "&Delete"
24:     BEGIN
25:        MENUITEM "&Line", CM_EDITDELETE
26:        MENUITEM "&Block", CM_EDITDELETE_BLOCK
27:     END
28:     MENUITEM "&Clear", CM_EDITCLEAR
29:   END
30:   MENUITEM "&Help", CM_HELP
31: END
```

Type **Listing 14.4. Source code for the MENU1.H header file.**

```
 1: #define CM_FILENEW              (WM_USER + 100)
 2: #define CM_FILEOPEN             (WM_USER + 101)
 3: #define CM_FILESAVE             (WM_USER + 102)
 4: #define CM_FILESAVEAS           (WM_USER + 103)
 5: #define CM_EXIT                 (WM_USER + 104)
 6: #define CM_EDITUNDO             (WM_USER + 105)
 7: #define CM_EDITCUT              (WM_USER + 106)
 8: #define CM_EDITCOPY             (WM_USER + 107)
 9: #define CM_EDITPASTE            (WM_USER + 108)
10: #define CM_EDITDELETE           (WM_USER + 109)
11: #define CM_EDITDELETE_BLOCK     (WM_USER + 110)
12: #define CM_EDITCLEAR            (WM_USER + 111)
13: #define CM_HELP                 (WM_USER + 112)
```

14

Type **Listing 14.5. Source code for the MENU1.CPP program.**

```
 1: #include <afxwin.h>
 2: #include "menu1.h"
 3:
 4: // Define a window class derived from CFrameWnd
 5: class CAppWindow : public CFrameWnd
 6: {
 7: public:
 8:   CAppWindow()
 9:   { Create(NULL, "A Menu-Driven MFC Application",
10:           WS_OVERLAPPEDWINDOW, rectDefault, NULL, "OPTIONS"); }
11:
12: protected:
13:   // handle the left mouse button click
14:   afx_msg void OnLButtonDown(UINT nFlags, CPoint point);
15:   // handle the right mouse button click
16:   afx_msg void OnRButtonDown(UINT nFlags, CPoint point);
17:   // handle the Exit menu option
18:   afx_msg void OnExit();
19:
20:   // message map macro
21:   DECLARE_MESSAGE_MAP()
22: };
23:
24: // Define an application class derived from CWinApp
25: class CWindowApp : public CWinApp
26: {
27: public:
28:   virtual BOOL InitInstance();
29: };
30:
31: void CAppWindow::OnLButtonDown(UINT nFlags, CPoint point)
32: {
33:   MessageBox("You clicked the left button!",
34:             "Mouse Click Event!", MB_OK);
35: }
36:
37: void CAppWindow::OnRButtonDown(UINT nFlags, CPoint point)
38: {
39:   MessageBeep(0); // beep
40:   // prompt user if he or she want to close the application
41:   if (MessageBox("Want to close this application", "Query",
42:                 MB_YESNO | MB_ICONQUESTION) == IDYES)
43:       SendMessage(WM_CLOSE);
44: }
45:
46: void CAppWindow::OnExit()
47: { SendMessage(WM_CLOSE); }
48:
```

```
49: BEGIN_MESSAGE_MAP(CAppWindow, CFrameWnd)
50:     ON_WM_LBUTTONDOWN()
51:     ON_WM_RBUTTONDOWN()
52:     ON_COMMAND(CM_EXIT, OnExit)
53: END_MESSAGE_MAP()
54:
55: // Construct the CWindowApp's m_pMainWnd data member
56: BOOL CWindowApp::InitInstance()
57: {
58:   m_pMainWnd = new CAppWindow();
59:   m_pMainWnd->ShowWindow(m_nCmdShow);
60:   m_pMainWnd->UpdateWindow();
61:   return TRUE;
62: }
63:
64: // application's constructor initializes and runs the app
65: CWindowApp WindowApp;
```

Figure 14.2 shows a sample session with program MENU1.EXE.

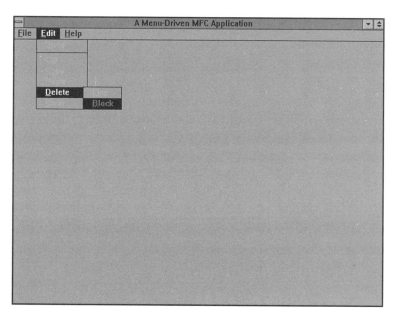

Figure 14.2. A sample session with program MENU1.EXE.

14

The program in Listing 14.5 declares a descendant of CFrameWnd to implement the desired options. Line 5 contains the declaration of class CAppWindow, a descendant of CFrameWnd. This descendant class declares a constructor, three message response member functions, and the DECLARE_MESSAGE_MAP macro. The CAppWindow constructor works in a manner similar to that in program MINWINAP.CPP. Notice that the call to the function Create statement in lines 9 and 10 has a list of arguments that ends with the string OPTIONS. This string specifies the name of the menu resource to load. The menu resource name matches the one in line 5 in Listing 14.3. The member functions OnLButtonDown and OnRButtonDown respond to the Windows messages WM_LBUTTONDOWN and WM_RBUTTONDOWN, respectively. This response is also echoed in the BEGIN_MESSAGE_MAP macro which specifies the messages handled by the various member functions. The CAppWindow class also declares the member function OnExit to respond to the Exit menu selection.

Lines 31 through 35 define the member function OnLButtonDown. This function merely calls the inherited CWnd::MessageBox member function to display the string You clicked the left button! in a message box with the caption Mouse Click Event!. The box has the OK button that you click to resume program execution.

Lines 46 and 47 define the member function OnExit. This function responds to the CM_EXIT command generated by the Exit menu selection. This command is associated with the Windows message command WM_COMMAND.

Lines 37 through 44 define the member function OnRButtonDown. The function first invokes the MessageBeep Windows API function to sound a beep. The function then calls the CWnd::MessageBox function to display a box with the caption Query, the message Want to close this application, Yes and No buttons, and a question mark icon. The if statement in line 41 compares the result of function MessageBox with the predefined constant IDYES. When the two values match, the function calls the CWnd::SendMessage member function to close the window using the WM_CLOSE message.

Lines 49 through 53 define the macros BEGIN_MESSAGE_MAP and END_MESSAGE_MAP. These macros contain the message-mapping macros ON_WM_LBUTTONDOWN, ON_WM_RBUTTONDOWN, and ON_COMMAND. The first two macros have no arguments and therefore they resort to the default mapping. Consequently, the OnLButtonDown and OnRButtonDown member functions respond to the WM_LBUTTONDOWN and WM_RBUTTONDOWN messages, respectively. The ON_COMMAND macro traps the CM_EXIT menu command and invokes the member function OnExit to handle it.

Note: Microsoft has promoted Visual C++ and its Workbench by empha-
sizing the AppWizard, ClassWizard, and App Studio tools, which make it
very easy to develop Windows applications and create resources. These
wizard tools are great for automating repetitive work involved in creating
MFC-based Windows applications. They build nontrivial Windows
applications by generating several kinds of source files. However, if you
are a novice, you need to learn the basic components of an MFC application before using AppWizard and ClassWizard. Once you learn to program MFC-based Windows manually, you can then use the AppWizard
because you can distinguish between primary and secondary code.

Responding to Menu Selections

The last program demonstrates how to build a nested menu and loads it in an
application. However, selecting the menu items (except for Exit) produces no action.
This section basically answers the question, "How does an application respond to a
menu selection, and can that response load a different menu?"

Let's look at the contents of resource file MENU2.RC, shown in Listing 14.6. The
resource file defines two menus, tagged LONGMENU and SHORTMENU. As the names
suggest, the first menu is the longer version of the second one. These menus differ from
the ones in MENU1.RC in that they are not as nested and use the INACTIVE and GRAYED
options. Notice that these two options do not appear with every menu item—they are
assigned to the menu items which I include but keep inactive. As a result, the names
of the menu items appear in a gray color and cannot be selected. From the C++ coding
aspect, there are no corresponding message response member functions. By contrast,
the menu items that do not have the INACTIVE and GRAYED options can be selected and
will generate a response, albeit a simple one. The CM_*xxxx* constants used by the menu
resource are all defined in the MENU2.H header file, shown in Listing 14.7.

The menu items in Listing 14.6 contain two interesting members. The Short &Menus
item in menu LONGMENU results in the CM_SHORTMENU command that selects the short
menu. The SHORTMENU menu has a complementary menu item, &Long Menu, that results
in the CM_LONGMENU command which selects the long menu.

Create the directory MENU2 as a subdirectory of \MSVC\VC21DAY and store all
the project's files in the new directory. The project's .MAK file should contain the files
MENU2.CPP, MENU2.RC, and MENU2.DEF. The latter file resembles file

14

MINWINAP.DEF in Listing 14.2. When you run the application, use the Long Menu and Short Menu selections to toggle between the two forms of menus. In addition, select the Help item to get the one-line help message box. Select the Edit Cut, Edit Copy, and Edit Paste items to view the response. Notice the inactive menu items when you navigate through the various menus. The program in Listing 14.8 includes the header file MENU2.H. This inclusion enables the program to use the user-defined CM_xxxx constants in the message response member functions. The source code declares the application class CWindowApp and the window class CAppWindow. The second class has the task of responding to the various Windows messages. The CAppWindow class declares a constructor, destructor, and a series of message response member functions. The class constructor creates a window and then creates a CMenu instance. The instance is accessed by the pAppMenu pointer which is a data member of the CAppWindow class. The constructor then loads the LONGMENU menu resource, associates the menu object with the window, and invokes the DrawMenuBar member function. Consequently, the application's window starts up with the long menu.

Type **Listing 14.6. Resource script in file MENU2.RC.**

```
 1: #include <windows.h>
 2: #include <afxres.h>
 3: #include "menu2.h"
 4:
 5: LONGMENU MENU LOADONCALL MOVEABLE PURE DISCARDABLE
 6: BEGIN
 7:   POPUP "&File"
 8:   BEGIN
 9:     MENUITEM "&New", CM_FILENEW, INACTIVE, GRAYED
10:     MENUITEM "&Open", CM_FILEOPEN, INACTIVE, GRAYED
11:     MENUITEM "&Save", CM_FILESAVE, INACTIVE, GRAYED
12:     MENUITEM "Save&As", CM_FILESAVEAS, INACTIVE, GRAYED
13:     MENUITEM SEPARATOR
14:     MENUITEM "Short &Menus", CM_SHORTMENU
15:     MENUITEM SEPARATOR
16:     MENUITEM "E&xit", CM_EXIT
17:   END
18:   POPUP "&Edit"
19:   BEGIN
20:     MENUITEM "&Undo", CM_EDITUNDO, INACTIVE, GRAYED
21:     MENUITEM SEPARATOR
22:     MENUITEM "C&ut", CM_EDITCUT
23:     MENUITEM "C&opy", CM_EDITCOPY
24:     MENUITEM "&Paste", CM_EDITPASTE
```

```
25:    MENUITEM "&Delete", CM_EDITDELETE, INACTIVE, GRAYED
26:    MENUITEM "&Clear", CM_EDITCLEAR, INACTIVE, GRAYED
27:  END
28:  MENUITEM "&Help", CM_HELP
29: END
30:
31: SHORTMENU MENU LOADONCALL MOVEABLE PURE DISCARDABLE
32: BEGIN
33:  POPUP "&File"
34:  BEGIN
35:    MENUITEM "&Open", CM_FILEOPEN, INACTIVE, GRAYED
36:    MENUITEM "Save&As", CM_FILESAVEAS, INACTIVE, GRAYED
37:    MENUITEM SEPARATOR
38:    MENUITEM "&Long Menus", CM_LONGMENU
39:    MENUITEM SEPARATOR
40:    MENUITEM "E&xit", CM_EXIT
41:  END
42:  POPUP "&Edit"
43:  BEGIN
44:    MENUITEM "C&ut", CM_EDITCUT
45:    MENUITEM "C&opy", CM_EDITCOPY
46:    MENUITEM "&Paste", CM_EDITPASTE
47:  END
48:  MENUITEM "&Help", CM_HELP
49: END
```

Type **Listing 14.7. Contents of the MENU2.H header file.**

```
 1: #define CM_FILENEW             (WM_USER + 100)
 2: #define CM_FILEOPEN            (WM_USER + 101)
 3: #define CM_FILESAVE            (WM_USER + 102)
 4: #define CM_FILESAVEAS          (WM_USER + 103)
 5: #define CM_EXIT                (WM_USER + 104)
 6: #define CM_EDITUNDO            (WM_USER + 105)
 7: #define CM_EDITCUT             (WM_USER + 106)
 8: #define CM_EDITCOPY            (WM_USER + 107)
 9: #define CM_EDITPASTE           (WM_USER + 108)
10: #define CM_EDITDELETE          (WM_USER + 109)
11: #define CM_EDITDELETE_BLOCK    (WM_USER + 110)
12: #define CM_EDITCLEAR           (WM_USER + 111)
13: #define CM_HELP                (WM_USER + 112)
14: #define CM_SHORTMENU           (WM_USER + 113)
15: #define CM_LONGMENU            (WM_USER + 114)
```

14

Listing 14.8. Source code in the file MENU2.CPP.

```
1: #include <afxwin.h>
2: #include "menu2.h"
3:
4: // Define a window class derived from CFrameWnd
5: class CAppWindow : public CFrameWnd
6: {
7: public:
8:     CMenu* pAppMenu;
9:     CAppWindow();
10:     ~CAppWindow() { if (pAppMenu) delete pAppMenu; }
11: protected:
12:     // handle the left mouse button click
13:     afx_msg void OnLButtonDown(UINT nFlags, CPoint point);
14:     // handle the right mouse button click
15:     afx_msg void OnRButtonDown(UINT nFlags, CPoint point);
16:     // load the long menu
17:     afx_msg void OnLongMenu();
18:     // load the short menu
19:     afx_msg void OnShortMenu();
20:     // exit the application
21:     afx_msg void OnExit();
22:     // get on-line help
23:     afx_msg void OnHelp();
24:     // handle the Cut menu option
25:     afx_msg void OnEditCut();
26:     // handle the Copy menu option
27:     afx_msg void OnEditCopy();
28:     // handle the Paste menu option
29:     afx_msg void OnEditPaste();
30: private:
31:     // display a message "Feature not implemented"
32:     void notImplemented();
33:     // prompt user to quit the application
34:     void promptToQuit();
35:     // Assign new menu
36:     void assignMenu(const char FAR* lpMenuName);
37:     // message map macro
38:     DECLARE_MESSAGE_MAP()
39: };
40:
41: // Define an application class derived from CWinApp
42: class CWindowApp : public CWinApp
43: {
44: public:
45:   virtual BOOL InitInstance();
46: };
47:
48: CAppWindow::CAppWindow()
```

```
49: {
50:    Create(NULL, "Multi-Menu Application",
51:             WS_OVERLAPPEDWINDOW, rectDefault);
52:    pAppMenu = new CMenu;
53:    pAppMenu->LoadMenu("LONGMENU");
54:    SetMenu(pAppMenu);
55:    DrawMenuBar();
56: }
57:
58: void CAppWindow::OnLButtonDown(UINT nFlags, CPoint point)
59: {
60:    MessageBox("You clicked the left button!",
61:             "Mouse Click Event!", MB_OK);
62: }
63:
64: void CAppWindow::OnRButtonDown(UINT nFlags, CPoint point)
65: { promptToQuit(); }
66:
67: void CAppWindow::OnLongMenu()
68: { assignMenu("LONGMENU"); }
69:
70: void CAppWindow::OnShortMenu()
71: { assignMenu("SHORTMENU"); }
72:
73: void CAppWindow::OnExit()
74: { SendMessage(WM_CLOSE); }
75:
76: void CAppWindow::OnHelp()
77: {
78:    MessageBox("This is a sample one line help",
79:      "Help", MB_OK | MB_ICONINFORMATION);
80: }
81:
82: void CAppWindow::OnEditCut()
83: { notImplemented(); }
84:
85: void CAppWindow::OnEditCopy()
86: { notImplemented(); }
87:
88: void CAppWindow::OnEditPaste()
89: { notImplemented(); }
90:
91: void CAppWindow::notImplemented()
92: {
93:    MessageBox("This feature is not implemented",
94:             "Information", MB_OK);
95: }
96: void CAppWindow::promptToQuit()
97: {
98:    MessageBeep(0); // beep
```

14

continues

Listing 14.8. continued

```
 99:     // prompt user if he or she want to close the application
100:     if (MessageBox("Want to close this application", "Query",
101:                    MB_YESNO | MB_ICONQUESTION) == IDYES)
102:        SendMessage(WM_CLOSE);
103: }
104:
105: void CAppWindow::assignMenu(const char FAR* lpMenuName)
106: {
107:    SetMenu(NULL);
108:    pAppMenu->DestroyMenu();
109:    pAppMenu->LoadMenu(lpMenuName);
110:    SetMenu(pAppMenu);
111:    DrawMenuBar();
112: }
113:
114: BEGIN_MESSAGE_MAP(CAppWindow, CFrameWnd)
115:     ON_WM_LBUTTONDOWN()
116:     ON_WM_RBUTTONDOWN()
117:     ON_COMMAND(CM_LONGMENU, OnLongMenu)
118:     ON_COMMAND(CM_SHORTMENU, OnShortMenu)
119:     ON_COMMAND(CM_EXIT, OnExit)
120:     ON_COMMAND(CM_HELP, OnHelp)
121:     ON_COMMAND(CM_EDITCUT, OnEditCut)
122:     ON_COMMAND(CM_EDITCOPY, OnEditCopy)
123:     ON_COMMAND(CM_EDITPASTE, OnEditPaste)
124: END_MESSAGE_MAP()
125:
126: // Construct the CWindowApp's m_pMainWnd data member
127: BOOL CWindowApp::InitInstance()
128: {
129:   m_pMainWnd = new CAppWindow();
130:   m_pMainWnd->ShowWindow(m_nCmdShow);
131:   m_pMainWnd->UpdateWindow();
132:   return TRUE;
133: }
134:
135: // application's constructor initializes and runs the app
136: CWindowApp WindowApp;
```

Figure 14.3 shows a sample session with program MENU2.EXE.

Figure 14.3. A sample session with program MENU2.EXE.

 The CAppWindow class declares three private functions, notImplemented, promptToQuit, and assignMenu. The first function displays a message box that contains the message This feature is not implemented. In fact, this is the common response to most menu items. The promptToQuit function prompts you to close the application using a message box with Yes and No buttons. The assignMenu member function deletes the current menu and loads a new one. The program uses this function to alternate between the short and long menus.

Now let's look at the message response member functions of CAppWindow. The first two functions are the same as those in the previous applications—they respond to mouse clicks on the window. The new version of function OnRButtonDown merely calls the promptToQuit function.

The member function OnLongMenu responds to the user-defined CM_LONGMENU command. The message map macro ON_COMMAND(CM_LONGMENU, OnLongMenu) indicates that the OnLongMenu function responds to the CM_LONGMENU command message. The OnLongMenu calls the assignMenu member function with the "LONGMENU" argument to load the long menu. The OnShortMenu member function is coded similarly and responds to the CM_SHORTMENU command to load the short menu.

14

The OnExit member function provides a new response to the Exit menu selection (which generates the CM_EXIT command). The function sends the Windows message WM_CLOSE using the inherited function SendMessage.

The OnHelp member function responds to the user-defined CM_HELP command by providing a one-line help message box. The message box appears with an OK button and an information icon (an i enclosed in a circle).

The member functions OnEditCut, OnEditCopy, and OnEditPaste all invoke the private member function notImplemented. This is the common (and symbolic) response that I provide for the CM_EDITCUT, CM_EDITCOPY, and CM_EDITPASTE commands.

The message loop macros include several ON_COMMAND macros that associate the various CM_xxxx command messages with their corresponding message response member functions.

Creating Multiple Instances

One of the powerful aspects of Windows is the ability to run multiple instances of the same application. This feature is backed by a smart scheme that saves on memory and other system resources by pooling the common code and data segments. Thus, you can load, for example, three instances of a scientific calculator and work with them independently. This section looks at creating multiple instances of an MFC application. To make the example application more interesting, the first instance has a different window title and menu from the other instances. All instances respond the same way to the left and right mouse button clicks. Listing 14.9 shows the resource script file MENU3.RC which defines the menu resources for the various program instances. The file MENU3.RC defines two menu resources, a MAINMENU and a SECONDMENU. These menu resources are similar to the menus LONGMENU and SHORTMENU, found in MENU2.RC, except they do not have the toggle menu items. Listing 14.10 contains the header file MENU3.H. Listing 14.11 shows the source code for the MENU3.CPP MFC application file.

Create the directory MENU3 as a subdirectory of \MSVC\VC21DAY and store all the project's files in the new directory. The project's .MAK file should contain the files MENU3.CPP, MENU3.RC, and MENU3.DEF. The latter file resembles file MINWINAP.DEF in Listing 14.2. Run multiple instances of the program MENU3.EXE. The first instance has the window title of Main Window, whereas the other instances have the title of A Secondary Window. In addition, the first instance has more selections, in the File menu option, than the remaining instances.

Listing 14.9. Resource script in file MENU3.RC.

```
 1: #include <windows.h>
 2: #include <afxres.h>
 3: #include "menu3.h"
 4:
 5: MAINMENU MENU LOADONCALL MOVEABLE PURE DISCARDABLE
 6: BEGIN
 7:   POPUP "&File"
 8:   BEGIN
 9:     MENUITEM "&New", CM_FILENEW, INACTIVE, GRAYED
10:     MENUITEM "&Open", CM_FILEOPEN, INACTIVE, GRAYED
11:     MENUITEM "&Save", CM_FILESAVE, INACTIVE, GRAYED
12:     MENUITEM "Save&As", CM_FILESAVEAS, INACTIVE, GRAYED
13:     MENUITEM SEPARATOR
14:     MENUITEM "E&xit", CM_EXIT
15:   END
16:   POPUP "&Edit"
17:   BEGIN
18:     MENUITEM "&Undo", CM_EDITUNDO, INACTIVE, GRAYED
19:     MENUITEM SEPARATOR
20:     MENUITEM "C&ut", CM_EDITCUT
21:     MENUITEM "C&opy", CM_EDITCOPY
22:     MENUITEM "&Paste", CM_EDITPASTE
23:     MENUITEM "&Delete", CM_EDITDELETE, INACTIVE, GRAYED
24:     MENUITEM "&Clear", CM_EDITCLEAR, INACTIVE, GRAYED
25:   END
26:   MENUITEM "&Help", CM_HELP
27: END
28:
29: SECONDMENU MENU LOADONCALL MOVEABLE PURE DISCARDABLE
30: BEGIN
31:   POPUP "&File"
32:   BEGIN
33:     MENUITEM "&Open", CM_FILEOPEN, INACTIVE, GRAYED
34:     MENUITEM "Save&As", CM_FILESAVEAS, INACTIVE, GRAYED
35:     MENUITEM SEPARATOR
36:     MENUITEM "E&xit", CM_EXIT
37:   END
38:   POPUP "&Edit"
39:   BEGIN
40:     MENUITEM "C&ut", CM_EDITCUT
41:     MENUITEM "C&opy", CM_EDITCOPY
42:     MENUITEM "&Paste", CM_EDITPASTE
43:   END
44:   MENUITEM "&Help", CM_HELP
45: END
```

14

Listing 14.10. Source code for the MENU3.H header file.

```
 1: #define CM_FILENEW            (WM_USER + 100)
 2: #define CM_FILEOPEN           (WM_USER + 101)
 3: #define CM_FILESAVE           (WM_USER + 102)
 4: #define CM_FILESAVEAS         (WM_USER + 103)
 5: #define CM_EXIT               (WM_USER + 104)
 6: #define CM_EDITUNDO           (WM_USER + 105)
 7: #define CM_EDITCUT            (WM_USER + 106)
 8: #define CM_EDITCOPY           (WM_USER + 107)
 9: #define CM_EDITPASTE          (WM_USER + 108)
10: #define CM_EDITDELETE         (WM_USER + 109)
11: #define CM_EDITDELETE_BLOCK   (WM_USER + 110)
12: #define CM_EDITCLEAR          (WM_USER + 111)
13: #define CM_HELP               (WM_USER + 112)
14: #define CM_SHORTMENU          (WM_USER + 113)
15: #define CM_LONGMENU           (WM_USER + 114)
```

Listing 14.11. Source code for the file MENU3.CPP.

```
 1: #include <afxwin.h>
 2: #include "menu3.h"
 3:
 4: // Define a window class derived from CFrameWnd
 5: class CAppWindow : public CFrameWnd
 6: {
 7: public:
 8:     CAppWindow(BOOL IsMainWindow);
 9:
10: protected:
11:     // handle the left mouse button click
12:     afx_msg void OnLButtonDown(UINT nFlags, CPoint point);
13:     // handle the right mouse button click
14:     afx_msg void OnRButtonDown(UINT nFlags, CPoint point);
15:     // exit the application
16:     afx_msg void OnExit();
17:     // get on-line help
18:     afx_msg void OnHelp();
19:     // handle the Cut menu option
20:     afx_msg void OnEditCut();
21:     // handle the Copy menu option
22:     afx_msg void OnEditCopy();
23:     // handle the Paste menu option
24:     afx_msg void OnEditPaste();
25:
26: private:
```

```
27:     // display a message "Feature not implemented"
28:     void notImplemented();
29:     // prompt user to quit the application
30:     void promptToQuit();
31:     // message map macro
32:     DECLARE_MESSAGE_MAP()
33: };
34:
35: // Define an application class derived from CWinApp
36: class CWindowApp : public CWinApp
37: {
38: public:
39:   BOOL IsFirst;
40:   virtual BOOL InitInstance();
41:   virtual BOOL InitApplication();
42: };
43:
44: CAppWindow::CAppWindow(BOOL IsMainWindow)
45: {
46:   if (IsMainWindow)
47:     Create(NULL, "Main Window",
48:            WS_OVERLAPPEDWINDOW, rectDefault, NULL, "MAINMENU");
49:   else
50:     Create(NULL, "A Secondary Window",
51:            WS_OVERLAPPEDWINDOW, rectDefault, NULL, "SECONDMENU");
52: }
53:
54: void CAppWindow::OnLButtonDown(UINT nFlags, CPoint point)
55: {
56:   MessageBox("You clicked the left button!",
57:              "Mouse Click Event!", MB_OK);
58: }
59:
60: void CAppWindow::OnRButtonDown(UINT nFlags, CPoint point)
61: { promptToQuit(); }
62:
63: void CAppWindow::OnExit()
64: { SendMessage(WM_CLOSE); }
65:
66: void CAppWindow::OnHelp()
67: {
68:   MessageBox(
69:     "This a sample one line help",
70:     "Help", MB_OK | MB_ICONINFORMATION);
71: }
72:
73: void CAppWindow::OnEditCut()
74: { notImplemented(); }
75:
76: void CAppWindow::OnEditCopy()
```

14

continues

Listing 14.11. continued

```
77: { notImplemented(); }
78:
79: void CAppWindow::OnEditPaste()
80: { notImplemented(); }
81:
82: void CAppWindow::notImplemented()
83: {
84:   MessageBox("This feature is not implemented",
85:             "Information", MB_OK);
86: }
87:
88: void CAppWindow::promptToQuit()
89: {
90:   MessageBeep(0); // beep
91:
92:   // prompt user if he or she want to close the application
93:   if (MessageBox("Want to close this application", "Query",
94:                  MB_YESNO | MB_ICONQUESTION) == IDYES)
95:       SendMessage(WM_CLOSE);
96: }
97:
98: BEGIN_MESSAGE_MAP(CAppWindow, CFrameWnd)
99:     ON_WM_LBUTTONDOWN()
100:     ON_WM_RBUTTONDOWN()
101:     ON_COMMAND(CM_EXIT, OnExit)
102:     ON_COMMAND(CM_HELP, OnHelp)
103:     ON_COMMAND(CM_EDITCUT, OnEditCut)
104:     ON_COMMAND(CM_EDITCOPY, OnEditCopy)
105:     ON_COMMAND(CM_EDITPASTE, OnEditPaste)
106: END_MESSAGE_MAP()
107:
108: // Construct the CWindowApp's m_pMainWnd data member
109: BOOL CWindowApp::InitInstance()
110: {
111:   m_pMainWnd = new CAppWindow(IsFirst);
112:   IsFirst = FALSE;
113:   m_pMainWnd->ShowWindow(m_nCmdShow);
114:   m_pMainWnd->UpdateWindow();
115:   return TRUE;
116: }
117:
118: // Initialize the application
119: BOOL CWindowApp::InitApplication()
120: {
121:   IsFirst = TRUE;
122:   return IsFirst;
123: }
124:
125: // application's constructor initializes and runs the app
126: CWindowApp WindowApp;
```

Figure 14.4 shows a sample session with multiple instances of the MENU3.EXE application.

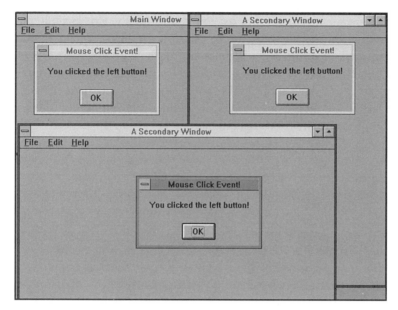

Figure 14.4. A sample session with the application MENU3.EXE.

How does the program in Listing 14.3 create a different first instance? In this case, the first instance has a different window title and menu from all other instances. To implement this feature, the program declares a Boolean data member, IsFirst, in the application class CWindowApp. The class also declares the InitApplication and InitInstance member functions. The CWindowApp::InitApplication member function, defined in lines 119 through 123, assigns TRUE to the IsFirst data member. This assignment allows the application to determine if the instance created is the first one. The CWindowApp::InitInstance member function, defined in lines 109 through 116, creates a window instance using the argument IsFirst (which is initialized with TRUE). The function then assigns FALSE to member IsFirst. This value is not altered by the subsequent instances.

The program declares the CAppWindow constructor to have the Boolean parameter IsMainWindow. If the argument of parameter IsMainWindow is TRUE, the constructor creates a window with the "Main Window" title and the MAINMENU menu resource. Otherwise, the constructor creates a window with the "A Secondary Window" title and the SECONDMENU menu resource.

14

Closing a Window

You may recall that programs MENU1.EXE through MENU3.EXE allow you to exit the application and close its window by simply selecting the Exit menu item. These applications use the default response to perform a quick program termination. Although this type of abrupt exit is harmless for the previous programs, it is a feature that, if maintained, drowns software developers with hate letters from application users! Therefore, Windows applications should close their windows only after making sure that the user does not lose data. In addition, the application should make any other appropriate shutdown operations.

Note: Both Windows and MFC offer a sophisticated sequence for carefully closing down an application to include all the child windows. In fact, the process resembles a query of all related objects that can veto closing the target window in response to the WM_CLOSE message. By declaring a member function OnClose in your custom window classes, you provide your application with an additional say (or vote, if you prefer) in the matter of closing down a window. The OnClose member function that you declare focuses on the special closing criteria of your own application. In most cases, you should make sure that the user does not exit the application if there is new and altered data that was not saved. Other criteria might include deallocating special dynamic data.

Let's look at a program which streamlines closing the application's window. Listing 14.12 shows the source code for the program MENU4.CPP. I derived this program from MENU1.CPP. Consequently, the MENU4.H and MENU4.RC files are identical to the MENU1.H and MENU1.RC files, and are therefore not listed.

Create the directory MENU4 as a subdirectory of \MSVC\VC21DAY and store all the project's files in the new directory. The project's .MAK file should contain the files MENU4.CPP, MENU4.RC, and MENU3.DEF. The latter file resembles file MINWINAP.DEF in Listing 14.2. Run the program and choose the Exit menu selection. The program responds by displaying a message box, with Yes and No buttons, that asks you if you wish to close the application. You obtain the same message box by clicking the right mouse button. Thus, program MENU4.EXE supports consolidated management for exiting an application.

Listing 14.12. Source code for the MENU4.CPP program file.

```
 1: #include <afxwin.h>
 2: #include "menu4.h"
 3:
 4: // Define a window class derived from CFrameWnd
 5: class CAppWindow : public CFrameWnd
 6: {
 7: public:
 8:   CAppWindow()
 9:     { Create(NULL, "A Menu-Driven MFC Application",
10:       WS_OVERLAPPEDWINDOW, rectDefault, NULL, "OPTIONS"); }
11:
12: protected:
13:   // handle the left mouse button click
14:   afx_msg void OnLButtonDown(UINT nFlags, CPoint point);
15:   // handle the right mouse button click
16:   afx_msg void OnRButtonDown(UINT nFlags, CPoint point);
17:   // handle the Exit menu option
18:   afx_msg void OnExit();
19:   // handle closing the window
20:   afx_msg void OnClose();
21:
22:   // message map macro
23:   DECLARE_MESSAGE_MAP()
24: };
25:
26: // Define an application class derived from CWinApp
27: class CWindowApp : public CWinApp
28: {
29: public:
30:   virtual BOOL InitInstance();
31: };
32:
33: void CAppWindow::OnLButtonDown(UINT nFlags, CPoint point)
34: {
35:   MessageBox("You clicked the left button!",
36:              "Mouse Click Event!", MB_OK);
37: }
38:
39: void CAppWindow::OnRButtonDown(UINT nFlags, CPoint point)
40: { SendMessage(WM_CLOSE); }
41:
42: void CAppWindow::OnExit()
43: { SendMessage(WM_CLOSE); }
44:
45: void CAppWindow::OnClose()
46: {
47:   if (MessageBox("Want to close this application",
```

continues

Listing 14.12. continued

```
48:                        "Query", MB_YESNO | MB_ICONQUESTION) == IDYES)
49:       DestroyWindow();
50: }
51:
52: BEGIN_MESSAGE_MAP(CAppWindow, CFrameWnd)
53:       ON_WM_LBUTTONDOWN()
54:       ON_WM_RBUTTONDOWN()
55:       ON_COMMAND(CM_EXIT, OnExit)
56:       ON_WM_CLOSE()
57: END_MESSAGE_MAP()
58:
59: // Construct the CWindowApp's m_pMainWnd data member
60: BOOL CWindowApp::InitInstance()
61: {
62:   m_pMainWnd = new CAppWindow();
63:   m_pMainWnd->ShowWindow(m_nCmdShow);
64:   m_pMainWnd->UpdateWindow();
65:   return TRUE;
66: }
67:
68: // application's constructor initializes and runs the app
69: CWindowApp WindowApp;
```

Figure 14.5 shows a sample session with the program MENU4.EXE.

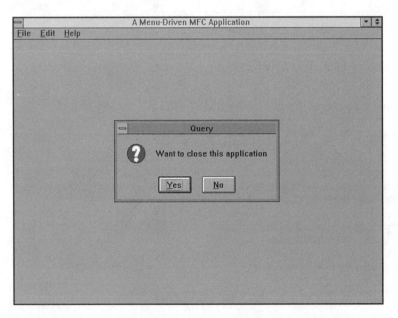

Figure 14.5. A sample session with the program MENU4.EXE.

The most important difference between programs MENU4.CPP and MENU1.CPP is the declaration of the member function `OnClose` in the custom window class `CAppWindow`:

```
void CAppWindow::OnClose()
{
  if (MessageBox("Want to close this application",
               "Query", MB_YESNO | MB_ICONQUESTION) == IDYES)
    DestroyWindow();
}
```

The function `OnClose` contains an `if` statement which calls the inherited member function `MessageBox`. The message box displays its querying message along with Yes and No buttons and an information icon. The `OnClose` function compares the result of `MessageBox` with the constant `IDYES`. If the condition is true, the function calls the inherited member function `DestroyWindow`.

Declaring the `OnClose` member function also allows you to rewrite the statement for the `OnRButtonDown` member function. The new version, in lines 41 and 42, has a simple code—one that relies on the `OnClose` function. The `OnRButtonDown` simply sends a `WM_CLOSE` message using the `SendMessage` member function and lets the `OnClose` member function worry about handling that message.

Summary

Today's lesson looks at the basics of creating MFC applications. You learn about the following topics:

☐ You can create a minimal MFC application that offers the predefined operations and default responses.

☐ Extending the window operations handles mouse clicks that result in displaying simple message boxes.

☐ A menu with nested menu structures can be added to illustrate how to use the resource script files to build sophisticated menus.

☐ There are ways to respond to menu selections that include changing menu structures at run-time.

☐ You can create multiple instances of an MFC application and give the first instance a different window title and menu structure.

☐ The `OnClose` member function confirms closing a window.

14

Today's lesson begins to give you a feel of how MFC models the components of its applications after the employees of a company. The simple interaction provided by each Day's programs only scratches the surface of the complex world of Windows and MFC. Tomorrow's lesson focuses more on the window classes and presents applications that place text in the windows.

Q&A

Q. What happens if the `Create` member function attempts to load a nonexisting menu resource?

A. The run-time system loads the application whose window may not appear. In addition, the offending application may cause a Windows run-time error.

Q. Why are the message-handling member function declarations protected?

A. The declarations prohibit the function `CWindowApp::InitInstance` from directly invoking the message-handling function through the pointer `m_pMainWnd`.

Q. What are the predefined message response maps?

A. The `BEGIN_MESSAGE_MAP` macro may include `ON_WM_XXXX` macros that automatically invoke `OnXxxx` member functions to handle the `WM_XXXX` messages. For example, the `ON_WM_CLOSE` macro maps the `OnClose` function to handle message `WM_CLOSE`.

Q. Must the message-mapping macro show the map entries in the same order of declaring the corresponding member functions in the window class?

A. No. Such an order is optional.

Workshop

The Workshop provides quiz questions to help you solidify your understanding of the material covered and exercises to provide you with experience in using what you've learned. Try to understand the quiz and exercise answers before continuing on to the next day's lesson. Answers are provided in Appendix B, "Answers."

Quiz

1. True or false? The `ON_WM_CREATE` message map entry associates the function `OnCreate` with the `WM_CREATE` Windows message.

2. True or false? The `ON_WM_ACTIVATE` message map entry associates the function `Onactivate` with the `WM_CREATE` Windows message.

3. True or false? The `ON_COMMAND(CM_CLEAR, OnClear)` message map entry associates the function `OnClear` with the `CM_CLEAR` command Windows message.

4. True or false? In program MENU4.CPP, if I replace line 40 with

   ```
   { SendMessage(WM_COMMAND, CM_EXIT); }
   ```

   I do not alter the program's interaction.

Exercise

Use App Studio, AppWizard, and ClassWizard to create a program that is similar to MENU1.CPP. Follow the instructions in the Microsoft manuals to use these wizard tools. Notice the difference between the number, size, and contents of the files generated by the wizard tools and the ones in today's lesson.

14

Week 2 in Review

As you end the second week of learning about programming with Visual C++, let's look at an enhanced version of the number-guessing game. Listing R2.1 shows the source code for the GAME2.CPP program. Although this version interacts with you the same way GAME1.CPP does, it uses a class and an enumerated type.

Type   **Listing R2.1. Source code for program GAME2.CPP.**

```
1: #include <stdlib.h>
2: #include <iostream.h>
3: #include <time.h>
4:
5: enum boolean { false, true };
6:
7: // declare a global random number generating function
8: int random(int maxVal)
9: { return rand() % maxVal; }
10:
11: class game
12: {
13:   protected:
14:     int n;
15:     int m;
16:     int MaxIter;
17:     int iter;
18:     boolean ok;
19:     void prompt();
20:     void examineInput();
21:
22:   public:
23:     game();
```

continues

Listing R2.1. continued

```
24:     void play();
25: };
26:
27: game::game()
28: {
29:   MaxIter = 11;
30:   iter = 0;
31:   ok = true;
32:
33:   // reseed random-number generator
34:   srand((unsigned)time(NULL));
35:   n = random(1001);
36:   m = -1;
37: }
38:
39: void game::prompt()
40: {
41:   cout << "Enter a number between 0 and 1000 : ";
42:   cin >> m;
43:   ok = (m < 0) ? false : true;
44: }
45:
46: void game::examineInput()
47: {
48:   // is the user's guess higher?
49:   if (m > n)
50:     cout << "Enter a lower guess\n\n";
51:   else if (m < n)
52:     cout << "Enter a higher guess\n\n";
53:   else
54:     cout << "You guessed it! Congratulations.";
55: }
56:
57: void game::play()
58: {
59:   // loop to obtain the other guesses
60:   while (m != n && iter < MaxIter && ok) {
61:     prompt();
62:     iter++;
63:     examineInput();
64:   }
65:   // did the user guess the secret number
66:   if (iter >= MaxIter || ok == 0)
67:     cout << "The secret number is " << n << "\n";
68: }
69:
70: main()
71: {
72:   game g;
```

```
73:
74:    g.play();
75:    return 0;
76: }
```

Here is a sample session with the program in Listing R2.1:

```
Enter a number between 0 and 1000 : 500
Enter a lower guess

Enter a number between 0 and 1000 : 250
Enter a higher guess

Enter a number between 0 and 1000 : -1
Enter a higher guess

The secret number is 324
```

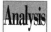

The program in Listing R2.1 declares the enumerated type boolean to model Boolean values. The program also declares the class game which models the number-guessing game. The class has a number of data members, including the Boolean variable ok. In addition, the class declares the protected member functions prompt and examineInput, and the public constructor and member function play.

The constructor initializes the data members and reseeds the random-number generator. The member function prompt, defined in lines 39 through 44, prompts you for input, obtains your input, and assigns a true/false value to the variable ok, based on your input.

The function examineInput, defined in lines 46 through 55, compares your guess (stored in the data member m) with the secret number (stored in the data member n) and displays the appropriate message.

The member function play, defined in lines 57 through 68, contains the while loop which plays the game. The loop statements invoke the member functions prompt and examineInput, and also increment the data member iter. In addition, the function contains the if statement which displays the secret number if you fail to guess it or if you quit the game.

The function main declares the instance g of class game and sends the message play to that instance.

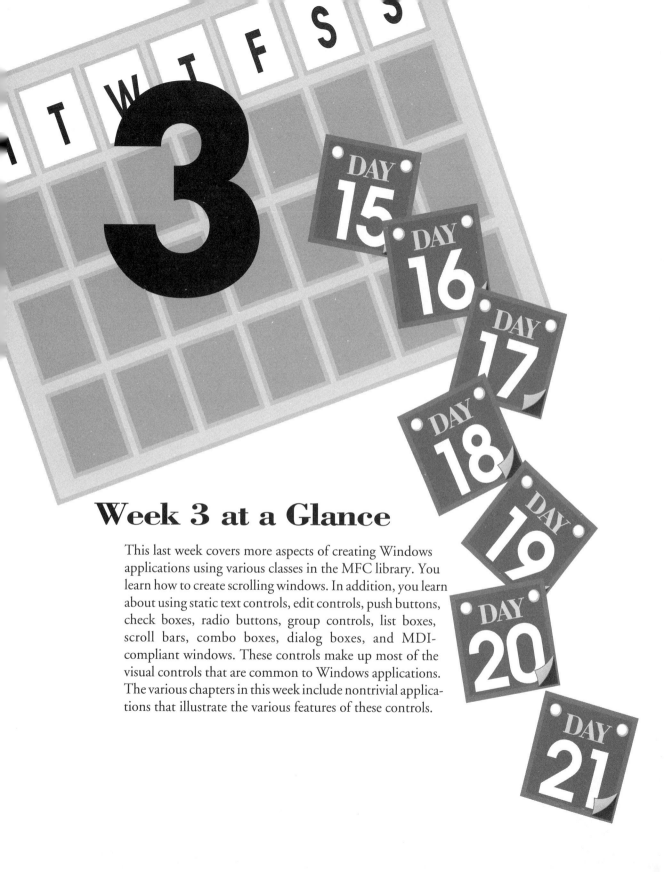

Week 3 at a Glance

This last week covers more aspects of creating Windows applications using various classes in the MFC library. You learn how to create scrolling windows. In addition, you learn about using static text controls, edit controls, push buttons, check boxes, radio buttons, group controls, list boxes, scroll bars, combo boxes, dialog boxes, and MDI-compliant windows. These controls make up most of the visual controls that are common to Windows applications. The various chapters in this week include nontrivial applications that illustrate the various features of these controls.

DAY
15

Basic Windows

The most relevant aspect of the Windows environment, as the name suggests, is the use of windows.

NEW☞ TERM Typically, a *window* is a visible part of the screen that contains specific information.

Windows are the placeholders of information. The application is responsible for maintaining that information when you resize, move, or use existing scroll bars. In today's lesson, you learn about the following:

☐ Creating read-only text windows

☐ Scrolling through text using scroll bars

☐ Changing the scroll bar metrics (units, line size, page size, and ranges)

☐ Optimizing the `OnPaint` member function

Creating a Read-Only Text Window

In Day 14, I present a number of menu-driven MFC applications. However, these programs do not display any information inside their windows. In this section I present an MFC application which displays read-only text in its windows. The basic notion of the application is similar to that of the read-only on-line help windows.

The purpose of the program is to demonstrate how to display text and maintain that text after one or more of the following has occurred:

☐ Resizing the window

☐ Minimizing and then normalizing or maximizing the window

☐ Moving a modal dialog box over the text area

The main tools to implement the application's features are the member functions `CDC::TextOut` and `CWnd::OnPaint`. The function `TextOut` draws a character string on the specified display. The text appears in the currently selected font and at the specified window coordinates.

The *OutText* Function

The declaration for the overloaded member function `OutText` is

```
BOOL TextOut(int X, int Y, char FAR* lpString, int nCount);
BOOL TextOut(int X, int Y, CString& str);
```

The X and Y parameters identify the window location where the first character appears. The lpString parameter points to the string to be displayed in the window. The nCount parameter indicates the leading number of characters of lpString to display. The argument for the last parameter is usually the size of the displayed string argument. In the second version of function TextOut, the str parameter is a reference to a CString instance. The function returns a nonzero value when successful and zero when it fails.

Examples:

```
char s[81] = "Hello";
CString cs = "Bon Jour!";
TextOut(10, 20, s, strlen(s));
TextOut(20, 10, cs);
```

Note: The MFC library offers the class CString which models string objects. Although the class CString is particular to Visual C++, I encourage you to read about the class in the MFC library reference book which is included in the Visual C++ package.

As expected, the function TextOut displays text once. This means that altering the viewing area of the window or moving another window over the displayed text erases that text. What is needed is a mechanism that updates the display of text in the window. Enter the member function CWnd::OnPaint! This function enables you to display and maintain the contents of a window (both text and graphics). The versatility of the function Paint comes from the fact that it responds to a WM_PAINT message when the UpdateWindow function is called. This update feature includes the initial creation of the window—after all, it is resized from nothing. Consequently, the versatility of OnPaint includes setting the initial display as well as maintaining it.

Note: You need to declare an OnPaint member function in your window application class. The code you place inside your version of the OnPaint function determines what information appears, remains, and disappears.

In the case of this MFC application, the same information is displayed from start to finish. The general form of the `CWnd::OnPaint` member function is

```
void _CAppWindow_::OnPaint()
{
  CPaintDC dc(this);
  // other declarations

  // statements using the TextOut member function
  // e.g.
  //        dc.TextOut(x, y, s, strlen(s));
}
```

The local variable `dc` declares an instance of the `CPaintDC` and is initialized with the argument `this` to point to the application window. This declaration is sufficient to set up the device-context object. The `OnPaint` function can then use `dc.TextOut` function calls as needed. Interestingly, if you come across a C-coded Windows application that uses the `TextOut` API function, you note that a similar text output requires initializating the device-context object and then promptly releasing it once it has finished its task. These steps are automatically performed by the CDC class in an MFC application.

Let's now look at the code for the MFC application. Listing 15.1 shows the WINDOW1.H header file with its single declaration of `CM_EXIT`. Listing 15.2 contains the script for the resource file WINDOW1.RC. This resource file defines a menu with a single menu item, Exit, to exit the application. Listing 15.3 shows the source code for the WINDOW1.CPP program.

Create the directory WINDOW1 as a subdirectory of \MSVC\VC21DAY and store all the project's files in the new directory. The project's .MAK file should contain the files WINDOW1.CPP, WINDOW1.RC, and WINDOW1.DEF. The latter file resembles file MINWINAP.DEF in Day 14, Listing 14.2.

Compile and run the application. Notice that the lines of text appear when the window is created. Alter the size of the window by resizing it, minimizing it, and then restoring it back to normal. The lines of text are always visible (or at least a portion of them) as long as the upper-left portion of the screen is not obscured by another window. You can also click the left mouse button to display a message box. Drag that message box over the text lines and release the mouse. Then, drag the message box away from the text location. What do you see? The text lines reappear—`OnPaint` is constantly at work.

Listing 15.1. Source code for the WINDOW1.H header file.

```
1:    1: #define CM_EXIT (WM_USER + 100)
```

15

 Listing 15.2. Script for the WINDOW1.RC resource file.

```
1: #include <windows.h>
2: #include <afxres.h>
3: #include "window1.h"
4:
5: EXITMENU MENU LOADONCALL MOVEABLE PURE DISCARDABLE
6: BEGIN
7:     MENUITEM "E&xit", CM_EXIT
8: END
```

 Listing 15.3. Source code for the WINDOW1.CPP program file.

```
1: #include <afxwin.h>
2: #include <stdio.h>
3: #include <string.h>
4: #include "window1.h"
5:
6: // Define a window class derived from CFrameWnd
7: class CAppWindow : public CFrameWnd
8: {
9: public:
10:    CAppWindow()
11:    { Create(NULL, "A Simple Read-Only Text Window",
12:            WS_OVERLAPPEDWINDOW, rectDefault, NULL, "EXITMENU"); }
13:
14: protected:
15:    // handle the left mouse button click
16:    afx_msg void OnLButtonDown(UINT nFlags, CPoint point);
17:    // handle the Exit menu option
18:    afx_msg void OnExit();
19:    // handle closing the window
20:    afx_msg void OnClose();
21:    // handle painting the window
22:    afx_msg void OnPaint();
23:
24:    // message map macro
25:    DECLARE_MESSAGE_MAP();
26: };
27:
```

continues

423

Listing 15.3. continued

```
28: // Define an application class derived from CWinApp
29: class CWindowApp : public CWinApp
30: {
31: public:
32:   virtual BOOL InitInstance();
33:
34: };
35:
36: void CAppWindow::OnLButtonDown(UINT nFlags, CPoint point)
37: {
38:   MessageBox("You clicked the left button!",
39:              "Mouse Click Event!", MB_OK);
40: }
41:
42:
43: void CAppWindow::OnExit()
44: { SendMessage(WM_CLOSE); }
45:
46: void CAppWindow::OnClose()
47: {
48:   if (MessageBox("Want to close this application",
49:                  "Query", MB_YESNO | MB_ICONQUESTION) == IDYES)
50:     DestroyWindow();
51: }
52:
53: void CAppWindow::OnPaint()
54: {
55:   const MAX_LINES = 30;
56:   const LINE_INCR = 20;
57:   char s[81];
58:   CPaintDC dc(this);
59:   BOOL ok = 1;
60:
61:   for (int i = 0; i < MAX_LINES && ok; i++) {
62:     sprintf(s, "This is line number %d", i);
63:     ok = dc.TextOut(0, i * LINE_INCR, s, strlen(s));
64:   }
65: }
66:
67: BEGIN_MESSAGE_MAP(CAppWindow, CFrameWnd)
68:     ON_WM_LBUTTONDOWN()
69:     ON_WM_RBUTTONDOWN()
70:     ON_COMMAND(CM_EXIT, OnExit)
71:     ON_WM_CLOSE()
72:     ON_WM_PAINT()
73: END_MESSAGE_MAP()
74:
75: // Construct the CWindowApp's m_pMainWnd data member
76: BOOL CWindowApp::InitInstance()
```

```
77: {
78:    m_pMainWnd = new CAppWindow();
79:    m_pMainWnd->ShowWindow(m_nCmdShow);
80:    m_pMainWnd->UpdateWindow();
81:    return TRUE;
82: }
83:
84: // application's constructor initializes and runs the app
85: CWindowApp WindowApp;
```

Figure 15.1 shows a sample session with the program WINDOW1.EXE.

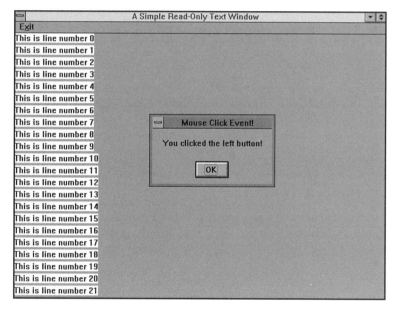

Figure 15.1. A sample session with the program WINDOW1.EXE.

Analysis
Listing 15.3 shows the source code for the WINDOW1.CPP program file. The part of the program that is relevant to this application is the CAppWindow class and its member functions. The window class declares a constructor and three member functions, namely, OnLButtonDown, OnClose, and OnPaint. The constructor creates a window with the title "A Simple Read-Only Text Window" that has default size and location, and uses the EXITMENU menu resource.

The main point of interest is the OnPaint function which is defined in lines 53 through 65. The function declares the two constants MAX_LINES and LINE_INCR, the string variable s, the device-context instance dc, and the BOOL-typed variable ok. The

OnPaint function displays the lines using the for loop in lines 61 through 64. Each loop iteration executes two statements. The first statement, in line 62, calls the sprintf function (prototyped in the STDIO.H header file) to create the image of a formatted output and store it in the variable s. The statement in line 63 calls the TextOut function. Notice the arguments of the TextOut function. The first two arguments are 0 (for parameter X) and i * LINE_INCR (for parameter Y). These values result in displaying the text starting with the left margin of the window. The constant LINE_INCR represents the total height of a line, taking into account both the height of the displayed characters and the line spacing. The third and fourth arguments are the string variable s and its length, strlen(s), respectively.

Scrolling Through Text

One of the versatile features of windows is the ability to scroll information if that information cannot be contained in the current viewing portion of the screen. The scroll bars are the visual components of a window that assist in scrolling through the window's contents. Recall that a window can have a vertical scroll bar, horizontal scroll bar, or both. A scroll bar has an arrow box at each end and a scroll thumb. The arrow boxes allow you to scroll the window's contents to either end or either side. In today's lesson, you learn about scrolling windows that contain text drawn using device-context objects.

NEW☞ TERM The *scroll thumb* serves two purposes. First, it indicates where you are relative to the entire width or length of the viewed information. Second, when you drag the thumb with the mouse, it quickly moves in or zooms on a portion of the viewed information.

The scrolling effect that I mention at the beginning of today's lesson is supported by a visual interface and an internal "engine." You can easily include the visual scroll bars in a window by incorporating the WS_VSCROLL and WS_HSCROLL styles in the dwStyle parameter of the Create member function. For example, to create a window with both vertical and horizontal scroll bars, use the following statement:

```
// both vertical and horizontal scroll bars
AStyle = WS_OVERLAPPEDWINDOW | WS_VSCROLL | WS_HSCROLL;
```

The WS_VSCROLL and WS_HSCROLL constants add the visual aspect of the scroll bars. The functionality is supported by the OnVScroll, OnHScroll, OnPaint, OnSize, SetScrollRange, SetScrollPos, and ScrollWindow functions, all inherited from class CWnd. Of course, your applications need to override the first four member functions to implement the custom scrolling features.

The SetScrollRange member function defines the minimum and maximum range, in device units, for the vertical and horizontal scroll bars. The SetScrollPos member function sets the position of the scroll bar. The ScrollWindow member function scrolls the contents of a window vertically and/or horizontally. The OnVScroll member function responds to the WM_VSCROLL message to vertically scroll a scroll bar. The OnHScroll member function responds to the WM_HSCROLL message to horizontally scroll a scroll bar.

The *SetScrollRange* Function

The declaration of the SetScrollRange function is

```
void SetScrollRange(int nBar, int nMinPos, int nMaxPos,
                    BOOL bRedraw = TRUE);
```

The nBar parameter is a numeric switch that specifies the scroll bar to set. The arguments for the nBar parameter can be one of the following predefined values:

☐ SB_VERT to set the range of the vertical scroll bar

☐ SB_HORZ to set the range of the horizontal scroll bar

☐ SB_CTL to set the ranges of a scroll bar control

The nMinPos and nMaxPos parameters define the scroll bar range. If you pass a 0 argument for each of these parameters, you hide the scroll bar. The range of scroll bar values cannot exceed the upper value of the int type, namely, 32767. The Boolean bRedraw parameter indicates whether or not the scroll bar should be redrawn to reflect the new scroll bar range. The default argument value causes the scroll bar to be redrawn. A FALSE value prevents the scroll bar from being redrawn.

Examples:

```
// set range for vertical scroll bar
SetScrollRange(SB_VERT, 0, 250);

// set range for horizontal scroll bar
SetScrollRange(SB_HORZ, 0, 500);
```

The *SetScrollPos* Function

The declaration of the SetScrollPos function is

```
int SetScrollPos(int nBar, int nPos, BOOL bRedraw = TRUE);
```

The nBar parameter is a numeric switch that specifies the scroll bar to set. The arguments for the nBar parameter can be one of the following predefined values:

☐ SB_VERT to set the position of the vertical scroll bar

☐ SB_HORZ to set the position of the horizontal scroll bar

☐ SB_CTL to set the position of a scroll bar control

The nPos parameter specifies the new scroll bar position which must be within the range of values defined by calling the function SetScrollRange. The Boolean bRedraw parameter indicates whether or not the scroll bar should be redrawn to reflect the new scroll bar range. The default argument value causes the scroll bar to be redrawn. A FALSE value prevents the scroll bar from being redrawn. The SetScrollPos function returns the previous position of the scroll bar.

Example:

```
prevPos = SetScrollPos(SB_VERT, 75);
```

The *ScrollWindow* Function

The declaration of the ScrollWindow function is

```
void ScrollWindow(int xAmount, int yAmount,
                LPRECT lpRect = NULL,
                LPRECT lpClipRect = NULL);
```

The xAmount indicates the amount of horizontal scrolling. Positive arguments for xAmount scroll the window to the right, and negative arguments scroll it to the left. The yAmount specifies the amount of vertical scrolling. Positive arguments for yAmount scroll the window downward, and negative arguments scroll it upward. The lpRect parameter is a pointer to CRect or RECT variable that defines the position of the client area to scroll. The default value of NULL causes the entire client area to scroll. The lpClipRect parameter is a pointer to a pointer to a CRect or RECT variable that defines the clipping rectangle to be scrolled. The default value of NULL results in scrolling the entire window. Calling the ScrollWindow function results in generating a WM_PAINT message which is handled by the OnPaint member function. You must define the OnPaint member function in your MFC application.

Example:

```
ScrollWindow(nDeltaX, nDeltaY);
```

The *OnVScroll* Function

The declaration of the OnVScroll function is

```
void OnVScroll(UINT nSBCode, UINT nPos, CWnd* pScrollBar);
```

The nSBCode is an integer code that specifies the vertical scrolling request. Table 15.1 shows the predefined constants for the various scrolling requests. The nPos parameter specifies the position of the thumb box when the argument for nSBCode is either SB_THUMBPOSITION or SB_THUMBTRACK. The pScrollBar parameter is a pointer to the control that has sent the WM_VSCROLL message.

Example:

```
OnVScroll(SB_LINEDOWN, 23, NULL);
```

Table 15.1. Predefined constants for vertical scrolling requests.

Value	Meaning
SB_BOTTOM	Scroll to the bottom.
SB_ENDSCROLL	End scroll.
SB_LINEDOWN	Scroll one line down.
SB_LINEUP	Scroll one line up.
SB_PAGEDOWN	Scroll one page down.
SB_PAGEUP	Scroll one page up.
SB_THUMBPOSITION	Scroll to the nPos position.
SB_THUMBTRACK	Drag the scroll thumb box to the nPos position.
SB_TOP	Scroll to the top.

The *OnHScroll* Function

The declaration of the OnHScroll function is

```
void OnHScroll(UINT nSBCode, UINT nPos, CWnd* pScrollBar);
```

The nSBCode is an integer code that specifies the horizontal scrolling request. Table 15.2 shows the predefined constants for the various scrolling requests. The nPos parameter specifies the position of the thumb box when the argument for nSBCode is SB_THUMBPOSITION. The pScrollBar parameter is a pointer to the control that has sent the WM_HSCROLL message.

Example:

```
OnHScroll(SB_LINEDOWN, 14, NULL);
```

Table 15.2. Predefined constants for horizontal scrolling requests.

Value	Meaning
SB_BOTTOM	Scroll to the right end.
SB_ENDSCROLL	End scroll.
SB_LINEDOWN	Scroll one line down.
SB_LINEUP	Scroll one line up.
SB_PAGEDOWN	Scroll one page down.
SB_PAGEUP	Scroll one page up.
SB_THUMBPOSITION	Scroll to the nPos position.
SB_TOP	Scroll to the left end.

The OnSize member function responds to the WM_SIZE message sent when a window is resized. The OnSize function has the task of updating the scrolling parameter (or metrics).

The *OnSize* Function

Syntax

The declaration of the OnSize function is

```
void OnSize(UINT nType, int nCx, int nCy);
```

The nType parameter indicates the type of resizing request. Table 15.3 shows the predefined values for the various sizing requests. The nCx and nCy parameters specify the new width and height of the client area.

Example:

```
OnSize(SIZEFULLSCREEN, 13, 55);
```

Table 15.3. Predefined values for sizing requests.

Value	Meaning
SIZEFULLSCREEN	Window is maximized.
SIZEICONIC	Window is minimized.
SIZENORMAL	Window is normal.

Value	Meaning
SIZEZOOMHIDE	Message is sent to pop-up windows when another window is maximized.
SIZEZOOMSHOW	Message is sent to pop-up windows when another window is restored to its prior size.

The parameterless OnPaint member function responds to the WM_PAINT message that requests the repainting of the window client area. The OnPaint function is responsible for displaying the updated contents of the window.

A Scrolling Window

This section presents a program that defines general scrollable windows. WINDOW2.EXE has two main menu items, Exit and Char Sets. The second menu item is a pop-up menu that has three selections: Set 1, Set 2, and Set 3. These options produce text lines that have a different line spacing and different maximum number of lines. The text fonts are the same for all three sets. Initially, the client area of the application window is clear. Therefore, you must select one of the three character sets. The application also supports the cursor movement keys to scroll the text. The Home and End keys scroll vertically to the top and bottom, respectively. The PageUp and PageDown keys scroll one page up or down, respectively. The up and down arrow keys scroll one line up or down, respectively. The left and right arrow keys scroll horizontally one page left and right, respectively.

This program illustrates two main aspects of scrolling windows:

1. Declaring a scrolling window class with additional member functions that manage the assignment, access, and use of scrolling-related data

2. Using assigned values to control vertical scrolling, and relying on the current window metrics to control the horizontal scrolling

Let's look at the code for the general text scroller window application. Listings 15.4 and 15.5 show the header file WINDOW2.H and the resource file WINDOW2.RC, respectively. Listing 15.6 contains the source code for the WINDOW2.CPP program.

Create the directory WINDOW2 as a subdirectory of \MSVC\VC21DAY and store all the project's files in the new directory. The project's .MAK file should contain the files WINDOW2.CPP, WINDOW2.RC, and WINDOW2.DEF. The latter file resembles file MINWINAP.DEF in Day 14, Listing 14.2.

Listing 15.4. Source code for the WINDOW2.H header file.

```
1: #define CM_EXIT (WM_USER + 100)
2: #define CM_SET1 (WM_USER + 101)
3: #define CM_SET2 (WM_USER + 102)
4: #define CM_SET3 (WM_USER + 103)
```

Listing 15.5. Script for the resource file WINDOW2.RC.

```
 1: #include <windows.h>
 2: #include <afxres.h>
 3: #include "window2.h"
 4:
 5: MAINMENU MENU LOADONCALL MOVEABLE PURE DISCARDABLE
 6: BEGIN
 7:     MENUITEM "E&xit", CM_EXIT
 8:     POPUP "&Char Sets"
 9:     BEGIN
10:       MENUITEM "Set &1", CM_SET1
11:       MENUITEM "Set &2", CM_SET2
12:       MENUITEM "Set &3", CM_SET3
13:     END
14: END
```

Listing 15.6. Source code for the WINDOW2.CPP program file.

```
 1: #include <afxwin.h>
 2: #include <stdio.h>
 3: #include <stdlib.h>
 4: #include <string.h>
 5: #include "window2.h"
 6:
 7: // declare the initial arguments for the window class constructor
 8: const DefYMax = 100;
 9: const DefXLine = 1;
10: const DefYLine = 1;
```

```
11: const DefXPage = 5;
12:
13: // Define a window class derived from CFrameWnd
14: class CAppWindow : public CFrameWnd
15: {
16: public:
17:     CAppWindow();
18:
19: protected:
20:     // declare data members to store character and page metrics
21:     int nCharWidth;
22:     int nCharHeight;
23:     int nXLine;
24:     int nYLine;
25:     int nXPage;
26:     int nYPage;
27:     int nVScrollMax;
28:     int nHScrollMax;
29:     int nVScrollPos;
30:     int nHScrollPos;
31:     int nxClient;
32:     int nyClient;
33:     BOOL bNoPaint;
34:     BOOL bNoInitPaint;
35:
36:     // handle vertical scrolling
37:     afx_msg void OnVScroll(UINT nSBCode, UINT nPos,
38:                            CScrollBar* pScrollBar);
39:     // handle horizontal scrolling
40:     afx_msg void OnHScroll(UINT nSBCode, UINT nPos,
41:                            CScrollBar* pScrollBar);
42:     // handle pressing keys
43:     afx_msg void OnKeyDown(UINT nChar, UINT nRepCnt, UINT Flags);
44:     // handle selecting character set # 1
45:     afx_msg void OnSet1();
46:     // handle selecting character set # 2
47:     afx_msg void OnSet2();
48:     // handle selecting character set # 3
49:     afx_msg void OnSet3();
50:     // handle the Exit menu option
51:     afx_msg void OnExit();
52:     // member functions to set the scroll parameters
53:     void SetCharHeight(int nCharHeightVal);
54:     void SetLineSize(int nXLineVal, int nYLineVal);
55:     void SetVScrollMax(int nVScrollMaxVal);
56:     void SetPageSize(int nXPageVal);
57:     // member functions to get the scroll parameters
58:     void GetCharHeight(int& nCharWidth, int& nCharHeightVal);
59:     void GetLineSize(int& nXLineVal, int& nYLineVal);
60:     void GetScrollMaxSize(int& nHScrollMaxVal,
61:                           int& nVScrollMaxVal);
```

continues

Listing 15.6. continued

```
 62:        void GetPageSize(int& nXPageVal, int& nYPageVal);
 63:        // handle closing the window
 64:        afx_msg void OnClose();
 65:        // handle resizing the window
 66:        afx_msg void OnSize(UINT nTypes, int nCx, int nCy);
 67:        // handle painting the window
 68:        afx_msg void OnPaint();
 69:
 70: private:
 71:        void makeSet(int nX, int nY);
 72:        int GetVScrollPos(int nVpos)
 73:        { return int(long(nVpos) * long(nyClient) / nVScrollMax);}
 74:
 75:        // message map macro
 76:        DECLARE_MESSAGE_MAP();
 77: };
 78:
 79: // Define an application class derived from CWinApp
 80: class CWindowApp : public CWinApp
 81: {
 82: public:
 83:        virtual BOOL InitInstance();
 84: };
 85:
 86: CAppWindow::CAppWindow()
 87: {
 88:     DWORD AttrStyle = WS_OVERLAPPEDWINDOW | WS_VSCROLL
 89:                          | WS_HSCROLL;
 90:     UINT ClassStyle = CS_VREDRAW | CS_HREDRAW;
 91:     const char FAR* lpszClassName;
 92:     HBRUSH hColor = (HBRUSH)(COLOR_HIGHLIGHTTEXT + 1);
 93:
 94:     // disable initial painting
 95:     bNoInitPaint = TRUE;
 96:     // get the registration class name
 97:     lpszClassName = AfxRegisterWndClass(ClassStyle, NULL, hColor,
 98:                                          NULL);
 99:     // create the window
100:     Create(lpszClassName, "A General Text Scroller Window",
101:            AttrStyle, rectDefault, NULL, "MAINMENU");
102:     // set the vertical and horizontal line heights
103:     SetLineSize(DefXLine, DefYLine);
104: }
105:
106: void CAppWindow::OnVScroll(UINT nSBCode, UINT nPos,
107:                            CScrollBar* pScrollBar)
108: {
109:     short nScrollInc;
110:     int nNewPos;
111:
```

```
112:    switch (nSBCode) {
113:      case SB_TOP: // move to the top
114:       nScrollInc = -nVScrollPos;
115:       break;
116:      case SB_BOTTOM: // move to the bottom
117:        nScrollInc = nVScrollMax - nVScrollPos;
118:       break;
119:      case SB_LINEUP: // move one line up
120:         nScrollInc = -nYLine;
121:       break;
122:      case SB_LINEDOWN: // move one line down
123:         nScrollInc = nYLine;
124:       break;
125:      case SB_PAGEUP: // move one page up
126:         nScrollInc = -nYPage;
127:       break;
128:      case SB_PAGEDOWN: // move one page down
129:         nScrollInc = nYPage;
130:       break;
131:      case SB_THUMBPOSITION: // track the thumb box
132:       nScrollInc = nPos - nVScrollPos;
133:       break;
134:      default:
135:       nScrollInc = 0;
136:    }
137:    // calculate new vertical thumb position so that:
138:    //      0 <= nNewPos <= nVScrollMax
139:    nNewPos = max(0, min(nVScrollPos + nScrollInc, nVScrollMax));
140:    // adjust scroll increment
141:    nScrollInc = nNewPos - nVScrollPos;
142:    // is nScrollInc not zero?
143:    if (nScrollInc) {
144:      nVScrollPos = nNewPos; // update vertical thumb position
145:      // scroll the window
146:      ScrollWindow(0, -nScrollInc * nCharHeight);
147:      // move the thumb box
148:      SetScrollPos(SB_VERT, GetVScrollPos(nVScrollPos));
149:      // repaint the window
150:      UpdateWindow();
151:    }
152: }
153:
154: void CAppWindow::OnHScroll(UINT nSBCode, UINT nPos,
155:                            CScrollBar* pScrollBar)
156: {
157:    short nScrollInc;
158:    int nNewPos;
159:
160:    switch (nSBCode) {
161:      case SB_LINEUP: // move to the left by one character
162:         nScrollInc = -nXLine;
```

continues

435

Listing 15.6. continued

```
163:        break;
164:        case SB_LINEDOWN: // move to the right by one character
165:            nScrollInc = nXLine;
166:        break;
167:        case SB_PAGEUP: // move to the left
168:            nScrollInc = -nXPage;
169:        break;
170:        case SB_PAGEDOWN: // move to the right
171:            nScrollInc = nXPage;
172:        break;
173:        case SB_THUMBPOSITION: // track the thumb box
174:        nScrollInc = nPos - nHScrollPos;
175:        break;
176:        default:
177:        nScrollInc = 0;
178:    }
179:    // calculate new horizontal thumb position so that:
180:    //      0 <= nNewPos <= nHScrollMax
181:    nNewPos = max(0, min(nHScrollPos + nScrollInc, nHScrollMax));
182:    // adjust scroll increment
183:    nScrollInc = nNewPos - nHScrollPos;
184:    // is nScrollInc not zero?
185:    if (nScrollInc) {
186:        nHScrollPos = nNewPos; // update thumb position
187:        // scroll window
188:        ScrollWindow(-nScrollInc * nCharWidth, 0);
189:        // set the thumb box position
190:        SetScrollPos(SB_HORZ, nHScrollPos * nCharWidth);
191:        // repaint the window
192:        UpdateWindow();
193:    }
194: }
195:
196: void CAppWindow::OnKeyDown(UINT nChar, UINT nRepCnt, UINT Flags)
197: {
198:    switch(nChar) {
199:      case VK_HOME:
200:         OnVScroll(SB_TOP, 0, NULL);
201:         break;
202:      case VK_END:
203:         OnVScroll(SB_BOTTOM, 0, NULL);
204:         break;
205:      case VK_PRIOR:
206:         OnVScroll(SB_PAGEUP, 0, NULL);
207:         break;
208:      case VK_NEXT:
209:         OnVScroll(SB_PAGEDOWN, 0, NULL);
210:         break;
211:      case VK_UP:
```

```
212:          OnVScroll(SB_LINEUP, 0, NULL);
213:          break;
214:      case VK_DOWN:
215:          OnVScroll(SB_LINEDOWN, 0, NULL);
216:          break;
217:      case VK_LEFT:
218:          OnHScroll(SB_PAGEUP, 0, NULL);
219:          break;
220:      case VK_RIGHT:
221:          OnHScroll(SB_PAGEDOWN, 0, NULL);
222:          break;
223:    }
224: }
225:
226: void CAppWindow::OnSet1()
227: { makeSet(0, DefYMax); }
228:
229: void CAppWindow::OnSet2()
230: { makeSet(-5, 2 * DefYMax); }
231:
232: void CAppWindow::OnSet3()
233: { makeSet(-10, DefYMax / 2); }
234:
235: void CAppWindow::makeSet(int nX, int nY)
236: {
237:   // enable painting
238:   bNoInitPaint = FALSE;
239:   // set default character height
240:   SetCharHeight(nX);
241:   // set maximum vertical scrolling range
242:   SetVScrollMax(nY);
243:   // set the page size
244:   SetPageSize(DefXPage);
245:   // clear the window client area
246:   InvalidateRect(NULL, TRUE);
247: }
248:
249: void CAppWindow::OnExit()
250: { SendMessage(WM_CLOSE); }
251:
252: void CAppWindow::SetCharHeight(int nCharHeightVal)
253: {
254:   TEXTMETRIC tm;
255:   CRect r;
256:   CDC* dc = GetDC();
257:
258:   // get the text metrics
259:   dc->GetTextMetrics(&tm);
260:   ReleaseDC(dc);
261:   // get the client area coordinates
262:   GetWindowRect(&r);
```

continues

Listing 15.6. continued

```
263:    nxClient = r.right - r.left;
264:    nyClient = r.bottom - r.top;
265:    // obtain the character height
266:    if (nCharHeightVal == 0)
267:      nCharHeight = tm.tmHeight + tm.tmExternalLeading;
268:    else if (nCharHeightVal > 0)
269:      nCharHeight = nCharHeightVal;
270:    else
271:      nCharHeight = tm.tmHeight + tm.tmExternalLeading -
272:                      nCharHeightVal;
273:    // set the range of the vertical scroll bar
274:    SetScrollRange(SB_VERT, 0, nyClient, TRUE);
275:    // get the character width
276:    nCharWidth =  tm.tmAveCharWidth;
277:    // set the range of the horizontal scroll bar
278:    SetScrollRange(SB_HORZ, 0, nxClient, TRUE);
279: }
280:
281: void CAppWindow::SetLineSize(int nXLineVal, int nYLineVal)
282: {
283:    // set the vertical and horizontal line heights
284:    nXLine = nXLineVal;
285:    nYLine = nYLineVal;
286: }
287:
288: void CAppWindow::SetVScrollMax(int nVScrollMaxVal)
289: {
290:    // set the vertical and horizontal limits
291:    nVScrollMax = nVScrollMaxVal;
292:    // set the initial line position
293:    nVScrollPos = 0;
294:    // set the position of the vertical scroll bar
295:    SetScrollPos(SB_VERT, 0, TRUE);
296:    // calculate the maximum number of characters
297:    nHScrollMax = nxClient / nCharWidth;
298:    // set the initial column position
299:    nHScrollPos = 0;
300:    // set the position of the horizontal scroll bar
301:    SetScrollPos(SB_HORZ, 0, TRUE);
302:    UpdateWindow();
303: }
304:
305: void CAppWindow::SetPageSize(int nXPageVal)
306: {
307:    // set the vertical and horizontal page up/down sizes
308:    nXPage = nXPageVal;
309:    nYPage = nyClient / nCharHeight;
310: }
311:
```

```
312: void CAppWindow::GetCharHeight(int& nCharHeightVal,
313:                      int& nCharWidthVal)
314: {
315:   nCharHeightVal = nCharHeight;
316:   nCharWidthVal = nCharWidth;
317: }
318:
319: void CAppWindow::GetLineSize(int& nXLineVal, int& nYLineVal)
320: {
321:   nXLineVal = nXLine;
322:   nYLineVal = nYLine;
323: }
324:
325: void CAppWindow::GetScrollMaxSize(int& nHScrollMaxVal,
326:                      int& nVScrollMaxVal)
327: {
328:   nHScrollMaxVal = nHScrollMax;
329:   nVScrollMaxVal = nVScrollMax;
330: }
331:
332: void CAppWindow::GetPageSize(int& nXPageVal, int& nYPageVal)
333: {
334:   nXPageVal = nXPage;
335:   nYPageVal = nYPage;
336: }
337:
338: void CAppWindow::OnClose()
339: {
340:   if (MessageBox("Want to close this application",
341:       "Query", MB_YESNO | MB_ICONQUESTION) == IDYES)
342:     DestroyWindow();
343: }
344:
345: void CAppWindow::OnSize(UINT nTypes, int nCx, int nCy)
346: {
347:    // disable painting?
348:   bNoPaint = nTypes == SIZEICONIC || nTypes == SIZEZOOMHIDE;
349:   // exit if painting is disabled
350:   if (bNoPaint || bNoInitPaint) return;
351:
352:   // update the client area
353:   nxClient = nCx;
354:   nyClient = nCy;
355:   // update the vertical page size
356:   nYPage = nyClient / nCharHeight;
357:   // set the new vertical scroll bar range
358:   SetScrollRange(SB_VERT, 0, nyClient,  FALSE);
359:   // set the new vertical thumb box position
360:   SetScrollPos(SB_VERT, GetVScrollPos(nVScrollPos), TRUE);
361:   // calculate the new maximum width
362:   nHScrollMax = max(1, nxClient / nCharWidth);
```

continues

439

Listing 15.6. continued

```
363:     //  set the new horizontal scroll bar range
364:     nHScrollPos = min(nHScrollPos, nHScrollMax);
365:     // set the new horizontal scroll bar range
366:     SetScrollRange(SB_HORZ, 0, nxClient, FALSE);
367:     // set the new horizontal thumb box position
368:     SetScrollPos(SB_HORZ,  nHScrollPos * nCharWidth, TRUE);
369:     // clear and repaint the window
370:     Invalidate(TRUE);
371: }
372:
373: void CAppWindow::OnPaint()
374: {
375:     CPaintDC dc(this);
376:     char aStr[80];
377:     char* pStr;
378:
379:     // exit if OnPaint is disabled
380:     if (bNoPaint ¦¦ bNoInitPaint) return;
381:
382:     // draw lines of text
383:     for (int i = 0, j = i + nVScrollPos;
384:         i < nYPage && j < nVScrollMax;
385:         i++, j++) {
386:       sprintf(aStr, "This is line number %d   ", j+1);
387:       // is the line visible?
388:       if (nHScrollPos < (int)(strlen(aStr))) {
389:         pStr = aStr + nHScrollPos;
390:         dc.TextOut(0, i * nCharHeight, pStr, strlen(pStr));
391:       }
392:     }
393: }
394:
395: BEGIN_MESSAGE_MAP(CAppWindow, CFrameWnd)
396:     ON_WM_VSCROLL()
397:     ON_WM_HSCROLL()
398:     ON_WM_KEYDOWN()
399:     ON_COMMAND(CM_SET1, OnSet1)
400:     ON_COMMAND(CM_SET2, OnSet2)
401:     ON_COMMAND(CM_SET3, OnSet3)
402:     ON_COMMAND(CM_EXIT, OnExit)
403:     ON_WM_CLOSE()
404:     ON_WM_SIZE()
405:     ON_WM_PAINT()
406: END_MESSAGE_MAP()
407:
408: // Construct the CWindowApp's m_pMainWnd data member
409: BOOL CWindowApp::InitInstance()
410: {
411:   m_pMainWnd = new CAppWindow();
```

```
412:    m_pMainWnd->ShowWindow(m_nCmdShow);
413:    m_pMainWnd->UpdateWindow();
414:    return TRUE;
415: }
416:
417: // application's constructor initializes and runs the app
418: CWindowApp WindowApp;
```

Figure 15.2 shows a sample session with the program WINDOW2.EXE.

Figure 15.2. A sample session with the program WINDOW2.EXE.

 The program in Listing 15.6 declares a set of global constants that serve as default (or initial) values to some of the character and page metrics. The program declares two classes: an application class and a window class. The latter is by far the most relevant one.

The CAppWindow window class declares a number of data members and member functions (public, protected, and private). The data members, which appear in lines 20 through 34, manage the display of text and can be divided into the following subgroups:

441

☐ The nCharHeight and nCharWidth members store the character height and width, respectively. Basically, these members obtain their data from the Windows text metrics. However, the program is coded to include additional line spacing to the nCharHeight data member. Consequently, the window class allows you to influence the character height.

☐ The nXLine and nYLine members store the number of characters and lines used in horizontal and vertical line scrolling, respectively. Each of these data members is assigned 1, the typical value.

☐ The nXPage and nYPage members store the number of characters and lines used in horizontal and vertical page scrolling, respectively. The nXPage member is assigned a value, and the nYPage member obtains its value by dividing the client window height by the character height. Consequently, the vertical page size depends on the size of the window, the character height, and the character spacing.

☐ The nVScrollMax and nHScrollmax members store the vertical and horizontal maximum scroll bar ranges, respectively. The member nVScrollMax is assigned a value. By contrast, the nHScrollMax has its value calculated as the ratio between the client window width and the character width.

☐ The nVScrollPos and nHScrollPos members store the vertical and horizontal scroll bar positions, respectively. The values stored in these members change with scrolling their respective bars.

☐ The nCxClient and nCyClient members store the width and height of the client area, respectively. The values of these members are updated by the OnSize member function.

☐ The Boolean bNoPaint member is used as a flag to prevent repainting the window when the window is either minimized or hidden by another window that is maximized.

☐ The Boolean bNoInitPaint member disables painting before you select any character from the Char Sets menu.

The class constructor, which appears in lines 86 through 104, performs the following tasks that initialize and build the application's window:

☐ Declares a number of initialized variables which assist in the window class (read as category) registration process

☐ Assigns the value TRUE to the Boolean data member bNoInitPaint, initially disabling painting

- [ ] Obtains the registration class (read as category) name by calling the global function `AfxRegisterWndClass`, enabling you to fine-tune the creation of a window

- [ ] Creates a window instance

- [ ] Sets the line sizes by calling the `SetLineSize` member function

 Note: The `CAppWindow` class declares the private inline member function `GetVScrollPos`. This function, which appears in lines 72 and 73, converts the number of the first line displayed into device units. This function is important in correctly positioning the scroll bar thumb box. Keep in mind that the text drawn in the window and the vertical thumb box *do not* scroll by the same number of device units.

The member function `OnVScroll`, which is defined in lines 106 through 152, responds to the `WM_VSCROLL` message and moves the vertical scroll bar. The function declares two local variables, `nScrollInc` and `nNewPos`. The `nScrollInc` variable stores the number of lines to scroll, and the `nNewPos` stores the *anticipated* new scroll bar position. The `OnVScroll` function carries out the following tasks:

- [ ] Uses a `switch` statement to determine the kind of vertical scroll request (notice that the line and page scroll requests now use the `nYLine` and `nYPage` data members rather than literal constants)

- [ ] Calculates the anticipated new scroll bar position, using the `min` and `max` functions (declared in stdlib.h) to ensure that the new position lies in the range of 0 to `nVScrollMax`

- [ ] Calculates the adjusted number of scrolled lines and stores the result in `nScrollInc`

- [ ] Vertically scrolls the window if the adjusted value of `nScrollInc` is not zero (the `if` statement assigns the new value for `nVScrollPos`, vertically scrolls the window by calling the `ScrollWindow` function, updates the vertical scroll bar position by calling the `SetScrollPos` and `GetVScrollPos` functions, and repaints the window by calling the `UpdateWindow` function)

Notice that the window is vertically scrolled by (`-nScrollInc * nCharHeight`) device units, and the vertical scroll bar is moved to the position `GetVScrollPos(nVScrollPos)`.

The member function OnHScroll, which is defined in lines 154 through 194, responds to the WM_HSCROLL message and scrolls the window horizontally. The code for this function is similar to that of OnVScroll. The main difference is that the horizontal scroll bar is moved to the (nHScrollPos * nCharWidth) position. This value is calculated using an expression that is quite different from that in function OnVScroll.

The member function OnKeyDown, which is defined in lines 196 through 224, handles the WM_KEYDOWN message to determine if and how to respond to keyboard input. The function uses a switch statement to handle the Home, End, PageUp, PageDown, up arrow, down arrow, left arrow, and right arrow keys. The statements in the various case labels invoke either function OnVScroll or function OnHScroll. These calls use the predefined SB_*xxxx* constants to determine the kind of scroll requests. All the calls supply 0 and NULL to the nPos and pScrollBar parameters of functions OnVScroll and OnHScroll.

The window class declares three similar member functions, OnSet1, OnSet2, and OnSet3, to load different sets of lines. These functions, which are defined in lines 226 through 233, in turn, call member function makeSet, with different arguments, to perform the required tasks. The makeSet function, which is defined in lines 235 through 247, performs the following tasks:

☐ Enables painting by assigning FALSE to bNoInitPaint

☐ Sets the character height

☐ Sets the maximum limit for the vertical scroll bar

☐ Sets the horizontal page size, using the same arguments for all three OnSet*x* functions

☐ Clears the window and requests repainting the client window area

The member function SetCharHeight, which is defined in lines 252 through 279, sets the character height and updates the character width. The function has one parameter, nCharHeightVal, because you are allowed to set or influence only the character height. The character width is computed based on current text metrics. The function carries out the following tasks:

☐ Obtains the text metrics by calling the GetTextMetrics function and passing the reference argument tm, which obtains the current text metrics

☐ Obtains the window width and height and stores them in the nCxClient and nCyClient members, respectively

☐ Obtains the character height

- [ ] Sets the vertical scroll bar range as 0 to nCyClient
- [ ] Calculates the character width using the related data given by the tm structure
- [ ] Sets the horizontal scroll bar range as 0 to nCxClient

There are three possibilities when SetCharHeight obtains the character height. If the argument for nCharHeightVal is zero, the function calculates the value for nCharHeight using only the text metrics data obtained by the local structure tm. If the argument for nCharHeightVal is positive, the function simply assigns nCharHeightVal to member nCharHeight. If the argument for nCharHeightVal is negative, the function adds that argument value to the height of the character obtained by the tm structure. In other words, negative arguments for nCharHeightVal are interpreted as additional line spacing, in device units.

Warning: Be careful if you experiment with the program! If the argument for nCharHeightVal is positive, the function assigns nCharHeightVal to member nCharHeight.

The member function SetLineSize, which is defined in lines 281 through 286, sets the sizes of the vertical and horizontal lines. The values passed to the function's parameters are assigned to their corresponding data members.

The member function SetVScrollMax, which is defined in lines 288 through 303, sets the maximum range for the vertical and horizontal scroll bar and resets these scroll bars to the 0 position. The function has one parameter, nVScrollMaxVal, indicating that the caller can assign a new value only to data member nVScrollMax. The function carries out the following tasks:

- [ ] Assigns the argument of the nVScrollMaxVal to the nVScrollMax data member
- [ ] Assigns 0 to the data member nVScrollPos
- [ ] Scrolls the vertical scroll bar to the position 0
- [ ] Calculates the maximum range for the horizontal scroll bar and stores the result in member nHScrollMax
- [ ] Assigns 0 to the data member nHScrollPos
- [ ] Scrolls the horizontal scroll bar to the position 0

445

The member function SetPageSize, which is defined in lines 305 through 310, sets the size of the vertical and horizontal page sizes. The function has one parameter, nXPageVal, indicating that a caller can assign a value only to the nXPage data member. The new value for the nYPage member is calculated as the ratio between the client window height and the character height (including any additional spacing).

The window class declares the member functions GetCharHeight, GetLineSize, GetScrollMax, and GetPageSize in lines 312 through 336. These functions use reference parameters to return the various queried data members. Although the program does not use these functions, I have included them for the sake of the example—your own scrolling windows may well need such functions.

The member function OnSize, which is defined in lines 345 through 371, handles the WM_SIZE request and updates the scroll bar ranges and positions. The OnSize function performs the following tasks:

☐ Verifies that the window can be painted, using the bNoPaint member to store the no-paint state (the function exits if either bNoPaint or bNoInitPaint data members is TRUE)

☐ Assigns the width and height of the resized client area (passed by the arguments of parameters nCx and nCy) to the data members nCxClient and nCyClient, respectively

☐ Updates the value of vertical page size, stored in nYPage (the new value is calculated as the ratio between the client window height and the character height)

☐ Sets the new vertical scroll bar range as 0 to nCyClient

☐ Sets the new vertical scroll bar position by calling the SetScrollPos function, using the GetVScrollPos member function to convert vertical lines into device units

☐ Sets the new vertical scroll bar position by calling the SetScrollPos function

☐ Calculates the new maximum width as the greater value of 1 and the ratio between the client area width and the character width

☐ Sets the new horizontal scroll bar position member, nHScrollPos, as the least of the old position and the maximum number of characters

☐ Sets the new horizontal scroll bar range as 0 to nCxClient, by calling the SetScrollPos function

☐ Sets the new horizontal scroll bar position by calling the SetScrollPos function

☐ Clears and repaints the client area by calling the Invalidate function

The member function OnPaint, which is defined in lines 373 through 393, responds to the WM_PAINT message requesting to repaint the window. The code for function OnPaint is simple, short, and needs no statements that obtain the current number of visible lines. That information is readily available from the nYPage data member. Notice that the loop termination condition uses the data member nVScrollMax.

Summary

Today's lesson discusses the mechanics of creating windows which show fixed and scrollable text, and includes the following topics:

☐ Read-only text windows that display information are the basis of help screens.

☐ You can write text in a window using the versatile CDC::TextOut member function.

☐ Scrollable windows can be created with vertical and horizontal scroll bars. These windows scroll using either the mouse or the cursor control keys. The classes of scrollable windows use the member functions OnVScroll, OnHScroll, OnPaint, and OnSize, as well as other functions to manage the text metrics.

Q&A

Q. Does the MFC library have a scrollable window class?

A. Yes, the MFC library has the CScrollView class which implements a scrollable view—a child window which can scroll its contents.

Q. Is the member function OnPaint needed to maintain windows with visual controls like command buttons?

A. No. You need only to write the function OnPaint to maintain windows that draw text and graphics. In the case of windows with controls you need not declare your own version of function OnPaint.

Workshop

The Workshop provides quiz questions to help you solidify your understanding of the material covered and exercises to provide you with experience in using what you've learned. Try to understand the quiz and exercise answers before continuing on to the next day's lesson. Answers are provided in Appendix B, "Answers."

Quiz

1. True or false? The member function `OnPaint` redraws the window only when needed.

2. True or false? The inherited `CWnd::OnVScroll` and `CWnd::OnHScroll` member functions offer default scrolling features.

3. True or false? If you declare the `OnPaint` member function in your window class, you must also declare the `OnSize` member function.

4. True or false? Omitting the `OnKeyDown` member function in program WINDOW2.CPP disables the vertical scrolling feature altogether.

Exercise

Experiment with modifying the WINDOW2.CPP program by altering the arguments of the member functions `OnSet1`, `OnSet2`, and `OnSet3`. In addition, you can experiment with adding more `OnSetx` menu selections and the corresponding member functions.

DAY
16
MFC Controls

Interacting with Windows applications often involves dialog boxes that contain various types of controls, such as the list box, the edit control (also called edit box), and the push button. These controls can be included in windows or, more frequently, in dialog boxes. Today's lesson and the next three look at the controls as they appear in windows and focus on the basic properties of these controls. Day 20 presents dialog boxes and views how the controls work with these boxes. Today, you learn about the following topics:

☐ Static text control

☐ Edit control

☐ Push button control

Understanding the various controls and mastering how they behave and interact enables you to implement highly interactive Windows applications. Today's lesson and the two that follow discuss the constructors and relevant member functions for the control classes.

The Static Text Control

The static text control provides a window or a dialog box with static text. The `CStatic` class implements the static text control. Let's look at the class constructor and members.

NEW☞ TERM *Static text* is text that the application user cannot easily and readily change. Static text does not necessarily mean text etched in stone! In fact, static text controls allow your MFC applications to alter the text at will. You can still specify that the text be permanent and unchangeable. The choice is ultimately yours.

The `CStatic` class, a descendant of `CWnd`, offers static text that is defined by a display area, text to display, and text attributes. Of these three components, you can alter only the displayed text during run-time.

The *Create* Function
The declaration of the `Create` member function is

```
BOOL Create(const char FAR* lpText, // control text
            DWORD dwStyle,           // control style
            const RECT& rect,        // control area
            CWnd* pParentWnd,        // parent window
            UINT nID = 0xffff);      // control ID
```

The lpText parameter specifies the text for the static text control. The dwStyle parameter designates the control style. The arguments for style typically include the WS_CHILD and WS_VISIBLE styles. Table 16.1 shows the set of SS_*xxxx* static text styles. The creation of static text control includes one or more of these styles. The rect parameter specifies the rectangular area occupied by the control. The pParentWnd parameter is the pointer to the parent window. The nID parameter specifies the control's ID. The Create function assigns a default parameter of 0xffff, because a static text control typically does not send notification messages to its parent window. The Create function returns TRUE if it succeeds and yields FALSE if it fails.

Example:

```
CStatic* pText;
// create control...

pText->Create("Operand 1", SS_SIMPLE, r, NULL);
```

Table 16.1. Values for static text styles.

Value	Meaning
SS_BLACKFRAME	Designates a box with a frame drawn with the color matching that of the window frame (black in the default Windows color scheme)
SS_BLACKRECT	Specifies a rectangle filled with the color matching that of the window frame (black in the default Windows color scheme)
SS_CENTER	Centers the static text characters; text is wrappable
SS_GRAYFRAME	Specifies a box with a frame that has the same color as the screen background (gray in the default Windows color scheme)
SS_GRAYRECT	Selects a rectangle filled with the same color as the screen background (gray in the default Windows color scheme)
SS_LEFT	Indicates left-justified text; text is wrappable
SS_LEFTNOWORDWRAP	Indicates left-justified text that cannot be wrapped

continues

Table 16.1. continued

Value	Meaning
SS_NOPREFIX	Specifies that the ampersand character (&) in the static text string should not be a hot-key designator character, but rather part of the static text character
SS_RIGHT	Selects right-justified text that is wrappable
SS_SIMPLE	Indicates that the static text characters cannot be altered at run-time and that the static text is displayed on a single line with line breaks ignored
SS_GRAYFRAME	Specifies a box with a frame that has the same color as the window background (white in the default Windows color scheme)
SS_GRAYRECT	Selects a rectangle filled with the same color as the window background (white in the default Windows color scheme)

The string accessed by the lpText pointer in the Create function may include the ampersand (&) to visually specify a hot-key—to actually support the hot-key your application needs to load accelerator keys. The hot-key character appears as an underlined character. The ampersand should be placed before the hot-key character. If the string contains multiple ampersand characters, only the last occurrence is effective. The other occurrences of the ampersand are not displayed and are ignored. To display the & character, you need to specify the SS_NOPREFIX style. The price to pay for using this style is the inability to display a hot-key character.

Now, let's focus on the component of the static text control that you can change during run-time, namely, the text itself. If you specify the SS_SIMPLE style during the creation of a CStatic instance, you cannot alter its text. In this sense, the instance of CStatic is indeed etched in stone. The CStatic class allows you to set, query, and clear the characters of the static text using the functions GetWindowTextLength, GetWindowText and SetWindowText, inherited from class CWnd:

SAMS
Sams Learning Center
SAMS PUBLISHING

The *GetWindowTextLength* Function

Syntax

The parameterless GetWindowTextLength member function returns the length of the control's text:

```
int GetWindowTextLength();
```

Example:

```
int nLen;
CStatic* pText;
// create control...

nLen = pText->GetWindowTextLength();
```

The *GetWindowText* Function

Syntax

The GetWindowText member function allows you to access the static text characters. The declaration of the GetWindowText function is

```
int GetWindowText(LPSTR lpString, int nMaxCount) const;
```

The lpString parameter is a pointer to the string that receives a copy of the static text characters. The nMaxCount parameter specifies the maximum number of static text characters to copy. The function result returns the actual number of characters copied to the string accessed by the pointer lpString.

Example:

```
const int MAX_LEN = 80;
char s[MAX_LEN+1];
int nLen;
CStatic* pText;
// create control...

nLen = pText->GetWindowText(s, MAX_LEN);
```

The *SetWindowText* Function

Syntax

The SetWindowText member function overwrites the current static text characters with those of a new string. The declaration of the SetWindowText function is

```
void SetWindowText(const char FAR* lpString);
```

The lpString parameter is the pointer to the new text for the control. If the new text is an empty string, the SetWindowText function call simply clears the text in the static text control instance.

Example:

```
char s[81] = "New window text";
CStatic* pText;
// create control...

pText->SetWindowText(s);
```

The Edit Control

Microsoft Foundation Class offers the CEdit class that implements an edit control. You have encountered this control in some of the earlier programs that use the input dialog box. The edit control allows you to type in and edit the text in the input dialog box. In this section I discuss the functionality of class CEdit in more detail, because implementing customized text editors in your MFC application requires you to become quite familiar with the CEdit member functions.

The *CEdit* Class

The CEdit class, a child of class CWnd, implements a versatile edit control that supports single-line and multiline text, as well as the ability to cut, paste, copy, delete, and clear text. The edit control can also undo the last text changes and exchange text with the clipboard. The CEdit class has a constructor and a Create member function used in building the various class instances.

The *Create* Function

The declaration of the Create function is

```
BOOL Create(DWORD dwStyle,          // control style
            const RECT& rect,        // control area
            CWnd* pParentWnd,        // parent window
            UINT nID);               // control ID
```

The dwStyle parameter designates the control style. The arguments for style typically include the WS_CHILD and WS_VISIBLE styles. Table 16.2 shows the set of ES_xxxx edit control styles. The creation of edit control includes one or more of these styles. The rect parameter specifies the rectangular area occupied by the control. The pParentWnd parameter is the pointer to the parent window. The nID parameter specifies the control's ID. The Create function returns TRUE if it succeeds and yields FALSE if it fails.

Example:

```
const ID_EDIT_TXT;
dwEditStyle = WS_CHILD ¦ WS_VISIBLE ¦ WS_TABSTOP ¦ WS_BORDER
                  ¦ WS_LEFT ¦ ES_AUTOHSCROLL;
Crect r = Crect(100, 30);
CEdit* pEdit;

pEdit->Create(dwEditStyle, r, this, IS_EDIT_TXT);
```

The typical styles for CEdit instances are WS_CHILD, WS_VISIBLE, WS_TABSTOP, ES_LEFT, ES_AUTOHSCROLL, and WS_BORDER. These styles produce an edit control that has a frame and shows left-justified text that can be scrolled horizontally if the entire text does not fit in the frame. When you create multiline edit controls you need to include the following styles: ES_MULTILINE, ES_AUTOVSCROLL, WS_HSCROLL, and WS_VSCROLL. These additional default styles support multiple text lines, make the text scroll vertically, and include vertical and horizontal scroll bars.

16

Table 16.2. Values for edit control styles.

Value	Meaning
ES_AUTOHSCROLL	Enables the text to automatically scroll to the right by 10 characters when the user enters a character at the end of the line; when the user presses the Enter key, text scrolls back to the left
ES_AUTOVSCROLL	Permits the text to scroll up by one page when the user presses the Enter key on the last visible line
ES_CENTER	Centers the text in a multiline edit control
ES_LEFT	Justifies the text to the left
ES_LOWERCASE	Converts all the letters that the user types into lowercase
ES_MULTILINE	Specifies a multiline edit control that recognizes line breaks (designated by the sequence of carriage return and line feed characters)
ES_NOHIDESEL	By default, hides the selected text when it loses focus and shows the selection when it gains focus again; prevents edit control from restoring the selected text

continues

Table 16.2. continued

Value	Meaning
ES_RIGHT	Justifies the text to the right
ES_UPPERCASE	Converts all the letters that the user types into uppercase

Clipboard-Related Editing Functions

The CEdit class includes a set of member functions that handle clipboard-related text editing commands. These commands are available in typical menu options: Cut, Copy, Paste, Clear, Undo, and Delete. Table 16.3 shows the CEdit member functions and their purpose. These functions work with the clipboard in the CF_TEXT format.

Table 16.3. CEdit member functions that support clipboard-related editing menu commands.

Member Function(s)	Purpose
Cut	Deletes the current selection in the edit control and copies the text to the clipboard
Copy	Copies the current selection to the clipboard
Paste	Inserts the text from the clipboard to the current cursor position in the edit control
Clear	Deletes the current selection; does not affect the clipboard
Undo	Undoes the last change made to the text of the edit control

Query of Edit Controls

The CEdit class has a family of text query member functions. These functions enable you to retrieve either the entire control text or parts of it, or permit you to obtain information on the text statistics (number of lines, length of lines, and so on). The relevant query member functions are

☐ The parameterless `GetWindowTextLength` member function returns the length of the control's text. This member function is inherited from the parent class, `CWnd`.

☐ The `GetWindowText` member function allows you to access the edit control characters. This function is also inherited from the parent class.

☐ The `GetLineCount` member function returns the number of lines in a multiline edit control.

☐ The `LineFromChar` member function returns the line number of a specified character index.

☐ The `LineIndex` member function returns the character index of a specific line. The character index is also the size of the text in the edit control up to the specified line number.

☐ The `LineLength` member function returns the length of a line for a specific character index.

☐ The `GetSel` member function returns the starting and ending character positions of the selected text. The starting character position is the index of the first selected character. The ending position is the index of the first character *after* the selected text.

☐ The overloaded `GetLine` member function returns a line from a multiline edit control.

The *GetWindowText* Function

The declaration of the `GetWindowText` function is

```
int GetWindowText(LPSTR lpString, int nMaxCount) const;
```

The `lpString` parameter is a pointer to the string that receives a copy of the static text characters. The `nMaxCount` parameter specifies the maximum number of static text characters to copy. The function `result` returns the actual number of characters copied to the string accessed by the pointer `lpString`.

Example:

```
const MAX_SIZE = 80;
char s[MAX_SIZE+1];
int nLen;
CEdit* pEdit;
// create control...
nLen = pEdit->GetWindowText(s, MAX_SIZE);
```

Syntax

The *GetLineCount* Function

The declaration of the GetLineCount function is

```
int GetLineCount() const;
```

Example:

```
CEdit* pEdit;
// create control...
nLineCount = pEdit->GetLineCount();
```

Note: In the case of multiline edit controls, take into account the characters involved in either the soft or hard line breaks. Hard line breaks use pairs of carriage return and line feed characters at the end of each line. Soft line breaks use two carriage returns and a line feed at line breaks. This information is relevant when you are counting the number of characters to process.

Syntax

The *LineFromChar* Function

The declaration of the LineFromChar function is

```
int LineFromChar(int nIndex = -1) const;
```

The function returns the line number for character nIndex. The default argument value of -1 is interpreted as a request to return either of these values:

☐ If there is selected text, the function yields the line number where the first selected character is located.

☐ If there is no selected text, the function returns the line number where character insertion occurs.

Example:

```
int nIdx = 3;
int nLineNum;
CEdit* pEdit;
// create control...

nLineNum = pEdit->LineFromChar(nIdx);
```

The *LineIndex* Function

The declaration of the LineIndex function is

```
int LineIndex(int nLine = -1) const;
```

The nLine parameter specifies the line index. The -1 argument indicates the current line. The function returns the number of characters from the first line and up to the specified line. If the argument of nLine is greater than the actual number of lines, the function yields -1.

Example:

```
CEdit* pEdit;
// create control...

nCharIndex = pEdit->LineIndex();
```

16

The *LineLength* Function

The declaration of the LineLength function is

```
int LineLength(int nLine = -1) const;
```

The nLine parameter specifies the character index. A -1 argument results in returning the length of the current line. In the case of a single-line edit control, the LineLength function yields the total number of characters in the control.

Example:

```
int nLineNum = 1;
int nLen;
CEdit* pEdit;
// create control...

nLen = pEdit->LineLength(nLineNum);
```

The *GetSel* Function

The declaration of the GetSel function is

```
DWORD GetSel() const;
```

The function returns a 32-bit integer that contains the starting position in the low word and the ending position in the high word. Use the predefined HIWORD and LOWORD macros to extract the high and low words, respectively. If these two words are equal, there is no selected text, because both words are the character indices to the current insertion point.

Example:

```
DWORD dwSelPos;
CEdit* pEdit;
// create control...
dwSelPos = pEdit->GetSel();
```

The *GetLine* Function

The declaration of the two versions of GetLine function is

```
int GetLine(int nIndex, LPSTR lpBuffer) const;
int GetLine(int nIndex, LPSTR lpBuffer, int nMaxLength) const;
```

The nIndex parameter specifies the index of the line to retrieve. The lpBuffer is a buffer that stores the retrieved line. The first two bytes of lpBuffer contain the length of the line. The nMaxLength parameter specifies the maximum number of bytes to copy to the buffer lpBuffer. When the second version of GetLine is used, it copies the argument of nMaxLength to the first two bytes of lpBuffer.

Example:

```
const MAX_STR = 80;
int nLineIndex;
int nNumChars;
char s[MAX_STR+1];
CEdit* pEdit;
// create control...
nNumChars = pEdit->GetLine(nLineIndex, s, MAX_STR);
```

 Note: Because lpBuffer is *not* an ASCIIZ string, you might prefer writing another version of GetLine that returns an ASCIIZ string. Of course, the new version of GetLine must be added to a descendant class of CEdit.

Altering the Edit Controls

Let's now focus on the member functions of CEdit that alter the edit control text. The operations of these member functions include writing new text to the control, selecting text, and replacing the selected text:

☐ The `SetWindowText` member function, which is inherited from the parent class, overwrites the current edit control characters with those of a new string.

☐ The overloaded `SetSel` member function defines a block of characters as the new selected text.

☐ The `ReplaceSel` member function replaces the selected text with new characters.

The *SetWindowText* Function

The declaration of the `SetWindowText` function is

```
void SetWindowText(const char FAR* lpString);
```

The `lpString` parameter is the pointer to the new text for the control. If the new text is an empty string, the `SetWindowText` call simply clears the text in the edit control instance.

Example:

```
CEdit* pEdit;
// create control...
pEdit->SetWindowText("Calculate");
```

The *SetSel* Function

The declaration of the `SetSel` function is

```
void SetSel(DWORD dwSelection);
void SetSel(int nStartChar, int nEndChar);
```

The `dwSelection` parameter contains the starting position in its low word and the ending position in its high word. The parameters `nStartChar` and `nEndChar` define the range of characters that make up the new selected text. In either version of `SetSel`, if the starting and ending positions are 0 and -1, respectively, the entire text in the edit control is selected.

Example:

```
int nStart = 10, nEnd = 20;
CEdit* pEdit;
// create control...
pEdit->SetSel(nStart, nEnd);
```

461

Syntax

The *ReplaceSel* Function

The declaration of the `ReplaceSel` function is

```
void ReplaceSel(const char FAR* lpNewText);
```

The `lpNewText` parameter is the pointer to the new selected text that replaces the current selection. If there is no selected text, the function simply inserts the text accessed by `lpNewText` at the current insertion point.

Example:

```
CEdit* pEdit;
// create control...
pEdit->ReplaceSel("New text");
```

Note: You can use the `ReplaceSel` function to delete parts of the edit control text by first selecting that part and then replacing it with an empty string.

The Push Button Control

The push button control is perhaps psychologically the most powerful control (you never hear about the nuclear list box or the nuclear check box). In a sense, the push button control represents the fundamental notion of a control—you click on the control and something happens.

NEW☞
TERM
The push button is also known as the *command button*.

Note: The MFC library implements the `CButton` class whose instances create push button controls, group boxes, check boxes, and radio buttons. These controls are created by specifying the button style. This multiplicity is considered by many practicing OOP programmers as an odd (or poor) design. The reason for the current form of class `CButton` is that the MFC library is an OOP shell around the Windows API functions.

The rest of today's lesson focuses on the aspects of class CButton that deal with the push button controls. Day 17 presents the aspects of CButton that are related to the group box, check box, and radio button controls.

NEW☞ TERM There are basically two types of push button controls: *default buttons* and *nondefault buttons.* Default buttons have slightly thicker edges than nondefault buttons. Pressing the Enter key is equivalent to clicking on the default button in a dialog box. There can be only one default button in a group. You can select a new default button by pressing the Tab key. This feature works only when the buttons are in a dialog box. If a nondialog box window owns push button control, it can only visually display a default button—the functionality is not supported.

The *CButton* Class

The CButton class, a descendant of CWnd, declares a rather small number of member functions. The following are CButton member functions that are relevant to the push button controls:

☐ The Create member function works with the class constructor to create a push button instance.

☐ The GetButtonStyle and SetButtonStyle member functions allow you to query and set the style of a push button. These functions enable you to determine whether or not, for example, a button is a default push button.

The *Create* Function

The declaration of the Create function is

```
BOOL Create(const char FAR* lpCaption,   // button label
            DWORD dwStyle,               // style
            const RECT& rect,            // area
            CWnd* pParentWnd,            // parent window
            UINT nID);                   // control ID
```

The lpCaption parameter specifies the button's label or caption. The dwStyle parameter determines the exact type of button. This parameter plays a more important role in class CButton's Create function than in the Create function of any other class. Typical styles for push buttons include WS_CHILD, WS_VISIBLE, BS_PUSHBTTON (or BS_DEFPUSHBUTTON), and WS_TABSTOP (when the parent window is a dialog box). The rect parameter specifies the area and location of the control. The pParent parameter is the pointer to the owner window which can be either a window or a dialog box. The nID parameter specifies a unique control ID.

Example:

```
CButton* pBtn;
dwBtnStyle = WS_CHILD | WS_VISIBLE | BS_PUSHBTTON;
pBtn->Create("Calc", dwBtnStyle, rect, NULL, ID_CALC_BTN);
```

The *GetButtonStyle* and *SetButtonStyle* Functions

The declarations for the GetButtonStyle and SetButtonStyle functions are

```
UINT GetButtonStyle() const;
void SetButtonStyle(UINT nStyle, BOOL bRedraw = TRUE);
```

The nStyle parameter specifies the new style of the CButton instance. The Boolean bRedraw parameter indicates whether or not to redraw the control.

Example:

```
UNIT nBtnStyle;
CButton* pBtn1;
CButton* pBtn2;
// create controls...
nBtnStyle = pBtn1->GetButtonStyle();
pBtn2->SetButtonStyle(nBtnStyle);
```

Handling Button Messages

When you click on a button, the control sends the BN_CLICKED notification message to its parent window. The parent window responds to this message by invoking a message response member function based on the ID of the button. For example, if you have a button that was created with an ID of ID_EXIT_BTN, the message handler function is

```
// other declarations
afx_msg void HandleExitBtn();
// other declarations

BEGIN_MESSAGE_LOOP(_CAppWindow_, CFrameWnd)
    // other possible message mapping macros
    ON_BN_CLICKED(ID_EXIT_BTN, HandleExitBtn)
    // other possible message mapping macros
END_MESSAGE_LOOP()
```

This example shows that the message map macro ON_BN_CLICKED is used to map the ID_EXIT_BTN notification message with the HandleExitBtn member function.

Manipulating Buttons

You can disable, enable, show, and hide a button by using the `CWnd::EnableWindow` function. A disabled button has a faded gray caption and does not respond to mouse clicks. The `CWnd::EnableWindow` function allows you to enable or disable a button. The function accepts a single argument, a Boolean argument that specifies whether the button is enabled (when the argument is `TRUE`) or disabled (when the argument is `FALSE`). Sample calls to the `EnableWindow` function are

```
AButton->EnableWindow(FALSE); // disable button
AButton->EnableWindow(TRUE);  // enable button
```

You can query the enabled state of a button by using the `Boolean CWnd::IsWindowEnabled` function which takes no arguments. A sample call to `IsEnabledWindow` is

```
// toggle the enabled state of a button
if (AButton->IsWindowEnabled()
    AButton->EnableWindow(FALSE); // disable button
else
    AButton->EnableWindow(TRUE); // enable button
```

You can also hide and show a button using the `CWnd::ShowWindow` function. The function takes one argument: either the `SW_HIDE` constant to hide the button or the `SW_SHOW` constant to show the button. The `Boolean CWnd::IsWindowVisible` function queries the visibility of a button. This function takes no arguments. A sample call to the `ShowWindow` and `IsWindowVisible` functions is

```
// toggle the visibility of a button
if (AButton->IsWindowVisible()
    AButton->ShowWindow(SW_HIDE); // hide button
else
    AButton->ShowWindow(SW_SHOW); // show button
```

The Command-Line Calculator

Let's look at an application that uses static text, single-line edit controls, multiline edit controls, and push buttons—the *Command-Line Calculator Application (COCA)*. This nontrivial application implements a floating-point calculator that uses edit controls instead of buttons. This type of interface is somewhat visually inferior to the typical button-populated calculator Windows applications. However, this interface can support more mathematical functions without requiring the addition of the buttons for these extra functions. In COCA, the calculator is made up of the following controls:

☐ Two edit controls for the first and second operands accept integers, floating-point numbers, and the names of single-letter variables, A to Z.

☐ One edit control for the operator supports the calculator's four basic math operations and the exponentiation (using a caret, ^).

☐ One edit control displays the result of the math operation.

☐ One edit control displays any error messages.

☐ One multiline edit control enables you to store a number in the Result edit control in one of 26 single-letter variables, A to Z. The multiline edit displays the current values stored in these variables and allows you to view and edit these numbers. You can use the vertical scroll bar to inspect the values in the different variables.

☐ Multiple static text controls serve to label the various edit controls. Of particular interest is the static control for the Error Message box. If you click on the accompanying static text, the Error Message is cleared of any text.

☐ A menu has the single Exit option.

☐ A push button with the caption Calc performs the operation specified in the Operator edit control, using the operands in the operand edit controls.

☐ A push button with the caption Store stores the contents of the result edit control in the currently selected line of the multiline edit control.

☐ A push button with the caption Exit exits the application after asking you for a confirmation.

The program supports the following special features for the Store button control:

☐ The Store push button is disabled if the application attempts to execute an invalid operator. This feature illustrates an example of disabling a push button when a certain condition arises (in this case, a specific calculation error).

☐ The Store push button is enabled if you click on the Error Message static text. The same button is enabled when you successfully execute a math operation.

The calculator application demonstrates the following tasks:

☐ Using single-line edit controls for simple input

☐ Using a multiline edit control to view and edit information

☐ Accessing and editing line-oriented text

☐ Simulating static text that responds to mouse clicks

☐ Writing custom `GetLine` and `GetLineLength` member functions

☐ Extending the `CEdit` class to accommodate the previous two member functions

☐ Using push buttons

☐ Disabling and enabling push buttons

☐ Associating accelerator keys with push buttons (this feature allows the program to use keys)

16

Create the directory CTLBTN1 as a subdirectory of \MSVC\VC21DAY and store all the project's files in the new directory. The project's .MAK file should contain the files CTLBTN1.CPP, CTLBTN1.RC, and CTLBTN1.DEF. The latter file resembles file MINWINAP.DEF in Day 14, Listing 14.2.

First compile and run the application to get a good feel of how the calculator application works. Experiment with typing different numeric operands and the supported operators and click on the Calc button. Each time, the result appears in the Result box, overwriting the previous result. Try dividing a number by zero to experiment with the error handling features.

Using the single-letter variables is easy. All these variables are initialized with 0. Therefore, the first step to using them is to store a nonzero value. Perform an operation and then click inside the Variables edit box. Select the first line that contains the variable A. Now click the Store button (or press Alt-S) and watch the number in the Result box appear in the first line of the Variables edit box. The name of the variable and the colon and space characters that follow reappear with the new text line. Now replace the contents of the Operand1 edit box with the variable A, and then click the Calc button. The Result edit box displays the result of the latest operation.

Listing 16.1 shows the source code for the CTLBTN1.H header file. The header file declares the command constants for the menu item and the push button accelerator keys. These accelerator keys associate the Alt-C, Alt-S, and Alt-E keys with their respective push button IDs. Listing 16.2 contains the script for the CTLBTN1.RC resource file. Listing 16.3 contains the source code for the CTLBTN1.CPP program file.

Listing 16.1. Source code for the CTLBTN1.H header file.

```
1: #define CM_EXIT  (WM_USER + 100)
2:
3: #define ID_CALC_BTN  107
4: #define ID_STORE_BTN 108
5: #define ID_EXIT_BTN  109
```

Listing 16.2. Script for the CTLBTN1.RC resource file.

```
 1: #include <windows.h>
 2: #include <afxres.h>
 3: #include "ctlbtn1.h"
 4:
 5: BUTTONS ACCELERATORS
 6: BEGIN
 7:    "c", ID_CALC_BTN, ALT
 8:    "s", ID_STORE_BTN, ALT
 9:    "e", ID_EXIT_BTN, ALT
10: END
11:
12: EXITMENU MENU LOADONCALL MOVEABLE PURE DISCARDABLE
13: BEGIN
14:     MENUITEM "E&xit", CM_EXIT
15: END
```

Listing 16.3. Source code for the CTLBTN1.CPP program file.

```
 1: #include <stdlib.h>
 2: #include <ctype.h>
 3: #include <stdio.h>
 4: #include <math.h>
 5: #include <string.h>
 6: #include <afxwin.h>
 7: #include "ctlbtn1.h"
 8:
 9: // declare the constants that represent the sizes of the controls
10: const Wlbl = 100;
11: const Hlbl = 20;
12: const LblVertSpacing = 5;
13: const LblHorzSpacing = 40;
14: const Wbox = 100;
15: const Hbox = 30;
16: const BoxVertSpacing = 40;
```

```
17: const BoxHorzSpacing = 40;
18: const WLongbox = 4 * (Wbox + BoxHorzSpacing);
19: const Wvarbox = 2 * Wbox;
20: const Hvarbox = 3 * Hbox;
21: const Hbtn = 30;
22: const Wbtn = 80;
23: const BtnHorzSpacing = 30;
24: const MaxEditLen = 30;
25: const MAX_MEMREG = 26;
26:
27: // declare the ID_XXXX constants for the edit boxes
28: #define ID_OPERAND1_EDIT 101
29: #define ID_OPERATOR_EDIT 102
30: #define ID_OPERAND2_EDIT 103
31: #define ID_RESULT_EDIT 104
32: #define ID_ERRMSG_EDIT 105
33: #define ID_VARIABLE_EDIT 106
34:
35: class CxButton : public CButton
36: {
37: public:
38:
39:    BOOL Create(const char FAR* lpCaption, const RECT& rect,
40:            CWnd* pParentWnd, UINT nID, BOOL bIsDefault);
41:    6p 42: };
43:
44: class CxEdit : public CEdit
45: {
46: public:
47:    // get an ASCIIZ string from a line
48:    BOOL GetLine(LPSTR lpString, int nStrSize, int nLineNumber);
49:    // get the line length given a line number
50:    int GetLineLength(int nLineNumber);
51:
52: };
53:
54: class CWindowApp : public CWinApp
55: {
56: public:
57:    virtual BOOL InitInstance();
58: };
59:
60: // expand the functionality of CFrameWnd by deriving
61: // class CAppWindow
62: class CAppWindow : public CFrameWnd
63: {
64: public:
65:
66:   CAppWindow();
67:
```

continues

Listing 16.3. continued

```
 68:    ~CAppWindow();
 69:
 70: protected:
 71:    // declare the pointers to the various controls
 72:    // first, the edit box controls
 73:    CEdit* Operand1Box;
 74:    CEdit* OperatorBox;
 75:    CEdit* Operand2Box;
 76:    CEdit* ResultBox;
 77:    CEdit* ErrMsgBox;
 78:    CxEdit* VariableBox;
 79:    // then the static text controls
 80:    CStatic* Operand1Txt;
 81:    CStatic* OperatorTxt;
 82:    CStatic* Operand2Txt;
 83:    CStatic* ResultTxt;
 84:    CStatic* ErrMsgTxt;
 85:    CStatic* VariableTxt;
 86:    // then the push buttons
 87:    CxButton* CalcBtn;
 88:    CxButton* StoreBtn;
 89:    CxButton* ExitBtn;
 90:    // math error flag
 91:    BOOL bInError;
 92:    // coordinates for the Error Message static text area
 93:    int nXulc, nYulc, nXlrc, nYlrc;
 94:
 95:    // handle clicking the left mouse button
 96:    afx_msg void OnLButtonDown(UINT nFlags, CPoint point);
 97:    // handle the calculation
 98:    afx_msg void HandleCalcBtn();
 99:    // handle the calculation
100:    afx_msg void CMCalc() { HandleCalcBtn(); }
101:    // handle storing the result in a variable
102:    afx_msg void HandleStoreBtn();
103:    // handle storing the result in a variable
104:    afx_msg void CMStore() { HandleStoreBtn(); }
105:    // handle exiting the application
106:    afx_msg void HandleExitBtn()
107:      { SendMessage(WM_CLOSE); }
108:    // handle exiting the application
109:    afx_msg void CMExit() { SendMessage(WM_CLOSE); }
110:    // handle exiting the application
111:    afx_msg void OnExit() { SendMessage(WM_CLOSE); }
112:    // enable a push button control
113:    virtual void EnableButton(CxButton* pBtn)
114:      { pBtn->EnableWindow( TRUE); }
115:    // disable a push button control
116:    virtual void DisableButton(CxButton* pBtn)
117:      { pBtn->EnableWindow(FALSE); }
```

```
118:    // handle creating the controls
119:    afx_msg int OnCreate(LPCREATESTRUCT lpCS);
120:    // handle keydown events
121:    afx_msg void OnKeyDown(UINT nChar, UINT nRepCnt, UINT nFlags);
122:    // handle closing the window
123:    afx_msg void OnClose();
124:    // return a reference to member r based on individual
125:    // coordinates and dimensions
126:    void makeRect(int X, int Y, int W, int H, CRect& r);
127:    // obtain a number of a Variable edit box line
128:    double getVar(int lineNum);
129:    // store a number in the selected text of
130:    // the Variable edit box line
131:    void putVar(double nX);
132:
133:    // declare message map macro
134:    DECLARE_MESSAGE_MAP();
135: };
136:
137: BOOL CxButton::Create(const char FAR* lpCaption, const RECT& rect,
138:                 CWnd* pParentWnd, UINT nID, BOOL bIsDefault)
139:
140: {
141:    DWORD dwBtnStyle = (bIsDefault == TRUE) ?
142:                 BS_DEFPUSHBUTTON : BS_PUSHBUTTON;
143:
144:    return CButton::Create(lpCaption, WS_CHILD | WS_VISIBLE |
145:          WS_TABSTOP | dwBtnStyle, rect, pParentWnd, nID);
146: }
147:
148: BOOL CxEdit::GetLine(LPSTR lpString, int nStrSize,
149:                     int nLineNumber)
150: {
151:    int nCopyCount;
152:    BOOL bResult;
153:
154:    if (nStrSize <= 0)
155:       return FALSE;
156:    bResult = (nStrSize >= GetLineLength(nLineNumber) + 1) ? TRUE
157:                                                : FALSE;
158:    if (nStrSize == 1)
159:    {
160:       lpString[0] = '\0';
161:       return bResult;
162:    }
163:    ((WORD FAR *)lpString)[0] = nStrSize;
164:    nCopyCount = (WORD)(SendMessage(EM_GETLINE, nLineNumber,
165:                                    long(lpString)));
166:    if (nCopyCount)
167:    {
```

continues

471

Listing 16.3. continued

```
168:      // Windows returns non-null-terminated string
169:      lpString[nCopyCount] = '\0';
170:      return bResult;
171:    }
172:    return FALSE;
173: }
174:
175: int CxEdit::GetLineLength(int nLineNumber)
176: {
177:    int nStartPos = -1;
178:
179:    if (nLineNumber > -1)
180:      nStartPos = LineIndex(nLineNumber);
181:    return (WORD) SendMessage(EM_LINELENGTH, nStartPos);
182: }
183:
184: CAppWindow::CAppWindow()
185: {
186:    // load accelerator resources
187:    LoadAccelTable("BUTTONS");
188:    // create the window
189:    Create(NULL,
190:      "Command-Oriented Calculator Application (COCA)",
191:        WS_OVERLAPPEDWINDOW | WS_MAXIMIZE,
192:          rectDefault, NULL, "EXITMENU");
193:    // clear the bInError flag
194:    bInError = FALSE;
195: }   6p196:      6p197: int CAppWindow::OnCreate(LPCREATESTRUCT lpCS)
198: {
199:    char s[81];
200:    char bigStr[6 * MAX_MEMREG + 1];
201:    char chC;
202:    int nX0 = 20;
203:    int nY0 = 30;
204:    int nX = nX0, nY = nY0;
205:    CRect r;
206:    DWORD dwStaticStyle = WS_CHILD | WS_VISIBLE | SS_LEFT;
207:    DWORD dwBoxStyle = WS_CHILD | WS_VISIBLE | WS_TABSTOP |
208:                       WS_BORDER | ES_LEFT | ES_AUTOHSCROLL |
209:                       ES_UPPERCASE;
210:
211:    // create the first set of labels for the edit boxes
212:    makeRect(nX, nY, Wlbl, Hlbl, r);
213:    Operand1Txt = new CStatic();
214:    Operand1Txt->Create("Operand1", dwStaticStyle, r, this);
215:    strcpy(s, "Operator");
216:    nX += Wlbl + LblHorzSpacing;
217:    makeRect(nX, nY, Wlbl, Hlbl, r);
218:    OperatorTxt = new CStatic();
219:    OperatorTxt->Create(s, dwStaticStyle, r, this);
```

```
220:    nX += Wlbl + LblHorzSpacing;
221:    makeRect(nX, nY, Wlbl, Hlbl, r);
222:    Operand2Txt = new CStatic();
223:    Operand2Txt->Create("Operand2", dwStaticStyle, r, this);
224:    nX += Wlbl + LblHorzSpacing;
225:    makeRect(nX, nY, Wlbl, Hlbl, r);
226:    ResultTxt = new CStatic();
227:    ResultTxt->Create("Result", dwStaticStyle, r, this);
228:    // create the operand1, operator, operand2, and result
229:    // edit boxes
230:    nX = nX0;
231:    nY += Hlbl + LblVertSpacing;
232:    makeRect(nX, nY, Wbox, Hbox, r);
233:    Operand1Box = new CEdit();
234:    Operand1Box->Create(dwBoxStyle, r, this, ID_OPERAND1_EDIT);
235:    Operand1Box->LimitText(); // set no limit for text
236:    nX += Wbox + BoxHorzSpacing;
237:    makeRect(nX, nY, Wbox, Hbox, r);
238:    OperatorBox = new CEdit();
239:    OperatorBox->Create(dwBoxStyle, r, this, ID_OPERATOR_EDIT);
240:    OperatorBox->LimitText(); // set no limit for text
241:    nX += Wbox + BoxHorzSpacing;
242:    makeRect(nX, nY, Wbox, Hbox, r);
243:    Operand2Box = new CEdit();
244:    Operand2Box->Create(dwBoxStyle, r, this, ID_OPERAND2_EDIT);
245:    Operand2Box->LimitText(); // set no limit for text
246:    nX += Wbox + BoxHorzSpacing;
247:    makeRect(nX, nY, Wbox, Hbox, r);
248:    ResultBox = new CEdit();
249:    ResultBox->Create(dwBoxStyle, r, this, ID_RESULT_EDIT);
250:    ResultBox->LimitText(); // set no limit for text
251:    // create the static text and edit box for the error message
252:    nX = nX0;
253:    nY += Hbox + BoxVertSpacing;
254:    // store the coordinates for the static text area
255:    nXulc = nX;
256:    nYulc = nY;
257:    nXlrc = nX + Wlbl;
258:    nYlrc = nY + Hlbl;
259:    makeRect(nX, nY, Wlbl, Hlbl, r);
260:    ErrMsgTxt = new CStatic();
261:    ErrMsgTxt->Create("Error Message", dwStaticStyle, r, this);
262:    nY += Hlbl + LblVertSpacing;
263:    makeRect(nX, nY, WLongbox, Hbox, r);
264:    ErrMsgBox = new CEdit();
265:    ErrMsgBox->Create(dwBoxStyle, r, this, ID_ERRMSG_EDIT);
266:    ErrMsgBox->LimitText(); // set no limit for text
267:    // create the static text and edit box for the single-letter
268:    // variable selection
269:    nY += Hbox + BoxVertSpacing;
```

16

continues

Listing 16.3. continued

```
270:   makeRect(nX, nY, Wlbl, Hlbl, r);
271:   VariableTxt = new CStatic();
272:   VariableTxt->Create("Variables", dwStaticStyle, r, this);
273:   nY += Hlbl + LblVertSpacing;
274:   bigStr[0] = '\0';
275:   // build the initial contents of the Variable edit box
276:   for (chC = 'A'; chC <= 'Z'; chC++) {
277:     sprintf(s, "%c: 0\r\n", chC);
278:     strcat(bigStr, s);
279:   }
280:   makeRect(nX, nY, Wvarbox, Hvarbox, r);
281:   VariableBox = new CxEdit();
282:   VariableBox->Create(dwBoxStyle | ES_MULTILINE | WS_HSCROLL
283:                 | WS_VSCROLL | ES_AUTOVSCROLL,
284:                     r, this, ID_VARIABLE_EDIT);
285:   VariableBox->LimitText(); // set no limit for text
286:   VariableBox->SetWindowText(bigStr);
287:   // create the Calc push button
288:   nX += Wvarbox + BtnHorzSpacing;
289:   CalcBtn = new CxButton();
290:   makeRect(nX, nY, Wbtn, Hbtn, r);
291:   CalcBtn->Create("&Calc", r, this, ID_CALC_BTN, TRUE);
292:   // create the Store Btn
293:   nX += Wbtn + BtnHorzSpacing;
294:   makeRect(nX, nY, Wbtn, Hbtn, r);
295:   StoreBtn = new CxButton();
296:   StoreBtn->Create("&Store", r, this, ID_STORE_BTN, FALSE);
297:   // Create the Exit Btn
298:   nX += Wbtn + BtnHorzSpacing;
299:   makeRect(nX, nY, Wbtn, Hbtn, r);
300:   ExitBtn = new CxButton();
301:   ExitBtn->Create("&Exit", r, this, ID_EXIT_BTN, FALSE);
302:   return CFrameWnd::OnCreate(lpCS);
303: }
304:
305: CAppWindow::~CAppWindow()
306: {
307:   // delete the controls 6p308:    delete Operand1Box;
309:   delete OperatorBox;
310:   delete Operand2Box;
311:   delete ResultBox;
312:   delete ErrMsgBox;
313:   delete VariableBox;
314:   delete Operand1Txt;
315:   delete OperatorTxt;
316:   delete Operand2Txt;
317:   delete ResultTxt;
318:   delete ErrMsgTxt;
319:   delete VariableTxt;
320:   delete CalcBtn;
```

```
321:    delete StoreBtn;
322:    delete ExitBtn;
323: }    6p324:
325: void CAppWindow::OnLButtonDown(UINT nFlags, CPoint point)
326: {
327:    int nX = point.x;
328:    int nY = point.y;
329:
330:    if (nX >= nXulc && nX <= nXlrc &&
331:        nY >= nYulc && nY <= nYlrc) {
332:        ErrMsgBox->SetWindowText("");
333:        EnableButton(StoreBtn);
334:    }
335: }
336:
337: void CAppWindow::HandleCalcBtn()
338: {
339:    double x, y, z;
340:    char opStr[MaxEditLen+1];
341:    char s[MaxEditLen+1];
342:
343:    // obtain the string in the Operand1 edit box
344:    Operand1Box->GetWindowText(s, MaxEditLen);
345:    // does the Operand1Box contain the name
346:    // of a single-letter variable?
347:    if (isalpha(s[0]))
348:      // obtain value from the Variable edit control
349:      x = getVar(s[0] - 'A');
350:    else
351:      // convert the string in the edit box
352:      x = atof(s);
353:
354:    // obtain the string in the Operand2 edit box
355:    Operand2Box->GetWindowText(s, MaxEditLen);
356:    // does the Operand2Box contain the name
357:    // of a single-letter variable?
358:    if (isalpha(s[0]))
359:      // obtain value from the Variable edit control
360:      y = getVar(s[0] - 'A');
361:    else
362:      // convert the string in the edit box
363:      y = atof(s);
364:
365:    // obtain the string in the Operator edit box
366:    OperatorBox->GetWindowText(opStr, MaxEditLen);
367:    // clear the error message box
368:    ErrMsgBox->SetWindowText("");
369:    bInError = FALSE;
370:    // determine the requested operation
371:    if (strcmp(opStr, "+") == 0)
```

continues

Listing 16.3. continued

```
372:     z = x + y;
373:   else if (strcmp(opStr, "-") == 0)
374:     z = x - y;
375:   else if (strcmp(opStr, "*") == 0)
376:     z = x * y;
377:   else if (strcmp(opStr, "/") == 0) {
378:     if (y != 0)
379:       z = x / y;
380:     else {
381:       z = 0;
382:       bInError = TRUE;
383:       ErrMsgBox->SetWindowText("Division-by-zero error");
384:     }
385:   }
386:   else if (strcmp(opStr, "^") == 0) {
387:     if (x > 0)
388:       z = exp(y * log(x));
389:     else {
390:       bInError = TRUE;
391:       ErrMsgBox->SetWindowText(
392:         "Cannot raise the power of a negative number");
393:     }
394:   }
395:   else {
396:     bInError = TRUE;
397:     ErrMsgBox->SetWindowText("Invalid operator");
398:   }
399:   // display the result if no error has occurred
400:   if (!bInError) {
401:     sprintf(s, "%g", z);
402:     ResultBox->SetWindowText(s);
403:     // enable the Store button
404:     EnableButton(StoreBtn);
405:   }
406:   else
407:     // disable the Store button
408:     DisableButton(StoreBtn);
409: }
410:
411: void CAppWindow::HandleStoreBtn()
412: {
413:   char result[MaxEditLen+1];
414:
415:   // get the string in the Result edit box
416:   ResultBox->GetWindowText(result, MaxEditLen);
417:   // store the result in the selected text of
418:   // the Variable edit box
419:   putVar(atof(result));
420: }
421:
```

```
422: void CAppWindow::makeRect(int nX, int nY, int nW,
423:                                 int nH, CRect& r)
424: {
425:   r.top = nY;
426:   r.left = nX;
427:   r.bottom = nY + nH;
428:   r.right = nX + nW;
429: }
430:
431: double CAppWindow::getVar(int nLineNum)
432: {
433:   int nLineSize;
434:   char s[MaxEditLen+1];
435:
436:   if (nLineNum >= MAX_MEMREG) return 0;
437:   // get the size of the target line
438:   nLineSize = VariableBox->GetLineLength(nLineNum);
439:   // get the line
440:   VariableBox->GetLine(s, nLineSize, nLineNum);
441:   // delete the first three characters
442:   strcpy(s, (s+3));
443:   // return the number stored in the target line
444:   return atof(s);
445: }
446:
447: void CAppWindow::putVar(double x)
448: {
449:   DWORD dwSelPos;
450:   WORD wStartPos, wEndPos;
451:   int nLineNum;
452:   int nLineSize;
453:   char s[MaxEditLen+1];
454:
455:   // locate the character position of the cursor
456:   dwSelPos = VariableBox->GetSel();
457:   wStartPos = LOWORD(dwSelPos);
458:   wEndPos = HIWORD(dwSelPos);
459:   // turn off the selected text
460:   if (wStartPos != wEndPos) {
461:     dwSelPos = MAKELONG(wStartPos, wStartPos);
462:     VariableBox->SetSel(dwSelPos);
463:   }
464:   // get the line number where the cursor is located
465:   nLineNum = VariableBox->LineFromChar(-1);
466:   // get the line size of line lineNum
467:   nLineSize = VariableBox->GetLineLength(nLineNum);
468:   // obtain the text of line lineNum
469:   VariableBox->GetLine(s, nLineSize, nLineNum);
470:   // build the new text line
471:   sprintf(s, "%c: %g", s[0], x);
472:   // get the character positions for the deleted line
```

Listing 16.3. continued

```
473:    wStartPos = (WORD) (VariableBox->LineIndex(-1));
474:    wEndPos = (WORD) (wStartPos + VariableBox->LineLength(-1));
475:    // select the current line
476:    dwSelPos = MAKELONG(wStartPos, wEndPos);
477:    VariableBox->SetSel(dwSelPos);
478:    // replace the current line with the new line
479:    VariableBox->ReplaceSel(s);
480: }
481:
482: void CAppWindow::OnKeyDown(UINT nChar, UINT nRepCnt, UINT nFlags)
483: {
484:    if (nFlags & 0x2000 == 1)
485:      switch (nChar) {
486:        case 'c':
487:          HandleCalcBtn();
488:          break;
489:        case 's':
490:          HandleStoreBtn();
491:          break;
492:        case 'e':
493:          HandleExitBtn();
494:          break;
495:        default:
496:          MessageBeep(0);
497:      }
498: }
499:
500: void CAppWindow::OnClose()
501: {
502:    if (MessageBox("Want to close this application",
503:                   "Query", MB_YESNO | MB_ICONQUESTION) == IDYES)
504:      DestroyWindow();                6p505: }
506:
507: BEGIN_MESSAGE_MAP(CAppWindow, CFrameWnd)
508:      ON_WM_LBUTTONDOWN()
509:      ON_BN_CLICKED(ID_CALC_BTN, HandleCalcBtn)
510:      ON_COMMAND(ID_CALC_BTN, CMCalc)
511:      ON_BN_CLICKED(ID_STORE_BTN, HandleStoreBtn)
512:      ON_COMMAND(ID_STORE_BTN, CMStore)
513:      ON_BN_CLICKED(ID_EXIT_BTN, HandleExitBtn)
514:      ON_COMMAND(ID_EXIT_BTN, CMExit)
515:      ON_COMMAND(CM_EXIT, OnExit)
516:      ON_WM_CREATE()
517:      ON_WM_KEYDOWN()
518:      ON_WM_CLOSE()
519: END_MESSAGE_MAP()
520:
521: // Construct the CWindowApp's m_pMainWnd data member
522: BOOL CWindowApp::InitInstance()
```

```
523: {
524:    m_pMainWnd = new CAppWindow();
525:    m_pMainWnd->ShowWindow(m_nCmdShow);
526:    m_pMainWnd->UpdateWindow();
527:    return TRUE;
528: }
529:
530: // application's constructor initializes and runs the app
531: CWindowApp WindowApp;
```

Figure 16.1 shows a sample session with the program CTLBTN1.EXE.

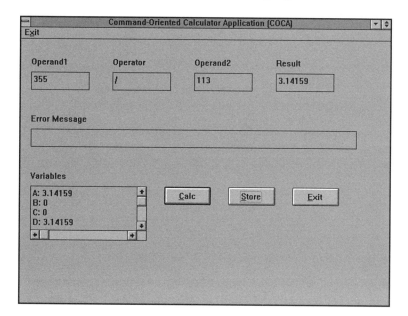

16

Figure 16.1. A sample session with the program CTLBTN1.EXE.

Analysis

The program in Listing 16.3 contains three sets of constants in lines 10 through 33. The first set, in lines 10 through 23, declares the constants for height, width, vertical spacing, and horizontal spacing that are used to dimension the various controls. The second set of constants, in lines 24 and 25, declares maximum characters in the edit control and the number of variables in the multiline edit control. The third set of constants, in lines 28 through 33, declares the ID_*xxxx* values used in creating the various edit control instances. The ID_*xxxx* for the push button controls are declared in the header file CTLBTN1.H which is included in the program.

The COCA program declares the application class, CWindowApp, the window class, CAppWindow, the extended button class CxButton, and the extended edit box class, CxEdit.

 Note: The program declares class CxButton that in turn declares a more specialized version of function Create. This version creates a push normal or default push button control by specifying the typical push button styles. Assigning these styles makes it easier for client windows or dialog boxes to create push button controls.

The CxEdit class is a descendant of CEdit that declares the GetLine and GetLineLength member functions. The GetLine function works with ASCIIZ arguments. The function is declared as follows:

```
BOOL GetLine(LPSTR lpString, int nStrSize, int nLineNumber);
```

The lpString is the pointer to an ASCIIZ string. The nStrSize parameter specifies the maximum number of characters to copy. The nLineNumber designates the target line number. The function returns TRUE if it succeeds, and yields FALSE if it fails.

The GetLineLength member function returns the length of a specified line. The declaration of the GetLineLength function is

```
int GetLineLength(int nLineNumber);
```

The nLineNumber parameter specifies the number of the line whose length is sought.

The CAppWindow window class is the owner of the static text and edit controls. The class declares a number of data members and member functions.

The CAppWindow contains the following groups of data members:

☐ Pointers to the various CStatic, CEdit, CxEdit, and CxButton instances (each pointer accesses one of the edit controls that appear in the program)

☐ The Boolean data member bInError, which flags any error

☐ The data members nXulc, nYulc, nXlrc, and nYlrc, which store the coordinates for the rectangle that contains the Error Message static text (the mouse click response member function OnLButtonDown examines whether the mouse is clicked inside that rectangle, and if so, clears the Error Message edit control text)

The CAppWindow class contains a constructor, a destructor, and a number of message response member functions that handle the mouse click and respond to the menu options.

The window class constructor performs the following tasks:

- ☐ Loads the menu resource by invoking the LoadAccelTable function and specifying the BUTTONS accelerator resource

- ☐ Builds the window instance by invoking the Create member function

- ☐ Assigns FALSE to the bInError data member

The call to Create specifies the window title, the WS_OVERLAPPEDWINDOW and WS_MAXIMIZE style, and the EXITMENU menu resource. The WS_MAXIMIZE style produces a maximized window. The call to function Create also creates the instances for the static text, edit box, and push buttons.

The EnableButton and DisableButton member functions enable and disable a push button, respectively, by calling the CWnd::EnableWindow function. The functions are called by other member functions with the StoreBtn argument.

The makeRect member function produces the values for the rectangular area occupied by a control, given the following values:

- ☐ The coordinates of the upper-left corner of the rectangular area

- ☐ The width of the rectangle

- ☐ The height of the rectangle

The OnCreate member function responds to the WM_CREATE message and builds the various controls attached to the window. The function carries out the following tasks:

- ☐ Creates the static text controls that label the operands, operator, and the result edit controls by invoking the CStatic constructor

- ☐ Creates the edit boxes for the operands, operator, and the result

- ☐ Creates the CxButton instances, each with a unique ID and caption

- ☐ Calculates the upper-left corner and lower-right corner of the rectangle containing the Error Message static text, and stores them in the nXulc, nYulc, nXlrc, and nYlrc data members

- ☐ Creates the error message static text control and edit control

☐ Creates the variables multiline edit control, by building the contents of the Variables box using the string variable `bigStr`

☐ Returns the expression `CFrameWnd::OnCreate(lpCS)`

The member function `OnCreate` uses the style `WS_CHILD | WS_VISIBLE | SS_LEFT` in creating the static text controls. The creation of the controls involves the private member function `makeRect` that generates the required `CRect` object. The local variable `nX` is increased by (`Wlbl + LblHorzSpacing`) to calculate the X-coordinate for the next static text control. This approach allows you to systematically increment the X and/or Y coordinates for the control's area.

The instances for the edit boxes for the operands, operator, and result are accessed by the `Operand1Box`, `OperatorBox`, `Operand2Box`, and `ResultBox` data members, respectively. Each `CEdit` instance is created with its own `ID_xxxx` constant, and an empty edit box. The edit boxes have the same size. The style of the edit controls include the `ES_UPPERCASE` style. This style results in automatically converting into uppercase the single-letter variable names that you type in these edit controls.

The caption for the `CxButton` instance uses the ampersand character to underline the hot-key. The first push button is created as the default control, by making the last argument of `CxButton:Create` a `TRUE`. The other two buttons are created as normal controls by specifying a `FALSE` argument to the last parameter of function `Create`. Consequently, the `Calc` button appears as the default push button. However, appearances can be deceiving—the `Calc` button totally lacks the functionality of a default button because its owner is a window and not a dialog box.

The Variables edit control is created with the additional styles of `ES_MULTILINE`, `WS_HSCROLL`, `WS_VSCROLL`, and `ES_AUTOVSCROLL`. These styles produce an edit control with fully functioning vertical and horizontal scroll bars. The `OnCreate` function writes the contents of `bigStr` in the edit control by calling the `SetWindowText` function.

The `OnLButtonDown` member function performs a simple task. It checks whether or not the mouse click occurs in the rectangle occupied by the error message static text control. If this condition is true, the function performs the following tasks:

☐ Clears the error message box by invoking the function `SetWindowText`

☐ Enables the Store button by invoking the function `EnableButton`

The `HandleCalcBtn` member function responds to the notification message emitted by the Calc button. The corresponding message map macro uses the message ID of `ID_CALC_BTN`. The latter is the ID of the Calc button that is also used in creating the Calc button instance. The function performs the following tasks:

☐ Obtains the first operand from the Operand1 edit box

☐ Obtains the second operand in a manner identical to the first one (the function stores the actual (numeric) second operand in variable y)

☐ Copies the text in the Operator edit box into the local variable opStr

☐ Clears the error message text box and sets the bInError data member to FALSE

☐ Determines the requested operation by using a series of if and if-else statements—operators supported are +, -, *, /, and ^ (power)—and, if the function detects an error, sets the bInError data member to TRUE and displays a message in the error message box

☐ Displays the result in the Result box if the bInError data member is FALSE (first converting the result from double to a string and then writing to the Result box using the SetWindowText function), and systematically enables the Store button (if member bInError is TRUE, it disables the Store push button by calling the member function DisableButton)

When the member function HandleCalcBtn obtains the first operand from the Operand1 edit box, the control may contain the name of a single-letter variable (A to Z) or a floating-point number. The function uses the GetWindowText function to store a copy of the edit control text in the local variable s. The function then examines the first character in variable s. If that character is a letter, the first operand is a single-letter variable. Consequently, the function calls the protected member function getVar to obtain the value associated with that variable. If the first character is not a letter, the function uses the atof function to convert the contents of variable s into a double-typed number. In both cases, the function stores the actual (numeric) first operand in variable x.

The CMCalcBtn member function handles the command messages emitted by the Alt-C accelerator key. The corresponding macro message ID is specified as ID_CALC_BTN, the ID associated with the Alt-C in the resource file (which is also the ID for the Calc button). The CMCalcBtn function simply invokes the HandleCalcBtn member function to execute the requested calculation.

The HandleStoreBtn member function stores the contents of the Result box in a single-letter variable. The function first obtains the string in the Result edit box by calling the GetWindowText function. Then, the function invokes the protected member function putVar to actually store the result string at the current insertion point in the Variables edit box.

The CMStore member function intercepts the Alt-S hot-key in the form of the command message with the ID number ID_STORE_BTN. The CMStore function merely calls the HandleStoreBtn member function.

The getVar member function returns the number stored at line number lineNum of the Variables edit box. The function performs the following tasks:

☐ Exits and returns 0 if the lineNum is greater than or equal to the constant MAX_MEMREG

☐ Obtains the size of the target line by making the GetLineLength(nLineNum) call

☐ Retrieves the strings of line number nLineNum by calling the GetLine function

☐ Deletes the first three characters of the retrieved line (this step should leave the string with the number stored in the target line)

☐ Returns the double-typed number obtained by calling the atof function and supplying it argument s

The putVar member function stores the number in the Result box in the variable that is located on the same line that contains the text insert position. The function performs the following tasks:

☐ Locates the character position of the cursor by calling the GetSel function, which returns the start and end character positions in the local dwSelPos, and then uses the predefined macros HIWORD and LOWORD to store the starting and ending positions in the local variables wStartPos and wEndPos

☐ Turns off any selected text, comparing the values in the variables wStartPos and wEndPos and, if they do not match, calculating a new value for variable dwSelPos so that the low and high words are both wStartPos (the function then invokes the SetSel function and supplies it with the variable dwSelPos to turn off the selected text)

☐ Obtains the line number where the cursor is located using the GetLineFromChar function

☐ Obtains the size of the target line using the GetLineLength function

☐ Retrieves the text in the target line by calling the GetLine function

☐ Builds the new text line

☐ Obtains the starting and ending character positions for the line to be replaced

☐ Selects the line to be replaced using the SetSel function

☐ Replaces the current line with a new line

The HandleExitBtn member function responds to the notification message of the Exit button. The function sends the WM_CLOSE message to the parent window. The CMExit member function intercepts the Alt-E hot-key in the form of a command message with the ID number ID_EXIT_BTN. The CMExit function also sends a WM_CLOSE message to the parent window.

Summary

Today's lesson looks at the static text, edit box, and push button controls. Using these and other controls animate the Windows applications and provide a more consistent user interface. You learn about the following topics:

☐ You can create static text controls and manipulate their text at run-time.

☐ Single-line and multiline edit box controls allow you to type and edit the text in the input dialog box.

☐ The two types of push button controls—default and nondefault—give you instant power.

In Day 17, I present the grouped controls: the classes for group, check box, and radio controls. These controls are used to fine-tune the execution of a specific task, such as searching and replacing text in a text editor.

Q&A

Q. How do I create a string for a multiline static text control?

A. You build a multiline string, such as "This is\na multiline" (notice the imbedded \n character which breaks the line) and pass it as the first argument to the CStatic::Create member function.

Q. How important is selecting the correct control style?

A. Very important. The style fine-tunes the control appearance, optional components, and behavior.

Q. Why does program CTLBTN1.CPP use local variables such as nX and nY to specify the location of a control? Why not replace these variables with numeric constants?

A. Using variables, such as nX and nY, allows you to specify the location of the controls relative to one another. This method enables you to shift controls very easily. By contrast, using numeric constants specifies the absolute values for the control locations. Shifting controls, in this case, means plugging a new set of numbers!

Workshop

The Workshop provides quiz questions to help you solidify your understanding of the material covered and exercises to provide you with experience in using what you've learned. Try to understand the quiz and exercise answers before continuing on to the next day's lesson. Answers are provided in Appendix B, "Answers."

Quiz

1. True or false? The text for all static text controls are unchangeable.

2. True or false? The SS_CENTER centers each line of a multiline static text control.

3. True or false? A static text control needs an accompanying pointer to access only when the program needs to set or query the text in the control.

4. True or false? Every edit control needs an accompanying pointer to access it.

5. True or false? The API Windows functions EnableWindow and DisableWindow can disable any control.

6. True or false? The Windows messages emitted by a push button can be mapped using the ON_COMMAND map.

Exercises

1. Experiment with the program CTLBTN1.CPP to add trigonometric functions, inverse trigonometric functions, hyperbolic functions, and inverse hyperbolic functions.

2. Experiment with a copy of program CTLBTN1.CPP by changing values assigned to the constants which specify the size and spacing of the various controls.

DAY
17

Grouped Controls

Windows supports check box and radio button controls that act as software switches. These controls appear in typical search and replace dialog boxes and influence certain aspects of the text search or replacement. These aspects include the scope, direction, and case-sensitivity of searching or replacing text. In today's lesson, you learn about the following topics:

☐ The check box control

☐ The radio button control

☐ The group control

Today's lesson also shows you how to respond to the messages emitted by these controls as well as how to use the ForEach iterators to manipulate the check box and radio button controls.

 NEW TERM The *group box control* is a special control that visually and logically groups the check box and radio button controls.

The Check Box Control

The check box control is a special button that toggles a check mark. The control instances appear with a small rectangular button and a title that appears, by default, to the right side of the square. When you click on the square, you toggle the control's check mark. Think of the check box as a binary digit that can be either set or cleared. The instances of a check box can appear inside or outside a group box and are mutually nonexclusive—toggling any check box does not affect the check state of other check boxes.

 Note: Placing check boxes inside groups (inside a dialog box) serves two purposes. First, the group box provides a visual grouping that clarifies the purpose of the check boxes to the application user. Second, you can streamline the notification messages emitted by the check boxes in a group to detect any change in the checked state of the check boxes.

NEW TERM Windows allows you to specify a check box with three states: checked, unchecked, and *grayed.* Table 5.1 in Day 5 shows the styles for the check box control. The grayed state fills the control's rectangular button with a gray color. This third state can serve to indicate that the check box control is in an indeterminate (or call it "don't care") state.

The *CButton* Class and Check Boxes

Microsoft Foundation Class offers the CButton class, a descendant of CWnd, as the class that provides the instances of check box controls (as well as other controls). Day 16 introduces you to the CButton class and discusses the aspects of that class that are related to the push button controls. In this section I focus on the aspects of class CButton that are relevant to the check box controls. Of course, the check box instances need the class constructor and the Create member function to come to life. The check box styles shown in Table 17.1 indicate that there are two basic modes for managing the check state of a check box control: automatic, and nonautomatic (manual, if you prefer). In automatic mode (specified by BS_AUTOCHECK and BS_AUTO3STATE), Windows toggles the check state when you click on the control. In manual mode, your application code is responsible for managing the check state of the check box.

Table 17.1. Check box control styles.

Style	Meaning
BS_CHECKBOX	Specifies a check box with the title to the right of the rectangular button
BS_AUTOCHECKBOX	Same as BS_CHECKBOX, except the button is automatically toggled when you click on it
BS_3STATE	Same as BS_CHECKBOX, except that the control has three states: checked, unchecked, and grayed
BS_AUTO3STATE	Same as BS_3STATE, except the button is automatically toggled when you click on it
BS_LEFTTEXT	Sets the control's title to the left of the button

The CButton class provides member functions to set and query the state of the check box. The GetCheck member function returns a state of the check box control and is declared as follows:

```
int GetCheck() const;
```

The function returns an int-typed value that represents the check state. A value of 0 indicates that the control is not checked. A value of 1 signals that the control is checked. A value of 2 indicates that the control is in an indeterminate state. The latter value is valid for the BS_3STATE and BS_AUTO3STATE styles.

17

The SetCheck member function allows you to set the check state of a check box control. The declaration of the SetCheck function is

```
void SetCheck(int nCheck);
```

The nCheck parameter specifies the new state of the check box control.

Responding to Check Box Messages

Because check boxes are instances of CButton with a BS_CHECKBOX or BS_AUTOCHECKBOX style, your MFC application responds to the messages emitted by check boxes in a manner similar to the push buttons. The BN_CLICKED macro maps the message sent by the check box control with the member function that responds to that message.

The Radio Button Control

Radio button controls typically allow you to select an option from two or more options. This kind of control comes with a circular button and a title that appears, by default, to the right of the button. When you check a radio button, a tiny filled circle appears inside the circular button. Radio buttons need to be placed in group boxes that visually and logically group them. In each group of radio buttons, only one button can be selected. Therefore, radio buttons are mutually exclusive.

The *CButton* Class and Radio Buttons

The MFC applications use the CButton class to create radio button controls by specifying the BS_RADIOBUTTON or BS_AUTORADIOBUTTON. Table 17.2 contains the radio button styles. The constructor creates a radio button with the BS_AUTORADIOBUTTON style. Creating these controls involves the class constructor and the Create member function. Like the check box controls, the radio buttons use the GetCheck and SetCheck member functions to query and set the state. Unlike the check box, the radio button has only two states: checked and unchecked.

Table 17.2. Radio button control styles.

Style	Meaning
BS_RADIOBUTTON	Specifies a radio button with the title to the right of the circular button
BS_AUTORADIOBUTTON	Same as BS_RADIOBUTTON, except the button is automatically toggled when you click on it
BS_LEFTTEXT	Sets the control's title to the left of the button

The radio button controls send the same type of notification messages to their parent windows as do the check box controls. Handling these messages for radio buttons is identical to that of check box and push button controls.

The Group Control

The group box control encloses radio buttons and check boxes. The group box performs the following tasks:

☐ Visually groups radio buttons and/or check boxes, which makes relating these controls to each other clearer for the application user

☐ Logically groups multiple radio buttons so that when you select one radio button, the other buttons in the same group are automatically deselected

NEW☞ TERM The group box control is a special type of control known as a *container control*.

You can code your MFC application so that the controls inside a group box notify the parent of the group box that you have changed the state of its controls.

The *CButton* Class and Group Boxes

Your MFC applications can create group boxes by specifying the BS_GROUPBOX style when creating a CButton instance. Unlike the check box, radio button, and push button controls, there is no state for the group box controls. In addition, group boxes do not send messages.

The Updated Calculator Application

The operations of the calculator application that are presented in Day 16 can be expanded to include trigonometric functions. Using trigonometric functions frequently offers you the choice of angle modes: radians, degrees, or gradians (100 gradians equal 90 degrees). Using a group box that contains angle mode radio buttons seems suitable to illustrate the operations of these controls. Check boxes are added to fine-tune other operational aspects of the calculator. More about this later in this section.

Create the directory CTLGRP1 as a subdirectory of \MSVC\VC21DAY and store all the project's files in the new directory. The project's .MAK file should contain the files CTLGRP1.CPP, CTLGRP1.RC, and CTLGRP1.DEF. The latter file resembles file MINWINAP.DEF in Day 14, Listing 14.2.

Note: I choose to present nontrivial applications to illustrate nontrivial features that involve the radio button, check box, and edit text controls. Although the program in Listing 17.3 is long, you can create it by starting with a copy of program CTLBTN1.CPP and adding the new functions and statements.

The Illustrated Aspects

The updated calculator application (COCA version 2) illustrates the following:

- ☐ The basic use of check box controls
- ☐ The basic use of radio buttons
- ☐ Responding to radio button notification messages
- ☐ Echoing the changes in the selected radio button control to the group box control
- ☐ Using a check box control to alter the action of a response message function (this function handles the group box response to select a new radio button)
- ☐ Manipulating multiple check boxes and edit boxes using the ForEach iterator

☐ Making initial check box selections

☐ Making initial radio button selections

The new version of the calculator application contains the following controls:

☐ The single-line edit controls labeled Operand1, Operator, Operand2, Result, and Error Message

☐ The multiline edit control labeled Variables

☐ The static text controls that label these edit boxes

☐ The Calc, Store, and Exit push buttons

☐ The Angle Mode group box that contains the Radians, Degrees, and Gradians radio buttons

☐ The Substitute variable name check box that replaces the names of the single-letter variables appearing in either operand edit box with their values (the replacement occurs after you click the Calc push button)

☐ The Echo Group box message check box that permits the group notification message handler to display a message box when you select another radio button

☐ The menu that contains the Exit and Clear main menu items

The Clear pop-up menu has the Edit Controls and Check Boxes menu items. The Edit Controls menu item clears the contents of the edit controls, except the Variables edit box. The Check Boxes menu item unchecks the three check boxes.

Experimenting with the Application

Listing 17.1 contains the source code for the CTLGRP1.H header file and Listing 17.2 shows the script for the CTLGRP1.RC resource file. The resource file contains the accelerator keys and the menu resources. Listing 17.3 contains the source code for the CTLGRP1.CPP program file. The program contains #include statements, declarations of constants, iterated functions, and the classes for the application, its window, and its controls.

Compile and run the calculator application to get a good feel for the features supported by the radio buttons, check boxes, and the group box. When the application's window appears, maximize it to get a full view. The Angle Mode group box shows the initial selection of the Degrees radio button. The current application version supports the SIN, COS, TAN, ASIN, ACOS, and ATAN trigonometric functions that you can enter in the Operator edit box. Enter the number 45 in the Operand1 edit box and type TAN in the Operator edit box. Click the Calc button to obtain the tangent of 45 degrees in the Result edit box (a value of 1). Store the result in variable A by clicking the Store button. Now replace the number 45 with the # character in the Operand1 edit box. Then insert an A before the string TAN in the Operator box, and click the Calc button. The # character is replaced by 1, the previous number in the Result edit box. The Result edit box now shows the number 45, the arctangent of 1. Using the # character is a new feature that I added to the program—the ability to use the result from the previous calculation in either or both operand edit boxes by typing in the # character. Next, click the Store button again. The application stores the number 45 in variable A, overwriting the previous result. Now, the number in the Result edit box is stored in multiple variables.

Check the Echo Group message box check box and then click on any radio button. The application displays a message box that contains information on converting between different angles. Selecting a different radio button yields a different message. These messages are responses to the Angle Mode group notification message.

Experiment with selecting different angle modes. Each time, enter a value in the Operand1 edit box and type in a trigonometric function. Observe how the results differ for the same arguments although the angle mode varies. Keep in mind that the inverse sine and cosine functions accept arguments between -1 and 1. The application detects invalid arguments for these two functions and displays error messages.

Finally, use the Clear | Edit Control and Clear | Check Boxes menu items to clear the edit boxes (except the Variables edit box) and the check boxes.

I omit the feature that clears the error message and enables the Store button when you click on the Error Message label. This omission should shorten the program a bit.

Listing 17.1. Source code for the CTLGRP1.H header file.

```
1: #define CM_EXIT     (WM_USER + 100)
2: #define CM_CLEARBOX (WM_USER + 101)
3: #define CM_CLEARCHK (WM_USER + 102)
4:
5: #define ID_CALC_BTN  107
6: #define ID_STORE_BTN 108
7: #define ID_EXIT_BTN  109
```

Listing 17.2. Script for the CTLGRP1.RC resource file.

```
 1: #include <windows.h>
 2: #include <afxres.h>
 3: #include "ctlgrp1.h"
 4:
 5: BUTTONS ACCELERATORS
 6: BEGIN
 7:   "c", ID_CALC_BTN, ALT
 8:   "s", ID_STORE_BTN, ALT
 9:   "e", ID_EXIT_BTN, ALT
10: END
11:
12: EXITMENU MENU LOADONCALL MOVEABLE PURE DISCARDABLE
13: BEGIN
14:     MENUITEM "E&xit", CM_EXIT
15:     POPUP "C&lear"
16:     BEGIN
17:       MENUITEM "&Edit Controls", CM_CLEARBOX
18:       MENUITEM "&Check Boxes", CM_CLEARCHK
19:     END
20: END
```

 Listing 17.3. Source code for the CTLGRP1.CPP program file.

```
 1: #include <stdlib.h>
 2: #include <ctype.h>
 3: #include <stdio.h>
 4: #include <math.h>
 5: #include <string.h>
 6: #include <afxwin.h>
 7: #include "ctlgrp1.h"
 8:
 9: // declare the constants that represent the sizes of the controls
10: const Wlbl = 100;
11: const Hlbl = 20;
12: const LblVertSpacing = 5;
13: const LblHorzSpacing = 40;
14: const Wbox = 100;
15: const Hbox = 30;
16: const BoxVertSpacing = 10;
17: const BoxHorzSpacing = 40;
18: const WLongbox = 4 * (Wbox + BoxHorzSpacing);
19: const Wvarbox = 2 * Wbox;
20: const Hvarbox = 3 * Hbox;
21: const Hbtn = 30;
22: const Wbtn = 80;
```

continues

Listing 17.3. continued

```
23: const BtnHorzSpacing = 30;
24: const BtnVertSpacing = 10;
25: const Hgrp = 150;
26: const Wgrp = 180;
27: const GrpHorzSpacing = 30;
28: const GrpVertSpacing = 10;
29: const Hchk = 30;
30: const Wchk = 200;
31: const ChkHorzSpacing = 30;
32: const ChkVertSpacing = 10;
33: const Hrbt = 30;
34: const Wrbt = 80;
35: const RbtHorzSpacing = 30;
36: const RbtVertSpacing = 30;
37: const RbtLeftMargin = 30;
38: // non-ctrol related constants
39: const MaxEditLen = 30;
40: const MAX_MEMREG = 26;
41: // declare the ID_XXXX constants for the various controls
42: // (except the push buttons)
43: #define ID_OPERAND1_EDIT 101
44: #define ID_OPERATOR_EDIT 102
45: #define ID_OPERAND2_EDIT 103
46: #define ID_RESULT_EDIT 104
47: #define ID_ERRMSG_EDIT 105
48: #define ID_VARIABLE_EDIT 106
49: #define ID_SUBST_CHK 110
50: #define ID_ECHO_CHK 111
51: #define ID_ANGLE_GRP 112
52: #define ID_RADIAN_RBT 113
53: #define ID_DEGREE_RBT 114
54: #define ID_GRADIAN_RBT 115
55: // declare constants for the check box and radio button states
56: const BF_CHECKED = 1;
57: const BF_UNCHECKED = 0;
58: // declare angle-related constants
59: const double pi = 4 * atan(1);
60: const double DegToRad = pi / 180;
61: const double GradToRad = 0.9 * DegToRad;
62:
63: // declare extended button class
64: class CxButton : public CButton
65: {
66: public:
67:
68:     BOOL Create(const char FAR* lpCaption, const RECT& rect,
69:             CWnd* pParentWnd, UINT nID)
70:     {
71:         return CButton::Create(lpCaption,
```

```
72:                                         WS_CHILD | WS_VISIBLE |
73:                                         WS_TABSTOP | BS_PUSHBUTTON,
74:                                         rect, pParentWnd, nID);
75:     }
76: };
77:
78: // declare check box class
79: class CCheckBox : public CButton
80: {
81: public:
82:     BOOL Create(const char FAR* lpCaption, const RECT& rect,
83:                 CWnd* pParentWnd, UINT nID)
84:     {
85:         return CButton::Create(lpCaption,
86:                                 WS_CHILD | WS_VISIBLE |
87:                                 WS_TABSTOP | BS_AUTOCHECKBOX,
88:                                 rect, pParentWnd, nID);
89:     }
90:     // check control
91:     void Check() { SetCheck(BF_CHECKED); }
92:     // uncheck control
93:     void UnCheck() { SetCheck(BF_UNCHECKED); }
94: };
95:
96: // declare radio button class
97: class CRadioButton : public CButton
98: {
99: public:
100:    BOOL Create(const char FAR* lpCaption, const RECT& rect,
101:                CWnd* pParentWnd, UINT nID)
102:    {
103:        return CButton::Create(lpCaption,
104:                                WS_CHILD | WS_VISIBLE |
105:                                WS_TABSTOP |
106:                                BS_AUTORADIOBUTTON,
107:                                rect, pParentWnd, nID);
108:    }
109:    // check control
110:    void Check() { SetCheck(BF_CHECKED); }
111:    // uncheck control
112:    void UnCheck()
113:      { SetCheck(BF_UNCHECKED); }
114: };
115:
116: // declare group box class
117: class CGroupBox : public CButton
118: {
119: public:
120:    BOOL Create(const char FAR* lpCaption, const RECT& rect,
121:                CWnd* pParentWnd, UINT nID)
122:    {
```

continues

Listing 17.3. continued

```
123:          return CButton::Create(lpCaption,
124:                              WS_CHILD | WS_VISIBLE |
125:                              WS_TABSTOP | BS_GROUPBOX,
126:                              rect, pParentWnd, nID);
127:     }
128: };
129:
130:
131: class CxEdit : public CEdit
132: {
133: public:
134:
135:    BOOL GetLine(LPSTR ATextString, int nStrSize, int nLineNumber);
136:    int GetLineLength(int nLineNumber);
137: };
138:
139: class CWindowApp : public CWinApp
140: {
141: public:
142:      virtual BOOL InitInstance();
143: };
144: // expand the functionality of CFrameWnd by deriving class
145: // CAppWindow
146: class CAppWindow : public CFrameWnd
147: {
148: public:
149:
150:    CAppWindow();
151:    ~CAppWindow();
152:
153: protected:
154:    // declare the pointers to the various controls
155:    // first, the edit box controls
156:    CEdit* Operand1Box;
157:    CEdit* OperatorBox;
158:    CEdit* Operand2Box;
159:    CEdit* ResultBox;
160:    CEdit* ErrMsgBox;
161:    CxEdit* VariableBox;
162:    // then the static text controls
163:    CStatic* Operand1Txt;
164:    CStatic* OperatorTxt;
165:    CStatic* Operand2Txt;
166:    CStatic* ResultTxt;
167:    CStatic* ErrMsgTxt;
168:    CStatic* VariableTxt;
169:    // then the push buttons
170:    CxButton* CalcBtn;
171:    CxButton* StoreBtn;
```

```
172:    CxButton* ExitBtn;
173:    // then the angle group box
174:    CGroupBox* AngleModeGrp;
175:    // then the radio buttons
176:    CRadioButton* RadianRbt;
177:    CRadioButton* DegreeRbt;
178:    CRadioButton* GradianRbt;
179:    // then the check boxes
180:    CCheckBox* AutoVarSubstChk;
181:    CCheckBox* EchoGroupChk;
182:    // math error flag
183:    BOOL bInError;
184:    // the factor that converts between angles the
185:    // currently selected angle mode and radians
186:    double angleFactor;
187:
188:    // handle clearing the edit controls
189:    afx_msg void CMClearBox();
190:    // handle clearing the check box controls
191:    afx_msg void CMClearChk();
192:    // handle the calculation
193:    afx_msg void HandleCalcBtn();
194:    // handle the calculation
195:    afx_msg void CMCalc() { HandleCalcBtn(); }
196:    // handle storing the result in a variable
197:    afx_msg void HandleStoreBtn();
198:    // handle storing the result in a variable
199:    afx_msg void CMStore() { HandleStoreBtn(); }
200:    // handle exiting the application
201:    afx_msg void HandleExitBtn() { SendMessage(WM_CLOSE); }
202:    // hanlde exiting the application
203:    afx_msg void CMExit() { SendMessage(WM_CLOSE); }
204:    // handle exiting the application
205:    afx_msg void OnExit() { SendMessage(WM_CLOSE); }
206:    // handle the Angle Mode group box message
207:    // this member is called only by the radio button
208:    // controls; it therefore need not be included in the
209:    // message map
210:    void HandleAngleModeGrp();
211:    // handle selecting the Radians radio button
212:    afx_msg void HandleRadianRbt();
213:    // handle selecting the Degrees radio button
214:    afx_msg void HandleDegreeRbt();
215:    // handle selecting the Gradians radio button
216:    afx_msg void HandleGradianRbt();
217:    // enable a push button control
218:    virtual void EnableButton(CxButton* pBtn)
219:      { pBtn->EnableWindow( TRUE); }
220:    // disable a push button control
221:    virtual void DisableButton(CxButton* pBtn)
222:      { pBtn->EnableWindow(FALSE); }
```

continues

Listing 17.3. continued

```
223:    // handle creating the controls
224:    afx_msg int OnCreate(LPCREATESTRUCT lpCS);
225:    // handle closing the window
226:    afx_msg void OnClose();
227:    // initialize the instances of CAppWindow
228:    virtual void InitAppWindow();
229:    // return a reference to member r based on individual
230:    // coordinates and dimensions
231:    void makeRect(int nX, int nY, int nW, int nH, CRect& r);
232:    // obtain a number of a Variable edit box line
233:    double getVar(int nLineNum);
234:    // store a number in the selected text of
235:    // the Variable edit box line
236:    void putVar(double x);
237:    // declare the iterator for the check boxes
238:    void ForEachCheckBox(void (FAR *f)(CCheckBox*));
239:    // declare the iterator for the edit controls
240:    void ForEachEditCtl(void (FAR *f)(CEdit*));
241:
242:    // declare message map macro
243:    DECLARE_MESSAGE_MAP();
244: };
245:
246: // declare an iterated function to clear all edit controls
247: // except the Variables edit control
248: void FAR ClearEditControls(CEdit* P)
249: { P->SetWindowText(""); }
250:
251: // declare the iterated function to clear the check boxes
252: void FAR ClearCheckBoxes(CCheckBox* P)
253: { P->UnCheck(); }
254:
255: BOOL CxEdit::GetLine(LPSTR ATextString, int nStrSize,
256:                      int nLineNumber)
257: {
258:    int nBytesCopied;
259:    BOOL bSuccess;
260:
261:    if (nStrSize <= 0)
262:      return FALSE;
263:    bSuccess = (nStrSize >= GetLineLength(nLineNumber) + 1) ? TRUE
264:                                                   : FALSE;
265:    if (nStrSize == 1)
266:    {
267:      ATextString[0] = '\0';
268:      return bSuccess;
269:    }
270:
271:    ((WORD FAR *)ATextString)[0] = nStrSize;
```

```
272:
273:    nBytesCopied = (WORD)(SendMessage(EM_GETLINE, nLineNumber,
274:                                      long(ATextString)));
275:    if (nBytesCopied)
276:    {
277:      // Windows returns non-null-terminated string
278:      ATextString[nBytesCopied] = '\0';
279:      return bSuccess;
280:    }
281:    else
282:      return FALSE;
283: }
284:
285: int CxEdit::GetLineLength(int nLineNumber)
286: {
287:    int nStartPos = -1;
288:
289:    if (nLineNumber > -1)
290:      nStartPos = LineIndex(nLineNumber);
291:    return (WORD) SendMessage(EM_LINELENGTH, nStartPos);
292: }
293:
294: CAppWindow::CAppWindow()
295: {
296:    // load accelerator resources
297:    LoadAccelTable("BUTTONS");
298:    // create the window
299:    Create(NULL,
300:      "Command-Oriented Calculator Application (COCA) Version 2",
301:       WS_OVERLAPPEDWINDOW | WS_MAXIMIZE,
302:          rectDefault, NULL, "EXITMENU");
303:    // perform initialization
304:    InitAppWindow();
305:    // clear the bInError flag
306:    bInError = FALSE;
307: }
308:
309: CAppWindow::~CAppWindow()
310: {
311:    // delete the controls
312:    delete Operand1Box;
313:    delete OperatorBox;
314:    delete Operand2Box;
315:    delete ResultBox;
316:    delete ErrMsgBox;
317:    delete VariableBox;
318:    delete Operand1Txt;
319:    delete OperatorTxt;
320:    delete Operand2Txt;
321:    delete ResultTxt;
322:    delete ErrMsgTxt;
```

continues

Listing 17.3. continued

```
323:    delete VariableTxt;
324:    delete CalcBtn;
325:    delete StoreBtn;
326:    delete ExitBtn;
327:    delete AngleModeGrp;
328:    delete RadianRbt;
329:    delete DegreeRbt;
330:    delete GradianRbt;
331:    delete AutoVarSubstChk;
332:    delete EchoGroupChk;
333: }
334:
335: int CAppWindow::OnCreate(LPCREATESTRUCT lpCS)
336: {
337:    char s[81];
338:    char bigStr[6 * MAX_MEMREG + 1];
339:    char chC;
340:    int nX0 = 20;
341:    int nY0 = 30;
342:    int nX = nX0, nY = nY0;
343:    int nX1, nY1;
344:    CRect r;
345:    DWORD StatStyle = WS_CHILD ¦ WS_VISIBLE ¦ SS_LEFT;
346:    DWORD BoxStyle = WS_CHILD ¦ WS_VISIBLE ¦ WS_TABSTOP ¦ WS_BORDER
347:                      ¦ ES_LEFT ¦ ES_AUTOHSCROLL ¦ ES_UPPERCASE;
348:
349:    // create the first set of labels for the edit boxes
350:    makeRect(nX, nY, Wlbl, Hlbl, r);
351:    Operand1Txt = new CStatic();
352:    Operand1Txt->Create("Operand1", StatStyle, r, this, -1);
353:    nX += Wlbl + LblHorzSpacing;
354:    makeRect(nX, nY, Wlbl, Hlbl, r);
355:    OperatorTxt = new CStatic();
356:    OperatorTxt->Create("Operator", StatStyle, r, this, -1);
357:    nX += Wlbl + LblHorzSpacing;
358:    makeRect(nX, nY, Wlbl, Hlbl, r);
359:    Operand2Txt = new CStatic();
360:    Operand2Txt->Create("Operand2", StatStyle, r, this, -1);
361:    nX += Wlbl + LblHorzSpacing;
362:    makeRect(nX, nY, Wlbl, Hlbl, r);
363:    ResultTxt = new CStatic();
364:    ResultTxt->Create("Result", StatStyle, r, this, -1);
365:
366:    // create the operand1, operator, operand2, and result
367:    // edit boxes
368:    nX = nX0;
369:    nY += Hlbl + LblVertSpacing;
370:    makeRect(nX, nY, Wbox, Hbox, r);
371:    Operand1Box = new CEdit();
```

```
372:    Operand1Box->Create(BoxStyle, r, this, ID_OPERAND1_EDIT);
373:    Operand1Box->LimitText(); // set no limit for text
374:    nX += Wbox + BoxHorzSpacing;
375:    makeRect(nX, nY, Wbox, Hbox, r);
376:    OperatorBox = new CEdit();
377:    OperatorBox->Create(BoxStyle, r, this, ID_OPERATOR_EDIT);
378:    OperatorBox->LimitText(); // set no limit for text
379:    nX += Wbox + BoxHorzSpacing;
380:    makeRect(nX, nY, Wbox, Hbox, r);
381:    Operand2Box = new CEdit();
382:    Operand2Box->Create(BoxStyle, r, this, ID_OPERAND2_EDIT);
383:    Operand2Box->LimitText(); // set no limit for text
384:    nX += Wbox + BoxHorzSpacing;
385:    makeRect(nX, nY, Wbox, Hbox, r);
386:    ResultBox = new CEdit();
387:    ResultBox->Create(BoxStyle, r, this, ID_RESULT_EDIT);
388:    ResultBox->LimitText(); // set no limit for text
389:    // create the static text and edit box for the error message
390:    nX = nX0;
391:    nY += Hbox + BoxVertSpacing;
392:    makeRect(nX, nY, Wlbl, Hlbl, r);
393:    ErrMsgTxt = new CStatic();
394:    ErrMsgTxt->Create("Error Message", StatStyle, r, this, -1);
395:    nY += Hlbl + LblVertSpacing;
396:    makeRect(nX, nY, WLongbox, Hbox, r);
397:    ErrMsgBox = new CEdit();
398:    ErrMsgBox->Create(BoxStyle, r, this, ID_ERRMSG_EDIT);
399:    ErrMsgBox->LimitText(); // set no limit for text
400:    // create the static text and edit box for the single-letter
401:    // variable selection
402:    nY += Hbox + BoxVertSpacing;
403:    makeRect(nX, nY, Wlbl, Hlbl, r);
404:    VariableTxt = new CStatic();
405:    VariableTxt->Create("Variables", StatStyle, r, this, -1);
406:    nY += Hlbl + LblVertSpacing;
407:    bigStr[0] = '\0';
408:    // build the initial contents of the Variable edit box
409:    for (chC = 'A'; chC <= 'Z'; chC++) {
410:      sprintf(s, "%c: 0\r\n", chC);
411:      strcat(bigStr, s);
412:    }
413:    makeRect(nX, nY, Wvarbox, Hvarbox, r);
414:    VariableBox = new CxEdit();
415:    VariableBox->Create(BoxStyle | ES_MULTILINE | WS_HSCROLL
416:                    | WS_VSCROLL | ES_AUTOVSCROLL,
417:                        r, this, ID_VARIABLE_EDIT);
418:    VariableBox->LimitText(); // set no limit for text
419:    VariableBox->SetWindowText(bigStr);
420:
421:    // create the Calc push button
422:    nX += Wvarbox + BtnHorzSpacing;
```

continues

Listing 17.3. continued

```
423:    nX1 = nX;
424:    nY1 = nY;
425:    makeRect(nX, nY, Wbtn, Hbtn, r);
426:    CalcBtn = new CxButton();
427:    CalcBtn->Create("&Calc", r, this, ID_CALC_BTN);
428:
429:    // create the Store Btn
430:    nX += Wbtn + BtnHorzSpacing;
431:    makeRect(nX, nY, Wbtn, Hbtn, r);
432:    StoreBtn = new CxButton();
433:    StoreBtn->Create("&Store", r, this, ID_STORE_BTN);
434:
435:    // create the Exit Btn
436:    nX += Wbtn + BtnHorzSpacing;
437:    makeRect(nX, nY, Wbtn, Hbtn, r);
438:    ExitBtn = new CxButton();
439:    ExitBtn->Create("&Exit", r, this, ID_EXIT_BTN);
440:
441:    // create the "Substitute variable name" check box
442:    nX = nX0;
443:    nY += Hvarbox + BoxVertSpacing;
444:    makeRect(nX, nY, Wchk, Hchk, r);
445:    AutoVarSubstChk = new CCheckBox();
446:    AutoVarSubstChk->Create("Substitute variable name", r,
447:                            this, ID_SUBST_CHK);
448:
449:    // create the "Echo Group box message" check box
450:    nY += Hchk + ChkVertSpacing;
451:    makeRect(nX, nY, Wchk, Hchk, r);
452:    EchoGroupChk = new CCheckBox();
453:    EchoGroupChk->Create("Echo Group box message", r,
454:                         this, ID_ECHO_CHK);
455:
456:    // create the Angle Mode group box
457:    nY = nY1 + Hbtn + BtnVertSpacing;
458:    nX = nX1;
459:    makeRect(nX, nY, Wgrp, Hgrp, r);
460:    AngleModeGrp = new CGroupBox();
461:    AngleModeGrp->Create(" Angle Mode ", r, this, ID_ANGLE_GRP);
462:
463:    // create the Radians radio button
464:    nY += RbtVertSpacing;
465:    makeRect(RbtLeftMargin + nX, nY, Wrbt, Hrbt, r);
466:    RadianRbt = new CRadioButton();
467:    RadianRbt->Create("Radians", r, this, ID_RADIAN_RBT);
468:
469:    // create the Degrees radio button
470:    nY += RbtVertSpacing;
```

```
471:    makeRect(RbtLeftMargin + nX, nY, Wrbt, Hrbt, r);
472:    DegreeRbt = new CRadioButton();
473:    DegreeRbt->Create("Degrees", r, this, ID_DEGREE_RBT);
474:
475:    // create the Gradians radio button
476:    nY += RbtVertSpacing;
477:    makeRect(RbtLeftMargin + nX, nY, Wrbt, Hrbt, r);
478:    GradianRbt = new CRadioButton();
479:    GradianRbt->Create("Gradians", r, this, ID_GRADIAN_RBT);
480:
481:    return CFrameWnd::OnCreate(lpCS);
482: }
483:
484: void CAppWindow::InitAppWindow()
485: {
486:
487:    // disable the Store button control
488:    EnableButton(StoreBtn);
489:
490:    // check the Degrees radio button
491:    DegreeRbt->Check();
492:    angleFactor = DegToRad;
493:
494:    // check the "Echo Group message box" check button
495:    EchoGroupChk->Check();
496: }
497:
498: void CAppWindow::CMClearBox()
499: {
500:    ForEachEditCtl(ClearEditControls);
501: }
502:
503: void CAppWindow::CMClearChk()
504: {
505:    ForEachCheckBox(ClearCheckBoxes);
506: }
507:
508: void CAppWindow::HandleCalcBtn()
509: {
510:    double x, y, z, result;
511:    char opStr[MaxEditLen+1];
512:    char s[MaxEditLen+1];
513:
514:    // convert the string in the Result box to a double
515:    ResultBox->GetWindowText(s, MaxEditLen);
516:    result = atof(s);
517:
518:    // obtain the string in the Operand1 edit box
519:    Operand1Box->GetWindowText(s, MaxEditLen);
```

continues

Listing 17.3. continued

```
520:   // does the Operand1Box contain the name
521:   // of a single-letter variable?
522:   if (isalpha(s[0])) {
523:     // obtain value from the Variable edit control
524:     x = getVar(s[0] - 'A');
525:     // substitute the variable name with its value
526:     if (AutoVarSubstChk->GetCheck() == BF_CHECKED) {
527:       sprintf(s, "%g", x);
528:       Operand1Box->SetWindowText(s);
529:     }
530:   }
531:   // translate the # character into the value in the Result box
532:   else if (s[0] == '#')
533:     x = result;
534:   else
535:     // convert the string in the edit box
536:     x = atof(s);
537:
538:   // obtain the string in the Operand2 edit box
539:   Operand2Box->GetWindowText(s, MaxEditLen);
540:   // does the Operand2Box contain the name
541:   // of a single-letter variable?
542:   if (isalpha(s[0])) {
543:     // obtain value from the Variable edit control
544:     y =getVar(s[0] - 'A');
545:     // substitute the variable name with its value
546:     if (AutoVarSubstChk->GetCheck() == BF_CHECKED) {
547:       sprintf(s, "%g", y);
548:       Operand2Box->SetWindowText(s);
549:     }
550:   }
551:   // translate the # character into the value in the Result box
552:   else if (s[0] == '#')
553:     y = result;
554:   else
555:     // convert the string in the edit box
556:     y = atof(s);
557:
558:   // obtain the string in the Operator edit box
559:   OperatorBox->GetWindowText(opStr, MaxEditLen);
560:
561:   // clear the error message box
562:   ErrMsgBox->SetWindowText("");
563:   bInError = FALSE;
564:
565:   // determine the requested operation
566:   if (strlen(opStr) == 1) {
```

```
567:        if (strcmp(opStr, "+") == 0)
568:          z = x + y;
569:        else if (strcmp(opStr, "-") == 0)
570:          z = x - y;
571:        else if (strcmp(opStr, "*") == 0)
572:          z = x * y;
573:        else if (strcmp(opStr, "/") == 0) {
574:          if (y != 0)
575:            z = x / y;
576:          else {
577:            z = 0;
578:            bInError = TRUE;
579:            ErrMsgBox->SetWindowText("Division-by-zero error");
580:          }
581:        }
582:        else if (strcmp(opStr, "^") == 0) {
583:          if (x > 0)
584:            z = exp(y * log(x));
585:          else {
586:            bInError = TRUE;
587:            ErrMsgBox->SetWindowText(
588:              "Cannot raise the power of a negative number");
589:          }
590:        }
591:        else {
592:          bInError = TRUE;
593:          ErrMsgBox->SetWindowText("Invalid operator");
594:        }
595:      }
596:      else if (strcmp(opStr, "SIN") == 0) {
597:        z = sin(angleFactor * x);
598:      }
599:      else if (strcmp(opStr, "COS") == 0) {
600:        z = cos(angleFactor * x);
601:      }
602:      else if (strcmp(opStr, "TAN") == 0) {
603:        z = tan(angleFactor * x);
604:      }
605:      else if (strcmp(opStr, "ASIN") == 0) {
606:        if (fabs(x) <= 1)
607:          z = asin(x) / angleFactor;
608:        else {
609:          bInError = TRUE;
610:          ErrMsgBox->SetWindowText(
611:              "Invalid argument for the asin(x)  function");
612:        }
613:      }
614:      else if (strcmp(opStr, "ACOS") == 0) {
615:        if (fabs(x) <= 1)
```

continues

Listing 17.3. continued

```
616:        z = acos(x) / angleFactor;
617:      else {
618:        bInError = TRUE;
619:        ErrMsgBox->SetWindowText
620:                        ("Invalid argument for the acos(x) function");
621:      }
622:    }
623:    else if (strcmp(opStr, "ATAN") == 0) {
624:      z = atan(x) / angleFactor;
625:    }
626:    else {
627:      bInError = TRUE;
628:      ErrMsgBox->SetWindowText("Invalid math function");
629:    }
630:
631:    // display the result if no error has occurred
632:    if (!bInError) {
633:      sprintf(s, "%g", z);
634:      ResultBox->SetWindowText(s);
635:      // enable the Store button
636:      EnableButton(StoreBtn);
637:    }
638:    else
639:      // disable the Store button
640:      DisableButton(StoreBtn);
641: }
642:
643: void CAppWindow::HandleStoreBtn()
644: {
645:    char result[MaxEditLen+1];
646:
647:    // get the string in the Result edit box
648:    ResultBox->GetWindowText(result, MaxEditLen);
649:
650:    // store the result in the selected text of
651:    // the Variable edit box
652:    putVar(atof(result));
653: }
654:
655: void CAppWindow::HandleAngleModeGrp()
656: {
657:    char angleStr[81];
658:
659:    // exit if the EchoGroup check box is not checked
660:    if (EchoGroupChk->GetCheck() != BF_CHECKED) return;
661:    // build the text of the message
662:    if (DegreeRbt->GetCheck() == BF_CHECKED)
```

```
663:        sprintf(angleStr, "1 radian = %g degrees", 1 / DegToRad);
664:      else if (GradianRbt->GetCheck() == BF_CHECKED)
665:        sprintf(angleStr, "1 radian = %g gradians", 1 / GradToRad);
666:      else
667:        sprintf(angleStr, "1 radian = %g degrees = %g gradians",
668:                1 / DegToRad, 1 / GradToRad);
669:      MessageBox(angleStr, "Group Box Message",
670:                MB_OK | MB_ICONINFORMATION);
671: }
672:
673: void CAppWindow::HandleRadianRbt()
674: {
675:    angleFactor = 1;
676:    HandleAngleModeGrp();
677: }
678:
679: void CAppWindow::HandleDegreeRbt()
680: {
681:    angleFactor = DegToRad;
682:    HandleAngleModeGrp();
683: }
684:
685: void CAppWindow::HandleGradianRbt()
686: {
687:    angleFactor = GradToRad;
688:    HandleAngleModeGrp();
689: }
690:
691: void CAppWindow::makeRect(int X, int Y, int W, int H, CRect& r)
692: {
693:    r.top = Y;
694:    r.left = X;
695:    r.bottom = Y + H;
696:    r.right = X + W;
697: }
698:
699: double CAppWindow::getVar(int nLineNum)
700: {
701:    int nLineSize;
702:    char s[MaxEditLen+1];
703:
704:    if (nLineNum >= MAX_MEMREG) return 0;
705:    // get the size of the target line
706:    nLineSize = VariableBox->GetLineLength(nLineNum);
707:    // get the line
708:    VariableBox->GetLine(s, nLineSize, nLineNum);
709:    // delete the first three characters
710:    strcpy(s, (s+3));
711:    // return the number stored in the target line
```

continues

Listing 17.3. continued

```
712:    return atof(s);
713: }
714:
715: void CAppWindow::putVar(double x)
716: {
717:    DWORD dwSelPos;
718:    WORD wStartPos, wEndPos;
719:    int nLineNum;
720:    int nLineSize;
721:    char s[MaxEditLen+1];
722:
723:    // locate the character position of the cursor
724:    dwSelPos = VariableBox->GetSel();
725:    wStartPos = LOWORD(dwSelPos);
726:    wEndPos = HIWORD(dwSelPos);
727:    // turn off the selected text
728:    if (wStartPos != wEndPos) {
729:      dwSelPos = MAKELONG(wStartPos, wStartPos);
730:      VariableBox->SetSel(dwSelPos);
731:    }
732:    // get the line number where the cursor is located
733:    nLineNum = VariableBox->LineFromChar(-1);
734:    // get the line size of line nLineNum
735:    nLineSize = VariableBox->GetLineLength(nLineNum);
736:    // obtain the text of line nLineNum
737:    VariableBox->GetLine(s, nLineSize, nLineNum);
738:    // build the new text line
739:    sprintf(s, "%c: %g", s[0], x);
740:    // get the character positions for the deleted line
741:    wStartPos = (WORD) (VariableBox->LineIndex(-1));
742:    wEndPos = (WORD) (wStartPos + VariableBox->LineLength(-1));
743:    // select the current line
744:    dwSelPos = MAKELONG(wStartPos, wEndPos);
745:    VariableBox->SetSel(dwSelPos);
746:    // replace the current line with the new line
747:    VariableBox->ReplaceSel(s);
748: }
749:
750: void CAppWindow::OnClose()
751: {
752:    if (MessageBox("Want to close this application",
753:                   "Query", MB_YESNO | MB_ICONQUESTION) == IDYES)
754:      DestroyWindow();
755: }
756:
757: void CAppWindow::ForEachCheckBox(void (FAR *f)(CCheckBox*))
758: {
759:    CCheckBox* P;
760:
```

```
761:    for (int nID = ID_SUBST_CHK; nID <= ID_ECHO_CHK; nID++) {
762:        // get the pointer to the next button
763:        P = (CCheckBox*) (this->GetDlgItem(nID));
764:        // process the button
765:        (*f)(P);
766:    }
767: }
768:
769: void CAppWindow::ForEachEditCtl(void (FAR *f)(CEdit*))
770: {
771:    CEdit* P;
772:
773:    for(int nID = ID_OPERAND1_EDIT; nID <= ID_ERRMSG_EDIT; nID++) {
774:        // get the pointer to the next button
775:        P = (CEdit*) (this->GetDlgItem(nID));
776:        // process the button
777:        (*f)(P);
778:    }
779: }
780:
781: BEGIN_MESSAGE_MAP(CAppWindow, CFrameWnd)
782:     ON_COMMAND(CM_CLEARBOX, CMClearBox)
783:     ON_COMMAND(CM_CLEARCHK, CMClearChk)
784:     ON_BN_CLICKED(ID_CALC_BTN, HandleCalcBtn)
785:     ON_COMMAND(ID_CALC_BTN, CMCalc)
786:     ON_BN_CLICKED(ID_STORE_BTN, HandleStoreBtn)
787:     ON_COMMAND(ID_STORE_BTN, CMStore)
788:     ON_BN_CLICKED(ID_EXIT_BTN, HandleExitBtn)
789:     ON_COMMAND(ID_EXIT_BTN, CMExit)
790:     ON_COMMAND(CM_EXIT, OnExit)
791:     ON_BN_CLICKED(ID_RADIAN_RBT, HandleRadianRbt)
792:     ON_BN_CLICKED(ID_DEGREE_RBT, HandleDegreeRbt)
793:     ON_BN_CLICKED(ID_GRADIAN_RBT, HandleGradianRbt)
794:     ON_WM_CREATE()
795:     ON_WM_KEYDOWN()
796:     ON_WM_CLOSE()
797: END_MESSAGE_MAP()
798:
799: // Construct the CWindowApp's m_pMainWnd data member
800: BOOL CWindowApp::InitInstance()
801: {
802:    m_pMainWnd = new CAppWindow();
803:    m_pMainWnd->ShowWindow(m_nCmdShow);
804:    m_pMainWnd->UpdateWindow();
805:    return TRUE;
806: }
807:
808: // application's constructor initializes and runs the app
809: CWindowApp WindowApp;
```

17

Figure 17.1 shows a sample session with program CTRLGRP1.EXE.

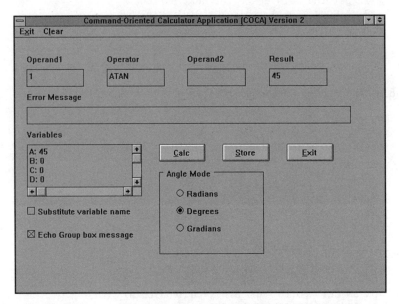

Figure 17.1. A sample session with program CTLGRP1.EXE.

The application declares the following sets of controls:

☐ A set of constants, in lines 10 through 37, specifies the sizes and spacings between the various controls.

☐ The macro-based constants, in lines 43 through 54, define the IDs of the various controls.

☐ The constants, in lines 56 and 57, are for the check box and radio button states.

☐ The last set of constants, in lines 59 through 61, specifies the value of pi and the angle conversion factors between radians and degrees and between radians and gradians.

The CTLGRP1.CPP program declares the following classes:

☐ The CxButton class, a descendant of CButton, to model push button controls (the declaration for this class starts at line 64)

☐ The CCheckBox class, a descendant of CButton, to model check box controls (the declaration for this class starts at line 79)

- [ ] The `CRadioButton` class, a descendant of `CButton`, to model radio button controls (the declaration for this class starts at line 97)

- [ ] The `CGroupBox` class, a descendant of `CButton`, to model group box controls (the declaration for this class starts at line 117)

- [ ] The `CxEdit` class, a descendant of `CEdit`, to model an enhanced version of the edit controls (the declaration for this class starts at line 131)

- [ ] The `CWindowApp` application class (the declaration for this class starts at line 139)

- [ ] The `CAppWindow` window class (the declaration for this class starts at line 146)

The `CCheckBox` and `CRadioButton` classes declare the member functions `Check` and `UnCheck` to set and clear the check state of these controls.

The `CAppWindow` window class contains a good number of data members in lines 156 through 186. Most of these members are pointers to the instances of the various controls used by the application. The application adds the `angleFactor` data member to store the angle conversion factor between the currently selected angle mode and radians.

The `CAppWindow` class declares a constructor, a destructor, and a number of member functions to support the nontrivial program operations and special initialization. The constructor loads the menu resource and creates the various controls, with the help of member function `OnCreate`. Of interest are the statements in function `OnCreate` that create the check boxes, the group box, and the radio buttons. Each instance of `CCheckBox` involves a unique control ID, title, and coordinates. These `CCheckBox` instances are created without the `WS_GROUP` style to indicate that each check box is created outside a group box. The group box instance is created with its own ID, title, and coordinates. Each radio button control is created with a unique ID, title, and coordinates. Notice that these radio buttons have the main window as their parent and not the group box, even though they are visually located inside the group box.

The `CAppWindow` class declares the various member functions needed to implement the program's operations. The `CMClearBox` function clears the text in all the edit controls, except the Variables edit control. The function uses the `ForEachEditCtl` member function as the iterator to perform the required task. Similarly, the `CMClearChk` member function clears the check boxes by invoking the `ForEachCheckBox` member function as the iterator.

The `HandleCalcBtn` member function performs the calculations and any character substitution. The member function performs the following tasks:

□ Converts the string in the Result edit control to a double and stores that value in the local variable result

□ Obtains the value for the first operand stored in variable x; the Operand1 edit control contains either a string image of a number, the name of a single-letter variable, or the # character:

  □ The statements that support the first option determine whether or not the Operand1 box contains a letter. If this condition is true, the statements invoke the getVar member function and assign the result to variable x. In addition, the code checks whether the Substitute variable name check box is checked. If so, the name of the variable in the Operand1 box is replaced with its value.

  □ The statements that support the second option compare the first character in the Operand1 box with the # character. If the two characters match, the value stored in the local variable result is assigned to the variable x.

  □ The statements that support the third option simply convert the string in the Operand1 edit box to a double and assign it to the local variable x.

□ Obtains the second operand in a manner very similar to the first one (the second operand is stored in the local variable y)

□ Acquires the operator or function from the Operator edit box

□ Performs the requested operation or function evaluation, with a set of `if` statements used to determine the requested operation (the statements also include argument error checking, and if there is any error, the function assigns `TRUE` to the `bInError` data member and displays an error message in the error message edit box)

□ Displays the result in the Result edit box if no error has occurred

The member functions `CMCalcBtn`, `HandleStoreBtn`, `CMStoreBtn`, `HandleExitBtn`, `CMExitBtn`, `putVar`, and `getVar` are the same as in the second version of the COCA program file CTLBTN1.CPP.

The `HandleAngleModeGrp` member function, defined in lines 655 through 671, is called by the response message functions of the radio buttons. The function first verifies whether the Echo Group message check box is not checked. If this condition is true, the member function simply exits. Otherwise, the function determines which radio button is checked and accordingly builds an angle-conversion message. The function then invokes the MessageBox function to display this message.

The HandleRadianRbt, HandleDegreeRbt, and HandleGradianRbt member functions, defined in lines 673 through 689, respond to the individual notification messages sent by the three radio buttons. Each member function assigns an angle-conversion factor to the angleFactor data member and then calls function HandleAngleModeGrp. Using these member functions is more efficient than systematically examining the check states of the radio buttons in the HandleCalcBtn member function. This approach alters the value in angleFactor *only* when you select a new angle mode.

Note: When you run the application and select another radio button, the previous radio button is automatically unchecked. It seems that the MFC library regards the radio buttons that are owned by a window as a single group. Therefore, deselecting the previous radio button requires no code within the program.

The CAppWindow class includes the InitAppWindow member function that initializes the following controls:

- ☐ Disables the Store button
- ☐ Checks the Degrees radio button
- ☐ Checks the Echo Group message box check box

Note: The window class also defines two iterator functions, namely, ForEachEditCtl and ForEachCheckBox in lines 757 through 779. Both functions use a for loop to iterate over the range of the target control ID. Each loop iteration obtains the pointer to the control based on its ID and then applies the iterated function to that control. The iterated (nonmember) functions themselves are ClearEditControls and ClearCheckBoxes, defined in lines 248 through 253. Each function has one statement that performs the sought task. This example shows that specialized iterators offer more control and require iterated functions with short code. The comparison is made with a C++ compiler sold by another major vendor.

Summary

Today's lesson discusses the special switch controls: group box, check box, and radio button. You learn about the following:

☐ Check box and radio button controls act as software switches.

☐ You can set and query the check state for the check box and radio button controls.

☐ You can respond to notification messages sent by these controls to their parent window.

☐ Group box controls enclose radio buttons and check boxes.

☐ Switch controls can be selectively manipulated.

Day 18 presents the scroll bar, list box, and combo box controls. These controls are value selectors, because they enable you to select from a list or range of values.

Q&A

Q. The check box has the states `BF_UNCHECKED`, `BF_CHECKED`, and `BF_GRAYED`. What can I use the third state for?

A. You can use the `BF_GRAYED` state as a "don't care" or undetermined state.

Q. Should I use the classes `CxButton`, `CRadioButton`, and `CCheckBox` that appear in program CTLGRP1.CPP? Why are such classes not part of the MFC library?

A. Using these classes enhances the readability of your programs because you can readily tell what kind of controls they generate. Such classes are not part of the MFC library because of a design decision. The developers of MFC wanted to consolidate multiple controls in the class `CButton`.

Q. Does it make any difference if I place check box controls in a group control?

A. Placing check box controls in a group control affects the logical grouping of such controls. Consequently, this enhances the interface for the user.

Workshop

The Workshop provides quiz questions to help you solidify your understanding of the material covered and exercises to provide you with experience in using what you've learned. Try to understand the quiz and exercise answers before continuing on to the next day's lesson. Answers are provided in Appendix B, "Answers."

Quiz

1. True or false? A check box can replace any two radio buttons in a group control.

2. True or false? You should use radio buttons in a group control when you have three or more options.

3. True or false? A set of check boxes parallel the bits in a byte or word.

4. True or false? Radio buttons, in a group control, are mutually nonexclusive.

Exercise

Expand on program CTLGRP1.CPP by adding more mathematical functions, such as the hyperbolic functions sinh, cosh, and tanh, and their inverse functions.

DAY
18

List Boxes

List controls are input tools that conveniently provide you with the items to choose. This feature makes list controls popular because they absolve you from remembering the list members—especially when computer programs expect exact spelling. Experience with DOS programs has shown that the various DOS utilities which display lists of files and directories are far easier and friendlier to use than their counterparts that assume you know all the names of your files and directories. Using list controls has gradually become a routine method for retrieving information. Today's lesson discusses the single-selection and multiple-selection list boxes. You learn about the following topics:

☐ The list box control

☐ Handling single-selection list boxes

☐ Handling multiple-selection list boxes

The List Box Control

List boxes are typically framed and include a vertical scroll bar. When you select an item by clicking on it, the selection is highlighted. Microsoft suggests the following guidelines for making a selection:

☐ Use a single mouse click to select a new or an additional item. A separate button control retrieves the selected item.

☐ Use a double-click as a shortcut for selecting an item and retrieving it.

NEW☛ TERM The *list box* is an input control which permits the application user to select from a list of items.

A list box control supports multiple selections only if you specify the multiple-selection style when you create the control. Making multiple selections is convenient when you want to process the selected items in a similar manner. For example, selecting multiple files for deletion speeds up the process and reduces the effort you have to make.

The *CListBox* Class

The Microsoft Foundation Class library offers the CListBox class, a descendant of CWnd, to implement list box controls. The CListBox class has a set of member functions that enable you to easily manipulate and query both the contents of the list box as well as the selected item. As with many other classes in the MFC library, the class CListBox uses a default constructor and the Create member function to create list box instances.

Syntax

The *Create* Function

The declaration of the Create function is

```
BOOL Create(DWORD dwStyle,        // control style
            const RECT& rect,     // location and dimensions
            CWnd* pParentWnd,     // pointer to parent window
            UINT nID);            // control ID
```

The dwStyle parameter specifies the style of the list box control. The list box styles include the usual WS_*xxxx* window styles as well as the special LBS_*xxxx* list box styles (shown in Table 18.1). The rect parameter specifies the location and dimensions of the control. The pParentWnd parameter is the pointer to the parent window. The nID parameter specifies the unique ID of the scroll bar instance.

Example:

```
CListBox* pList;
pList->Create(LBS_STANDARD, rectDefault, this, ID_FILES_LST);
```

> **Note:** The LBS_STANDARD style is equivalent to the WS_BORDER, WS_VSCROLL, LBS_SORT, and LBS_NOTIFY styles. You can remove the LBS_SORT style from the list box controls to maintain a list of items that is not automatically sorted. Such a list allows you to maintain items in a chronological fashion. You can also use this type of list to maintain the items sorted in descending order. Of course, you are responsible for maintaining the list items in that order. Removing the WS_VSCROLL style gives you a list box without the vertical scroll bar. The next section presents a demonstration program that uses this type of list box to implement the synchronized scrolling of multiple list boxes.

Table 18.1. List box control styles.

Style	Meaning
LBS_EXTENDESEL	Allows the extension of multiple-selections in the list box by using the Shift key
LBS_MULTICOLUMN	Designates a multicolumn list box that scrolls horizontally, and requires the use of Windows API functions (the number of columns is set by sending the message LB_SETCOLUMNWIDTH)

continues

Table 18.1. continued

Style	Meaning
LBS_MULTIPLESEL	Supports multiple selections in a list box
LBS_NOINTEGRALHEIGHT	Suppresses showing parts of an item
LBS_NOREDRAW	Prevents the list box from being updated when the selection is changed (the message WM_SETREDRAW alters this style at will)
LBS_NOTIFY	Notifies the parent window when you click or double-click in the list box
LBS_SORT	Specifies that the items inserted in the list box be automatically sorted in ascending order
LBS_STANDARD	Sets the WS_BORDER, WS_VSCROLL, LBS_SORT, and LBS_NOTIFY styles
LBS_WANTKEYBOARDINPUT	Permits the list box owner to receive WM_VKEYTOITEM or WM_CHARTOITEM messages when a key is pressed while the list box has the focus (allows the application to manipulate the items in the list box)

The CListBox class allows you to refer to the items in a list box by index. The index of the first item is 0. The CListBox class offers the following member functions to set and query ordinary and selected list members:

☐ The AddString member function adds a string to the list box.

☐ The DeleteString member function removes a list member from a specified position.

☐ The parameterless ResetContent member function clears the list of strings in the list box control in one swoop. This function serves to reset the contents of a list box before building up a new list.

☐ The FindString member function performs a case-insensitive search for an item in the list box.

☐ The parameterless GetCount member function returns the number of items in the list box. The function returns the LB_ERR value if there is an error.

- [ ] The parameterless `GetCurSel` member function returns the position of the selected item in a single-selection list box. If there is no selected item, the function yields a negative value. This function is aimed at single-selection list boxes only.

- [ ] The `GetSel` member function returns the selection state of a list box item, specified by index.

- [ ] The parameterless `GetSelCount` member function returns the number of selected items in the list box. For single-selection list boxes, the function returns `LB_ERR`.

- [ ] The `GetSelItems` member function returns the number and positions of the selected items in a multiple-selection list box.

- [ ] The overloaded `GetText` member function obtains an item in a list box by specifying its index.

- [ ] The `GetTextLen` member function returns the length of a list item specified by its position in the list.

- [ ] The parameterless `GetTopIndex` member function returns the index of the first visible list box item.

- [ ] The `InsertString` member function inserts a string in a list box.

- [ ] The `SelectString` member function selects a list box item that matches a search string.

- [ ] The `SelItemRange` member function is another function that allows you to select a range of items in one call.

- [ ] The `SetCurSel` member function chooses a list item as the new selection in a single-selection list box.

- [ ] The `SetSel` member function makes or clears a selection in a multiple-selection list box.

- [ ] The `SetTopIndex` member function selects the list box that becomes the first visible item in the list box control.

- [ ] The `Dir` member function is a special member function that allows you to insert filenames in a list box.

The *AddString* Function

The declaration of the AddString member function is

```
int AddString(const char FAR* lpItem);
```

The lpItem parameter is the pointer to the added string. The function also returns the position of the added string in the control. If there is any error in adding the string, the function yields an LB_ERR or LB_ERRSPACE value (out-of-memory error). If the LBS_SORT style is set, the string is inserted so that the list order is maintained. If the LBS_SORT style is not set, the added string is inserted at the end of the list.

Example:

```
CListBox* pList;
// create control...
pList->AddString("MS-DOS");
```

The *DeleteString* Function

The declaration of the DeleteString member function is

```
int DeleteString(int nIndex);
```

The nIndex parameter specifies the position of the item to delete. The function returns the number of remaining list members. If an error occurs, DeleteString yields the value LB_ERR.

Example:

```
CListBox* pList;
// create control...
// add names to the list...
pList->DeleteString("MS-DOS");
```

The *FindString* Function

The declaration of the FindString function is

```
int FindString(int nStartAfter, const char FAR* lpItem) const;
```

The nStartAfter parameter specifies the index of the first list box member to be searched. The lpItem parameter is the pointer to the searched string. The function searches *the entire* list, beginning with position nStartAfter and resuming at the beginning of the list if needed. The search stops when either a list member matches the search string or the entire list is searched. Passing an argument of -1 to nStartAfter forces the function to start searching from the beginning. The function returns the position of the matching list item, or yields the LB_ERR value if no match is found or when an error occurs.

Example:

```
CListBox* pList;
int nIdx;
// create control...
// add names to the list...
nIdx = pList->FindString(-1, "MS-DOS");
```

> **Note:** The interesting search method used by `FindString` enables you to speed up the search by specifying a position that comes closely before the most likely location for a match. The beauty of this method is that if you specify a position that is *actually* beyond that of the string you seek, you cannot miss finding that string because the function resumes searching at the beginning of the list. Another benefit of `FindString` is its ability to find duplicate strings.

The *GetSel* Function

The declaration of the function `GetSel` is

```
int GetSel(int nIndex) const;
```

The `nIndex` parameter specifies the index of the queried list box item. The function returns a positive number if the item is selected, yields 0 if the item is not selected, and returns `LB_ERR` if an error occurs.

Example:

```
CListBox* pList;
// create control...
// add names to the list...
if (pList->GetSel(0))
    // process information
```

The *GetSelItems* Function

The declaration of the `GetSelItems` function is

```
int GetSelItems(int nMaxItems, LPINT rgIndex) const;
```

The `nMaxItems` parameter specifies the size of the array accessed by the `rgIndex` pointer. The `rgIndex` parameter is the pointer to an array of integers that stores the positions of the selected items. The function returns the current number of selections. The function yields `LB_ERR` with single-selection list boxes.

18

Example:

```
const int MAX_ARRAY = 100;
CListBox* pList;
int intArr[MAX_ARRAY];
int nCount;
// create control...
// add names to the list...
nCount = pList->GetSelItems(MAX_ARRAY, intArr);
```

The *GetText* Function

The declaration for the GetText function is

```
int GetText(int nIndex, char FAR* lpBuffer) const;
void GetText(int nIndex, CString& rString) const;
```

The nIndex parameter specifies the index of the retrieved items. The first list box item has the index of 0. The lpBuffer parameter points to a buffer that receives the retrieved item. You are responsible for ensuring that the buffer has enough space for the retrieved item. The rString parameter is a reference to the CString object that receives a copy of the list box item. The first form of the function returns the number of characters retrieved from the list box.

Example:

```
const STR_SIZE = 80;
char s[STR_SIZE+1];
CListBox* pList;
// create control...
// add names to the list...
if (pList->GetText(0, s) > 0)
    MessageBox(s, MB_OK, "Information");
```

The *GetTextLen* Function

The declaration of the GetTextLen function is

```
int GetTextLen(int nIndex) const;
```

The parameter nIndex specifies the index of the target list item. The function returns the length of the target item, or the LB_ERR result if an error occurs.

Example:

```
int nLen;
CListBox* pList;
// create control...
// add names to the list...
nLen = pList->GetTextLen(0);
```

Syntax

The *InsertString* Function

The declaration of the InsertString function is

```
int InsertString(int nIndex, const char FAR* lpItem);
```

The nIndex parameter specifies the requested insertion position. The lpItem parameter is the pointer to the inserted string. The function returns the actual insertion position, or yields the LB_ERR value if an error occurs. If the argument for Index is -1, the string is simply appended to the end of the list.

Example:

```
CListBox* pList;
// create control...
// add names to the list...
if (pList->InsertString(0, "Windows") == 0)
    MessageBox("Inserted at index 0", MB_OK, "Information");
```

Warning: In general, do not use the InsertString member function with list boxes that have the LBS_SORT style set. Using this function with ordered list boxes will most likely corrupt the sort order of the list.

Syntax

The *SelectString* Function

The declaration of the SelectString function is

```
int SelectString(int nStartAfter, const char FAR* lpItem);
```

The parameters and search mechanism of SelectString are identical to those of FindString. The difference is that SelectString selects the list box item that matches the string accessed by parameter lpItem.

Example:

```
CListBox* pList;
int nIdx;
// create control...
// add names to the list...
nIdx = pList->SelectString(-1, "MS-DOS");
```

The *SelItemRange* Function

The declaration of the SelItemRange function is

```
int SelItemRange(BOOL bSelect, int nFirstItem, int nLastItem);
```

The bSelect parameter acts as a switch used to select or deselect the range of list box items defined by parameters nFirstItem and nLastItem.

Example:

```
CListBox* pList;
int nNumSel;
// create control...
// add names to the list...
nNumSel = pList->SelectItemRange(TRUE, 0, 10);
```

The *SetCurSel* Function

The declaration of the SetCurSel function is

```
int SetCurSel(int nSelect);
```

The parameter nSelect specifies the position of the new selection. To clear a list box from any selection, pass a -1 argument to the nSelect parameter. The function returns LB_ERR if an error occurs.

Example:

```
CListBox* pList;
// create control...
// add names to the list...
pList->SetCurSel(-1); // clear current selection
```

The *SetSel* Function

The declaration of the SetSel function is

```
int SetSel(int nIndex, BOOL bSelect = TRUE);
```

The nIndex parameter specifies the list box item to either select, if bSelect is TRUE, or deselect, if bSelect is FALSE. The function returns LB_ERR if an error occurs. The function result serves only to flag a selection/deselection error. You can use the SetSel function to toggle the selection of multiple items in a multiple-selection list box, one at a time.

Example:

```
CListBox* pList;
// create control...
// add names to the list...
pList->SetSel(0, TRUE); // select first item in list
```

The *SetTopIndex* Function

Syntax

The declaration of the function SetTopIndex is

```
int SetTopIndex(int nIndex);
```

The nIndex parameter specifies the index of the list box item that becomes the first visible item. This selection scrolls the list box, unless item nIndex is already the first visible item. The function returns LB_ERR if an error occurs. Otherwise, the result is meaningless.

Example:

```
CListBox* pList;
int nIdxTop;
// create control...
// add names to the list...
nIdxTop = pList->SetTopIndex(10); // select 11th item
if (nIdxTop != 10)
    MessageBox("Selection failed!", MB_OK, "Error!");
```

18

The *Dir* Function

Syntax

The declaration of the Dir function is

```
int Dir(UINT attr, const char FAR* lpWildCard);
```

The attr parameter specifies the combination of attributes, shown in Table 18.2. The table also shows the equivalent file attribute constants that are declared in the DOS.H header file. The lpWildCard parameter is the pointer to the filename wildcard, such as *.*, L*.EXE, or A???.CPP.

Example:

```
int nNumFiles;
CListBox* pList;
// create control...
// get all CTL*.CPP files
nNumFiles = pList->Dir(_A_ARCH, "CTL*.CPP");
```

Table 18.2. Attributes for the `attr` parameter in the `Dir` member function.

Attribute Value	Equivalent Constant in DOS.H Header File	Meaning
0x0000	_A_NORMAL	File can be used for input and output
0x0001	_A_RDONLY	File is read only
0x0002	_A_HIDDEN	File is hidden
0x0004	_A_SYSTEM	File is system file
0x0010	_A_SUBDIR	Name indicated by parameter `lpWildCard` also supplies the directory
0x0020	_A_ARCH	File has the archive bit set
0x4000		Include all the drives that match the filename supplied by `lpWildCard`
0x8000		Exclusive flag (prevents normal files to be included with specified files)

Responding to List Box Notification Messages

The list box control emits various types of messages, shown in Table 18.3. The table also shows the message-mapping macros that are associated with the various command and notification messages. Each type of command or notification message requires a separate member function declared in the control's parent window class.

Table 18.3. List box notification messages.

Message	Macro	Meaning
WS_COMMAND	ON_COMMAND	A Windows command message

Message	Macro	Meaning
LBN_CHANGE	ON_LBN_SELCHANGE	A list item is selected with a mouse click
LBN_DBLCLK	ON_LBN_DBLCLK	A list item is selected with a mouse double-click
LBN_SETFOCUS	ON_LBN_SETFOCUS	The list box has gained focus
LBN_KILLFOCUS	ON_LBN_KILLFOCUS	The list box has lost focus
LBN_ERRSPACE	ON_LBNERRSPACE	The list box cannot allocate more dynamic memory to accommodate new list items

The List Manipulation Tester

The next program demonstrates how to set and query normal and selected strings, and how to set and query the current selection in a single-selection list box—a simple list manipulation tester. This program focuses on illustrating how to use most of the CListBox member functions presented earlier in this section. The program contains the following controls which offer the indicated test features:

☐ A list box control

☐ A String Box edit control that allows you to type in and retrieve a list member

☐ An Index Box edit control that enables you to key in and retrieve the position of the current selection

☐ An Add String push button to add the content of the String Box to the list box (the program does not allow you to add duplicate names, and, if you attempt to do so, the program displays a warning message)

☐ A Delete String push button to delete the current selection in the list box (the program automatically selects another list member)

☐ The Get Selected String push button that copies the current list selection to the String Box

☐ The Set Selected String push button that overwrites the current selection with the string in the String box

18

☐ The Get Selected Index push button that writes the position of the current selection in the Index Box

☐ The Set Selected Index push button that uses the integer value in the Index Box as the position of the new list box selection

☐ The Get String button that copies the string whose position appears in the Index Box into the String Box

☐ The Exit push button

These controls exercise various aspects of manipulating a sorted list box and its members. The program is coded to retain a current selection and to prevent the insertion of duplicate names.

Listings 18.1, 18.2, and 18.3 show the header file CTLLST1.H, the script for the CTLLST1.RC resource file, and the source code for the CTLLST1.CPP program file, respectively. The resource file contains a single-item menu resource. I purposely avoid using accelerator keys to make the program a bit shorter.

Create the directory CTLLST1 as a subdirectory of \MSVC\VC21DAY and store all the project's files in the new directory. The project's .MAK file should contain the files CTLLST1.CPP, CTLLST1.RC, and CTLLST1.DEF. The latter file resembles file MINWINAP.DEF in Day 14, Listing 14.2.

Compile and run the program. When the program starts running, it places a set of names in the list box. Experiment with the various push button controls to add, delete, and obtain strings. The program is straightforward and easy to run.

Listing 18.1. Source code for the CTLLST1.H header file.

```
1: #define CM_EXIT (WM_USER + 100)
```

Listing 18.2. Script for the CTLLST1.RC resource file.

```
1: #include <windows.h>
2: #include <afxres.h>
3: #include "ctllst1.h"
4:
5: EXITMENU MENU LOADONCALL MOVEABLE PURE DISCARDABLE
6: BEGIN
7:     MENUITEM "E&xit", CM_EXIT
8: END
```

Listing 18.3. Source code for the CTLLST1.CPP program file.

```
 1: #include <stdio.h>
 2: #include <string.h>
 3: #include <afxwin.h>
 4: #include "ctllst1.h"
 5:
 6: // declare constants for the size and spacing of controls
 7: const LowVertSpacing = 5;
 8: const HiVertSpacing = 25;
 9: const HorzSpacing = 50;
10: const Wctl = 150;
11: const Hctl = 30;
12: const Wbox = 2 * Wctl + HorzSpacing;
13: const Hlst = Hctl + LowVertSpacing + 4 * (Hctl + HiVertSpacing);
14: const MaxEditLen = 10;
15:
16: // declare the ID constants for the various controls
17: #define ID_STRING_LST 101
18: #define ID_STRING_EDIT 102
19: #define ID_INDEX_EDIT 103
20: #define ID_ADDSTR_BTN 104
21: #define ID_DELSTR_BTN 105
22: #define ID_GETSELSTR_BTN 106
23: #define ID_SETSELSTR_BTN 107
24: #define ID_GETSELIDX_BTN 108
25: #define ID_SETSELIDX_BTN 109
26: #define ID_EXIT_BTN 110
27: #define ID_GETSTR_BTN 111
28:
29: class CxButton : public CButton
30: {
31: public:
32:
33:     BOOL Create(const char FAR* lpCaption, const RECT& rect,
34:                 CWnd* pParentWnd, UINT nID)
35:     {
36:       return CButton::Create(lpCaption,
37:             WS_CHILD ¦ WS_VISIBLE ¦ BS_PUSHBUTTON,
38:             rect, pParentWnd, nID);
39:     }
40: };
41:
42: class CWindowApp : public CWinApp
43: {
44: public:
45:     virtual BOOL InitInstance();
46: };
47:
```

continues

Listing 18.3. continued

```
48: // expand the functionality of CFrameWnd by deriving
49: // class CAppWindow
50: class CAppWindow : public CFrameWnd
51: {
52: public:
53:
54:   CAppWindow();
55:   ~CAppWindow();
56:
57: protected:
58:   // handle creating the controls
59:   // declare the pointers to the controls
60:   CStatic* StringListTxt;
61:   CStatic* StringBoxTxt;
62:   CStatic* IndexBoxTxt;
63:   CListBox* StringLst;
64:   CEdit* StringBox;
65:   CEdit* IndexBox;
66:   CxButton* AddStrBtn;
67:   CxButton* DelStrBtn;
68:   CxButton* GetSelStrBtn;
69:   CxButton* SetSelStrBtn;
70:   CxButton* GetSelIdxBtn;
71:   CxButton* SetSelIdxBtn;
72:   CxButton* GetStrBtn;
73:   CxButton* ExitBtn;
74:   char dataStr[MaxEditLen+1];  // string for StringBox
75:   char indexStr[MaxEditLen+1]; // string for IndexBox
76:
77:   afx_msg int OnCreate(LPCREATESTRUCT lpCS);
78:   // initialize the String list box
79:   void InitStringLst();
80:   // handle adding a string to the list box
81:   afx_msg void HandleAddStrBtn();
82:   // handle deleting a string from the list box
83:   afx_msg void HandleDelStrBtn();
84:   // handle getting the selected text
85:   afx_msg void HandleGetSelStrBtn();
86:   // handle setting the selected text
87:   afx_msg void HandleSetSelStrBtn();
88:   // handle getting the index of the selected text
89:   afx_msg void HandleGetSelIdxBtn();
90:   // handle setting the index of the selected text
91:   afx_msg void HandleSetSelIdxBtn();
92:   // handle getting a string from the list box
93:   afx_msg void HandleGetStrBtn();
94:   // handle setting a string in the list box
95:   afx_msg void HandleExitBtn()
96:     { SendMessage(WM_CLOSE); }
97:   // handle exiting the application
```

```
 98:    afx_msg void OnExit()
 99:      { SendMessage(WM_CLOSE); }
100:    // handle closing the window
101:    afx_msg void OnClose();
102:    void makeRect(int nX, int nY, int nW, int nH, CRect& r);
103:
104:    // declare message map macro
105:    DECLARE_MESSAGE_MAP();
106: };
107:
108: CAppWindow::CAppWindow()
109: {
110:    // create the window
111:    Create(NULL, "Simple List Box Tester Application",
112:       WS_OVERLAPPEDWINDOW | WS_MAXIMIZE,
113:       rectDefault, NULL, "EXITMENU");
114:    // insert the initial list of names
115:    InitStringLst();
116: }
117:
118: CAppWindow::~CAppWindow()
119: {
120:    delete StringListTxt;
121:    delete StringBoxTxt;
122:    delete IndexBoxTxt;
123:    delete StringLst;
124:    delete StringBox;
125:    delete IndexBox;
126:    delete AddStrBtn;
127:    delete DelStrBtn;
128:    delete GetSelStrBtn;
129:    delete SetSelStrBtn;
130:    delete GetSelIdxBtn;
131:    delete SetSelIdxBtn;
132:    delete GetStrBtn;
133:    delete ExitBtn;
134: }
135:
136: int CAppWindow::OnCreate(LPCREATESTRUCT lpCS)
137: {
138:    int nX0 = 30;
139:    int nX1 = nX0 + Wctl + HorzSpacing;
140:    int x2 = nX1 + Wctl + HorzSpacing;
141:    int nY0 = 50;
142:    int nX = nX0;
143:    int nY = nY0;
144:    int nY1;
145:    DWORD dwStaticStyle = WS_CHILD | WS_VISIBLE | SS_LEFT;
146:    DWORD dwEditStyle = WS_CHILD | WS_VISIBLE | ES_LEFT |
147:                        WS_BORDER;
```

continues

Listing 18.3. continued

```
148:   DWORD dwScrollStyle = WS_CHILD | WS_VISIBLE | SBS_VERT;
149:   DWORD dwListBoxStyle = WS_CHILD | WS_VISIBLE | WS_VSCROLL |
150:                         LBS_STANDARD;
151:   CRect r;
152:
153:   // create the list box and its label
154:   makeRect(nX, nY, Wctl, Hctl, r);
155:   StringListTxt = new CStatic();
156:   StringListTxt->Create("List Box", dwStaticStyle, r, this);
157:   nY += Hctl + LowVertSpacing;
158:   makeRect(nX, nY, Wctl, Hlst, r);
159:   StringLst = new CListBox();
160:   StringLst->Create(dwListBoxStyle, r, this, ID_STRING_LST);
161:
162:   // create the edit boxes and their labels
163:   nX = nX1;
164:   nY = nY0;
165:   makeRect(nX, nY, Wctl, Hctl, r);
166:   StringBoxTxt = new CStatic();
167:   StringBoxTxt->Create("String Box", dwStaticStyle, r, this);
168:   nY += Hctl + LowVertSpacing;
169:   makeRect(nX, nY, Wbox, Hctl, r);
170:   StringBox = new CEdit();
171:   StringBox->Create(dwEditStyle, r, this, ID_STRING_EDIT);
172:
173:   nY += Hctl + HiVertSpacing;
174:   makeRect(nX, nY, Wctl, Hctl, r);
175:   IndexBoxTxt = new CStatic();
176:   IndexBoxTxt->Create("Index Box", dwStaticStyle, r, this);
177:   nY += Hctl + LowVertSpacing;
178:   makeRect(nX, nY, Wbox, Hctl, r);
179:   IndexBox = new CEdit();
180:   IndexBox->Create(dwEditStyle, r, this, ID_INDEX_EDIT);
181:
182:   // create the button controls
183:   nY += Hctl + HiVertSpacing;
184:   nY1 = nY;
185:   makeRect(nX, nY, Wctl, Hctl, r);
186:   AddStrBtn = new CxButton();
187:   AddStrBtn->Create("Add String", r, this, ID_ADDSTR_BTN);
188:
189:   nY += Hctl + HiVertSpacing;
190:   makeRect(nX, nY, Wctl, Hctl, r);
191:   DelStrBtn = new CxButton();
192:   DelStrBtn->Create("Delete String", r, this, ID_DELSTR_BTN);
193:
194:   nY += Hctl + HiVertSpacing;
195:   makeRect(nX, nY, Wctl, Hctl, r);
196:   GetSelStrBtn = new CxButton();
197:   GetSelStrBtn->Create("Get Selected String", r, this,
```

```
198:                               ID_GETSELSTR_BTN);
199:
200:    nY += Hctl + HiVertSpacing;
201:    makeRect(nX, nY, Wctl, Hctl, r);
202:    SetSelStrBtn = new CxButton();
203:    SetSelStrBtn->Create("Set Selected String", r, this,
204:                               ID_SETSELSTR_BTN);
205:
206:    // create the second row of buttons
207:    nY  = nY1;
208:    nX = x2;
209:    makeRect(nX, nY, Wctl, Hctl, r);
210:    GetSelIdxBtn = new CxButton();
211:    GetSelIdxBtn->Create("Get Selected Index", r, this,
212:                               ID_GETSELIDX_BTN);
213:
214:    nY += Hctl + HiVertSpacing;
215:    makeRect(nX, nY, Wctl, Hctl, r);
216:    SetSelIdxBtn = new CxButton();
217:    SetSelIdxBtn->Create("Set Selected Index", r, this,
218:                               ID_SETSELIDX_BTN);
219:
220:    nY += Hctl + HiVertSpacing;
221:    makeRect(nX, nY, Wctl, Hctl, r);
222:    GetStrBtn = new CxButton();
223:    GetStrBtn->Create("Get String by Index", r, this,
224:                            ID_GETSTR_BTN);
225:
226:    nY += Hctl + HiVertSpacing;
227:    makeRect(nX, nY, Wctl, Hctl, r);
228:    ExitBtn = new CxButton();
229:    ExitBtn->Create("Exit", r, this, ID_EXIT_BTN);
230:
231:    return CFrameWnd::OnCreate(lpCS);
232:
233: }
234:
235: void CAppWindow::HandleAddStrBtn()
236: {
237:    int nIdx;
238:    // get the string in the String box
239:    StringBox->GetWindowText(dataStr, MaxEditLen);
240:    // exit if the string empty?
241:    if (dataStr[0] == '\0') return;
242:    // add the string if it is not already in the list box
243:    if (StringLst->FindString(-1, dataStr) < 0) {
244:      // add the string and store the position of the new string
245:      nIdx = StringLst->AddString(dataStr);
246:      // make the added string the new selection
247:      StringLst->SetCurSel(nIdx);
248:    }
```

18

continues

537

Listing 18.3. continued

```
249:    else
250:      // handle the duplicate-data error
251:      MessageBox("Cannot add duplicate names", "Bad Data", MB_OK);
252: }
253:
254: void CAppWindow::HandleDelStrBtn()
255: {
256:    // get the index of the currently selected list member
257:    int nIdx = StringLst->GetCurSel();
258:    // delete the currently selected list member
259:    StringLst->DeleteString(nIdx);
260:    // select another list member
261:    StringLst->SetCurSel((nIdx > 0) ? (nIdx-1) : 0);
262: }
263:
264: void CAppWindow::HandleGetSelStrBtn()
265: {
266:    // get the selected list item
267:    StringLst->GetText(StringLst->GetCurSel(), dataStr);
268:    /// store it in the String box
269:    StringBox->SetWindowText(dataStr);
270: }
271:
272: void CAppWindow::HandleSetSelStrBtn()
273: {
274:    // get the index of the currently selected list member
275:    int nIdx = StringLst->GetCurSel();
276:    // get the string to be replace the currently selected
277:    // list item
278:    StringBox->GetWindowText(dataStr, MaxEditLen);
279:    // is the candidate string not in the list?
280:    if (StringLst->FindString(-1, dataStr) < 0) {
281:      // delete the current selection
282:      StringLst->DeleteString(nIdx);
283:      // insert the new selection
284:      nIdx = StringLst->AddString(dataStr);
285:      // select the inserted string
286:      StringLst->SetCurSel(nIdx);
287:    }
288:    else
289:      MessageBox("Cannot add duplicate names", "Bad Data", MB_OK);
290: }
291:
292: void CAppWindow::HandleGetSelIdxBtn()
293: {
294:    sprintf(indexStr, "%d", StringLst->GetCurSel());
295:    IndexBox->SetWindowText(indexStr);
296: }
297:
298: void CAppWindow::HandleSetSelIdxBtn()
```

```
299: {
300:     IndexBox->GetWindowText(indexStr, MaxEditLen);
301:     StringLst->SetCurSel(atoi(indexStr));
302: }
303:
304: void CAppWindow::HandleGetStrBtn()
305: {
306:     int nIdx;
307:     // get the index from the Index box
308:     IndexBox->GetWindowText(indexStr, MaxEditLen);
309:     nIdx = atoi(indexStr);
310:     // get the target string from the list box
311:     StringLst->GetText(nIdx, dataStr);
312:     // write the list member in the String box
313:     StringBox->SetWindowText(dataStr);
314: }
315:
316: void CAppWindow::OnClose()
317: {
318:     if (MessageBox("Want to close this application",
319:             "Query", MB_YESNO | MB_ICONQUESTION) == IDYES)
320:       DestroyWindow();
321: }
322:
323: void CAppWindow::InitStringLst()
324: {
325:     // add data in the list box
326:     StringLst->AddString("Edward");
327:     StringLst->AddString("John");
328:     StringLst->AddString("Anne");
329:     StringLst->AddString("Elaine");
330:     StringLst->AddString("Joseph");
331:     StringLst->AddString("Clement");
332:     StringLst->AddString("Daisy");
333:     StringLst->AddString("Tony");
334:     // select the second item
335:     StringLst->SetCurSel(1);
336: }
337:
338: void CAppWindow::makeRect(int nX, int nY, int nW, int nH,
339:                           CRect& r)
340: {
341:     r.top = nY;
342:     r.left = nX;
343:     r.bottom = nY + nH;
344:     r.right = nX + nW;
345: }
346:
347: BEGIN_MESSAGE_MAP(CAppWindow, CFrameWnd)
348:     ON_WM_CREATE()
```

continues

Listing 18.3. continued

```
349:    ON_BN_CLICKED(ID_ADDSTR_BTN, HandleAddStrBtn)
350:    ON_BN_CLICKED(ID_DELSTR_BTN, HandleDelStrBtn)
351:    ON_BN_CLICKED(ID_GETSELSTR_BTN, HandleGetSelStrBtn)
352:    ON_BN_CLICKED(ID_SETSELSTR_BTN, HandleSetSelStrBtn)
353:    ON_BN_CLICKED(ID_GETSELIDX_BTN, HandleGetSelIdxBtn)
354:    ON_BN_CLICKED(ID_SETSELIDX_BTN, HandleSetSelIdxBtn)
355:    ON_BN_CLICKED(ID_GETSTR_BTN, HandleGetStrBtn)
356:    ON_BN_CLICKED(ID_EXIT_BTN, HandleExitBtn)
357:    ON_COMMAND(CM_EXIT, OnExit)
358:    ON_WM_CLOSE()
359: END_MESSAGE_MAP()
360:
361: // Construct the CWindowApp's m_pMainWnd data member
362: BOOL CWindowApp::InitInstance()
363: {
364:    m_pMainWnd = new CAppWindow();
365:    m_pMainWnd->ShowWindow(m_nCmdShow);
366:    m_pMainWnd->UpdateWindow();
367:    return TRUE;
368: }
369:
370: // application's constructor initializes and runs the app
371: CWindowApp WindowApp;
```

Figure 18.1 shows a sample session with the CTLLST1.EXE application.

The program in Listing 18.3 declares two sets of constants. The first, declared in lines 7 through 14, specifies the dimensions and sizes of the various controls used. The second set of constants, declared in lines 17 through 27, specifies the ID for the various controls.

The program declares the application class, CWindowApp, the window class, CAppWindow, and the button class, CxButton. The class CAppWindow declares a number of data members, in lines 60 through 73, that are pointers to the controls owned by the main window. The class also declares two strings to handle the contents of the String Box and Index Box edit controls. The CAppWindow class also declares a constructor, a destructor, and a number of member functions that respond to the notification messages emitted by the various push button controls.

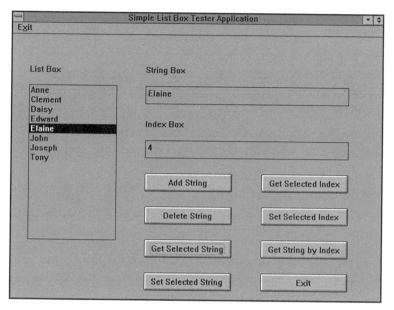

Figure 18.1. A sample session with the CTLLST1.EXE application.

The CAppWindow constructor performs two tasks:

☐ Invokes the member function Create to build the application window

☐ Calls the InitStringLst member function to initialize the Names list box with data

The member function OnCreate, defined in lines 136 through 233, creates the controls using the appropriate styles. For example, the list box control appears with a vertical scroll bar and automatically maintains a sorted list of strings.

The member function HandleAddStrBtn, defined in lines 235 through 252, adds the string of the String Box in the list box control. The function performs the following tasks:

☐ Obtains the string in the String Box edit control and stores it in the dataStr data member

☐ Exits if the dataStr member stores an empty string

☐ Verifies that the added string does not already exist in the list box, using the `FindString` function to detect an attempt to add duplicate strings (if `FindString` returns a negative number, `HandleAddStrBtn` resumes with the subsequent tasks, and if it doesn't return a negative number, `HandleAddStrBtn` displays a message informing you that you cannot add duplicate strings in the list box)

☐ Adds the string of the `dataStr` member to the list box and assigns the position of the string to the local variable `nIdx`, using the `AddString` member

☐ Makes the added string the current selection by invoking the `SetCurSel` function with the argument `nIdx`

The member function `HandleDelStrBtn`, defined in lines 254 through 262, deletes the current selection by carrying out the following tasks:

☐ Obtains the position of the current selection by invoking the `GetCurSel` function, and stores the selection position in the local variable `nIdx`

☐ Deletes the selection by calling the `DeleteString` function and supplying it the argument `nIdx`

☐ Selects another list item as the new selection at position `nIdx - 1` (if the variable `nIdx` already contains 0, the new first list item becomes the new selection)

The member function `HandleGetSelStrBtn`, defined in lines 264 through 270, copies the current selection to the String Box edit control. The function performs the following tasks:

☐ Copies the current selection to the `dataStr` member by calling the `GetText` and `GetCurSel` functions

☐ Overwrites the contents of the String Box with the characters of the `dataStr` member

The member function `HandleSetSelStrBtn`, defined in lines 272 through 290, overwrites the current selection with the string in the String Box edit control. Because the list maintains sorted items, the replacement string likely has a different position that the original selection. The function performs the following tasks:

☐ Obtains the position of the current selection, using the `GetCurSel` function, and assigns that value to the local variable `nIdx`

☐ Copies the text in the String Box to the `dataStr` member

☐ Verifies that the string in dataStr does not already exist in the list box, using the FindString function (if the string in dataStr is new to the list, the function uses the DeleteString function to delete the current selection, uses the AddString function to add the dataStr, and then uses the SetCurSel function to select the added string)

If the string in dataStr has a matching list item, the function displays a message informing you that you cannot add duplicate strings in the list box. This warning also appears if you attempt to overwrite the current selection with the same string!

The member function HandleGetSelIdxBtn, defined in lines 292 through 296, writes the position of the current selection to the Index Box edit box. The function uses the GetCurSel function to obtain the sought position.

The member function HandleSetSelIdxBtn, defined in lines 298 through 302, reads the value in the Index Box edit control and uses that value to set the new current selection. The function uses the SetCurSel function to make the new selection.

The member function HandleGetStrBtn, defined in lines 304 through 314, enables you to retrieve the list item whose position appears in the Index Box edit control. The function performs the following tasks:

☐ Copies the characters of the Index Box to the indxStr data member

☐ Converts the string in indexStr to the int-typed local variable nIdx

☐ Copies the characters of the list item at position nIdx to the dataStr member

☐ Writes the characters of dataStr in the String Box edit control

Handling Multiple-Selection Lists

This section demonstrates the use of multiple-selection lists and focuses on getting and setting the selection strings and their indices. There are two modes for making multiple selections in a list box. These modes depend on whether or not you set the LBS_EXTENDEDSEL style when you create a CListBox instance. Setting this style enables you to quickly extend the range of selected items by holding down the Shift key and clicking the mouse. The disadvantage for this style is that you are committed to selecting blocks of contiguous items in the list box manually (that is, using the mouse or cursor keys). Using the SetSel or SetItemRange member functions, you can make your program select noncontiguous items. However, this approach requires extra effort on behalf of the application user and a few extra controls. By contrast, if you do not set the LBS_EXTENDEDSEL style, you can make dispersed selections easily by clicking the mouse button on the individual items that you want to select. The disadvantage of this selection mode is that you must click on every item to select it, including neighboring items. Choose the selection mode that you feel best meets the user-interface requirements for your MFC applications.

The Multiple-Selection List Tester

Figure 18.2 shows a sample session with the CTLLST2.EXE application—a program that demonstrates how to set and query multiple selections in a list box—and also conveys the controls used by that application. The controls used by the test program and the operation they support are

- ☐ A multiple-selection list that has the LBS_MULTIPLESEL style selected, but not the LBS_EXTENDEDSEL style (the strings in the list box are sorted in ascending order)

- ☐ A multiline edit box control labeled Names Box that contains the names of the selected strings

- ☐ A push button with the caption Get Names to copy the list box selections in the Names Box edit control (each selection appears on a separate line in the edit box, and every time you click this button you lose the previous contents of the Names Box edit control)

- ☐ A push button with the caption Set Names to select, or deselect, the list box items that match those in the Names Box edit control (the match need not be exact, but the Names Box strings must match the leading characters of the list items)

- ☐ A multiline edit box control labeled Indices Box that contains the indices of the selected strings

- ☐ A push button with the caption Get Indices to copy the indices of the list box selections in the Indices Box edit control (the index of each selection appears on a separate line in the edit box, and every time you click this button you lose the previous contents of the Indices Box edit control)

- ☐ A push button with the caption Set Indices to select, or deselect, the list box items using the values in the Indices Box edit control

☐ A check box control with the caption Deselect mode that determines whether the Set Names and Set Indices buttons select or deselect list items

☐ The static text controls that label the list and edit boxes

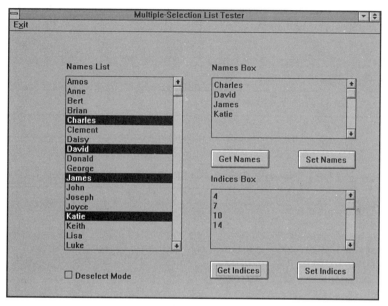

Figure 18.2. A sample session with the CTLLST2.EXE application.

The multiple-selection list tester application basically drills the `GetSelIndexes`, `GetSelStrings`, `SetSelIndexes`, and `SetSelStrings` member functions of class `CListBox`. Listings 18.4, 18.5, and 18.6 contain the source code for the CTLLST2.H, CTLLST2.RC, and CTLLST2.CPP files, respectively.

Create the directory CTLLST2 as a subdirectory of \MSVC\VC21DAY and store all the project's files in the new directory. The project's .MAK file should contain the files CTLLST2.CPP, CTLLST2.RC, and CTLLST2.DEF. The latter file resembles file MINWINAP.DEF in Day 14, Listing 14.2.

Compile and run the program. The application initializes the list box with many names. This feature saves you the time and effort needed to enter the names yourself. Select a few list items and click on the Get Names and Get Indices push buttons. The selected strings and indices appear in the Names Box and Indices Box edit controls. Now edit the lines on the Names Box by deleting one or two trailing characters from each line to create partial names. Click on the Set Names push button. What do you see? The selections have not changed because the strings in the Names Box still match the same list box selection. Type in a new set of indices in the Indices Box and click the Set Indices push button. The program now displays a new set of selected items in the list box. You can also make a new selection by deleting the text in the Names Box and typing in names that are found in the list box. Now click the Set Names button and view the new list box selections. When you are finished experimenting with the program, click on the Exit menu item or press the Alt-X keys.

Listing 18.4. Source code for the CTLLST2.H header file.

```
1: #define CM_EXIT (WM_USER + 100)
```

Listing 18.5. Script for the CTLLST2.RC resource file.

```
1: #include <windows.h>
2: #include <afxres.h>
3: #include "ctllst2.h"
4:
5: EXITMENU MENU LOADONCALL MOVEABLE PURE DISCARDABLE
6: BEGIN
7:     MENUITEM "E&xit", CM_EXIT
8: END
```

Listing 18.6. Source code for the CTLLST2.CPP program file.

```
 1: #include <stdio.h>
 2: #include <string.h>
 3: #include <afxwin.h>
 4: #include "ctllst2.h"
 5:
 6: // declare the constants for the dimensions and spacing
 7: // of the various controls
 8: const Wtxt = 100;
 9: const Htxt = 20;
10: const TxtVertSpacing = 5;
11: const Wlst = 200;
12: const Hlst = 300;
13: const LstHorzSpacing = 50;
14: const LstVertSpacing = 20;
15: const Wbox = 250;
16: const Hbox = 100;
17: const BoxVertSpacing = 20;
18: const Wbtn = 100;
```

```
19: const Hbtn = 30;
20: const BtnHorzSpacing = 50;
21: const BtnVertSpacing = 10;
22: const Wchk = 200;
23: const Hchk = 20;
24: // miscellaneous constants
25: const MaxString = 40;
26: const MaxSelections = 35; // maximum number of selections
27: // declare the ID constants for the various controls
28: #define ID_NAMES_LST 101
29: #define ID_NAMES_EDIT 102
30: #define ID_INDICES_EDIT 103
31: #define ID_GETNAMES_BTN 104
32: #define ID_SETNAMES_BTN 105
33: #define ID_GETINDICES_BTN 106
34: #define ID_SETINDICES_BTN 107
35: #define ID_SELECT_CHK 108
36: // declare constants for the check box and radio button states
37: const BF_CHECKED = 1;
38: const BF_UNCHECKED = 0;
39:
40: // declare extended edit control class
41: class CxEdit : public CEdit
42: {
43: public:
44:
45:   BOOL GetLine(LPSTR lpString, int nStrSize, int nLineNumber);
46:   int GetLineLength(int nLineNumber);
47:   int GetNumOfLines();
48: };
49:
50: // declare the extended button class
51: class CxButton : public CButton
52: {
53: public:
54:
55:   BOOL Create(const char FAR* lpCaption, const RECT& rect,
56:             CWnd* pParentWnd, UINT nID)
57:   {
58:       return CButton::Create(lpCaption,
59:                   WS_CHILD | WS_VISIBLE |
60:                   WS_TABSTOP | BS_PUSHBUTTON,
61:                   rect, pParentWnd, nID);
62:   }
63: };
64:
65: // declare the check box class
66: class CCheckBox : public CButton
67: {
68: public:
```

continues

Listing 18.6. continued

```
69:    BOOL Create(const char FAR* lpCaption, const RECT& rect,
70:              CWnd* pParentWnd, UINT nID)
71:    {
72:        return CButton::Create(lpCaption,
73:                        WS_CHILD ¦ WS_VISIBLE ¦
74:                        WS_TABSTOP ¦ BS_AUTOCHECKBOX,
75:                        rect, pParentWnd, nID);
76:    }
77:
78: };
79:
80:
81: // expand the functionality of CFrameWnd by deriving
82: // class CAppWindow
83: class CAppWindow : public CFrameWnd
84: {
85: public:
86:
87:    CAppWindow();
88:    ~CAppWindow();
89:
90: protected:
91:    // declare pointers to controls
92:    CStatic* NamesListTxt;
93:    CStatic* NamesBoxTxt;
94:    CStatic* IndicesBoxTxt;
95:    CListBox* NamesLst;
96:    CxEdit* NamesBox;
97:    CxEdit* IndicesBox;
98:    CxButton* GetNamesBtn;
99:    CxButton* SetNamesBtn;
100:   CxButton* GetIndicesBtn;
101:   CxButton* SetIndicesBtn;
102:   CCheckBox* SelectChk;
103:   // declare edit control insertion buffer
104:   CString insertBuffer;
105:   // array of string pointers
106:   LPSTR names[MaxSelections];
107:   // array of integers to store the selection indices
108:   int indices[MaxSelections];
109:
110:   // handle creating the controls
111:   afx_msg int OnCreate(LPCREATESTRUCT lpCS);
112:   // initialize the list box
113:   void InitNamesLst();
114:   // handle getting the selections
115:   afx_msg void HandleGetNamesBtn();
116:   // handle setting the selections
117:   afx_msg void HandleSetNamesBtn();
118:   // handle getting the selection indices
```

```
119:    afx_msg void HandleGetIndicesBtn();
120:    // handle setting the selection indices
121:    afx_msg void HandleSetIndicesBtn();
122:    // handle exiting the application
123:    afx_msg void OnExit()
124:      { SendMessage(WM_CLOSE); }
125:    // handle closing the window
126:    virtual void OnClose();
127:    void resetSelections();
128:    void makeRect(int nX, int nY, int nW, int nH, CRect& r);
129:
130:    // declare message map macro
131:    DECLARE_MESSAGE_MAP();
132: };
133:
134: class CWindowApp : public CWinApp
135: {
136: public:
137:    virtual BOOL InitInstance();
138: };
139:
140: BOOL CxEdit::GetLine(LPSTR lpString, int nStrSize,
141:                        int nLineNumber)
142: {
143:    int nCopyCount;
144:    BOOL bResult;
145:
146:    if (nStrSize <= 0)
147:      return FALSE;
148:    bResult = (nStrSize >= GetLineLength(nLineNumber) + 1) ? TRUE
149:                                                           : FALSE;
150:    if (nStrSize == 1) {
151:      lpString[0] = '\0';
152:      return bResult;
153:    }
154:    ((WORD FAR *)lpString)[0] = nStrSize;
155:    nCopyCount = (WORD)(SendMessage(EM_GETLINE, nLineNumber,
156:                                     long(lpString)));
157:    if (nCopyCount) {
158:      // Windows returns non-null terminated string
159:      lpString[nCopyCount] = '\0';
160:      return bResult;
161:    }
162:    else
163:      return FALSE;
164: }
165:
166: int CxEdit::GetLineLength(int nLineNumber)
167: {
168:    int nStartPos = -1;
```

18

continues

Listing 18.6. continued

```
169:
170:    if (nLineNumber > -1)
171:      nStartPos = LineIndex(nLineNumber);
172:    return (WORD) SendMessage(EM_LINELENGTH, nStartPos);
173: }
174:
175: int CxEdit::GetNumOfLines()
176: {
177:    // get the size of the text in the edit control
178:    int nSize = GetWindowTextLength();
179:    // initialize the function's result
180:    int nCount = (nSize == 0) ? 0 : 1;
181:    // return 0 if the edit box is empty
182:    if (nSize == 0)
183:      return 0;
184:    // create a string object of the same nSize
185:    CString s(' ', nSize);
186:    // copy the text in the edit control to the string object
187:    GetWindowText(s.GetBuffer(nSize), nSize);
188:    s.ReleaseBuffer(); // release any extra space
189:    // loop to nCount the number of lines by counting the number
190:    // of '\n' characters (assuming they only occur at a line
191:    // break)
192:    for (int i = 0; i < s.GetLength();)
193:      if (s[i++] == '\r' && s[i] == '\n') {
194:        nCount++;
195:        i++;
196:        }
197:    return nCount;
198: }
199:
200: CAppWindow::CAppWindow()
201: {
202:    // create the window
203:    Create(NULL, "Multiple-Selection List Tester",
204:        WS_OVERLAPPEDWINDOW | WS_MAXIMIZE,
205:        rectDefault, NULL, "EXITMENU");
206:    // insert the initial names in the lists
207:    InitNamesLst();
208: }
209:
210: CAppWindow::~CAppWindow()
211: {
212:    delete NamesListTxt;
213:    delete NamesBoxTxt;
214:    delete IndicesBoxTxt;
215:    delete NamesLst;
216:    delete NamesBox;
217:    delete IndicesBox;
218:    delete GetNamesBtn;
```

```
219:    delete SetNamesBtn;
220:    delete GetIndicesBtn;
221:    delete SetIndicesBtn;
222:    delete SelectChk;
223:    // deallocate the dynamic string space
224:    for (int i = 0; i < MaxSelections; i++)
225:      delete names[i];
226: }
227:
228: int CAppWindow::OnCreate(LPCREATESTRUCT lpCS)
229: {
230:    int nX0 = 100;
231:    int nY0 = 50;
232:    int nX = nX0;
233:    int nY = nY0;
234:    DWORD dwStaticStyle = WS_CHILD | WS_VISIBLE | SS_LEFT;
235:    DWORD dwEditStyle = WS_CHILD | WS_VISIBLE | WS_TABSTOP |
236:                   WS_BORDER | WS_VSCROLL | ES_LEFT |
237:                   ES_AUTOHSCROLL | ES_AUTOVSCROLL |
238:                   ES_MULTILINE;
239:    DWORD dwListBoxStyle = WS_CHILD | WS_VISIBLE | LBS_STANDARD |
240:                   LBS_MULTIPLESEL;
241:    CRect r;
242:
243:    // create the name list box and its label
244:    makeRect(nX, nY, Wtxt, Htxt, r);
245:    NamesListTxt = new CStatic();
246:    NamesListTxt->Create("Names List", dwStaticStyle, r, this);
247:    nY += Htxt + TxtVertSpacing;
248:    makeRect(nX, nY, Wlst, Hlst, r);
249:    NamesLst = new CListBox();
250:    NamesLst->Create(dwListBoxStyle, r, this, ID_NAMES_LST);
251:    // create the Deselect Mode check box
252:    nY += Hlst + LstVertSpacing;
253:    makeRect(nX, nY, Wchk, Hchk, r);
254:    SelectChk = new CCheckBox();
255:    SelectChk->Create("Deselect Mode", r, this, ID_SELECT_CHK);
256:    nX0 += Wlst + LstHorzSpacing;
257:    nX = nX0;
258:    nY = nY0;
259:    // creates the multiline Names Box edit control and its label
260:    makeRect(nX, nY, Wtxt, Htxt, r);
261:    NamesBoxTxt = new CStatic();
262:    NamesBoxTxt->Create("Names Box", dwStaticStyle, r, this);
263:    nY += Htxt + TxtVertSpacing;
264:    makeRect(nX, nY, Wbox, Hbox, r);
265:    NamesBox = new CxEdit();
266:    NamesBox->Create(dwEditStyle, r, this, ID_NAMES_EDIT);
267:    // create the Get Names button
268:    nY += Hbox + BoxVertSpacing;
```

continues

Listing 18.6. continued

```
269:    makeRect(nX, nY, Wbtn, Hbtn, r);
270:    GetNamesBtn = new CxButton();
271:    GetNamesBtn->Create("Get Names", r, this, ID_GETNAMES_BTN);
272:    // create the Set Names button
273:    nX += Wbtn + BtnHorzSpacing;
274:    makeRect(nX, nY, Wbtn, Hbtn, r);
275:    SetNamesBtn = new CxButton();
276:    SetNamesBtn->Create("Set Names", r, this, ID_SETNAMES_BTN);
277:    nX = nX0;
278:    nY += Hbtn + BtnVertSpacing;
279:    // create the multi=line Indices Box edit control and its label
280:    makeRect(nX, nY, Wtxt, Htxt, r);
281:    IndicesBoxTxt = new CStatic();
282:    IndicesBoxTxt->Create("Indices Box", dwStaticStyle, r, this);
283:    nY += Htxt + TxtVertSpacing;
284:    makeRect(nX, nY, Wbox, Hbox, r);
285:    IndicesBox = new CxEdit();
286:    IndicesBox->Create(dwEditStyle, r, this, ID_INDICES_EDIT);
287:    // create the GetIndices button
288:    nY += Hbox + BoxVertSpacing;
289:    makeRect(nX, nY, Wbtn, Hbtn, r);
290:    GetIndicesBtn = new CxButton();
291:    GetIndicesBtn->Create("Get Indices", r, this,
292:                              ID_GETINDICES_BTN);
293:    // create the Set Indices button
294:    nX += Wbtn + BtnHorzSpacing;
295:    makeRect(nX, nY, Wbtn, Hbtn, r);
296:    SetIndicesBtn = new CxButton();
297:    SetIndicesBtn->Create("Set Indices", r, this,
298:                              ID_SETINDICES_BTN);
299:    // allocate the dynamic space for the array of strings accessed
300:    // by the array of pointers names
301:    for (int i = 0; i < MaxSelections; i++)
302:      names[i] = new char[MaxString + 1];
303:    return CFrameWnd::OnCreate(lpCS);
304: }
305:
306: void CAppWindow::InitNamesLst()
307: {
308:    char* p[] = { "John", "Ribert", "Melody", "Charles", "Olivia",
309:                  "Richard", "James", "Anne", "Keith", "Brian",
310:                  "Lisa", "Margie", "Thomas", "Joseph", "Donald",
311:                  "Bert", "George", "Ronald", "Katie", "Susan",
312:                  "Joyce", "David", "Paul", "Mark", "Luke",
313:                  "Amos", "Matthew", "Mary", "Patrick", "Clement",
314:                  "Daisy", "EOL" };
315:    for (int i = 0; p[i] != "EOL"; i++)
316:      NamesLst->AddString(p[i]);
317: }
318:
```

```
319: void CAppWindow::HandleGetNamesBtn()
320: {
321:    char s[MaxString+1];
322:    // get the indices of the selected strings
323:    int n = NamesLst->GetSelItems(MaxSelections, indices);
324:
325:    // exit if n is not positive
326:    if (n <= 0) return;
327:    // clear the insertion buffer
328:    insertBuffer = "";
329:    // concatenate the selected strings in the insertion buffer
330:    for (int i = 0; i < n; i++) {
331:      NamesLst->GetText(indices[i], names[i]);
332:      sprintf(s, "%s\r\n", names[i]);
333:      insertBuffer += s;
334:    }
335:    // copy the insertion buffer to the Names Box edit control
336:    NamesBox->SetWindowText((const char*) insertBuffer);
337: }
338:
339: void CAppWindow::HandleSetNamesBtn()
340: {
341:    char s[MaxString+1];
342:    int j;
343:    // get the number of lines in the Names Box edit control
344:    int n = NamesBox->GetNumOfLines();
345:    // get the select status from the Deselect Mode check box
346:    BOOL bShouldSet =
347:      (SelectChk->GetCheck() == BF_UNCHECKED) ? TRUE : FALSE;
348:
349:    resetSelections();
350:    // read the lines from the Names Box control
351:    for (int i = 0; i < n; i++) {
352:      // get the i'th name from the Names Box edit control
353:      NamesBox->GetLine(s, MaxString, i);
354:      // find its match in the list box
355:      j = NamesLst->FindString(-1, s);
356:      // select the matching element
357:      if (j != LB_ERR)
358:        NamesLst->SetSel(j, bShouldSet);
359:    }
360: }
361:
362: void CAppWindow::HandleGetIndicesBtn()
363: {
364:    char s[MaxString+1];
365:    // get the selected indices
366:    int n = NamesLst->GetSelItems(MaxSelections, indices);
367:
368:    // exit if n is not positive
```

continues

Listing 18.6. continued

```
369:    if (n <= 0) return;
370:    // initialize the insertion buffer
371:    insertBuffer = "";
372:    // concatenate the selected indices in the insertion buffer
373:    for (int i = 0; i < n; i++) {
374:      sprintf(s, "%d\r\n", indices[i]);
375:      insertBuffer += s;
376:    }
377:    // copy the insertion buffer to the Names edit control
378:    IndicesBox->SetWindowText((const char*) insertBuffer);
379: }
380:
381: void CAppWindow::HandleSetIndicesBtn()
382: {
383:    char s[MaxString + 1];
384:    int j;
385:
386:    resetSelections();
387:    // get the number of lines in the Indices Box edit control
388:    int n = IndicesBox->GetNumOfLines();
389:    // get the select status from the Deselect Mode check box
390:    BOOL bShouldSet =
391:      (SelectChk->GetCheck() == BF_UNCHECKED) ? TRUE : FALSE;
392:
393:    // read the lines from the Names Box control and set the
394:    // corresponding names in the list box
395:    for (int i = 0; i < n; i++) {
396:      IndicesBox->GetLine(s, MaxString, i);
397:      j = atoi(s);
398:      NamesLst->SetSel(j, bShouldSet);
399:    }
400: }
401:
402: void CAppWindow::OnClose()
403: {
404:    if (MessageBox("Want to close this application",
405:               "Query", MB_YESNO | MB_ICONQUESTION) == IDYES)
406:      DestroyWindow();
407: }
408:
409: void CAppWindow::resetSelections()
410: {
411:    int n = NamesLst->GetSelItems(MaxSelections, indices);
412:
413:    for (int i = 0; i < n; i++)
414:        NamesLst->SetSel(indices[i], FALSE);
415: }
416:
417: void CAppWindow::makeRect(int nX, int nY, int nW, int nH,
418:                                   CRect& r)
```

```
419: {
420:   r.top = nY;
421:   r.left = nX;
422:   r.bottom = nY + nH;
423:   r.right = nX + nW;
424: }
425:
426: BEGIN_MESSAGE_MAP(CAppWindow, CFrameWnd)
427:   ON_WM_CREATE()
428:   ON_BN_CLICKED(ID_GETNAMES_BTN, HandleGetNamesBtn)
429:   ON_BN_CLICKED(ID_SETNAMES_BTN, HandleSetNamesBtn)
430:   ON_BN_CLICKED(ID_GETINDICES_BTN, HandleGetIndicesBtn)
431:   ON_BN_CLICKED(ID_SETINDICES_BTN, HandleSetIndicesBtn)
432:   ON_COMMAND(CM_EXIT, OnExit)
433:   ON_WM_CLOSE()
434: END_MESSAGE_MAP()
435:
436: // Construct the CWindowApp's m_pMainWnd data member
437: BOOL CWindowApp::InitInstance()
438: {
439:   m_pMainWnd = new CAppWindow();
440:   m_pMainWnd->ShowWindow(m_nCmdShow);
441:   m_pMainWnd->UpdateWindow();
442:   return TRUE;
443: }
444:
445: // application's constructor initializes and runs the app
446: CWindowApp WindowApp;
```

18

The program in Listing 18.6 declares the following sets of constants:

- The set in lines 8 through 23 specifies the dimensions and spacing for the various application controls.

- The set in lines 25 and 26 declares the maximum string size and maximum number of selections.

- The set in lines 28 through 35 establishes the ID numbers for the various controls.

- The set in lines 37 and 38 declares the check box state constants, BF_CHECKED and BF_UNCHECKED.

The test program declares the application class, CWindowApp, the window class, CAppWindow, the edit control class, CxEdit, the button class, CxButton, and the check box class, CCheckBox. The last three classes extend the CEdit and CButton classes in a manner similar to that shown in previous programs. The current implementation of class `CxEdit` introduces an additional member function, `GetNumOfLines`. This function counts the number of lines in an edit control. This result is required by the application to read individual lines in a multiline edit control.

The `CAppWindow` class declares two sets of data members. The first set represents pointers to the various controls used in the application. The second set of data members contains the array of string pointers, `Names`, and the array of integers, `Indices`. Both arrays have `MaxSelections` members.

The `CAppWindow` class declares a class constructor, a destructor, and a collection of member functions. The class destructor removes the dynamic control instances and the dynamic strings.

The `CAppWindow` constructor invokes the `Create` function and calls the `InitNamesLst` function to initialize the Names list box.

The member function `OnCreate`, defined in lines 228 through 304, creates the various controls and creates the array of dynamic strings. The function sets the style for `CListBox` instance to include the `LBS_MULTIPLESEL` style. If you want to make the application extend the list box selections with the Shift key, add ¦ `LBS_EXTENDEDSEL` to the expression that initializes the local variable `dwListBoxStyle`.

The member function `HandleGetNamesBtn`, defined in lines 319 through 337, responds to the notification message sent by clicking the Get Names push button. The function performs the following tasks:

☐ Invokes the `GetSelItems` function to obtain the list box selections, which are copied to the array of indices accessed by the `Indices` array of pointers, and specifies that up to `MaxSelections` indices can be copied (the function result is assigned to the local variable n)

☐ Exits the function if the variable n stores a negative value

☐ Initializes the insertion buffer `insertBuffer`

☐ Uses a loop to append the strings accessed by the names array to the insertion buffer `insertBuffer`

☐ Copies the contents of the insertion buffer to the Names Box control

The member function `HandleSetNamesBtn`, defined in lines 339 through 360, responds to the notification message of the Set Names push button control. The function carries out the following tasks:

- ☐ Obtains the number of lines in the Names Box control

- ☐ Obtains the check state of the Deselect Mode check box and assigns a Boolean value, equivalent to the check state, to the local variable shouldSet

- ☐ Calls the resetSelections member function to deselect the current selections

- ☐ Copies the lines of the Names Box control to the string array accessed by the array of pointer names

- ☐ Uses a loop to read each line from the Names Box control and then select that line (this involves using the FindString function to locate the index of the matching list box item and the SetSel function to select or deselect the matching element, based on the value stored in the local variable shouldSet)

The member function HandleGetIndicesBtn, defined in lines 362 through 379, responds to the notification message sent by the Get Indices push button control. The function performs the following tasks:

- ☐ Invokes the GetSelItems function to obtain the list box selections, copies these selections to the integer array indices, and specifies that up to MaxSelections indices can be copied (the function result is assigned to the local variable n)

- ☐ Exits the function if the variable n stores a negative value

- ☐ Initializes the insertion buffer insertBuffer with an empty string

- ☐ Uses a loop to convert the selection indices to their string images and concatenate these strings in the insertion buffer

- ☐ Copies the string of the insertion buffer to the Indices Box edit control

The member function HandleSetIndicesBtn, defined in lines 381 through 400, responds to the notification message of the Set Indices push button control. The function carries out the following tasks:

- ☐ Obtains the number of lines in the Indices Box control, using the CxEdit::GetNumOfLines() member function

- ☐ Obtains the check state of the Deselect Mode check box, assigning a Boolean value equivalent to the check state to the local variable shouldSet

- ☐ Copies each line of the Indices Box control to a temporary string, converts that string into an int value, and stores that integer in a member of the indices array

☐ Uses a loop to read each line from the Indices Box control, convert that line into an index, and then use that index to select (or deselect, depending on the value of the local variable shouldSet) a list box item

Summary

Today's lesson presents the list box control which allows an application user to choose from a fixed collection of values. You learn about the following topics:

☐ The single-selection list box control provides you with a list of items to select from. This kind of list box allows you to select only one item at a time.

☐ The multiple-selection list box permits you to select multiple items in a list box for collective processing. Setting the LBS_EXTENDEDSEL style when you create the list box enables you to quickly extend the range of selected items by holding down the Shift key and clicking the mouse.

Q&A

Q. Can the argument for the lpWildCard parameter in function CListBox::Dir contain multiple wildcards such as *.CPP *.H?

A. No, the argument for lpWildCard is limited to one filename wildcard.

Q. Does the MFC library support intercepting the messages related to the movement of the thumb box in a list box control?

A. No.

Q. What is the general approach to implementing a program with two list boxes that scroll simultaneously?

A. The general approach is to create the two list boxes with hidden scroll bars and then add a scroll bar control (see Day 19). The list boxes then are made to scroll in synch with the scroll bar control, because you can handle the messages emitted by this control and scroll the lists accordingly. You cannot intercept the messages sent by the scroll bars that are part of the list box itself.

Q. Should I use InsertString in a list box created with the LBS_SORT style?

A. No, because the LBS_SORT style maintains the list box items in order. Using InsertString corrupts the order in the list box. Instead, use the AddString member function.

Workshop

The Workshop provides quiz questions to help you solidify your understanding of the material covered and exercises to provide you with experience in using what you've learned. Try to understand the quiz and exercise answers before continuing on to the next day's lesson. Answers are provided in Appendix B, "Answers."

Quiz

1. True or false? The list box notification message LBN_SETFOCUS is suitable for optional initializing related to selecting a list box control.

2. True or false? The list box notification message LBN_KILLFOCUS is suitable for optional validation after you deselect a list box control.

3. True or false? The list box allows you to detect only the final selection, using the LBN_KILLFOCUS notification.

4. True or false? You should use LBN_CHANGE with a special flag to detect mouse double-clicks on a list box item.

5. True or false? LBS_STANDARD creates a list box control with unordered items.

Exercise

Write a program that displays a list of files (in a list box) that match the filename wildcard that appears in a text box.

DAY 19

Scroll Bars and Combo Boxes

Day 18 presents list box controls. Today's lesson presents two somewhat similar controls, the scroll bar and the combo box. The scroll bar control allows you to select a numeric value quickly, usually in a wide range of values. The combo box control combines the edit control and the list box, allowing the user to select a value from the list box component or enter a new value in the edit control part. You learn about the following topics:

☐ The scroll bar control

☐ The combo box control in its various styles

The Scroll Bar Control

Windows allows the scroll bar to exist as a separate control as well as to be incorporated in windows, lists, and combo boxes. The scroll bar control appears and behaves much like the scroll bar of a window. The control has a thumb box that keeps track of the current value and allows mouse clicks to move it either by single lines or by pages. This thumb box mechanism is supported by the `OnVScroll` or `OnHScroll` member functions. In addition, the scroll bar responds to cursor control keys, such as Home, End, PageUp, and PageDown. This feature is supported by the `OnKeyDown` member function. The main purpose of the scroll bar control is to enable you to quickly and efficiently select an integer value in a predefined range of values. Windows, for example, uses scroll bars to fine-tune the color palette, the keyboard rate, and the mouse sensitivity.

The *CScrollBar* Class

Microsoft Foundation Class offers the `CScrollBar`, a descendant of `CWnd`, as the class that models the scroll bar controls. The `CScrollBar` class declares a class constructor and a number of member functions to set and query the control's current position and range of values.

The class constructor, like other MFC classes, has no parameters. To create a scroll bar control you first invoke the constructor and then call the `Create` member function.

Syntax

The *Create* Function

The declaration of the function `Create` is

```
BOOL Create(DWORD dwStyle,        // control style
            const RECT& rect,     // location and dimensions
            CWnd* pParentWnd,     // pointer to parent window
            UINT nID);            // control ID
```

The dwStyle parameter specifies the style of the scroll bar control. Scroll bar styles include the WS_*xxxx* window styles as well as the special SBS_*xxxx* scroll bar styles. Table 19.1 shows the SBS_*xxxx* styles and indicates that you can make the CScrollBar instances as size boxes by specifying the SBS_SIZEBOX style. The rect parameter specifies the location and dimensions of the control. The pParentWnd parameter is the pointer to the parent window. The nID parameter specifies the unique ID of the scroll bar instance.

Example:

```
CScrollBar* pSB;
pSB->Create(SBS_HORZ, rectDefault, this, ID_SB_SCR);
```

Table 19.1. SBS_*xxxx* **styles for the scroll bar control.**

Value	Meaning
SBS_BOTTOMALIGN	Specifies a style used with SBS_HORZ to align the bottom of the scroll bar with the bottom edge of the rectangle specified in function Create
SBS_HORZ	Specifies a horizontal scroll bar whose location, width, and height are specified by the parameter rect in function Create, if neither SBS_BOTTOMALIGN nor SBS_TOPALIGN are specified
SBS_LEFTALIGN	Specifies a style used with the SBS_VERT to align the left edge of the scroll bar with the left edge of the rectangle specified in function Create
SBS_RIGHTALIGN	Specifies a style used with SBS_VERT to align the right edge of the scroll bar with the right edge of the rectangle specified in function Create

continues

19

Table 19.1. continued

Value	Meaning
SBS_SIZEBOX	Specifies a size box whose location, width, and height are specified by the parameter rect in function Create, if neither one of the next two SBS_*xxxx* styles is specified
SBS_SIZEBOXBOTTOMRIGHTALIGN	Specifies a style used with SBS_SIZEBOX to align the lower-right corner of the size box with the lower-right corner of the rectangle specified in the function Create
SBS_SIZEBOXTOPLEFTALIGN	Specifies a style used with the SBS_SIZEBOX style to align the upper-left corner of the size box with the upper-left corner of the rectangle specified in the function Create
SBS_TOPALIGN	Specifies a style used with SBS_HORZ to align the top of the scroll bar with the top edge of the rectangle specified in function Create
SBS_VERT	Specifies a vertical scroll bar whose location, width, and height are specified by parameter rect in function Create, if neither SBS_RIGHTALIGN nor SBS_LEFTALIGN is specified

The CScrollBar declares a number of member functions. The following are the relevant functions:

☐ The first member function that you most likely use after creating a CScrollBar instance is SetScrollRange. This function allows you to set the range of values for the scroll bar.

☐ The GetScrollRange member function enables you to query the current range of values for the scroll bar.

☐ The parameterless `GetScrollPos` member function returns the current position of the thumb box.

☐ The `SetScrollPos` member function moves the thumb box to the specified position. You are responsible for ensuring that the new thumb position is within the current scroll bar range.

The *SetScrollRange* Function

The declaration of the `SetScrollRange` function is

```
void SetScrollRange(int nMinPos, int nMaxPos,
                    BOOL bRedraw = TRUE);
```

The arguments for the `nMinPos` and `nMaxPos` parameters designate the new range of values for the scroll bar control. The Boolean parameter `bRedraw` indicates whether or not to redraw the scroll bar instance using the new range.

Example:

```
int nMin = 1, nMax = 100;
CScrollBar* pSB;
// create control...
pSB->SetScrollRange(nMin, nMax);
```

The *GetScrollRange* Function

The declaration of the `GetScrollRange` function is

```
void GetScrollRange(LPINT lpMinPos, LPINT lpMaxPos) const;
```

The parameters `lpMinPos` and `lpMaxPos` point to the current range of values for the scroll bar control.

Example:

```
int nMin, nMax;
CScrollBar* pSB;
// create control...
pSB->GetScrollRange(&nMin, &nMax);
```

The *SetScrollPos* Function

The declaration of the member function `SetScrollPos` is

```
void SetScrollPos(int nPos, BOOL bRedraw = TRUE);
```

The parameter `nPos` specifies the new thumb box position. The Boolean parameter `bRedraw` indicates whether or not to redraw the scroll bar instance using the new position.

19

Example:

```
CScrollBar* pSB;
// create control...
pSB->SetScrollPos(nMedianValue);
```

Responding to Scroll Bar Notification Messages

The instances of CScrollBar that implement scroll bar controls rely on the CWnd::OnVScroll or CWnd::OnHScroll member functions to support the actual scrolling of the thumb box. The MFC library requires you to declare the scrolling functions as members of the parent window. How is the connection made between the scroll bar and the parent window? The answer lies in the parameters of the OnVScroll and OnHScroll member functions:

```
afx_msg void OnVScroll(UINT nSBCode, UINT nPos,
                       CScrollBar* pScrollBar);
afx_msg void OnHScroll(UINT nSBCode, UINT nPos,
                       CScrollBar* pScrollBar);
```

The pScrollBar parameter is the pointer to the scroll bar control that is clicked by the user. In the scrolling windows examples in Day 15's lesson, I use the OnVScroll and OnHScroll functions but do not employ the pScrollBar parameter in the functions' statements. When you write an OnVScroll or OnHScroll member function to handle a scroll bar control, you must use the pScrollBar parameter along with other CScrollBar member functions. The run-time message-handling system makes the connection between the scroll bar control and the OnVScroll or OnHScroll member functions of the parent window. You need not be concerned about that aspect. The next example shows how this method works.

The Count-Down Timer

The count-down timer application contains the following controls:

☐ The Timer Input Box edit control that accepts input for the timer and displays the current timer value

☐ The Static text control that labels the edit box

☐ The Start button that triggers the count-down timer

☐ The Exit Button

☐ The timer scroll bar control that has a default range of 0 to 600 seconds

☐ The static text controls that label the range of values for the timer scroll bar

You can set the number of seconds in one of two ways: type in that value in the edit box, or use the scroll bar. When you move the scroll bar thumb box, the current thumb position appears in the edit box. To trigger the count-down process, click the Start button or press the Alt-S keys. The count-down process takes the value stored in the edit box and converts it into the maximum number of seconds to count down. If the edit box is empty, contains 0, or has nonnumeric text, the program assigns a default of 15 seconds. The program also assigns that value to the static text that specifies the maximum scroll bar value. During the count-down, the application decrements the number of seconds in the edit box and moves the scroll bar's thumb box upward. When the count-down ends, the program sounds a beep, restores the maximum limit of the scroll bar, and restores the maximum limit static text.

The count-down timer application illustrates the following scroll bar manipulations:

☐ Setting and altering the scroll bar range of values

☐ Moving and changing the scroll bar thumb box position (the program illustrates how these tasks are performed internally or with the mouse)

☐ Using the scroll bar to supply a value

Listing 19.1 shows the source code for the CTLSCRL1.H header file. Listing 19.2 shows the script for the CTLSCRL1.RC resource file. The resource file contains the accelerator keys and menu resources. Listing 19.3 shows the source code for the CTLSCRL1.CPP program file. The program uses a menu with the single menu item Exit.

19

Listing 19.1. Source code for the CTLSCRL1.H header file.

```
1: #define CM_EXIT      (WM_USER + 100)
2: #define ID_START_BTN (WM_USER + 101)
3: #define ID_EXIT_BTN  (WM_USER + 102)
4: #define ID_INPUT_BOX (WM_USER + 103)
5: #define ID_TIMER_SCR (WM_USER + 104)
```

Listing 19.2. Script for the CTLSCRL1.RC resource file.

```
 1: #include <windows.h>
 2: #include <afxres.h>
 3: #include "ctlscrl1.h"
 4:
 5: BUTTONS ACCELERATORS
 6: BEGIN
 7:   "s", ID_START_BTN, ALT
 8:   "e", ID_EXIT_BTN, ALT
 9: END
10:
11: EXITMENU MENU LOADONCALL MOVEABLE PURE DISCARDABLE
12: BEGIN
13:     MENUITEM "E&xit", CM_EXIT
14: END
15:
```

Listing 19.3. Source code for the CTLSCRL1.CPP program file.

```
 1: #include <stdio.h>
 2: #include <string.h>
 3: #include <afxwin.h>
 4: #include "ctlscrl1.h"
 5:
 6: // current timer limit is 10 minutes
 7: const MaxTimer = 600; // seconds
 8: const MaxEditLen = 10;
 9: const PageSize = 100;
10:
11: class CxButton : public CButton
12: {
13: public:
14:
15:     BOOL Create(const char FAR* lpCaption, const RECT& rect,
16:                 CWnd* pParentWnd, UINT nID)
17:     {
18:       return CButton::Create(lpCaption,
19:                 WS_CHILD | WS_VISIBLE | BS_PUSHBUTTON,
20:                 rect, pParentWnd, nID);
21:     }
22: };
23:
24: class CWindowApp : public CWinApp
25: {
26: public:
27:     virtual BOOL InitInstance();
```

```
28: };
29:
30: // expand the functionality of CFrameWnd by deriving
31: // class CAppWindow
32: class CAppWindow : public CFrameWnd
33: {
34: public:
35:
36:    CAppWindow();
37:    ~CAppWindow();
38:
39: protected:
40:    // declare the pointers to the various controls
41:    CEdit* InputBox;
42:    CxButton* StartBtn;
43:    CxButton* ExitBtn;
44:    CScrollBar* TimerScr;
45:    CStatic* InputTxt;
46:    CStatic* Timer1Txt;
47:    CStatic* Timer2Txt;
48:    // handle creating the controls
49:    afx_msg int OnCreate(LPCREATESTRUCT lpCS);
50:    // handle the vertical scrolling of the scroll bar
51:    afx_msg void OnVScroll(UINT nSBCode, UINT nPos,
52:                  CScrollBar* pScrollBar);
53:    // handle starting the timer
54:    afx_msg void HandleStartBtn();
55:    // handle starting the timer
56:    afx_msg void CMStartBtn()
57:       { HandleStartBtn(); }
58:    // handle exiting the program
59:    afx_msg void HandleExitBtn()
60:       { SendMessage(WM_CLOSE); }
61:    // handle exiting the program
62:    afx_msg void CMExitBtn()
63:       { SendMessage(WM_CLOSE); }
64:    // handle moving the scroll bar
65:    void HandleTimerScr();
66:    // handle exiting the application
67:    afx_msg void OnExit()
68:       { SendMessage(WM_CLOSE); }
69:    // handle closing the window
70:    afx_msg void OnClose();
71:    void makeRect(int nX, int nY, int nW, int nH, CRect& r);
72:
73: private:
74:    // delay the program for about ms milliseconds
75:    void delay(DWORD dwMs);
76:
77:    // declare message map macro
```

continues

Listing 19.3. continued

```
78:    DECLARE_MESSAGE_MAP();
79: };
80:
81: CAppWindow::CAppWindow()
82: {
83:    // load accelerator resources
84:    LoadAccelTable("BUTTONS");
85:    // create the window
86:    Create(NULL, "CountDown Timer", WS_OVERLAPPEDWINDOW,
87:        rectDefault, NULL, "EXITMENU");
88: }
89:
90: CAppWindow::~CAppWindow()
91: {
92:    delete InputBox;
93:    delete StartBtn;
94:    delete ExitBtn;
95:    delete TimerScr;
96:    delete InputTxt;
97:    delete Timer1Txt;
98:    delete Timer2Txt;
99: }
100:
101: int CAppWindow::OnCreate(LPCREATESTRUCT lpCS)
102: {
103:    char s[81];
104:    int nX = 50, nY = 50;
105:    DWORD dwStaticStyle = WS_CHILD | WS_VISIBLE | SS_LEFT;
106:    DWORD dwEditStyle = WS_CHILD | WS_VISIBLE | ES_LEFT |
107:                        WS_BORDER;
108:    DWORD dwScrollStyle = WS_CHILD | WS_VISIBLE | SBS_VERT;
109:    CRect r;
110:
111:    // create the timer input box and its label
112:    makeRect(nX, nY, 150, 30, r);
113:    InputTxt = new CStatic();
114:    InputTxt->Create("Timer Input Box", dwStaticStyle, r, this);
115:    nY += 30 + 5;
116:    makeRect(nX, nY, 150, 30, r);
117:    InputBox = new CEdit();
118:    InputBox->Create(dwEditStyle, r, this, ID_INPUT_BOX);
119:    InputBox->LimitText(MaxEditLen);
120:    // create the Start button
121:    nY += 30 + 20;
122:    makeRect(nX, nY, 60, 40, r);
123:    StartBtn = new CxButton();
124:    StartBtn->Create("&Start", r, this, ID_START_BTN);
125:    // create the Exit button
126:    nX += 60 + 20;
127:    makeRect(nX, nY, 60, 40, r);
```

```
128:    ExitBtn  = new CxButton();
129:    ExitBtn->Create("&Exit", r, this, ID_EXIT_BTN);
130:    // create the timer scroll bar
131:    nX = 300;
132:    nY = 100;
133:    makeRect(nX, nY, 20, 150, r);
134:    TimerScr = new CScrollBar();
135:    TimerScr->Create(dwScrollStyle, r, this, ID_TIMER_SCR);
136:    // create the static text controls that label the
137:    // minimum and maximum values
138:    nX += 20 + 10;
139:    makeRect(nX, nY, 80, 20, r);
140:    Timer1Txt = new CStatic();
141:    Timer1Txt->Create("0", dwStaticStyle, r, this);
142:    nY += 130;
143:    makeRect(nX, nY, 80, 20, r);
144:    sprintf(s, "%d", MaxTimer);
145:    Timer2Txt = new CStatic();
146:    Timer2Txt->Create(s, dwStaticStyle, r, this);
147:    // initialize the timer range
148:    TimerScr->SetScrollRange(0, MaxTimer);
149:    return CFrameWnd::OnCreate(lpCS);
150: }
151:
152: void CAppWindow::HandleStartBtn()
153: {
154:    char s[MaxEditLen+1];
155:    int nX;
156:
157:    // get the text in the edit box
158:    InputBox->GetWindowText(s, MaxEditLen);
159:    // convert the string into an integer
160:    nX = atoi(s);
161:    // if nX is 0 assign it 15
162:    nX = (nX != 0) ? nX : 15;
163:    // set the maximum timer static text
164:    sprintf(s, "%d", nX);
165:    Timer2Txt->SetWindowText(s);
166:    // set the new range
167:    TimerScr->SetScrollRange(0, nX);
168:    // set the thumb position to the maximum position
169:    TimerScr->SetScrollPos(nX);
170:    // countdown loop
171:    while (nX— > 0) {
172:      delay(980);
173:      // update the thumb position
174:      TimerScr->SetScrollPos(TimerScr->GetScrollPos() - 1);
175:      sprintf(s, "%d", nX);
176:      // echo thumb position in the edit box
177:      InputBox->SetWindowText(s);
```

continues

19

Listing 19.3. continued

```
178:      InputBox->UpdateWindow();
179:    }
180:    MessageBeep(0); // beep
181:    // restore the default timer limits
182:    sprintf(s, "%d", MaxTimer);
183:    TimerScr->SetScrollRange(0, MaxTimer);
184:    TimerScr->SetScrollPos(MaxTimer);
185:    Timer2Txt->SetWindowText(s);
186: }
187:
188: void CAppWindow::OnVScroll(UINT nSBCode, UINT nPos,
189:                            CScrollBar* pScrollBar)
190: {
191:    short nScrollInc;
192:    int nNewPos;
193:    int nVScrollMin, nVScrollMax;
194:    int nVScrollPos = pScrollBar->GetScrollPos();
195:
196:    // get the scroll bar range
197:    pScrollBar->GetScrollRange(&nVScrollMin, &nVScrollMax);
198:    switch (nSBCode) {
199:      case SB_TOP: // move to the top
200:          nScrollInc = -nVScrollPos;
201:          break;
202:      case SB_BOTTOM: // move to the bottom
203:          nScrollInc = nVScrollMax - nVScrollPos;
204:          break;
205:      case SB_LINEUP: // move one line up
206:          nScrollInc = -1;
207:          break;
208:      case SB_LINEDOWN: // move one line down
209:          nScrollInc = 1;
210:          break;
211:      case SB_PAGEUP: // move one page up
212:          nScrollInc = -PageSize;
213:          break;
214:      case SB_PAGEDOWN: // move one page down
215:          nScrollInc = PageSize;
216:          break;
217:      case SB_THUMBPOSITION: // track the thumb box
218:          nScrollInc = nPos - nVScrollPos;
219:          break;
220:      default:
221:          nScrollInc = 0;
222:    }
223:    // calculate new vertical thumb position so that:
224:    //            0 <= nNewPos <= nVScrollMax
225:    nNewPos = max(0, min(nVScrollPos + nScrollInc, nVScrollMax));
226:    // adjust scroll increment
227:    nScrollInc = nNewPos - nVScrollPos;
```

```
228:    // is nScrollInc not zero?
229:    if (nScrollInc) {
230:      // move the thumb box
231:      pScrollBar->SetScrollPos(nNewPos);
232:      // scroll the list boxes
233:      HandleTimerScr();
234:    }
235: }
236:
237: void CAppWindow::HandleTimerScr()
238: {
239:    int nX = TimerScr->GetScrollPos();
240:    char s[MaxEditLen+1];
241:    // convert the thumb position into a string
242:    sprintf(s, "%d", nX);
243:    // insert the string in the edit box
244:    InputBox->SetWindowText(s);
245: }
246:
247: void CAppWindow::OnClose()
248: {
249:    if (MessageBox("Want to close this application",
250:             "Query", MB_YESNO | MB_ICONQUESTION) == IDYES)
251:      DestroyWindow();
252: }
253:
254: void CAppWindow::delay(DWORD dwMs)
255: {
256:    DWORD dwTime = GetTickCount();
257:    do { ; } while ((GetTickCount() - dwTime) < dwMs);
258: }
259:
260: void CAppWindow::makeRect(int nX, int nY, int nW, int nH,
261:                           CRect& r)
262: {
263:    r.top = nY;
264:    r.left = nX;
265:    r.bottom = nY + nH;
266:    r.right = nX + nW;
267: }
268:
269: BEGIN_MESSAGE_MAP(CAppWindow, CFrameWnd)
270:    ON_WM_CREATE()
271:    ON_WM_VSCROLL()
272:    ON_BN_CLICKED(ID_START_BTN, HandleStartBtn)
273:    ON_COMMAND(ID_START_BTN, CMStartBtn)
274:    ON_BN_CLICKED(ID_EXIT_BTN, HandleExitBtn)
275:    ON_COMMAND(ID_EXIT_BTN, CMExitBtn)
276:    ON_COMMAND(CM_EXIT, OnExit)
277:    ON_WM_CLOSE()
```

19

continues

Listing 19.3. continued

```
278: END_MESSAGE_MAP()
279:
280: // Construct the CWindowApp's m_pMainWnd data member
281: BOOL CWindowApp::InitInstance()
282: {
283:   m_pMainWnd = new CAppWindow();
284:   m_pMainWnd->ShowWindow(m_nCmdShow);
285:   m_pMainWnd->UpdateWindow();
286:   return TRUE;
287: }
288:
289: // application's constructor initializes and runs the app
290: CWindowApp WindowApp;
```

Figure 19.1 shows a sample session with the CTLSCRL1.EXE application.

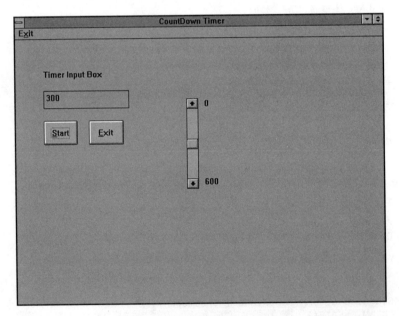

Figure 19.1. A sample session with the CTLSCRL1.EXE application.

Analysis   The program in Listing 19.3 contains the declaration for the application class, CWindowApp, the window classes, CAppWindow, and the button control class, CxButton. The window class CAppWindow declares a number of data members that are pointers to the application's controls. The class CAppWindow declares a constructor, a destructor, and ten member functions.

The `CAppWindow` class constructor creates the application window and performs the following tasks:

- ☐ Loads the accelerator keys resource

- ☐ Creates the application window, specifying a title, a default size, a default location, and the `EXITMENU` menu resource

The member function `OnCreate`, defined in lines 101 through 150, creates the various controls used by the application. The function carries out the following tasks:

- ☐ Creates the timer edit box and the static text that labels it

- ☐ Creates the push button controls marked Start and Exit

- ☐ Creates the timer scroll bar control (the function `CScrollBar::Create` specifies a vertical scroll using the `SBS_VERT` style, and assigns the argument `ID_TIMER_SCR` as the control's ID)

- ☐ Creates the static text controls that label the range of scroll bar values, the lower always 0 and the upper initially set using the global constant `MaxTimer` (the program changes the upper limit for the count-down process)

- ☐ Returns the function's result

The member function `HandleStartBtn`, defined in lines 152 through 186, implements the functionality that triggers the timer count-down. The function carries out the following tasks:

- ☐ Retrieves the text in the edit box and stores it in the local variable `s`

- ☐ Converts the characters in variable `s` into an `int` type and stores the result in the local variable `x`

- ☐ Examines the value of `x` (if it is zero, the function assigns 15 to variable `x`)

- ☐ Sets the maximum timer limit static text to the string image of the value in variable `x`

- ☐ Sets the range of the timer scroll bar by invoking the `CScrollBar::SetScrollRange` member function with the arguments of `0` and `x`

- ☐ Moves the thumb position all the way to the bottom of the scroll bar by using the `CScrollBar::SetScrollPos` member function (the argument for that function call is `x`)

19

☐ Starts the count-down loop, which invokes the delay function, requests that the program wait for 980 milliseconds, changes the thumb box position by moving it one value upward (using the member functions `CScrollBar::GetScrollPos` and `CScrollBar::SetScrollPos`), and writes the string image of the current thumb box position in the edit box (this simulates the edit box showing the count-down time in seconds)

☐ Beeps when the previous loop terminates

☐ Restores the default upper range of the scroll bar timer to 600 and updates the maximum limit static text accordingly

The `CMStartBtn` member function traps the command message generated by the Alt-S keys. The function merely calls the `HandleStartBtn` member function.

The `HandleExitBtn` and `CMExitBtn` member functions send a `WM_CLOSE` message to the application window.

Note: The member function `OnVScroll`, defined in lines 188 through 235, has the task of vertically scrolling the thumb box of the scroll bar control. The statements in the function use the `pScrollBar` parameter to query and set the thumb box position, and also to query the current scroll bar range.

The member function `HandleTimerScr`, defined in lines 237 through 245, is called by the `OnVScroll` member function. The function converts the current thumb box position into a string and writes it in the edit box. Thus, function `HandleTimerScr` is responsible for updating the contents of the edit box when you move the thumb box.

The delay member function uses the `GetTickCount` API function to simulate the requested delay.

The Combo Box Control

Windows supports the combo box control which combines an edit box with a list box. Thus, a combo box allows you to select either an item in the list box component (or part, if you prefer) or type in your own input. In a sense, the list box part of the combo box contains convenient or frequently used selections. A combo box, unlike a list box, does not confine you to choosing items in the list box. There are three kinds of combo boxes: simple, drop-down, and drop-down list.

NEW⟶
TERM
The *simple combo box* includes the edit box and the list box that is always displayed. The *drop-down combo box* differs from the simple type by the fact that the list box appears only when you click on the down scroll arrow. The *drop-down list combo box* provides a drop-down list that appears when you click on the down scroll arrow. There is no edit box in this kind of combo box!

The *CComboBox* Class

MFC offers the CComboxBox class, a descendant of CWnd, to support the combo box controls. The CComboBox class declares a constructor and a rich set of member functions to support both the list box and edit control components. The Create member function assists the class constructor in building class instances.

The *Create* Function

The declaration of the Create function is

```
BOOL Create(DWORD dwStyle,        // control style
            const RECT& rect,     // location and dimensions
            CWnd* pParentWnd,     // pointer to parent window
            UINT nID);            // control ID
```

The dwStyle parameter specifies the style of the list box control. The list box styles include the usual WS_*xxxx* window styles as well as the special CBS_*xxxx* combo box styles (shown in Table 19.2). The rect parameter specifies the location and dimensions of the control. The pParentWnd parameter is the pointer to the parent window. The nID parameter specifies the unique ID of the scroll bar instance.

Example:

```
DWORD dwStyle = WS_CHILD ¦ WS_VISIBLE ¦ WS_GROUP ¦ WS_TABSTOP
              ¦ CBS_SORT ¦ CBS_AUTOHSCROLL ¦ WS_VSCROLL[
CComboBox pCB;
pCB->Create(dwStyle, rectDefault, this, ID_CTL_CMB);
```

The arguments the dwStyle parameter may include either CBS_SIMPLE for a simple combo box, CBS_DROPDOWN for a drop-down combo box, or CBS_DROPDOWNLIST for a drop-down list combo box. Typical instances of CComboBox are created with styles WS_CHILD, WS_VISIBLE, WS_GROUP, WS_TABSTOP, CBS_SORT, CBS_AUTOHSCROLL, and WS_VSCROLL.

19

Table 19.2. Combo box control styles.

Style	Meaning
CBS_AUTOHSCROLL	Automatically scrolls the text in the edit control to the right when you enter a character at the end of the line (removing this style limits the text to the characters that fit inside the rectangular boundary of the edit control)
CBS_DROPDOWN	Specifies a drop-down combo box
CBS_DROPDOWNLIST	Specifies a drop-down list combo box
CBS_SIMPLE	Specifies a simple combo box
CBS_SORT	Automatically sorts the items in the list box

The CComboBox class declares member functions to manage the list box and the edit control components. Most of these functions are similar to members of the CEdit and CListBox class. Because the MFC library does not declare the CComboBox as a descendant of the CListBox and CEdit (using multiple inheritance), these functions must be redeclared.

Among the functions that handle the list box components are the following:

☐ The parameterless GetCount member function returns the number of items in the list box.

☐ The parameterless GetCurSel member function yields the index of the current selection. If there is no current selection, the function returns CB_ERR.

☐ The SetCurSel member function selects the current selection.

☐ The overloaded GetLBText member function is similar to the function CListBox::GetText. The function returns the item of the list box.

☐ The GetLBTextLen member function returns the length of list box items specified by an index.

☐ The ShowDropDown member function shows or hides the list box components of a combo box control.

☐ The AddString member function adds a string to the list box component of a combo box control.

☐ The DeleteString member function removes an item from the list box.

☐ The InsertString member function inserts a string at a specified location in the list box.

☐ The parameterless ResetContent member function clears the list box components of a combo box control.

☐ The Dir member function is a special member function that allows you to insert filenames in the list box component.

☐ The FindString member function performs a case-insensitive search for an item in the list box.

☐ The SelectString member function selects a list box item that matches a search string.

The *SetCurSel* Function

Syntax

The declaration of the SetCurSel function is

```
int SetCurSel(int nSelect);
```

The nSelect parameter specifies the index of the new selection in the list box. The function returns the index of the selected item, or yields CB_ERR if there is an error.

Example:

```
CComboBox* pCB;
// create control...
pCB->SetCurSel(0); // select the first item
```

19

The *GetLBText* Function

Syntax

The declaration of the GetLBText function is

```
int GetLBText(int nIndex, char FAR* lpItem) const;
void GetLBText(int nIndex, CString& rString) const;
```

The nIndex parameter specifies the index of the retrieved item. The lpItem parameter is the pointer to the buffer (which must be large enough) that receives the list box item. The rString parameter is the reference to a CString object that receives a copy of the list box item. The first form of the function returns the length of the retrieved list box item, or yields CB_ERR if there is an error.

Example:

```
char* s[81];
CComboBox* pCB;
// create control...
pCB->GetLBText(0, s); // get string in first list box item
```

The *GetLBTextLen* Function

The declaration of the function GetLBTextLen is

```
int GetLBTextLen(int nIndex) const;
```

The nIndex parameter specifies the list box item. The function returns the length of the sought list box item, or yields CB_ERR if the argument for nIndex is not valid. Use the GetLBTextLen to ensure that the buffer used with function GetLBText is large enough.

Example:

```
int nLen;
CComboBox* pCB;
// create control...
nLen = pCB->GetLBTextLen(0); // get length of first item
```

The *ShowDropDown* Function

The declaration of the function ShowDropDown is

```
void ShowDropDown(BOOL bShowIt = TRUE);
```

The Boolean bShowIt parameter is a switch that is used to show (when TRUE) or hide (when FALSE) the drop-down list box. Use the ShowDropDown member function when you want to toggle the visibility of the drop-down list box from within a program.

Example:

```
CComboBox* pCB;
// create control...
pCB->ShowDropDown();
```

The *AddString* Function

The declaration of the AddString function is

```
int AddString(const char FAR* lpString);
```

The lpString parameter is the pointer to the added string. The function returns the index of the inserted item, when successful. Otherwise, the function yields the negative CB_ERR

580

value. If the CBS_SORT style is set, the added string is placed in the appropriate location to maintain a sorted list. Otherwise, the string is added at the end of the list.

Example:

```
CComboBox* pCB;
// create control...
pCB->AddString("MS-DOS");
```

The *DeleteString* Function

Syntax

The declaration of the DeleteString function is

```
int DeleteString(int nIndex);
```

The nIndex parameter specifies the index of the deleted list box item. The function returns the number of remaining strings if the deletion is successful. Otherwise, the function yields the negative CB_ERR value.

Example:

```
CComboBox* pCB;
// create control...
// add strings to control...
pCB->DeleteString(0); // delete first item
```

The *InsertString* Function

Syntax

The declaration of the InsertString function is

```
int InsertString(int nIndex, const char FAR* lpString);
```

The nIndex parameter specifies the insertion index. The lpString parameter is the pointer to the inserted string. Do not use InsertString while the CBS_SORT style is set, unless you are inserting an item so that the order of the list box is not corrupted. The function returns the index of the inserted string, or yields CB_ERR if an error occurs. If the list box runs out of memory space, the function returns CB_ERRSPACE.

Example:

```
CComboBox* pCB;
// create control...
// add strings to control...
pCB->InsertString(0, "Windows"); // insert as new first item
```

19

The *Dir* Function

The declaration of the Dir function is

```
int Dir(UINT attr, const char FAR* lpWildCard);
```

The attr parameter specifies the combination of attributes. The file attributes are the same ones for the CListBox::Dir function, shown in Day 18, Table 18.2. The lpWildCard parameter is the pointer to the filename wildcard, such as *.*, L*.EXE, or A???.CPP.

Example:

```
int nNumFiles;
CComboBox* pCB;
// create control...
nNumFiles = pCB->Dir(_A_ARCH, "*.*");
```

The *FindString* Function

The declaration of the FindString function is

```
int FindString(int nStartAfter, const char FAR* lpItem) const;
```

The nStartAfter parameter specifies the index of the first list box member to be searched. The lpItem parameter is the pointer to the searched string. The function searches *the entire* list beginning with position nStartAfter and resuming at the beginning of the list if needed. The search stops when either a list member matches the search string or the entire list is searched. Passing an argument of -1 to nStartAfter forces the function to start searching from the beginning. The function returns the position of the matching list item, or LB_ERR if no match is found or when an error occurs.

Example:

```
int nIndex;
CComboBox* pCB;
// create control...
// add strings to control...
nIndex = pCB->FindString(-1, "MS-DOS");
```

The *SelectString* Function

The declaration of function SelectString is

```
int SelectString(int nStartAfter, const char FAR* lpItem);
```

The parameters and search mechanism of SelectString are identical to those of FindString. The difference is that SelectString selects the list box item that matches the string accessed by parameter lpItem.

Example:

```
CComboBox* pCB;
// create control...
// add strings to control...
pCB->SelectString(-1, "MS-DOS");
```

The following are among the functions that manage the edit control component:

☐ The parameterless GetEditSel member function returns a DWORD value containing the starting and ending character positions for the selected text. The lower word contains the starting character position (that is, the index of the first selected character) and the higher word contains the ending character position (that is, the index of the first character that is not in the selected text).

☐ The LimitText member function limits the number of characters that you can type in the edit box of a combo box control.

☐ The parameterless Clear member function clears the selected text.

☐ The parameterless Copy member function copies the selected text to the clipboard.

☐ The Cut member function clears the selected text and copies it to the clipboard.

☐ The Paste member function copies the contents of the clipboard to the current insertion point of the edit box.

The *LimitText* Function

The declaration of the LimitText function is

```
BOOL LimitText(int nMaxChars);
```

The parameter nMaxChars specifies the limit of the text in the edit box. The function returns TRUE if successful, and yields FALSE otherwise.

Example:

```
const int MAX_STR_SIZE = 81;
CComboBox* pCB;
// create control...
pCB->LimitText(MAX_STR_SIZE);
```

Responding to Combo Box Notification Messages

The combo box control emits various types of messages, shown in Table 19.3. The table also shows the message-mapping macros that are associated with the various command and notification messages. Each type of command or notification message requires a separate member function declared in the control's parent window class.

Table 19.3. Combo box notification messages.

Message	Macro	Meaning
WS_COMMAND	ON_COMMAND	A Windows command message
CBN_SELCHANGE	ON_CBN_SELCHANGE	A combo item is selected with a mouse click
CBN_DBLCLK	ON_CBN_DBLCLK	A combo item is selected with a mouse double-click
CBN_SETFOCUS	ON_CBN_SETFOCUS	The combo box has gained focus
CBN_KILLFOCUS	ON_CBN_KILLFOCUS	The combo box has lost focus
CBN_ERRSPACE	ON_CBN_ERRSPACE	The combo box cannot allocate more dynamic memory to accommodate new list items
CBN_EDITCHANGE	ON_CBN_EDITCHANGE	The contents of the edit box are changed
CBN_EDITUPDATE	ON_CBN_EDITUPDATE	The contents of the edit box are updated

Combo Boxes as History List Boxes

A combo box can also be a history list box. History list boxes typically follow these rules of operations:

1. The combo list box removes the CBS_SORT style to insert the list items in a chronological fashion. New items are inserted at position 0, pushing the older items farther down the list. The oldest item is the one at the bottom of the list.

2. History boxes usually have a limit on the number of items you can insert, to prevent bleeding memory. This conservative scheme requires that oldest list items be removed once the number of list items reaches a maximum limit.

3. If the edit control contains a string that does not have an exact match in the accompanying list box, the edit control string is inserted as a new member at position 0.

4. If the edit control contains a string that has an exact match in the accompanying list box, the matching list member is moved to position 0, the top of the list. Of course, this process involves first deleting the matching list member from its current position and then reinserting it at position 0.

NEW☞ TERM A *history list box* is a special combo box that inserts new edit control strings in the list box in chronological order.

A history list box is really a combo box that manipulates its edit control and list box items in a certain way. There is no need to derive a descendant of CComboBox to add new member functions.

NEW☞ TERM The history list box behaves like a *queue data structure*, with new items inserted at position 0, pushing the older items farther down the list.

The COCA Version 4 Application

Let me present the fourth version of the calculator application (COCA). This new version is actually derived from the second version, not the third one (except that the feature of substituting the # character in the operand controls with the previous result is also included). Figure 19.2 shows a sample session with the CTLCOMB1.EXE application and indicates the controls that are used:

☐ An Operand1 drop-down combo box that operates like a history list box

☐ An Operator simple combo box that contains the list of supported operators and functions log, exp, and sqrt (the program handles the LBN_KILLFOCUS notification messages sent by this control to select these functions by typing in the letters l, e, and s, respectively)

☐ An Operand2 drop-down combo box that operates like a history list box

19

☐ A Result drop-down combo box that operates like a history list box

☐ The error message edit box

☐ The Calc push button control

☐ The Exit push button control

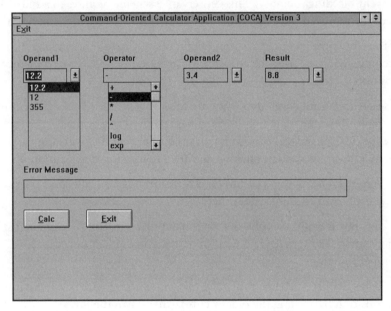

Figure 19.2. A sample session with the CTLCOMB1.EXE application.

Compile and run the program. Experiment with entering and executing numbers and operators or functions. Notice that combo boxes for the operands and the result enter in their accompanying list boxes in a chronological order. The operand combo boxes remember the last 30 different operands you entered. The Result combo box remembers the last 30 different results calculated. In a way, the Result combo box acts as a temporary transient memory.

Listing 19.4 shows the source code for the CTLCOMB1.H header file. Listing 19.5 shows the script for the CTLCOMB1.RC resource file. Listing 19.6 contains the source code for the CTLCOMB1.CPP program file. The resource file defines the accelerator keys and menu resources.

Listing 19.4. Source code for the CTLCOMB1.H header file.

```
1: #define CM_EXIT (WM_USER + 100)
2: #define ID_CALC_BTN 110
3: #define ID_EXIT_BTN 111
```

Listing 19.5. Script for the CTLCOMB1.RC resource file.

```
 1: #include <windows.h>
 2: #include <afxres.h>
 3: #include "ctlcomb1.h"
 4:
 5: BUTTONS ACCELERATORS
 6: BEGIN
 7:   "s", ID_START_BTN, ALT
 8:   "e", ID_EXIT_BTN, ALT
 9: END
10:
11: EXITMENU MENU LOADONCALL MOVEABLE PURE DISCARDABLE
12: BEGIN
13:     MENUITEM "E&xit", CM_EXIT
14: END
15:
```

Listing 19.6. Source code for the CTLCOMB1.CPP program file.

19

```
 1: #include <stdlib.h>
 2: #include <ctype.h>
 3: #include <stdio.h>
 4: #include <math.h>
 5: #include <string.h>
 6: #include <afxwin.h>
 7: #include "ctlcomb1.h"
 8:
 9: // declare the constants that represent the sizes of the controls
10: const Wlbl = 100;
11: const Hlbl = 20;
12: const LblVertSpacing = 5;
13: const LblHorzSpacing = 40;
14: const Wbox = 100;
15: const Hbox = 30;
16: const BoxVertSpacing = 20;
17: const BoxHorzSpacing = 40;
```

continues

Listing 19.6. continued

```
18: const WLongbox = 4 * (Wbox + BoxHorzSpacing);
19: const Hbtn = 30;
20: const Wbtn = 80;
21: const BtnHorzSpacing = 30;
22: const BtnVertSpacing = 10;
23: const Wcmb = 100;
24: const Hcmb = 150;
25: const CmbVertSpacing = 10;
26: const CmbHorzSpacing = 40;
27: // declare maximum size of text in edit control
28: const MaxEditLen = 30;
29: // maximum number of items in a combo box that doubles up as
30: // history list box
31: const MaxHistory = 30;
32: // declare the ID_XXXX constants for the edit boxes
33: #define ID_OPERAND1_CMB 101
34: #define ID_OPERATOR_CMB 102
35: #define ID_OPERAND2_CMB 103
36: #define ID_RESULT_CMB 104
37: #define ID_ERRMSG_EDIT 105
38:
39: class CxButton : public CButton
40: {
41: public:
42:
43:     BOOL Create(const char FAR* lpCaption, const RECT& rect,
44:                 CWnd* pParentWnd, UINT nID)
45:     { return CButton::Create(lpCaption,
46:                 WS_CHILD | WS_VISIBLE | WS_TABSTOP,
47:                 rect, pParentWnd, nID);
48:     }
49: };
50:
51: // expand the functionality of CFrameWnd by deriving
52: // class CAppWindow
53: class CAppWindow : public CFrameWnd
54: {
55: public:
56:
57:   CAppWindow();
58:   ~CAppWindow();
59:
60: protected:
61:   // declare the pointers to the controls
62:   CStatic* Operand1Txt;
63:   CStatic* OperatorTxt;
64:   CStatic* Operand2Txt;
65:   CStatic* ResultTxt;
66:   CStatic* ErrMsgTxt;
67:   CComboBox* Operand1Cmb;
```

```
68:     CComboBox* OperatorCmb;
69:     CComboBox* Operand2Cmb;
70:     CComboBox* ResultCmb;
71:     CEdit* ErrMsgBox;
72:     CxButton* CalcBtn;
73:     CxButton* ExitBtn;
74:     // math error flag
75:     BOOL bInError;
76:
77:     // handle notification messages from the Operator combo box
78:     afx_msg void HandleOperatorCmb();
79:     // handle the calculation
80:     afx_msg void HandleCalcBtn();
81:     // handle the accelerator key for the Calculate button
82:     afx_msg void CMCalcBtn()
83:         { HandleCalcBtn(); }
84:     // handle exiting the application
85:     afx_msg void HandleExitBtn()
86:         { SendMessage(WM_CLOSE); }
87:     // handle the accelerator key for the Exit button
88:     afx_msg void CMExitBtn()
89:         { SendMessage(WM_CLOSE); }
90:     // handle exiting the application
91:     afx_msg void OnExit()
92:         { SendMessage(WM_CLOSE); }
93:     // handle creating the controls
94:     afx_msg int OnCreate(LPCREATESTRUCT lpCS);
95:     // initialize the instances of CAppWindow
96:     void InitAppWindow();
97:     // handle closing the window
98:     afx_msg void OnClose();
99:     // return a reference to member r based on individual
100:    // coordinates and dimenions
101:    void makeRect(int nX, int nY, int nW, int nH, CRect& r);
102:    // update the combo box with the text in the
103:    // accompanying edit box, assuming that the text
104:    // is not already in the box
105:    void updateComboBox(CComboBox* pComboBox);
106:
107:    // declare message map macro
108:    DECLARE_MESSAGE_MAP();
109: };
110:
111: class CWindowApp : public CWinApp
112: {
113: public:
114:     virtual BOOL InitInstance();
115: };
116:
117: CAppWindow::CAppWindow()
118: {
```

continues

Listing 19.6. continued

```
119:   // load accelerator resources
120:   LoadAccelTable("BUTTONS");
121:   // create the window
122:   Create(NULL,
123:     "Command-Oriented Calculator Application (COCA) Version 3",
124:       WS_OVERLAPPEDWINDOW | WS_MAXIMIZE,
125:         rectDefault, NULL, "EXITMENU");
126:   // clear the bInError flag
127:   bInError = FALSE;
128:   // initialize application
129:   InitAppWindow();
130: }
131:
132: CAppWindow::~CAppWindow()
133: {
134:   // delete the controls
135:   delete Operand1Txt;
136:   delete OperatorTxt;
137:   delete Operand2Txt;
138:   delete ResultTxt;
139:   delete ErrMsgTxt;
140:   delete Operand1Cmb;
141:   delete OperatorCmb;
142:   delete Operand2Cmb;
143:   delete ResultCmb;
144:   delete ErrMsgBox;
145:   delete CalcBtn;
146:   delete ExitBtn;
147: }
148:
149: int CAppWindow::OnCreate(LPCREATESTRUCT lpCS)
150: {
151:   int nX0 = 20;
152:   int nY0 = 30;
153:   int nX = nX0, nY = nY0;
154:   DWORD dwStaticStyle = WS_CHILD | WS_VISIBLE | SS_LEFT;
155:   DWORD dwEditStyle = WS_CHILD | WS_VISIBLE | WS_BORDER |
156:                  ES_LEFT | ES_AUTOHSCROLL | ES_UPPERCASE;
157:   DWORD dwComboStyle = WS_CHILD | WS_VISIBLE | WS_VSCROLL;
158:   CRect r;
159:
160:   // create the first set of labels for the edit boxes
161:   makeRect(nX, nY, Wlbl, Hlbl, r);
162:   Operand1Txt = new CStatic();
163:   Operand1Txt->Create("Operand1", dwStaticStyle, r, this);
164:   nX += Wlbl + LblHorzSpacing;
165:   makeRect(nX, nY, Wlbl, Hlbl, r);
166:   OperatorTxt = new CStatic();
167:   OperatorTxt->Create("Operator", dwStaticStyle, r, this);
```

```
168:    nX += Wlbl + LblHorzSpacing;
169:    makeRect(nX, nY, Wlbl, Hlbl, r);
170:    Operand2Txt = new CStatic();
171:    Operand2Txt->Create("Operand2", dwStaticStyle, r, this);
172:    nX += Wlbl + LblHorzSpacing;
173:    makeRect(nX, nY, Wlbl, Hlbl, r);
174:    ResultTxt = new CStatic();
175:    ResultTxt->Create("Result", dwStaticStyle, r, this);
176:    // create the Operand1, Operator, Operand2, and Result
177:    // combo list boxes
178:    nX = nX0;
179:    nY += Hlbl + LblVertSpacing;
180:    makeRect(nX, nY, Wcmb, Hcmb, r);
181:    Operand1Cmb = new CComboBox();
182:    Operand1Cmb->Create(dwComboStyle | CBS_DROPDOWN, r,
183:                        this, ID_OPERAND1_CMB);
184:    // create the Operator combo box
185:    nX += Wcmb + CmbHorzSpacing;
186:    makeRect(nX, nY, Wcmb, Hcmb, r);
187:    OperatorCmb = new CComboBox();
188:    OperatorCmb->Create(dwComboStyle | CBS_SIMPLE, r,
189:                        this, ID_OPERATOR_CMB);
190:    nX += Wcmb + CmbHorzSpacing;
191:    makeRect(nX, nY, Wcmb, Hcmb, r);
192:    Operand2Cmb = new CComboBox();
193:    Operand2Cmb->Create(dwComboStyle | CBS_DROPDOWN, r,
194:                        this, ID_OPERAND2_CMB);
195:    nX += Wcmb + CmbHorzSpacing;
196:    makeRect(nX, nY, Wcmb, Hcmb, r);
197:    ResultCmb = new CComboBox();
198:    ResultCmb->Create(dwComboStyle | CBS_DROPDOWN, r,
199:                        this, ID_RESULT_CMB);
200:    // create the static text and edit box for the error message
201:    nX = nX0;
202:    nY += Hcmb + CmbVertSpacing;
203:    makeRect(nX, nY, Wlbl, Hlbl, r);
204:    ErrMsgTxt = new CStatic();
205:    ErrMsgTxt->Create("Error Message", dwStaticStyle, r, this);
206:    nY += Hlbl + LblVertSpacing;
207:    makeRect(nX, nY, WLongbox, Hbox, r);
208:    ErrMsgBox = new CEdit();
209:    ErrMsgBox->Create(dwEditStyle, r, this, ID_ERRMSG_EDIT);
210:    // create the Calc push button
211:    nY += Hbox + BoxVertSpacing;
212:    makeRect(nX, nY, Wbtn, Hbtn, r);
213:    CalcBtn = new CxButton();
214:    CalcBtn->Create("&Calc", r, this, ID_CALC_BTN);
215:    // Create the Exit Btn
216:    nX += Wbtn + BtnHorzSpacing;
217:    makeRect(nX, nY, Wbtn, Hbtn, r);
```

continues

Listing 19.6. continued

```
218:     ExitBtn = new CxButton();
219:     ExitBtn->Create("&Exit", r, this, ID_EXIT_BTN);
220:     // clear the bInError flag
221:     bInError = FALSE;
222:     return CFrameWnd::OnCreate(lpCS);
223: }
224:
225: void CAppWindow::InitAppWindow()
226: {
227:     char* p[] = { "+", "-", "*", "/", "^",
228:                   "log", "exp", "sqrt", "EOL" };
229:
230:     // add the operators in the Operator combo box
231:     for (int i = 0; p[i] != "EOL"; i++)
232:       OperatorCmb->AddString(p[i]);
233: }
234:
235: void CAppWindow::HandleOperatorCmb()
236: {
237:     char s[MaxEditLen+1];
238:
239:     // get the text in the Operator combo box edit area
240:     OperatorCmb->GetWindowText(s, MaxEditLen);
241:     // use it to search for a matching list item
242:     OperatorCmb->SelectString(-1, s);
243: }
244:
245: void CAppWindow::HandleCalcBtn()
246: {
247:     int nOpIndex;
248:     double x, y, z;
249:     char opStr[MaxEditLen+1];
250:     char s[MaxEditLen+1];
251:
252:     // obtain the string in the Operand1 combo box
253:     Operand1Cmb->GetWindowText(s, MaxEditLen);
254:     // convert the string in the edit box area
255:     x = atof(s);
256:     // obtain the string in the Operand2 combo box
257:     Operand2Cmb->GetWindowText(s, MaxEditLen);
258:     // convert the string in the edit box area
259:     y = atof(s);
260:     // obtain the string in the Operator combo box
261:     OperatorCmb->GetWindowText(opStr, MaxEditLen);
262:     // clear the error message box
263:     ErrMsgBox->SetWindowText("");
264:     bInError = FALSE;
265:     // determine the requested operation using the FindString
266:     // member function of CListBox
267:     nOpIndex = OperatorCmb->FindString(-1, opStr);
```

```
268:    switch (nOpIndex) {
269:      case 0: // + operator
270:        z = x + y;
271:        break;
272:      case 1: // - operator
273:        z = x - y;
274:        break;
275:      case 2: // * operator
276:        z = x * y;
277:        break;
278:      case 3: // / operator
279:        if (y != 0)
280:          z = x / y;
281:        else {
282:          z = 0;
283:          bInError = TRUE;
284:          ErrMsgBox->SetWindowText("Division-by-zero error");
285:        }
286:        break;
287:      case 4: // ^ operator
288:        if (x > 0)
289:          z = exp(y * log(x));
290:        else {
291:          bInError = TRUE;
292:          ErrMsgBox->SetWindowText(
293:            "Cannot raise the power of a negative number");
294:        }
295:        break;
296:      case 5: // the natural logarithm function
297:        if (x > 0)
298:          z = log(x);
299:        else {
300:          bInError = TRUE;
301:          ErrMsgBox->SetWindowText(
302:            "Invalid argument for the log(x) function");
303:        }
304:        break;
305:      case 6: // the exponential function
306:        if (x < 230)
307:          z = exp(x);
308:        else {
309:          bInError = TRUE;
310:          ErrMsgBox->SetWindowText(
311:            "Invalid argument for the exp(x) function");
312:        }
313:        break;
314:      case 7: // the square root function
315:        if (x >= 0)
316:          z = sqrt(x);
317:        else {
```

19

continues

Listing 19.6. continued

```
318:          bInError = TRUE;
319:          ErrMsgBox->SetWindowText(
320:            "Invalid argument for the sqrt(x) function");
321:        }
322:      break;
323:    default:
324:      bInError = TRUE;
325:      ErrMsgBox->SetWindowText("Invalid operator");
326:      break;
327:   }
328:   // display the result if no error has occurred
329:   if (!bInError) {
330:     sprintf(s, "%g", z);
331:     ResultCmb->SetWindowText(s);
332:     updateComboBox(ResultCmb);
333:   }
334:   // update the operand combo boxes
335:   updateComboBox(Operand1Cmb);
336:   updateComboBox(Operand2Cmb);
337: }
338:
339:
340: void CAppWindow::makeRect(int nX, int nY, int nW, int nH,
341:                           CRect& r)
342: {
343:   r.top = nY;
344:   r.left = nX;
345:   r.bottom = nY + nH;
346:   r.right = nX + nW;
347: }
348:
349: void CAppWindow::updateComboBox(CComboBox* pComboBox)
350: {
351:   char s[MaxEditLen+1];
352:   int nIdx;
353:
354:   pComboBox->GetWindowText(s, MaxEditLen);
355:   // is string s in the combo list
356:   nIdx = pComboBox->FindString(-1, s);
357:   if (nIdx == 0) return;
358:   else if (nIdx < 0) {
359:     pComboBox->InsertString(0, s);
360:     // delete extra history list members?
361:     while (pComboBox->GetCount() >= MaxHistory)
362:       pComboBox->DeleteString(pComboBox->GetCount()-1);
363:   }
364:   else {
365:     // delete the current selection
366:     pComboBox->DeleteString(nIdx);
367:     // insert the string s at the first position
```

```
368:        pComboBox->InsertString(0, s);
369:        // select the first combo box item
370:        pComboBox->SetCurSel(0);
371:    }
372: }
373:
374: void CAppWindow::OnClose()
375: {
376:    if (MessageBox("Want to close this application",
377:                   "Query", MB_YESNO | MB_ICONQUESTION) == IDYES)
378:       DestroyWindow();
379: }
380:
381: BEGIN_MESSAGE_MAP(CAppWindow, CFrameWnd)
382:    ON_CBN_EDITUPDATE(ID_OPERATOR_CMB, HandleOperatorCmb)
383:    ON_BN_CLICKED(ID_CALC_BTN, HandleCalcBtn)
384:    ON_COMMAND(ID_CALC_BTN, CMCalcBtn)
385:    ON_BN_CLICKED(ID_EXIT_BTN, HandleExitBtn)
386:    ON_COMMAND(ID_EXIT_BTN, CMExitBtn)
387:    ON_COMMAND(CM_EXIT, OnExit)
388:    ON_WM_CREATE()
389:    ON_WM_CLOSE()
390: END_MESSAGE_MAP()
391:
392: // Construct the CWindowApp's m_pMainWnd data member
393: BOOL CWindowApp::InitInstance()
394: {
395:    m_pMainWnd = new CAppWindow();
396:    m_pMainWnd->ShowWindow(m_nCmdShow);
397:    m_pMainWnd->UpdateWindow();
398:    return TRUE;
399: }
400:
401: // application's constructor initializes and runs the app
402: CWindowApp WindowApp;
```

Analysis

The program in Listing 19.6 declares three sets of constants. The first set specifies the dimensions and spacing for the various application controls. The second set of constants declares the maximum string size and maximum number of selections. The third set of constants establishes the ID numbers for the various controls.

The calculator program declares the application class, CWindowApp, the window class, CAppWindow, and the button class, CxButton. The CAppWindow class declares two sets of data members. The first set represents pointers to the various controls used in the application. The second set of members merely contains the bInError data member that flags any computational errors.

The `CAppWindow` class declares a constructor, a destructor, and a collection of member functions to handle the various messages. The `CAppWindow` constructor performs the following tasks:

- ☐ Loads the accelerator keys resource

- ☐ Invokes the `Create` function to create the application window (the window is maximized and uses the `EXITMENU` resource menu)

- ☐ Assigns `FALSE` to the `bInError` data member

- ☐ Calls the `InitAppWindow` function to initialize the application

The member function `OnCreate`, defined in lines 149 through 223, creates the instances for the various controls. The operand and result combo boxes are created with the `CBS_DROPDOWN` style. These same combo boxes avoid including the `CBS_SORT` style to enable them to work as history list boxes. The function creates the Operator combo box with the `CBS_SIMPLE` style and maintains the ordered items in the accompanying list box.

The member function `InitAppWindow`, defined in lines 225 through 233, initializes the window instance by adding the supported operators and math functions in the list box component of the Operator combo box. This task uses a `for` loop which invokes the member function `AddString`.

The member function `HandleOperatorCmb`, defined in lines 235 through 243, responds to the `CBN_EDITUPDATE` notification message sent by the Operator combo box. The function carries out the following tasks:

- ☐ Obtains the text from the edit box using the `GetText` function

- ☐ Invokes the `SelectString` function to search for a list box member that matches the retrieved string (if it finds a match, the matching item appears as selected text in the edit control area of the combo box)

The member function `HandleCalcBtn`, defined in lines 245 through 337, responds to the notification message of the Calc button and performs the requested calculation. The function performs these subsequent tasks:

- ☐ Retrieves the string in the edit box of the Operand1 combo box

- ☐ Converts this retrieved string into a numeric value and stores this value in the local variable `x`

- ☐ Retrieves the string in the edit box of the Operand2 combo box

☐ Converts this retrieved string into a numeric value and stores this value in the local variable y

☐ Obtains the string in the edit control of the Operator combo box

☐ Clears the Error Message edit control and assigns FALSE to the bInError data member

☐ Finds the position of the invoked operator or math function in the Operator combo box list, using the member function CComboBox::FindString

☐ Uses a switch statement to determine the requested operation or math function evaluation, then performs the requested task and assigns the result to variable z, or flags an error (this is the first time a version of the COCA program uses the switch statement, which should execute faster than the cascaded if statements that use the strcmp function found in earlier versions)

☐ If no error occurs, displays the result of the operation or function evaluation in the edit control box of the Result combo box, then inserts the new result in the list box of the Result combo box by calling the updateComboBox member function

☐ Inserts the new operands in the list boxes of their respective combo boxes, calling the updateComboBox member function twice to update both operand combo boxes (this update occurs regardless of the error condition, and, if you request to evaluate a math function, the list box of the Operand2 combo box remains unchanged unless you enter a new and superfluous operand in that combo box)

19

The function CMCalcBtn responds to the command message invoked by the Alt-C accelerator key. The function merely calls the HandleCalcBtn member function to provide the needed response.

The member function updatedComboBox, defined in lines 349 through 372, inserts the string of the edit control part in the list box part. This insertion occurs only if the string is not already in the list box part. In this case, the string is inserted at index 0 and becomes the new top-of-the-list item. If the targeted string is already in the list box part, the function deletes the existing item in the list box and reinserts it at index 0. Thus, the targeted string appears to have moved up to the top of the list box part.

The HandleExitBtn and CMExitBtn member functions offer the same response to the messages sent by the Exit button and the Alt-E accelerator key. Both functions send the WM_CLOSE message to the parent window.

Summary

Today's lesson presents the scroll bar and combo box controls. These controls share the common factor of being input objects. You learn about the following topics:

☐ The scroll bar control enables you to select quickly from a wide range of integers.

☐ There are various types of combo box controls: simple, drop-down, and drop-down list. You can use the `CBN_EDITUPDATE` notification message to make the combo boxes more interactive.

☐ You can make a history list box out of a drop-down combo box.

Q&A

Q. Do the scroll bars strictly select integers?

A. Yes. However, these integers can be indices to arrays, items in list box controls, and other integer codes to various attributes such as colors. Therefore, in a sense, the scroll bar can be used to select nonintegers.

Q. Can I create a scroll bar control with an excluded subrange of values?

A. No. You may want to use a list box control instead and have that control list the value numbers.

Workshop

The Workshop provides quiz questions to help you solidify your understanding of the material covered and exercises to provide you with experience in using what you've learned. Try to understand the quiz and exercise answers before continuing on to the next day's lesson. Answers are provided in Appendix B, "Answers."

Quiz

1. True or false? If you do not include the `CBS_AUTOHSCROLL` style in creating a combo list box, you limit the text to the characters that fit inside the rectangular boundary of the edit control.

2. True or false? You can handle the `CBN_SELCHANGE` notification message to monitor every keystroke in the edit control of a combo box.

3. True or false? Setting CBS_SORT creates a combo box whose list box items are sorted and unique.

4. True or false? To emulate a history list box, a combo box must be created without the CBS_SORT style.

5. True or false? A history list may have duplicate items.

6. True or false? CTLSCRL1.CPP demonstrates how to implement a two-way connection between the current value of a scroll bar control and the numeric value in a text box.

7. True or false? The range of values for a scroll bar control are fixed when you create the control.

Exercises

1. Modify the CTLCOMB1.CPP program by adding a Variables multiline box and a Store push button.

2. Modify the CTLCOMB1.CPP program by adding a Variables list box and a Store push button.

19

DAY 20

20

Dialog Boxes

M T W T F

Dialog boxes are special child windows that contain controls serving to display information or to input data. Windows applications use dialog boxes to exchange information with the user. Today's lesson looks at the modal and modeless dialog boxes supported by Windows.

**NEW☞
TERM**   *Modal dialog boxes* require you to close them before you can proceed any further with the application, because they are meant to perform a critical exchange of data. In fact, modal dialog boxes disable their parent windows while they have the focus. *Modeless dialog boxes* do need to be closed to continue using the application.

Today you learn about the following topics:

☐ Constructing instances of class `CDialog`

☐ Executing a modal dialog box

☐ Transferring control data

☐ Transferring data for modal dialog boxes

☐ Transferring data for modeless dialog boxes

Constructing Dialog Boxes

The MFC library declares the `CDialog` class to support both modeless and modal dialog boxes. The `CDialog` class, a descendant of `CWnd`, has a class constructor and a number of member functions, including the `Create` function. The `CDialog` constructor is declared as a protected member to force you to create your own modeless dialog box classes. These derived classes can declare either set of members to supplement your custom dialog box classes:

☐ Declare only a public constructor that invokes the `CDialog::Create` member function. This approach creates dialog box instances in one step.

☐ Declare both a public constructor and a `Create` member function. This scheme creates dialog box instances in two steps, by first calling the class constructor and then invoking the `Create` member function.

The declaration of the overloaded `CDialog::Create` member function is

```
BOOL Create(LPCSTR lpTemplateName, CWnd* pParentWnd = NULL);
BOOL Create(UINT nIDTemplate, CWnd* pParentWnd = NULL);
```

The `lpTemplateName` and `nIDTemplate` parameters are the dialog box resource name and ID, respectively. The `pParentWnd` parameter is the pointer to the parent window.

You can use the default argument when the dialog box instance is also the main application window.

> **Note:** Using resources to define dialog boxes and their controls allows you to define the location, dimensions, style, and caption of a control outside the Windows application source code. Thus, you can change the resource file, recompile it, and then incorporate it in the .EXE application file without recompiling the source file itself. This approach enables you to develop different resource versions with varying colors, styles, and even languages while maintaining a single copy of the application code.

> **Note:** The Visual C++ package includes the App Studio that enables you to create dialog boxes by drawing the controls in the dialog boxes, Visual Basic style. The App Studio creates .RC resource files that are then bound in your Windows applications. If you are a novice Windows programmer, first learn about the .RC file and its script. Using the App Studio is very easy and intuitive. Knowing about the .RC resource script makes working with the output of the App Studio even easier.

Executing Modal Dialog Boxes

Typically, modal dialog boxes are created and removed more frequently than modeless dialog boxes and much more frequently than windows. Executing modal dialog boxes involves the following steps:

1. Create a dialog box instance by using the dialog box class constructor.

2. Call the DoModal() member function, declared in class CDialog, to bring up the dialog box. Typically, dialog boxes contain the OK and Cancel push buttons, with the OK button as the default button. The OK and Cancel buttons have the predefined ID of IDOK and IDCANCEL, respectively. You may use push button controls with different captions than OK and Cancel. However, you should still use the IDOK and IDCANCEL with these renamed buttons. Using these IDs allows you to take advantage of the automatic response to IDOK and IDCANCEL provided by the OnOK and OnCancel member

functions defined in your dialog box class. Clicking OK or pressing the Enter key usually signals your acceptance of the current (that is, the default and/or edited) data in the dialog box. By contrast, clicking the Cancel button signals your dissatisfaction with the current data. The declaration of the `DoModal()` function is

```
int DoModal();
```

The function returns an integer that represents the outcome. Typical outcome values are `IDOK` or `IDCANCEL`.

3. Compare the result of the `DoModal` function with `IDOK` (or, less frequently, `IDCANCEL`). The outcome of this comparison determines the steps to take. Such steps usually involve accessing data that you entered in the dialog box controls.

The `OnInitDialog` (inherited from class `CDialog`), `OnOK`, and `OnCancel` member functions support the execution of the modal dialog boxes. These parameterless functions are declared as virtual, requiring that overriding functions be void of any parameters. The `OnInitDialog` member function serves to initialize the dialog box and its controls. The declaration of the `OnInitDialog` is

```
virtual BOOL OnInitDialog();
```

The function returns a Boolean result to indicate the success of the dialog box initialization. Typically, the `OnInitDialog` function initializes the controls of the dialog box. This initialization usually involves copying data from buffers or data members.

The `OnOK` member function handles pressing the OK button. The declaration of the `OnOK` function is

```
virtual void OnOK();
```

The `OnOK` function serves to copy data from the dialog box controls to data members or buffers. Using the `EndDialog` member function, the `OnOk` function is able to provide the `DoModal` function with its return value. Usually, the last statement in the `OnOK` member function definition is `EndDialog(IDOK)`. The latter function call causes the `DoModal` function to return `IDOK`.

The `OnCancel` member function handles pressing the Cancel button. The declaration of the `OnCancel` function is

```
virtual void OnCancel();
```

The OnCancel function serves to clean up before the dialog box is closed, which may involve closing data files, for example. Usually, the last statement in the OnCancel member function definition is EndDialog(IDCANCEL). The latter function call causes the DoModal function to return IDCANCEL.

The next example is a simple MFC program that uses a dialog box defined in resource files. It also uses resource files to create alternate forms of the same dialog box—the first uses modern English and the second uses old English. The application is simple and is made up of an empty window with a single menu item, Exit. When you click the Exit menu item (or press the Alt-X keys) you get a dialog box that asks you whether or not you want to exit the application. The dialog box has a title, a message, and the two buttons (in fact, I purposely made it to resemble the dialog boxes spawned by the CWnd::MessageBox function). The program alternates between the two versions of the dialog box. When you first click the Exit menu, you get the modern English version (with OK and Cancel buttons), shown in Figure 20.1. If you click the Cancel button and then click the Exit menu again, you get the old English version of the dialog box (with Yea and Nay buttons), shown in Figure 20.2. Every time you select the Cancel or Nay button and then click the Exit menu, you toggle between the two versions of the dialog box. To exit the application, click the OK or Yea button, depending on the current dialog box version.

Listing 20.1 shows the DIALOG1.H header file. Listing 20.2 contains the script for the DIALOG1.RC resource file. Listing 20.3 shows the source code for the DIALOG1.CPP program.

Listing 20.1. Source code for the DIALOG1.H header file.

```
1: #define CM_EXIT (WM_USER + 100)
```

Listing 20.2. Script for the DIALOG1.RC resource file.

```
1: #include <windows.h>
2: #include <afxres.h>
3: #include "dialog1.h"
4:
5: EXITMENU MENU LOADONCALL MOVEABLE PURE DISCARDABLE
6: BEGIN
7:     MENUITEM "E&xit", CM_EXIT
8: END
9:
```

continues

Listing 20.2. continued

```
10: NEW DIALOG DISCARDABLE LOADONCALL PURE MOVEABLE 30, 50, 200, 100
11: STYLE WS_POPUP | DS_MODALFRAME
12: CAPTION "Message"
13: BEGIN
14:   CTEXT "Exit the application?", 1, 10, 10, 170, 15
15:   CONTROL "OK", IDOK, "BUTTON", WS_CHILD | WS_VISIBLE |
16:     WS_TABSTOP | BS_DEFPUSHBUTTON, 20, 50, 70, 15
17:   CONTROL "Cancel", IDCANCEL, "BUTTON", WS_CHILD | WS_VISIBLE |
18:     WS_TABSTOP | BS_PUSHBUTTON, 110, 50, 70, 15
19: END
20:
21: OLD DIALOG DISCARDABLE LOADONCALL PURE MOVEABLE 30, 50, 200, 100
22: STYLE WS_POPUP | DS_MODALFRAME
23: CAPTION "A Word With Thou"
24: BEGIN
25:   CTEXT "Thou leavest now?", 1, 10, 10, 170, 15
26:   CONTROL "Yea", IDOK, "BUTTON", WS_CHILD | WS_VISIBLE |
27:     WS_TABSTOP | BS_DEFPUSHBUTTON, 20, 50, 70, 15
28:   CONTROL "Nay", IDCANCEL, "BUTTON", WS_CHILD | WS_VISIBLE |
29:     WS_TABSTOP | BS_PUSHBUTTON, 110, 50, 70, 15
30: END
```

Type

Listing 20.3. Source code for the DIALOG1.CPP program file.

```
1: #include <afxwin.h>
2: #include "dialog1.h"
3:
4: class CWindowApp : public CWinApp
5: {
6: public:
7:     virtual BOOL InitInstance();
8: };
9: // expand the functionality of CFrameWnd by deriving
10: // class CAppWindow
11: class CAppWindow : public CFrameWnd
12: {
13: public:
14:
15:   CAppWindow();
16:
17: protected:
18:   // handle exiting the application
19:   afx_msg void OnExit()
20:     { SendMessage(WM_CLOSE); }
21:   // Handle closing the window
22:   afx_msg void OnClose();
23:
```

```
24:    DECLARE_MESSAGE_MAP();
25:
26: };
27:
28: CAppWindow::CAppWindow()
29: {
30:    // create the window
31:    Create(NULL, "A Bare-Bones Dialog Box Tester",
32:           WS_OVERLAPPEDWINDOW, rectDefault, NULL, "EXITMENU");
33:
34: }
35:
36: void CAppWindow::OnClose()
37: {
38:    static BOOL bFlag = FALSE;
39:    CDialog* pDialogBox;
40:    BOOL bCloseIt;
41:
42:    // toggle flag that selects alternate dialog box resources
43:    bFlag = (bFlag == TRUE) ? FALSE : TRUE;
44:    if (bFlag) {
45:      pDialogBox = new CDialog("NEW", this);
46:      // use Modern English dialog box
47:      bCloseIt = (pDialogBox->DoModal() == IDOK) ? TRUE : FALSE;
48:    }
49:    else {
50:      pDialogBox = new CDialog("OLD", this);
51:      // use Old English dialog box
52:      bCloseIt = (pDialogBox->DoModal() == IDOK) ? TRUE : FALSE;
53:    }
54:    if (bCloseIt)
55:       DestroyWindow();
56: }
57:
58: BEGIN_MESSAGE_MAP(CAppWindow, CFrameWnd)
59:   ON_COMMAND(CM_EXIT, OnExit)
60:   ON_WM_CLOSE()
61: END_MESSAGE_MAP()
62:
63: // Construct the CWindowApp's m_pMainWnd data member
64: BOOL CWindowApp::InitInstance()
65: {
66:   m_pMainWnd = new CAppWindow();
67:   m_pMainWnd->ShowWindow(m_nCmdShow);
68:   m_pMainWnd->UpdateWindow();
69:   return TRUE;
70: }
71:
72: // application's constructor initializes and runs the app
73: CWindowApp WindowApp;
```

20

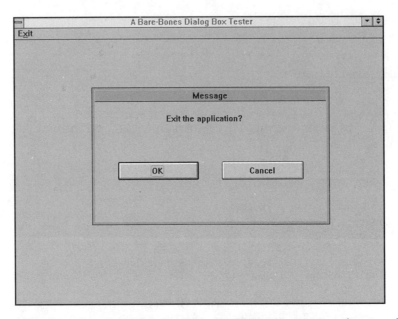

Figure 20.1. A sample session with the DIALOG1.EXE application showing the dialog box with modern English wording.

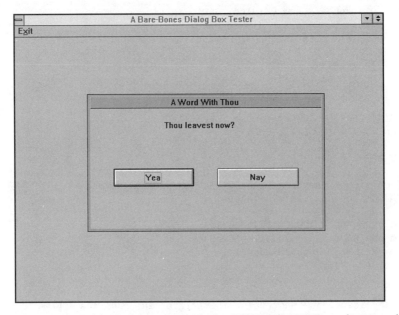

Figure 20.2. A sample session with the DIALOG1.EXE application showing the dialog box with old English wording.

Analysis

Listing 20.2 shows the script for the DIALOG1.RC resource file which defines the following resources:

☐ The menu resource, EXITMENU, displays a single menu with the single item Exit.

☐ The dialog box resource, NEW, has a defined style, caption, and list of child controls. The specified style indicates that the dialog box is a modal pop-up child window. The caption specified is the string Message. The dialog box contains three controls: a centered static text (for the dialog box message), a default OK push button, and an ordinary Cancel button. The OK button has the resource ID of the predefined IDOK constant. The Cancel button has the resource ID of the predefined IDCANCEL constant.

☐ The dialog box resource, OLD, is similar to the NEW dialog box resource, except it uses old English wording. The Yea button has the resource ID of the predefined IDOK constant. The Nay button has the resource ID of the predefined IDCANCEL constant. These buttons are examples of exit buttons with atypical captions.

The resource definition of the dialog box and controls may be new to you. Appendix A discusses the resource files for dialog boxes and their controls in more detail. The CTEXT is a keyword that specifies centered text. The CONTROL keyword allows you to define any control and requires the caption, ID, control class, control style, location, and dimensions of the control.

Listing 20.3 shows the source code for the DIALOG1.CPP program file. The source code declares two classes: an application class and a window class. The application uses the CDialog class, because no additional dialog box functionality is required.

The most relevant member function is CAppWindow::OnClose which responds to the WM_CLOSE command message sent by the Exit menu item. The function uses the Boolean static local variable, flag, to toggle between the two dialog box resources NEW and OLD. The new English dialog box is invoked in the following statement:

```
pDialogBox = new CDialog("NEW", this);
```

The dialog box is executed using the DoModal function, disabling the parent window until you click on either push button control. The value returned by the DoModal member function is compared with the IDOK constant to assign either TRUE or FALSE to the local Boolean variable bCloseIt. The OnClose function examines the value in bCloseIt to determine whether or not to close the application window.

The instance of the old English version of the dialog box is similarly created, as shown in the following statement:

```
pDialogBox = new CDialog("OLD", this);
```

The `CDialog::OnOK` member function responds to the `IDOK` command by closing the dialog boxes and returning the `IDOK` result.

Transferring Control Data

Dialog boxes serve mainly as pop-up windows to request input from the application user. This input often includes a variety of settings that use radio buttons, check boxes, and edit boxes. Because dialog boxes are frequently created, it makes sense to preserve the latest values in the dialog's controls for the next time it appears. Search and Replace dialog boxes that are found in many Windows editors are typical examples. These dialog boxes remember the settings of all or some of their controls from the last time the dialog box was executed.

To implement this feature in dialog boxes, you need a data transfer mechanism between the dialog box and a buffer. This buffer is usually a data member of the parent window. Therefore, the first step in supporting data transfer is to define a transfer buffer type. The buffer declares the data fields to buffer the controls that transfer their data. These controls typically include the static text, edit box, list box, combo box, scroll bar, check box, and radio button. The group box and push button controls have no data to transfer and therefore do not enter in the declaration of the data transfer buffer type. A sample data buffer type that includes a single instance of each allowable control is

```
struct TAppTransferBuffer {
    char StaticText[MaxStaticLen];
    char EditBox[MaxEditLen];
    CListBoxData ListBoxData;       // user-defined class
    CComboBoxData ComboBoxData;     // user-defined class
    CScrollBarData ScrollBarData;   // user-defined class
    int CheckBox;
    int RadioButton;
};
```

The buffer structure needs only to include the controls that participate in the data transfer. You do not need to declare the fields of the buffer structure in any particular order. This sample buffer type includes three special user-defined classes that transfer data between dialog boxes and list boxes, combo boxes, and scroll bars. More about these classes later in this section.

Let's look at the various members of the data transfer buffer type:

- [ ] The StaticText member helps in transferring data between a static text control and the data buffer. The data member defines a character array that should be equal to or greater than the number of characters in the static text control.

- [ ] The EditBox member assists in moving data between the edit box control and the data buffer. The data member defines a character array that should be equal to or greater than the number of characters in the edit box control.

- [ ] The ListBoxData member helps to transfer data between a list box control and the data buffer. The ListBoxData is an instance of the class that you declare to manage the data transfer between a dialog box and a list box. Why use a special data transfer class? Such a class successfully encapsulates the data and operations related to the transferred data. A typical declaration for the CListBoxData class is

```
class CListBox
{
public:
    // array of CString to store the list box items
    CStringArray DataList;
    CListBoxData();
    // transfer data to the buffer
    void GetListBoxData(CListBox* pListBox);
    // transfer data to the list box
    void SetListBoxData(CListBox* pListBox);
};
```

The DataList member is a dynamic array of CString objects that stores the list box items. The MFC library declares the CStringArray class and provides adequate operations to manipulate the array of strings. The absence of a data member to keep track of the number of list box items is justified by the fact

20

that the `CStringArray` class offers the `GetSize` member function to provide the number of string objects in a `CStringArray` instance.

The `GetListBoxData` and `SetListBoxData` member functions provide the two-way data transfer between a list box control and the data buffer.

☐ The `ComboBoxData` member helps to move data between a combo box control and the data buffer. The `ComboBoxData` is an instance to the `CComboBoxData` class that you declare. Here is a typical declaration for class `CComboBoxData`:

```
class CComboBox
{
public:
     // the combo box selection
     CString Selection;
     // array of CString to store the list box items
     CStringArray DataList;

     CComboBoxData();
     // transfer data to the buffer
     void GetComboBoxData(CListBox* pComboBox);
     // transfer data to the combo box
     void SetComboBoxData(CListBox* pComboBox);
};
```

The suggested declaration of class `CComboBoxData` is similar to that of class `CListBoxData`. The class `ComboBoxData` has an additional data member, `Selection`, to store the combo box selection located in its edit control.

☐ The `ScrollBarData` member assists in transferring data between a scroll bar control and the data buffer. This member has the suggested `CScollBarData` class, defined as follows:

```
class CScrollBarData
{
public:
     int LowValue;
     int HighValue;
     int Position;

     CScrollBarData();
     // move data to the buffer
```

```
        void GetScrollBarData(CScrollBar* pScrollBar);
        // move data to the scroll bar
        void SetScrollBarData(CScrollBar* pScrollBar);
    };
```

The `LowValue`, `HighValue`, and `Position` members store the scroll bar range and the current thumb position.

☐ The `CheckBox` member stores the current check state of a check box in an `int` type.

☐ The `RadioButton` member stores the current check state of a radio button in an `int` type.

Data Transfer for Modal Dialog Boxes

The next application is a simple example of transferring data between the controls of a modal dialog box and a buffer. It creates a typical dialog box that is used in replacing characters in a text editor. The dialog box contains the following controls:

☐ The Find edit box

☐ The Replace edit box

☐ The Scope group box that contains the Global and Selected Text radio button controls

☐ The Case-Sensitive check box

☐ The Whole Word check box

☐ The OK push button control

☐ The Cancel push button control

The application has a main menu with the Exit and Dialog menu items. To invoke the dialog box, click on the Dialog menu item or press the Alt-D keys. When you invoke the dialog box for the first time, the controls have the following initial values and states:

☐ The Find edit box contains the string DOS.

☐ The Replace edit box has the string Windows.

20

☐ The Global radio button is checked.

☐ The Case-Sensitive check box is checked.

☐ The Whole Word check box is checked.

Type in new strings in the edit box and alter the check states of the radio buttons and check boxes. Now, click on the OK button (or press the Alt-O keys) to close the dialog box. Invoke the Dialog menu item again to pop up the dialog box. Notice that the controls of the dialog box have the same values and states as when you last closed the dialog box.

Listing 20.4 shows the source code for the DIALOG2.H header file. Listing 20.5 contains the script for the DIALOG2.RC resource file. Listing 20.6 shows the source code for the DIALOG2.CPP program file.

Type

Listing 20.4. Source code for the DIALOG2.H header file.

```
 1: #define CM_EXIT   (WM_USER + 100)
 2: #define CM_DIALOG (WM_USER + 101)
 3:
 4: #define ID_FIND_TXT       201
 5: #define ID_FIND_EDIT      202
 6: #define ID_REPLACE_TXT    203
 7: #define ID_REPLACE_EDIT   204
 8: #define ID_SCOPE_GRP      205
 9: #define ID_GLOBAL_RBT     206
10: #define ID_SELTEXT_RBT    207
11: #define ID_CASE_CHK       208
12: #define ID_WHOLEWORD_CHK 209
```

Type

Listing 20.5. Script for the DIALOG2.RC resource file.

```
 1: #include <windows.h>
 2: #include <afxres.h>
 3: #include "dialog2.h"
 4:
 5: BUTTONS ACCELERATORS
 6: BEGIN
 7:   "o", IDOK, ALT
 8:   "c", IDCANCEL, ALT
 9: END
10:
11: SEARCH DIALOG DISCARDABLE LOADONCALL PURE MOVEABLE 10, 10,
12:                                              200, 150
```

```
13: STYLE WS_POPUP ¦ WS_CLIPSIBLINGS ¦ WS_CAPTION ¦ WS_SYSMENU ¦
14:      DS_MODALFRAME
15: CAPTION "Controls Demo"
16: BEGIN
17:   CONTROL "Find", ID_FIND_TXT, "STATIC", WS_CHILD ¦ WS_VISIBLE ¦
18:     SS_LEFT, 20, 10, 100, 15
19:   CONTROL "", ID_FIND_EDIT, "EDIT", WS_CHILD ¦ WS_VISIBLE ¦
20:     WS_BORDER ¦ WS_TABSTOP, 20, 25, 100, 15
21:   CONTROL "Replace", ID_REPLACE_TXT, "STATIC", WS_CHILD ¦
22:     WS_VISIBLE ¦ SS_LEFT, 20, 45, 100, 15
23:   CONTROL "", ID_REPLACE_EDIT, "EDIT", WS_CHILD ¦ WS_VISIBLE ¦
24:     WS_BORDER ¦ WS_TABSTOP, 20, 60, 100, 15
25:   CONTROL " Scope ", ID_SCOPE_GRP, "BUTTON", WS_CHILD ¦
26:     WS_VISIBLE ¦ WS_GROUP ¦ BS_GROUPBOX, 20, 80, 90, 50
27:   CONTROL "Global", ID_GLOBAL_RBT, "BUTTON", WS_CHILD ¦
28:     WS_VISIBLE ¦ WS_TABSTOP ¦ BS_AUTORADIOBUTTON, 30, 90, 50, 15
29:   CONTROL "Selected Text", ID_SELTEXT_RBT, "BUTTON", WS_CHILD ¦
30:     WS_VISIBLE ¦ WS_TABSTOP ¦ BS_AUTORADIOBUTTON, 30, 105, 60, 15
31:   CONTROL "Case Sensitive", ID_CASE_CHK, "BUTTON", WS_CHILD ¦
32:     WS_VISIBLE ¦ WS_TABSTOP ¦ BS_AUTOCHECKBOX, 20, 130, 80, 15
33:   CONTROL "Whole Word", ID_WHOLEWORD_CHK, "BUTTON", WS_CHILD ¦
34:     WS_VISIBLE ¦ WS_TABSTOP ¦ BS_AUTOCHECKBOX, 100, 130, 80, 15
35:   CONTROL, "&OK", IDOK, "BUTTON", WS_CHILD ¦ WS_VISIBLE ¦
36:     WS_TABSTOP ¦ WS_GROUP ¦ BS_DEFPUSHBUTTON, 120, 90, 30, 20
37:   CONTROL "&Cancel", IDCANCEL, "BUTTON", WS_CHILD ¦ WS_VISIBLE ¦
38:     WS_TABSTOP ¦ WS_GROUP ¦ BS_PUSHBUTTON, 160, 90, 30, 20
39: END
40:
41: MAINMENU MENU LOADONCALL MOVEABLE PURE DISCARDABLE
42: BEGIN
43:     MENUITEM "E&xit", CM_EXIT
44:     MENUITEM "&Dialog", CM_DIALOG
45: END
```

Type

Listing 20.6. Source code for the DIALOG2.CPP program file.

20

```
1: #include <string.h>
2: #include <afxwin.h>
3: #include "dialog2.h"
4:
5: // declare constants
6: const MaxEditLen = 30;
7: const BF_CHECKED = 1;
8: const BF_UNCHECKED = 0;
9: // declare the application buffer
10: struct TAppTransferBuf {
11:   char FindBoxBuff[MaxEditLen+1];
```

continues

Listing 20.6. continued

```
12:    char ReplaceBoxBuff[MaxEditLen+1];
13:    int GlobalRbtBuff;
14:    int SelTextRbtBuff;
15:    int CaseChkBuff;
16:    int WholeWordChkBuff;
17: };
18:
19: class CWindowApp : public CWinApp
20: {
21: public:
22:     virtual BOOL InitInstance();
23: };
24:
25: // expand the functionality of CDialog by
26: // deriving class CAppDialog
27: class CAppDialog : public CDialog
28: {
29: public:
30:
31:    CAppDialog(const char FAR* lpTemplateName,
32:            CWnd* pParentWnd = NULL) :
33:            CDialog(lpTemplateName, pParentWnd) {}
34:
35: protected:
36:
37:    // handle initializing the dialog box
38:    virtual BOOL OnInitDialog();
39:    // handle pressing the OK button
40:    virtual void OnOK();
41:    // pointer to data buffer in parent window
42:    TAppTransferBuf* pAppBuffer;
43: };
44:
45: // expand the functionality of CFrameWnd by deriving class
    CAppWindow
46: class CAppWindow : public CFrameWnd
47: {
48:
49:    friend CAppDialog;
50:
51: public:
52:
53:    // declare data transfer buffer
54:    TAppTransferBuf AppBuffer;
55:
56:    CAppWindow();
57:    // handle the dialog command
58:    afx_msg void CMDialog();
```

```
59:    // handle exiting the application
60:    afx_msg void OnExit()
61:      { SendMessage(WM_CLOSE); }
62:
63: protected:
64:
65:    // handle closing the window
66:    afx_msg void OnClose();
67:
68:    // declare message map macro
69:    DECLARE_MESSAGE_MAP();
70:
71: };
72:
73: BOOL CAppDialog::OnInitDialog()
74: {
75:    CAppWindow* pW = (CAppWindow*)(GetParent());
76:    pAppBuffer = &pW->AppBuffer;
77:    // copy data from the buffer to the dialog box controls
78:    SetDlgItemText(ID_FIND_EDIT, pAppBuffer->FindBoxBuff);
79:    SetDlgItemText(ID_REPLACE_EDIT, pAppBuffer->ReplaceBoxBuff);
80:    CButton* pBtn = (CButton*)(GetDlgItem(ID_GLOBAL_RBT));
81:    pBtn->SetCheck(pAppBuffer->GlobalRbtBuff);
82:    pBtn = (CButton*)(GetDlgItem(ID_SELTEXT_RBT));
83:    pBtn->SetCheck(pAppBuffer->SelTextRbtBuff);
84:    pBtn = (CButton*)(GetDlgItem(ID_CASE_CHK));
85:    pBtn->SetCheck(pAppBuffer->CaseChkBuff);
86:    pBtn = (CButton*)(GetDlgItem(ID_WHOLEWORD_CHK));
87:    pBtn->SetCheck(pAppBuffer->WholeWordChkBuff);
88:    return TRUE;
89: }
90:
91: void CAppDialog::OnOK()
92: {
93:    // copy data from the dialog box controls to the buffer
94:    GetDlgItemText(ID_FIND_EDIT, pAppBuffer->FindBoxBuff,
95:                   MaxEditLen);
96:    GetDlgItemText(ID_REPLACE_EDIT, pAppBuffer->ReplaceBoxBuff,
97:             MaxEditLen);
98:    CButton* pBtn = (CButton*)(GetDlgItem(ID_GLOBAL_RBT));
99:    pAppBuffer->GlobalRbtBuff = pBtn->GetCheck();
100:   pBtn = (CButton*)(GetDlgItem(ID_SELTEXT_RBT));
101:   pAppBuffer->SelTextRbtBuff = pBtn->GetCheck();
102:   pBtn = (CButton*)(GetDlgItem(ID_CASE_CHK));
103:   pAppBuffer->CaseChkBuff = pBtn->GetCheck();
104:   pBtn = (CButton*)(GetDlgItem(ID_WHOLEWORD_CHK));
105:   pAppBuffer->WholeWordChkBuff = pBtn->GetCheck();
106:   // return dialog box value
107:   EndDialog(IDOK);
```

continues

Listing 20.6. continued

```
108: }
109:
110: CAppWindow::CAppWindow()
111: {
112:     // load the accelerator keys resource
113:     LoadAccelTable("BUTTONS");
114:
115:     // create the window
116:     Create(NULL, "Modal Dialog Box Data Transfer Tester",
117:            WS_OVERLAPPEDWINDOW, rectDefault, NULL, "MAINMENU");
118:
119:     // fill buffer with 0's
120:     memset(&AppBuffer, 0x0, sizeof(AppBuffer));
121:     strcpy(AppBuffer.FindBoxBuff, "DOS");
122:     strcpy(AppBuffer.ReplaceBoxBuff, "Windows");
123:     AppBuffer.GlobalRbtBuff = BF_CHECKED;
124:     AppBuffer.CaseChkBuff = BF_CHECKED;
125:     AppBuffer.WholeWordChkBuff = BF_CHECKED;
126: };
127:
128: void CAppWindow::CMDialog()
129: {
130:     CString msgStr;
131:     CAppDialog* pDlg = new CAppDialog("SEARCH", this);
132:
133:     if (pDlg->DoModal() == IDOK) {
134:       msgStr = "Find String: ";
135:       msgStr += AppBuffer.FindBoxBuff;
136:       msgStr += "\n\nReplace String:";
137:       msgStr += AppBuffer.ReplaceBoxBuff;
138:       MessageBox((const char*) msgStr, "Dialog Box Data", MB_OK);
139:     }
140: }
141:
142: void CAppWindow::OnClose()
143: {
144:     if (MessageBox("Want to close this application",
145:                    "Query", MB_YESNO | MB_ICONQUESTION) == IDYES)
146:       DestroyWindow();
147: }
148:
149: BEGIN_MESSAGE_MAP(CAppWindow, CFrameWnd)
150:   ON_COMMAND(CM_DIALOG, CMDialog)
151:   ON_COMMAND(CM_EXIT, OnExit)
152:   ON_WM_CLOSE()
153: END_MESSAGE_MAP()
154:
155: // Construct the CWindowApp's m_pMainWnd data member
156: BOOL CWindowApp::InitInstance()
```

```
157: {
158:   m_pMainWnd = new CAppWindow();
159:   m_pMainWnd->ShowWindow(m_nCmdShow);
160:   m_pMainWnd->UpdateWindow();
161:   return TRUE;
162: }
163:
164: // application's constructor initializes and runs the app
165: CWindowApp WindowApp;
```

Figure 20.3 shows a sample session with the DIALOG2.EXE program.

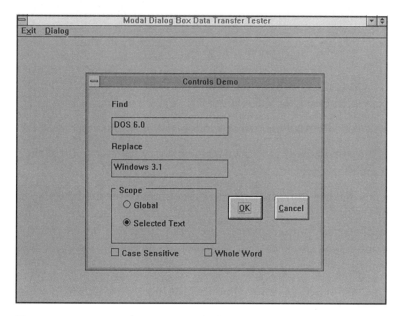

Figure 20.3. A sample session with the DIALOG2.EXE application.

Listing 20.5 contains the script for the DIALOG2.RC resource file. This file defines the resources for the accelerator keys, the menu, and the dialog box, including its controls. In the dialog box resource definition, the OK and Cancel push buttons have the predefined IDOK and IDCANCEL IDs, respectively. The OK button has the default push button style, and the Cancel button has the normal push button style. The group box, radio buttons, and check boxes have the BUTTON class name. The styles associated with these controls determine their final form. Appendix A gives you more details about declaring the resources for controls that are owned by dialog boxes.

Listing 20.6 shows the source code for the DIALOG2.CPP program file. The program declares the data transfer type `TAppTransferBuf` and includes members for the edit boxes, radio buttons, and check boxes.

The program listing declares three classes: an application class, a window class, and a modal dialog box class.

The application's dialog box class `CAppDialog` declares a class constructor, a few member functions, and the `pAppBuffer` data member. This data member is the pointer to the data buffer `AppBuffer`, a member of the parent window. This is a data-hiding scheme applied to manage the data buffer. You can simplify the code by declaring the transfer buffer as a global variable. Keep in mind that this approach makes the buffer accessible (and also vulnerable) to all sorts of objects in a full-blown Windows application. The class constructor creates the instances by invoking the parent class constructor.

The `OnInitDialog` member function, defined in lines 73 through 89, initializes the dialog box by performing the following tasks:

☐ Assigns the address of the parent window to the local pointer `pW`

☐ Uses the `pW` pointer to have the data member `pAppBuffer` point to the parent window's `AppBuffer` member

☐ Obtains the data from the buffer to the controls of the modal dialog box, using the `CWnd::SetDlgItemText` function and a local pointer, `pBtn`, to access the various push button controls (the `pBtn` pointer and the `SetCheck()` function set the check state for the various radio button and check box controls)

The `OnOK` member function, defined in lines 91 through 108, transfers data from the dialog box to the data buffer. The transfer takes place using the `CWnd::GetDlgItemText` function and a local pointer, `pBtn`, to the push button controls. The `pBtn` pointer and the `GetCheck()` function obtain the check state for the various radio button and check box controls.

The application window class, `CAppWindow`, declares a public data transfer buffer, `AppBuffer`, a class constructor, and three member functions. The class also declares class `CAppDialog` to be a friend. Making the `AppBuffer` member public and making `CAppDialog` a friend are steps necessary to give the dialog box member functions access to the `AppBuffer` member.

The `CAppWindow` constructor creates the window (which also loads the menu resource) and then initializes the data buffer. The call to the `memset` function fills the `AppBuffer` member with zeros. I recommend that you systematically call the `memset` function to perform a basic initialization of the buffer before assigning specific values to its controls. The constructor then assigns the `"DOS"` and `"Windows"` strings to the Find and Replace edit box buffers, respectively. The constructor also assigns the constant `BF_CHECKED` to the `GlobalRbtBuff`, `CaseChkBuff`, and `WholeWordChkBuf` members.

The `CAppWindow` class defines the `CMDialog` member function, in lines 128 through 140, to handle the command message emitted by the Dialog menu item. This function invokes an instance of the dialog box using the `DoModal` member function and compares the result of that function with `IDOK`. If the two items match, the `CMDialog` function builds and displays a message string that reflects the current Find and Replace text.

Transferring Data for Modeless Dialog Boxes

This section presents an MFC application that transfers data for a modeless dialog box. Thus, the program shows how to create a modeless dialog box and how to transfer data at will by using a special push button control. The next application uses a modified version of program DIALOG2.CPP. This new version, DIALOG3.EXE, is very similar to that presented in DIALOG2.EXE but differs in the following aspects:

☐ The dialog box is modeless.

☐ The dialog box has an extra Send push button.

☐ The main window has two edit boxes labeled Find and Replace.

When you click the Send button, the dialog box copies the text in its Find and Replace edit boxes to the edit boxes in the parent window that are also labeled Find and Replace.

When you click the Dialog menu item in the program, the application pops up a modeless dialog box. The dialog box has the `"DOS"` and `"Windows"` strings appearing in the Find and Replace edit boxes, respectively. The Global radio button, Case-Sensitive check box, and Selected check box are all initially selected. Type in new text in either or both edit boxes and click the OK push button. This action closes the dialog box and echoes the text of the dialog box in the edit boxes of the window. Reinvoke the dialog box to check that it retains your last input. Now type in new text in both edit boxes and then click the Send button. Watch the text echoed in the window's edit boxes.

20

Listing 20.7 shows the source code for the DIALOG3.H header file. Listing 20.8 contains the script for the DIALOG3.RC resource file. Listing 20.9 shows the source code for the DIALOG3.CPP program file.

Listing 20.7. Source code for the DIALOG3.H header file.

```
 1: #define CM_EXIT    (WM_USER + 100)
 2: #define CM_DIALOG  (WM_USER + 101)
 3: #define ID_FIND_TXT        201
 4: #define ID_FIND_EDIT       202
 5: #define ID_REPLACE_TXT     203
 6: #define ID_REPLACE_EDIT    204
 7: #define ID_SCOPE_GRP       205
 8: #define ID_GLOBAL_RBT      206
 9: #define ID_SELTEXT_RBT     207
10: #define ID_CASE_CHK        208
11: #define ID_WHOLEWORD_CHK   209
12: #define ID_FIND_BOX        301
13: #define ID_REPLACE_BOX     302
14: #define ID_SEND_BTN        303
```

Listing 20.8. Script for the DIALOG3.RC resource file.

```
 1: #include <windows.h>
 2: #include <afxres.h>
 3: #include "dialog3.h"
 4:
 5: BUTTONS ACCELERATORS
 6: BEGIN
 7:   "o", IDOK, ALT
 8:   "c", IDCANCEL, ALT
 9:   "s", ID_SEND_BTN, ALT
10: END
11:
12: SEARCH DIALOG DISCARDABLE LOADONCALL PURE MOVEABLE 10, 10,
13:                                              200, 150
14: STYLE WS_POPUP ¦ WS_CLIPSIBLINGS ¦ WS_CAPTION ¦ WS_SYSMENU ¦
15:     WS_DLGFRAME ¦ WS_VISIBLE
16: CAPTION "Controls Demo"
17: BEGIN
18:   CONTROL "Find", ID_FIND_TXT, "STATIC", WS_CHILD ¦ WS_VISIBLE ¦
19:     SS_LEFT, 20, 10, 100, 15
20:   CONTROL "", ID_FIND_EDIT, "EDIT", WS_CHILD ¦ WS_VISIBLE ¦
21:     WS_BORDER ¦ WS_TABSTOP, 20, 25, 100, 15
22:   CONTROL "Replace", ID_REPLACE_TXT, "STATIC", WS_CHILD ¦
```

```
23:     WS_VISIBLE ¦ SS_LEFT, 20, 45, 100, 15
24:   CONTROL "", ID_REPLACE_EDIT, "EDIT", WS_CHILD ¦ WS_VISIBLE ¦
25:     WS_BORDER ¦ WS_TABSTOP, 20, 60, 100, 15
26:   CONTROL " Scope ", ID_SCOPE_GRP, "BUTTON", WS_CHILD ¦
27:     WS_VISIBLE ¦ WS_GROUP ¦ BS_GROUPBOX, 20, 80, 90, 50
28:   CONTROL "Global", ID_GLOBAL_RBT, "BUTTON", WS_CHILD ¦
29:     WS_VISIBLE ¦ WS_TABSTOP ¦ BS_AUTORADIOBUTTON, 30, 90, 50, 15
30:   CONTROL "Selected Text", ID_SELTEXT_RBT, "BUTTON", WS_CHILD ¦
31:     WS_VISIBLE ¦ WS_TABSTOP ¦ BS_AUTORADIOBUTTON, 30, 105, 60, 15
32:   CONTROL "Case Sensitive", ID_CASE_CHK, "BUTTON", WS_CHILD ¦
33:     WS_VISIBLE ¦ WS_TABSTOP ¦ BS_AUTOCHECKBOX, 20, 130, 80, 15
34:   CONTROL "Whole Word", ID_WHOLEWORD_CHK, "BUTTON", WS_CHILD ¦
35:     WS_VISIBLE ¦ WS_TABSTOP ¦ BS_AUTOCHECKBOX, 100, 130, 80, 15
36:   CONTROL, "&OK", IDOK, "BUTTON", WS_CHILD ¦ WS_VISIBLE ¦
37:     WS_TABSTOP ¦ BS_DEFPUSHBUTTON, 120, 90, 30, 20
38:   CONTROL "&Cancel", IDCANCEL, "BUTTON", WS_CHILD ¦ WS_VISIBLE ¦
39:     WS_TABSTOP ¦ BS_PUSHBUTTON, 160, 90, 30, 20
40:   CONTROL "&Send", ID_SEND_BTN, "BUTTON", WS_CHILD ¦ WS_VISIBLE ¦
41:     WS_TABSTOP ¦ BS_PUSHBUTTON, 160, 60, 30, 20
42: END
43:
44: MAINMENU MENU LOADONCALL MOVEABLE PURE DISCARDABLE
45: BEGIN
46:     MENUITEM "E&xit", CM_EXIT
47:     MENUITEM "&Dialog", CM_DIALOG
48: END
```

**Listing 20.9. Source code
for the DIALOG3.CPP program file.**

```
1: #include <string.h>
2: #include <afxwin.h>
3: #include "dialog3.h"
4:
5: // declare constants for sizing and dimensioning the
6: // application window's controls
7: const Wtxt = 200;
8: const Htxt = 20;
9: const TxtVertSpacing = 10;
10: const Wbox = 200;
11: const Hbox = 30;
12: const BoxHorzSpacing = 40;
13: // declare other constants
14: const MaxEditLen = 30;
15: const BF_CHECKED = 1;
16: const BF_UNCHECKED = 0;
17:
18: // declare the application buffer
```

continues

Listing 20.9. continued

```
19: struct TAppTransferBuf {
20:   char FindBoxBuff[MaxEditLen+1];
21:   char ReplaceBoxBuff[MaxEditLen+1];
22:   int GlobalRbtBuff;
23:   int SelTextRbtBuff;
24:   int CaseChkBuff;
25:   int WholeWordChkBuff;
26: };
27:
28: class CWindowApp : public CWinApp
29: {
30: public:
31:     virtual BOOL InitInstance();
32: };
33:
34: // expand the functionality of CDialog by
35: // deriving class CAppDialog
36: class CAppDialog : public CDialog
37: {
38: public:
39:
40:   CAppDialog(const char FAR* lpTemplateName,
41:           CWnd* pParentWnd);
42:   // handle pressing the OK button
43:   afx_msg void OnOK();
44:   afx_msg void CMOK() { OnOK(); }
45:   // handle pressing the Cancel button
46:   afx_msg void OnCancel();
47:   afx_msg void CMCancel() { OnCancel(); }
48:   // handle sending data without closing the modal dialog box
49:   afx_msg void HandleSendBtn();
50:   afx_msg void CMSendBtn() { HandleSendBtn(); }
51:
52: protected:
53:
54:   // pointer to data buffer in parent window
55:   TAppTransferBuf* pAppBuffer;
56:
57:   // handle initializing the dialog box
58:   virtual BOOL OnInitDialog();
59:   // transfer data from the controls to the buffer
60:   void TransferData();
61:
62:   // declare message map macro
63:   DECLARE_MESSAGE_MAP();
64: };
65:
66: // expand the functionality of CFrameWnd by deriving
67: // class CAppWindow
```

```
68: class CAppWindow : public CFrameWnd
69: {
70: public:
71:
72:    // declare data transfer buffer
73:    TAppTransferBuf AppBuffer;
74:    // flag to indicate whether or not the
75:    // modeless dialog box is active
76:    BOOL bDialogActive;
77:
78:    CAppWindow();
79:    ~CAppWindow();
80:    // handle the dialog command
81:    afx_msg void CMDialog();
82:    // handle a message sent by the Send button of
83:    // the dialog box
84:    afx_msg void HandleSendBtn();
85:    // handle exiting the application
86:    afx_msg void OnExit()
87:      { SendMessage(WM_CLOSE); }
88:
89: protected:
90:
91:    // declare the pointers to the window's controls
92:    // and the modeless dialog box
93:    CStatic* FindTxt;
94:    CEdit* FindBox;
95:    CStatic* ReplaceTxt;
96:    CEdit* ReplaceBox;
97:    CAppDialog* pDlg;
98:
99:    // handle creating the controls
100:   afx_msg int OnCreate(LPCREATESTRUCT lpCS);
101:   // handle closing the window
102:   afx_msg void OnClose();
103:   // return a reference to member r based on individual
104:   // coordinates and dimensions
105:   void makeRect(int nX, int nY, int nW, int nH, CRect& r);
106:
107:   // declare message map macro
108:   DECLARE_MESSAGE_MAP();
109:
110: };
111:
112: CAppDialog::CAppDialog(const char FAR* lpTemplateName,
113:                   CWnd* pParentWnd)
114: {
115:    Create(lpTemplateName, pParentWnd);
116: }
117:
```

continues

Listing 20.9. continued

```
118: BOOL CAppDialog::OnInitDialog()
119: {
120:   CAppWindow* pW = (CAppWindow*)(GetParent());
121:   pAppBuffer = &pW->AppBuffer;
122:   // copy data from the buffer to the dialog box controls
123:   SetDlgItemText(ID_FIND_EDIT, pAppBuffer->FindBoxBuff);
124:   SetDlgItemText(ID_REPLACE_EDIT, pAppBuffer->ReplaceBoxBuff);
125:   CButton* pBtn = (CButton*)(GetDlgItem(ID_GLOBAL_RBT));
126:   pBtn->SetCheck(pAppBuffer->GlobalRbtBuff);
127:   pBtn = (CButton*)(GetDlgItem(ID_SELTEXT_RBT));
128:   pBtn->SetCheck(pAppBuffer->SelTextRbtBuff);
129:   pBtn = (CButton*)(GetDlgItem(ID_CASE_CHK));
130:   pBtn->SetCheck(pAppBuffer->CaseChkBuff);
131:   pBtn = (CButton*)(GetDlgItem(ID_WHOLEWORD_CHK));
132:   pBtn->SetCheck(pAppBuffer->WholeWordChkBuff);
133:   return TRUE;
134: }
135:
136: void CAppDialog::OnOK()
137: {
138:   CAppWindow* pParent = (CAppWindow*)(GetParent());
139:   // transfer data to the buffer
140:   TransferData();
141:   // notify parent of transfer
142:   pParent->SendMessage(WM_COMMAND, ID_SEND_BTN);
143:   // clear active dialog flag
144:   pParent->bDialogActive = FALSE;
145:   // close the modeless dialog box
146:   DestroyWindow();
147: }
148:
149: void CAppDialog::OnCancel()
150: {
151:   CAppWindow* pParent = (CAppWindow*)(GetParent());
152:   // clear active dialog flag
153:   pParent->bDialogActive = FALSE;
154:   // close the modeless dialog box
155:   DestroyWindow();
156: }
157:
158: void CAppDialog::HandleSendBtn()
159: {
160:   CAppWindow* pParent = (CAppWindow*)(GetParent());
161:
162:   // transfer data to the buffer
163:   TransferData();
164:   // notify parent of transfer
165:   pParent->SendMessage(WM_COMMAND, ID_SEND_BTN);
166: }
167:
```

```
168: void CAppDialog::TransferData()
169: {
170:    // copy data from the dialog box controls to the buffer
171:    GetDlgItemText(ID_FIND_EDIT, pAppBuffer->FindBoxBuff,
172:                   MaxEditLen);
173:    GetDlgItemText(ID_REPLACE_EDIT, pAppBuffer->ReplaceBoxBuff,
174:             MaxEditLen);
175:    CButton* pBtn = (CButton*)(GetDlgItem(ID_GLOBAL_RBT));
176:    pAppBuffer->GlobalRbtBuff = pBtn->GetCheck();
177:    pBtn = (CButton*)(GetDlgItem(ID_SELTEXT_RBT));
178:    pAppBuffer->SelTextRbtBuff = pBtn->GetCheck();
179:    pBtn = (CButton*)(GetDlgItem(ID_CASE_CHK));
180:    pAppBuffer->CaseChkBuff = pBtn->GetCheck();
181:    pBtn = (CButton*)(GetDlgItem(ID_WHOLEWORD_CHK));
182:    pAppBuffer->WholeWordChkBuff = pBtn->GetCheck();
183: }
184:
185: CAppWindow::CAppWindow()
186: {
187:    // load the accelerator keys resource
188:    LoadAccelTable("BUTTONS");
189:
190:    // create the window
191:    Create(NULL, "Modeless Dialog Box Data Transfer Tester",
192:          WS_OVERLAPPEDWINDOW, rectDefault, NULL, "MAINMENU");
193:
194:    // fill buffer with 0's
195:    memset(&AppBuffer, 0x0, sizeof(AppBuffer));
196:    strcpy(AppBuffer.FindBoxBuff, "DOS");
197:    strcpy(AppBuffer.ReplaceBoxBuff, "Windows");
198:    AppBuffer.GlobalRbtBuff = BF_CHECKED;
199:    AppBuffer.CaseChkBuff = BF_CHECKED;
200:    AppBuffer.WholeWordChkBuff = BF_CHECKED;
201:    // clear the active dialog flag
202:    bDialogActive = FALSE;
203: };
204:
205: CAppWindow::~CAppWindow()
206: {
207:    delete FindTxt;
208:    delete FindBox;
209:    delete ReplaceTxt;
210:    delete ReplaceBox;
211: }
212:
213: int CAppWindow::OnCreate(LPCREATESTRUCT lpCS)
214: {
215:    int nX0 = 30;
216:    int nY0 = 20;
```

continues

Listing 20.9. continued

```
217:    int nX = nX0;
218:    int nY = nY0;
219:
220:    CRect r;
221:    DWORD dwStaticStyle = WS_CHILD ¦ WS_VISIBLE ¦ SS_LEFT;
222:    DWORD dwEditStyle = WS_CHILD ¦ WS_VISIBLE ¦ WS_BORDER ¦
223:                   ES_LEFT ¦ ES_AUTOHSCROLL;
224:    // create Find static text
225:    makeRect(nX, nY, Wtxt, Htxt, r);
226:    FindTxt = new CStatic();
227:    FindTxt->Create("Find", dwStaticStyle, r, this);
228:    // create Find edit control
229:    nY += Htxt + TxtVertSpacing;
230:    makeRect(nX, nY, Wbox, Hbox, r);
231:    FindBox = new CEdit();
232:    FindBox->Create(dwEditStyle, r, this, ID_FIND_BOX);
233:    // create Replace static text
234:    nX += Wbox + BoxHorzSpacing;
235:    nY = nY0;
236:    makeRect(nX, nY, Wtxt, Htxt, r);
237:    ReplaceTxt = new CStatic();
238:    ReplaceTxt->Create("Replace", dwStaticStyle, r, this);
239:    // create Replace edit control
240:    nY += Htxt + TxtVertSpacing;
241:    makeRect(nX, nY, Wbox, Hbox, r);
242:    ReplaceBox = new CEdit();
243:    ReplaceBox->Create(dwEditStyle, r, this, ID_REPLACE_BOX);
244:    return CFrameWnd::OnCreate(lpCS);
245: }
246:
247: void CAppWindow::CMDialog()
248: {
249:    if (bDialogActive) return;
250:    pDlg = new CAppDialog("SEARCH", this);
251:    bDialogActive = TRUE;
252:    pDlg->SendMessage(WM_INITDIALOG);
253: }
254:
255: void CAppWindow::HandleSendBtn()
256: {
257:    FindBox->SetWindowText(AppBuffer.FindBoxBuff);
258:    ReplaceBox->SetWindowText(AppBuffer.ReplaceBoxBuff);
259: }
260:
261: void CAppWindow::OnClose()
262: {
```

```
263:    if (MessageBox("Want to close this application",
264:                   "Query", MB_YESNO | MB_ICONQUESTION) == IDYES)
265:      DestroyWindow();
266: }
267:
268: void CAppWindow::makeRect(int nX, int nY, int nW, int nH,
269:                          CRect& r)
270: {
271:    r.top = nY;
272:    r.left = nX;
273:    r.bottom = nY + nH;
274:    r.right = nX + nW;
275: }
276:
277: BEGIN_MESSAGE_MAP(CAppDialog, CDialog)
278:    ON_BN_CLICKED(IDOK, OnOK)
279:    ON_COMMAND(IDOK, CMOK)
280:    ON_BN_CLICKED(IDCANCEL, OnCancel)
281:    ON_COMMAND(IDCANCEL, CMCancel)
282:    ON_BN_CLICKED(ID_SEND_BTN, HandleSendBtn)
283:    ON_COMMAND(ID_SEND_BTN, CMSendBtn)
284: END_MESSAGE_MAP()
285:
286: BEGIN_MESSAGE_MAP(CAppWindow, CFrameWnd)
287:    ON_COMMAND(CM_DIALOG, CMDialog)
288:    ON_COMMAND(ID_SEND_BTN, HandleSendBtn)
289:    ON_COMMAND(CM_EXIT, OnExit)
290:    ON_WM_CREATE()
291:    ON_WM_CLOSE()
292: END_MESSAGE_MAP()
293:
294: // Construct the CWindowApp's m_pMainWnd data member
295: BOOL CWindowApp::InitInstance()
296: {
297:    m_pMainWnd = new CAppWindow();
298:    m_pMainWnd->ShowWindow(m_nCmdShow);
299:    m_pMainWnd->UpdateWindow();
300:    return TRUE;
301: }
302:
303: // application's constructor initializes and runs the app
304: CWindowApp WindowApp;
```

20

Figure 20.4 shows a sample session with the DIALOG3.EXE application.

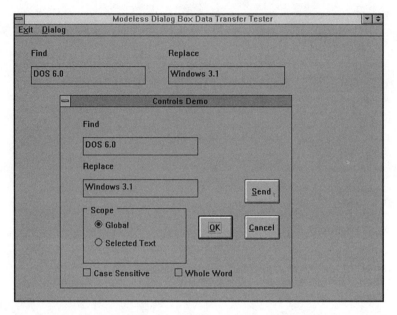

Figure 20.4. A sample session with the DIALOG3.EXE application.

Listing 20.8 shows the script for the DIALOG3.RC resource file. The resource file defines the resources for the accelerator keys, menu, and modeless dialog box.

Listing 20.9 contains the source code for the DIALOG3.CPP program file. The listing declares a group of constants for sizing and spacing the controls in the window application. The listing also contains the declaration of the data transfer buffer type—which is identical to that shown in program DIALOG2.EXE.

The application declares three classes: the application class, the window class, and the dialog box class. The CAppDialog constructor simply invokes the inherited Create function to build a dialog box. The CAppDialog class declares member functions to handle each push button. The dialog class declares the TransferData member function to transfer data from the dialog box controls to the buffer. This function is called by the OnOK and HandleSendBtn member functions.

The virtual OnOK member function, defined in lines 136 through 147, responds to the IDOK notification message emitted by the OK button. The function performs the following tasks:

☐ Transfers the data from the controls to the buffer by calling the TransferData member function

☐ Sends an ID_SEND_BTN message to the parent window using the SendMessage function

☐ Sets the parent window data member, bDialogActive, to FALSE

☐ Closes the dialog box by invoking the DestroyWindow function

The OnCancel member function, defined in lines 149 through 156, handles the IDCANCEL notification message sent by the Cancel button. The function performs the following two tasks:

☐ Sets the parent window data member, bDialogActive, to FALSE

☐ Closes the dialog box by invoking the DestroyWindow function

The HandleSendBtn member function, defined in lines 255 through 259, handles the ID_SEND_BTN notification message emitted by the Send button. The function carries out the following tasks:

☐ Transfers the data from the controls to the buffer by calling the TransferData member function

☐ Sends an ID_SEND_BTN message to the parent window using the SendMessage function

The CMSendBtn member function handles the ID_SEND_BTN command message generated by the accelerator key Alt-S. The function simply calls the HandleSendBtn member function.

The application window class CAppWindow declares two public data members, five protected data members, a constructor, a destructor, and six member functions. The Boolean bDialogActive data member indicates whether or not the dialog box instance exists. Using this flag ensures that there is one instance of the modeless dialog box. The AppBuffer data member is the data transfer buffer. The window class declares five protected pointers. The FindBox and ReplaceBox pointers access the edit box instances. The pDlg pointer is the pointer to the dialog box instance.

The CAppWindow constructor performs the following tasks:

☐ Loads the menu resource

☐ Creates the application window by calling the Create function

☐ Initializes the buffer by filling it with zeros

20

☐ Assigns values to the edit box buffers, the check box buffers, and the Global radio button buffer

☐ Sets the `bDialogActive` data member to `FALSE`

The `OnCreate` member function, defined in lines 213 through 245, actually creates the controls that are attached to the application window. The function carries out the following tasks:

☐ Creates the static text instance that labels the Find edit box

☐ Creates the Find edit box

☐ Creates the static text instance that labels the Replace edit box

☐ Creates the Replace edit box

☐ Returns the function value

The application window class declares the `CMDialog` member function to create a modeless dialog box. The function carries out these subsequent tasks:

☐ Exits if the `bDialogActive` member is `TRUE`

☐ Creates a `CAppDialog` instance that is accessed by the `pDlg` pointer

☐ Sets the `bDialogActive` data member to `TRUE`

☐ Brings up the modeless dialog box on the screen by sending it a `WM_INITDIALOG` message (this task involves using the `pDlg` pointer to make the dialog box receive the intended message)

The `HandleSendBtn` member function, defined in lines 255 through 259, responds to the message sent by the Send button in the dialog box by copying the `FindBoxBuff` and `ReplaceBoxBuff` buffer members to the Find and Replace edit boxes in the window.

Summary

Today's lesson presents you with powerful dialog boxes that serve as input tools. You learn about the following topics:

☐ You can construct instances of class `CDialog` to create modeless or modal dialog boxes.

☐ Modal dialog boxes are executed with the `DoModal` member function.

☐ The basics of transferring control data include declaring the data transfer buffer type, declaring the buffer, creating the controls in a sequence that matches their buffers, and establishing the buffer link.

☐ The first step in supporting data transfer is to define a transfer buffer type. You can transfer data for modal dialog boxes and modeless dialog boxes.

Q&A

Q. Does MFC support specialized dialog boxes?

A. Yes. The MFC library has a set of classes that implement dialog boxes for selecting files, selecting colors, selecting fonts, printing, and searching/replacing text. The classes that model these dialog boxes are all descendants of class CDialog.

Q. Does the MFC version 1.0 implement dialog box classes differently?

A. Yes, version 1.0 implements the CModalDialog box as a descendant of class CDialog. Version 2 uses class CDialog for both kinds of dialog boxes. The compiler is aware of class CModalDialog and treats listings where it appears as though it were CDialog.

Q. Can I create a set of modeless dialog boxes followed by a modal dialog box?

A. Yes. Interestingly, the modal dialog box allows you to select the modeless dialog boxes created before it. However, you cannot create any additional modeless dialog boxes until you close the modal dialog box.

Q. Is the data transfer buffer necessary for modeless dialog boxes?

A. Not always. You can have an application which pops up multiple modeless dialog boxes and have them communicate with each other directly, without the need of a data transfer buffer.

Q. Are there any advantages to writing my own .RC resource files now that a tool such as App Studio is available?

A. Yes. The .RC resource file documents the exact dimensions, styles, and other attributes of the controls in a dialog box or any kind of resource.

Q. What do .RC resource files compile into?

A. The resouce compiler, RC.EXE, compiles .RC files into .RES files.

Workshop

The Workshop provides quiz questions to help you solidify your understanding of the material covered and exercises to provide you with experience in using what you've learned. Try to understand the quiz and exercise answers before continuing on to the next day's lesson. Answers are provided in Appendix B, "Answers."

Quiz

1. True or false? You must compile all the .RC files into .RES before or during the creation of the application.

2. True or false? The OK and Cancel buttons in a dialog box are optional.

3. True or false? You can create a dialog box with buttons labeled Yes and No.

4. True or false? Nested dialog boxes are not allowed by Windows.

5. True or false? Dialog boxes must always have a nondialog window parent.

Exercises

1. Create a version of the Command-Line Calculator Application (COCA) that uses a dialog box as a stand-alone window.

2. Use the Studio App to create the dialog box resources for program DIALOG2.CPP.

3. Use the Studio App to create the dialog box resources for program DIALOG3.CPP.

DAY
21

MDI Windows

Recall that many Windows applications, such as the Windows Program Manager, Windows File Manager, and many Windows-text editors, implement a special windows interface—the Multiple Document Interface (MDI). The MDI standard is also part of the Common User Access (CUA) standard set by IBM. Each MDI-compliant application allows you to open child windows for file-specific tasks such as editing text, managing a database, and working with a spreadsheet. In today's lesson, you learn about the following topics relative to managing MDI windows and objects:

- [ ] Basic features and components of an MDI-compliant application

- [ ] Building an MDI-compliant application

- [ ] The `CMDIFrameWnd` class

- [ ] Building MDI frame windows

- [ ] The `CMDIChildWnd` class

- [ ] Building MDI child windows

MDI Application Features and Components

An MDI-compliant application is made up of the following objects:

- [ ] The MDI frame window is an instance of class `CMDIFrameWnd` or its descendants. Each MDI application has one MDI frame window.

- [ ] The MDI client window is created by the `CreateClient` member function. Each MDI application has one MDI client window.

- [ ] The MDI child window is an instance of `CMDIChildWNd` or its descendant. An MDI application dynamically creates and removes multiple instances of MDI child windows. At any given time (and while there is at least one MDI child window), there is only one active MDI child window.

NEW   The visible *MDI frame window* contains all other MDI objects. The invisible
TERM   *MDI client window* performs underlying management of the MDI child windows that are dynamically created and removed. The dynamic and visible *MDI child window* is located, moved, resized, maximized, and minimized inside the area defined by the MDI frame window.

When you maximize an MDI child window, it occupies the area defined by the MDI frame window. When you minimize an MDI child window, the icon of that window appears at the bottom of the MDI frame window.

> **Note:** The MDI frame window has a menu that manipulates the MDI child windows and their contents. The MDI child windows cannot have a menu, but may contain controls. The MFC library supports the ability to change the menu attached to the MDI frame window when you select a different MDI child window. This feature supports MDI child windows that have different uses and data.

Building an MDI Application

In the last section you learn that the basic ingredients for an MDI application are the CMDIFrameWnd and CMDIChildWnd classes. The CMDIFrameWnd class supports the following tasks:

☐ Creating and handling the MDI client window

☐ Creating and handling the MDI child windows

☐ Managing menu selections

The *CMDIFrameWnd* Class

MFC offers the CMDIFrameWnd class, a descendant of CFrameWnd to implement the MDI frame window of an MDI application.

The CMDIFrameWnd class declares a constructor, a Create function, and a number of member functions to manipulate MDI child windows.

The class constructor and the inherited Create function work together in creating the instances of class CMDIFrameWnd. The Create function takes a number of arguments that define the Windows class (a WNDCLASS structure), the MDI window title, the window style, the window location and position (specified using the CRect parameter), the pointer to the parent window, and the name of the associated menu resource. When the MDI frame window is the top-level window, the argument for the parent pointer is NULL.

21

The CreateClient member function has the role of creating the invisible MDI client window. The function takes two arguments: an LPCREATESTRUCT parameter and a CMenu* menu pointer parameter.

The member functions of CMDIFrameWnd support a number of operations for the MDI child windows. These operations include the following:

☐ Activating an MDI child window with the MDIActive member function

☐ Obtaining the pointer to the currently active MDI child window, using the MDIGetActive member function

☐ Maximizing and restoring an MDI child window, using the MDIMaximize and MDIRestore member functions, respectively

☐ Cascading and tiling MDI child windows, using the MDICascade and MDITile member functions, respectively

☐ Selecting the next MDI child window (the one right behind the currently active MDI child window)

Building MDI Frame Windows

The usual approach for creating the objects that make up an MFC application is to create the application instance and then its main window instance. In the case of an MDI-compliant application, the application's main window is typically a descendant of class CMDIFrameWnd. The InitInstance member function of the application class creates this window. The constructor of the MDI frame window class, together with the Create function, builds the MDI frame and MDI client windows. It is also possible to create an initial or default MDI child window. For example, some Windows text editors open the last edited file (if possible), and other editors display an empty MDI child window.

The *CMDIChildWnd* Class

MFC offers the CMDIChildWnd class, a descendant of CFrameWnd, to implement the MDI child windows. The CMDIChildWnd class declares a constructor, a Create function, a set of member functions, and a data member. The member functions allow you to destroy, activate, maximize, restore, and obtain the pointer to the parent window.

Building MDI Child Windows

Building MDI child windows is similar to building application windows in the previous programs in this book, with the following differences:

- [ ] An MDI child window is an instance of `CMDIChildWnd` or its descendants.

- [ ] An MDI child window cannot have its own menu. The menu of the MDI frame window is the one that manipulates the currently active MDI child window or all of the MDI child windows.

- [ ] An MDI child window can have controls—unusual but certainly allowed.

Managing MDI Messages

The message loop directs the command messages first to the active MDI child window to allow it to respond. If that window does not respond, the message is then sent to the parent MDI frame window. Of course, the active MDI child window responds to the notification messages sent by its controls, just as any window or dialog box would.

A Simple Text Viewer

Let's look at a simple MDI-compliant application. MDI applications are frequently used as text viewers and text editors. This application emulates a simple text viewer—the application actually displays random text rather than text that you can retrieve from a file. This approach keeps the program simple and helps you focus on implementing the various MDI objects. The MDI application has a simple menu containing the Exit and MDI Children menu items.

Compile and run the application. Experiment with creating MDI children. Notice that the text in odd-numbered MDI child windows is static, and the text in even-numbered windows can be edited. This feature illustrates how to create a simple form of text viewer and text editor (with no load and save options, to keep the example short). Try to tile, cascade, maximize, and minimize these windows. Also test closing individual MDI child windows as well as closing all the MDI children.

Listing 21.1 shows the source code for the MDIWIN1.H header file. Listing 21.2 contains the script for the MDIWIN1.RC resource file. Listing 21.3 shows the source code for the MDIWIN1.CPP program.

21

Listing 21.1. Source code for the MDIWIN1.H header file.

```
 1: #define CM_EXIT            (WM_USER + 100)
 2: #define CM_COUNTCHILDREN   (WM_USER + 101)
 3: #define CM_CREATECHILD     (WM_USER + 102)
 4: #define CM_CASCADECHILDREN (WM_USER + 103)
 5: #define CM_TILECHILDREN    (WM_USER + 104)
 6: #define CM_ARRANGEICONS    (WM_USER + 105)
 7: #define CM_CLOSECHILDREN   (WM_USER + 106)
 8: #define WM_CHILDDESTROY    (WM_USER + 200)
 9:
10: #define ID_TEXT_EDIT    100
```

Listing 21.2. Script for the MDIWIN1.RC resource file.

```
 1: #include <windows.h>
 2: #include <afxres.h>
 3: #include "mdiwin1.h"
 4:
 5: MAINMENU MENU LOADONCALL MOVEABLE PURE DISCARDABLE
 6: BEGIN
 7:   MENUITEM "E&xit", CM_EXIT
 8:   POPUP "&MDI Children"
 9:   BEGIN
10:     MENUITEM  "C&reate", CM_CREATECHILD
11:     MENUITEM  "&Cascade", CM_CASCADECHILDREN
12:     MENUITEM  "&Tile", CM_TILECHILDREN
13:     MENUITEM  "Arrange &Icons", CM_ARRANGEICONS
14:     MENUITEM  "C&lose All", CM_CLOSECHILDREN
15:     MENUITEM  "C&ount Children", CM_COUNTCHILDREN
16:   END
17: END
```

Listing 21.3. Source code for the MDIWIN1.CPP program file.

```
 1: #include <stdlib.h>
 2: #include <stdio.h>
 3: #include <string.h>
 4: #include <afxwin.h>
 5: #include "mdiwin1.h"
 6:
 7: const char* MenuRezName = "MAINMENU";
 8: const Hctl = 200;
```

```
 9: const Wctl = 400;
10: const MaxWords = 200;
11: const WordsPerLine = 10;
12: const NumWords = 10;
13: char* Words[NumWords] = { "The ", "man ", "ate ", "the ",
14:                           "food ", "in ", "hurry ", "girl ",
15:                           "cake ", "bread " };
16: // declare a global random-number generating function
17: int random(int maxVal)
18: { return rand() % maxVal; }
19:
20: // declare global function to calculate the size and
21: // location of a control
22: void makeRect(int nX, int nY, int nW, int nH, CRect& r)
23: {
24:   r.top = nY;
25:   r.left = nX;
26:   r.bottom = nY + nH;
27:   r.right = nX + nW;
28: }
29:
30: // Define an application class derived from CWinApp
31: class CWindowApp : public CWinApp
32: {
33: public:
34:
35:   virtual BOOL InitInstance();
36: };
37:
38: class CAppMDIChild : public CMDIChildWnd
39: {
40: public:
41:   int nChildNum;
42:   // pointer to the edit box control
43:   CEdit* TextBox;
44:   CStatic* TextTxt;
45:
46:   CAppMDIChild();
47:   ~CAppMDIChild();
48:   BOOL Create(LPSTR szTitle, int nChildNum);
49:
50: protected:
51:   // handle closing the MDI child window
52:   afx_msg void OnClose();
53:   // handle destroying an MDI child window
54:   afx_msg void OnDestroy();
55:   afx_msg int OnCreate(LPCREATESTRUCT lpCS);
56:
57:   // declare message map macro
58:   DECLARE_MESSAGE_MAP()
```

21

continues

Listing 21.3. continued

```
59: };
60:
61: class CAppMDIFrame : public CMDIFrameWnd
62: {
63:    //DECLARE_DYNCREATE(CAppMDIFrame)
64: public:
65:    // flag to quickly close all MDI children windows
66:    BOOL bExpressClose;
67:    int nLastMDIChild;
68:
69:    CAppMDIFrame();
70:    ~CAppMDIFrame() { delete pMenu; }
71:    // create a new client window area
72:    afx_msg int OnCreate(LPCREATESTRUCT lpCS);
73:    // create an MDI child window
74:    afx_msg void CMCreateChild();
75:    // cascade MDI children
76:    afx_msg void CMCascadeChildren() { MDICascade(); }
77:    // tile MDI children
78:    afx_msg void CMTileChildren() { MDITile(); }
79:    // arrange MDI children icons
80:    afx_msg void CMArrageIcons() { MDIIconArrange(); }
81:    // close all MDI children
82:    afx_msg void CMCloseChildren();
83:    // get the number of MDI children
84:    int GetChildCount() { return nNumMDIChildren; }
85:    // handle the command for counting the MDI children
86:    afx_msg void CMCountChildren();
87:    // handle the child destroy message
88:    afx_msg LONG OnChildDestroy(UINT wParam, LONG lParam);
89:    // handle exiting the application
90:    afx_msg void OnExit()
91:      { SendMessage(WM_CLOSE); }
92:
93: protected:
94:    CMenu* pMenu;
95:    int nNumMDIChildren;
96:    // handle closing the MDI frame window
97:    virtual void OnClose();
98:
99:    // declare message map macro
100:    DECLARE_MESSAGE_MAP();
101: };
102:
103: CAppMDIChild::CAppMDIChild()
104: {
105:    TextBox = NULL;
106:    TextTxt = NULL;
107: }
108:
```

```
109:  CAppMDIChild::~CAppMDIChild()
110:  {
111:    if (TextBox)
112:      delete TextBox;
113:    else
114:      delete TextTxt;
115:  }
116:
117:  BOOL CAppMDIChild::Create(LPSTR szTitle, int nChildNumber)
118:  {
119:    nChildNum = nChildNumber;
120:    return CMDIChildWnd::Create(NULL, szTitle);
121:  }
122:
123:  CAppMDIChild::OnCreate(LPCREATESTRUCT lpCS)
124:  {
125:    CString s;
126:    CRect r;
127:    DWORD dwStaticStyle = WS_CHILD | WS_VISIBLE | SS_LEFT;
128:    DWORD dwEditStyle = WS_CHILD | WS_VISIBLE | ES_LEFT |
129:                        ES_MULTILINE | ES_AUTOHSCROLL |
130:                        ES_AUTOVSCROLL;
131:
132:    // randomize seed for the random-number generator
133:    srand((unsigned)time(NULL));
134:    // build the list of random words
135:    for (int i = 0; i < MaxWords; i++) {
136:      if (i > 0 && i % WordsPerLine == 0)
137:        s += "\r\n";
138:      s += Words[random(NumWords)];
139:    }
140:    // obtain the size and location of the control to create
141:    makeRect(10, 10, Wctl, Hctl, r);
142:    // create a static text object in the child window if the
143:    // nChildNum variable stores an odd number.  Otherwise,
144:    // create an edit box control
145:    if (nChildNum % 2 == 0) {
146:      // create the edit box
147:      TextBox = new CEdit();
148:      TextBox->Create(dwEditStyle, r, this, ID_TEXT_EDIT);
149:      TextBox->SetWindowText((const char*) s);
150:    }
151:    else {
152:      // create static text
153:      TextTxt = new CStatic();
154:      TextTxt->Create((const char*)s, dwStaticStyle, r,  this);
155:    }
156:    return 0;
157:  }
158:
```

continues

Listing 21.3. continued

```
159: void CAppMDIChild::OnClose()
160: {
161:   CAppMDIFrame* pParent = (CAppMDIFrame*)(GetParentFrame());
162:
163:   // return TRUE if the bExpressClose member of the
164:   // is the express-close flag of the parent window set?
165:   if (pParent->bExpressClose == TRUE)
166:     return;
167:   else
168:     // prompt the user and return the prompt result
169:     if (MessageBox("Close this MDI window?",
170:               "Query", MB_YESNO | MB_ICONQUESTION) == IDYES) {
171:       MDIDestroy();
172:   }
173: }
174:
175: void CAppMDIChild::OnDestroy()
176: {
177:   CAppMDIFrame* pParent = (CAppMDIFrame*)(GetParentFrame());
178:   pParent->SendMessage(WM_CHILDDESTROY, (UINT)m_hWnd, 0);
179: }
180:
181: CAppMDIFrame::CAppMDIFrame()
182: {
183:   Create(NULL, "MDI Text Viewer",
184:          WS_OVERLAPPEDWINDOW | WS_MAXIMIZE, rectDefault,
185:          NULL, MenuRezName);
186:   // clear the express-close flag
187:   bExpressClose = FALSE;
188:   // initialize the number of MDI children
189:   nLastMDIChild = 0;
190:   nNumMDIChildren = 0;
191: }
192:
193: int CAppMDIFrame::OnCreate(LPCREATESTRUCT lpCS)
194: {
195:   pMenu = new CMenu();
196:   pMenu->LoadMenu(MenuRezName);
197:   CreateClient(lpCS, pMenu->GetSubMenu(0));
198:   return 0;
199: }
200:
201: void CAppMDIFrame::CMCreateChild()
202: {
203:   char s[81];
204:   CRect r;
205:   CAppMDIChild* pChild = new CAppMDIChild();
206:   makeRect(10 * nNumMDIChildren, 10 * nNumMDIChildren,
207:            Wctl, Hctl, r);
```

```
208:    nLastMDIChild++;
209:    sprintf(s, "Child # %d", nLastMDIChild);
210:    if (!pChild->Create(s, nLastMDIChild)) {
211:      delete pChild;
212:      nLastMDIChild--; // decrement highest child index
213:      return;
214:    }
215:    nNumMDIChildren++;
216:    // show the new MDI child window
217:    pChild->ShowWindow(SW_SHOW);
218: }
219:
220: void CAppMDIFrame::CMCloseChildren()
221: {
222:    CAppMDIChild* pChild = (CAppMDIChild*) MDIGetActive();
223:
224:    // set the bExpressClose flag
225:    bExpressClose = TRUE;
226:    while (pChild) {
227:      // close the active MDI child
228:      pChild->MDIDestroy();
229:      MDINext; // get the next MDI child
230:      pChild = (CAppMDIChild*) MDIGetActive();
231:    }
232:    // clear the bExpressClose flag
233:    bExpressClose = FALSE;
234: }
235:
236: //  display a message box which shows the number of children
237: void CAppMDIFrame::CMCountChildren()
238: {
239:    char msgStr[81];
240:
241:    sprintf(msgStr, "There are %d MDI children", nNumMDIChildren);
242:    MessageBox(msgStr, "Information", MB_OK | MB_ICONINFORMATION);
243: }
244:
245: LONG CAppMDIFrame::OnChildDestroy(UINT wParam, LONG lParam)
246: {
247:    nNumMDIChildren-;
248:    // reset nLastMDIChild to 0, if there are no MDI children
249:    nLastMDIChild = (nNumMDIChildren == 0) ? 0 : nLastMDIChild;
250:    return 0;
251: }
252:
253: void CAppMDIFrame::OnClose()
254: {
255:    if (MessageBox("Want to close this application",
256:                   "Query", MB_YESNO | MB_ICONQUESTION) == IDYES)
257:      DestroyWindow();
```

continues

Listing 21.3. continued

```
258: }
259:
260: BEGIN_MESSAGE_MAP(CAppMDIChild, CMDIChildWnd)
261:   ON_WM_CREATE()
262:   ON_WM_CLOSE()
263:   ON_WM_DESTROY()
264: END_MESSAGE_MAP()
265:
266: BEGIN_MESSAGE_MAP(CAppMDIFrame, CMDIFrameWnd)
267:   ON_WM_CREATE()
268:   ON_COMMAND(CM_CREATECHILD, CMCreateChild)
269:   ON_COMMAND(CM_CASCADECHILDREN, CMCascadeChildren)
270:   ON_COMMAND(CM_TILECHILDREN, CMTileChildren)
271:   ON_COMMAND(CM_ARRANGEICONS, CMArrageIcons)
272:   ON_COMMAND(CM_CLOSECHILDREN, CMCloseChildren)
273:   ON_COMMAND(CM_COUNTCHILDREN, CMCountChildren)
274:   ON_MESSAGE(WM_CHILDDESTROY, OnChildDestroy)
275:   ON_COMMAND(CM_EXIT, OnExit)
276:   ON_WM_CLOSE()
277: END_MESSAGE_MAP()
278:
279: // Construct the CWindowApp's m_pMainWnd data member
280: BOOL CWindowApp::InitInstance()
281: {
282:   m_pMainWnd = new CAppMDIFrame();
283:   m_pMainWnd->ShowWindow(m_nCmdShow);
284:   m_pMainWnd->UpdateWindow();
285:   return TRUE;
286: }
287:
288: // application's constructor initializes and runs the app
289: CWindowApp WindowApp;
```

Figure 21.1 shows a sample session with the MDIWIN1.EXE program.

 Listing 21.2 contains the script for the MDIWIN1.RC resource file. The file defines the menu resource required by the MDI frame window. The menu has two menu items, Exit and MDI Children. The latter menu item is a pop-up menu with several options. These options include creating a new MDI child window, cascading the MDI child windows, tiling the MDI child windows, arranging the icons for the MDI child windows, closing all MDI child windows, and displaying the number of MDI child windows.

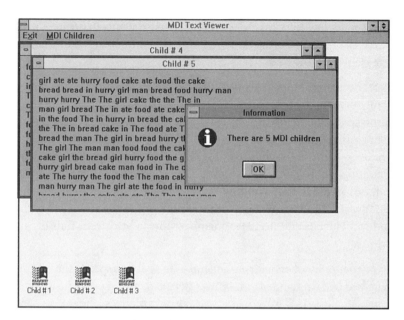

Figure 21.1. A sample session with the MDIWIN1.EXE program.

Listing 21.3 shows the source code for the MDIWIN1.CPP program file. The program listing declares the following sets of constants:

☐ The MenuRezName constant defines the name of the menu resource used in calling the Create and CreateClient functions.

☐ The Hctl and Wctl constants are used to size up the static text and edit controls that are attached to the MDI child windows.

☐ The constants MaxWords, WordsPerLine, and NumWords are used in generating the random text in each MDI child window.

The global array of pointers, Words, contains the program's rather limited vocabulary. The listing also declares the global functions random and makeRect. The random function generates the random number between 0 and maxVal (the function's only parameter). The makeRect function is similar to the makeRect member functions that are used in many examples shown in previous Days in this book. Because both MDI frame and child window classes need this function, I made it global rather than declaring in each class.

The program listing declares three classes: the application class CWindowApp, the MDI frame class CAppMDIFrame, and the MDI child window class CAppMDIChild.

21

The code for the application class looks very much like the ones in previous programs, with one exception. The InitInstance member function creates an instance of the MDI frame class CAppMDIFrame.

The CAppMDIFrame class, a descendant of CMDIFrameWnd, declares four data members, a constructor, a destructor, and a group of member functions. There are two public and two protected data members. The public data members are bExpressClose and nLastMDIChild. The Boolean data member bExpressClose assists in quickly closing all the windows—this process bypasses the confirmation normally requested when you close an individual MDI child window. The nLastMDIChild member stores the highest index of an MDI child window. The protected data members are pMenu and nNumMDIChildren. The pMenu member is the pointer to the menu attached to the MDI frame window. The nNumMDIChildren member stores the current number of MDI child windows.

The class constructor invokes the Create member function to specify the window title, style (maximized and overlapped), and the MAINMENU menu resource (using the global constant MenuRezName). The constructor also initializes the bExpressClose, nLastMDIChild, and nNumMDIChildren data members. The class destructor deletes the dynamic menu accessed by the pMenu pointer.

The member function OnCreate, defined in lines 193 through 199, responds to the WM_CREATE message sent by the Create function (which itself is called by the class constructor). The function performs the following tasks:

☐ Creates a new instance of CMenu, the menu class, and links that instance with the pMenu data member

☐ Attaches the resource menu MAINMENU to the MDI frame window by calling the CMenu::LoadMenu function, using the pMenu pointer

☐ Creates the invisible MDI client window by calling the CreateClient member function (the first argument of the CreateClient function is the parameter of the OnCreate function itself; the second argument of the CreateClient function is the pointer to the first menu item, accessed by the expression pMenu->GetSubMenu(0))

☐ Returns zero as the function result

The member function CMCreateChild, defined in lines 201 through 218, creates an MDI child window. The function carries out the following tasks:

☐ Creates a new instance of class CAppMDIChild and accesses that instance with the local pointer pChild

☐ Calculates the size and location of the MDI child window by calling the global function makeRect

☐ Increments the nLastMDIChild data member

☐ Builds the MDI child window title, using the value stored in nLastMDIChild, and stores the title in the local string s

☐ Builds the MDI child window by calling the member function CAppMDIFrame::Create (the function call supplies the MDI child window title and child number; if the Create function returns FALSE, the CMCreateChild function deletes the dynamic instance of CAppMDIChild, decrements the nLastMDIChild member, and then exits)

☐ Increments the number of current MDI child windows that is stored in data member nNumMDIChildren

☐ Displays the new MDI child window by invoking the ShowWindow function

The member function CMCloseChildren, defined in lines 220 through 234, closes all the MDI child windows. The function performs the following tasks:

☐ Obtains the pointer to the currently active MDI child window by calling the MDIGetActive member function (the local pointer pChild accesses the active window)

☐ Assigns TRUE to the data member bExpressClose

☐ Uses a while loop statement to close each MDI child window, starting with the currently active window (using the pChild pointer, the loop statements close the currently active window by calling the MDIDestroy function; then, the loop selects the next MDI child by calling the MDINext function, and uses the MDIGetActive function to assign the address of the new active child to pointer pChild)

☐ Assigns FALSE to the bExpressClose data member

When the while loop closes all MDI child windows, the MDIGetActive function assigns a NULL to the pChild pointer. This NULL value ends the loop iteration.

The member function CMCountChildren, defined in lines 237 through 243, displays the current number of MDI child windows in a message box. The function converts the value stored in the nNumMDIChildren into a formatted string displayed by a message box.

21

The member function OnChildDestroy, defined in lines 245 through 251, responds to the messages sent by an MDI child window when it is destroyed. The function decrements the value stored in member nNumMDIChildren and resets the value of member nLastMDIChild to 0 if nNumMDIChildren is 0. Therefore, when you close all the MDI child windows, the next MDI child window you create has a Child #1 caption.

The member functions CMCascadeChildren, CMTileChldren, and CMArrangeIcons invoke the inherited member functions MDICascade, MDITile, and MDIIconArrange, respectively.

The CAppMDIChild class declares two public members, TextBox and TextTxt, and a protected member, nChildNum. The TextBox and TextTxt members are pointers to the edit control and static text control that are created (the instances of CAppMDIChild create either one but not both). The class also declares a constructor, a destructor, a Create function, and a number of member functions. The nChildNum data member stores the child number of an MDI child window for self-identification.

The class constructor assigns NULL values to the TextBox and TextTxt pointers. The class destructors delete the dynamic instance of the control accessed by either TextBox or TextTxt.

The member function Create, defined in lines 117 through 121, is a short version of the inherited Create function, and has two parameters: szText and nChildNumber. The function assigns the argument of nChildNumber to the member nChildNum and then calls the Create member function of the parent class.

The member function OnCreate, defined in lines 123 through 157, responds to the WM_CREATE message emitted by the Create function. The OnCreate function carries out the following tasks:

☐ Randomizes the seed for the random-number generator

☐ Builds the list of random words using the CString object s (this task uses a for loop statement and inserts a line break after generating each WordsPerLine random word)

☐ Calculates the size and location of the edit control or static text control to be created in the next task

☐ Creates an edit control accessed by member TextBox if the value stored in nChildNum is even; otherwise, creates a static text control accessed by member TextTxt

☐ Returns zero as the function value

The member function OnClose, defined in lines 159 through 173, closes an MDI child window with or without user confirmation. The function uses the local pointer pParent to access the parent MDI frame window. This access allows the function to then obtain the Boolean value of bExpressClose and, depending on that value, determine whether or not to prompt the user before closing the window.

The member function OnDestroy, defined in lines 175 through 179, sends the parent MDI frame window a WM_CHILDDESTROY message when an MDI child window is removed. This allows the parent MDI frame window to take appropriate action, which in this case is the decrement of the nNumMDIChildren member.

Summary

Today's lesson presents the Multiple Document Interface (MDI) which is an interface standard in Windows. You learn about the following subjects:

☐ The basic features and components of an MDI-compliant application include the MDI frame window, the invisible MDI client window, and the dynamically created MDI child window.

☐ The basic ingredients for an MDI application are the CMDIFrameWnd and CMDIChildWnd classes.

☐ The CMDIFrameWnd class manages the MDI client window, the MDI child window, and the execution of the menu commands.

☐ You can build MDI frame windows as objects that are owned by the application and that own the MDI children.

☐ The CMDIChildWnd class is used in building MDI child windows.

Q&A

Q. Should each MDI-child window have an ID?

A. Yes. Associating each MDI-child window with an ID gives you more control over managing these windows, especially if they vary in relevance. Thus, you can use the ID to exclude special MDI-child windows from collective operations.

21

Q. Can I hide MDI-child windows?

A. Yes, you can use the inherited member function `CWnd::ShowWindow` to show and hide one or more MDI-child windows.

Workshop

The Workshop provides quiz questions to help you solidify your understanding of the material covered and exercises to provide you with experience in using what you've learned. Try to understand the quiz and exercise answers before continuing on to the next day's lesson. Answers are provided in Appendix B, "Answers."

Quiz

1. True or false? MDI child windows can have their own menus.

2. True or false? MDI child windows can be moved outside the area of the frame window.

3. True or false? The MFC library supports nested MDI-child windows.

4. True or false? This is the last quiz question in this book.

Exercise

Experiment with program MDIWIN1.CPP by adding command buttons in each MDI child window. Make these command buttons toggle the case of the text in the static text or edit controls associated with each MDI child window.

Week 3 in Review

As you end the last week of learning about programming with Visual C++, let's look at a Windows version of the number-guessing game. Listing R3.1 shows the source code for the INPUTDIA.H header file. Listing R3.2 contains the script for the INPUTDIA.RC resource file. Listing R3.3 shows the source code for the GAME3.H header file. Listing R3.4 contains the script for the GAME3.RC resource file. Listing R3.5 shows the source code for the GAME3.CPP program file. Create the GAME3.MAK project file in the directory \MSVC\VC21DAY\GAME3 and include the files GAME3.CPP, GAME3.DEF (which resembles the MINWINAP.DEF file in Day 14, Listing 14.2), and GAME3.RC. The INPUTDIA.RC is automatically included with file GAME3.RC using the rcinclude statement in the latter file.

Type **Listing R3.1. Source code for the INPUTDIA.H header file.**

```
1: #define ID_INPUT_TXT 100
2: #define ID_INPUT_EDIT 101
```

Type **Listing R3.2. Script for the INPUTDIA.RC resource file.**

```
1: #include <windows.h>
2: #include <afxres.h>
3: #include "inputdia.h"
4:
5: GAME DIALOG 44, 34, 200, 80
6: STYLE DS_MODALFRAME | WS_CAPTION | WS_VISIBLE | WS_SYSMENU
7: CAPTION "Hi-Lo Guessing Game"
```

continues

Listing R3.2. continued

```
 8: BEGIN
 9:    LTEXT "Enter a string:", ID_INPUT_TXT, 20, 10, 160, 12,
10:         NOT WS_GROUP
11:    EDITTEXT ID_INPUT_EDIT, 20, 25, 160, 12, ES_AUTOHSCROLL
12:    DEFPUSHBUTTON "OK", IDOK, 20, 45, 65, 14, WS_GROUP
13:    PUSHBUTTON "Cancel", IDCANCEL, 110, 45, 65, 14, WS_GROUP
14: END
```

Listing R3.3. Source code for the GAME3.H header file.

```
1: #define CM_EXIT (WM_USER + 100)
2: #define CM_GAME (WM_USER + 101)
```

Listing R3.4. Script for the GAME3.RC resource file.

```
 1: #include <windows.h>
 2: #include <afxres.h>
 3: #include "game3.h"
 4:
 5: MAINMENU MENU LOADONCALL MOVEABLE PURE DISCARDABLE
 6: BEGIN
 7:     MENUITEM "E&xit", CM_EXIT
 8:     MENUITEM "&Game", CM_GAME
 9: END
10:
11: rcinclude inputdia.rc
```

Listing R3.5. Source code for the GAME3.CPP program file.

```
 1: #include <stdlib.h>
 2: #include <stdio.h>
 3: #include <string.h>
 4: #include <afxwin.h>
 5: #include "game3.h"
 6: #include "inputdia.h"
 7:
 8: const MaxBuffer = 81;
 9:
10: // declare a global random number generating function
```

```
11: int random(int maxVal)
12: { return rand() % maxVal; }
13:
14: class CWindowApp : public CWinApp
15: {
16: public:
17:     virtual BOOL InitInstance();
18: };
19:
20: // expand the functionality of CFrameWnd by deriving
21: // class CAppWindow
22: class CAppWindow : public CFrameWnd
23: {
24: public:
25:
26:   CAppWindow();
27:
28: protected:
29:   // handle the Game menu item
30:   afx_msg void CMGame();
31:   afx_msg void OnExit()
32:     { SendMessage(WM_CLOSE); }
33:   // handle closing the window
34:   afx_msg void OnClose();
35:
36:   // declare message map macro
37:   DECLARE_MESSAGE_MAP();
38: };
39:
40: // declare a class for the line input dialog box
41: class CInputDialog : public CDialog
42: {
43: public:
44:   CInputDialog(CWnd* pParent) : CDialog("GAME", pParent) {}
45:   // handle invoking the dialog box
46:   int DoModal(CString& Message, CString& Text);
47:   // handle initializing the dialog box
48:   virtual BOOL OnInitDialog();
49:   // handle the OK button
50:   virtual void OnOK();
51:   // access input
52:   CString& GetInput() { return szText; }
53:
54: protected:
55:   CString szText;
56:   CString szMessage;
57: };
58:
59: int CInputDialog::DoModal(CString& Message, CString& Text)
60: {
```

continues

Listing R3.5. continued

```
61:    // copy parameters to data members
62:    szText = Text;
63:    szMessage = Message;
64:    return CDialog::DoModal();
65: }
66:
67: BOOL CInputDialog::OnInitDialog()
68: {
69:    // assign the message a default input to the dialog
70:    // box static and edit box controls
71:    SetDlgItemText(ID_INPUT_TXT, (const char*) szMessage);
72:    SetDlgItemText(ID_INPUT_EDIT, (const char*) szText);
73:    return TRUE;
74: }
75:
76: void CInputDialog::OnOK()
77: {
78:     // obtain the user's input
79:     GetDlgItemText(ID_INPUT_EDIT, szText.GetBuffer(MaxBuffer),
80:                    MaxBuffer);
81:     szText.ReleaseBuffer();
82:     EndDialog(IDOK);
83: }
84:
85: CAppWindow::CAppWindow()
86: {
87:    // create the window
88:    Create(NULL, "Hi-Lo Game", WS_OVERLAPPEDWINDOW,
89:           rectDefault, NULL, "MAINMENU");
90: }
91:
92: void CAppWindow::CMGame()
93: {
94:    CString Message = "Enter a number between 0 and 1000";
95:    CString Input = "500";
96:    int nNum, nGuess;
97:    int MaxIter = 11;
98:    int nIter = 0;
99:    BOOL bOk = TRUE;
100:    CInputDialog GameDlg(this);
101:
102:
103:    // reseed random-number generator
104:    srand((unsigned)time(NULL));
105:    nNum = random(1001);
106:    // execute the opening dialog box
107:    if (GameDlg.DoModal(Message, Input) == IDOK) {
108:        Input = GameDlg.GetInput();
109:        nGuess = atoi((const char*) Input);
```

```
110:        nIter++;
111:        // loop to obtain the other guesses
112:        while (nGuess != nNum && nIter < MaxIter && bOk ==
           TRUE) {
113:          // is the user's guess higher?
114:          Message = (nGuess > nNum) ? "Enter a lower guess" :
115:                             "Enter a higher guess";
116:          bOk = (GameDlg.DoModal(Message, Input) == IDOK) ?
           TRUE :

117:
           FALSE;
118:          Input = GameDlg.GetInput();
119:          nGuess = atoi((const char*) Input);
120:          nIter++;
121:        }
122:
123:        // did the user guess the secret number
124:        if (nIter < MaxIter && bOk == TRUE) {
125:          MessageBeep(0);
126:          MessageBeep(0);
127:          MessageBox("You guessed it!", "Congratulations!",
128:                     MB_OK);
129:        }
130:        else {
131:          sprintf(Message.GetBuffer(MaxBuffer),
132:                  "The secret number is %d", nNum);
133:          Message.ReleaseBuffer();
134:          MessageBox((const char*) Message, "Sorry!", MB_OK);
135:        }
136:    }
137: }
138:
139: void CAppWindow::OnClose()
140: {
141:   if (MessageBox("Want to close this application",
142:                  "Query", MB_YESNO | MB_ICONQUESTION) ==
                  IDYES)
143:     DestroyWindow();
144: }
145:
146: BEGIN_MESSAGE_MAP(CAppWindow, CFrameWnd)
147:   ON_COMMAND(CM_GAME, CMGame)
148:   ON_COMMAND(CM_EXIT, OnExit)
149:   ON_WM_CLOSE()
150: END_MESSAGE_MAP()
151:
152: // Construct the CWindowApp's m_pMainWnd data member
153: BOOL CWindowApp::InitInstance()
154: {
```

continues

Listing R3.5. continued

```
155:    m_pMainWnd = new CAppWindow();
156:    m_pMainWnd->ShowWindow(m_nCmdShow);
157:    m_pMainWnd->UpdateWindow();
158:    return TRUE;
159: }
160:
161: // application's constructor initializes and runs the app
162: CWindowApp WindowApp;
```

Figure R3.1 shows a sample session with the GAME3.EXE program.

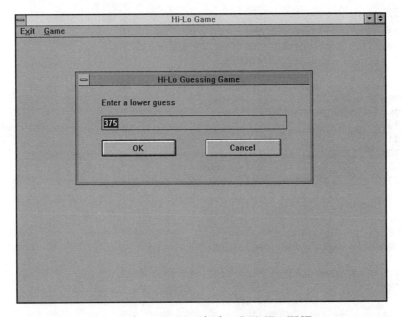

Figure R3.1. A sample session with the GAME3.EXE program.

 Listings R3.1 and R3.2 contribute in defining the GAME dialog box resource used to prompt you for a guess. Listings R3.3 and R3.4 define the menu resource used by the main window.

The program in Listing R3.5 declares the application class, CWindowApp, the window class, CAppWindow, and the input dialog box class, CInputDialog.

The input dialog box class, CInputDialog, declares a constructor, a number of member functions, and two CString data members. The member functions include DoModal, OnInitDialog, OnOK, and GetInput.

The member function DoModal, defined in lines 59 through 65, has two CString reference parameters: Message and Text. The function assigns the parameters Text and Message to the data members szText and szMessage. The function returns the value of the inherited CDialog::DoModal member function.

The member function OnInitDialog, defined in lines 67 through 74, calls the function SetDlgItemText twice. The first call assigns the string in member szMessage to the static text control of the input dialog box. The second call assigns the string in member szText to the edit control in the input dialog box. The Boolean function then returns TRUE.

The member function OnOK, defined in lines 76 through 83, copies the text in the edit control to the data member szText.

The member function GetInput returns the contents of the data member szText.

The class CAppWindow declares the member functions CMGame, OnExit, and OnClose. The function CMGame plays the number-guessing game and performs the following tasks:

- [ ] Declares and initializes a number of local variables and instances of classes CString and CInputDialog

- [ ] Reseeds the random-number generator

- [ ] Generates the secret number and stores it in the variable nNum

- [ ] Executes the modal dialog box instance GameDlg; when the examined condition in the if statement of line 107 is true, the function performs the following subtasks:

  Obtains the input text by sending the GetInput message to instance GameDlg (the result is stored in the string Input)

  Converts the string in variable Input into an integer and stores the integer in variable nGuess

  Increments the iteration counter, variable nIter

  Executes a while loop which redisplays the input dialog box and performs these subtasks

☐ Displays a congratulatory message if the user guesses the secret number; if the user does not guess the secret number, displays the secret number in a message dialog box

A

Controls
Resource Script

This appendix presents the syntax for the menu resource and the controls resource scripts. The resource script itself was defined by Microsoft long before it created the MFC class hierarchy. However, as you see in Day 19, dialog box instances are created using resources. In this appendix, you learn about the following resources:

☐ The menu resources

☐ The dialog box resource

☐ The DIALOG option statements

☐ The general control resource

☐ The resources for the default controls

Building Menu Resources

The menu resource file (which is usually stored in an .RC file extension) may contain the following statements:

☐ The MENU statement

☐ The MENUITEM statement

☐ The POPUP statement

☐ The MENUITEM SEPARATOR statement

☐ The ACCELERATORS statement

The MENU statement defines the contents of a menu resource. The general syntax for the MENU statement is

```
menuID MENU [load options] [mem options]
BEGIN
     item definitions
END
```

The *menuID* is the unique name or integer ID of the menu resource. The keywords associated with resource files appear in uppercase. This is optional—they are not case-sensitive. I maintain the uppercase letters to make it easier to distinguish between resource keywords and non-keywords. The following are the load options:

☐ PRELOAD loads the resource immediately.

☐ LOADONCALL loads the resource as needed (the default option).

The following are the memory options:

- ☐ FIXED keeps the resource in a fixed memory location.

- ☐ MOVABLE moves the resource when needed for the sake of memory compaction (the default option).

- ☐ DISCARDABLE discards the resource when no longer needed (this option is also selected by default).

The MENUITEM statement defines the name and attributes of an actual menu item. The general syntax for the MENUITEM statement is

```
MENUITEM text, result [, option list]
```

The text field accepts a string literal (enclosed in double quotes) that designates the name of the menu item. To define a hot-key for a menu item, place the ampersand character (&) before the letter you want to make the hot-key (the selection is case-insensitive). To display the ampersand as part of the menu name, use a sequence of two ampersand characters (that is, &&). You can also include the \t sequence to insert a tab in the menu item name. The \a sequence can be inserted to align all text that follows, by flushing it to the right.

The result field contains an integer, usually a CM_XXXX constant, that represents the command emitted by the menu item.

The option list may contain the following items:

- ☐ CHECKED displays a check mark next to the menu item.

- ☐ GRAYED displays the menu item in a gray color to indicate the menu item is not active.

- ☐ HELP puts a vertical separator bar to the left of the menu item.

- ☐ INACTIVE displays the menu item but prevents its selection. This option is usually combined with the GRAYED option to give a better visual indication that the menu item is inactive.

- ☐ MENUBARBREAK places the menu item on a new line for static menu bar items. In the case of pop-up menu items (presented next), it separates the new and old columns with a vertical line.

- ☐ MENUBREAK places the menu item on a new line for static menu bar items. In the case of pop-up menus, it places the menu item in a new column, without any dividing line between the columns.

The POPUP statement defines the beginning of a pop-up menu. The general syntax for the POPUP statement is

```
POPUP text [,option list]
BEGIN
      item definitions
END
```

The text and option list fields are similar to their counterparts in the MENUITEM statement. The item definitions are made up of MENUITEM and/or other POPUP statements. The latter statements enable you to create nested menus.

The MENUITEM SEPARATOR statement is a special form of the MENUITEM statement that creates an inactive menu item and displays a dividing bar between two active menu items.

The ACCELERATORS statement defines one or more accelerators for your MFC application.

NEW☛ TERM An *accelerator* is a key stroke defined to give the application user a quick way to select a menu item and carry out a specific task.

The general syntax for the ACCELERATORS statement is

```
accTableName ACCELERATORS
BEGIN
      event, idValue, [type] [NOINVERT] [ALT] [SHIFT] [CONTROL]
END
```

The accTableName field defines a unique name or integer ID that distinguishes an accelerator resource from any other type of resources. The event field specifies the key stroke used as an accelerator and can be one of the following:

☐ A single ASCII character is enclosed in double quotes. You can place a caret symbol before the character to signal that it is a control character. In this case, the type field is not required.

☐ An integer value designates an ASCII code of a character. In this case, the type field must be the keyword ASCII.

☐ An integer value represents a virtual key. In this case, the type field must be the keyword VIRTKEY.

The idValue field is an integer that identifies the accelerator. The type field is required only when the event field is an ASCII character code or a virtual key.

The NOINVERT option prevents a top-level menu item from being highlighted when the accelerator is used. The ALT, SHIFT, and CONTROL options activate the accelerator when the Alt, Shift, and Control keys are pressed down, respectively. The following is an example of an accelerator resource:

```
"EditKeys" ACCELERATORS
BEGIN
    "h",            IDDHEADING              ; the H key
    "H",            IDDHOLD                 ; the Shift-H keys
    "^B",   IDDBOLD                         ; the Control-B keys
    64,             IDDADD                  ; The Shift-A keys
    97,             IDDAPPEND               ; The A key
    "s",            IDDSEARCH, ALT          ;  The Alt-S keys
    VK_F7, IDDSAVE, VIRTKEY                 ; The F7 function key
    VK_F2, IDDLOAD, SHIFT, VIRTKEY          ; The Shift-F2 keys
    VK_F3, IDDSAVEAS, CONTROL, VIRTKEY      ; The Control-F3 keys
    VK_F1, IDDNEW, ALT, SHIFT, VIRTKEY      ; The Alt-Shift-F1
                                            ; keys
END
```

Dialog Box Resource

The DIALOG statement defines the resource that can be utilized in a Windows program to build dialog boxes. The general syntax for the DIALOG statement is

```
nameID DIALOG [load-option][mem-option] x, y, width, height
[option-statements]
BEGIN
    control-statements
END
```

The nameID is the unique name or integer ID of the dialog box resource. The keywords associated with resource files appear in uppercase. This is optional—they are not case-sensitive. I maintain the uppercase letters to make it easier to distinguish between resource keywords and non-keywords. The following are the load options:

☐ PRELOAD loads the resource immediately.

☐ LOADONCALL loads the resource as needed (the default option).

The following are the memory options:

☐ FIXED keeps the resource in a fixed memory location.

☐ MOVABLE moves the resource when needed for the sake of memory compaction (the default option).

☐ DISCARDABLE discards the resource when no longer needed (this option is also selected by default).

The x and y parameters specify the location of the upper-left corner of the dialog box. The width and height parameters define the dimensions of the dialog box.

An example of a dialog box resource definition is shown below. The example is taken from the DIALOG1.RC file:

```
#include <windows.h>
#include <afxres.h>

NEW DIALOG DISCARDABLE LOADONCALL PURE MOVEABLE 30, 50, 200, 100
STYLE WS_POPUP | DS_MODALFRAME
CAPTION "Message"
BEGIN
  CTEXT "Exit the application?", 1, 10, 10, 170, 15
  CONTROL "OK", IDOK, "BUTTON", WS_CHILD | WS_VISIBLE |
    WS_TABSTOP | BS_DEFPUSHBUTTON, 20, 50, 70, 15
  CONTROL "Cancel", IDCANCEL, "BUTTON", WS_CHILD | WS_VISIBLE |
    WS_TABSTOP | BS_PUSHBUTTON, 110, 50, 70, 15
END
```

DIALOG Option Statements

The DIALOG option statements designate the special attributes of the dialog box, such as style, caption, and menu. These statements are optional. If you do not incorporate any option statements in your dialog box resource definition, you end up with a dialog box that has default attributes. The DIALOG option statements include the following items:

- [ ] STYLE

- [ ] CAPTION

- [ ] MENU

- [ ] CLASS

- [ ] FONT

In the following subsections, I explain each of these dialog box attributes.

The *STYLE* Statement

The STYLE statement specifies the window style of the dialog box. This attribute indicates whether the dialog box is a child window or a pop-up window. The default style for the dialog box has the WS_POPUP, WS_BORDER, and WS_SYSMENU styles. The general syntax for the STYLE statement is

```
STYLE style
```

The *style* parameter takes an integer value made up of bitwise OR style attributes. The following is an example of the STYLE option statement:

```
STYLE WS_POPUP ¦ DS_MODALFRAME
```

The *CAPTION* Statement

The CAPTION statement defines the title for the dialog box. This title appears in the caption bar of the dialog box, if the box has that bar. By default, the title is an empty string. The general syntax for the CAPTION statement is

```
CAPTION title
```

The *title* parameter is a string literal. The following is an example of the CAPTION statement:

```
CAPTION "Replace Text"
```

The *MENU* Statement

The MENU statement specifies the menu attached to the dialog box. By default, the dialog box has no menu. The general syntax for the MENU statement is

```
MENU menuName
```

The *menuName* parameter is the name or number of the menu resource. The following is an example of the MENU statement:

```
#include <windows.h>
#include <afxres.h>

YesNo MENU LOADONCALL MOVEABLE PURE DISCARDABLE
BEGIN
    MENUITEM "&Ok", IDOK
    MENUITEM "&Cancel", IDCANCEL
END

NEW DIALOG DISCARDABLE LOADONCALL PURE MOVEABLE 30, 50, 200, 100
STYLE WS_POPUP ¦ DS_MODALFRAME
CAPTION "Message"
MENU YesNo
BEGIN
  CTEXT "Exit the application?", 1, 10, 10, 170, 15
  CONTROL "OK", IDOK, "BUTTON", WS_CHILD ¦ WS_VISIBLE ¦
    WS_TABSTOP ¦ BS_DEFPUSHBUTTON, 20, 50, 70, 15
  CONTROL "Cancel", IDCANCEL, "BUTTON", WS_CHILD ¦ WS_VISIBLE ¦
    WS_TABSTOP ¦ BS_PUSHBUTTON, 110, 50, 70, 15
END
```

The *CLASS* Statement

The CLASS statement specifies the Windows registration class (and not the MFC library class) of the dialog box. The general syntax for the CLASS statement is

CLASS *className*

The *className* parameter defines the integer or string name of the registration class. The following is an example of the CLASS statement:

CLASS "ChitChat"

The *FONT* Statement

The FONT statement specifies the font used by Windows to draw text in the dialog box. The specified font must be already loaded, either from WIN.INI or by invoking the LoadFont API function. The general syntax for the FONT statement is

FONT *pointSize*, *typeface*

The *pointSize* parameter is an integer that specifies the size of the font in points. The *typeface* parameter is a string that indicates the name of the font. The following is an example of the FONT statement:

FONT 10, "Helv"

Dialog Box Control Resources

The resource script supports two types of controls resource. The first one is the CONTROL statement which provides a general way for declaring the resource of a control. The other type of resource controls are the modifiable default control resources. These resources use statements with keywords that are descriptive of the control they define. For example, the RADIOBUTTON statement defines the resource for a radio button. In the next section I present the CONTROL statement. In the sections after the next one I present the statements that define the resources for specific controls.

The General Control Resource

The CONTROL statement allows you to define the resource for any standard or user-defined control that is owned by a dialog box. The general syntax for the CONTROL statement is

A

```
CONTROL text, id, class, style, x, y, width, height
```

The *text* parameter specifies a string literal for the text that appears in the control.

The *id* parameter declares the control's unique ID.

Note: The *class* parameter is a string that indicates the name of the Windows registration class for the control. Table A.1 shows the Windows registration class names for the various standard controls. Notice that the push button, check box, radio button, and group box all share the same registration class name! How are they distinguished from each other? The answer lies with the *style* parameter.

Note: The *style* parameter, which is usually a bitwise OR expression, sets all the styles associated with the control. There are *no default style values!*

The *x*, *y*, *width*, and *height* parameters specify the location and dimensions of the control. These parameters are typically integer constants. You can also use the addition operator to build simple expressions.

Table A.1. Windows registration class names for the various standard controls.

Control	Registration Class Name
Check box	BUTTON
Combo box	COMBOBOX
Edit box	EDIT
Group box	BUTTON
List box	LISTBOX
Push button	BUTTON
Radio button	BUTTON

continues

669

Table A.1. continued

Control	Registration Class Name
Scroll bar	SCROLLBAR
Static text	STATIC

Examples of using the CONTROL statement to create dialog box controls are shown below. These examples are taken from the DIALOG6.RC resource file:

```
ID_DIALOG DIALOG DISCARDABLE LOADONCALL PURE MOVEABLE 10, 10, 200, 150
STYLE WS_POPUP ¦ WS_CLIPSIBLINGS ¦ WS_CAPTION ¦ WS_SYSMENU ¦
DS_MODALFRAME
CAPTION "Controls Demo"
BEGIN
  CONTROL "Find", ID_FIND_TXT, "STATIC", WS_CHILD ¦ WS_VISIBLE ¦
    SS_LEFT, 20, 10, 100, 15

  CONTROL "", ID_FIND_CMB, "COMBOBOX", WS_CHILD ¦ WS_VISIBLE ¦
    WS_BORDER ¦ WS_TABSTOP ¦ CBS_DROPDOWN, 20, 25, 100, 50

  CONTROL "Replace", ID_REPLACE_TXT, "STATIC", WS_CHILD ¦ WS_VISIBLE ¦
    SS_LEFT, 20, 45, 100, 15

  CONTROL "", ID_REPLACE_CMB, "COMBOBOX", WS_CHILD ¦ WS_VISIBLE ¦
    WS_BORDER ¦ WS_TABSTOP ¦ CBS_DROPDOWN, 20, 60, 100, 50

  CONTROL " Scope ", ID_SCOPE_GRP, "BUTTON", WS_CHILD ¦ WS_VISIBLE
    ¦ WS_GROUP ¦ BS_GROUPBOX, 20, 80, 90, 50

  CONTROL "Global", ID_GLOBAL_RBT, "BUTTON", WS_CHILD ¦ WS_VISIBLE
    ¦ WS_TABSTOP ¦ BS_AUTORADIOBUTTON, 30, 90, 50, 15

  CONTROL "Selected Text", ID_SELTEXT_RBT, "BUTTON", WS_CHILD ¦
    WS_VISIBLE ¦ WS_TABSTOP ¦ BS_AUTORADIOBUTTON, 30, 105, 60, 15

  CONTROL "Case Sensitive", ID_CASE_CHK, "BUTTON", WS_CHILD ¦
    WS_VISIBLE ¦ WS_TABSTOP ¦ BS_AUTOCHECKBOX, 20, 130, 80, 15

  CONTROL "Whole Word", ID_WHOLEWORD_CHK, "BUTTON", WS_CHILD ¦
    WS_VISIBLE ¦ WS_TABSTOP ¦ BS_AUTOCHECKBOX, 100, 130, 80, 15

  CONTROL, "&OK", IDOK, "BUTTON", WS_CHILD ¦ WS_VISIBLE ¦ WS_TABSTOP
    ¦ BS_DEFPUSHBUTTON, 120, 90, 30, 20

  CONTROL "&Cancel", IDCANCEL, "BUTTON", WS_CHILD ¦ WS_VISIBLE ¦
    WS_TABSTOP, 160, 90, 30, 20
END
```

The *LTEXT* Statement

The LTEXT statement defines the resource of a static text control whose text is flush left. The general syntax for the LTEXT statement is

```
LTEXT text, id, x, y, width, height [, style]
```

The *text* parameter specifies the static control text. This text may include an & character to underline a hot-key character. The *id* parameter defines the ID of the static control. The *x*, *y*, *width*, and *height* parameters specify the location and dimensions of the control. The optional *style* parameter specifies the additional styles for the resource. The default style is SS_LEFT and WS_GROUP. The style parameter can be the WS_TABSTOP style, the WS_GROUP style, or both.

The characters of the *text* parameter are displayed left-justified. If the entire text does not fit in the specified width, the additional characters are wrapped to the beginning of the next line.

The following are examples of the LTEXT statement:

```
LTEXT "Current Drive:", ID_DRIVE_TXT, 10, 10, 50, 10

LTEXT "Current Dir:", ID_DIR_TXT, 10, 50, 50, 10, WS_TABSTOP
      ¦ WS_GROUP
```

The *RTEXT* Statement

The RTEXT statement defines the resource of a static text control whose text is flush right. The general syntax for the RTEXT statement is

```
RTEXT text, id, x, y, width, height [, style]
```

The *text* parameter specifies the static control text. This text may include an & character to underline a hot-key character. The *id* parameter defines the ID of the static control. The *x*, *y*, *width*, and *height* parameters specify the location and dimensions of the control. The optional *style* parameter specifies the additional styles for the resource. The default style is SS_RIGHT and WS_GROUP. The *style* parameter can be the WS_TABSTOP style, the WS_GROUP style, or both.

The characters of the text parameter are displayed right-justified. If the entire text does not fit in the specified width, the additional characters are wrapped to the next line and also appear right-justified.

The following is an example of the RTEXT statement:

```
RTEXT "Current Drive:", ID_DRIVE_TXT, 70, 10, 50, 10
```

The *CTEXT* Statement

The CTEXT statement defines the resource of a static text control whose text is centered. The general syntax for the CTEXT statement is

```
CTEXT text, id, x, y, width, height [, style]
```

The *text* parameter specifies the static control text. This text may include an & character to underline a hot-key character. The *id* parameter defines the ID of the static control. The *x*, *y*, *width*, and *height* parameters specify the location and dimensions of the control. The optional *style* parameter specifies the additional styles for the resource. The default style is SS_CENTER and WS_GROUP. The *style* parameter can be the WS_TABSTOP style, or the WS_GROUP style, or both.

The characters of the text parameter are displayed centered. If the entire text does not fit in the specified width, the additional characters are wrapped to the next line and also appear centered.

The following is an example of the CTEXT statement:

```
CTEXT "Current Drive:", ID_DRIVE_TXT, 10, 10, 50, 10
```

The *CHECKBOX* Statement

The CHECKBOX statement defines a check box control resource that has the BUTTON registration class. The general syntax for the CHECKBOX statement is

```
CHECKBOX text, id, x, y, width, height [, style]
```

The *text* parameter specifies the caption of the control. This text may include an & character to underline a hot-key character. The *id* parameter defines the ID of the check box control. The *x*, *y*, *width*, and *height* parameters specify the location and dimensions of the control. The optional style parameter specifies the additional styles for the resource. The default style is BS_CHECKBOX and WS_TABSTOP. The *style* parameter can be the WS_DISABLED style, the WS_TABSTOP style, or both.

The following is an example of the CHECKBOX statement:

```
CHECKBOX "Case-Sensitive", ID_CASE_CHK, 10, 10, 100, 10
```

The *PUSHBUTTON* Statement

The PUSHBUTTON statement defines a push button control resource that has the BUTTON registration class. The general syntax for the PUSHBUTTON statement is

```
PUSHBUTTON text, id, x, y, width, height [, style]
```

The *text* parameter specifies the caption of the control. This *text* may include an & character to underline a hot-key character. The *id* parameter defines the ID of the push button control. The *x*, *y*, *width*, and *height* parameters specify the location and dimensions of the control. The optional *style* parameter specifies the additional styles for the resource. The default style is BS_PUSHBUTTON and WS_TABSTOP. The style parameter can be the WS_TABSTOP style, the WS_DISABLED style, or the WS_GROUP style, or any bitwise OR combination of these styles.

The following is an example of the PUSHBUTTON statement:

```
PUSHBUTTON "Calculate", ID_CALC_BTN, 10, 10, 100, 10, WS_DISABLED
```

The *DEFPUSHBUTTON* Statement

The DEFPUSHBUTTON statement defines a default push button control resource that has the BUTTON registration class. The general syntax for the DEFPUSHBUTTON statement is

```
DEFPUSHBUTTON text, id, x, y, width, height [, style]
```

The *text* parameter specifies the caption of the control. This *text* may include an & character to underline a hot-key character. The *id* parameter defines the ID of the default push button control. The *x*, *y*, *width*, and *height* parameters specify the location and dimensions of the control. The optional *style* parameter specifies the additional styles for the resource. The default style is BS_DEFPUSHBUTTON and WS_TABSTOP. The *style* parameter can be the WS_TABSTOP style, the WS_DISABLED style, the WS_GROUP style, or any bitwise OR combination of these styles.

The following is an example of the DEFPUSHBUTTON statement:

```
DEFPUSHBUTTON "Calculate", ID_CALC_BTN, 10, 10, 100, 10
```

The *LISTBOX* Statement

The LISTBOX statement defines a list box control resource that has the LISTBOX registration class. The general syntax for the LISTBOX statement is

```
LISTBOX id, x, y, width, height [, style]
```

The *id* parameter defines the ID of the list box control. The *x*, *y*, *width*, and *height* parameters specify the location and dimensions of the control. The optional *style* parameter specifies the additional styles for the resource. The default style is LBS_NOTIFY, WS_VSCROLL, and WS_BORDER. The style parameter can be the WS_BORDER style, the WS_VSCROLL style, or both.

The following is an example of the LISTBOX statement:

```
LISTBOX ID_OPERAND_LST, 10, 10, 100, 100
```

The *GROUPBOX* Statement

The GROUPBOX statement defines a group box control resource that has the BUTTON registration class. The general syntax for the GROUPBOX statement is

```
GROUPBOX text, id, x, y, width, height [, style]
```

The *text* parameter specifies the caption of the control. This text may include an & character to underline a hot-key character. The *id* parameter defines the ID of the group box control. The *x*, *y*, *width*, and *height* parameters specify the location and dimensions of the control. The optional style parameter specifies the additional styles for the resource. The default style is BS_GROUPBOX and WS_TABSTOP. The style parameter can be the WS_TABSTOP style, the WS_DISABLED style, or both.

The following is an example of the GROUPBOX statement:

```
GROUPBOX "Angle", ID_ANGLE_GRP, 10, 10, 200, 200
```

The *RADIOBUTTON* Statement

The RADIOBUTTON statement defines a radio button control resource that has the BUTTON registration class. The general syntax for the RADIOBUTTON statement is

```
RADIOBUTTON text, id, x, y, width, height [, style]
```

The *text* parameter specifies the caption of the control. This text may include an &
character to underline a hot-key character. The *id* parameter defines the ID of the
radio button control. The *x*, *y*, *width*, and *height* parameters specify the location and
dimensions of the control. The optional style parameter specifies the additional styles
for the resource. The default style is BS_RADIOBUTTON and WS_TABSTOP. The *style*
parameter can be the WS_TABSTOP style, the WS_GROUP style, the WS_DISABLED style, or
any bitwise OR combination of these styles.

The following is an example of the RADIOBUTTON statement:

```
RADIOBUTTON "Degrees", ID_DEGREES_RBT, 10, 10, 100, 10
```

The *EDITTEXT* Statement

The EDITTEXT statement defines an edit box control resource that has the EDIT
registration class. The general syntax for the EDITTEXT statement is

```
EDITTEXT id, x, y, width, height [, style]
```

The *id* parameter defines the ID of the edit box control. The *x*, *y*, *width*, and *height*
parameters specify the location and dimensions of the control. The optional style
parameter specifies the additional styles for the resource. The default style is
WS_TABSTOP, ES_EDIT, and WS_BORDER. The style parameter can be the WS_TABSTOP, the
WS_GROUP, the WS_VSCROLL, the WS_HSCROLL, or the WS_DISABLED styles, or any bitwise
OR combination of these styles.

The following is an example of the EDITTEXT statement:

```
EDITTEXT ID_INPUT_BOX, 10, 10, 200, 200
```

The *COMBOBOX* Statement

The COMBOBOX statement defines a combo box control resource that has the COMBOBOX
registration class. The general syntax for the COMBOBOX statement is

```
COMBOBOX id, x, y, width, height [, style]
```

The *id* parameter defines the ID of the combo box control. The *x*, *y*, *width*, and *height*
parameters specify the location and dimensions of the control. The optional *style*
parameter specifies the additional styles for the resource. The default style is
WS_TABSTOP and CBS_SIMPLE. The *style* parameter can be the WS_TABSTOP, the
WS_GROUP, the WS_VSCROLL, or the WS_DISABLED styles, or any bitwise OR combination
of these styles.

The following is an example of the COMBOBOX statement:

```
COMBOBOX ID_INPUT_BOX, 10, 10, 200, 200
```

The *SCROLLBAR* Statement

The SCROLLBAR statement defines a scroll bar control resource that has the SCROLLBAR registration class. The general syntax for the SCROLLBAR statement is

```
SCROLLBAR id, x, y, width, height [, style]
```

The *id* parameter defines the ID of the scroll bar control. The *x*, *y*, *width*, and *height* parameters specify the location and dimensions of the control. The optional *style* parameter specifies the additional styles for the resource. The default style is SBS_HORZ. The *style* parameter can be the WS_TABSTOP, the WS_GROUP, the WS_DISABLED styles, or any bitwise OR combination of these styles.

The following is an example of the SCROLLBAR statement:

```
SCROLLBAR ID_INDEX_SCR, 10, 10, 20, 200
```

Summary

This appendix briefly introduces you to the resource statements used to create the dialog box and its controls. You learn about the following topics:

- [ ] The DIALOG statement defines a dialog box resource.

- [ ] The DIALOG option statements include the STYLE, CAPTION, MENU, CLASS, and FONT statements.

- [ ] The CONTROL statement defines the resources for both standard and user-defined controls.

- [ ] The LTEXT statement defines the resource for a left-justified static text control.

- [ ] The RTEXT statement defines the resource for a right-justified static text control.

- [ ] The CTEXT statement defines the resource for a centered-text static text control.

- [ ] The CHECKBOX statement defines the resource for a check box control.

☐ The PUSHBUTTON statement defines the resource for a push button control.

☐ The DEFPUSHBUTTON statement defines the resource for a default push button control.

☐ The LISTBOX statement defines the resource for a list box control.

☐ The GROUPBOX statement defines the resource for a group box control.

☐ The RADIOBUTTON statement defines the resource for a radio button control.

☐ The EDITTEXT statement defines the resource for an edit box control.

☐ The COMBOBOX statement defines the resource for a combo box control.

☐ The SCROLLBAR statement defines the resource for a scroll bar control.

B

Answers

> **Note:** Due to space limitations, not every Exercise is answered.

Answers to Day 1, "Getting Started"

Quiz

1. The program generates the string C++ in 21 Days?.

2. The program generates no output because the cout statement appears inside a comment! The function main simply returns 0.

3. The cout statement is missing the semicolon.

Exercise

```
// Exercise program

#include <iostream.h>

main()
{
  cout << "I am a C++ Programmer";
  return 0;
}
```

Answers to Day 2, "C++ Program Components"

Quiz

1. The following table indicates which identifiers are valid and which are not (and why):

Identifiers	Valid?	Reason (if Invalid)
numFiles	Yes	
n0Distance_02_Line	Yes	
0Weight	No	Starts with a digit
Bin Number	No	Contains a space
static	No	Reserved keyword
Static	Yes	

2. The output of the program is

   ```
   a = 10 and b = 3
   ```

   The function swap fails to swap the arguments a and b, because it only swaps a copy of their values.

3. The output of the program is

   ```
   a = 3 and b = 10
   ```

   The function swap succeeds in swapping the arguments a and b because it uses reference parameters. Consequently, the changes in the values of parameters i and j go beyond the scope of the function itself.

4. The second version of function inc has a default argument, which, when used, hinders the compiler from determining which version of inc to call. The compiler flags a compile-time error for such functions.

5. Because the second parameter has a default argument, the third one must also have a default argument. Here is one version of the correct definition of function volume:

   ```
   double volume(double length, double width = 1, double height = 1)
   {
     return length * width * height
   }
   ```

6. The parameter i is a lowercase letter. However, the function uses the uppercase I in the assignment statement. The compiler complains that the identifier I is not defined.

7. The function `main` requires a prototype of function `sqr`. The correct version of the program is

```
#include <iostream.h>

// declare prototype of function sqr
double sqr(double);

main()
{
  double x = 5.2;

  cout << x << "^2 = " << sqr(x);
  return 0;
}

double sqr(double x)
{ return x * x ; }
```

Exercise

Here is my version of program OVERLOD2.CPP:

```
// C++ program illustrates function overloading
// and default arguments

#include <iostream.h>

// inc version for int types
void inc(int& i, int diff = 1)
{
  i = i + diff;
}

// inc version for double types
void inc(double& x, double diff = 1)
{
  x = x + diff;
}

// inc version for char types
void inc(char& c, int diff = 1)
```

```
{
  c = c + diff;
}

main()
{
  char c = 'A';
  int i = 10;
  double x = 10.2;

  // display initial values
  cout << "c = " << c << "\n"
       << "i = " << i << "\n"
       << "x = " << x << "\n";
  // invoke the inc functions using default arguments
  inc(c);
  inc(i);
  inc(x);
  // display updated values
  cout << "After using the overloaded inc function\n";
  cout << "c = " << c << "\n"
       << "i = " << i << "\n"
       << "x = " << x << "\n";
  return 0;
}
```

B

Answers to Day 3, "Operators and Expressions"

Quiz

1. The output is

   ```
   12
   8
   2
   3.64851
   150.5
   ```

2. The output is

   ```
   12
   8
   2
   ```

3. The output is

    ```
    12
    27
    ```

4. The output is

    ```
    TRUE
    TRUE
    TRUE
    FALSE
    ```

Exercises

1. Here is my version of the function max:

    ```c
    int max(int i, int j)
    {
      return (i > j) ? i : j;
    }
    ```

2. Here is my version of the function min:

    ```c
    int min(int i, int j)
    {
      return (i < j) ? i : j;
    }
    ```

3. Here is my version of the function abs:

    ```c
    int abs(int i)
    {
      return (i > 0) ? i : -i;
    }
    ```

4. Here is my version of the function isOdd:

    ```c
    int isOdd(int i)
    {
      return (i % 2 != 0) ? 1 : 0;
    }
    ```

Answers to Day 4, "Managing I/O"

Quiz

B

1. The output statement cannot contain the inserter operator >>. The statement can be corrected as follows:

```
count << "Enter a number ";
cin >> x;
```

2. Because the variable x appears in the first and last items, the last number overwrites the first number.

Exercises

1. Here is my version of program OUT3.CPP:

```
// C++ program uses the printf function for formatted output

#include <stdio.h>
#include <math.h>

main()
{
  double x;

  // display table heading
  printf("     X          Sqrt(X)\n");
  printf("----------------------\n");
  x = 2;
  printf("    %3.0lf         %3.4lf\n", x, sqrt(x));
  x++;
  printf("    %3.0lf         %3.4lf\n", x, sqrt(x));
  x++;
  printf("    %3.0lf         %3.4lf\n", x, sqrt(x));
  x++;
  printf("    %3.0lf         %3.4lf\n", x, sqrt(x));
  x++;
  printf("    %3.0lf         %3.4lf\n", x, sqrt(x));
  x++;
  printf("    %3.0lf         %3.4lf\n", x, sqrt(x));
  x++;
  printf("    %3.0lf         %3.4lf\n", x, sqrt(x));
  x++;
  printf("    %3.0lf         %3.4lf\n", x, sqrt(x));
  x++;
  printf("    %3.0lf         %3.4lf\n", x, sqrt(x));
  return 0;
}
```

2. Here is my version of program OUT4.CPP:

```
// C++ program which displays octal and hexadecimal integers

#include <iostream.h>
#include <stdio.h>

main()
{
  long i;
  cout << "Enter an integer : ";
  cin >> i;

  printf("%ld = %lX (hex) = %lo (octal)\n", i, i, i);
  return 0;
}
```

Answers to Day 5, "The Decision-Making Constructs"

Quiz

1. The simpler version is

```
if (i > 0 && i < 10)
  cout << "i = " << i << "\n";
```

2. The simpler version is

```
if (i > 0) {
  j = i * i;
  cout << "j = " << j << "\n";
}
else if (i < 0) {
  j = 4 * i;
  cout << "j = " << j << "\n";
}
else {
  j = 10 + i;
  cout << "j = " << j << "\n";
}
```

3. False. When the variable i stores values between -10 and -1, the statements in the clauses of the two if statements execute. In this case, all the assignment statements are executed. By contrast, it is impossible to execute the statements in both the if and else clauses of the supposedly equivalent if-else statement.

4. The simplified version is

```
if (i > 0 && i < 100)
    j = i * i;
else if (i >= 100)
    j = i;
else
    j = 1;
```

Notice that I eliminate the original first else if clause because the tested condition is a subset of the first tested condition. Consequently, the condition in the first else if never gets examined and the associated assign statement never gets executed. This is an example of what is called *dead code*.

5. The tested condition is always false. Consequently, the statements in the clause are never executed. This is another example of dead code.

Exercises

1. Here is my version of program IF5.CPP:

```
// C++ program to solve quadratic equation

#include <iostream.h>
#include <math.h>

main()
{
  double A, B, C, discrim, root1, root2, twoA;

  cout << "Enter coefficients for equation A*X^2 + B*X + C\n";
  cout << "Enter A: ";
  cin >> A;
  cout << "Enter B: ";
  cin >> B;
  cout << "Enter C: ";
  cin >> C;
```

```
       if (A != 0) {
          twoA = 2 * A;
          discrim = B * B - 4 * A * C;
          if (discrim > 0) {
            root1 = (-B + sqrt(discrim)) / twoA;
            root2 = (-B - sqrt(discrim)) / twoA;
            cout << "root1 = " << root1 << "\n";
            cout << "root2 = " << root2 << "\n";
          }
          else if (discrim < 0) {

            discrim = -discrim;
            cout << "root1 = (" << -B/twoA
                 << ") + i (" << sqrt(discrim) / twoA <<")\n";
            cout << "root2 = (" << -B/twoA
                 << ") - i (" << sqrt(discrim) / twoA << ")\n";
          }
          else {
            root1 = -B / 2 / A;
            root2 = root1;
            cout << "root1 = " << root1 << "\n";
            cout << "root2 = " << root2 << "\n";
          }
       }
       else
         cout << "root = " << (-C / B) << "\n";


       return 0;
    }
```

2. Here is my version of program SWITCH2.CPP:

```
// C++ program which uses the switch statement to implement
// a simple four-function calculator program

#include <iostream.h>

const int TRUE = 1;
const int FALSE = 0;

main()
{
  double x, y, z;
  char op;
  int error = FALSE;

  cout << "Enter the first operand: ";
  cin >> x;
  cout << "Enter the operator: ";
  cin >> op;
```

```
        cout << "Enter the second operand: ";
        cin >> y;

        switch (op) {
          case '+':
            z = x + y;
            break;
          case '-':
            z = x - y;
            break;
          case '*':
            z = x * y;
            break;
          case '/':
            if (y != 0)
              z = x / y;
            else
              error = TRUE;
            break;
          default:
            error = TRUE;
        }

        if (!error)
          cout << x << " " << op << " " << y << " = " << z << "\n";
        else
          cout << "Bad operator or division-by-zero error\n";

        return 0;
}
```

Answers to Day 6, "Loops"

Quiz

1. The statements inside the loop fail to alter the value of I. Consequently, the tested condition is always true and the loop iterates endlessly.

2. The output of the program consists of the numbers 3, 5, and 7.

3. The output of the program is an endless sequence of lines that display the value of 3. The reason for the indefinite looping is that the loop control variable is not incremented.

4. The nested for loops use the same loop control variable. This program will not run.

5. Both `for` loops declare the variable `i` as their loop control variable. The compiler generates an error for this duplication.

6. The condition of the `while` loop is always true. Therefore, the loop iterates endlessly.

7. The program lacks a statement which explicitly initializes the variable `factorial` to 1. Without this statement, the program automatically initializes the variable `factorial` to 0—the wrong value. Consequently, the `for` loop ends up assigning 0 to the variable `factorial` in every iteration. Here is the correct version of the code:

```
int n;
double factorial = 1;
cout << "Enter positive integer : ";
cin >> n;
for (int i = 1; i <= n; i++)
  factorial *= i;
cout << n << "!= " << factorial;
```

Exercises

1. Here is my version of program FOR5.CPP:

```
// Program calculates a sum of odd integers in
// the range of 11 to 121

#include <iostream.h>

const int FIRST = 11;
const int LAST = 121;

main()
{
    double sum = 0;
    for (int i = FIRST; i <= LAST; i += 2)
      sum += (double)i;

    cout << "Sum of odd integers from "
         << FIRST << " to " << LAST << " = "
         << sum << "\n";
    return 0;
}
```

2. Here is my version of program WHILE2.CPP:

```cpp
// Program calculates a sum of squared odd integers in
// the range of 11 to 121

#include <iostream.h>

const int FIRST = 11;
const int LAST = 121;

main()
{
    double sum = 0;
    int i = FIRST;
    while (i <= LAST) {
      sum += double(i * i++);
    }
    cout << "Sum of squared odd integers from "
        << FIRST << " to " << LAST << " = "
        << sum << "\n";
    return 0;
}
```

3. Here is my version of program DOWHILE2.CPP:

```cpp
// Program calculates a sum of squared odd integers in
// the range of 11 to 121

#include <iostream.h>

const int FIRST = 11;
const int LAST = 121;

main()
{
    double sum = 0;
    int i = FIRST;
    do {
      sum += double(i * i++);
    } while (i <= LAST);
    cout << "Sum of squared odd integers from "
        << FIRST << " to " << LAST << " = "
        << sum << "\n";
    return 0;
}
```

Answers to Day 7, "Arrays"

Quiz

1. The program displays the factorials for the numbers 0 to 4:

   ```
   x[0] = 1
   x[1] = 1
   x[2] = 2
   x[3] = 6
   x[4] = 24
   ```

2. The program displays the square roots for the numbers 0 to 4:

   ```
   x[0] = 0
   x[1] = 1
   x[2] = 1.41421
   x[3] = 1.73205
   x[4] = 2
   ```

3. The first `for` loop should iterate between 1 and `MAX-1` and not between 0 and `MAX-1`. The first loop iteration uses an out-of-range index.

Exercise

Here is my version of program ARRAY7.CPP:

```
// C++ program that sorts arrays using the Comb sort method
#include <iostream.h>

const int MAX = 10;
const int TRUE = 1;
const int FALSE = 0;

int obtainNumData()
{
  int m;
  do { // obtain number of data points
    cout << "Enter number of data points [2 to "
         << MAX << "] : ";
    cin >> m;
    cout << "\n";
  } while (m < 2 || m > MAX);
  return m;
}

void inputArray(int intArr[], int n)
```

```
{
  // prompt user for data
  for (int i = 0; i < n; i++) {
    cout << "arr[" << i << "] : ";
    cin >> intArr[i];
  }
}

void showArray(int intArr[], int n)
{
  for (int i = 0; i < n; i++) {
    cout.width(5);
    cout << intArr[i] << " ";
  }
  cout << "\n";
}

void sortArray(int intArr[], int n)
{
  int offset, temp, inOrder;

  offset = n;
  while (offset > 1) {
    offset /= 2;
    do {
      inOrder = TRUE;
      for (int i = 0, j = offset; i < (n - offset); i++, ++) {
        if (intArr[i] > intArr[j]) {
          inOrder = FALSE;
          temp = intArr[i];
          intArr[i] = intArr[j];
          intArr[j] = temp;
        }
      }
    } while (!inOrder);
  }
}

main()
{
  int arr[MAX];
  int n;

  n = obtainNumData();
  inputArray(arr, n);
  cout << "Unordered array is:\n";
  showArray(arr, n);
  sortArray(arr, n);
  cout << "\nSorted array is:\n";
  showArray(arr, n);
  return 0;
}
```

Answers to Day 8, "User-Defined Types and Pointers"

Quiz

1. The enumerated values on and off appear in two different enumerated types. Here is a correct version of these statements:

```
enum Boolean { false, true };
enum State { state_on, state_off };
enum YesNo { yes, no };
enum DiskDriveStatus { drive_on , drive_off };
```

2. False. The enumerated type YesNo is correctly declared.

3. Here is my version of structure intArrStruct:

```
struct intArrStruct {
  int* dataPtr;
  unsigned size;
};
```

4. Here is my version of structure matStruct:

```
struct matStruct {
  double* dataPtr;
  unsigned rows;
  unsigned columns;
};
```

5. The program lacks a delete statement before the return statement. Here is the correct version:

```
#include <iostream.h>
main()
{
  int *p = new int;
  cout << "Enter a number : ";
  cin >> *p;
  cout << "The square of " << *p << " = " << (*p * *p);
  delete p;
  return 0;
}
```

Exercise

Here is my version of PTR6.CPP:

```cpp
/* C++ program that demonstrates pointers to structured types */

#include <iostream.h>
#include <stdio.h>
#include <math.h>

const MAX_RECT = 4;
const TRUE = 1;
const FALSE = -1;

struct point {
  double x;
  double y;
};

struct rect {
  point ulc; // upper left corner
  point lrc; // lower right corner
  double area;
  int id;
};

typedef rect rectArr[MAX_RECT];

main()
{
  rectArr r;
  rect temp;
  rect* pr = r;
  rect* pr2;
  double length, width;
  int offset;
  int inOrder;

  for (int i = 0; i < MAX_RECT; i++, pr++) {
    cout << "Enter (X,Y) coord. for ULC of rect. # "
         << i << " : ";
    cin >> pr->ulc.x >> pr->ulc.y;
    cout << "Enter (X,Y) coord. for LRC of rect. # "
         << i << " : ";
    cin >> pr->lrc.x >> pr->lrc.y;
    pr->id = i;
    length = fabs(pr->ulc.x - pr->lrc.x);
    width = fabs(pr->ulc.y - pr->lrc.y);
    pr->area = length * width;
  }
```

B

```
    // sort the rectangles by areas
offset = MAX_RECT;
do {
  offset = (8 * offset) / 11;
  offset = (offset == 0) ? 1 : offset;
  inOrder = TRUE;
  pr = r;
  pr2 = r + offset;
  for (int i = 0;
       i < MAX_RECT - offset;
       i++, pr++, pr2++)
    if (pr->area > pr2->area) {
      inOrder = FALSE;
      temp = *pr;
      *pr = *pr2;
      *pr2 = temp;
    }
} while (!(offset == 1 && inOrder));

pr = r; // reset pointer
// display rectangles sorted by area
for (i = 0; i < MAX_RECT; i++, pr++)
  printf("Rect # %d has area %5.4lf\n", pr->id, pr->area);
return 0;
}
```

Answers to Day 9, "Strings"

Quiz

1. The string s1 is smaller than string s2. Consequently, the call to function strcpy causes a program bug.

2. Using the function strncpy to include the constant MAX as the third argument ensures that string s1 receives MAX characters (excluding the null terminator) from string s1:

```
#include <iostream.h>
#include <string.h>
const in MAX = 10;
main()
{
  char s1[MAX+1];
  char s2[] = "12345678901234567890";
```

```
        strncpy(s1, s2, MAX);
        cout << "String 1 is " << s1
             << "\nString 2 is " << s2;
        return 0;
    }
```

3. Because the string in variable s1 is greater than that in variable s2, the statement assigns a positive number (1 to be exact) in variable i.

4. The call to function strcmp compares the substrings "C++" with "Basic" because the arguments include an offset value. Because "C++" is greater than "Basic", the statement assigns a positive number (1 to be exact) in variable i.

5. False! Although the basic idea for the function is sound, dimensioning the local variable requires a constant. One solution is to use the same constant, call it MAX_STRING_SIZE, to size up the arguments of parameter s:

```
int hasNoLowerCase(const char* s)
{
    char s2[MAX_STRING_SIZE+1];
    strcpy(s2, s);
    strupr(s2);
    return (strcmp(s1, s2) == 0) ? 1 : 0);
}
```

The other solution uses dynamic allocation to create a dynamic local string which stores a copy of the argument of parameter s. This solution works with all arguments of parameter s:

```
int hasNoLowerCase(const char* s)
{
    char *s2 = new char[strlen(s)+1];
    int i;
    strcpy(s2, s);
    strupr(s2);
    // store result in variable i
    i = (strcmp(s1, s2) == 0) ? 1 : 0);
    delete [] s2; // first delete local dynamic string
    return i; // then return the result of the function
}
```

Exercises

1. Here is my version of function strlen:

```
int strlen(const char* s)
{
  int i = 0;
  while (s[i] != '\0')
    i++;
  return i;
}
```

2. Here is the other version of function strlen:

```
int strlen(const char* s)
{
  char *p = s;
  while (p++ != '\0')
    /* do nothing */;
  return p - s;
}
```

3. Here is my version of program STRING5.CPP:

```
#include <stdio.h>
#include <string.h>

main()
{
  char str[] = "2*(X+Y)/(X+Z) - (X+10)/(Y-5)";
  char strCopy[41];
  char* tkn[3] = { "+-*/ ()", "( )", "+-*/ " };
  char* ptr;

  strcpy(strCopy, str); // copy str into strCopy
  printf("%s\n", str);
  printf("Using token string %s\n", tkn[0]);
  // the first call
  ptr = strtok(str, tkn[0]);
  printf("String is broken into: %s",ptr);
  while (ptr) {
    printf("  ,%s", ptr);
    // must make first argument a NULL character
    ptr = strtok(NULL, tkn[0]);
  }

  strcpy(str, strCopy); // restore str
  printf("\nUsing token string %s\n", tkn[1]);
  // the first call
  ptr = strtok(str, tkn[1]);
  printf("String is broken into: %s",ptr);
```

```
while (ptr) {
  printf("  ,%s", ptr);
  // must make first argument a NULL character
  ptr = strtok(NULL, tkn[1]);
}

strcpy(str, strCopy); // restore str
printf("\nUsing token string %s\n", tkn[2]);
// the first call
ptr = strtok(str, tkn[2]);
printf("String is broken into: %s",ptr);
while (ptr) {
  printf("  ,%s", ptr);
  // must make first argument a NULL character
  ptr = strtok(NULL, tkn[2]);
}
printf("\n\n");
return 0;
}
```

Answers to Day 10, "Advanced Functions Parameters"

Quiz

1. The function is

   ```
   double factorial(int i)
   { return (i > 1) ? double(i) * factorial(i-1) : 1; }
   ```

2. At first glance, the function may seem correct, though somewhat unusual. The case labels offer quick results for arguments of 0 to 4. However, the catch-all default clause traps arguments that are greater than 4 *and* are negative values! The latter kind of arguments causes the recursion to overflow the memory resources. Here is a corrected version which returns a very large negative number when the argument is a negative number:

   ```
   double factorial(int i)
   {
     if (i > -1)
       switch (i) {
           case 0:
   ```

```
            case 1:
                return 1;
                break;
            case 2:
                return 2;
                break;
            case 3:
                return 6;
                break;
            case 4:
                return 24;
                break;
            default:
                return double(i) * factorial(i-1);
    }
  else
    return -1.0e+30; // numeric code for a bad argument
}
```

3. The nonrecursive version of function Fibonacci is

```
double Fibonacci(int n)
{
  double Fib0 = 0;
  double Fib1 = 1;
  double Fib2;

  if (n == 0)
    return 0;
  else if (n == 1 || n == 2)
    return 1;
  else
    for (int i = 0; i <= n; i++) {
      Fib2 = Fib0 + Fib1;
      Fib0 = Fib1;
      Fib1 = Fib2;
    }
    return Fib2;
}
```

4. True. The first function uses a formal reference parameter, whereas the second parameter uses a pointer parameter.

Exercise

Here is my version of program ADVFUN9.CPP:

```
/*
   C++ program that uses pointers to functions to implement a
   a linear regression program that supports temporary
   mathematical transformations.
*/

#include <iostream.h>
#include <math.h>

const unsigned MAX_SIZE = 100;

typedef double vector[MAX_SIZE];

struct regression {
   double Rsqr;
   double slope;
   double intercept;
};

// declare array of function pointers
double (*f[2])(double);

// declare function prototypes
void initArray(double*, double*, unsigned);
double linear(double);
double sqr(double);
double reciprocal(double);
void calcRegression(double*, double*, unsigned, regression&,
                    double (*f[2])(double));
int select_transf(const char*);

main()
{
   char ans;
   unsigned count;
   vector x, y;
   regression stat;
   int trnsfx, trnsfy;

   do {
      cout << "Enter array size [2.."
           << MAX_SIZE << "] : ";
      cin >> count;
   } while (count <= 1 || count > MAX_SIZE);

   // initialize array
   initArray(x, y, count);
```

```
// transform data
do {
  // set the transformation functions
  trnsfx = select_transf("X");
  trnsfy = select_transf("Y");
  // set function pointer f[0]
  switch (trnsfx) {
   case 0 :
     f[0] = linear;
     break;
   case 1 :
     f[0] = log;
     break;
   case 2 :
     f[0] = sqrt;
     break;
   case 3 :
     f[0] = sqr;
     break;
   case 4 :
     f[0] = reciprocal;
     break;
   default :
     f[0] = linear;
     break;
  }
  // set function pointer f[1]
  switch (trnsfy) {
   case 0 :
     f[1] = linear;
     break;
   case 1 :
     f[1] = log;
     break;
   case 2 :
     f[1] = sqrt;
     break;
   case 3 :
     f[1] = sqr;
     break;
   case 4 :
     f[1] = reciprocal;
     break;
   default :
     f[1] = linear;
     break;
  }

  calcRegression(x, y, count, stat, f);
```

B

```cpp
        cout << "\n\n\n\n"
             << "R-square = " << stat.Rsqr << "\n"
             << "Slope = " << stat.slope << "\n"
             << "Intercept = " << stat.intercept << "\n\n\n";
        cout << "Want to use other transformations? (Y/N) ";
        cin >> ans;
    } while (ans == 'Y' || ans == 'y');
    return 0;
}

void initArray(double* x, double* y, unsigned count)
// read data for array from the keyboard
{
    for (unsigned i = 0; i < count; i++, x++, y++) {
        cout << "X[" << i << "] : ";
        cin >> *x;
        cout << "Y[" << i << "] : ";
        cin >> *y;
    }
}

int select_transf(const char* var_name)
// select choice of transformation
{

    int choice = -1;
    cout << "\n\n\n";
    cout << "select transformation for variable " << var_name
         << "\n\n\n"
         << "0) No transformation\n"
         << "1) Logarithmic transformation\n"
         << "2) Square root transformation\n"
         << "3) Square   transformation\n"
         << "4) Reciprocal transformation\n";
    while (choice < 0 || choice > 4) {
        cout << "\nSelect choice by number : ";
        cin >> choice;
    }
    return choice;
}

double linear(double x)
{ return x; }

double sqr(double x)
{ return x * x; }

double reciprocal(double x)
{ return 1.0 / x; }
```

703

```
void calcRegression(double* x,
                     double* y,
                     unsigned count,
                     regression &stat,
                     double (*f[2])(double))

{
    double meanx, meany, sdevx, sdevy;
    double sum = (double) count, sumx = 0, sumy = 0;
    double sumxx = 0, sumyy = 0, sumxy = 0;
    double xdata, ydata;

    for (unsigned i = 0; i < count; i++) {
        xdata = (*f[0])(*(x+i));
        ydata = (*f[1])(*(y+i));
        sumx += xdata;
        sumy += ydata;
        sumxx += sqr(xdata);
        sumyy += sqr(ydata);
        sumxy += xdata * ydata;
    }

    meanx = sumx / sum;
    meany = sumy / sum;
    sdevx = sqrt((sumxx - sqr(sumx) / sum)/(sum-1.0));
    sdevy = sqrt((sumyy - sqr(sumy) / sum)/(sum-1.0));
    stat.slope = (sumxy - meanx * meany * sum) /
                  sqr(sdevx)/(sum-1);
    stat.intercept = meany - stat.slope * meanx;
    stat.Rsqr = sqr(sdevx / sdevy * stat.slope);
}
```

Answers to Day 11, "Object-Oriented Programming and C++ Classes"

Quiz

1. By default, the members of a class are protected. Therefore the class declaration has no public member and cannot be used to create instances.

2. The third constructor has a default argument, which makes it redundant with the fourth constructor. The C++ compiler detects such an error.

3. True. `String("Hello Visual C++")` creates a temporary instance of class `String` and then assigns it to the instance s.

4. Yes. The new statements are valid.

Exercise

Here is the implementation of function main in my version of program CLASS7.CPP:

```
main()
{

    Complex c[5];
    c[1].assign(3, 5);
    c[2].assign(7, 5);
    c[4].assign(2, 3);

    c[3] = c[1] + c[2];
    cout << c[1] << " + " << c[2] << " = " << c[3] << "\n";
    cout << c[3] << " + " << c[4] << " = ";
    c[3] += c[4];
    cout << c[3] << "\n";
    return 0;
}
```

Answers to Day 12, "Basic Stream File I/O"

Quiz

1. False. The read and write functions cannot store and recall the dynamic data, which is accessed by a pointer member of a structure or a class.

2. True.

3. True.

4. False.

Exercise

Here is the code for member function binSearch and the updated function main in program IO4.CPP (the output also shows the new global constant NOT_FOUND and the updated class declaration):

```
const unsigned NOT_FOUND = 0xffff;

class VmArray
{
   protected:
     fstream f;
     unsigned size;
     double badIndex;

   public:
     VmArray(unsigned Size, const char* filename);
     ~VmArray()
       { f.close(); }
     unsigned getSize() const
       { return size; }
     boolean writeElem(const char* str, unsigned index);
     boolean readElem(char* str, unsigned index);
     void Combsort();
     unsigned binSearch(const char* search);
};

unsigned VmArray::binSearch(const char* search)
{
  unsigned low = 0;
  unsigned high = size - 1;
  unsigned median;
  char str[STR_SIZE+1];
  int result;

  do {
    median = (low + high) / 2;
    readElem(str, median);
    result = strcmp(search, str);
    if (result > 0)
      low = median + 1;
    else
      high = median - 1;
  } while (result != 0 && low <= high);
  return (result == 0) ? median : NOT_FOUND;
}

main()
{
  const unsigned NUM_ELEMS = 10;
  char* data[] = { "Michigan", "California", "Virginia", "Maine",
                   "New York", "Florida", "Nevada", "Alaska",
                   "Ohio", "Maryland" };
  VmArray arr(NUM_ELEMS, "arr.dat");
  char str[STR_SIZE+1];
  char c;
  unsigned index;
```

```
      // assign values to array arr
      for (unsigned i = 0; i < arr.getSize(); i++) {
        strcpy(str, data[i]);
        arr.writeElem(str, i);
      }
      // display unordered array
      cout << "Unsorted arrays is:\n";
      for (i = 0; i < arr.getSize(); i++) {
        arr.readElem(str, i);
        cout << str << "\n";
      }
      // pause
      cout << "\nPress any key and then Return to sort the array...";
      cin >> c;
      // sort the array
      arr.Combsort();
      // display sorted array
      cout << "Sorted arrays is:\n";
      for (i = 0; i < arr.getSize(); i++) {
        arr.readElem(str, i);
        cout << str << "\n"
      }
      // pause
      cout << "\nPress any key and then Return to search the array...";
      cin >> c;
      // search for array elements using the pointer data
      for (i = 0; i < NUM_ELEMS; i++) {
        index = arr.binSearch(data[i]);
        if (index != NOT_FOUND)
          cout << "Found " << data[i]
               << " at index " << index << "\n";
        else
          cout << "No match for " << data[i] << "\n";
      }
      return 0;
    }
```

Answers to Day 13, "Programming Windows Using the MFC Library"

Quiz

1. The message box needs the following MB_*xxxx* expression:

```
MB_YESNOCANCEL ¦ MB_ICONQUESTION
```

2. The message box needs the following MB_*xxxx* expression:

   MB_OK ¦ MB_ICONEXCLAMATION

3. The MessageBox function returns IDYES.

4. The MessageBox function returns IDCANCEL.

Answers to Day 14, "Creating Basic MFC Applications"

Quiz

1. True.

2. False. The associated function is OnActivate and not Onactivate.

3. True.

4. True.

Answers to Day 15, "Basic Windows"

Quiz

1. False. The function OnPaint also initially draws the window. Windows are drawn and redrawn when the application receives the Windows message WM_PAINT.

2. False. The inherited scrolling function offers no scrolling features.

3. False. The member function OnSize is only required when the window class scrolls its contents. In this case, the run-time system supplies the OnSize with the updated window dimensions.

4. False. The bascence of function OnKeyDown only disables using the cursor control keys, such as PageUp and PageDown.

Answers to Day 16, "MFC Controls"

Quiz

1. False. Only the text for static controls with the SS_SIMPLE style are unchangeable.

2. True.

3. False. The pointer is needed at least to delete the dynamic instance of the static control.

4. True.

5. True, because every control is a window.

6. False. The Windows messages emitted by a push button must be mapped using the ON_BTN_CLICKED map.

Answers to Day 17, "Grouped Controls"

Quiz

1. False. The check box can replace the two radio buttons only if these buttons offer opposite alternatives.

2. True.

3. True. Each check box can be independently toggled.

4. False. Radio buttons in a group control are mutually exclusive.

Answers to Day 18, "List Boxes"

Quiz

1. True.

2. True.

3. False. The list box notification message LBN_CHANGE indicates that a new item is selected.

4. False. The list box notification message LBN_DBLCLK indicates that a list item is selected with a double mouse click.

5. False. The LBS_STANDARD style does include the LBS_SORT style and therefore creates ordered list boxes.

Answers to Day 19, "Scroll Bars and Combo Boxes"

Quiz

1. True.

2. False. The correct notification message is CBN_EDITUPDATE.

3. False. The items in the list box components are sorted, but not unique. You can insert multiple copies of the same string.

4. True, otherwise the items inserted in the list box components are not in chronological order. Instead, they are in sorted order.

5. False.

6. True. The program illustrates this concept: when you alter the value of either control, the other control changes accordingly.

7. False. The program CTLSCRL1.CPP demonstrates that you can alter the range of values for a scroll bar at run-time.

Answers to Day 20, "Dialog Boxes"

Quiz

1. False. You may compile the .RC files after you compile your .CPP files.

2. False. The OK and Cancel buttons are mandatory.

3. True. However, these buttons must be treated in the program as the OK and Cancel buttons. In other words, you can alter the caption of standard OK and Cancel buttons.

4. False. The best examples of nested dialog boxes are those related to setting up the printer.

5. False. Dialog boxes can be stand-alone windows.

Answers to Day 21, "MDI Windows"

Quiz

1. False.

2. False.

3. False.

4. True! Congratulations on completing the book.

Glossary

address: The location of each memory byte in the computer's memory. The lowest memory address is 0. The highest memory address depends on the amount of memory in a computer.

ancestor class: A class that is one or more levels higher in the class hierarchy than a referenced class.

argument: The value that is passed to a parameter of a function or a procedure.

array: A collection of variables which share the same name and use one or more indices to access an individual member.

ASCII: Acronym for American Standard Code for Information Interchange.

ASCII file: A file which contains readable text. ASCII files are also called *text files*.

AUTOEXEC.BAT: A special batch file which the computer automatically executes if it finds it in the root directory of the boot disk.

backup file: A duplicate copy of a file which protects your work in case you damage the text or data in the main file.

.BAK: The common file extension for backup files.

base class: The root of a class hierarchy. A base class has no parent class.

batch file: An executable file which contains MS-DOS commands and other special commands. Batch files assist in automating various tasks.

binary: A numbering system which includes 0 and 1.

bit: The short name for *binary digit*. Bits are the smallest units of data storage. Programs commonly use groups of 8, 16, 32, and 64 bits to represent different kinds of data.

Boolean: Synonomous with logical (true or false). The word Boolean comes from the name of the English mathematician George Bool who studied logical values and created the truth table.

bubblesort: The slowest and simplest method for ordering the elements of an array in ascending or descending order.

buffer: A memory location where transient data flows in and out.

bug: A common name for a logical program error.

byte: A unit of data storage which contains 8 bits.

.C: The extension of a C file.

CGA: Acronym for Color Graphics Adapter. CGA screens have a resolution of 640 by 200 pixels.

class: A category of objects.

clipboard: A special memory area in the Windows environment which holds text that you copied or deleted.

clock tick: The duration based on the CPU's internal clock. One second has 18.2 clock ticks.

Comb sort: A new and efficient method for sorting the elements of an array. This method is based on improving the bubblesort method.

compiler: A tool which converts the source code of a program file into a binary object code (.OBJ) file. The object code must be linked with other object files and library files to generate an executable .EXE file.

concatenation: The process of joining two or more strings by chaining their characters.

conditional loop: A loop which iterates until or while a tested condition is true.

CONFIG.SYS: The name of the system configuration file. When a machine boots, it reads the CONFIG.SYS file in the root directory of the boot disk.

constant: Information that remains fixed during the execution of a program.

.CPP: The extension of a C++ source file.

CPU: Acronym for Central Processing Unit, the computer's brain.

crash: The state in which a computer seems to freeze and does not respond to the keyboard, mouse, or any other input device.

cursor: The blinking underline or block which appears on the screen to indicate where the next character insertion will occur.

data member: The fields in a class which store data.

data processing: The manipulating and/or managing of information.

data record: A collection of data items which convey meaningful information. Your mailing address, for example, is a data record.

debug: To detect and remove logical errors in the program.

debugger: A tool which assists you in debugging the program. The environment contains a powerful debugger.

.DEF: The extension of a Windows program definition file.

default: A preselected action or value that is used when no other action or value is offered.

descendant class: Any child class derived from a parent class.

dialog box: A special pop-up screen which prompts you for input.

directory: A section or compartment of a hard, floppy, or electronic disk which contains files.

disk: The magnetic medium which stores data.

disk drive: The device which reads and loads data and programs in a disk.

diskette: A removable thin disk. Also called *floppy disk.*

display: The screen, console, or monitor in a computer.

display adapter: The board inside a computer which assists in displaying text and graphics.

DOS: Acronym for Disk Operating System.

drag: The act of holding a mouse button down while moving the mouse. This action moves a window from one location in the screen to another.

EGA: Acronym for Enhanced Graphics Adapter. The resolution of an EGA display is 640 by 350 pixels.

element (of an array): The member of an array, which is accessed by specifying one or more indices.

file: The name of a location in a disk which contains a program, text, or other data.

file extension: The three letters used by DOS files to identify the type of a file. Programs have file extensions of .COM or .EXE.

file I/O: File input and/or output.

filename: The name of a DOS file.

floppy disk: *See* **diskette**.

format: The image or map used to output data.

function: A subprogram that executes one or more statements and returns a single value.

function key: The keys labeled F1 to F10 on a keyboard. Some keyboards also have keys labeled F11 and F12.

global variable: A variable that is accessible to all functions and procedures in a program.

graphics monitor: A monitor that is able to display high-resolution graphics.

.H: The extension of a header file.

header file: A file that contains the declarations of constants, data types, function prototypes, and class declarations.

hertz: The unit of measuring frequency. One hertz is one cycle per second. Abbreviated Hz.

HGA: Acronym for Hercules Graphics Adapter.

inheritance: The ability of a class to reuse data members and member functions in a parent class.

input: The data which a program obtains from the keyboard, disk drive, communication port, or any other input device.

I/O: Acronym for Input/Output.

kilobyte (K): A unit of measuring memory. 1K is 1024 bytes.

least significant bit: The rightmost bit in a byte, word, or any other unit of memory.

linker: A tool that combines the various .OBJ files generated by the compiler with the various library files to create the executable .EXE file.

local variable: A variable which is declared inside a function or procedure.

loop: A set of statements which are repeatedly executed.

main module: The program section containing the function `main`.

.MAK: The extension of a project make file.

make file: A special file which invokes the compiler and linker as needed to compile and link the source and/or object files.

math operator: A symbol which performs a mathematical operation, such as addition, subtraction, multiplication, division, and raising to powers.

matrix: A two-dimensional array. The elements of a matrix are accessed by specifying the row and column indices.

MCGA: Acronym for Multi-Color Graphics Adapter.

G

MDA: Acronym for Monochrome Display Adapter.

megabyte (M): The unit of memory. 1M is approximately one million bytes.

member function: A function that is a member in a class.

memory: The part of the computer that retains programs and data while the computer is on.

menu: A display which offers a set of options to select from.

menu-driven: A program which depends on one or more menus to perform its tasks, as guided by the user.

message: What an object-oriented program does to an object.

method: How an object-oriented program manipulates an object.

modulus: The integer remainder of a division.

monitor: The screen, console, or display.

monochrome: Single color. Monochrome monitors can display neither colors nor high-resolution graphics.

most significant bit: The leftmost bit in a byte, word, or other unit of memory.

MS-DOS: Acronym for Microsoft Disk Operator System.

multidimensional arrays: Arrays which have multiple subscripts.

nested loop: A loop inside another loop.

null string: An empty string.

numeric functions: A function which returns a numerical value.

object: An instance of a class.

object file: The output of the compiler. The linker combines various object and library files to create the executable .EXE file.

object-oriented programming (OOP): Programming techniques which focus on modeling objects and their operations.

open loop: A loop which in principle iterates indefinitely. In practice, most open loops use an exit mechanism located in a statement inside the loop.

order of operators: The priority of executing operations in an expression.

output device: A device which receives output. Common output devices are the screen, the printer, the disk drive, and the communication port. Some output devices also support input, such as the communication port and the disk drive.

palette: A set of possible colors.

parameter: A special variable which appears after the declaration of a function or procedure, and which fine-tunes the operations of the function or procedure.

passing by reference: The task of passing an argument to a function or procedure by providing its reference. Consequently, the parameter receiving the reference becomes an alias to the argument. Any changes made to the parameter inside the function or procedure also affects the argument.

passing by value: The task of passing an argument to a function or procedure by providing a copy of its value. Consequently, any changes made to the parameter inside the function or procedure do not affect the argument.

pixel: The short name for picture element.

pointer: A special variable which stores the address of another variable or system information.

polymorphism: The feature of object-oriented programming that supports abstract functionality.

precedence of operators: *See* **order of operators**.

program: A collection of executable statements or instructions.

programming language: The high-level human interface for communicating with a machine.

pseudocode: A text outline which describes in English the tasks of a program.

RAM: *See* **random access memory (RAM)**.

random access file: A file which permits you to access its fixed-length records for input and output by specifying the record number. Random access files are suitable for databases.

random access memory (RAM):   Memory that can be accessed by specifying an address.

.RC: The extension of a resource script file.

read only memory (ROM):   A class of memory which contains fixed data.

record: A unit of storing information in a data file. Typically, text files have variable-length records. Random access files contain fixed-length records.

G

relational operators: Symbols which compare two compatible data items and return a logical value.

.RES: The extension of a compiled resource file.

resolution: The sharpness of an image which appears on a screen.

resource file: A file which defines resources to be used by one or more Windows applications. Resource files can be shared by applications written in different programming languages. Resources include strings, keyboard, menu, controls, and dialog box resources.

ROM: *See* **read only memory (ROM).**

scientific notation: A special form for representing numbers by specifying the mantissa and the exponent. In a number such as 1.23E+44, the 1.23 is the mantissa and +44 is the exponent (the power of ten). Therefore 1.23E+44 is a more convenient way to write 1.23 x 10+44.

sequential file: A file which stores readable text using variable-length records.

single-dimensional arrays: An array which requires a single subscript to access its elements.

sorting: The task of arranging the elements of an array in either ascending or descending order. The array is ordered using part or all of the value in each element.

static variable: A variable with a fixed memory location. Usually, static variables are declared in functions and are able to retain their values between function calls.

string constant: A constant associated with a string literal.

string literal: A set of characters enclosed in a pair of double quotes.

string variable: A variable which stores a string of characters.

structure: A user-defined data type. C++ allows you to define a structure using the TYPE statement.

structured array: An array that contains elements that have a user-defined data type.

structured variable: A variable whose type is a user-defined data type.

subdirectory: A directory which is connected to a parent directory.

subscript: The index of an array.

SVGA: Acronym for Super Vector Graphics Array. *See also* VGA.

syntax error: An error in writing a statement.

system hang: *See* **crash**.

text file: *See* **ASCII file**.

unary operator: Symbols that require only one operand.

user-defined data type: *See* **structure**.

user-defined functions: A function defined by a programmer to conceptually extend the C++ language and serve the host program.

variable: A tagged memory location which stores data.

variable-length record: A record with a varying number of bytes or characters.

variable-length string variables: A string variable which can accommodate a varying number of characters.

variable scope: The visibility of a variable in the different components of a program.

VGA: Acronym for Vector Graphics Array. The resolution of VGA is 640 by 480 pixels.

virtual function: A function which, when overriden by a descendant class, must have the same purpose and parameter list as the one in an ancestor class.

Windows message: A message sent by one Windows component to another.

word: A unit of data storage which contains 2 bytes or 16 bits.

G

Index

Symbols

! overloaded operator, 334
&& operator, 80
& ampersand character
   hot-keys, 663
   in strings, 452
++ increment operators, 64-66
~ tilde, 304
*= operator, 69
-= operator, 69
/= operator, 69
<< extraction operator, 24, 334
= operator, 76
== operator, 76, 80
>> insertion operator, 37, 334
¦¦ operator, 80

A

abstract classes, 359
accelerators, 664-665
ACCELERATORS statement, 664
accTableName field, 664
adapters, display, 716
add friend function, 321
additive operators, 85
addresses, 206, 714
   nonreference pointer parameters, 275
AddString member function, 524, 580-581

ADVFUN1.CPP program, 261-263
ADVFUN2.CPP program, 263-265
ADVFUN3.CPP program, 265-267
ADVFUN4.CPP program, 268-269
ADVFUN5.CPP program, 270-271
ADVFUN6.CPP program, 272-274
ADVFUN7.CPP program, 275-278
ADVFUN8.CPP program, 281-287
AFXWIN.H header file, 386
ALT option, 665
American Standard Code for Information
   Interchange, see ASCII
ampersand character (&)
   hot-keys, defining, 663
   in strings, 452
ancestor class, 714
API functions, 362-366
   invoking, 367-370
App Studio, creating dialog boxes, 603
application classes, 383-387
   CWindowApp, 647
application-exec functions, 366
applications
   calculator, 492-515, 585-597
      Command-Line Calculator, 465-485
   count-down timer, 566-567
   CTLCOMB1.EXE, 585-597
   CTLLST2.EXE, 544-546
   MDI, 639
      building, 637
      features, 636-637

MFC, 382-387
   closing windows, 406-409
   menu selections, 393-400
   multiple instances, 400-405
   window operations, 387-393
MINWINAP.EXE, 387-393
WINDOW2.EXE, 431-447
Windows, developing, 356-379
AppWizard command (Project menu), 14
AppWizard dialog box, 14
`area()` member function, 311
arguments, 714
   default, 47-50
      `overloaded` functions, 50-51
   passing arrays as, 260-263
   passing by reference, 267
   strings as, 263-265
   structures as, 265-267
arithmetic
arithmetic expressions, 63
arithmetic operators, 60-63
array parameters in functions, 157-161
ARRAY1.CPP program, 152-154
ARRAY2.CPP program, 154-156
ARRAY3.CPP program, 156-157
ARRAY4.CPP program, 158-161
ARRAY5.CPP program, 162-165
ARRAY6.CPP program, 167-172
arrays, 714
   dynamic, 218
   function pointer, declaring, 279
   multidimensional, 718
   passing as arguments, 260-263
   pointers, 209-214
   searching, 165-172
   single-dimensional, 151-154, 720
      declaring, 150-151
      initializing, 154-157
   sorting, 161-165
   structured, 720
   three-dimensional, 172-176
      function parameters, 178-181
      initializing, 176-178

two-dimensional, 172-176
      function parameters, 178-181
      initializing, 176-178
   virtual, 347
ASCII (American Standard Code for Information Interchange), 714
   files, 714
`assign` member function, 300
assigning
   breakpoints, 17
   strings, 230-232
assignment operators, 66-69, 86
`assignMenu` private function, 399
`atom-management` functions, 366
AUTOEXEC.BAT file, 714
automatic data conversion, 72-75

B

backup files, 714
.BAK file extension, 714
`base` classes, 714
   declaring, 296-297
batch files, 714
`BEGIN_MESSAGE_MAP` macro, 374, 392
binary, 714
binary digits, *see* bits
binary object code files, *see* OBJ files
binary search method, 166
binary trees, accessing, 274-278
`binarySearch` function, 171
bit-manipulating operators, 81-83
`Bitmap` function, 364
bits, 714
BITS1.CPP program, 82-83
bitwise operators, 85
bitwise shift operators, 85
blocks, defining, 12
`bNoPaint` member function, 446
bookmarks, 13
Boole, George, 714

Boolean, 714
    data members, IsFirst, 405
    expressions, 77-81
    identifiers, predefined, 77
    parameters, IsMainWindow, 405
braces, curly, 12
break statement, 132, 141
breakpoints, assigning, 17
Browse menu, 16-17
bubblesorting, 714
buffers, 714
    data transfer, 610-613
    Undo, altering size, 9
bugs, 714
Build command (Project menu), 15, 20-21
building, menu resources, 662-665
button messages, 464
buttons, manipulating, 465
bytes, 714

C

.C file extension, 714
C++, programming, 4
C++ stream library, 332
    class hierarchies, 332
calcRegression function, 287
calculations, iterative, 137
calculator application, 492-515, 585-597
calling, functions, 41-42
CAppDialog class, 620, 630
CAppMDIChild window class, 647-650
CAppMDIFrame class, 647-648
CAppWindow constructor, 392, 405, 541, 556
CAppWindow window class, 441-442,
    480-481, 513-515, 556, 620-621, 631-632
CAPTION statement, 667
Caret function, 363
case-sensitive searches, 10-11
CButton class, 463-464, 489-490
    group boxes, 491
    radio button controls, 490-491

cCircle class, 311
CCmdTarget class, 359
CComboBox class, 577-583
CComboBoxData class, declaring, 612
cCylinder class, 311
CDataExchange class, 611
CDC class, 360
CDC subhierarchy, 360
CDialog class, constructing dialog boxes,
    602-603
CEdit class, 454-462
Central Processing Unit, see CPU
CGA (Color Graphics Adapter), 715
chaining, >> inserter operator, 94
char type, treatment, 75
characters
    ampersand (&), defining hot-keys, 663
    data type, printf function, 99-100
    in strings, locating, 246-248
check box control, 488-490
    styles, 489
check boxes, messages, 490
CheckBox member, 613
CHECKBOX statement, 672
CHECKED option, 663
class
    hierarchies, 294
        C++ stream library, 332
        declaring, 307-311
    parameters, 669
CLASS statement, 668
CLASS1.CPP program, 299-300
CLASS2.CPP program, 304-307
CLASS3.CPP program, 309-311
CLASS4.CPP program, 314-316
CLASS5.CPP program, 319-321
CLASS6.CPP program, 323-325
classes, 294-295, 715
    abstract, 359
    ancestor, 714
    application, CWindowApp, 647

classes (continued)
   base, 714
      declaring, 296-297
   CAppDialog, 620, 630
   CAppWindow, 441-442, 480-481,
      513-515, 620-621, 631-632
   CButton, 463-464, 489-490
      group boxes, 491
      radio button controls, 490-491
   cCircle, 311
   CCmdTarget, 359
   CComboBox, 577-583
   CComboBoxData, 612
   cCylinder, 311
   CDataExchange, 611
   CDC, 360
   CDialog, constructing dialog boxes,
      602-603
   CEdit, 454-462
   child window, CAppMDIChild, 647-650
   CListBox, 520-530
   CMDIChildWnd, 638-639
   CMDIFrameWnd, 636-638
   CMenu, 359
   CObject, 359
   Complex, 320-321, 325
   cRectangle, 315-316
   CScollBarData, 612
   CScrollBar, 562-566
   cSquare, 315-316
   CStatic, 450-454
   CStringArray, 611
   CWinApp, 359
   CxButton, 480
   CxEdit, 480
   data transfer, 611
   derived, 295-296, 307-311
   descendant, 308, 716
   file stream, 333
   MDI frame, 638
      CAppMDIFrame, 647-648
   sections, 297-300
   VmArray, 351
ClassWizard, 14

ClassWizard command (Browse menu), 17
ClassWizard dialog box, 17
Clear All Bookmarks command (View
   menu), 13
clipboard, 715
   CEdit member functions, 456
   functions, 363
   messages, 373
clipping functions, 364
CListBox class, 520-530
   indexes, 522
CListBox member functions, utilizing,
   531-544
clock ticks, 715
Close command
   File menu, 7, 20-21
   Project menu, 14, 25
close function, 334
closing, windows, 406-409
   MDI, 7
CM_EDITCOPY command, 400
CM_EDITCUT command, 400
CM_EDITPASTE command, 400
CM_EXIT command, 392
CM_HELP command, 400
CM_LONGMENU command, 393, 399
CM_SHORTMENU command, 393, 399
CMArrangeIcons member function, 650
CMCalc member function, 377
CMCalcBtn member function, 483, 597
CMCascadeChildren member function, 650
CMCloseChildren member function, 649
CMCountChildren member function, 649
CMCreateChild member function, 648-649
CMDialog member function, 621, 632
CMDIChildWnd class, 638-639
CMDIFrameWnd class, 636-638
CMenu class, 359
CMExit member function, 485
CMExitBtn member function, 576, 597
CMSendBtn member function, 631
CMStartBtn member function, 576
CMStore member function, 377, 484

CMTileChldren member function, 650
CObject class, 359
Collections subhierarchy, 361
Color command (Options menu), 19
Color Graphics Adapter, *see* CGA
color-palette functions, 364
colored syntax, selecting, 13
Colors dialog box, 19
Comb sorting, 161, 715
combination function, 273-274
combo box controls, 576-597
   styles, 578
combo boxes
   as history list boxes, 584-585
   notification messages, 584
COMBOBOX statement, 675-676
ComboBoxData member, 612
Combsort function, 351
comma operator, 83-84
Command-Line Calculator Application,
  465-485
   controls, 465-466
command-line switches, 5
commands
   Browse menu
      ClassWizard, 17
      Go to Definition, 16
      Go to Reference, 17
      Next, 17
      Open, 17
      Pop Context, 17
      Previous, 17
   CM_EDITCOPY, 400
   CM_EDITCUT, 400
   CM_EDITPASTE, 400
   CM_EXIT command, 392
   CM_HELP, 400
   CM_LONGMENU, 393, 399
   CM_SHORTMENU, 393, 399
   Edit menu
      Copy, 9
      Cut, 9
      Delete, 9
      Find, 9-10, 13
      Find Matching Brace, 12
      Paste, 9
      Read Only, 12
      Redo, 9
      Replace, 11
      Undo, 8-9
   File menu
      Close, 7, 20-21
      Exit, 8, 25
      New, 6, 20-21
      Open, 6
      Page Setup, 8
      Print, 8
      Save, 7
      Save All, 8
      Save As, 7, 20-21
   Options menu
      Color, 19
      Debug, 18
      Directories, 18
      Editor, 18
      Fonts, 19
      Project, 18
      Tools, 18, 19
      Workspace, 19
   Project menu
      AppWizard, 14
      Build, 15, 20-21
      Close, 14, 25
      Compile File, 15
      Edit, 14
      Execute, 15, 20-21
      Load Workspace, 16
      New, 14, 20-21
      Open, 14
      Project, 16
      Rebuild All, 15
      Save Workspace, 16
      Scan All Dependencies, 16
      Scan Dependencies, 16
      Stop Build, 15

commands (continued)
  View menu
    Clear All Bookmarks, 13
    Line, 12
    Mixed Source/Asm, 12
    Next Bookmark, 13
    Next Error, 12
    Previous Bookmark, 13
    Previous Error, 12
    Status Bar, 13
    Syntax Coloring, 13
    Toggle Bookmark, 13
    Toolbar, 13
    WM_COMMAND, 392
comments, 24
Common User Access standard, *see* CUA
communications function, 366
Compile File command (Project menu), 15
compiler directives, 24
compilers, 715
Complex class, 320-321, 325
concatenation, 715
  string, 233-237
conditional expressions, 77
conditional loops, 715
  do-while, 134-137
CONFIG.SYS file, 715
const parameters, 261
CONST1.CPP program, 37
CONST2.CPP program, 38-39
constants, 715
  declaring, 35-39
  formal, 35-39
  horizontal scrolling, 430
  macro-based, 35-38
  MAX_NUM, 143
  MIN_NUM, 143
  string, 720
  TOLERANCE, 136, 143
  vertical scrolling, 429
constructors, 298, 301-307
  CAppWindow, 405
  file stream classes, 333

constructs, decision-making, 106
  nested, 119-120
Control Bars subhierarchy, 360
control data, transferring
  dialog boxes, 610-613
    modal, 613-621
    modeless, 621-632
CONTROL keyword, 609
control manipulation messages, 373
control notification messages, 373
CONTROL option, 665
control resources, dialog box, 668
CONTROL statement, 668-670
control styles (list boxes), 521-559
Control subhierarchy, 360
controls
  check box, 488-490
  combo box, 576-597
  edit, 454-462
  format, effects, 101-102
  group box, 491
  list boxes, 520-543
  push button, 462-485
  radio button, 490-491
  scroll bar, 562-576
  static text, 450-454
  Windows registration class names,
    669-670
conventions, naming
  (Hungarian prefix), 358
conversion, 72-75
  string, 242-243
coordinate functions, 364
Copy command (Edit menu), 9
copy constructors, 301-303
count-down timer application, 566-567
cout stream, 92
.CPP file extension, 715
CPU (Central Processing Unit), 715
crashing, 715
Create member function, 450-457,
  463-464, 521-523, 562-565, 577-579,
  602-603, 637, 647-650
  dwStyle parameter, 563, 577

CreateClient member function, 636-638, 647-648
cRectangle class, 315-316
CScollBarData class, 612
CScrollBar class, 562-566
cSquare class, 315-316
CStatic class, 450-454
CString class, 421
CStringArray class, 611
CTEXT keyword, 609
CTEXT statement, 672
CTLBTN1.CPP program, 468-479
CTLBTN1.H header file, 468
CTLBTN1.RC resource file, 468
CTLCOMB1.CPP program, 587-595
CTLCOMB1.EXE application, 585-597
CTLCOMB1.H header file, 587
CTLCOMB1.RC resource file, 587
CTLGRP1.CPP program
    case declarations, 512-513
    source code, 495-511
CTLGRP1.H header file, 494
CTLGRP1.RC resource file, 495
CTLLST1.CPP program
    CAppWindow constructor, 541
    source code, 533-540
CTLLST1.H header file, 532
CTLLST1.RC resource file, 532
CTLLST2.CPP program, 546-555
CTLLST2.EXE application, 544-546
CTLLST2.H header file, 546
CTLLST2.RC resource file, 546
CTLSCRL1.CPP program, 568-574
CTLSCRL1.H header file, 567
CTLSCRL1.RC resource file, 568
CUA (Common User Access) standard, 636
cube functions, 47
curly braces, matching, 12
cursor functions, 363
cursors, 715
Cut command (Edit menu), 9
CWinApp class, 359
CWindowApp application class, 647

CxButton class, 480
CxEdit class, 480

D

data, non-key, 275
data buffer types, 610-613
data conversion, 72-75
data members, 715
    Boolean, IsFirst, 405
data processing, 715
data records, 715
data transfer classes, 611
data type modifiers, *see* modifiers
data types, 194-195
    enumerated, 195-199
    predefined, 30-31
        reading, 94
    Windows, 356-358
data validation, 137
DataList member, 611
DDE messages, 371
Debug command (Options menu), 18
Debug menu, 17-18
debuggers, 715
debugging functions, 366
decision-making constructs, 106, 119-120
DECLARE_DYNAMIC macro, 361
DECLARE_MESSAGE_MAP() macro, 373
DECLARE_SERIAL macro, 362
declaring
    arrays, single-dimensional, 150-151
    CComboBoxData class, 612
    constants, 35-39
    derived classes, 307-311
    DoModal() member function, 604
    function pointers, 279
    functions, 40-42
        friend, 318-321
        virtual, rules, 316-318
    parameters, open array, 260
    pointers to functions, 279
    variables, 33-35

decrement method, pointers, 212-214
decrement operators (- -), 64-66
.DEF file extension, 716
DEF files, 384
DEFARGS1.CPP program, 48-49
default arguments, 47-50
    overloaded functions, 50-51
defaults; 716
#define directive, 35-37, 75
    inline function alternatives, 46
defining
    blocks, 12
    hot-keys, 663
    member functions, 298-299
DEFPUSHBUTTON statement, 673
Delete command (Edit menu), 9
delete operator, 217
DeleteString member function, 524, 581
deleting
    bookmarks, 13
    text, 9
dependent files (lists, updating), 16
derived classes, 295-296
descendant classes, 308, 716
DestroyWindow function, 631
destructors, 298, 303-307
    virtual, 316
device-context functions, 364
device-control functions, 365
devices, output, 718
dialog box control resources, 668
dialog box resources, 665-666
    NEW, 609
    OLD, 609
dialog boxes, 716
    AppWizard, 14
    ClassWizard, 17
    Colors, 19
    constructing, 602-603
    control data, transferring, 610-632
    creating, RC resource files, 603-610
    Directories, 18
    Edit, 20-21
    Editor, 18
    Find, 9-10
    Fonts, 19
    modal, creating, 603-610
    modeless, 602
    New Project, 14
    Open File, 6
    Print, 8
    project, 20
    Project Options, 18
    Replace, 11
    Save As, 7-8, 20
    Tools, 19
    Workspace, 19
Dialog Boxes subhierarchy, 360
DIALOG option statements, 665-668
dialog-box functions, 363
DIALOG1.CPP program, 609-610
    source code, 606-607
DIALOG1.H header file, 605
DIALOG1.RC resource file, 605-606
DIALOG2.CPP program, 620-621
    source code, 615-619
DIALOG2.RC resource file, 614-615, 619
DIALOG3.CPP program, 630
    source code, 623-629
DIALOG3.H header file, 622
DIALOG3.RC resource file, 622-623, 630
Dir member function, 529-530, 582
    attr parameter attributes, 530
direction, evaluation, 84-86
directives
    #include, 24, 32-33, 35-37
    compiler, 24
    #define, 35-37, 75
        inline function alternatives, 46
directories, 716
Directories command (Options menu), 18
Directories dialog box, 18
DISCARDABLE option, 663-665
disk drives, 716
Disk Operating System, *see* DOS
diskettes, 716

disks, 716
display adapters, 716
display and movement functions, 362
displays, 716
distance function, 49-50
do-while loop, 134-137, 153, 160, 175
Document Architecture subhierarchy, 359
DoModal() member function, 603-604, 609
DOS (disk operating system), 716
dot operator, 268
DOWHILE1.CPP program source code, 135-137
dragging, 716
drawing-attribute functions, 364
drawing-tool functions, 364
drives, disk, 716
dual-alternative if-else statement, 108-111
dynamic arrays, 218
dynamic memory, pointers, 217-221
dynamic structures, passing pointers to, 274-278

E

edit boxes, 482
Edit command (Project menu), 14
edit controls, 454-462
    altering, 460-462
    styles, 455-456
Edit dialog box, 20-21
Edit menu, 8-12
EditBox member, 611
editing, undoing, 8
editing functions, 456
Editor command (Options menu), 18
Editor dialog box, 18
editors, text (replacing characters), 613-621
EDITTEXT statement, 675
EGA (Enhanced Graphics Adapter), 716
elements (of arrays), 716
    assigning functions to, 280
Ellipse function, 364

embedded numbers, 36
empty string, 24
EnableWindow function, 465
END_MESSAGE_MAP() macro, 374, 392
EndDialog member function, 604
Enhanced Graphics Adapter, see EGA
entering multiple items, 94
ENUM1.CPP program source code, 197-199
enumerated data types, 195-199
environment functions, 365
error functions, 363
errors, syntax, 721
escape sequences, 97-98
evaluation direction, 84-86
Exceptions subhierarchy, 361
.EXE program files, creating, 15
Execute command (Project menu), 15, 20-21
Exit command (File menu), 8, 25
exit function, 132
exiting
    functions, 47
    loops, 141
    workbench, 25
expressions
    arithmetic, 63
    Boolean, 77-81
    conditional, 77
extensions, file, 716
    .BAK, 714
    .C, 714
    .CPP, 715
    .DEF, 716
    .H, 717
    .MAK, 717
    .RC, 719
    .RES, 720
extractor operator, <<, 24

F

factorial functions, 271-274
`fail()` function, 334
fields
    accTableName, 664
    idValue, 664
file extensions
    .BAK, 714
    .C, 714
    .CPP, 715
    .DEF, 716
    .H, 717
    .MAK, 717
    .RC, 719
    .RES, 720
file I/O, 716
File menu, 5-8
File Services subhierarchy, 361
file stream classes, constructors, 333
file stream I/O
    random access, 347-352
    sequential binary, 339-346
filenames, 716
files, 716
    ASCII, 714
    AUTOEXEC.BAT, 714
    backup, 714
    batch, 714
    CONFIG.SYS, 715
    DEF, 384
    dependent, updating lists, 16
    header, 24, 717
        AFXWIN.H, 386
        CTLBTN1.H, 468
        CTLCOMB1.H, 587
        CTLGRP1.H, 494
        CTLLST1.H, 532
        CTLLST2.H, 546
        CTLSCRL1.H, 567
        DIALOG1.H, 605
        DIALOG2.H, 614
        DIALOG3.H, 622
        FSTREAM.H, 332
        IFSTREAM.H, 332
        IO.H, 333
        IOSTREAM.H, 24, 35-37, 332
        MATH.H, 49
        MDIWIN1.H, 639-640
        MENU1.H, 389
        MENU3.H, 402
        OFSTREAM.H, 332
        STDIO.H, 96
        WINDOW1.H, 423
        WINDOW2.H, 432
make, 717
menu resource, 662-665
MINWINAP.DEF, 385
.OBJ, 715
    generating, 15
object, 718
program, 4
    .EXE, 15
project, 4
    creating, 14
    opening, 14
random access, 719
recent, 8
resource, 720
    CTLBTN1.RC, 468
    CTLCOMB1.RC, 587
    CTLGRP1.RC, 495
    CTLLST1.RC, 532
    CTLLST2.RC, 546
    CTLSCRL1.RC, 568
    dialog boxes, creating, 603-610
    DIALOG1.RC, 605-606
    DIALOG2.RC, 614-615, 619
    DIALOG3.RC, 622-623, 630
    MDIWIN1.RC, 640
    MENU1.RC, 388-389
    MENU2.H, 395
    MENU2.RC, 394-395
    MENU3RC, 401
    WINDOW1.RC, 423
    WINDOW2.RC, 432

selecting, 6
sequential, 720
source, 15
text, 721
updating, 7
Find command (Edit menu), 9-10, 13
Find dialog box, 9-10
Find Matching Brace command
  (Edit menu), 12
`FindString` member function,
  524-525, 582
FIXED option, 663-665
fixed-array parameters, 157-161
fixed-length records, 719
flags, options (`printf` function), 97-98
floating-point numbers, 63
floppy disks, *see* diskettes
`FONT` statement, 668
Fonts command (Options menu), 19
Fonts dialog box, 19
`fonts` functions, 364
`for` loops, 128-131, 153, 160
  nested, 175
  open loops, 132-134
FOR1.CPP program source code, 129-131
FOR2.CPP program source code, 131
FOR3.CPP program source code, 132-134
FOR4.CPP program source code, 139-141
formal constants, 35-39
formats, 716
formatted stream output, 92-94
formatting, `printf` function, 96-102
Frames Windows subhierarchy, 359
friend functions, 318-321
  add friend, 321
friend operators, 321-325
FSTREAM.H header file, 332
function keys, 716
function overloading, 50-53
function parameters, multidimensional
  arrays, 178-181

function pointers
  initializing, 280
  invoking, 280
function signatures, 50
functions, 39, 260, 716
  API, 362-366
    invoking, 367-370
  application-exec, 366
  assigning to elements, 280
  atom-management, 366
  `binarySearch`, 171
  `Bitmap`, 364
  `calcRegression`, 287
  calling, 41-42
  `Caret`, 363
  clipboard, 363
  clipping, 364
  `close`, 334
  color-palette, 364
  combination, 273-274
  `Combsort`, 351
  communications, 366
  coordinate, 364
  cube, 47
  cursor, 363
  debugging, 366
  declaring, 40-42
  `DestroyWindow`, 631
  device-context, 364
  device-control, 365
  dialog-box, 363
  display and movement, 362
  `distance`, 49-50
  drawing-attribute, 364
  drawing-tool, 364
  editing, *see* editing functions
  `Ellipse`, 364
  `EnableWindow`, 465
  environment, 365
  error, 363
  `exit`, 132
  exiting, 47
  factorial, 271-274

functions (continued)
> fail(), 334
> fonts, 364
> friend, 318-321
> GDI (graphics device interface), 363-365
> GetCheck(), 620
> GetDlgItemText, 620
> getInputFilename, 338
> getline, 229
> getMedian, 267-271
> getNumber, 136
> getOutputFilename, 338
> good(), 334
> hardware, 363
> hook, 363
> information, 363
> initArray, 287
> initialization, 366
> inline, 45-47
> input, 362
> inputArray, 164
> inputMatrix, 181
> line-output, 364
> linear, 287
> linearSearch, 171
> LoadMenu, 648
> local variables in, 42-44
> main, 24-25, 136, 165, 198, 202-203,
>   273-274, 278, 346, 351-352
> makeRect, 647
> manager interface, 362-363
> mapping, 364
> MDIDestroy, 649
> MDIGetActive, 649
> MDINext, 649
> member, *see* member functions
> memory-management, 365
> menu, 363
> message, 362
> MessageBeep, 367-368
> MessageBox, 367-368, 605
>   identifiers, 369-370
> metafile, 364
> module-management, 365

nested, 41
non-inline, 46
nonvirtual, overriding, 312
numeric, 718
obtainNumData, 164
OnPaint, 425-426
open, 333
optimization-tool, 366
OS interrupt, 365
painting, 363
parameters, array, 157-161
passing arguments by reference, 267
passing arrays as arguments, 260-263
passing structures to by reference,
  268-269
permutation, 273-274
pointers, 278-287
Polygon, 364
Polyline (Boolean), 367-368
PostMessage (Boolean), 375-376
precision, 92
printer-control, 365
printer-escape, 365
printf, 96-102
private functions, *see* private functions
processLines, 338-339
property, 363
prototyping, 41-42
random, 647
read, 340-346
recall, 306
reciprocal, 287
rectangle, 363
recursive, 271-274
> showTree, 278
region, 364
resource-management, 366
results, 42
sayError, 198
scrolling, 363
searchInSortedArray, 172
searchInUnorderedArray, 171-172
seekg, 347

functions (continued)

segment, 365
select_transf, 287
SendDlgItemMessage, 375-376
SendMessage, 375-376, 631
SetCheck(), 620
SetDlgItemText, 620
showArray, 164
showColumnAverage, 181
ShowWindow, 465, 649
sortArray, 165
sound, 366
sprintf, 100
sqr, 47-49, 287
sqroot, 136
sqrt, 49
static variables in, 44-45
store, 306
strcat, 233
strchr, 246
strcmp, 237
strcspn, 248
strdup, 231
stream, overloaded, 339-346
stream I/O, 332-334
stricmp, 238
string-manipulation, 366
strings as arguments, using, 263-265
strlen, 232-233, 265
_strlw, 242
strncat, 233-234
strncmp, 238
strncpy, 231-232, 277
strnicmp, 239
strpbrk, 248
strrchr, 247
strrev, 243
strspn, 247
strstr, 249
strtok, 249-250
_strupr, 242
system, 363
system services interface, 365-366
task, 365
text, 364
transformation, 281-287
trimStr, 338
upperCase, 264-265
user-defined, *see* user-defined functions
virtual, *see* virtual functions
width, 92
window-creation, 362
WinMain, 382
write, 339-346

G

GDI (graphics device interface) functions, 363-365
GetButtonStyle member function, 464
GetCheck() function, 620
GetDlgItemText function, 620
getImag member function, 321
getInputFilename function, 338
GetLBText member function, 579-580
GetLBTextLen member function, 580
GetLine member function, 229, 460
GetLineCount member function, 458
GetListBoxData member function, 612
getMedian function, 267-271
getNumber function, 136
getOutputFilename function, 338
getReal member function, 321
GetScrollRange member function, 565
GetSel member function, 459-460, 525
GetSelItems member function, 525-526
GetSize member function, 306, 612
GetText member function, 526
GetTextLen member function, 526
getVar member function, 484
GetWindowText member function, 453, 457
GetWindowTextLength member function, 453
global constants, TOLERANCE, 136
global variables, 34, 717
Go to Definition command (Browse menu), 16

Go to Reference command
(Browse menu), 17
good() function, 334
Graphical Drawing Objects
subhierarchy, 361
Graphics device interface functions,
see GDI functions
graphics monitors, 717
GRAYED option, 663
group box control, 491
GROUPBOX statement, 674

H

.H file extension, 717
HandleAddStrBtn member functions,
541-542
HandleAngleModeGrp member
function, 514
HandleCalcBtn member function, 482-483,
513-514, 596-597
HandleDelStrBtn member function, 542
HandleExitBtn member function, 485,
576, 597
HandleGetIndicesBtn member
function, 557
HandleGetNamesBtn member functions, 556
HandleGetSelIdxBtn member
function, 543
HandleGetSelStrBtn member
function, 542
HandleGetStrBtn member function, 543
HandleOperatorCmb member function, 596
HandleSendBtn member function, 630-632
HandleSetIndicesBtn member function,
557-558
HandleSetNamesBtn member functions,
556-557
HandleSetSelIdxBtn member
function, 543
HandleSetSelStrBtn member function,
542-543

HandleStartBtn member function,
575-576
HandleStoreBtn member function, 483
HandleTimerScr member function, 576
hardware functions, 363
header files, 24, 717
AFXWIN.H, 386
CTLBTN1.H, 468
CTLCOMB1.H, 587
CTLGRP1.H, 494
CTLLST1.H, 532
CTLLST2.H, 546
CTLSCRL1.H, 567
DIALOG1.H, 605
DIALOG2.H, 614
DIALOG3.H, 622
FSTREAM.H, 332
IFSTREAM.H, 332
IO.H, arguments exported by, 333
IOSTREAM.H, 24, 35-37, 332
MATH.H, 49
MDIWIN1.H, 639-640
MENU1.H, 389
MENU3.H, 402
OFSTREAM.H, 332
STDIO.H, 96
WINDOW1.H, 423
WINDOW2.H, 432
heap sort, 161
HELLO.CPP program, 21-23
Help menu, 19
HELP option, 663
hertz, 717
hexadecimal numbers, 31
HGA (Hercules Graphics Adapter), 717
hierarchies
class, 294
C++ stream library, 332
declaring, 307-311
MFC, 359-362
HighValue member, 613
history list boxes, combo boxes as, 584-585
hook functions, 363

horizontal scrolling, constants, 430
hot-key characters, 452
hot-keys, defining, 663
Hungarian prefix naming convention, 358

I

I/O (Input/Output), 717
identifiers
    Boolean, 77
    names, 32
idValue field, 664
if statements, single alternative, 106-108
if-else statements
    dual-alternative, 108-111
    multiple-alternative, 111-114
IF1.CPP program, 107-108
IF2.CPP program, 109-111
IF3.CPP program, 113-114
IF4.CPP program, 119-120
IFSTREAM.H header file, 332
IMPLEMENT_DYNAMIC macro, 362
IMPLEMENT_SERIAL macro, 362
IN1.CPP program, 94-95
INACTIVE option, 663
#include directive, 24, 32-37
increment method, pointers, 212-214
increment operators (++), 64-66
inear search method, 166
information functions, 363
inheritance, 295-296, 307-311, 717
InitApplication member function, 405
InitAppWindow member function, 596
initArray function, 287
initialization function, 366
initialization messages, 371-372
initializing
    arrays
        single-dimensional, 154-157
        two-dimensional and
            three-dimensional, 176-178
    function pointers, 280
    strings, 230-231

InitInstance member function, 383-384,
    405, 648
inline functions, 45-47
INLINE1.CPP program, 46-47
input, 717
    stream, 94-96
    string, 229-230
input controls, list boxes, 520-543
input dialog boxes, 454
input functions, 362
input messages, 372
inputArray function, 164
inputMatrix function, 181
insertion operator >>, 37, 94
InsertString member function, 527, 581
    precautions, 527
IO.H header file, arguments exported
    by, 333
IO1.CPP program, 335-339
IO2.CPP program, 340-346
IO3.CPP program, 347-352
IOSTREAM.H header file, 24, 35-37, 332
IsFirst Boolean data member, 405
IsMainWindow Boolean parameter, 405
iterations, loop (skipping), 138-141
iterative calculations, 137

K

key strokes, accelerator, 664
keys, function, 716
keywords
    CONTROL, 609
    CTEXT, 609
    typedef, 194-195
    VIRTKEY, 664
kilobytes (K), 717

L

languages, programming, 719
LBS_EXTENDEDSEL style, 543-544
least significant bit, 717

length, string, 232-233
libraries, 4
    C++ stream, 332
        class hierarchies, 332
    MFC (Microsoft Foundation Classes),
      14, 356
        CButton class, 463-464, 489-491
        CComboBox class, 577-583
        CEdit class, 454-462
        CListBox class, 520-530
        CScrollBar class, 562-566
        CStatic class, 450-454
        CString class, 421
        hierarchy, 359-362
        messages, responding to, 373-374
    stream, 92
    STRING.H, 230
LimitText member function, 583
Line command (View menu), 12
line numbers, 21
line-output functions, 364
linear function, 287
linearized regression, 280-287
linearSearch function, 171
LineFromChar member function, 458
LineIndex member function, 459
LineLength member function, 459
linkers, 717
list boxes, 520-543
    CListBox class (member functions),
      520-530
    control styles, 521-559
    InsertString member function,
      precautions, 527
    notification messages, 530-531
    see also history list boxes
list manipulation tester, 531-544
LISTBOX statement, 674
ListBoxData member, 611
listings
    1.1. HELLO.CPP program, 23
    2.1. VAR1.CPP program, 34
    2.2. CONST1.CPP program, 37

2.3. CONST2.CPP program, 38-39
2.4. VAR2.CPP program, 43
2.5. STATIC1.CPP program, 44-45
2.6. INLINE1.CPP program, 46-47
2.7. DEFARGS1.CPP program, 48-49
2.8. OVERLOAD.CPP program, 51-52
3.1. OPER1.CPP program, 61-62
3.2. OPER2.CPP program, 65
3.3. OPER3.CPP program, 67-68
3.4. SIZEOF1.CPP program, 70-71
3.5. TYPCAST1.CPP program, 73-74
3.6. RELOP1.CPP program, 78-79
3.7. BITS1.CPP program, 82-83
4.1. OUT1.CPP program, 93
4.2. IN1.CPP program, 95
4.3. OUT2.CPP program, 100-101
5.1. IF1.CPP program, 107
5.2. IF2.CPP program, 109-110
5.3. IF3.CPP program, 113
5.4. SWITCH1.CPP program, 117
5.5. IF4.CPP program, 119
6.1. FOR1.CPP program, 129
6.2. FOR2.CPP program, 131
6.3. FOR3.CPP program, 132-133
6.4. DOWHILE1.CPP program, 135
6.5. WHILE1.CPP program, 137-138
6.6. FOR4.CPP program, 139-140
6.7. NESTFOR1.CPP program, 142
7.1. ARRAY1.CPP program, 152
7.2. ARRAY2.CPP program, 154-155
7.3. ARRAY3.CPP program, 156-157
7.4. ARRAY4.CPP program, 158-159
7.5. ARRAY5.CPP program, 162-163
7.6. ARRAY6.CPP program, 167-170
7.7. MAT1.CPP program, 174-175
7.8. MAT2.CPP program, 176-179
7.9. MAT3.CPP program, 179-180
8.1. ENUM1.CPP program, 197-198
8.2. STRUCT1.CPP program, 201-202
8.3. REFVAR1.CPP program, 205
8.4. PTR1.CPP program, 208
8.5. PTR2.CPP program, 210-211
8.6. PTR3.CPP program, 212-213

8.7. PTR4.CPP program, 214-216
8.8. PTR5.CPP program, 219-220
9.1. STRING1.CPP program, 235
9.2. STRING2.CPP program, 239-240
9.3. STRING3.CPP program, 244-245
9.4. STRING4.CPP program, 251-252
10.1. ADVFUN1.CPP program, 261-262
10.2. ADVFUN2.CPP program, 263-264
10.3. ADVFUN3.CPP program, 266
10.4. ADVFUN4.CPP program, 268-269
10.5. ADVFUN5.CPP program, 270-271
10.6. ADVFUN6.CPP, 272-273
10.7. ADVFUN7.CPP, 275-276
10.8. ADVFUN8.CPP program, 281-285
11.1. CLASS1.CPP program, 299
11.2. CLASS2.CPP program, 305
11.3. CLASS3.CPP program, 309-310
11.4. CLASS4.CPP program, 314-315
11.5. CLASS5.CPP program, 319-320
11.6. CLASS6.CPP program, 323-324
12.1. IO1.CPP program, 335-337
12.2. IO2.CPP program, 341-344
12.3. IO3.CPP program, 348-350
14.1. MINWINAP.CPP program, 385
14.2. MINWINAP.DEF file, 385
14.3. MENU1.RC resource file, 388-389
14.4. MENU1.H header file, 389
14.5. MENU1.CPP program, 390-391
14.6. MENU2.RC resource file, 394-395
14.7. MENU2.H header file, 395
14.8. MENU2.CPP program, 396-398
14.9. MENU3RC resource file, 401
14.10. MENU3.H header files, 402
14.11. MENU3.CPP program, 402-405
14.12. MENU4.CPP program, 407-408
15.1. WINDOW1.H header file, 423
15.2. WINDOW1.RC resource file, 423
15.3. WINDOW1.CPP program, 423-425
15.4. WINDOW2.H header file, 432
15.5. WINDOW2.RC resource file, 432
15.6. WINDOW2.CPP program, 432-441

16.1. CTLBTN1.CPP program, 468-479
16.2. CTLBTN1.RC resource file, 468
17.1. CTLGRP1.H header file, 494
17.2. CTLGRP1.RC resource file, 495
17.3. CTLGRP1.CPP program, 495-511
18.1. CTLLST1.H header file, 532
18.2. CTLLST1.RC resource file, 532
18.3. CTLLST1.CPP program, 533-540
18.4. CTLLST2.H header file, 546
18.5. CTLLST2.RC resource file, 546
18.6. CTLLST2.CPP program, 546-555
19.1. CTLSCRL1.H header file, 567
19.2. CTLSCRL1.RC resource file, 568
19.3. CTLSCRL1.CPP program, 568-574
19.4. CTLCOMB1.H header file, 587
19.5. CTLCOMB1.RC resource file, 587
19.6. CTLCOMB1.CPP program, 587-595
20.1. DIALOG1.H header file, 605
20.2. DIALOG1.RC resource file, 605-606
20.3. DIALOG1.CPP program, 606-607
20.4. DIALOG2.H header file, 614
20.5. DIALOG2.RC resource file, 614-615
20.6. DIALOG2.CPP program, 615-619
20.7. DIALOG3.H header file, 622
20.8. DIALOG3.RC resource file, 622-623
20.9. DIALOG3.CPP program, 623-629
21.1. MDIWIN1.H header file, 639-640
21.2. MDIWIN1.RC resource file, 640
21.3. MDIWIN1.CPP program, 640-646
lists, multiple-selection, 543-558
load options, 662, 665
LoadMenu function, 648
Load Workspace command (Project menu), 16
loading, Workbench, 5
LOADONCALL option, 662, 665
local variables, 717
    in functions, 42-44

locating
    characters in strings, 246-248
    strings, 248-253
logical operators, 75-77, 85
loop iterations, skipping, 138-141
looping, recursive functions, 272-274
loops, 83, 717
    conditional, 715
    do-while, 134-137, 153, 160, 175
    exiting, 141
    for, 128-134, 153, 160, 175
    nested, 142-143. 175, 718
    open, 132-134, 718
    while, 137-138
LowValue member, 613
lpTemplateName parameter, 602
LTEXT statement, 671

M

macro-based constants, 35-38
macros
    BEGIN_MESSAGE_MAP, 374, 392
    DECLARE_MESSAGE_MAP(), 373
    END_MESSAGE_MAP(), 374, 392
    MFC library, 361-362
    ON_COMMAND, 376-377
    ON_WM_CLOSE(), 374
    ON_WM_PAINT(), 374
    ON_WM_SIZE(), 374
    START_MESSAGE_MAP(), 374
    utility, 366
main function, 24-25, 136, 165, 198,
    202-203, 273-274, 278, 346, 351-352
main modules, 717
.MAK file extension, 717
.MAK project files, retrieving most recent,
    16
make files, 717
makeRect member function, 481, 647
manager interface functions, 362-363
manipulating buttons, 465

mapping functions, 364
MAT1.CPP program, 174-176
MAT2.CPP program, 176-178
MAT3.CPP program, 179-181
math operators, 717
MATH.H header file, 49
matrices, 717
MAX_NUM constant, 143
maximizing, MDI child windows, 637
MCGA (Multi-Color Graphics
  Adapter), 717
MDA (Monochrome Display Adapter), 718
MDI (Multiple Document Interface), 636
    applications, 639
        building, 637
        features, 636-637
    child windows, 636
        building, 639
        maximizing/minimizing, 637
        odd-numbered versus
          even-numbered, 639
        operations, 638
    client windows, 636
    frame classes, 638
        CAppMDIFrame, 647-648
    frame windows, 636, 639
    messages, 373, 639
    window classes
        CAppMDIChild, 647-650
        frame, 638
    windows, 5, 359
        blank, creating, 6
        closing, 7
MDICascade member function, 650
MDIDestroy function, 649
MDIGetActive function, 649
MDIIconArrange member function, 650
MDIMaximize member function, 638
MDINext function, 649
MDIRestore member function, 638
MDITile member function, 650
MDIWIN1.CPP program, 640-646
MDIWIN1.H header file, 639-640

MDIWIN1.RC resource file, 640
    script, 646
megabytes (M), 718
member functions, 295, 718
    AddString, 524, 580-581
    area(), 311
    assign, 300
    bNoPaint, 446
    CButton class, 463-464
    CComboBox class, 577-583
    CEdit class, 454-462
        Create, 454-457
        GetLine, 460
        GetLineCount, 458
        GetSel, 459-460
        GetWindowText, 453, 457
        GetWindowTextLength, 453
        LineFromChar, 458
        LineIndex, 459
        LineLength, 459
        ReplaceSel, 462
        SetSel, 461
        SetWindowText, 453-454, 461
        text query, 456-460
    clipboaard-related, 456
    CListBox class, 520-530
        AddString, 524
        Create, 521-523
        DeleteString, 524
        Dir, 529-530
        FindString, 524-525
        GetSel, 525
        GetSelItems, 525-526
        GetText, 526
        GetTextLen, 526
        InsertString, 527
        SelectString, 527
        SelItemRange, 528
        SetCurSel, 528
        SetSel, 528-529
        SetTopIndex, 529
    CMArrangeIcons, 650
    CMCalc, 377

    CMCalcBtn, 483, 597
    CMCascadeChildren, 650
    CMCloseChildren, 649
    CMCountChildren, 649
    CMCreateChild, 648-649
    CMDialog, 621, 632
    CMExit, 485
    CMExitBtn, 576, 597
    CMSendBtn, 631
    CMStartBtn, 576
    CMStore, 377, 484
    CMTileChldren, 650
    Create, 450-457, 463-464, 521-523,
        562-565, 577-579, 602-603, 637,
        647-650
    CreateClient, 636-638, 647–648
    CScrollBar class, 562-566
        AddString, 580-581
        Create, 562-565, 577-579
        DeleteString, 581
        Dir, 582
        FindString, 582
        GetLBText, 579-580
        GetLBTextLen, 580
        GetScroll Range, 565
        InsertString, 581
        LimitText, 583
        SelectString, 582-583
        SetCurSel, 579
        SetScroll Range, 565
        SetScrollPos, 565-566
        ShowDropDown, 580
    CStatic class, 450-454
        Create, 450-452, 463-464
        GetButtonStyle, 464
        SetButtonStyle, 464
    defining, 298-299
    DeleteString, 524, 581
    Dir, 529-530, 582
    DoModal(), 603-604, 609
    EndDialog, 604
    FindString, 524-525, 582
    getImag, 321

member functions (continued)
    GetButtonStyle, 464
    GetLBText, 579-580
    GetLBTextLen, 580
    GetLine, 460
    GetLineCount, 458
    GetListBoxData, 612
    getReal, 321
    GetScroll Range, 565
    GetSel, 459-460, 525
    GetSelItems, 525-526
    GetSize, 306, 612
    GetText, 526
    GetTextLen, 526
    getVar, 484
    GetWindowText, 453, 457
    GetWindowTextLength, 453
    HandleAddStrBtn, 541-542
    HandleAngleModeGrp, 514
    HandleCalcBtn, 482-483, 513-514,
      596-597
    HandleDelStrBtn, 542
    HandleExitBtn, 485, 576, 597
    HandleGetIndicesBtn, 557
    HandleGetNamesBtn, 556
    HandleGetSelIdxBtn, 543
    HandleGetSelStrBtn, 542
    HandleGetStrBtn, 543
    HandleOperatorCmb, 596
    HandleSendBtn, 630-632
    HandleSetIndicesBtn, 557-558
    HandleSetNamesBtn, 556-557
    HandleSetSelIdxBtn, 543
    HandleSetSelStrBtn, 542-543
    HandleStartBtn, 575-576
    HandleStoreBtn, 483
    HandleTimerScr, 576
    InitApplication, 405
    InitAppWindow, 596
    InitInstance, 383-384, 405, 648
    InsertString, 527, 581
    invoking in MFC applications, 383
    LimitText, 583

LineFromChar, 458
LineIndex, 459
LineLength, 459
makeRect, 481
MDICascade, 650
MDIIconArrange, 650
MDIMaximize, 638
MDIRestore, 638
MDITile, 650
MessageBox, 369, 409
OnCancel, 604-605, 631
OnChildDestroy, 650
OnClose, 409, 609, 651
OnCreate, 481-482, 541-542, 556, 575,
    596, 632, 648-650
OnDestroy, 651
OnEditCopy, 400
OnEditCut, 400
OnEditPaste, 400
OnExit, 392, 400
OnHelp, 400
OnHScroll, 429-430, 444
OnInitDialog, 604, 620
OnKeyDown, 444
OnLButtonDown, 392, 482
OnLongMenu, 399
OnOK, 604, 610, 620
    virtual, 630
OnPaint, 421-422, 447
OnRButtonDown, 392, 409
OnShortMenu, 399
OnSize, 430-431, 446-447
OnVScroll, 428-429, 443, 576
OutText, 420-427
overriding, 308
putVar, 484-485
readArray, 345
readElem, 345, 351
ReplaceSel, 462
ScrollWindow, 428
SelectString, 527, 582-583
SelItemRange, 528
SetButtonStyle, 464

SetCharHeight, 444-445
SetCheck, 490
SetCurSel, 528, 579
SetLineSize, 445
SetListBoxData, 612
SetPageSize, 446
SetScrollPos, 427-428, 565-566
SetScrollRange, 427, 565
SetVScrollMax, 445
SetSel, 461, 528-529
SetTopIndex, 529
SetWindowText, 453-454, 461
ShowDropDown, 580
text query, 456-460
TransferData, 630-631
updatedComboBox, 597
writeArray, 345
writeElem, 344, 351
memory, 718
  addresses, 206
  dynamic, pointers, 217-221
  options, 663-665
memory-management functions, 365
menu functions, 363
menu resource file, 662-665
menu resources, building, 662-665
MENU statement, 662, 667
menu-driven programs, 718
MENU1.CPP program
  CAppWindow constructor, 392
  source code, 390-391
MENU1.H header file, 389
MENU1.RC resource file, 388-389
MENU2.CPP program source code,
  396-400
MENU2.H resource file, 395
MENU2.RC resource file, 394-395
MENU3.CPP program source code,
  402-405
MENU3.H header file, 402
MENU3RC resource file, 401
MENU4.CPP program source code,
407-408

MENUBARBREAK option, 663
MENUBREAK option, 663
menuID, 662
MENUITEM SEPARATOR statement, 664
MENUITEM statement, 662-663
menus, 718
  Browse, 16-17
  Debug, 17-18
  Edit, 8-12
  File, 5-8
  Help, 19
  MDI child windows, 637-639
  Options, 18-19
  Project, 14-16
  responding to selections, 393-400
  Tools, 18
  View, 12-13
  Window, 19
message functions, 362
MessageBeep function, 367-368
MessageBox member function, 367-368,
  369, 409, 605
  identifiers, 369-370
messages, 718
  button messages, 464
  check boxes, 490
  clipboard, 373
  control manipulation, 373
  control notification, 373
  DDE, 371
  initialization, 371-372
  input, 372
  MDI, 373, 639
  nonclient-area, 373
  notification
    combo boxes, 584
    list boxes, 530-531
    scroll bars, 566
  OOP, 295
  ranges, Windows, 376
  scroll bar notification, 373
  sending, 375-376
  system, 373

user-defined, 376-377
user-generated, 370
Windows, 370-373, 721
metafile functions, 364
methods, 718
  binary search, 166
  linear search, 166
  sorting
    bubblesort, 714
    Comb, 715
MFC (Microsoft Foundation Class) library,
  14, 356
  applications, 382-387
    member function invocation, 383
    menu selections, 393-400
    multiple instances, 400-405
    window operations, 387-393
    windows, closing, 406-409
  hierarchy, 359-362
  library
    `CButton` class, 463-464, 489-491
    `CComboBox` class, 577-583
    `CEdit` class, 454-462
    `CListBox` class, 520-530
    `CScrollBar` class, 562-566
    `CStatic` class, 450-454
    `CString` class, 421
    macros, 361-362
    messages, responding to, 373-374
Microsoft Disk Operator System, *see*
  MS-DOS
Microsoft Foundation Class library, *see* MFC
Microsoft Foundation Classes, *see* MFC
`MIN_NUM` constant, 143
minimizing, MDI child windows, 637
MINWINAP.CPP program source
  code, 385
MINWINAP.DEF file, 385
MINWINAP.EXE application, 387-393
Mixed Source/Asm command (View
  menu), 12
modal dialog boxes, 602
  creating, 603-610

data transfer, 613-621
modeless dialog boxes, 602
  data transfer, 621-632
modes, parameter, 333
modifiers, 30-31
module-management functions, 365
modules, main, 717
modulus, 718
monadic operators, 84
monitors, 718
  graphics, 717
monochrome, 718
Monochrome Display Adapter, *see* MDA
most significant bit, 718
`MOVABLE` option, 663-665
MS-DOS, 718
MSVC.EXE program, 5
Multi-Color Graphics Adapter, *see* MCGA
Multi-Document Interface, *see* MDI
multidimensional arrays, 718
Multiple Document Interface, *see* MDI
multiple instances, applications, 400-405
multiple items, entering, 94
multiple-alternative `if-else` statement,
  111-114
multiple-selection lists, 543-558
multiplicative operators, 85

N

nameID, 665
names
  constants, 36
  identifier, 32
  recent files, displaying, 8
  static variables, 44
  Windows registration class, 669-670
naming conventions, Hungarian prefix, 358
nested decision-making constructs, 119-120
nested functions, 41
nested loops, 142-143, 718
  `for`, 175
NESTFOR1.CPP program source code,

142-143
New command
    File menu, 6, 20-21
    Project menu, 14, 20-21
NEW dialog box resource, 609
new operator, 217
New Project dialog box, 14
Next Bookmark command (View menu), 13
Next command (Browse menu), 17
Next Error command (View menu), 12
nIDTemplate parameter, 602
nodes, 275-277
NOINVERT option, 665
non-inline functions, 46
non-key data, 275
nonclient-area messages, 373
nonreference pointer parameters,
    addresses, 275
nonvirtual functions, overriding, 312
notation, scientific, 720
notification messages
    combo boxes, 584
    list boxes, 530-531
    scroll bars, 566
notImplemented private function, 399
null strings, 718
null terminators, 228
numbers
    embedded, 36
    floating-point, 63
    hexadecimal, 31
    real, 63
numeric functions, 718

O

.OBJ files, 715
    generating, 15
object files, 718
object-oriented programming, *see* OOP
objects, 294-295, 718
obtainNumData function, 164

odd-numbered MDI child windows, 639
OFSTREAM.H header file, 332
OLD dialog box resource, 609
OLE 1.0 Support subhierarchy, 361
ON_COMMAND macro, 376-377
ON_WM_CLOSE() macro, 374
ON_WM_PAINT() macro, 374
ON_WM_SIZE() macro, 374
OnCancel member function, 604-605, 631
OnChildDestroy member function, 650
OnClose member function, 409, 609, 651
OnCreate member function, 481-482, 541,
    556, 575, 596, 632, 648-650
OnDestroy member function, 651
OnEditCopy member function, 400
OnEditCut member function, 400
OnEditPaste member function, 400
OnExit member function, 392, 400
OnHelp member function, 400
OnHScroll member function, 429-430, 444
OnInitDialog member function, 604, 620
OnKeyDown member function, 444
OnLButtonDown member function, 392, 482
OnLongMenu member function, 399
OnOK member function, 604, 610, 620
    virtual, 630
OnPaint member function, 421-422,
    425-426, 447
OnRButtonDown member function, 392, 409
OnShortMenu member function, 399
OnSize member function, 430-431, 446-447
OnVScroll member function, 428-429,
    443, 576
OOP (object-oriented programming), 4
    classes, 294
    inheritance, 295-296
    messages, 295
    polymorphism, 296
open array parameters, declaring, 260
Open command
    Browse menu, 17
    File menu, 6
    Project menu, 14

Open File dialog box, 6
open function, 333
open loops, 132-134, 718
open-array parameters, 157-161
OPER1.CPP program, 61-62
OPER2.CPP program, source code, 65
OPER3.CPP program, source code, 67-68
operands, 60
operator precedence, 84-86
operators, 60
&&, 80
*=, 69
-=, 69
/=, 69
=, 76
==, 76, 80
¦¦, 80
additive, 85
arithmetic, 60-63
assignment, 66-69, 86
bit-manipulating, 81-83
bitwise, 85
bitwise shift, 85
comma, 83-84
decrement (- -), 64-66
delete, 217
dot, 268
extractor (<<), 24, 334
friend, 321-325
increment (++), 64-66
inserter (>>), 37, 94, 334
logical, 75-77, 85
math, 717
monadic, 84
multiplicative, 85
new, 217
OR, 83
order of, 718
overloaded !, 334
relational, 75-77, 85, 720
sizeof, 69-72
stream extractor, writing for classes, 325
ternary, 86

unary, 721
XOR, 75, 80, 83
optimization-tool functions, 366
options
load, 662, 665
memory, 663-665
searching, 9-12
see also menus
Options menu, 18-19
OR operator, 83
order of operators, 718
OS interrupt functions, 365
OUT1.CPP program, 93
OUT2.CPP program, 100-101
output, stream, 92-94
output devices, 718
output statement, 199
OutText member function, 420-427
OVERLOAD.CPP program, source code,
51-52
overloaded operator !, 334
overloaded stream functions, 339-346
overloading, function, 50-53
overriding
member functions, 308
virtual functions, 312

P

Page Setup command (File menu), 8
painting functions, 363
palettes, 719
parameter mode, arguments, 333
parameters, 719
array
in functions, 157-161
open, declaring, 260
Boolean, IsMainWindow, 405
class, 669
const, 261
function, multidimensional arrays,
178-181

lpTemplateName, 602
nIDTemplate, 602
pParentWnd, 602
reference, 268
style, 669
values, modifying, 35
with default arguments, listing, 48
passing by reference, 719
passing by value, 719
Paste command (Edit menu), 9
permutation function, 273-274
pixels, 719
placement, increment operators, 64
POINT structure, 357-358
pointers, 206, 719
dynamic memory, 217-221
function
initializing, 280
invoking, 280
increment/decrement method, 212-214
passing structures by, 270-271
passing to dynamic structures, 274-278
to arrays, 209-214
to functions, 278-287
to structures, 214-217
to variables, existing, 206-209
Polygon function, 364
polygons, plotting, 367-368
Polyline function (Boolean), 367-368
polymorphism, 296, 312-316, 719
Pop Context command (Browse menu), 17
POPUP statement, 664
Position member, 613
PostMessage function (Boolean), 375-376
pParentWnd parameter, 602
precedence, operator, 84-86
precision function, 92
precision option, printf function, 97
predefined data types, 30-31
reading, 94
predefined identifiers, Boolean, 77
PRELOAD option, 662, 665

Previous Bookmark command
(View menu), 13
Previous command (Browse menu), 17
Previous Error command (View menu), 12
Print command (File menu), 8
Print dialog box, 8
printer-control functions, 365
printer-escape functions, 365
printf function, 96-102
private functions
assignMenu, 399
promptToQuit, 399
private section, 297
processLines function, 338-339
program continuation, 137
program files, 4
.EXE, creating, 15
program variables, 209
programming
C++, 4
languages, 719
object-oriented, see OOP
programs, 719
ADVFUN1.CPP, 261-263
ADVFUN2.CPP, 263-265
ADVFUN3.CPP, 265-267
ADVFUN4.CPP, 268-269
ADVFUN5.CPP, 270-271
ADVFUN6.CPP, 272-274
ADVFUN7.CPP, 275-278
ADVFUN8.CPP, 281-287
application classes, 383-387
ARRAY1.CPP, 152-154
ARRAY2.CPP, 154-156
ARRAY3.CPP, 156-157
ARRAY4.CPP, 158-161
ARRAY5.CPP, 162-165
ARRAY6.CPP, 167-172
BITS1.CPP, 82-83
characteristics, 24-25
CLASS1.CPP, 299-300
CLASS2.CPP, 304-307
CLASS3.CPP, 309-311

programs (continued)
    CLASS4.CPP, 314-316
    CLASS5.CPP, 319-321
    CLASS6.CPP, 323-325
    CListBox class (member functions), 520-530
    CONST1.CPP, 37
    CONST2.CPP, 38-39
    creating, 15
    CTLBTN1.CPP, 468-479
    CTLCOMB1.CPP, 587-595
    CTLGRP1.CPP, 495-511
    CTLLST1.CPP, 533-540
    CTLLST2.CPP, 546-555
    CTLSCRL1.CPP, 568-574
    DEFARGS1.CPP, 48-49
    DIALOG1.CPP, 609-610
    DIALOG1.CPP, 606-607
    DIALOG2.CPP, 620-621
        source code, 615-619
    DIALOG3.CPP, 630
        source code, 623-629
    DOWHILE1.CPP, 135-137
    ENUM1.CPP, 197-199
    FOR1.CPP, 129-131
    FOR2.CPP, 131
    FOR3.CPP, 132-134
    FOR4.CPP, 139-148
    HELLO.CPP, 21-23
    IF1.CPP, 107-108
    IF2.CPP, 109-111
    IF3.CPP, 113-114
    IF4.CPP, 119-120
    IN1.CPP, 94-95
    INLINE1.CPP, 46-47
    input controls
        list boxes, 520-543
    IO1.CPP, 335-339
    IO2.CPP, 340-346
    IO3.CPP, 347-352
    LBS_EXTENDEDSEL style, 543-544
    MAT1.CPP, 174-176
    MAT2.CPP, 176-178

MAT3.CPP, 179-181
MDIWIN1.CPP, 640-646
menu-driven, 718
MENU1.CPP, 390-391
MENU2.CPP, 396-400
MENU3.CPP, 402-405
MENU4.CPP, 407-409
MINWINAP.CPP, 385
MSVC.EXE, 5
multiple-selection lists, 543-558
NESTFOR1.CPP, 142-143
notification messages, list boxes, 530-531
OPER1.CPP, 61-62
OPER2.CPP, 65
OPER3.CPP, 67-68
OUT1.CPP, 93
OUT2.CPP, 100-101
OVERLOAD.CPP, 51-52
PTR1.CPP, 208-209
PTR2.CPP, 210-212
PTR3.CPP, 212-214
PTR4.CPP, 214-217
PTR5.CPP, 219-221
querying strings, 531-544
QuickWin, creating, 19-21
REFVAR1.CPP, 205-206
RELOP1.CPP, 78-79
resources, 388
single-letter variables, 467
SIZEOF1.CPP, 70-71
STATIC1.CPP, 44-45
STRING1.CPP, 235-237
STRING2.CPP, 239-242
STRING3.CPP, 244-246
STRING4.CPP, 251-253
STRUCT1.CPP, 201-203
SWITCH1.CPP, 117-118
TYPCAST1.CPP, 73-74
VAR1.CPP, 34
VAR2.CPP, 43
WHILE1.CPP, 137-138
WINDOW1.CPP, 423-425
WINDOW2.CPP, 432-441

Project command
  Options menu, 18
  Project menu, 16
project dialog box, 20
project files, 4
  creating, 14
  .MAK, retrieving most recent, 16
  opening, 14
Project menu, 14-16
Project Options dialog box, 18
promptToQuit private function, 399
property functions, 363
protected section, 297
prototyping, 41-42
  functions, printf, 96
pScrollBar parameter, 566
pseudocodes, 719
PTR1.CPP program, 208-209
PTR2.CPP program, 210-212
PTR3.CPP program, 212-214
PTR4.CPP program, 214-217
PTR5.CPP program, 219-221
public section, 297
push button control, 462-485
PUSHBUTTON statement, 673
putVar member function, 484-485

Q

querying, strings, 531-544
QuickSort, 161
QuickWin applications, creating, 19-21

R

radio button controls, 490-491
  styles, 491
RadioButton member, 613
RADIOBUTTON statement, 668, 674-675
RAM (random access memory), 719
random access file stream I/O, 347-352
random access files, 719

random functions, 647
ranges, Windows messages, 376
.RC file extension, 719
.RC resource files, creating dialog boxes,
  603-610
read function, 340-346
Read Only check box, 6
Read Only command (Edit menu), 12
read-only memory, see ROM
read-only text windows, 420-426
readArray member function, 345
readElem member function, 345, 351
real numbers, 63
Rebuild All command (Project menu), 15
recall function, 306
recent files, displaying names, 8
reciprocal function, 287
records, 715, 719
  variable-length, 721
RECT structure, 357-358
rectangle functions, 363
recursive functions, 271-274
  showTree, 278
Redo command (Edit menu), 9
reference parameters, 268
reference, passing by, 719
reference variables, 204-206
REFVAR1.CPP program source code,
  205-206
region functions, 364
regression, linearized, 280-287
relational operators, 75-77, 85, 720
RELOP1.CPP program, 78-79
Replace command (Edit menu), 11
Replace dialog box, 11
ReplaceSel member function, 462
.RES file extension, 720
resolution, 720
resource files, 720
  CTLBTN1.RC, 468
  CTLCOMB1.RC, 587
  CTLGRP1.RC, 495
  CTLLST1.RC, 532

CTLLST2.RC, 546
CTLSCRL1.RC, 568
dialog boxes, creating, 603-610
DIALOG1.RC, 605-606
DIALOG2.RC, 614-615, 619
DIALOG3.RC, 622-623, 630
MDIWIN1.RC, 640
   script, 646
MENU1.RC, 388-389
MENU2.H, 395
MENU2.RC, 394-395
MENU3RC, 401
WINDOW1.RC, 423
WINDOW2.RC, 432
resource-management functions, 366
resources
   control, 668
   dialog box, 603, 605, 665-666
      NEW, 609
      OLD, 609
resources (programs), 388
Result box, 467
results, function, 42
reversing, strings, 243-246
ROM (read-only memory), 719-720
RTEXT statement, 671
rules
   class sections, 297-298
   constructors, 301-303
   default arguments, 48
   destructors, 304
   functions
      declaring, 40-41
      virtual, 316-318
Run-Time Object Model Support
  subhierarchy, 361
RUNTIME_CLASS macro, 361

S

Save All command (File menu), 8
Save As command (File menu), 7, 20-21
Save As dialog box, 7-8, 20
Save command (File menu), 7
Save Workspace command
  (Project menu), 16
sayError function, 198
Scan All Dependencies command (Project
  menu), 16
Scan Dependencies command (Project
  menu), 16
scientific notation, 720
scripts, MDIWIN1.RC resource files, 646
scroll bar controls, 562-576
   styles, 563-564
scroll bar notification messages, 373
scroll bars
   count-down timer application, 566-567
   notification messages, 566
   pScrollBar parameter, 566
scroll thumb, 426
SCROLLBAR statement, 676
ScrollBarData member, 612-613
scrolling
   functions, 363
   text, 426-431
   windows, 431-447
ScrollWindow member function, 428
SDI (single-document interface)
  windows, 359
searching
   arrays, 165-172
   options, 9-12
searchInSortedArray function, 172
searchInUnorderedArray function,
  171-172
sections, class, 297-300
seekg function, 347
segment functions, 365
select_transf function, 287
SelectString member function, 527,
  582-583
SelItemRange member function, 528
SendDlgItemMessage function, 375-376
sending, messages, 375-376
SendMessage function, 375-376, 631

sequences, escape, 97-98
sequential binary file stream I/O, 339-346
sequential files, 720
sequential text stream I/O, 334-339
SetButtonStyle member function, 464
SetCharHeight member function, 444-445
SetCheck member function, 490, 620
SetCurSel member function, 528, 579
SetDlgItemText function, 620
SetLineSize member function, 445
SetListBoxData member function, 612
SetPageSize member function, 446
SetScrollPos member function, 427-428, 565-566
SetScrollRange member function, 427, 565
SetSel member function, 461, 528-529
SetTopIndex member function, 529
SetVScrollMax member function, 445
SetWindowText member function, 453-454, 461
Shell-Metzner sort, 161
SHIFT option, 665
showArray function, 164
showColumnAverage function, 181
ShowDropDown member function, 580
showTree function, 278
ShowWindow function, 465, 649
signatures, function, 50
Simple Value Types subhierarchy, 361
single alternative if statement, 106-108
single-dimensional arrays, 151-154, 720
   declaring, 150-151
   initializing, 154-157
single-document interface (SDI) window, 359
single-letter variables, 467
sizeof operator, 69-72
SIZEOF1.CPP program source code, 70-71
sizes, variables, 70
sizing, windows, 430-431
sortArray function, 165

sorting, 720
   arrays, 161-165
   bubblesort method, 714
   Comb method, 161, 715
sound function, 366
source files, 15
sprintf function, 100
sqr function, 47-49, 287
sqroot function, 136
sqrt function, 49
START_MESSAGE_MAP() macro, 374
statements
   ACCELERATORS, 664
   blocks, defining, 12
   break, 132, 141
   CAPTION, 667
   CHECKBOX, 672
   CLASS, 668
   COMBOBOX, 675-676
   compiling, 15
   CONTROL, 668-670
   CTEXT, 672
   DEFPUSHBUTTON, 673
   DIALOG, 665
   EDITTEXT, 675
   FONT, 668
   GROUPBOX, 674
   if, single alternative, 106-108
   if-else
      dual-alternative, 108-111
      multiple-alternative, 111-114
   LISTBOX, 674
   LTEXT, 671
   MENU, 662, 667
   MENUITEM, 662-663
   MENUITEM SEPARATOR, 664
   option, DIALOG, 666-668
   output, 199
   POPUP, 664
   PUSHBUTTON, 673
   RADIOBUTTON, 668, 674-675
   RTEXT, 671
   SCROLLBAR, 676

STYLE, 666-667
switch, 114-118
static text, styles, 451-452
static text control, 450-454
static variables, 720
    in functions, 44-45
STATIC1.CPP program, 44-45
StaticText member, 611
Status Bar command (View menu), 13
STDIO.H header file, 96
Stop Build command (Project menu), 15
store function, 306
strcat function, 233
strchr function, 246
strcmp function, 237
strcspn function, 248
strdup function, 231
stream extractor operators <<, 334
    writing for classes, 325
stream functions, overloaded, 339-346
stream I/O
    random access file, 347-352
    sequential binary file, 339-346
    sequential text, 334-339
stream I/O functions, 332-334
stream input, 94-96
stream inserter operator >>, 334
stream libraries, 92
streams, 24
    output, formatted, 92-94
stricmp function, 238
string constants, 720
string input, 229-230
string literal, 720
string variables, 720
    variable-length, 721
string-manipulation functions, 366
STRING.H library, 230
STRING1.CPP program, 235
STRING2.CPP program, 239-242
STRING3.CPP program, 244-246
STRING4.CPP program, 251-253

strings, 228-229
    ampersand (&) in, 452
    as arguments, 263-265
    assigning, 230-232
    concatenating, 233-237
    converting, 242-243
    empty, 24
    initializing, 230-231
    length, 232-233
    libraries, STRING.H, 230
    locating, substrings, 248-253
    locating characters, 246-248
    null, 718
    querying, 531-544
    reversing, 243-246
strlen function, 232-233, 265
_strlwr function, 242
strncat function, 233-234
strncmp function, 238
strncpy function, 231-232, 277
strnicmp function, 239
Stroustrup, Bjarn, 4
strpbrk function, 248
strrchr functions, 247
strrev function, 243
strspn function, 247
strstr function, 249
strtok function, 249-250
STRUCT.CPP program source code,
    201-203
structured arrays, 720
structured variables, 720
structures, 199-203, 720
    dynamic, passing pointers to, 274-278
    passing, 265-267
        by pointers, 270-271
        to functions by reference, 268-269
    pointers, 214-217
    unions, 203-204
    untagged, 200
Structures subhierarchy, 361
_strupr function, 242
style parameter, 669
STYLE statement, 666-667

styles
  check box control, 489
  combo box control, 578
  edit control, 455-456
  LBS_EXTENDEDSEL, 543-544
  radio button control, 491
  scroll bar control, 563-564
  static text, 451-452
subdirectories, 720
  VC21DAY, 21
subhierarchies
  CDC, 360
  Collections, 361
  Control, 360
  Control Bars, 360
  Dialog Boxes, 360
  Document Architecture, 359
  Exceptions, 361
  File Services, 361
  Frames Windows, 359
  Graphical Drawing Objects, 361
  MFC, 359-362
  OLE 1.0 Support, 361
  Run-Time Object Model Support, 361
  Simple Value Types, 361
  Structures, 361
  Support Classes, 361
  Views, 360
subscripts, 720
substrings, locating, 248-253
Support Classes subhierarchy, 361
SVGA (Super Vector Graphics Array), 720
switch statement, 114-118
SWITCH1.CPP program source code,
  117-118
switches, command-line, 5
syntax boxes
  #define directive, 35-36
  #include directive, 33
  Accessing structure members, 214
  AddString member function, 524,
    580-581
  An array of function pointers, 279
  An array type name, 195

Assigning a function to an element, 280
A base class, 296
A derived class, 307
A dynamic array, 218
A structure, 199-200
An enumerated type, 195
break statement, 141
close function, 334
Comma operator, 84
Constructors, 301
continue statement, 139
Create member function, 450-457,
  463-464, 521-523, 562-565, 577-579
Declaring functions, 40
Declaring variables, 33
Decrement operators, 64
DeleteString member function,
  524, 581
Destructors, 303
Dir member function, 529-530, 582
do-while loop, 134
Dual-alternative if-else statement,
  108-109
FindString member function,
  524-525, 582
Fixed-array parameter, 158, 178-179
for loop, 128
Formal constant, 36
Friend functions, 318
Function pointer expression, 280
GetButtonStyle member function, 464
GetLBText member function, 579-580
GetLBTextLen member function, 580
GetLine member function, 229,
  335, 460
GetLineCount member function, 458
GetScrollRange member function, 565
GetSel member function, 459-460, 525
GetSelItems member function,
  525-526
GetText member function, 526
GetTextLen member function, 526
GetWindowText member function,
  453, 457

syntax boxes (continued)

GetWindowTextLength member function, 453

Increment operators, 64

Initializing a function pointer, 280

Initializing a string, 230-231

InsertString member function, 527, 581

LimitText member function, 583

LineFromChar member function, 458

LineIndex member function, 459

LineLength member function, 459

Multiple-alternative if-else statement, 111-112

new and delete operators, 217

open function, 333

Open-array parameter, 158

Operators and friend operators, 322

Pointer, 207

Pointer to a function, 279

Pointer-to-array parameter, 260

Reference variable, 204

ReplaceSel member function, 462

seekg function, 347

SelectString member function, 527, 582-583

SelItemRange member function, 528

SetButtonStyle member function, 464

SetCurSel member function, 528, 579

SetScrollPos member function, 565-566

SetScrollRange member function, 565

SetSel member function, 461, 528-529

SetTopIndex member function, 529

SetWindowText member function, 453-454, 461

ShowDropDown member function, 580

Single-alternative if statement, 106-107

Single-dimensional array, 150-151

sizeof operator, 69

strcat function, 233

strchr function, 246

strcmp function, 237

strcspn function, 248

strdup function, 231

stricmp function, 238

strlwr function, 242

strncat function, 233-234

strncmp function, 238

strncpy function, 231-232

strnicmp function, 239

strpbrk function, 248

strrchr function, 247

strrev function, 243

strspn function, 247

strstr function, 249

strtok function, 249-250

strupr function, 242

switch statement, 114-115

strlen function, 232-233

Two-dimensional and three-dimensional arrays, 172

Typecasting, 72

typedef keyword, 194

Unions, 203

Virtual functions, 313

while loop, 137

write function, 339

Syntax Coloring command (View menu), 13

syntax errors, 721

system functions, 363

system hangs, *see* crashing

system information messages, 373

system messages, 373

system services interface functions, 365-366

T

tabs, inserting in menu item name, 663

tags, 206

task functions, 365

terminal nodes, 275

ternary operators, 86

text
deleting, 9
hot-key characters, 452
in MDI windows, 639
replacing, 11
restoring, 9
scrolling, 426-431
searching for, 9-10
text editors, replacing characters, 613-621
text files, 721
text functions, 364
text query member functions, 456-460
text windows, read-only, 420-426
three-dimensional arrays, 172-176
function paramenters, 178-181
initializing, 176-178
thumb box, position, 429
tilde (~), 304
Toggle Bookmark command
(View menu), 13
TOLERANCE constant, 136, 143
Toolbar command (View menu), 13
Tools command (Options menu), 18-19
Tools dialog box, 19
Tools menu, 18
TransferData member function, 630-631
transferring control data, dialog boxes,
610-632
transformation functions, 281-287
trees, binary, 274-278
trimStr function, 338
two-dimensional arrays, 172-176
function parameters, 178-181
initializing, 176-178
TYPCAST1.CPP program, 73-74
type checking, 46
typecasting, 72-75
typedef keyword, 194-195

U

unary operators, 721
Undo command (Edit menu), 8-9
unions, 203-204
untagged structures, 200
updatedComboBox member function, 597
updating, files, 7
upperCase function, 264-265
user-defined data types, 721
user-defined functions, 721
user-defined messages, 376-377
user-generated messages, 370
utility macros, 366

V

validating, data, 137
value, passing by, 719
values
parameter, modifying, 35
passing structures by, 268
VAR1.CPP program, 34
VAR2.CPP program, 43
variable scope, 721
variable-length records, 719-721
variable-length string variables, 721
variables, 721
declaring, 33-35
global, 34, 717
local, 717
in functions, 42-44
pointers, 206-209
reference, 204-206
single-letter, 467
sizes, representing, 70
static, 720
in functions, 44-45
string, 720
structured, 720
VC21DAY subdirectory, 21
vertical scrolling, constants, 429

VGA (Vector Graphics Array), 721
View menu, 12-13
Views subhierarchy, 360
VIRTKEY keyword, 664
virtual destructors, 316
virtual arrays, 347
virtual functions, 312-316, 721
inheriting, 316
rules, 316-318
Visual C++, wizards, 393
VmArray class, 351
void data type, 30

W

while loop, 137-138
WHILE1.CPP program source code,
137-138
width function, 92
width option, printf function, 97
Window menu, 19
window operations, developing, 387-393
window-creation functions, 362
WINDOW1.CPP program, 423-425
WINDOW1.H header file, 423
WINDOW1.RC resource file, 423
WINDOW2.CPP program, 432-441
WINDOW2.EXE application, 431-447
WINDOW2.H header file, 432
WINDOW2.RC resource file, 432
Windows
API functions, 362-366
applications, developing, 356-379
data types, 356-358
DEF files, 384
manager interface functions, 362-363
messages, 370-373
ranges, 376
WinMain function, 382

windows, 420
closing, 406-409
contents, saving, 7
MDI (Multi-Document Interface), 5, 359
blank, creating, 6
child, *see* MDI child windows
closing, 7
frame, *see* MDI frame windows
multiple scroll bars, 426
OnPaint member functions, 421-422
read-only, 420-426
scroll thumb, 426
scrolling, 431-447
text, 426-431
SDI (single-document interface), 359
sizing, 430-431
Windows messages, 370-371, 721
Windows registration class names, 669-670
WinMain function, 382
wizards (Visual C++), 393
WM_COMMAND command, 392
words, 721
Workbench
exiting, 25
features, 5
loading, 5
Workspace command (Options menu), 19
Workspace dialog box, 19
write function, 339-346
writeArray member function, 345
writeElem member function, 344, 351

X-Z

XOR operator, 75, 80, 83

Disk Offer

The programs in *Teach Yourself Visual C++ in 21 Days* are available on disk from the author. Fill out this form and enclose a check for only $10.00 to receive a copy. Outside the U.S., please enclose a check for $14.00 in U.S. currency, drawn on a U.S. bank. Please make the check payable to **Namir C. Shammas**. Sorry, no credit card orders. Mail this form to

Namir C. Shammas
3928 Margate Drive
Richmond, VA 23235

Name _____

Company (for company address) _____

Street _____

City _____

State/Province _____

ZIP or Postal Code _____

Country (outside USA) _____

Disk format (check one):

5.25 inch _____ 3.5 inch _____

Add to Your Sams Library Today with the Best Books for Programming, Operating Systems, and New Technologies

The easiest way to order is to pick up the phone and call

1-800-428-5331

between 9:00 a.m. and 5:00 p.m. EST.
For faster service please have your credit card available.

ISBN	Quantity	Description of Item	Unit Cost	Total Cost
0-672-30168-7		Advanced C (Book/Disk)	$39.95	
0-672-30158-X		Advanced C++ (Book/Disk)	$39.95	
0-672-30287-X		Tom Swan's Code Secrets (Book/Disk)	$39.95	
0-672-30309-4		Programming Sound for DOS and Windows (Book/Disk)	$39.95	
0-672-30240-3		OS/2 2.1 Unleashed (Book/Disk)	$34.95	
0-672-30288-8		DOS Secrets Unleashed (Book/Disk)	$39.95	
0-672-30299-3		Uncharted Windows Programming (Book/Disk)	$34.95	
0-672-30274-8		Mastering Borland C++ (Book/Disk)	$39.95	
0-672-30226-8		Windows Programmer's Guide to OLE/DDE (Book/Disk)	$34.95	
0-672-30236-5		Windows Programmer's Guide to DLLs & Memory Management (Book/Disk)	$34.95	
0-672-30030-3		Windows Programmer's Guide to Serial Communications (Book/Disk)	$39.95	
0-672-30177-6		Windows Programmer's Guide to Borland C++ Tools (Book/Disk)	$39.95	
0-672-30097-4		Windows Programmer's Guide to Resources (Book/Disk)	$34.95	
0-672-30067-2		Windows Programmer's Guide to MS Foundation Class Library (Book/Disk)	$34.95	
0-672-30106-7		Windows Programmer's Guide to ObjectWindows Library (Book/Disk)	$34.95	
0-672-30249-7		Multimedia Madness (Book/Disk/CD-ROM)	$44.95	
0-672-30137-7		Secrets of the Borland C++ Masters (Book/Disk)	$44.95	
0-672-30190-3		Windows Resource and Memory Management (Book/Disk)	$29.95	
❏ 3 ½" Disk		Shipping and Handling: See information below.		
❏ 5 ¼" Disk		TOTAL		

Shipping and Handling: $4.00 for the first book, and $1.75 for each additional book. Floppy disk: add $1.75 for shipping and handling. If you need to have it NOW, we can ship product to you in 24 hours for an additional charge of approximately $18.00, and you will receive your item overnight or in two days. Overseas shipping and handling adds $2.00 per book and $8.00 for up to three disks. Prices subject to change. Call for availability and pricing information on latest editions.

11711 N. College Avenue, Suite 140, Carmel, Indiana 46032

1-800-428-5331 — Orders   1-800-835-3202 — FAX   1-800-858-7674 — Customer Service

Book ISBN 0-672-30372-8